The 500 Best Ways for Teens to Spend the Summer

Learn about Programs for College-Bound High School Students

Neill Seltzer

The 500 Best Ways for Teens to Spend the Summer

Learn about Programs for College-Bound High School Students

Random House, Inc., New York
www.PrincetonReview.com

Princeton Review Publishing, L.L.C.
2315 Broadway
New York, NY 10024
Email: bookeditor@review.com

ISBN: 0-375-76372-4
ISSN: 1015-8880

Editor: Erik Olson
Production Editor: Vivian Gomez
Production Coordinator: Greta Blau
Account Manager: Ben Zelevansky

Manufactured in the United States of America on partially recycled paper.

9 8 7 6 5 4 3 2 1

2004 Edition

The letter from Deer Hill Expeditions is reprinted with the permission of Doug Capelin.

DEDICATION

This book is dedicated to Neil Bull, the original Mr. Rourke. In addition to having more wisdom in one finger than most of us will find in a lifetime, Neil helped me find unique experiences and inspired me to jump into many of the challenges that have contributed to the person I am today.

ACKNOWLEDGMENTS

For help on the book, the author would like to thank:

In particular: Richard Webb; Keri Hoyt; Zack White; Holly Bull; Kim Eddy; Anne, Mitch, and Marna Seltzer, all of whom contributed wisdom, support, and skills without which I, and by extension this book, could not exist.

Of the many great summer programs and program directors dedicated to putting kids in the path of oncoming wisdom, these few were especially generous, patient, insightful, and essential to the creation of this book: Joanne Pinaire, Doug Capelin, Bert Rogers, Chris Yager, and Marc Simon.

At the college level, David Borus, Tom Marlett, Jen Stein, Mike Mills, Andrea Thomas, Nancy Meislahn, Martha Merrill, and Joan Adams were all very generous with their time and wisdom.

Of the many folks providing great guidance to teens at the high school level, these in particular also provided guidance for me: Ted de Villafranca, Phyllis Steinbrecher, Bob Rhett, and in particular, Madeline Selden and Bill Cole.

Contents

PART ONE

INTRODUCTION

Chapter 1

School's Out

Summer is special. It can't come soon enough and it always ends too quickly. There is some strange alchemy afoot, a combination of temperature and flavor, laziness and adventure, long days and even longer evenings that make it a particularly special time of year. Moviemakers, songwriters, poets, artists—even chefs—have been trying for years to capture its special essence, and yet it still eludes most attempts to pin it down. Indeed, the difficulty of defining it, or perhaps its very lack of definition, is a large part of its magic. However ineffable, the magic is potent and summer seems to have its own rules. At no point is summer's effect more concentrated, more evocative, more intoxicating, than when we are young. Who, upon hearing the chime of a shackle against an aluminum mast, or catching sight of a yard bejeweled with fireflies in the twilight, is not transported back to another summer in another time when the same sounds adorned a few months of refulgent freedom?

Summer is everything that school is not. Where school days often seem to drag on during the summer whole months slip by before we know it. Days during the school year have a rigid schedule, packed full of deadlines and obligations. Summers are deliciously unstructured. During the year, there is always someone looking over your shoulder. It might be a teacher, a coach, a boss, or a parent, but whoever it is, he or she is always checking up on your work. In the summer, however, once you get the lawn mowed, the rest of the afternoon is all yours to spend as you please. During the year we are told what to read, what to write, when to work, and when to relax. In the summer, the choice is ours. Generally, no homework or term papers are due in the summer. If you set foot in a library, it probably has more to do with the quality of the air-conditioning than the quality of the books. Still, there is plenty of learning that takes place when school is out.

The learning that takes place in summer is of a different sort than the kind you find in school. In school, teachers fill your head with information. Summers fill your head with dreams. Summer is about lack of structure. It's about filling your time the way you choose. It is about discovering your own interests, at your own pace, and in your own way.

When we're younger, summer often means day camp, sleepover camp, or long days at the pool. At twelve years old, that's all the excitement or entertainment we need. In college, the pressures of the school year can begin to encroach on summer's freedom, as students work to make money for tuition or compete for internships that might eventually turn into careers. After college, of course, summer no longer exists in quite the same way. So it's during those few summers in high school, when we are grown up and independent enough to take on or find authentic challenges, but still young enough to retain that imaginative quality, which allows us to immerse ourselves completely in the moment and in the experience, that an enormous amount of our learning takes place.

Of course, from an emotional standpoint, the high school years can be rough. They are full of angst and vulnerability as we begin to define ourselves as individuals. Our roles as sons or daughters, students, peers, employees, friends, and members of different communities are in flux. Most of the time we are just making it up as we go along, hoping that it all works out. Somehow, summer lends itself to this process. In the absence of the structure and pressures of the school year, we are freer to explore our individual needs and identities. This leads to all kinds of firsts, adventures . . . and a few messes as well. If during the year we are too often told how to behave as students, siblings, athletes, or college applicants, in summer we have greater opportunity to be what we want to be. It is a blank page, and we're holding the crayon. This makes it potentially scary, but certainly exciting.

It's all of these factors that make the high school summers a particularly priceless, but scarce, commodity. We only have a few of them with which to work. It doesn't take too much imagination to see these three precious summers as the three magic beans given to Jack in the fairy tale about the beanstalk. Jack plants his beans in the garden, and out grows a magic beanstalk that reaches far beyond Jack's limited horizons. Needless to say, anytime you go beyond your own horizons, you have an adventure. It is worth noting that Jack was originally sent by his mother to the market to sell his cow. While he *did* sell the cow, he didn't quite do it the way he was supposed to. Jack took a chance on a few magic beans. He took a chance on his own dreams. When he began to climb that beanstalk, he had no idea what was at the other end. As we all know, it wasn't easy. It was even downright scary at times, but in the end he got his mother's approval *and* the golden goose. Your high school summers are like Jack's magic beans. If you plant them in fertile ground, they will lead to adventure. At times it will be scary, at times difficult, and at times thrilling. The only guarantee is that you will come back enriched in unexpected ways. The catch is, however, that you only have a few beans with which to work and not all ground is equally fertile.

Here's another way to think about it: Each summer, like youth, is like a coin that you can spend exactly once. The ways you can spend them are practically limitless. You can choose to view what you do with your coins as an investment. Some people invest them in the hopes of reaping a benefit at college admissions time. Other people invest them in longer-term accounts by doing internships or skill building for a future career. Many people squander them by sitting on the couch watching TV, playing video games, or driving to the mall. The good old-fashioned summer job is a traditional and often valuable investment. There is a lot to be learned from working hard and contributing to an organization. For many parents, exotic summer adventures seem too expensive for too little quantifiable gain. It's not a job, the logic goes; it's not necessarily going to help with college admissions; it's not guaranteed to improve your grades in chemistry; and it's really expensive. Where's the return on investment?

The beauty of summer and good summer programs is that they are not formulaic, predictable, or quantifiable. The benefits, however, are very real. Investing these coins in a good summer program is like giving them to the few experts that really understand their value: the few people whose sole mission is to ensure that the reward you reap exceeds your expectations and has true lasting value.

The opportunity to reinvent yourself, to discover that you are capable of so much more than you ever thought possible, to discover that other people hold the same fears and dreams that you never dared to share out loud, to collide with another culture, to work as a team, to overcome authentic challenges, to face questions of personal and cultural identity, to expand your view and understanding of the world, and most of all to discover who you are and where you come from by stepping out of your world and out of your comfort zone, can only be described in one way: priceless. These are the benefits you reap by jumping in a deeper deep end than you previously would have considered.

It just so happens that those direct benefits lead to residual benefits: You become a more interesting and thoughtful person, which can help with college admissions. You may have a clearer sense of your own personal interests and learning styles, which will lead to a more fulfilling and more successful academic career. You will have a greater sense of self-confidence, which will help overcome peer pressure, loneliness, and the feeling of being trapped. You will be better equipped to deal with the transitions that we all face from high school to college—or from dependent to independent—and better equipped to deal with the unexpected crises that come up in all lives.

To tap into any of these benefits, however, you must first engage. You must take the plunge. This is both the beginning and the purpose of the journey itself. Engage, and everything else will follow. While there are lots of things that you can do to ensure that your journey is everything you are hoping for, it's the things you can't anticipate that are likely to mean the most. With this in mind, the details or type of program, from service to adventure, from home stay to dorm, from domestic to abroad, are secondary to the simple act of committing yourself to a new experience and fully engaging while you're there.

If there are two pieces of advice you should take from this book, the first is that summers are an amazing gift. Find the magic inherent in these respites from prescribed learning. The second is, once you get there, burn all of the guidebooks, including this one. Forget about what you're supposed to do. Dig up your most outrageous dreams. This is where you should begin. Find yourself on that blank page, or at least give yourself a chance to find you. If your first step is genuine—if it comes from you—you need not worry where it will end.

Engage, and see what happens. The rest will take care of itself.

2003 Leading Edge students take a break while climbing Mt. Massive, one of Colorado's 14,000-foot peaks.

Chapter 2

Why Go?

Summer programs are hard. They're not comfortable. The people can be weird. They mean leaving behind your home, your friends, and the lifestyle you are used to. You will miss some epic parties. You're friends will all be home learning how to drive and hitting on you significant other (successfully, you're sure). Where you're going there's no TV, no internet, no mall, and worst of all, you will miss out on all of the fun and intrigue your friends will have while you're gone.

Your parents said that they're willing to pay for it, but only if you're sure, because it's expensive. They're worried that it will be too hard, that you'll want to come home early, or that you're better off living at home and taking classes at the local community college.

So why go? Is it really worth it? The chances are good that, in your heart, you already know the answer to this question. Summer in your hometown is really not all that exciting. Yeah, summer programs are hard, but you have a sneaking suspicion that there is something to them.

Everyone knows that finding and surmounting new challenges makes you stronger. It teaches you new skills, gives you a greater wealth of experience, and increases your understanding of the world around you. How many new challenges do you think you are likely to bump into while sitting on your couch at home?

When you really think about it, the reason you don't go is not because you are afraid of what you might miss, but because you are afraid of what you might find. What if it's too hard? What if you can't make friends? It's just so much effort. In case you don't already have some in mind, let's look at some reasons *to* go.

CHANGING YOUR PERSPECTIVE

Did you ever go back and visit your old grade school or middle school? If you did, you might have noted a change in scale. Hallways that once seemed miles long now seem shorter and strangely without drama. Classrooms and even chairs seem smaller, and how about the cafeteria? It was once a sea of interpersonal issues; now it's just a roomful of tables and lots of noisy kids.

Guess what. The school hasn't changed, but you have. Environments that were once so challenging now seem so simple, almost innocent. This all comes from a change in perspective. And the benefits of changing your perspective are nearly limitless. Understanding another walk of life not only enriches your understanding of the world, but also it makes you a more capable person, ready to tackle and solve complex problems that involve real human beings.

When you bring this change in perspective from your summer experience home with you, it will act equally on those truths that you thought you knew. Your will see your friends, your family, your town, your high school, even your country in a new way. This is especially true of students returning form particularly intense service programs. Richard Webb, the founder of ProPeru, puts it this way: "Returning students often describe to me a newly found sense of what is important and what is not important. The interpersonal dramas that once consumed their lives no longer seem to have any significance. Students experience a new sense of peace and balance as a result of understanding how petty [their] previous issues were when seen in relation to the hunger and poverty—but also joy—that they have seen over the summer."

Vladimir Nabokov, a famous writer, once likened our lives to a house in which the doors are locked and the windows have been replaced with mirrors. In his analogy, anytime we try to look beyond the bounds of our lives, all we can see is a reflection of ourselves. We base our expectations for the future on our experiences in the past. When we are in middle school, we know that high school will be different but it is hard to imagine anything other than a bigger, more complex middle school. That may be enough to get us through the transition to high school, but if you imagine college to be just a bigger more complex high school, you're missing some major pieces of the picture. When we look back at middle school, however, it is not nearly as large or dramatic as it seemed at the time. One of the values of stepping out of our present life is that it is an opportunity to see beyond the mirrors, or at least to make them two-way mirrors. In so doing, we increase the ways that we can describe our lives and the world around us. This is what understanding and insight are all about.

DRY RUN FOR COLLEGE

One change that you know is coming is the transition from high school to college. When you get to college you will have to walk into an unfamiliar environment and spend long periods of time away from home. You will be leaving your friends and the comforts of home behind. You will have to face new challenges emotionally, physically, academically, and socially. Your personal weaknesses will be tested, and you will have to find new strengths to pull you through. In order to succeed you will need to find a way to embrace this new adventure and find ways to make it enjoyable and productive. Sound familiar?

A good summer program will test you in all of the same ways, but the length of commitment is shorter, the environment is smaller (20 kids as opposed to 2,000), and the support groups are better. Putting yourself in this challenging environment now is a perfect way to learn to manage more dramatic, unsupervised, unsupported transitions later. Like in college. You can start to develop these skills now, in a safer environment, where the stakes are lower and the activities are more fun.

TRYING ON A LIFE FOR SIZE

Did you ever dream of being a filmmaker? Some parts of the profession are creative and very glamorous, right? But how do you feel about making sure that your cast and crew are on the set at 6:00 A.M., shooting the same scene 27 times because something keeps going wrong; loading and unloading hundreds of pounds of equipment on and off a van every day; and then spending hours upon hours upon hours in the editing room? You might find that you love it. You might also find that it makes for a great summer when you're seventeen, but it's not the way you want to spend the rest of your life.

In college admissions they call it "developing nonacademic interests." We prefer to think of it as living out your fantasies, or at very least, trying on a new life for size. If you've always had a hankering to be a filmmaker, try it out for a summer. Even if you hate it, you will have developed a much greater insight into the process than your average moviegoer, and you have learned something about yourself along the way.

Summer programs offer you the opportunity to try out skills, job descriptions, or fantasies that normally require years of commitment to achieve. They also provide an opportunity to travel to exotic places, meet people from different countries, develop arcane but interesting skills, and generally to do things that you could never do at home.

REINVENT YOURSELF

High school is tough. Small towns can be tough. Did you ever wish that you could be someone else? Maybe you'd like to trade places with someone in your school that you know. Maybe you'd just like a chance to start over. Perhaps your life is fine, but you have a sneaking suspicion that if given the chance, you could do better. Or maybe you wish that everyone would stop trying to be cool and just be honest about what is really going on.

It's hard, however, to do this in high school. You can't just be a geek one day and decide to be a jock the next. Besides, if it were up to you, you'd get rid of categories like these altogether.

Summer programs provide you with that magic wand. They give you a chance to be whoever you want to be. Many challenging programs even create an environment where teamwork is a survival skill, and it doesn't matter who you are or what your abilities are. Everyone on the team has something to contribute. Other programs focus on creating an atmosphere of open, honest communication. No posturing, no being cool, no playing to the audience, just talking about the issues that are confronting the entire group.

If you are feeling typecast, pigeonholed, or trapped in a particular peer group, summer programs allow you to change the channel. A lot of times a high school student has a specific role in his or her peer group: You are the serious one, the funny one, the slacker, and so on. Summer programs that push the whole student—mentally, physically, emotionally, and socially—create a space in which a teenager can develop skills and personality traits that may have been stifled in school.

PUSH PERSONAL LIMITS

Have you ever finished a science project or an English paper and found yourself surprised by the quality of what you had created? Did you ever decide not to try out for an activity because you were worried that you couldn't do it? Summer programs, whether they are cultural, physical, or intellectual, will provide you with bigger and/or different challenges than you have faced before. They will also, however, help you overcome those challenges.

If the notion of challenging or expanding your personal limits sounds scary to you, don't worry. Good summer programs are not in the business of setting people up for failure. If they confronted students with challenges, but did not help them to succeed, no one would come back. You may not believe it, but they are not created for mythical, superhuman students. They are created for students just like you. If you're not sure, call the references that they give you. They will all tell you the same thing: "If you think that it won't work, don't worry. You can do it. I didn't think that I would ever do it, but I did, and now I'll never forget it!"

IT'S FUN

Come on, is sitting in summer school really that fun? Your summer baby-sitting job or house-painting job may not be that bad, but is it the greatest time of your life? Do you really want to spend the entire summer going to the pool, hanging out with the same old faces, and doing all of the same things that you've done a hundred times before?

There is nothing boring about sitting in a kayak off the coast of Alaska. Rebuilding old Romanesque chapels in the south of France is way more interesting than painting houses in Pennsylvania. Spend a summer with twenty of your peers doing community service in Peru where just walking down the street is fun. (So what if you only get a five-minute shower every other day. At least everyone is in the same boat.) Most of the students we've spoken to tell us that the programs they went on made for the dirtiest, hottest, hungriest, most exhausting—but quite possibly the happiest—summers they ever spent. What more do you need to know? These are people just like you.

A SPECIAL NOTE TO PARENTS:

THE TEENAGE TURNING POINT

Your daughter has rounded a developmental corner. A summer at home that was once delightfully full of odd jobs and trips to the pool now looms as unbearably boring. She has told you, either directly or indirectly, that she is ready for something new, something challenging, something real. Her world at home suddenly feels confining. Your town, your house, her social options all fit a bit too tightly. Going to the mall no longer holds the same allure. More than likely, some of her friends are starting to do some interesting things, and she is beginning to have a sneaking suspicion that she might be left behind.

Your daughter is looking for adventure. She may not be able to put a finger on it, but she is hungry for an authentic experience. She is ready to face some challenges and decisions on her own. When this time comes, most teenagers will find excitement they crave one way or another. They will test the boundaries of their own comfort zone by pushing the boundaries of their families, their hometown, or their friends. This is simply part of what it means to be a teenager.

Chances are pretty good that you will know when it is time. If mood swings are escalating, it is probably time. If you are dying to get her out of the house, it is probably time. If she has started getting into trouble and testing limits, it's probably time. She may also simply tell you, "Mom, my friend Mike is going to this theater camp over the summer. They get to produce their own plays and lots of famous actors went there. Can I go?" If she says something like this to you, it is probably time. If the usual summer activities sound "boring." If her friends are starting to venture farther afield during the summer, or if she simply tells you that she wants to do something different for the summer, it is time.

Be wary, however, of the reluctant adventurer. Even when the time has come, the natural inclination of many teenagers is to stay right where they are in the company of their friends. This may seem contradictory, but it remains true. In many cases, no matter how pigeonholed, isolated, or pressured your daughter may feel by her peers, it may still take a distinct shove to get her out the door. Paradoxically, her thirst for authentic challenges is no less.

It is not only the students who are sometimes reluctant adventurers. Many parents allow excuses like cost or time to mask their own reluctance to let their sons or daughters go. Frequently parents feel guilty about sending their kids away for the summer because they have not been able to spend much time with them during the year. Often the student says that they do not want to go and parents are reluctant to push any harder. Fears about travel including terrorism and infectious diseases contribute to an inclination to keep the kids close to home.

None of this erases the fact that a healthy part of being a teenager is the search for personal identity, or that you, as a parent, should contribute to this process. It is finding the language and the stance with which you are going to interact with the world. Good summer programs for teenagers, be they cultural, physical, or intellectual, exist to create challenges and scenarios that will help students to find their voice. It is a shorter and more controlled version than the process that they will go through when they leave home to go to college. All of this is a long way of saying: Don't be afraid to insist that your daughter does something more interesting with her summer than sit on the couch. By the end of the summer, both of you will be glad that you weren't.

So the time has come to help them find some authentic experiences away from home. The challenge may be physical, it may be cultural, or it may be intellectual, depending on the inclination of your child. It may be all three. As Doug Capelin of Deer Hill Expeditions puts it, "To really provide a life-changing experience we must get a student out of his or her comfort zone and into the learning zone." By facing and overcoming these challenges, away from home, students learn that they can do, be, and achieve more.

It is important to note that when teenagers reach this turning point, they are hungry for challenges and authentic experiences. More than likely, they will find them, with or without you. There are lots of ways for them to find adventure close to home, some wholesome, and some not. All too frequently teenagers look to forbidden or adult activities such as alcohol, drugs, or physical relationships to provide excitement, adventure, and a method of altering their surroundings. When your child appears to be testing her limits, it is crucially important to help her find authentic experiences that will push her, but that will also help her to grow and learn. For your own peace of mind, known challenges provided by responsible programs are a far better option than challenges that she may find on her own.

There are two primary themes here: Authentic and Challenge. "Authentic" means that the challenges faced are real. The ocean is real, a mountain is real, interacting with another culture is real, engaging in actual scientific research is real, making your own movie is real. Learning biology or Spanish from a textbook, while potentially challenging, is not an "authentic" experience.

The second theme is challenge. Getting out of the comfort zone puts you into the learning zone automatically. Of course this comfort zone is deeply subjective. Some people are out of their comfort zone by the time they get three lines into a Chinese take-out menu. For others, that line is not crossed until they have to shop for food in the snake market in Guanzhou. There is also a zone beyond the learning zone where students are in over their heads. Manageable risk is an important learning tool, unmanageable risk is irresponsible at best, and can be downright dangerous.

Nevertheless, the only way to feed that need for adventure, that hunger for something authentic is with challenge. Easy won't do it, mundane won't do it, and more of the same won't do it. It is through challenges that we learn about ourselves, and our limits. It is how we find new strengths and build new abilities. It also provides a different sort of peer interaction that is important for developing a voice. These things are hard to come by during the school year, but often they are at the heart of a good summer program's mission.

Like most worthwhile pursuits, there are few quick or easy solutions. When the time comes to help your teenager broaden his or her horizons, you'll need to have a few discussions. One or two over dinner won't do it. A long one on a Sunday won't do it. Even a few productive car rides won't do it. You will need to start the discussion early, and carry it over a period of months. This is a process of peeling away layers of "shoulds" and "oughts" and digging down to "wants" and "coulds" for both you and your would-be adventurer. The range of possibilities makes for a large and complicated discussion that will touch on strengths and weaknesses as well as hopes and fears. These are all, of course, great discussions to be having with your kids anyway. You are already reaping benefits and you haven't even picked program yet.

Here is another way to think about: Those few years in high school but before college represent a unique and powerful window of opportunity. When she gets to college, her time becomes more and more dominated by jobs, sports, and other activities (not that her time is not packed full in her junior year of high school). She will take on more and more of the burden of decision-making and more of her path will be determined by opportunity and circumstance. In early high school and before, she is not quite ready or informed enough to tackle adult situations or to really take advantage of cultural opportunities. Not to sell any younger students short, but there is a world of difference between twelve and seventeen. For a teenager, these years are characterized by angst and vulnerability. Almost by definition, teenagers are people experiencing personality crises. It is this very vulnerability that makes her special. There is no better time to give a kid an opportunity to reinvent herself, or to help her to understand who she is and where she comes from by taking her out of her world and showing her something different. Pick her favorite activity, swap out her peer group, change the backdrop, and give her some challenges. She will come back changed.

A participant savors a moment with his students at a rural monastery in the Nepal Himalaya during the volunteer service phase of his Cultural Immersion Experience program. **International Cultural Adventures** organizes extraordinary cultural, educational and volunteer service experiences in Asia and South America. Please see our profile for more information.

Chapter 3

Spending Your Magic Beans: Where do You Want to Go?

The good news is that there are absolutely no limits to the things that you can do with your summer. Dream your wildest dream and then find a way to make it happen. You would be amazed how many doors a little bit of ingenuity, an ounce or two of self-confidence, and a whole lot of genuine enthusiasm can open for you.

Ben from Toledo loves opera. He can't sing a note, doesn't speak Italian, and he knew that opera would never be a career move for him, but still, it made him happy. For the summer between his junior and senior year of high school, his best options were mowing the lawn and working at the Baskin Robbins. At least during the school year he didn't have to have a job. On a whim one day, he picked up the phone and called the New York Metropolitan Opera. Fortunately, he knew his stuff. He knew the name of the director, he knew which operas they would be staging that summer, and he knew that he had nothing to lose. As you might guess, he did not get the director on the phone. In fact, he was lucky just to get his secretary. Not knowing what else to do, however, he left a message. He told the secretary that he was calling from Toledo, that he loved the opera, in particular the one they would be staging that summer, and would they take an intern for the summer to do anything that needed doing?

Two days later the phone rang, and to his enormous surprise, it was the executive director of the Metropolitan Opera calling. He had received Ben's message and was intrigued. He had never gotten a phone call from a high school student before, much less one from Toledo, Ohio, so he returned the call. After chatting for about ten minutes, the director found that Ben really did love the opera, and he was won over by Ben's enthusiasm. He offered him an unpaid internship on the set for the summer. Ben's parents were also quite surprised. Had he asked them if he could forgo his usual summer job and spend the summer in New York City, they would have checked him for a fever. Getting offered a job by the executive director of the Metropolitan Opera, on the other hand, was a whole different story. After much pleading, promising, and cajoling, Ben's parents agreed. The fact that Ben's father's college roommate lived in New York City and agreed to put Ben up for the summer helped. Ben did such a good job while he was there that the company even invited him to tour with them. Ben works in the arts to this day. His wildest dream came true before he even got to college.

Jessica from New Jersey didn't have such an easy time of it. Jess is a theater buff and also loves sci-fi movies. She was hoping to get an internship on a movie set for the summer. She knew some people who knew some people at a few of the studios, and she had plenty of theater experience. Every studio she called, however, told her no way. They didn't do that sort of thing, it was an insurance liability, she had to be union, etc. Hollywood and New York both turned out to be dead ends. The only other studio she'd even heard of was in Australia. It produced a show that she liked on the sci-fi channel. A little web surfing yielded a phone number, and one night she called. The phone was answered by a production person who put her on with a costume person who passed her to an assistant producer, who was flattered that someone was calling from America about his show. Thinking that it would never happen, he told her that if she showed up, he would put her to work. One of her teachers had a brother-in-law who worked in Australia who knew a family with two high school–age kids who agreed to put her up. They were an hour by bus from the soundstage, but Jess didn't care. She borrowed the money for her plane ticket from her dad and went. Ultimately, she decided that TV production was not for her. She had no idea how stressful and chaotic it was. There were so many people required just to put on one low-budget TV show, and the hours were crazy. Actors showed up at 4 A.M. to start getting into costume and worked until nine at night! Nevertheless, it was the greatest summer of her life. She has tapes of the episodes that she worked on and can tell you right where she was standing (off camera) and what she was doing on every scene.

Justin from Manhattan had a great summer planned. His best friend's parents were going to be away for most of the summer. His own parents would be away for many of the weekends. He planned to take that SAT course his mother had been bothering him about, which would necessitate his staying in the city. When his parents were out of town, he could stay out as late as he wanted, and when they were in town, he could crash at his buddy's place anytime he wanted. It was going to be a good summer. Justin's mom, however, had other plans. She didn't care what he did, as long as he did something. She had spoken to some other parents who'd all had their kids enrolled in community service programs abroad because it got them out of the house and it was good for college. She got a list of programs from Justin's guidance counselor and told him to pick one. He picked the shortest one he could fine, four weeks in Ecuador, but he wasn't happy about it. His first night was spent on a gym floor in Manhattan with 200 other kids that he didn't know. He found his group, but he didn't say much. They all looked strange. They were the kind of happy kids that teachers always liked. He was already annoyed. They were up at 5 A.M. the next morning. By noon they were in Miami and by 5 P.M. they were touching down in Quito. As soon as he got a chance, he pulled one of the leaders aside and gave it to her straight. "Look," he said, "I don't really want to be here. My mom signed me up for this thing. I didn't have a choice. Do me a favor and just leave me alone. I won't cause any trouble and we won't have to talk again until it's time to go home." "Justin," she replied, "I can't really do that. If you're on the program, you've got to pull your weight. This isn't like summer camp where you can sign up for different activities. We're here to work. But I'll make you a deal. Give me two weeks of commitment. After two weeks, if you don't like it, you can get on the next plane out. I'll take you there myself." Justin reluctantly agreed, mostly because he was nervous about what his parents would say if he came home early.

The forthright approach he showed with his leaders, and his willingness to question everything, actually turned out to be the very qualities that made all the difference. On this program, students engaged in a variety of service projects within the community. Often students were encouraged to seek out their own places to add value. The group convened regularly in the evenings to share experiences and compare progress. Justin's observations were taken seriously, and his leaders—who were well-trained service veterans who had put a lot of thought into the philosophy behind their program and their approach with high school students—Generally had serious and insightful answers to most of his questions. By the second week he was running the evening meetings, and by the third week he had found his own service projects to work on. At the end of four weeks, he was not ready to go home.

You have these two or three wonderful blank spaces between when you begin high school and when you graduate, and you have to fill them in somehow. But where do you start? The first and most obvious question is "What do you want to do?" and the second is "How much time do you have to work with?" We'll deal with the question of cost in Chapter 4.

TIME

Let's start with time. There is the time that you will spend on your program, but there is also the time that you need to spend on research. If you are developing your own program arrangements, including dead ends, immunizations, and living arrangements, plan on spending a good three hours a week for most of your spring semester. Warning: no matter what kind of summer you are planning, start early. If you're designing your own, bear in mind that it's hard to take someone seriously when they cold call you two weeks before they are about to start. Also, your plan for the summer is likely to change a few times, depending upon the roadblocks and unexpected opportunities that you come across. If you are looking for an established program, you'll still need to give it some due diligence. There are lots of programs out there. Some programs will send a course leader to your house to discuss the program. You'll have to check to see when they are in town. The more selective programs will require essays, recommendations, and will have deadlines. The more popular programs may even fill up.

The next thing to look at is the amount of time you have available during the summer itself. What else needs to take place during the same summer? Do you need a job? Do you have to be back early for pre-season sports? Is the family taking a vacation together in June? Once you've blocked out those immovable objects in your summer schedule, you can focus on length of engagement. Two weeks, four weeks, six, ten? If possible, longer is better. You can always come home early, if absolutely necessary, but you can't turn a six-week program into an eight-week program, no matter how much you may want to. Since part of the goal is to push yourself in new ways, here's a rule of thumb: Pick the longest amount of time with which you are comfortable, and then add two weeks. The longer the engagement, the more you are likely to accomplish. This is especially true for language, arts, or service programs.

If you don't think that you can handle living in a tent, or showering every other day in a jury-rigged outdoor shower for six weeks, consider this: Alaska has some of the biggest, most aggressive, and most ruthless mosquito swarms in the world. There is no escaping them. In fifteen years of running programs for high school students in Alaska, however, Joanne Pinaire, the executive director of Visions, which runs an outdoor program in Alaska, has yet to receive a single evaluation that even mentions the word "mosquito."

Sound strange? Maybe. But what seems strange or exotic or terribly uncomfortable in the brochure will come to seem quite normal when it's part of your everyday life. In fact, this is part of why you go, to take on and live out an entirely different reality. While sleeping in a tent that is tethered to the side of a cliff is not for everyone, talk to people who have done it, and they are all likely to say the same thing: "Yeah, it was a little bit scary at first, but once you get used to it, it's no big deal." Discomfort—whether physical, cultural, or intellectual, is what *makes* the adventure—but once it fades into the background, you can pat yourself on the back because it means you have achieved something. It means that you have grown.

CHOOSING AN ACTIVITY

Now on to the more important question: What are you going to do? The good news is that it's pretty hard to go wrong. There is no such thing as a program designed to torture high school students with the goal of giving them a miserable summer. If you go with an open mind, no matter where you go or what you end up doing, there will be something to take from it or something to learn. On the other hand, you only have a few summers to play with, so it's worth your time to choose wisely. Let's start with the broad strokes. Here are two big categories:

- Are you going to chase an existing passion or delve more deeply into an existing skill?

- Are you going to try something new, try on a different life for size, or just do something you've never done before?

CHASING YOUR PASSION

In the first category you take an existing passion or skill and push it further by immersing yourself in it completely. A typical school day can make you feel intensely schizophrenic. In one day you are working on math, history, playing sports, and writing English papers, with maybe some time left over to see your friends. While this approach keeps you on your toes and gives you only short doses of subjects that you may not like, it is difficult to accomplish really intensive work in the subjects that you *do* like. Total concentration or a complete focus brings its own unique intellectual rewards.

Forget about the stuff that you don't like. Dedicate all of your time to the things that you like best. Unless it is something that you eventually base a career around, these next few summers may be the only time in your life when you get to do this. You enrich your knowledge and add to your skills, and you will also surprise yourself with what you can accomplish.

You may have lots of existing passions, or you may have only one or two. If you can't think of any, that doesn't mean that they're not there. They may simply be embedded in some other activities. Can you name one thing that you've done in the last week, month, or year, during which you completely lost track of time? You started doing it, and before you knew it, the sun had gone down, it was three hours later, and you were late for dinner. That's a pretty good sign that you were intensely engaged in that activity. If you hated it, you'd have been checking your watch every ten minutes. What are your hobbies? What kind of elective classes look interesting to you in school? If you were designing your own school, what would every student be allowed to do or be required to do? Start paying attention to the things that make you happy, the accomplishments of which you are most proud, and the activities you'd rather be doing when you're doing the ones you don't like. When it comes time to design a summer plan, this is a good place to start.

The same holds true for a skill that you'd like to develop. What are some nonacademic activities that you enjoy that are based upon a particular talent or body of knowledge? Is it acting, playing the clarinet, writing, or drawing? Do you read books about horses? Dogs? Sailing captains? Let's say that an activity that you particularly enjoy is baby-sitting. Basically, you do it for the money, but you also actually like it. You're also pretty good at it and the families for whom you work trust you with their children, their house, and their pets for extended periods of time. If this is the case, perhaps you should look at some service programs in which you are working with children. There are hundreds of these, some probably in your own town, some around the United States, and many around the world. You can combine travel, language study, and community service with a skill that you already enjoy and at which you already excel.

You can dedicate your summers to things that you love. The key is to make sure that you are actively involved. Use the summer as an opportunity to take your skill or passion further than you could during the school year or further than you ever believed that you could at any time of the year. If you love to climb mountains, find a bigger one to climb. Commit to a program or activity that will force you down this road.

NEW TERRITORY

The second route is to try something new and different. You are challenging yourself by engaging in an activity that you've never done before. You are test-driving hobbies, potential careers, or just things that you've always thought looked fun. This approach is so wide open that it helps to ask yourself a few questions:

Physical
What is my physical comfort level? Do I want to live in a tent, in a dorm, in a house? Do I want to eat foods I've never heard of, or do I want three square meals from a cafeteria? Is part of the adventure to test myself physically, or is that not what I'm after?

Cultural
What makes it an adventure? Are the exchange students at school fascinating, or just plain weird? Do you secretly like to observe different groups of students at school, like a cultural anthropologist, fascinated by what makes them, them? Are you comfortable with a wide range of people in a diverse set of situations? You can see another country through the window of a bus and the pages of a museum catalog, or you can live in their homes, eat their food, and find out what constitutes a big night out in rural Grenada. Is this the kind of adventure you want?

Intellectual
Not all adventures take place on white water canoe trips or small jungle villages. Adventures can take place in the mind as well. You could spend your summer playing chamber music, designing clothes, learning to draw nature, counting seaweed species in tidal areas, or cataloging pottery in a museum. Is it an intellectual adventure that you're after? Will your summer be made special by delving deeply into a subject or an indoor skill, rather than an exotic locale or activity?

There is one very important thing to keep in mind here. The point is adventure. The point is to challenge yourself. The point is to stretch yourself in new ways, develop new muscles and appreciations. You want to jump in the deep end, but it is important that it is either a deeper deep end than you've jumped in before, or a different one.

Intellectual vs. cultural vs. physical are very different types of adventures. It is important for you to identify the type of adventure you want, but ruling out bungee-jumping doesn't necessarily mean playing it safe.

A NOTE ON SERVICE PROGRAMS

Community service programs are becoming increasingly popular as a summer option. One reason is that more and more schools, both high schools and colleges, are requiring students to dedicate some time to community service. But why is community service so important to college admissions officers?

The answer is that community service is not necessarily important to college admissions officers at all, but interesting, mature, motivated, aware students are. Often the two go hand in hand. As we already know, pleasing some theoretical Admissions Office is not a good reason to commit one of your precious summers to a service adventure. But there are some very compelling reasons to spend a summer working on behalf of another community.

The difference between studying another culture in school and actually living in that culture is similar to the difference between reading about a dish in a cookbook and actually eating it. Service is a readily available way for students to gain firsthand knowledge of what it is like to live in a place very different from their own, with people very different from them, in a community with a culture and values that are different from the ones to which they are accustomed. This is an education second to none, and the only way to find it is to do it. There is no substitute for cultural immersion. It is one of the very best reasons to go.

Of course, community service is also about giving. Spending an extended period of time in a scenario in which you are there specifically to give, rather than to take, can be a profound shift in perspective for many students. The act of giving is often a very new experience for teenagers. For most of us, it is a strange new skill that must be learned. Once students get it in their blood, however, it usually stays. People respond to you in different ways. Opportunities come up that would not have otherwise, and you make wonderful friendships.

A NOTE ON ACADEMIC PROGRAMS

Nearly every college campus in the country plays host to some kind of academic enrichment program over the summer. It is a great way for schools to generate revenue from their facilities during the off-season. These programs range from super-challenging to remedial. Many advertise "college-level work" and may even be taught by college professors.

Here's a myth that a lot of high school students buy into: Succeeding at a summer academic program at the school in which you would eventually like to enroll will help you get in. Not true. If you are a freshman or a sophomore, it's too early to even be choosing a school, and so much will have gone on between the time you finish your summer program and the time you apply to college that your performance in the program is not going to have much relevance. If you are a junior and you blew it in chemistry, doing better the second time around during the summer may help, but it won't vault you to the top of the class, nor will it change your GPA on your official transcript, which is the most important component of any college application.

In many cases, the summer institutes on college campuses are, in fact, third-party contractors that do nothing but rent space from the school and are not affiliated in any other way. The grades that you receive will be seen by college admissions folks only if you send them. They may help, but even straight A's does not make acceptance into the same school automatic. On the upside, if your grades in the program are terrible, they're unlikely to hurt your chances of acceptance.

Some students truly have a passion for literature, writing, or maybe even advanced applied mathematics (hard to believe, but true). If nothing would make you happier than spending a summer in a writing workshop or eating organic chemistry formulas for lunch, then these are the programs for you. Following a personal passion as far as it may lead is an ideal use for any summer (any winter, weekend, or any other block of time for just about any person anywhere, for that matter). If you are doing it for you, then it is right.

If you are doing it for any other reason, college admissions for example, you might want to think again. You may have only one or two magic beans left to spend: do you really want to spend them on more academics? You have nine months of school a year to hone your writing, math, reading, or science skills. In fact, for most of the year, you don't have any choice. In the summer there are no rules or requirements. Make a list of everything that you think that you "should" do and throw it out the window. If you were on a strict diet of green vegetables and brown rice for three months and you were given one day to splurge and eat anything that you want, would you order more broccoli? Summer is the same way. Use it to do what you want, or better yet, to find out what you want.

College admissions officers tell us over and over again that you shouldn't do things you think they want you to do; do the things that *you* want to do. They want to see students with genuine interests, real enthusiasm, and lots of initiative. They don't want to see students who are going to burn out before they turn nineteen, or students who are blindly following the all-too-generic recipe for college admissions that seems to determine so many of the actions of college-bound high school students today.

Many students choose academic summer programs in order to generate college credit. They hope to check off a few pre-med requirements, to get a head start on some language requirements, or simply to amass enough credits to graduate college early. Whoa! Where's the fire? What's the rush? You're going to miss high school when it's gone, you're going to miss college when it's gone, and unlike college and high school, the "real world" doesn't have three months of summer vacation built in. Neither college, nor your post-college future, is going anywhere. They are both right there where they've always been. If you need to start school in January rather than in September because you chose to spend three months on a ship at sea rather than taking that SAT course, that's okay. It may help you get into a better school than you might have had you made more traditional choices. What it will do for sure is make you a more interesting person, with a better sense of your own strengths, weaknesses, and values.

A NOTE TO PARENTS ON PUSHING

We asked a dozen summer program directors to tell us where parents go right and where they can go wrong in this process. One thing that emerged was a very fine line between encouraging their children to commit to a program that they will ultimately love and pushing them to commit to a program that does not fit. Unfortunately, but not unexpectedly, there are no simple formulas to follow; and, of course, there are exceptions to every rule. Here are a few things to think about along the way:

Your dreams or his?
For many parents, these kinds of opportunities just didn't exist when they were growing up. In fact, lots of adults wouldn't mind being sixteen again, just to get to go on one of these trips. But programs that look exciting to you may not appear the same way to your kid. One place where parents go wrong is projecting their enthusiasm for a particular opportunity onto their child.

"What's your most popular program? I'll take that one."
Let's face it: if you left everything up to your teenager, there are a lot of things, like the laundry, that would never get done. Still, the beauty of summer is choice. You can pick a great program, but that doesn't mean that it is a great program for your son or daughter. When you are with a small group in unusual circumstances, having a positive attitude can be critical. Students are far more likely to show up ready to engage if they feel as though they have picked the program. Of course, this doesn't mean that you can't drop brochures on their desk, give them deadlines, or mandate that they will not be spending the summer on the couch in front of the TV. The bottom line is, do what you need to do to make sure the legwork gets done, but the more involved in the choice your child is, the better.

Step back and let engagement happen.
Most students will find a way to let you know that they are ready for something different. Sooner or later they all seem to feel like they're a little bit too big for their

container. They may not be able to describe it exactly, but there's a hunger for adventure, something different, something challenging, something new. Once they let you know, push them to explore their options, let them know what your comfort barriers are, and feel free to challenge them to dig deeper, but let them do the digging. Even if it is a simple as calling to schedule the appointment or to request the brochure, let them do the legwork. The more they do, the more programs they will find, and the more engaged they will become. The more engaged they are, the more value they are likely to get from their summer. Ultimately, this sense of ownership is an important step on their road to independence. Once again, feel free to give them deadlines, but, as problems arise—and they will—let them do the solving. You may be surprised at how much ingenuity and effort they can muster when needed.

Send them away and hope they come back fixed.

Summer programs are not therapy. Do not send your son or daughter away and expect them to come back fixed. A good program will certainly expand a student's horizons, but it won't change a personality. If your child needs discipline, send them somewhere that specializes in discipline. The same is true for emotional problems, weight loss, smoking, social problems, etc. Students who can't manage these issues in school are not likely to do any better on a wilderness hike. You may be setting them up for failure if you are expecting things that the program is not designed to deliver. Programs can work with an enormous range of issues from diabetes to Tourette's Syndrome, but you must be upfront with the programs and realistic with your own expectations. A failure to do so is not fair to your child, the other students on the program, or the program itself.

Likewise, all good programs take their mission seriously, whether it's service, research, or wilderness adventure. If you are looking for a parking place for your teenager over the summer, there are plenty of programs that will fit that bill. Students can kayak, bike, visit European capitals, prepare for the SATs, you name it. Good programs will take the time to explain their mission to you. Listen. Read the material. Talk to the parents of alumni. They will tell you. Most of all, be honest with yourself and your child about what you both want from a summer.

Counting on a specific result

The folks who lead students on these learning journeys often talk about "being there when the lights go on." This is the moment when the student, who has left his comfort zone and slipped into his learning zone, drops some of his reserve and engages emotionally with the program activities. It will happen at a different pace and for different reasons for just about every student. For some students, it may not happen until they are confronted with personal challenges years later and suddenly realize that they are capable of facing these challenges because of the hurdles they overcame while involved in an especially challenging summer program.

This moment, this transition, makes up much of the core lasting value of these summers. This is why people who run summer programs for high school students see themselves as educators, not as camp directors, baby-sitters, or tour guides. If this moment occurs, it is not important whether the student played in the master class orchestra or completed the community center they were building.

Many participants fixate on a particular result or expectation. But fixating on that goal may blind students or parents to the less visible, but infinitely more valuable, lessons of adaptation, different cultural pace, and finding value or worth in the face of adversity.

Some people fixate on personal expectations. They may be looking for community service credit, resume building, weight loss, change of peer group, or an intellectual awakening. Unless one of these things is a stated primary objective of the program, measuring a program's success against these objectives is using the wrong yard-stick.

Don't get derailed.

You'll run into some resistance along the way. It might come form your son or daughter: "But I won't know anyone"; "I don't know if I can do it"; "I'd rather stay home with my friends". Or it might come from you. The cost appears prohibitive; you may be planning a family vacation for the middle of the summer, or you know that your child has worked his or her tail off in school all year and you'd like him or her to have a chance to relax for a while. These are all legitimate objections, but when you see the spark in your child when he or she comes home, you will know that you made the right choice. Don't get derailed. Let your child finish what he or she started. It's a good habit to develop.

In short

As a parent, your comfort level is important, too. Your expectations need to be met as well. Think about the kinds of experiences you would like your child to have. Talk to him or her about the kinds of things that he or she would like to do. If you feel like you need to get the ball rolling, do your due diligence and find a wide selection of programs with which you are comfortable. Ask questions about length of time, cost, degree of supervision, program goals, philosophy, leader training, communication policy, etc. Once you have a shorter list of programs that work for you, present it to your children and let them choose. Better yet, take them to a summer program fair and turn them loose. You'd be surprised at what they come back with. They might go in reluctantly, but chances are that they'll come out with some ideas. Most high school students are ready for some adventure. The process of helping your child identify his interests and match them with the appropriate summer program is good practice for the process you'll go through when choosing a college. It's just a question of degree.

JUST ENGAGE

This is really the number-one golden rule. Do something. Do it with an open mind and a free spirit. Don't hold back or play it safe. Give yourself to the experience. Volunteer, ask questions, forge relationships. This is how we learn and what makes the difference between an interesting summer activity and an experience that will change your life.

Westcoast Connection

Chapter 4

Evaluating a Program

ASSESSING QUALITY

Let's start with the basics.

COST

This includes not only the price of the program, but also may include travel, equipment, insurance, medical checkups, visas, and spending money. The program should be able to provide a comprehensive list of all costs you might incur. Remember also that many programs provide scholarships. Even those that don't will often find a way to help really enthusiastic students participate in the program. If cost is out of your parents' range, don't be afraid to put some of the responsibility on yourself. You also have earning power. And if you're paying for most or part of the program with the money you've earned yourself through a part-time job, you are more likely to choose one wisely and put forward your best effort to get the most out of it while you're there.

TIME

Summers can be busy. Family vacations may already be planned, an SAT course may already be scheduled, and pre-season training may be looming, but whenever possible, longer is better. As we said before, a two-week program will not have the same impact as a two-month program. You must set your own priorities, but carve out as much time for this experience as possible. Also, start the process early. There is a lot of research to be done, and a lot of discussions to be had. If you leave it to the last minute, you may limit your options. "How long is the program?" and "When does it start?" are key questions when planning your summer. Many programs will have multiple sessions. Know your options as far as timing goes.

PROGRAM REQUIREMENTS

Some programs are highly selective. They will require essays and references. This will take some legwork. Other programs have physical requirements. You may need to schedule a physical or get some shots. This will also take some time. Other programs may require a level of physical fitness or academic preparation.

CURRICULUM

What are the main activities? Are students sailing, hiking, researching, playing an instrument, doing community service, or some combination of the above? How intensive is it? Can a student opt out of activities? If kayaking is the main focus, what are the secondary activities? Camping? Natural history? Leadership skills?

DRUG/ALCOHOL/SMOKING POLICY

What is it? This is especially important for programs that are far away and/or in another country. Drinking is hard to police in places with no underage drinking laws, but with the right staff, despite the surroundings, these rules can be enforced. Most programs have a zero tolerance policy, but will pass to parents the extra cost of sending a kid home early. Also, a zero tolerance policy may exist on paper, but how aggressively it is enforced can vary considerably. Ask around, and you can find out the word on the street regarding how serious a program is about their "rules."

SAFETY

Adventure programs in particular like to call it "risk management." Does a program subcontract out the adventure portions of their trips? This can be a good thing or a bad thing, but either way you want to know. For example, if they have trained professionals leading their SCUBA diving and that subcontracted company has a good reputation, this is probably better than your summer staff teaching the diving. However, if it is a basic hike and the staff is taking the day off and they have hired other people to hike with the group, this is probably not ideal, as the hired help doesn't know the students as well. No matter what program you are looking at, at least one program staff person should always be with the participants.

Safety, therefore, will rely on the training, experience, and judgment of the staff. Ask programs how they manage risk. Can they evacuate a student if necessary? Safety can also be an issue on academic programs, especially ones based in major cities. Are students supervised 24/7? Is the place they are staying secure? How many adults per student are on duty at night? Can students go into town alone? Ask as many questions as you need to feel comfortable, but do not expect perfect guarantees. Whether at home or abroad, there will always be some risk.

Communication Policy

What is it? Can parents of participants call their children and vice versa? Can parents send care packages? Will participants receive mail? Can they send mail? Can they check e-mail? How often? Depending upon the program, these answers may vary widely. Programs that try to minimize their participants' contact with their parents are not bad; they are just trying to help the kids have a purer experience. So as a parent you need to step back and check your need to talk to your kid.

The Intangibles

Programs come in so many shapes and sizes that comparing them can get complicated. Once you've covered the basics, how do you separate the truly meaningful programs from those that are just average? It is useful to develop a set of questions to ask each of the programs. Some will be designed to elicit precise responses that will allow you to compare similar attributes of very different programs. Other questions are designed simply to stimulate conversation. With good questions you should be able to asses the differences between programs with a real mission and those that simply deliver a range of exciting activities to a large number of students.

Here are some questions you should ask any summer program director prior to signing up with them. Any program worth your money and time should have thorough, sensible answers to these questions:

1. **What is the mission of your company or program?** This is a very important question. The best programs are almost always run by people who see themselves as educators rather than tour guides or camp counselors. Look for programs with a clear set of values and a concise, well-articulated mission statement. At a good program, this mission should be clear to just about anyone who asks for it. You shouldn't need them to translate it for you.

2. **What is your staff return rate?** The single largest factor in the quality of a participant's experience is the staff. The people on staff are the ones who will be spending the most time with the participants and who make all of the difference. Good programs tend to attract people who are motivated by the mission and quality of the company. If they are able to achieve that mission and maintain that quality, the leaders will love their job and usually stick around for a few summers. Generally, the more they've done it, the better they get. Imagine how much easier it is to guarantee the quality of the experience when 70 percent of the leader corps has done it all before. If 70 percent of the leaders are brand-new, do you really know what you're getting?

3. **What percentage of the participants completes your program?** Completion rates can vary from year to year or from program to program for a variety of reasons, some good and some bad. If a large number of participants came home early (1 to 5 percent is reasonable) from last year's program, it is fair to ask why. Did the program do a poor job setting expectations? Was the program not well designed? Was it too

hard? Too easy? Did they do a poor job selecting the students? Did they do a poor job managing them? Do a lot of students get sent home for alcohol, drugs, or smoking? On a good program, there should be minimal downtime, and students should be stretched enough that there is little time, opportunity, or need to go looking for ways to make things more interesting. Students should have known the physical, intellectual, and cultural rigors going in, but a good program will help students find ways to overcome those challenges when they come up.

4. **How do you spend your budget?** A program may or may not share exact numbers with you, but you can still get an inkling of their values depending on how they answer this question. What percentage of the tuition is being spent on the student experience (staff-to-student ratio, equipment, travel, materials, etc.), versus overhead, or risk-management or marketing? Look for programs that invest in leader training, in-field experience, and a low student-to-staff ratio, as opposed to programs that use third-party contractors, send out really large groups, or that spend more on their brochures than their equipment.

5. **Are students allowed to bring friends?** Programs that are more concerned with revenue than with quality will want all of the enrollments that they can possibly get. Programs where learning takes place by getting students out of their comfort zone, on the other hand, know that joining with friends tends to limit personal growth. Students traveling in a pack are less likely to go out on an emotional limb and forge new relationships. Most good adventure or service programs will limit the number friends a participant can bring to one or two, maximum.

6. **Do you use third-party contractors?** If your program is in Colorado and part of the experience includes white-water rafting, there are hundreds of outfits around the major rivers that will take groups from point A, through some rapids, to point B. Often it is more cost effective for a program to drop their kids off at point A, hand them over to a local outfit that has the equipment and the expertise, and pick them back up again at point B. This is not necessarily dangerous and may have no impact on the quality of the experience, but it may also be a tip-off that a program is making cost-based decisions where quality is concerned. Quality programs will be reluctant to give up their time to a third party.

7. **What hasn't worked for you in the past, and what have you done to fix it?** Has the program become formulaic, or are they always looking for ways to improve? Are they actively responding to student, parent, and leader feedback? The most common factors that programs tend to adjust are program length and group size. Many programs have been forced to shorten their duration to accommodate growing pre-season athletics, additional academic programs, and family vacations. This is problematic for programs that really seek to have an impact on students' lives. Can it be done in three weeks? How about eighteen days? The size of the group is another experimental factor. Larger groups carry a higher profit for the program, but more challenging dynamics. Groups that are too small can become dominated by a few students, and/or isolate others. How many leaders are cost-effective, but also provide

adequate supervision? All programs struggle with these questions, and the ideal solutions will vary widely depending on the demands of the program. Nevertheless, these questions will have a dramatic effect on the quality of the experience. How programs solve them, therefore, is worth your attention.

8. **What makes your program special?** When comparing programs with similar features, your decision will likely rest on those things that make one program stand out. As a question, this should be easy for any program director to answer. As a point of comparison when you're making your own decision, however, it might make a big difference.

9. **Can I talk to past students and parents?** This is a must. In fact, it may be the most important question on the list. Not only should you be asking this question, but when they give you names, call them. Nobody is going to give out a bad reference, so the thing to look for is the size of the list, their willingness to send it, and current names. Good programs should be able to give you at least twenty names, at least, from recent programs. Any less than that and you have to wonder why. It is also instructive to look for families who have sent multiple kids. Another thing to remember is that the people on the reference list are there because they will say that they had a good time, so you need to tease out the good times from the extraordinary experiences. To do this you need to be intelligent about the questions that you ask. Vague questions get vague or inconclusive answers.

TALKING TO REFERENCES

Expect to call a number of a program's references. Ask to speak to both the parents and the children. Be prepared with some appropriate questions. Here are some "Do's" and some "Don'ts" you should follow when talking to these references:

*Don't

Was it fun? This is an extremely relative term and may not be the point of the program. Getting up at 4 A.M. for three hours of deck watch followed by three hours of deck mopping is not fun, but that doesn't mean that it wasn't an intensely rewarding summer.

*Don't

Was it hard? Same as above. If it was not hard, is that good or bad? Hard is generally good because students will find the most value when they are stretched, but too hard can be demoralizing.

∗Do

Would you do it again? Would you recommend it to a friend? This should account for the students who found it to be a challenging summer that they absolutely loved.

∗Do

Did you feel challenged? "Challenged" gets to the heart of the kind of "hard" that is good for personal growth. Challenging goes hand in hand with learning; therefore, it is almost always part of any good program.

∗Do

Did the staff engage you? The quality of the staff makes all the difference. They are more than just supervisors, more than just guides, and more than just leaders. As energy ebbs and flows along with challenge and downtime, it is critical that they know how to handle a group of teenagers.

∗Do

Was there a lot of downtime? A rule of thumb for staff leaders is that downtime is an invitation for trouble. It's okay for students to have some personal time to walk into town or to write in their journals; but if there is too much downtime, students will find a way to fill in that time, and you might not like what they find.

∗Do

What project did you work on, and what was the level of community involvement? (For service projects.) It is important that students on service programs feel like the work they are doing is making a difference. Work that makes a difference is rewarding; work that doesn't is just work. If the community values the project, you can bet that they'll be involved. It's also a lot more interesting as a participant if you are working alongside someone from a completely different culture. You want to hear stories about students floundering through with their tenth-grade Spanish in order to mix cement or build a wall.

∗Do

Did you feel like your child was in safe hands? (When parents talk to other parents.) You might not need the details, but did the people running the program give you the impression that they were professional, knowledgeable, reliable, and prudent? When parents and children are 4,000 miles apart, surprises are not necessarily a good thing. If you are talking to someone who has been through it all before, he or she should have a strong impression of the relative professionalism of the outfit.

BAD MATCHES

The summer program market is tough and getting tougher. (It is tough if you are in the business; if not, then it is just full of choices.) Whether you are an academic program, a study abroad program, a service program, or a summer sailing camp, you've got competition. Unless you have a really large marketing budget (most don't), it would be very difficult to survive if your students didn't come home happy. Happy, howeer

Happy, however, is a relative term. Certainly some programs are better at what they do than others. There may be differences in staff training, housing, food, program design, etc. For alternative programs that really seek to make a difference in students' lives, the comment that they most dread is, "It was okay." When asked how their summer went, they want students to get all choked up and say, "It was the greatest six weeks of my life!" If a student says that their program was just "okay," there are three possible reasons why.

The first reason is that the program truly was not very inspiring. Really good programs manage to produce emotional responses with remarkable consistency. Even middle-of-the-road programs have their happy students. Middle-of-the-road might be what some students want.

The second reason may be the student. Even the best programs can't get through to all students, and not all students will take advantage of everything that a program has to offer. Whether it is meeting your peers, using your language skills, or taking advantage of elective weekend trips, some students are more comfortable sticking to home base, or more tentative when it comes to forging bonds with the other participants in the program. This may mean that they have just an "okay" summer, or it may mean that they have about as good a summer as they are ready for.

The single most likely reason for an "okay" summer, however, is a bad match. Bad matches come from bad communication. Here are common places where students go wrong:

1. No research or last-minute research.

It's the beginning of June and you suddenly realize that all of your friends are going away for the summer and you're stuck at home on the couch. You call a few friends, but their programs are closed, too expensive, or conflict with your schedule. You desperately pick the first thing that fits your schedule, only to find out that it's a Bible study camp for students with eating disorders. You meet some wonderful people, but it's not your cup of tea.

2. Your mom signed you up.

Hey, if you don't take the initiative and do the legwork, you're going to have to live with what you get. Your mom tells you that she will not put up with you sitting on the couch all summer. You fully intend to do some research, but somehow it slips your mind. So your mom calls her friend, who recommends a program that her niece went on in eighth grade ("She loved it!"). Your mom calls up the company running that particular program ("What's your most popular program? How much does it cost? Yeah, I'll take that one. Does he need mosquito repellant?"), checks the dates, and you are committed to making lanyard key chains and nameplates out of Popsicle sticks. Tough luck, pal. You called her bluff and lost.

3. Somebody isn't listening.

Your mom wants something that will look good for college, your dad found something about river rafting that he thinks sounds really cool (you don't), and you would prefer cheerleading camp. You end up with a choice between summer school and a two-week canoe trip in the Pine Barrens (you hate camping and hate canoes). Unless you speak up, the net result will be that you will not enjoy your summer and your parents will end up spending too much money on something that you don't even want. It is a hard balance really, because every summer there are hundreds of stories about kids who were encouraged to go on this or that trip by their parents and ended up loving it. Then there are the ones who went to Alaska to ice-fish because their fathers always wanted to go there and want to come visit them after the program. The trick in a situation like this is talking to your dad about why he thinks you should go to Alaska. If you can get to the bottom of that, then you can make a better decision about whether to listen to him.

4. You didn't read the brochure.

You picked the program with your parents because it fit your schedule, fit their price range, and it's in Jamaica, which sounds really cool. You knew that it involved community service, but you didn't realize that you would spend six weeks in Jamaica and never see a beach! There are fifteen of you in a three-bedroom place with very little running water in a not-so-nice section of town. It's not a bad program, but it's not at all what you were expecting. When you get a chance to call your parents, a week into the program, you tell them that life sucks. Now they're worried, but it's going to cost more money to get you home early, and everyone on the program knows that you want to leave. Suddenly it's all a mess. This could have been avoided had you read the material and talked to a few former program participants.

5. You're doing it because it will look good on your college application.

You got your SAT I out of the way as a junior so that you can take your SAT II Subject Tests in October and November. You figure that you can take AP chemistry and AP biology over the summer because you want to take those tests as soon as possible because you want to apply early. You pick a summer-school program on the campus of the school to which you want to apply. Everything goes as planned. You get good grades in your summer courses, you get home in time for pre-season, and you are ready to take up the reins as the editor of the school newspaper. Disaster doesn't strike until around Thanksgiving of your senior year. You didn't get in early to your first-choice school. Suddenly, you're crushed. You thought you could avoid writing all of those other applications because you figured you were a shoo-in at your first-choice school. Now you're committed to all of these extracurricular activities, you've got all of these tests to take, and you've go ten applications to fill out. You've got an ulcer and your hair is falling out and you're only seventeen. You put in all of this effort and made all of these sacrifices to get into the college of your choice, and then didn't. The college didn't think you were good enough, but what more could you possibly have done? Was it all wasted? Is life over? Was it all worth it?

When it comes time to pick a program, there are a few things that you can do to ensure that your experience is everything you hope it will be.

Start early.

Start your research early, start your discussions with your parents early, and start your own assessment of what you want early.

Look inside before you look outside.

Before you so much as turn on your computer, spend some time thinking about the things that make you happy. Forget about what you should do or ought to do. Forget about what your parents want you to do. What is it that you want for your summer? If you could do anything in the entire world, what would it be? This is a good place to start.

Once you've identified some programs that look good, read the literature, talk to the program directors, and talk to past participants.

You wouldn't dream of taking your biology final without studying. Why in the world would you commit to an entire summer program without doing the research? Your folks are a lot more likely to let you go on some wild adventure if you have done your homework and can show that you have thought it through and appreciate the program for more than the cool beaches.

Discuss it with your parents and be honest.

This will take some time. You might not see eye-to-eye with them at first, but you won't get anywhere if they don't agree. If it is important to you, hold your ground, but be prepared to do some more research and be ready to meet them halfway. This will take some time.

Once you've picked a program and committed to it, the research doesn't end.

Do you need special equipment? Do you need to be in shape? Is there anything that you can read about the place that you are going? The more you know and the more prepared you are, the easier you will adjust and the more you will get out of your summer.

Chapter 5

Being a Good Participant

You've spent a lot of time researching your summer, you've found just the right program, and your expectations are high. How do you ensure that you get the most out of the summer? What makes a good participant?

A good participant reads the program literature. This is number one. Program organizers want you to have a great summer. They've seen hundreds, even thousands of students before you, and they usually have a pretty good sense of what works. In many cases there will be things that you can do to prepare for your summer so that when you get there, you spend less time adjusting and more time engaging. Some of the things might seem minor or superfluous. That's not for you to decide. If a program has sent you suggestions, it is in your best interest to follow them. Eating yogurt for two weeks before you head for a third-world country may seem silly, but it just might save you from two days of extreme intestinal discomfort. (We don't know if it works, but the folks who do this for a living are much more likely to know.) Walking up and down the stairs with a backpack full of rocks might seem silly to you; after all, you're as fit as the next guy, right? Wrong. Tents, gear, and food for three weeks in the wilderness are heavy. You can spend your first week miserable because your ankles are sore and your shoulders hurt, or you can follow their advice and show up prepared. You only have three weeks on the trip; you might as well enjoy all three of them instead of just two. This extends to reading material as well. Books on natural history, current events, or cultural history may not be your cup of tea, but the more you know, the more you will understand. Cultural barriers are hard to overcome under the best of circumstances. Give yourself a leg up. It will help.

A good participant prepares herself for discomfort and newness. In fact, much of what you are paying for when you do an adventure program/community service program is to be put in new situations. Frankly, if you could do it yourself, why would you pay at all? The challenge for any good program is to find limits and push participants a little beyond them without overwhelming the students so that they shut down and stop learning.

It is remarkable how often students will understand this intellectually but then be blown away by the actual experience of a program.

Often the assimilation process follows predictable steps. First is wonder and excitement, then comes annoyance and resentment for the difference and difficulty of things, then comes the final appreciation of the difference. Efforts to continue living one's normal lifestyle in new territory subside and he or she gives in to the new culture and enjoys it for what it is.

Richard Webb of ProWorld Service Corps describes this process as two icebergs colliding. "I give all my students the Iceberg Lecture on their first day," he says. "I describe cultures as icebergs. And there you are, Student X floating along on your American iceberg. You see the Peruvian iceberg and a Peruvian on it. You wave, you take in the differences, you see cultural differences like language, food, dress, religion, personal space, etc., and you think you pretty much get it; you prepare yourself for this encounter as you float toward each other on your program. What you don't know is that 90 percent of the iceberg is underwater, as is 90 percent of culture. It is how people react to lateness or what inspires, offends, and attracts people. It is the sense of humor, it is what death feels like, it is so many things that you cannot see. And frankly, when those huge sections of iceberg collide below the surface, it can be quite a jolt for someone standing by the edge who wasn't expecting much, someone who thought they knew what they were looking at when they sized up the foreign culture."

A good participant begins with the end in mind. It's pretty safe to assume that by the end of the summer, you're going to be as close to some of the kids in your group as you are to your current best friends, or even closer. You will certainly know everyone in the group very well. Therefore, on the first day, treat everyone you meet as the friends they will soon become. This means be open, be honest, be friendly. If you are naturally shy in new situations or when meeting new people, a simple smile goes a long, long way. This does not mean be fake, or overly cheery. It just means being open to the natural process of getting to know people and making friends. It starts on day one. If you assume that it will all work out, it will all work out that much faster. It's also helpful to remember that everyone is in the same boat. If you're feeling it (nervous, awkward, etc.) they probably are as well.

Good participants seek out one-on-one relationships. No matter what kind of program you are going on, you are bound to come across some interesting people. It may be peers in the group, a leader, a teacher, or someone in the community. Whether you are in a classroom, on a boat, in a village, or on a mountainside, it is often easier to be one more person in the crowd. If this is your natural inclination, force yourself to engage people in conversation. It is these small (or large) efforts that lead to opportunities and enrichments. The really special and memorable moments in a summer experience are often the result of a small effort like this to extend oneself. Remember that you are only likely to go on this program once; it is important to make the most of it.

A good participant keeps a journal. Many of us are not natural journal writers. It's not that it is hard to find the time; it's just that there are often many things that you'd rather do with that time. It might be sleeping, packing, chatting with your new friends, reading, or writing postcards home. The ten to thirty minutes a day it takes to keep your journal up-to-date is well worth the effort. You use your camera to record activities, people, events, and views that are important to you. When you look back, your photos will help you remember those things that you captured on film. Think of your journal as a way of capturing those things that you can't record on film: things like conversations, feelings, impressions, fears, or moments of important insight. These are details that will fade from your memory over time but that are every bit as important as your snapshots. Journals are also useful for recording change over time. Things that seem big, unusual, uncomfortable, or weird at first may come to seem perfectly normal over the course of the summer. Chances are that you will remember them as you last saw them or thought of them, but you may not remember how they appeared at first.

A good program will encourage students to set goals at the start. And the people running it will check in with students throughout the program to see how they are doing in achieving those goals. A goal could be to hike up to a high point every morning. It could be to do regularly any of the aforementioned tasks (seeking out relationships, journaling, etc.). But goals will help you maximize your time and get more out of the program than is being offered to everyone. Any staff can push a group, but a good staff must always adhere to the axiom of functioning on the lowest threshold of the weakest link in the program. If you are not that person, then there is more for you. Sit down with a staff member early on and set some goals with him or her. Your leader may not let you go ice climbing alone, but who knows? Maybe you'll take on more responsibility, or maybe you'll just develop your own ideas in talking about it.

No matter what kind of summer you are in for, look for opportunities to give. Opportunities to give actually come up a hundred times a day, once you know how to look for them. There are lots of things that you can give and lots of different ways to do it. You might wait for someone who has fallen behind the group, offer to share a snack with someone who is hungry, volunteer for less popular jobs, sit next to someone who looks lonely, or offer to carry some extra gear when everyone (including you) is tired. Make a bet with yourself that you will find one extra way to give every day. You'd be amazed how simple actions like this can transform your whole summer. On many summer programs, groups are small and everyone is being challenged physically, mentally, and emotionally. Small gestures of generosity often have a huge impact, especially when everyone is feeling stressed or tired. One of the exciting things about summer programs is the opportunity they offer you to reinvent yourself. In high school, it's easy to feel trapped, typecast, pigeonholed, or labeled in some other way. Maybe that label fits you, but maybe it doesn't. When you sign on for a summer program, you instantly get a new group, new peers, a new place, and new activities. Take this opportunity to be consciously generous and then pay attention to how it affects your own satisfaction. We promise you won't regret it.

Chapter 6

Summer Programs and College Admissions

WHAT EXACTLY IS IT THAT YOU'RE APPLYING TO?

Let's start with where you are going: college. Just in case you weren't sure, college is the greatest invention ever. Think about it. You go to this beautiful place with hundreds of people your own age, and not only are you are encouraged to study whatever you want, the people there will also help you do it. Do you want to play sports? Great. They will give you a team, equipment, a coach, a field, competition, and even someone to pick up after you when you're done. That's not to mention fans, a newspaper to write about you, and often a trophy or two—or at least a sweatshirt. Would you prefer to be a DJ? Great. Here's a radio station. Go nuts. Looking for a boyfriend or girlfriend? Here are a couple thousand people your own age and no parents. If you would like to learn something, the college will find some of the leading experts in the country (maybe even the world) on your chosen subject and pay them to teach it to you. Did we mention the parties, the food, housing, plays, live music, trips to anything interesting that's close by, probably even your own museum on campus, too? Are you starting to get the picture?

Should you feel a bit overwhelmed, there are academic counselors, mental health centers, support groups, residential advisors, and a host of other support services. Although the truth is that you have to work pretty hard to get in any kind of serious trouble on a college campus.

College campuses are places of discovery, places where students can try out different personas, different politics, different social roles. You will be exposed to a whole range of academic subjects and teachers. Some you will love, and some you will hate. Discovering which is which is a large part of the point of college. The only thing standing between you and a great, enriching, rewarding, awakening college experience is you.

HOW TO NOT BE A VICTIM IN COLLEGE ADMISSIONS

Everyone wants to go to a "top" school, but what does that mean? Most people assume that it means that you're getting a "top" education. Regardless of what the diploma or the sticker on the back of your mom's car says, however, the quality of the education that you receive depends a hundred times more on you, the student, than it does on the school that you attend. There are some great professors at Harvard, but some really terrible ones, too. Likewise, there are some great professors at your local community college and some that are distinctly uninspiring. The question is not "Where are you going to go?" but "What are you going to do when you get there?" "Top" depends on you. Are you going to feel comfortable taking chances on unknown adventures, or is the environment going to be too overwhelming, forcing you to hide in your room and take only the safest paths?

There are a few things that you can do to optimize your college experience before you even get there. The most important thing is spending some time paying attention to the things that make you happy and the things that you hate. There are thousands of colleges in the U.S., and the vast majority of them would love to have you as a student. These colleges come in different shapes and sizes. Picking which one is right for you is the surest path to a quality education.

Students who spend a lot of time worrying about acceptance to a "top" school are making themselves victims of the system. You spend all of this time and effort doing things that you believe will make you look good in their eyes, praying that you will be accepted. Sounds more like some nightmare popularity contest than the road to your future. In many ways, chasing after a "name-brand" college is little different than placing too much importance on wearing the right "name-brand" clothes or living in the right zip code. It's got very little to do with education.

Why Picking the Right School is Important for You

Does your school have a football team? Is it a big deal? Do you have cheerleaders, night games, and pep rallies? Does everyone show up for the games? Is there a homecoming dance? How do you feel about the whole scene? Some people love it. It's a chance to get involved. They love the school spirit and ceremony. For some students, on the other hand, the whole thing makes them want to puke. At a lot of colleges, social life revolves around the football team (or the basketball team, or the baseball team) and every weekend everyone is at the game. If you don't like this scene, and you pick a college like this, you are likely to spend the fall of your freshman year sitting in your dorm room thinking about how much the place sucks. Is that a good way to take advantage of everything that college has to offer?

WHAT WE MEAN BY "THE RIGHT SCHOOL FOR YOU"

It is important to remember that college is not just a place where you will go to school for four years (or five, or six). It is also a place where you will *live* for four years. Here are some good questions to ask yourself:

Do you want to go somewhere close to home or as far away from your parents as you can possibly get?

Do you care about the weather? Some places are cold and rainy half the year, and some never have a day below 80 degrees.

Do you want a big school or a small school?

Do you want to go to school in a city, near a city, or in the middle of a cornfield somewhere?

When you think of college, do you think of a green lawn surrounded by old-looking buildings, some kid playing Frisbee, and a few big trees? That is available at many schools, but not all. If you are looking for a traditional campus, but you want to be in a city, there are only a few schools that you have to choose from.

What kind of distribution requirements can you handle? One factor that students frequently overlook is a college's distribution requirements. Almost every school has them. Distribution requirements are a prescribed number of courses in a certain set of subjects that a student *must* take in order to graduate. At some schools they are very specific. You might have to take at least two years of a foreign language, two years of U.S. history, one year of European history, courses covering at least three historical time periods outside of your major, and, maybe by the time you get to be a senior, you have time for an elective of your choice. At other schools they are less strict. You need to pass 42 credits and write a thesis and you're done. Hello basket-weaving, good-bye homework! Distribution requirements will have a major impact on your college experience and the direction of your education. If they're not important to you now, they will be later. They should also be important to your parents.

PERSONAL PREFERENCES

WHAT DO YOU LIKE? WHAT DO YOU HATE?

Is there a subject in school that you are taking now that you never want to see again for the rest of your life? For me it was math. I hated it then, and I still hate it now. When I applied to school I deliberately picked a school with very loose distribution requirements that allowed me to avoid math altogether. Now, although I can't balance my checkbook, I haven't seen a math class since my junior year of high school, and I couldn't be happier. If I was forced to take a math class, I probably would not have done too well. I'd have hated it, and my parents would not have been too pleased either.

Another interesting thing about my school is that all of the bathrooms on campus were coed. When you wandered into the bathroom in the morning, there was usually some guy taking a shower and a woman next to you brushing her teeth. For most students, this was no big deal. There was one student on my floor, however, who was not comfortable with this arrangement. She used to get up at four every morning to take a shower (of course she never realized that the people that you run into at 4 A.M. in the bathroom are much scarier than the people that you run into at 8 A.M.). Nevertheless, is it likely that you are going to be comfortable, happy, and in a position to take advantage of a tremendous range of possibilities if you have to get up at four every morning to take a shower? I don't think so. I think that she eventually dropped out or transferred. Had she visited the school before she decided, or had she spent as much time worrying about whether she liked the school as she spent worrying about whether the school liked her, she would have had a far more positive and productive college experience.

THE "HOT" SCHOOL

Another common trend is the "hot" school. When I lived in Miami, the hot school that year was Dartmouth College. Maybe it's because it's an often-overlooked Ivy League school, or perhaps it's because it was mentioned on *Friends*, but that year every student I spoke to wanted to go to Dartmouth. When this happens, a school's application pool can double and that school can be harder to get into than the hardest schools in the country. One of my students was determined to get in and dedicated most of her high school life to making it happen. The funny thing was that she grew up in Miami. She had never seen snow and she was a city girl. She loved Miami's cosmopolitan energy and diverse culture. Dartmouth is a great school, but it's not cosmopolitan, it's not in a warm place, and it's not particularly diverse when compared to Miami. She eventually got in, but last I heard she had transferred back to the University of Miami. Think about the time and energy she wasted by being seduced by what was "hot."

PICKING A COLLEGE

Spend the time leading up to your senior year paying attention to the things that make you happy, the times and situations where you feel the most alive and fulfilled. Write these down. Pay attention also to the things that make you miserable, or the times when you feel stressed, uncomfortable, or unhappy. Write these down as well. When it comes time to start picking colleges, start with the list of things that are important to you, and look for college that matches your criteria. Doing this has three benefits. The first is that you will find some great colleges, some that you may never even have heard of, but that are, in fact, great colleges for you. Many of these schools would love to have you as a student. The second benefit comes from knowing what you are looking for. If the school is highly selective, you can make a very compelling and well-informed case to the admissions committee for why you are a great match for the school. Matchmaking is really important to highly selective schools, and it will improve your chances of getting into them. The third benefit is that you have just exponentially increased the chances that you find college to be an exciting, enriching time of personal growth—in short, a good education.

Picture your first day at school. When you show up at the college of your choice (not the only options left to you after you've applied to twenty) you will see some students who are already disappointed. For some it is because it is their second-choice school. For other students it's because they have no idea what to expect and are feeling a bit lost and out of place. Many students will eventually take valuable semesters, even years, to discover all of the resources that the college has to offer. You, on the other hand, will arrive on campus excited about your choice, confident that you are in the right place, and with a list of things that you already know that you want to investigate. Those four years will go by pretty quickly. How would you prefer to start your college career?

Notice that the subject is college admissions, but we to this point we have only been talking about you. We haven't yet said a word about the admissions committee, or the requirements of the school. This is a shift in perspective. *You* have the power to choose. Once you realize that, the only hard part is finding out what you want. Once you know that, admissions becomes a lot easier. This approach puts you in the driver's seat and allows you to be as selective of the school as they are of you. It is worth your time to think hard and objectively about what you want out of college before you ever look at a school. The benefits of this approach are limitless.

COLLEGES LIKE SELECTIVE STUDENTS

It is to the college's advantage to have students jumping through hoops and worrying about their qualifications. It allows them to set the terms of the interaction. Wouldn't it be nice, however, if it were the other way around? It can be. In fact, it is up to you to be as selective of the colleges as they are of you. Not only does this increase the likelihood that you get accepted, but more important, it also increases the likelihood that you end up somewhere that is right for you.

HOW PICKING THE RIGHT SCHOOL HELPS THE SCHOOL (AND THEREFORE YOUR CHANCES OF BEING ACCEPTED)

The college admissions officer has two jobs. The first is to select qualified candidates for the school. Their second job is to ensure that all of the beds, especially for first-year students, are full. Empty beds mean lost revenue. When you look at the cost of four years of tuition, it's easy to see how important it is for a college to be sure that all of their beds are full. They do this by accepting more students than they have beds. A lot more. For a freshman class of 600, the Admissions Office might send out 1,800 acceptances, because they know that roughly a third of the students that they accept will eventually choose their college. Of that 1,800 they will accept a few superstars that they'd love to get their hands on, but for whom they know that they are probably a "safety school." They will accept a bunch of students who would be lucky to have been accepted because they can be fairly certain that these students will choose to attend. Most of the students who they accept, however, are in the middle range. They have applied to this college and a number of others like it.

With good selection and consistent relationship-building, a portion of these middle-range students will eventually attend. They always over-accept because they always lose a few students during the course of the first year. As a result, in the first few months of the first semester, you may hear about a few new students who will be packed three to a double room, or housed in the alumni house, perhaps in upperclassman housing, or maybe in a lounge somewhere. The school knows that a small percentage of their students will drop out or transfer in the first semester, and it's a lot harder to replace students (and replace tuition) after that first round of acceptance.

That's the Admissions Office's job. The reason that early decision works so well is that you agree to attend that school if you are accepted. Colleges love this because it guarantees that one bed will be filled. If you are within their qualified range, or have a particular skill for which the school is looking, and you can convince them that you are serious about attending their school, they will take you much more seriously as a candidate. It solves a problem for them by taking some of the guesswork out of their process. If September rolls around and a college does not have 100 percent of its incoming beds filled, the college is losing major revenue and the admissions officer is probably losing his or her job. They like to pick students that they know will attend.

Sooner or later, in one way or another, each school will ask you one central question, "Why do you want to attend our school?" Compare these two responses:

STUDENT A: "I want to go to your school because it's a really good school, and I really like the campus."

STUDENT B: "I wanted a school with a traditional campus, but I wanted to be near a major city. I want to stay on the East Coast, because my parents want me to be within driving distance. I love to play field hockey, but I'm not a superstar. I know that you're a good Division III school which means that I'll be challenged, but hopefully won't sit the bench. I think that I want to be an English major, but I'm not sure; I may want to go the political science route and go on to law school after college. I know that I don't have to declare my major with you until my junior year and both departments are strong. I'd like to live in my own apartment and I know that you have on-campus student apartments, but I know that if I live off-campus, the town is safe."

Student A's answer is not very impressive or distinct. There are lots of good schools with nice campuses. How do they know that you will pick theirs if you are accepted to more than one?

Student B's answer, on the other hand is impressive and happens all too infrequently. "Whoa!" thinks the college admissions officer while listening to Student B. "Here's a student who has done her research. She knows what she wants. She asked good questions. She's a great match for our school. Her scores are a bit low, but she seems to have her act together. I like her." Most importantly, you have convinced the admissions team that this is where you want to go and it is the only school that fits the bill. That works for them. You've gotten their attention and solved a problem for them.

WHAT ARE THEY REALLY LOOKING FOR?

While it is possible to put yourself in the driver's seat, and to be as selective of the schools as they are of you, it helps to understand what actually goes on in the admissions office. Imagine, for a moment, that you are an admissions officer. Actually, imagine that you are the president of a university, U. of You. You are in the process of selecting students for next year's freshman class. On Monday morning you come in to the office and find two folders on your desk. Student A and Student B.

Student A, you read, plays soccer, volleyball, and lacrosse. She is on the student counsel, a member of the French Club, and recently took up the cello. She is also the photo editor of the school newspaper and volunteers for community service once a month. In other words, she is a very well-rounded student.

You open up the second folder. Student B doesn't do any of those things. In fact, student B hates students who do all of those things. Although Student B has the same GPA and the same SAT scores as Student A, Student B prefers to spend as little time in school as possible. When she's not in school she rides horses. She loves to ride horses. She's been doing it since she was about seven, and, needless to say, she's gotten pretty good at it. She's got a whole closet full of big blue horse ribbons and tall gold trophies.

As the President of U. of You, which student would you choose? Student A, the super well-rounded student with the eye towards college admissions, or Student B, the nonacademic horse lover?

Now, let's assume that we are talking about those highly selective schools that actually take the time to get to know their applicants. Which one do you think actually has the best chance of getting into the university of her choice? You can answer this question by looking around at your own school. Do you know anybody, in your school, that is doing something right now simply because it will look good on his or her application? Student A just took up the cello in her junior year of high school. In the unlikely event that her cello actually makes it to college with her, what are the odds that she actually takes it out of its case? Remember, college is full of more pressures, opportunities, and activities than you can possibly anticipate while daydreaming in study hall.

What's obvious to you about Student A's choice of activities is just as obvious to the person reading her file. College Admissions officers are a pretty savvy bunch. They get pretty good at spotting people who have more things down as interests than the people possibly have hours in the day to pursue. Colleges much prefer to see a proven genuine interest, preferably an interest that has been taken to a higher level. They would rather see a team captain, an editor, a manager, an organizer, a state or national competitor, than simply a participant.

Many students (and some guidance counselors) believe that the well-rounded student, Student A, has the best chance at getting accepted to the college of her choice. To be sure, all of her activities will certainly help. They show her to be responsible, active in her school community, and relatively accomplished. These are all very good things and are viewed favorably by most admissions officers. The choices that she has made, because she is smart, hard-working, and doing her best to build an attractive college bound resume, are the same choices made by thousands of other students across the country in thousands of other high schools. In seeking to tailor "endeavors" to the imagined admissions requirements of the country's top schools, however, she has, in fact made herself look like all of the other students aiming for the same schools. Ironically, her efforts to make herself stand out have made her less likely to stand out from her peers across the country. Standing out is a big part of the game.

Student B will stand out. She will stand out the only way that any student can in the college bound herd. It will happen precisely because she is not trying to stand out, she is trying only to be herself. She has found a passion and has been pursuing it for years, not for the sake of an imagined admissions committee, but for her own satisfaction. As opposed to Student A's cello, what are the chances that Student B is going to suddenly drop the horseback riding after five years of national competition? Slim, right? Not only is she likely to continue to ride, but she will continue to improve and will bring all of that wealth of experience with her to the campus that she eventually chooses. A diverse student body is created by bringing together a diverse group of unique individuals, not by bringing together a homogeneous group of people, each with a diverse set of interests. Student B is a more attractive candidate because she has a proven track record of excellence, demonstrated interests and abilities, and because she offers up memorable portrait of a real person with real interests. She is not a generic laundry list of interests. She is an identifiable individual. That makes her stand out because it makes her memorable.

Remember that colleges are communities. Students on campus learn as much from each other as they do from their classes. If the school thinks that Student B is a loner, or hides in the stable with her horses and cannot contribute to her community, all of her hard-earned expertise won't count for much (unless the school has a pressing need to beef up their equestrian team). Interests need to be attached to values and values to self-knowledge. The head bone needs to be connected to the heart bone, and all of this needs to be presented convincingly on your application.

TELLING YOUR STORY

But what if you've made it halfway through high school and don't have a closet full of blue ribbons? What if, like most of us, you haven't yet identified your one true passion? What if you're not an all-star athlete and don't really want to join the Latin Club or try out for the school musical? It's okay. You are still you. There is no one else on the planet quite like you. All you have to do is find a way to communicate it.

Every student in the country will have a GPA somewhere between 1 and 4 (if it's not weighted). Every student will have an SAT score somewhere between 400 and 1600, or an ACT score somewhere between 1 and 36, but not every student does the same thing at three o'clock in the afternoon, on Thursday nights, or dreams about the same things during study hall. In many ways, the extracurricular section of your college application is the most important part because it is the only section that allows you to be you. Managing this section is a bit like dating. If you try to be someone you're not, you might have some short-term success, but in the long term, it will never work out. You will end up with someone who is attracted to the person you were trying to be, not the person you are. College is much the same way. If you try to be someone your not, first of all, it's not very convincing, and second of all, if you *are* unfortunately convincing, you run the very real risk of ending up somewhere that is not right for you.

SO HOW DO YOU DO IT?

Your three most important tools are your essays, your recommendations, and your summers. Pick a theme, a story, or a portrait that is unique to you. What makes you tick? What catches your eye when you're channel surfing? What web pages are saved under your favorites? What subjects in school, or out of school, actually hold your attention? This theme is the unique identifier that you want to project to the readers of your application. Once you've chosen it, you then want to weave it throughout your application. Show the reader where to find these things in your life. Playing soccer may not be a unique activity, but explaining why it has value to you probably is. The teamwork that you find on the soccer field may be similar to the satisfaction that you got putting together a project with two of your pals for your AP biology class. When it was done, it was actually kind of cool, and much better than you could have done on your own. You also happen to see how teamwork can be successful as a broader skill when you spent a summer building a community center in Peru. There the whole village had to work together to survive. Now, not only do you have your essay topic, but you can objectively support your story by getting recommendations from your coach, your team leader in Peru and your biology teacher. You've picked an identifiable trait that is a unique thread in your life, you've shown it to be objectively true, and you've shown it to be a motivating factor in your life not only academically, but in your choice of summer activities as well. Remember that there is one subject on which you are the world's leading expert. That subject is you.

ESSAYS

Many people believe that you have to write your essay with the skill of William Shakespeare about your life as the next Albert Einstein on the weekdays and your life as the next Mother Teresa on the weekends. Hey, if that happens to be an accurate description of your life, go for it. For the rest of us mortals, an essay like that is pure fiction and a very bad idea. It is virtually impossible, even for Hemingway, to write a convincing essay on a subject about which you know very little and care even less. Remember the time you tried to write an English paper on that book that you never quite finished? It didn't come out too well, did it? That same approach won't work any better when it comes to your college essays.

Fortunately, in this case, the easier approach is the better approach. Pick something that you care about, something that you like, something that you hate, something about which you have strong opinions, and then just show why it's important to you. If it happens to be the *Simpsons,* or the dangly thing in the back of your throat, or why Jackie Chan is so much cooler than Jet Li, so be it. If you care, it will be a better essay by definition. When you do this, the essay practically writes itself because you have lots to say on the subject. In fact, the hardest part of this approach is often sticking within the word limit. Better still, if it is really something about which you have strong personal opinions, you will end up with an essay that only you could have written. It will have your unique voice, and, because of this, it will have a far stronger chance of standing out from the crowd.

REFERENCES

You will be asked to submit references. The traditional approach is to get a reference from your English teacher, your math teacher, and your guidance counselor. Remember that you have only limited opportunities to tell your story your way. Make sure that you think hard about how you use them. You want to craft your story and then tell it in the most compelling way possible. If your story is about expanding your horizons, get a reference from someone who was around when your horizons were getting their makeover. It could be your Spanish teacher or your host family in Spain (translated by you). If your story is about being someone who organizes, gets involved, and makes things happen, get a reference from the faculty advisor to the fund-raiser that you ran, your boss at the ice-cream shop where you work, and the director of the camp where you are a counselor each summer. Colleges rely heavily upon these recommendations. Tens of thousands of students play soccer in high school. Many of them are the captains of their teams. How should a school know which team is good and which students display good leadership or a strong work ethic? They don't. They rely instead on the coach to tell them that a particular student is special. So choose wisely. Finding someone who can convincingly support your story, someone you know, will have far more impact than picking someone "important." One caveat: whomever you choose to ask to write a letter of recommendation for you should have a decent handle on the English language and be able to communicate efficiently through writing.

SO HOW DOES ALL THIS RELATE TO SUMMER PROGRAMS?

Summer programs are the ace up your sleeve. They are the true point of differentiation. One role of summer programs is to offer students the opportunity to build their story. If you tell colleges that you are passionate about Spanish and believe in community service, taking AP Spanish and volunteering once a month will support that story. How much more effective is it, however, to have spent a summer or two in South America engaged in some kind of community service? Talk about displaying commitment over time, showing initiative, and standing out from the crowd. Anyone can take high school Spanish. Far fewer students have put themselves in a position where they needed that Spanish to get food every day at the market.

Another way that summer programs are useful for admissions is that they can help you find the story that you want to tell. If you think that you might want to be a biology major, spending a summer counting seaweed varieties off the coast of Florida will not only support that assertion, but also it will help you to discover if it is true or not. Think of all of the time and effort you could save. If you have tried the life of a biologist on for size, and it fits, you can pick a college with a strong program, arrive on campus with a focused mission, and get a jump start on a long and glorious career. You may find that field biology is not really your thing. You can now say that you've tried it and learned something about yourself in the process, but you can save yourself the pain of taking lots of genetics and statistics courses.

If you really have no idea what your "story" is; if picking a major sounds to you about as random as picking a number out of a hat; if you don't necessarily have a burning desire to be a biologist, learn Spanish, or save the world from poverty; then go anyway. Pick a program that looks interesting, and go for it. The simple process of choosing, engaging, taking action, plunging into something new, will teach you something. It's tough to predict what that something is now, but we can guarantee that you'll feel different when you come back. When it comes to college admissions, you'll have a few more experiences to choose from, a slightly more unique perspective, and perhaps a bit more insight into yourself, and none of these is ever a bad thing.

Do not, however, pick a program that you think the admissions committee might like. You don't know them, and they don't care. They are looking for interesting students, which doesn't automatically mean students who spent two weeks in Bali digging trenches. Interesting students don't care what some crusty old admissions dean wants. Interesting students are too busy living life to waste time on activities just because they will "look good on an application." Besides, your summers are too precious to waste on something that is not going to engage your own personal passions. Do it for you, not for them.

HOW TO DESCRIBE YOUR SUMMER ON YOUR APPLICATION

If the greatest summer in the world falls in a forest and there is no one around to hear it, it won't help you get into college. You have to tell your story. Here are the three golden rules for putting your experience into context:

1. Keep it real.

   What was the first story you told your parents? How about your friends? When you close your eyes and picture your summer, what is the first thing to come to mind? This is where you start. What did it mean to *you*? What made it special for *you*? Forget about what you are supposed to have learned. Forget about what might sound impressive. Forget about trying to make it sound more dramatic or more essay-worthy than it actually was. The people reading the essay want to know about you. Honestly. They're not interested in hearing what you think they want to hear. They get plenty of that. Talk about the aspects of your summer that you think you will never forget, no matter how trivial or dull they may sound. It could be the best thing about the summer, the worst, or the scariest. This makes it easier because you could probably talk about these things all day. But it also ensures that your essay will be unique and believable because it's true and there's no one quite like you.

2. Do not talk about how privileged you are to have had the opportunity to go do whatever it is that you did.

   They don't care. They don't reward privilege. They read twenty essays every day about how lucky we are here in America, and how we don't realize how much we have, and how you have learned to appreciate the SUV in your driveway since seeing how people live elsewhere. If you were on an academic program, do not write about the sense of satisfaction you got from doing more chemistry. They won't buy it.

If you went to a program on their campus, don't tell them what a wonderful school they have. They know more about the place than you do. They're not children or the culture police. They don't need a history lesson. Talk about you.

3. Find a way to relate your experiences over the summer to your day-to-day life.

History seems a lot more interesting since you worked on some building originally built by the Romans. You now can appreciate how advanced they were. You had to hike over a ridge for fifteen miles with a full pack. You didn't think that you could do it, but you had no choice. Now you'll think twice about complaining when you are faced with a challenge like writing a ten-page paper. Or your favorite word used to be "awesome." You used to apply it to everything, but ever since seeing a glacier up close, you now know what it really means. You might see a great outfit in the store, but it doesn't even come close to qualifying as awesome. You get the picture. Talk about you, your daily life, and the impact of your summer experience.

A NOTE ON EXPLAINING PROGRAMS

If your summer was significant, whether you write your essay about it or not, admissions folks need to know about it. If it is a large mainstream program, they are probably familiar with it and you don't have to worry. Just say that you completed the program, when, and where, and that should be enough. If the program was smaller or more out of the way, however, they may need more information.

Be careful, however, these folks are very busy and have a lot to read. We're talking hundreds of essays, hundreds of recommendations, and hundreds of applications. The last thing they need is more reading material. If they will accept a brochure, send them that. If not, it is ok to include a brief description of the program, but keep it brief. Brief means one to two paragraphs, nothing more.

If your summer experience was so unusual or so central to your application that you need more than a paragraph or two to explain it, you've got yourself an essay topic. That's where it belongs.

Chapter 7

Reentry

REENTRY FOR PARENTS

It's been six weeks since she left. You had one phone call in which she said that she was tired, the people were all nice, and she had to go. You got one postcard in which she said that she was nervous about "hiking the pass" the next day. That's it. You've read all about the program and talked to some alums and their parents. Your hopes are high for a great summer for your daughter. You can't wait to hear all about it. Be forewarned. Homecoming may not be what you expect.

Your child has just returned from a very intense experience amongst some very passionate people. When she says, "Mom, you wouldn't understand," she's probably right. Reentry may not be easy. For some students, the stories will start spilling out as soon as they get in the car. For others, it might take a little longer. A shift in perspective, a change in values, no matter how minute (or major) will automatically provoke a host of questions. They left a life they never questioned, they changed, and they returned with fresh eyes. Nothing will look the same.

We've heard lots of stories. We've heard about lots of students that insisted on sleeping on the floor for the first week back. Others wanted to dig a hole in the backyard instead of using the toilet. Chelsea Clinton, when she returned from a program in this book, told her entire extended family (more than 80 people) that she would no longer love them if they did not each make a personal commitment to recycling. We've heard about other students who castigated their parents for employing a maid. At the very least, some reticence is normal. A period of readjustment is only expected. One thing that you can count on is a spike in phone bills or Internet usage as your kid communicates with his new friends from the program.

Be patient. The harder the adjustment, the more likely it is that the program achieved some of its goals. Speaking personally, for a year after a particularly intensive program in France with students much older than me, I found myself incapable of interacting with my high school peers. To this day, I still sleep with eyeshades as a result of two summer months spent in Alaska during which the sun never set and we all slept in orange tents. Good programs are designed for this purpose. They stick with you.

Doug Capelin, the cofounder and codirector of Deer Hill, sums it up in this letter that he sends home to parents before the students return:

Summer of 2003

Dear _____,

Greetings from southwestern Colorado. I hope that this summer has been as enjoyable and rewarding for you as it has been for all of us here. I know that I can speak for Beverly and for all of our staff in wishing your family a happy reunion.

Over the years, many parents have asked me to send home a letter about what we at Deer Hill call "re-entry." This is a broad subject and every family's experience is different, but I am hoping that the following general remarks may be of some value to you.

Your son or daughter is returning home from a very powerful experience. He or she has been away from home and familiar routines for an extended period of time. Deer Hill life is challenging, but simple. The focus is on food, clothing, shelter, and having fun. The pace is geared for living in the outdoors and being an integral member of a closely knit group of peers.

Some return home with huge smiles on their faces, ready to tell tales of their adventures, and glad to see friends and family; others return home with some uncertainty and a quiet demeanor. There are many variations on this theme, all of which are quite normal. It is impossible for me to tell you exactly what to expect.

Mainly, I want you to understand that your son or daughter has more than likely been profoundly affected, in a good way, by his or her program at Deer Hill. He or she has developed new skills, forged new friendships, and lived outdoors for weeks. These challenges, shared in a supportive group setting, deepen self-esteem, foster respect for others, and promote a broader world view. However, he or she may or may not be ready to tell you about it right away. You are eager to hear all about it, but your son or daughter may need just a little time before opening up and sharing this experience with you. Your patience and understanding will be rewarded.

Our groups exercise vigorously for many weeks at elevations ranging from 5,000 to 14,000 feet. Expect insect bites and scratches on tanned skin, and lots of dirty laundry. Your son or daughter may very well need to catch up on sleep.

Don't worry about his or her big appetite. This is totally normal. Appetites tend to be modest at the beginning of a program. After about a week, metabolisms kick into a higher gear to compensate for the level of exercise. Your son or daughter will bring home this appetite because it takes at least a few days for a metabolism to return to normal. He or she may act like they have not eaten for a month! Please don't think that we don't feed them well. We do!

Lastly, I encourage you to enjoy these first few days home together. Allow this fine young individual to share his or her Deer Hill adventure with you as a flower unfolds.

All of us at Deer Hill send our best wishes to you. Thank you for your choosing Deer Hill this summer. Please call us anytime if we can be of any service.

Sincerely,

Doug and Beverly and the entire Deer Hill staff

REENTRY FOR STUDENTS

So how are you going to explain your summer to your parents? It's going to be frustrating. They're going to ask, "How was it?", "Who were the other kids?", "What was your favorite part?", and "Where did you get that T-shirt?" You can tell them that you traded the T-shirt with a friend from the program, but that's not really the whole story, is it? To tell the whole story you'd have to start with the first day when you met your friend and then you'd have to walk them through the whole incident with the tents, and the night of the bonfire, and the day the two of you got to go into town, etc. It could take all night to explain the T-shirt, and they probably still won't get it. So better to just say that it was fun and that you got the T-shirt from some kid on the program, right? Wrong.

You may not have realized it, but your parents were as excited about the program as you were. All summer long they wondered what you were doing at a particular moment. They helped make your summer experience possible. Like it or not, you're going to have to share. They may never totally understand. At the very least, however, they deserve to hear about some of the highlights.

Your program probably had a different set of values, a different standard of communication, and a different level of involvement than you have at home or at school. In other words, you may have changed, but the environment that you left has not. You may have difficulty reconnecting with your old friends. If you were on an intensive academic program, the same subject in school may seem impossibly dry. If you were on a service program, your eyes may have been opened to the level of affluence in which many Americans live. You cannot blame your friends, your family, or your schoolmates for not having had the same intense experience that you have had. You are the lucky one.

Oftentimes intense experiences lead to a different kind of sharing. Students in extreme conditions must work together as a group. The leaders at most wilderness programs believe in strong commitment to the environment. When you get home, people may not share the same belief. They may not see the benefits of teamwork quite the way you do. They may not live out the same values that you have learned in another place. This doesn't mean that they are wrong. It is great that you want to teach them what you have learned, or that you want to help them see things from your newly achieved perspective, but you must respect their perspective, too. Some compromises may have to be struck. You can't expect your mom or dad to sell the car and convert their entire diet to organically produced food just because you think that it's a better way to live. People who get up on soapboxes annoy other people. So unless you want to annoy people, don't get up on yours.

On the other hand, you do not have to give up what you have learned, either. Teach your friends and family to share in a circle the way you did on your program. Help foster a greater commitment to recycling in your community, or encourage your teachers to let you create a hands-on science project as part of your grade. When you get home and no one understands where you've been or what you've learned, don't slide back into your old habits. If your old habits are no longer satisfying, find new ones. You are now an emissary, a pioneer, and a bridge to another culture. That is bound to set you apart; but don't worry, your old world will catch up, or you will move on.

Your friends from the program may be a great resource in your transition back into your old life. You probably don't need to be told to keep in touch. Remember, however, that life has a way of asserting itself. As you get back into the school year and your life begins to get busy again, you might not have time for the same long e-mails or phone calls that you exchanged when you first returned. They might not, either. If your level of communication begins to decrease, cut them some slack. They are dealing with their lives just like you are dealing with yours.

So welcome back. Be patient. You are a slightly different person from the one you were when you left. It may take some time for your friends and family to adjust to the new you, and for you to readjust to them. Don't worry. It will all have been worth it.

Chapter 8

Paying for It

THE PRICE TAG—WHY SO HIGH?

Most summer programs aren't cheap, and you may wonder where the money is going. The kids live in tents. They stay in rural villages. They work their tails off in third-world countries. How could that be so expensive?

While the price tag of a five-week summer experience can be expensive, it is necessary to put it into perspective. Summer programs are not inexpensive to run. Just imagine, for a moment, what the insurance costs are for an organization whose business is doing something—*anything*—with large groups of teenagers. Then add to that the cost of paying for the staff, housing, equipment, training, and travel.

The better the program is, the more they are likely to invest in the student experience. This means better equipment, better sites, a higher staff to student ratio, more staff training, and better staff. This does not mean full color ads in national magazines and a full time sales force. Most summer programs—especially the really good ones—don't turn a very large profit. Generally, the people running these programs are motivated by more than just money—and that should make you feel more comfortable. When it comes time for you to think about cost, ask the program directors questions about how they spend the money they make. The bottom line is that the majority of the money should go directly into the quality of the experience.

WHEN YOU PUT THINGS INTO PERSPECTIVE...

Consider the cost of college. The cost of the program you're considering seems like a drop in the bucket compared to what most four-year colleges are charging, right? Now consider the impact of a summer program on the college experience. Students who are veterans of intensive summer programs are more self-confident and therefore they are less likely to succumb to peer pressure. They also gain a better sense of what is most important to them. This greater self-awareness better prepares them to take full advantage of the college experience.

NEED SOME DIRECTION?

Parents and their children should consult with a summer programs advisor. An advisor can help match students with programs and may also be a good resource for finding lesser-known high quality programs. Advisors can help ensure that the money you invest in a summer program is well spent.

NO MONEY, NO PROBLEM

There are options for families who cannot afford the full price of most summer programs. Most good programs offer financial aid, although they don't necessarily advertise it. Each program profile in this book will tell you whether the program offers financial aid. If a program doesn't offer financial aid at all, or if what they offer is insufficient, all is not lost. Good programs want good kids; a program will often find a way to make sure that cost is no barrier to attendance and will help out kids who have done their homework, have good recommendations, and are enthusiastic about the program.

WHERE THERE'S A WILL, THERE'S A WAY

There are often community groups that will support students who have shown the initiative to seek them out. These groups include Rotary International, Elks clubs, local churches, chambers of commerce, the school board, the local hospital, and even the local fire department. With the remarkably effective combination of enthusiasm and initiative, you may be able to convince such groups to support your cause. We have heard plenty of stories about students who started looking for help, kept trying new angles when old ones came up short, and generally refused to take no for an answer. These kids succeeded in finding ways to fund their summer program experience. What we have *not* heard are any stories of good kids who tried everything they could think of and still failed to get where they wanted to go.

EXPLORE ALL YOUR OPTIONS

Students should not forget about their own earning power. Working for the first six weeks of summer may enable you to earn enough to cover your plane fare and expenses to a program offered during the second half of your summer break. Not only is this approach enormously impressive to program directors, but also it is enormously impressive to college admissions officers. Many college admissions officers told us they were deeply suspicious of students who paid a lot of money to spend two weeks in an exotic locale doing community service. They were impressed by students who made sacrifices or contributed their own money toward the cost of a summer program. They found that students such as these definitely stood out from the crowd. When you pay for a summer program with money you earned, you are more likely to appreciate your experience and take the opportunities it presents very seriously.

NO PROGRAM, NO PROBLEM

What do you want to do with your summer? Does it involve community service, being in the wilderness, making movies, or even trying out field biology? Regardless of what area interests you, there is probably someone right now who could use your help. You don't need to fly to Belize to perform community service—there are plenty of places to volunteer in your neighborhood. For example, there are wilderness conservation organizations that rely on volunteers to get their job done. Unlike a summer program, you don't have to pay any money to volunteer your time at an organization; you just have to offer them your services.

It is true that the Internet is an incredible tool for finding people and organizations. But once you've done your basic research, don't shy away from picking up the phone. People can ignore an email message, but they have a harder time ignoring an enthusiastic-sounding student. Let them hear who you are and what you're prepared to do. End every conversation with the question, "Can you think of anyone else that I should talk to?" Be brave, be bold, be genuine, and be enthusiastic. You'll find that not only is this good practice for college, but also for the rest of your life.

Chapter 9

How to Use This Book

It's pretty self-explanatory.

The first part—you are reading it now—is a fairly thorough primer on searching for the right summer program for you; being a good participant and getting the most out of that program; coming back to your normal life without driving yourself and everyone around you crazy; and the role your summer program experience can play in college admissions. Basically, it's a game plan for going about the whole summer program experience in the smartest way possible.

The second—and larger—part houses the actual summer program profiles. There are 522 of them, appearing in alphabetical order according to the name of the sponsor institution of the program. What that means is that if a sponsoring institution runs more than one summer program, you will only see the institution's general information once; specific data for all programs run by the institution appear after the institution's general information and contact information. While many of the data fields for both the sponsoring institution and the programs they run are largely self-explanatory, here's what you can expect to see. Keep in mind that not every category will appear for every summer program, since in some cases the information is not reported or not applicable. The data that appears in this book was collected from the sponsoring institutions in 2003.

Sponsoring Institution Information

Here you will find a general overview of the sponsoring institution; any religious affiliation it has; the number of years it has been in operation; the price range for all of the programs it offers; and all relevant contact information, including its website, phone and fax numbers, and e-mail and postal addresses. We also provide the name of the primary contact person, and the position that person holds within the sponsoring institution. If you have a question (that this guide can't answer) about any of the programs a sponsoring institution offers, talk to this person.

PROGRAM INFORMATION

The real meat and potatoes of the book.

Description
The sponsoring institution explains the overall theme of the program.

Specialty
The sponsoring institutions briefly tell us what makes their program special.

Goals
What the sponsoring institution wants participants to get out of their experience on the program.

Focus
In descending order of importance, this lists the themes that the program is designed to help participants explore. Up to three focuses may appear.

Activities Centered On
In descending order according to how much students can expect to do them, this lists the actual types of activities in which participants will be engaged.

Location
This is where participants can expect to be for (most of) the duration of the program.

Duration
This is how long the program lasts.

Years in Operation
Programs that have been operating for many years have established track records. If it has been around for a long time, it usually means that the program is safe and that participants get out of it what they expect to get out of it. (And, after all, that's the whole point.)

Average Number of Participants
Self-explanatory. Smaller groups usually mean more personal attention from the staff for each participant.

Type
This describes whether the program is single-sex or coeducational, residential or day.

Housing
If the program is residential, this lists the types of accommodations available to participants.

When Offered
Some programs aren't just offered in the summer. They may have programs one can attend during the winter break from school.

INTENSITY LEVEL

This is a truly unique and very helpful piece of information that you will not find in any other guide.

We asked the sponsoring institutions to rate their programs on the scale described below. The categories are based on physical extremes, intellectual rigor, or cultural challenges.

This rating scale is independent of age. Some ninth graders may find quite enough authentic challenge in a long program that rates itself a number two.

5

Physically, think high school pre-season, but subtract the trainer, the locker room, and the water breaks. A level-five program is physically challenging. Students may be climbing an ice face, hiking many miles through difficult terrain, or climbing the rigging of a ship in rough seas. Food may be inconsistent. A prepared hot meal is probably a luxury rather than the norm. A specific physical skill set may be required.

If it's not physical challenges that make this program a level five, it may be intellectual. It is likely that this is a program dedicated to research or some other intellectual pursuit to which a small handful of high school students have been invited. They are welcome on the program, but the program does not exist for them. It is not a dedicated summer program. Students should expect college- or graduate-level work.

Cultural challenges may also contribute to a level five rating. Cultural challenges may include demanding community service work, substandard (by U.S. standards) living conditions, minimal program supervision, or unique political situations. It is likely that students are living and working amongst a group of diverse ages and nationalities. Programs will be coed in both working and living arrangements, with potentially European standards applying to things like alcohol consumption. Without exception, students will be treated like and expected to act like adults.

Do not expect a regular schedule, defined role, or 24/7 supervision. These programs are level five for a reason.

4

A level-four program may still be physically challenging. If it is rated a level-four program for physical reasons, students who are healthy and in active physical condition can expect to meet the physical demands, but should not expect it to be easy. Level five may demand a specific physical expertise. Level four does not require expertise in a specific skill set, but honing that expertise may be part of the point. Good physical condition and ability will be essential.

If the program has an intellectual focus, students should attend because of a specific passion for this activity. This is why they will be there. Whether it is filmmaking, intensive journal-writing, or biological research, it is the dedicated focus of the program. Students can try this activity on for size, but it is not an elective that can be dropped in favor of other pursuits.

Culturally, it could still be community service, foreign countries, or a mixed age group that puts this at one end of the Intensity Index. Students may be supervised during the day, but their evenings and weekends are not scheduled for them. There may be some behavioral expectations, but it is unlikely that there will be any chaperones.

3

Whether it's sailing a square-rigged sloop or hiking through the Pyrenees, students will not have to show up equipped with the skills, but they will certainly have to learn them. In fact, learning them may be part of the point. Students of average physical fitness will be challenged. Triathletes will not.

Intellectually, some of the more intensive "pre-college preparatory" programs fall into this category. Students will be doing academic work that is more intensive than they will find at most public high schools; it will, however, be interspaced by weekend trips and evening activities. It is like high school, but with more interesting subjects, better classes, and more motivated students. If it is not a school setting, the level of intellectual rigor required will still be the same.

Culturally, students may be in another country, but they will still be amongst a group of their peers. They should be careful, though; this is an adventure, and their social, diplomatic, and maturity skills will be tested. There may not be direct supervision at all times, but help is never far away.

2

While there may be plenty of physical activities, physical challenges are not the primary focus of this program. Think bunk beds and mosquito repellent rather than subzero sleeping bags and freeze-dried rations. Some physical activities, such as a Sunday hike to the top of a mountain for vespers, or lots of walking through European cities, may not be optional.

If it is a pre-college preparatory program with an academic focus, it will be characterized by SAT preparation and high school–level programs. Students looking for AP-level calculus will not be challenged. A program in Europe may include some European history and art history, but this will be background information rather than a dedicated focus.

Foreign currency or weekend trips into New York, San Francisco, or other metropolitan areas separate a level two from a level one. A more structured environment, regular supervision, and lights out at 11:00 separate it from level three.

1

Physically, let's face it: you don't have to be Lance Armstrong to enjoy a bike ride. Students might try waterskiing, but then again, they might just elect to stay in the boat. Either way, they will have plenty of company. This program has physical activities because they are fun, but anyone can opt out. For those determined to not to break a sweat, there is always an indoor option.

Intellectually, students should bring a good book, find a few fossils, or get involved in the annual End of Summer Follies. Those looking for challenges may be called upon to help out with the younger students.

Culturally, sometimes just getting away from home is enough. In this program students may elect a shorter three-week stay rather than six or eight weeks. A bonfire and a three-day horseback trek can feel pretty exotic for younger participants, and may yield a year's worth of pictures and stories for many students.

Student/Staff
The lower the student/staff ratio, the more personal attention and closer supervision participants will have.

Staff Qualifications
The people running the day-to-day aspects of the program are really what makes for the experience of the participants. Good programs try to hire and retain the brightest and most reliable people. When following up directly with a program, you should make it a point to find out what percentage of their staff returns to help run the program the following year. A high staff return rate is a good sign.

For Participants Aged
Self-explanatory.

The Ideal Candidate
We asked program sponsors to describe the best kind of participant for the specific program. Don't worry if you don't feel like you fit the ideal. You probably will after going on the program.

Special Requirements for Participation
Self-explanatory. Pay attention to these, however. Requirements are in place for a reason, often to keep you from being injured, embarrassed, or feeling like the program is a profound waste of your time.

Average Cost
You might end up spending more if you live farther from the program location than most other program participants.

Included in Cost
All the program expenses you cover when you send your check to the sponsoring institution. Most times your travel costs to and from the program location are up to you to meet. It's always a good idea to overbudget for a summer program, especially if the program location is overseas.

Financial Aid Available
If it is, be sure to ask the contact person of the sponsoring institution what the qualifications are for it and how you can apply.

Nota Bene

We have chosen not to include sports and musical camps in our listings. We figured that anyone looking for a "quarterback camp" has plenty of expert resources, such as coaches, athletic directors, and teammates to call on when looking for such an appropriate summer opportunity. And we assume that students of music who can qualify for a summer conservatory probably know more about what makes a good or bad conservatory than we do.

PART TWO
THE PROFILES

4 STAR SUMMER CAMPS AT UNIVERSITY OF VIRGINIA

Offering academic programs for middle and high school students such as writing and math courses and PSAT/SAT prep. Instruction in golf and tennis is also provided.

Years in Operation: 28

Religious Affiliation: Not relevant

Price Range of Programs: $2,295–$4,545

For More Information:
Contact: Marietta Naramore, Administrative Director
PO Box 3387
Falls Church, VA 22043
Phone: 800-334-7827
Fax: 703-866-7775
Email: info@4starcamps.com
Website: www.4starcamps.com

4 STAR SUMMER CAMPS SCHOLARS PROGRAM

THE PROGRAM

Description: This program is designed for motivated students completing grades 10 through 12 who wish to earn college credit from University of Virginia. Choose from a great selection of courses. Can be combined with instruction in tennis or golf.

Specialty: A unique opportunity to experience college life at one of the most highly regarded academic institutions in the country while earning college credits and participating in world-class sports instruction.

Program Type: Academic/pre-college enrichment

Classification: Coeducational, residential, day program

Goals: Students will have the opportunity to experience college life in a highly prestigious university while earning college credits.

Focus: Academic/pre-college enrichment

Activities Center On: Academic, SAT prep, and study skills

Intensity Level: 3

Duration: 4–6 weeks

Program Offered: Summer

Location: Charlottesville, Virginia

Accommodations: Dormitory

Years in Operation: 2

Religious Affiliation: Not relevant

STAFF

Student/Staff Ratio: 15:1

Staff Qualifications: College courses are designed and taught by university faculty.

PARTICIPANTS

Average Number of Participants: 50

For Participants Aged: 16–18

The Ideal Candidate: Students must be mature and motivated.

Special Requirements for Participation: High school transcripts and recommendation from guidance counselors or principals are required.

COSTS

Average Cost: $5,500

Included in Cost: Tuition includes course instruction, room and board, most afternoon activities, and all evening activities.

Financial Aid Available: No

4 STAR SUMMER CAMPS SENIOR PROGRAM

THE PROGRAM

Description: Designed for students entering grades 10 through 12; offers stimulating and fun classes, world-class sports instruction in tennis and golf, recreational activities, or seminars.

Specialty: A summer filled with fun, stimulating classes, and new friendships on the campus of one of the most presitigious universities in the country.

Program Type: Academic/pre-college enrichment

Classification: Coeducational, residential, day program

Goals: Students will benefit from a well-designed curriculum that targets skills needed for success in high school and beyond.

Focus: Academic/pre-college enrichment and skill-building

Activities Center On: Academic, SAT prep, and writing

Intensity Level: 2

Duration: 2–4 weeks

Program Offered: Summer

Location: Charlottesville, Virginia

Accommodations: Dormitory

Years in Operation: 13

Religious Affiliation: Not relevant

STAFF

Student/Staff Ratio: 15:1

Staff Qualifications: Instructors are experienced secondary school teachers and advanced graduate students.

PARTICIPANTS

Average Number of Participants: 50

For Participants Aged: 14–18

The Ideal Candidate: An ideal candidate would be a mature and motivated student.

Special Requirements for Participation: None.

COSTS

Average Cost: $2,400

Included in Cost: Courses, room and board, most afternoon activities, and all evening activities.

Financial Aid Available: No

ACADEMIC STUDY ASSOCIATES, INC.

ASA is celebrating its 20th year running summer programs. We offer pre-college and language immersion programs for high school students. Our pre-college locations are: University of Massachusetts—Amherst, University of California—Berkeley, Emory University, and Oxford University; our language immersion locations are in France and Spain.

Years in Operation: 20

Religious Affiliation: Not relevant

Price Range of Programs: $2,495–$6,395

For More Information:
Contact: Grace Chang, Marketing Director
10 New King Street
White Plains, NY 10604
Phone: 914-686-7730
Fax: 914-686-7740
Email: summer@asaprograms.com
Website: www.asaprograms.com

ASA AT UNIVERSITY OF MASSACHUSETTS— AMHERST

THE PROGRAM

Description: Students in grades 9 through 12 get a taste of the New England college experience with ASA at UMass—Amherst's three- or five-week program! Explore interesting subjects from our wide selection of college credit or enrichment courses. After class, choose from a jam-packed calendar of activities to suit whatever your interest and mood: relax and enjoy UMass' sports facilities, explore Amherst and the Berkshires, or participate in RA-organized activities. Complete the experience with trips to attractions including Boston.

Specialty: ASA bridges students' transition from high school to college. We enable them to experience the social and academic aspects of college life while providing resources such as caring RAs and group activities that ensure camaraderie and success!

Program Type: Academic/pre-college enrichment, community service, music/arts, sports/athletic

Classification: Coeducational, residential, day program

Goals: Students leave ASA programs socially and intellectually enriched and prepared for college. In class, students collaborate with college professors and experience different collegiate teaching methods. They explore and gain a deeper knowledge of interesting subjects. Outside of class, students learn to adjust to the freedoms of college life. They learn to live in a dorm with others and gain interpersonal skills, independence, and time management skills that are essential for college and beyond.

Focus: Academic/pre-college enrichment, skill-building, and travel

Activities Center On: Academic and touring

Intensity Level: 2

Duration: 2–4 weeks, 4–6 weeks

Program Offered: Summer

Location: Amherst, Massachusetts

Accommodations: Dormitory

Religious Affiliation: Not relevant

STAFF

Student/Staff Ratio: 10:1

Staff Qualifications: Mary Lynn Alton, the program director, has been with ASA for 10 years. She has a BA from Rice University and worked as assistant director of admissions there for several years. Currently, she works year-round in the ASA office directing all the ASA pre-college programs. Resident assistants, essential to student life, are rigorously selected and trained college students. They live on the floor with students, organize activities, and support students with academics and social issues.

PARTICIPANTS

Average Number of Participants: 220

For Participants Aged: 15–18

The Ideal Candidate: Our students are looking for a fun and productive summer. They are intellectually motivated and are excited about the prospect of making new friends from all over the world.

Special Requirements for Participation: Applicants must be students currently in grades 9 through 12.

COSTS

Average Cost: $4,495

Financial Aid Available: Yes

ASA AT UNIVERSITY OF CALIFORNIA— BERKELEY

THE PROGRAM

Description: Students in grades 10 through 12 get a taste of the California college experience in just five or six weeks with ASA at UC—Berkeley! Explore interesting subjects from our wide selection of college credit or enrichment courses. After class, choose from a variety of activities that suit whatever your mood is: enjoy Berkeley's world-class facilities, explore the surrounding neighborhoods and San Francisco, or participate in RA-organized activities. Complete the experience with trips to top regional attractions.

Specialty: ASA bridges students' transition from high school to college. We enable them to experience the social and academic aspects of college life while providing resources such as caring RAs and group activities that ensure camaraderie and success!

Program Type: Academic/pre-college enrichment, community service, music/arts, sports/athletic

Classification: Coeducational, residential, day program

Goals: Students leave ASA programs socially and intellectually enriched and prepared for college. In class, students collaborate with college professors and experience different collegiate teaching methods. They explore and gain a deeper knowledge of interesting subjects. Outside of class, students learn to adjust to the freedoms of college life. They learn to live in a dorm with others and gain interpersonal skills, independence, and time management skills that are essential for college and beyond.

Focus: Academic/pre-college enrichment, skill-building, and travel

Activities Center On: Academic and touring

Intensity Level: 2

Duration: 4–6 weeks

Program Offered: Summer

Location: Berkeley, California

Accommodations: Dormitory

Years in Operation: 3

Religious Affiliation: Not relevant

STAFF

Student/Staff Ratio: 10:1

Staff Qualifications: Willem Vroegh, the program director for ASA at UC Berkeley, has been with ASA for eight years. He has a master's degree in Education from Smith College and an undergraduate degree from Miami University of Ohio. Willem currently teaches in San Francisco and has taught for Teach for America. Resident assistants, essential to student life, are rigorously selected and trained college students. They live on the floor with students, organize activities, and support students with academics and social issues.

PARTICIPANTS

Average Number of Participants: 100

For Participants Aged: 16–18

The Ideal Candidate: Our students are looking for a fun and productive summer. They are intellectually motivated and are excited about the prospect of making new friends from all over the world.

Special Requirements for Participation: Applicants must be students currently in grades 10 through 12.

COSTS

Average Cost: $5,895

Financial Aid Available: Yes

ASA AT EMORY UNIVERSITY

THE PROGRAM

Description: Students in grades 9 through 12 get a taste of college in cosmopolitan Atlanta in ASA at Emory's four-week program! Spend part of your day exploring interesting subjects from our wide selection of enrichment courses—from photography to SAT. After class, choose from a jam-packed selection of activities to suit whatever your mood is: relax and enjoy Emory's sports facilities, explore nearby college towns and Atlanta, or participate in RA-organized activities. Complete the experience with trips to top regional attractions.

Specialty: ASA bridges students' transition from high school to college. We enable them to experience the social and academic aspects of college life while providing resources such as caring RAs and group activities that ensure camaraderie and success!

Program Type: Academic/pre-college enrichment, community service, music/arts, sports/athletic

Classification: Coeducational, residential, day program

Goals: Students leave ASA programs socially and intellectually enriched and prepared for college. In class, students collaborate with college professors and experience different collegiate teaching methods. They explore and gain a deeper knowledge of interesting subjects. Outside of class, students learn to adjust to the freedoms of college life. They learn to live in a dorm with others and gain interpersonal skills, independence, and time management skills that are essential for college and beyond.

Focus: Academic/pre-college enrichment, skill-building, and travel

Activities Center On: Academic and touring

Intensity Level: 2

Duration: 2–4 weeks

Program Offered: Summer

Location: Atlanta, Georgia

Accommodations: Dormitory

Years in Operation: 2

Religious Affiliation: Not relevant

STAFF

Student/Staff Ratio: 10:1

Staff Qualifications: James Hughes, the program director for ASA at Emory, has been with ASA for nine years. He has a master's degree in education and English from Stanford University and a BA from the University of San Diego. Currently, he teaches English at Sacred Heart Preparatory School in Atherton. Resident assistants, essential to student life, are rigorously selected and trained college students. They live on the floor with students, organize activities, and support students with academics and social issues.

PARTICIPANTS

Average Number of Participants: 100

For Participants Aged: 15–18

The Ideal Candidate: Our students are looking for a fun and productive summer. They are intellectually motivated and are excited about the prospect of making new friends from all over the world.

Special Requirements for Participation: Applicants must be students currently in grades 9 through 12.

COSTS

Average Cost: $4,895

Financial Aid Available: Yes

OXFORD EXPERIENCE

THE PROGRAM

Description: Students in grades 10 through 12 get a taste of English life with ASA's four-week Oxford Experience. Explore interesting subjects taught by Oxford faculty from our wide selection of enrichment courses. After class, choose from a jam-packed calendar of activities that suit whatever your mood is: relax on campus, explore Oxford, or participate in RA-organized activities including trips to the theater and other entertainment. Complete the experience with excursions to nearby attractions including London and Stonehenge.

Specialty: ASA bridges students' transition from high school to college. We enable them to experience the social and academic aspects of college life while providing resources such as caring RAs and group activities that ensure camaraderie and success!

Program Type: Academic/pre-college enrichment, travel and cultural

Classification: Coeducational, residential, day program

Goals: Students leave ASA programs socially and intellectually enriched and prepared for college. In class, students collaborate with college professors and experience different collegiate teaching methods. They explore and gain a deeper knowledge of interesting subjects. Outside of class, students learn to adjust to the freedoms of college life. They learn to live in a dorm with others and gain interpersonal skills, independence, and time management skills that are essential for college and beyond.

Focus: Academic/pre-college enrichment, cultural, and travel

Activities Center On: Academic, cultural, and travel

Intensity Level: 2

Duration: 4–6 weeks

Program Offered: Summer

Location: Oxford, United Kingdom

Accommodations: Dormitory

Religious Affiliation: Not relevant

STAFF

Student/Staff Ratio: 10:1

Staff Qualifications: Paul Saville, the program director for ASA at Oxford, has been with ASA for 17 years. He was educated at Glasgow and Oxford. Currently, he heads the Department of Art and Art History and the Liberal Arts Program for overseas students at St. Clare's. Resident assistants, essential to student life, are rigorously selected and trained college students. They live on the floor with students, organize activities, and support students with academics and social issues.

PARTICIPANTS

Average Number of Participants: 150

For Participants Aged: 15–18

The Ideal Candidate: Our students are looking for a fun and productive summer. They are intellectually motivated and are excited about the prospect of making new friends from all over the world.

Special Requirements for Participation: Applicants must be students currently in grades 10 through 12.

COSTS

Average Cost: $5,495

Financial Aid Available: Yes

ASA IN NICE

THE PROGRAM

Description: Discover Nice with ASA's four-week residential program. As a resident of the Lycee Massena, located in the heart of the old town, you're steps away from major sites and campus facilities. Part of your day will be spent in language class and cultural workshops. After class you're free to choose from all Nice has to offer, including scuba diving, cultural outings, and exploration of Nice's attractions. Your experience is completed by trips through the Riviera including Monaco and Cannes.

Program Type: Travel/cultural

Classification: Coeducational, residential

Focus: Cultural, travel, and skill-building

Activities Center On: Language, cultural, and touring

Intensity Level: 2

Duration: 2–4 weeks

Program Offered: Summer

Location: Nice, France

Accommodations: Dormitory

Religious Affiliation: Not relevant

PARTICIPANTS

Average Number of Participants: 40

For Participants Aged: 15–18

Special Requirements for Participation: None.

COSTS

Average Cost: $5,195

Financial Aid Available: No

ASA IN PARIS

THE PROGRAM

Description: Discover Paris in ASA's four-week homestay program. You will live with a family in St. Germain-enLaye, an affluent town 20 minutes from Paris, and gain a unique perspective of French life. Your days will be spent in the heart of Paris in language class, field trips, and tours of Parisian attractions. In the evenings, you can unwind in St. Germain and participate in organized activities. Your Paris experience is completed with overnight excursions to the Loire Valley and Chantilly.

Program Type: Travel/cultural

Classification: Coeducational, residential

Focus: Cultural, travel, and skill-building

Activities Center On: Language, cultural, and touring

Intensity Level: 3

Duration: 2–4 weeks

Program Offered: Summer

Location: Paris, France

Accommodations: Family-stay/host-family

Religious Affiliation: Not relevant

PARTICIPANTS

Average Number of Participants: 50

For Participants Aged: 15–18

Special Requirements for Participation: None.

COSTS

Average Cost: $4,295

Financial Aid Available: No

ASA IN ROYAN

THE PROGRAM

Description: Discover French country living in Royan, a popular resort town located in the Bordeaux region. In this four-week homestay program you will gain a unique perspective of French life and improve your language skills. Part of your days will be spent at the CAREL language school and in cultural workshops. In your leisure time, you're free to choose from activities including sailing, art, and outings to neighboring towns. Your experience is completed with excursions through the beautiful countryside.

Program Type: Travel/cultural

Classification: Coeducational, residential

Focus: Cultural, travel, and skill-building

Activities Center On: Language, cultural, and touring

Intensity Level: 4

Duration: 2–4 weeks

Program Offered: Summer

Location: Royan, France

Accommodations: Family-stay/host-family

Religious Affiliation: Not relevant

PARTICIPANTS

Average Number of Participants: 25

For Participants Aged: 15–18

Special Requirements for Participation: None.

COSTS

Average Cost: $4,995

Financial Aid Available: Yes

ASA IN BARCELONA

THE PROGRAM

Description: Discover Barcelona in ASA's residential program at the Universitat Autonoma de Barcelona. In four weeks you will improve your language skills and experience the unique Spanish culture. Spend part of your day in the heart of the city in language class, cultural workshops, and field trips. In your free time, choose from several activities: unwind at a tapas bar or cafe, explore the city, or relax on campus or the sports facilities. Complete your experience with trips to unforgettable attractions.

Program Type: Travel/cultural

Classification: Coeducational, residential

Focus: Cultural, travel, and skill-building

Activities Center On: Language, cultural, and touring

Intensity Level: 2

Duration: 2–4 weeks

Program Offered: Summer

Location: Barcelona, Spain

Accommodations: Dormitory

Years in Operation: 2

Religious Affiliation: Not relevant

PARTICIPANTS

Average Number of Participants: 45

For Participants Aged: 15–18

Special Requirements for Participation: None.

COSTS

Average Cost: $5,195

Financial Aid Available: No

SPANISH IN ESPAÑA

THE PROGRAM

Description: Experience the authentic Spanish way of life at our homestay programs held in the Andalusia region of southern Spain. Choose from four locations. In this four-week homestay program you will gain a unique perspective of Spanish life and improve your language skills. Your immersion consists of daily language class, cultural activities such as Flamenco dancing and Spanish cooking, workshops such as Soccer and Watercolor, and excursions to regional attractions such as Seville, Cadiz, and Gibraltar.

Program Type: Travel/cultural

Classification: Coeducational, residential

Focus: Cultural, travel, and skill-building

Activities Center On: Language, cultural, and touring

Intensity Level: 3

Duration: 2–4 weeks

Program Offered: Summer

Location: Conil, Cadiz, Nerja, or Tarifa, Spain

Accommodations: Family-stay/host-family

Religious Affiliation: Not relevant

PARTICIPANTS

For Participants Aged: 15–18

Special Requirements for Participation: None.

COSTS

Average Cost: $5,095

Financial Aid Available: No

COLLEGE ADMISSIONS ADVANTAGE

THE PROGRAM

Description: College Admissions Advantage at Pepperdine University or Amherst College helps students in grades 10 through 11 prepare for the competitive college admissions process. This intensive 11-day program offers one-on-one counseling, daily writing workshops focused on the Personal Statement of applications, SAT prep with The Princeton Review, and valuable workshops on college admissions topics. At the end of the program, students will have a complete admissions portfolio ready to guide them in the college admissions process.

Program Type: Academic/pre-college enrichment

Classification: Coeducational, residential, day program

Goals: Students learn about every element in the college application process and leave with a completed college admissions portfolio, which includes targeted schools list, model application, two personal statements, resume, and personalized calendar.

Intensity Level: 4

Duration: 1–2 weeks

Program Offered: Summer

Location: Malibu, California; Amherst, Massachusetts

Accommodations: Dormitory

Years in Operation: 1

Religious Affiliation: Not relevant

PARTICIPANTS

Average Number of Participants: 50

For Participants Aged: 15–18

Special Requirements for Participation: For students completing grades 10–11.

COSTS

Average Cost: $2,495

Financial Aid Available: No

ADVENTURE TREKS, INC.

Offers 16- to 28-day wilderness adventure programs featuring a variety of exciting activities in the North American West. A 1:4 instructor/student ratio ensures a focus on fun, safety, community, and personal growth.

Years in Operation: 25

Religious Affiliation: Not relevant

Price Range of Programs: $2,095–$3,695

For More Information:
 Contact: John Dockendorf, Director
   PO Box 1321
   Flat Rock, NC 28731
 Phone: 888-954-5555
 Fax: 828-696-1663
 Email: info@advtreks.com
 Website: www.adventuretreks.com

ALASKA ADVENTURES

THE PROGRAM

Description: A 28-day wilderness adventure in Alaska featuring sea kayaking, backpacking, whitewater rafting, and ice climbing for 16- to 18-year-olds.

Specialty: A focus on safety, community living, and personal growth in a wilderness setting; an immeasurable amount of fun and interaction with powerful role models; a 1:4 instructor/student ratio.

Program Type: Outdoors/adventure

Classification: Coeducational, residential

Goals: Teamwork, community living, and outdoor skills.

Focus: Leadership/teamwork, skill-building, and travel

Activities Center On: Backpacking, kayaking, and camping

Intensity Level: 4

Duration: 2–4 weeks

Program Offered: Summer

Location: Anchorage, Alaska

Accommodations: Tent

Years in Operation: 6

Religious Affiliation: Not relevant

STAFF

Student/Staff Ratio: 4:1

Staff Qualifications: Minimum age of 23; previous instructional experience with Adventure Treks; Wilderness First Responder or higher medical training; five years experience working with students in the outdoors.

PARTICIPANTS

Average Number of Participants: 0.2

For Participants Aged: 16–18

The Ideal Candidate: A great young person with previous outdoor experience.

Special Requirements for Participation: Previous outdoor experience required.

COSTS

Average Cost: $3,695

Included in Cost: All inclusive including equipment. Airfare is not included.

Financial Aid Available: Yes

ADVENTURES AFLOAT/ ODYSSEY EXPEDITIONS

Co-ed residential academic program, outdoor program, and adventure program established in 1995; for ages 15–19. College credit may be earned.

Years in Operation: 8

Religious Affiliation: Not relevant

Price Range of Programs: $3,950–$4,050

For More Information:
  Contact: Jason Buchheim, Director
      650 Southeast Paradise Point Road, #100
      Crystal River, FL 34429
  Phone: 800-929-7749
  Fax: 801-340-5000
  Email: odyssey@usa.net
  Website: www.odysseyexpeditions.org

ODYSSEY EXPEDITIONS TROPICAL MARINE BIOLOGY VOYAGES (BRITISH VIRGIN ISLANDS)

THE PROGRAM

Description: Summer program for teenagers. Live aboard 46-foot catamarans in the Caribbean. Enjoy coral reef discoveries, rainforest hikes, and wilderness exploration. Features marine biology, PADI scuba instruction, sail training, and island exploration during 21-day voyages of discovery. There are three sessions beginning in mid-June and going into August.

Specialty: Students learn teamwork while living aboard a 45-foot catamaran. Students are responsible for all day-to-day activites of the vessel. Scuba and sailing instruction are supplemented with hands-on marine biology exploration.

Program Type: Outdoors/adventure

Classification: Coeducational, residential

Goals: Marine science, scuba certifications (open water), and higher introductory sailing experience.

Focus: Academic/pre-college enrichment, skill-building, and travel

Activities Center On: Sailing, science, and sports/athletic

Intensity Level: 3

Duration: 2–4 weeks

Program Offered: Summer

Location: British Virgin Islands

Accommodations: Catamaran

Years in Operation: 8

Religious Affiliation: Not relevant

STAFF

Student/Staff Ratio: 4:1

Staff Qualifications: USCG-licensed sailing master; BS or higher in marine biology; PADI scuba instructor.

PARTICIPANTS

Average Number of Participants: 170

For Participants Aged: 14–24

The Ideal Candidate: High school or college student interested in learning about the underwater environment; should be interested in a fully participatory experience.

Special Requirements for Participation: Good health, no asthma.

COSTS

Average Cost: $4,000

Included in Cost: All meals, berths aboard the catamaran, diving expenses and equipment, transportation from the airport, fees, and instruction are included.

Financial Aid Available: No

ALFRED UNIVERSITY

Each summer students from all over the country come to our beautiful campus for exciting programs in astronomy, creative writing, entrepreneurial leadership, and swimming. We're located in a peaceful village in the Finger Lakes area, where summer days are warm, and nights, cool. It's a great place for students to spend an enjoyable week or two learning more about a favorite subject and meeting other students with similar interests. Classes are taught by AU faculty. Students stay in modern residence halls and have meals in the dining hall. When not in class, they enjoy recreational activities and relaxation. Living, dining, and learning together, they have ample opportunity to get to know each other well and develop lasting friendships.

Years in Operation: 6

Religious Affiliation: Not relevant

Price Range of Programs: $425–$995

For More Information:
   Contact: Melody McLay, Director of Summer Programs
           Alfred University
           One Saxon Drive
           Alfred, NY 14802
   Phone: 607-871-2612
   Fax: 607-871-2045
   Email: mclaym@alfred.edu

   Website: www.alfred.edu/summer

SUMMER INSTITUTE IN ASTRONOMY

THE PROGRAM

Description: This program is held at the Stull Observatory on the AU campus, considered one of the best teaching observatories in the country. Students choose an intermediate or advanced track. Topics include variable star photometry, asteroid astrometry and photometry, astronomical imaging of nebulae, clusters and galaxies, observation and analysis of solar activity, lunar and planetary science, solar flares, stellar evolution, CCD imaging, galactic structure, and cosmology and spectroscopy.

Specialty: The program held in the Stull Observatory, judged one of the best teaching observatories in the country. It is staffed by members of our physics and astronomy faculty. Its small size allows for individualized attention and optimal use of observatory equipment.

Program Type: Academic/pre-college enrichment

Classification: Coeducational, residential

Goals: Students will learn more about astronomy, sample life on a college campus, and meet other students with similar interests and levels of academic ability.

Focus: Academic/pre-college enrichment

Activities Center On: Academic and science

Intensity Level: 3

Duration: Less than 1 week, 1–2 weeks

Program Offered: Summer

Location: Alfred, New York

Accommodations: Dormitory

Years in Operation: 6

Religious Affiliation: Not relevant

STAFF

Student/Staff Ratio: 10:1

Staff Qualifications: Programs are taught by Alfred University full-time faculty.

PARTICIPANTS

Average Number of Participants: 25

For Participants Aged: 14–17

The Ideal Candidate: A high school student with a keen interest in astronomy, interested in pursuing an education in the phsycial sciences or math, who has completed his/her freshman, sophomore, or junior year.

Special Requirements for Participation: Students considering the advanced-level track should have had at least one course in astronomy or have done a lot of serious reading on the subject.

COSTS

Average Cost: $500

Included in Cost: The cost for the institute covers room and board from dinner on the first day through lunch on the last day, tuition, and program materials.

Financial Aid Available: No

SUMMER INSTITUTE IN ENTREPRENEURIAL LEADERSHIP

THE PROGRAM

Description: This program is designed for students interested in learning how to be successful entrepreneurs. Students participate in hands-on workshops covering a wide variety of topics such as marketing, financial planning, e-commerce, and business plans.

Specialty: This program is staffed by distinguished members of our business faculty and provides instruction in entrepreneurial leadership.

Program Type: Academic/pre-college enrichment

Classification: Coeducational, residential

Goals: Participants will learn more about entrepreneurship and the world of business, will sample life on a college campus, and meet other students with similar interests.

Focus: Academic/pre-college enrichment and leadership and teamwork

Activities Center On: Academic

Intensity Level: 3

Duration: Less than 1 week, 1–2 weeks

Program Offered: Summer

Location: Alfred, NY

Accommodations: Dormitory

Years in Operation: 6

Religious Affiliation: Not relevant

STAFF

Student/Staff Ratio: 10:1

Staff Qualifications: The program is staffed by members of the Alfred University College of Business Faculty.

PARTICIPANTS

Average Number of Participants: 20

For Participants Aged: 14–17

The Ideal Candidate: This program is for students interested in learning how to be successful entrepreneurs and who have completed their freshman, sophomore, or junior years of high school.

Special Requirements for Participation: Students must have completed their freshman, sophomore, or junior year of high school, and must provide two letters of recommendation from high school teachers, a recent transcript, and an essay explaining why they want to attend.

COSTS

Average Cost: $500

Included in Cost: The cost for the institute covers room and board from dinner on the first day through lunch on the last day, tuition, and recreational activities.

Financial Aid Available: No

Summer Institutes in Creative Writing

The Program

Description: These institutes provide an introduction to some of the most powerful and important genres: poetry, short fiction, creative nonfiction, and drama. In both morning and afternoon sessions, students participate in writing-intensive exercises and workshops.

Specialty: Programs are staffed by English professors who work with students in group and individual settings, presenting a detailed introduction to poetry, short fiction, creative nonfiction, and drama, and helping the students develop and refine their own writing skills.

Program Type: Academic/pre-college enrichment

Classification: Coeducational, residential

Goals: Students will learn ways to improve their writing skills and will come away with a greater understanding of the genres explored.

Focus: Academic/pre-college enrichment and skill-building

Activities Center On: Academic, writing, and liberal arts

Intensity Level: 3

Duration: 1–2 weeks

Program Offered: Summer

Location: Alfred, New York

Accommodations: Dormitory

Years in Operation: 4

Religious Affiliation: Not relevant

Staff

Student/Staff Ratio: 10:1

Staff Qualifications: The program is staffed by distinguished members of the Alfred University English faculty.

Participants

Average Number of Participants: 25

For Participants Aged: 14–17

The Ideal Candidate: A high school student with a keen interest creative writing, who has completed his/her freshman, sophomore, or junior year, and who wishes to improve his/her writing skills.

Special Requirements for Participation: Applicants must have completed their freshman, sophomore, or junior year of high school, and must submit an essay, two letters of recommendation from high school teachers, and a recent transcript.

Costs

Average Cost: $500

Included in Cost: The costs range from about $500 for the 6-day institute to about $1,000 for the 11-day institute. This covers room and board, tuition, and program materials.

Financial Aid Available: No

American Association of Teachers of German

AATG is a nonprofit membership organization dedicated to the advancement and improvement of the teaching of the language, literature, and cultures of the German-speaking world.

Years in Operation: 76

Religious Affiliation: Not relevant

Price Range of Programs: $2,500–$2,750

For More Information:
  Contact: Helene Zimmer-Loew, Executive Director
                112 Haddontowne Court #104
                Cherry Hill, NJ 08034
  Phone: 856-795-5553
  Fax: 856-795-9398
  Email: headquarters@aatg.org
  Website: www.aatg.org/programs/hssstudentprogs/sum-stud.html

German Summer Study Program

The Program

Description: Travel to Germany with an American teacher of German, live with a host family, attend school, and go on excursions. Prerequisite: Two years of German language study. Enrollment begins on December 1. Cost includes international air fare.

Specialty: Living with host families and attending school/excursions. Participants are accompanied by American teachers of German. The program is directed by local teachers at German high schools, is coordinated by AATG, and is sponsored by Pedagogical Exchange Service of the German government.

Program Type: Academic/pre-college enrichment, travel/cultural

Classification: Coeducational, residential

Goals: Students gain confidence in their language proficiency through immersion in Germany and acquire a deeper understanding and appreciation of customs, values, and viewpoints of both Germans and Americans.

Focus: Academic/pre-college enrichment, cultural, and travel

Activities Center On: Language, cultural, and travel

Intensity Level: 3

Duration: 2–4 weeks

Program Offered: Summer

Location: Various locations in Germany

Accommodations: Family-stay/host-family

Years in Operation: 30

Religious Affiliation: Not relevant

STAFF

Student/Staff Ratio: 14:1

Staff Qualifications: American teachers of German serve as chaperones and liaisons with the German program director (a teacher at the academic high school that students attend).

PARTICIPANTS

Average Number of Participants: 100

For Participants Aged: 15–18

The Ideal Candidate: A student with two years of high school German who is mature and ready for a study abroad experience.

Special Requirements for Participation: Prerequisite: two years of high school German and teacher recommendation.

COSTS

Average Cost: $2,600

Included in Cost: Included: international airfare from departure airport, transfer to course site, home stay with families, academic program, and excursions. Not included: passport fees, excess baggage charges, transportation to/from departure airport, spending money.

Financial Aid Available: Yes

AMERICAN FARM SCHOOL

The American Farm School of Thessaloniki, Greece, is a private, nonprofit educational institution founded in 1904 to serve the rural population of Greece and the Balkans. It is a 501(c)(3) organization registered in the State of New York. Major divisions include the Secondary School, the Dimitris Perrotis College of Agricultural Studies, the Department of Lifelong Learning, and a cultural exchange program for U.S. and international high school students known as Greek Summer.

Years in Operation: 100

Religious Affiliation: Not relevant

For More Information:
Contact: Hilary Goldstein, Development Asso./Program Coordinator
1133 Broadway, Suite 1625
New York, NY 10010
Phone: 212-463-8434
Fax: 212-463-8208
Email: nyoffice@amerfarm.org
Website: www.afs.edu.gr

GREEK SUMMER

THE PROGRAM

Description: Greek Summer is a six-week community service, cultural immersion, and travel odyssey for high school students. Each year students complete a community service project while living with a host family in a small Greek village. In addition students spend close to two weeks traveling throughout Greece, visiting such sites as the Oracle at Delphi, the Acropolis, and a selection of the Greek Isles. The culmination of the trip is marked by a two-day hike to the summit of Mount Olympus.

Specialty: In its 33-year history, Greek Summer has become one of the top summer programs available. The program combines the exhileration of adventure travel with the joy of true cultural immersion through a village homestay and a community service project.

Program Type: Community Service, outdoors/adventure, travel/cultural

Classification: Coeducational, residential

Goals: Participants will be completely immersed in the Greek culture for the duration of the program. They should expect to learn a great deal about the Greek culture and about themselves as they proceed through the program.

Focus: Cultural, community service, and travel

Activities Center On: Cultural, volunteer, and travel

Intensity Level: 4

Duration: 4–6 weeks

Program Offered: Summer

Location: Thessaloniki, Greece

Accommodations: Dormitory, family-stay/host-family, tent, bunk/cabin, hotels, youth hostels

Years in Operation: 33

Religious Affiliation: Not relevant

STAFF

Student/Staff Ratio: 5:1

Staff Qualifications: Counselors: four-year university graduates with prior camp counselor experience; director: a former counselor; assistant director: member of the staff of the American Farm School in Greece; program coordinator: runs the program year round from New York, then travels with the program for its duration in Greece.

PARTICIPANTS

Average Number of Participants: 35

For Participants Aged: 15–19

The Ideal Candidate: Our ideal candidate is someone who is open to other cultures, willing to learn, and looking for an adventure.

Special Requirements for Participation: Students must be age 15–19 and have completed their sophomore, junior, or senior year in high school.

COSTS

Average Cost: $4,300

Included in Cost: Does not include airfare. Does include all expenses while in Greece: housing, travel, hotels, food, educational experiences, most entertainment.

Financial Aid Available: Yes

AMERICAN INSTITUTE FOR FOREIGN STUDY

AIFS is America's leading study abroad organization. We offer high quality high school summer study abroad programs to five countries across Europe. Our comprehensive programs include housing, meals, tuition, airfare, 24/7 on-location support services, transcripts, medical/travel insurance, and great cultural activities and excursions. AIFS has enriched the lives of more than 1 million students since we were founded in 1964. AIFS also offers college study abroad programs for the spring or fall semester, academic year, and summer to 13 countries. To find out more about our college programs, visit www.aifsabroad.com.

Years in Operation: 39

Religious Affiliation: Not relevant

Price Range of Programs: $4,799–$5,999

For More Information:
Contact: Drew Scott, Admissions Officer
River Plaza
9 West Broad Street
Stamford, CT 06902
Phone: 800-727-2437
Fax: 203-399-5597
Email: scott@aifs.com
Website: www.summer-enrichment.com

SUMMER ENRICHMENT ABROAD— CANNES, FRANCE

THE PROGRAM

Description: Receive four college credits studying French through the College International de Cannes. Includes cultural activities and overnight tours of London and Cannes.

Specialty: Most experience, comprehensive programs.

Program Type: Academic/pre-college enrichment

Classification: Coeducational, residential

Goals: French language/culture.

Focus: Academic/pre-college enrichment, cultural, and travel

Activities Center On: Academic, cultural, and travel

Intensity Level: 3

Duration: 4–6 weeks

Program Offered: Summer

Location: Cannes, France

Accommodations: Dormitory

Religious Affiliation: Not relevant

STAFF

Student/Staff Ratio: 15:1

Staff Qualifications: Must have master's degree.

PARTICIPANTS

Average Number of Participants: 25

For Participants Aged: 16–19

The Ideal Candidate: Motivated, independent high school juniors and seniors.

Special Requirements for Participation: 2.5 GPA; minimum age: 16 years.

COSTS

Average Cost: $5,599

Included in Cost: Round-trip airfare; tuition; room and board; cultural activities; services of on-site resident director; two-day sightseeing visit to London, England; three-day sightseeing visit to Paris, France; services of pre-departure Advisory Center.

Financial Aid Available: No

SUMMER ENRICHMENT ABROAD— LONDON, ENGLAND

THE PROGRAM

Description: Earn up to six college credits studying in London.

Specialty: Most experience, comprehesive program.

Program Type: Academic/pre-college enrichment

Classification: Coeducational, residential

Focus: Academic/pre-college enrichment, cultural, and travel

Activities Center On: Academic, cultural, and travel

Intensity Level: 3

Duration: 4–6 weeks

Program Offered: Summer

Location: London, United Kingdom

Accommodations: Dormitory

Religious Affiliation: Not relevant

STAFF

Student/Staff Ratio: 15:1

Staff Qualifications: Must have master's degree

PARTICIPANTS

Average Number of Participants: 60

For Participants Aged: 15–18

The Ideal Candidate: Motivated, independent 15- to 18-year-olds.

Special Requirements for Participation: 2.5 GPA; minimum age: 15 years.

COSTS

Average Cost: $5,299

Included in Cost: Round-trip airfare, tuition, room and board, cultural activities, services of on-site resident director, weekend excursion to Stratford-Upon-Avon, student-travel card for London buses and subway, services of pre-departure Advisory Center.

Financial Aid Available: No

SUMMER ENRICHMENT ABROAD — ROME, ITALY

THE PROGRAM

Description: Earn up to six college credits studying in Rome, Italy.

Specialty: Most experience, comprehensive program.

Program Type: Academic/pre-college enrichment

Classification: Coeducational, residential

Goals: Italian language, art history, history, and studio art.

Focus: Academic/pre-college enrichment, cultural, and travel

Activities Center On: Academic, cultural, and travel

Intensity Level: 3

Duration: 4–6 weeks

Program Offered: Summer

Location: Rome, Italy

Accommodations: Dormitory

Religious Affiliation: Not relevant

STAFF

Student/Staff Ratio: 15:1

Staff Qualifications: Must have master's degree

PARTICIPANTS

Average Number of Participants: 35

For Participants Aged: 16–19

The Ideal Candidate: Motivated high school juniors and seniors.

Special Requirements for Participation: 2.5 GPA.

COSTS

Average Cost: $5,999

Included in Cost: Round-trip airfare; tuition; room and board; cultural activities; services of on-site resident director; two-day sightseeing visit to London, England; visit to Florence, Italy; services of pre-departure Advisory Center.

Financial Aid Available: No

SUMMER ENRICHMENT ABROAD — SALAMANCA, SPAIN

THE PROGRAM

Description: Earn up to four college credits studying Spanish language and culture in Spain.

Specialty: Most experience, comprehensive program.

Program Type: Academic/pre-college enrichment

Classification: Coeducational, residential

Goals: Spanish language and culture

Focus: Academic/pre-college enrichment, cultural, and travel

Activities Center On: Academic, cultural, and travel

Intensity Level: 3

Duration: 4–6 weeks

Program Offered: Summer

Location: Salamanca, Spain

Accommodations: Family-stay/host-family

Religious Affiliation: Not relevant

STAFF

Student/Staff Ratio: 15:1

Staff Qualifications: Must have master's degree

PARTICIPANTS

Average Number of Participants: 50

For Participants Aged: 16–19

Special Requirements for Participation: 2.5 GPA; minimum age: 16 years.

COSTS

Average Cost: $4,799

Included in Cost: Round-trip airfare; tuition; room and board; cultural activities; services of on-site resident director, two-day sightseeing visit to London, England; sightseeing tour of Madrid, Spain; services of pre-departure Advisory Center

Financial Aid Available: No

Summer Enrichment Abroad — St. Petersburg, Russian Federation

The Program

Description: Earn up to eight college credits studying in St. Petersburg, Russia.

Specialty: Most experience, comprehensive program.

Program Type: Academic/pre-college enrichment

Classification: Coeducational, residential

Goals: Russian language, art history, and political science.

Focus: Academic/pre-college enrichment, cultural, and travel

Activities Center On: Academic, cultural, and travel

Intensity Level: 3

Duration: 4–6 weeks

Program Offered: Summer

Location: St. Petersburg, Russia

Accommodations: Dormitory

Religious Affiliation: Not relevant

Staff

Student/Staff Ratio: 15:1

Staff Qualifications: Must have master's degree

Participants

Average Number of Participants: 10

For Participants Aged: 16–19

Special Requirements for Participation: 2.5 GPA; minimum age: 16 years.

Costs

Average Cost: $4,999

Included in Cost: Round-trip airfare; tuition; room and board; cultural activities; services of on-site resident director; two-day sightseeing visit to London, England; excursion to Moscow, Russia; visa; services of pre-departure Advisory Center.

Financial Aid Available: No

AMERICAN TRAILS WEST

A summer of travel with American Trails West is a broadening experience in discovering new places, and an opportunity to make friends with fellow travelers from across the United States, Canada, and Europe. Many teenagers come on their own, and compatible age groupings and a wide geographic mix assure that each one will feel comfortable. Traveling on an American Trails West trip means being part of the group, a member of the ATW family. ATW's philosophy, staff, and activities make that goal a reality.

Years in Operation: 38

Religious Affiliation: Not relevant

Price Range of Programs: $2,745–$7,795

For More Information:
Contact: Director
92 Middle Neck Road
Great Neck, NY 11021
Phone: 800-645-6260
Fax: 516-487-2855
Email: info@americantrailswest.com
Website: www.americantrailswest.com

ActionAmerica West

The Program

Description: A summer of travel with American Trails West is a broadening experience in discovering new places, and an opportunity to make friends with fellow travelers from across the United States, Canada, and Europe.

Specialty: The most camping of any one-month program, with NO one-night stops!

Program Type: Outdoors/adventure, travel/cultural

Classification: Coeducational, residential

Focus: Travel

Activities Center On: Travel, outdoors/adventure, and camping

Intensity Level: 1

Duration: 2–4 weeks

Program Offered: Summer

Location: Arizona, California, Nevada, Utah, Wyoming

Accommodations: Dormitory, hotels, tent

Years in Operation: 38

Religious Affiliation: Not relevant

Staff

Student/Staff Ratio: 6:1

Staff Qualifications: College grads over 21 years of age; background and references are checked.

Participants

Average Number of Participants: 45

For Participants Aged: 14–18

Special Requirements for Participation: None.

Costs

Average Cost: $4,595

Included in Cost: Includes three meals daily, all entertainment and recreation, all lodging, gratuities, and taxes. Round-trip airfare not included.

Financial Aid Available: No

AMERICAN HORIZONS

THE PROGRAM

Description: A summer of travel with American Trails West is a broadening experience in discovering new places, and an opportunity to make friends with fellow travelers from across the United States, Canada, and Europe.

Specialty: The only all-motorcoach cross-country trip with NO one-night camping stops!

Program Type: Outdoors/adventure, travel/cultural

Classification: Coeducational, residential

Focus: Travel

Activities Center On: Travel, outdoors/adventure, and camping

Intensity Level: 1

Duration: 6–8 weeks

Program Offered: Summer

Location: Arizona, California, Colorado, Illinois, Kansas, Michigan, Minnesota, Missouri, Nevada, New York, Ohio, Pennsylvania, South Dakota, Utah, Wisconsin, Wyoming

Accommodations: Dormitory, hotels, tent

Years in Operation: 38

Religious Affiliation: Not relevant

STAFF

Student/Staff Ratio: 6:1

Staff Qualifications: College grads over 21 years of age; background and references are checked.

PARTICIPANTS

Average Number of Participants: 45

For Participants Aged: 14–18

Special Requirements for Participation: None.

COSTS

Average Cost: $6,895

Included in Cost: Three meals daily, all entertainment and recreation, all lodging, gratuities, and taxes.

Financial Aid Available: No

CALIFORNIA SUNSET

THE PROGRAM

Description: A summer of travel with American Trails West is a broadening experience in discovering new places, and an opportunity to make friends with fellow travelers from across the United States, Canada, and Europe.

Specialty: The luxury of California and Canyon Country, with NO one-night stops!

Program Type: Outdoors/adventure, travel/cultural

Classification: Coeducational, residential

Focus: Travel

Activities Center On: Travel and outdoors/adventure

Intensity Level: 1

Duration: 2–4 weeks

Program Offered: Summer

Location: Arizona, California, Nevada

Accommodations: Dormitory, hotels

Years in Operation: 38

Religious Affiliation: Not relevant

STAFF

Student/Staff Ratio: 6:1

Staff Qualifications: College grads over 21 years of age; background and references are checked.

PARTICIPANTS

Average Number of Participants: 45

For Participants Aged: 14–18

Special Requirements for Participation: None.

COSTS

Average Cost: $4,995

Included in Cost: Includes three meals daily, all entertainment and recreation, all lodging, gratuities, and taxes. Round-trip airfare not included.

Financial Aid Available: No

CAMP INN 42

THE PROGRAM

Description: A summer of travel with American Trails West is a broadening experience in discovering new places, and an opportunity to make friends with fellow travelers from across the United States, Canada, and Europe.

Specialty: The U.S. West, Canadian Rockies, and Hawaiian Islands luxury, with NO one-night stops!

Program Type: Outdoors/adventure, travel/cultural

Classification: Coeducational, residential

Focus: Travel

Activities Center On: Travel, outdoors/adventure, and camping

Intensity Level: 1

Duration: 4–6 weeks

Program Offered: Summer

Location: Alberta and British Columbia, Canada; Arizona, California, Montana, Nevada, Utah, Washington, and Wyoming

Accommodations: Dormitory, hotels, tent

Years in Operation: 38

Religious Affiliation: Not relevant

STAFF

Student/Staff Ratio: 6:1

Staff Qualifications: College grads over 21 years of age; background and references are checked.

PARTICIPANTS

Average Number of Participants: 45

For Participants Aged: 14–18

Special Requirements for Participation: None.

COSTS

Average Cost: $7,495

Included in Cost: Includes three meals daily, all entertainment and recreation, all lodging, gratuities, and taxes. Round-trip airfare not included.

Financial Aid Available: No

DISCOVERER

THE PROGRAM

Description: A summer of travel with American Trails West is a broadening experience in discovering new places, and an opportunity to make friends with fellow travelers from across the United States, Canada, and Europe.

Specialty: Best of the West, with NO one-night stops!

Program Type: Outdoors/adventure, travel/cultural

Classification: Coeducational, residential

Focus: Travel

Activities Center On: Travel, outdoors/adventure, and camping

Intensity Level: 1

Duration: 2–4 weeks

Program Offered: Summer

Location: Arizona, California, Colorado, Nevada, South Dakota, Utah, Wyoming

Accommodations: Dormitory, hotels, tent

Years in Operation: 38

Religious Affiliation: Not relevant

STAFF

Student/Staff Ratio: 6:1

Staff Qualifications: College grads over 21 years of age; background and references are checked.

PARTICIPANTS

Average Number of Participants: 45

For Participants Aged: 14–18

Special Requirements for Participation: None.

COSTS

Average Cost: $5,795

Included in Cost: Includes three meals daily, all entertainment and recreation, all lodging, gratuities, and taxes. Round-trip airfare not included.

Financial Aid Available: No

EUROPEAN ADVENTURES

THE PROGRAM

Description: A summer of travel with American Trails West is a broadening experience in discovering new places, and an opportunity to make friends with fellow travelers from across the United States, Canada, and Europe.

Specialty: Wimbledon, Tuscan cooking school, snow skiing in Zermatt, Mediterranean water-skiing, two Action Centers, and NO one-night stops!

Program Type: Travel/cultural

Classification: Coeducational, residential

Focus: Travel and cultural

Activities Center On: Travel and cultural

Intensity Level: 1

Duration: 2–4 weeks

Program Offered: Summer

Location: France, Italy, Switzerland, United Kingdom

Accommodations: Hotels

Years in Operation: 38

Religious Affiliation: Not relevant

STAFF

Student/Staff Ratio: 8:1

PARTICIPANTS

Average Number of Participants: 40

For Participants Aged: 16–18

Special Requirements for Participation: None.

COSTS

Average Cost: $7,295

Included in Cost: Includes three meals daily, all entertainment and recreation, all lodging, gratuities, and taxes. Round-trip airfare not included.

Financial Aid Available: No

FIRE AND ICE

THE PROGRAM

Description: A summer of travel with American Trails West is a broadening experience in discovering new places, and an opportunity to make friends with fellow travelers from across the United States, Canada, and Europe.

Specialty: The action and excitement of Alaska, the luxury of Hawaii, with NO one-night stops!

Program Type: Outdoors/adventure, travel/cultural

Classification: Coeducational, residential

Focus: Travel

Activities Center On: Travel and outdoors/adventure

Intensity Level: 1

Duration: 4–6 weeks

Program Offered: Summer

Location: Alaska, California, Hawaii, Washington; British Columbia, Canada

Accommodations: Hotels

Years in Operation: 38

Religious Affiliation: Not relevant

STAFF

Student/Staff Ratio: 6:1

Staff Qualifications: College grads over 21 years of age; background and references are checked.

PARTICIPANTS

Average Number of Participants: 45

For Participants Aged: 14–18

Special Requirements for Participation: None.

COSTS

Average Cost: $7,795

Included in Cost: Includes three meals daily, all entertainment and recreation, all lodging, gratuities, and taxes. Round-trip airfare not included.

Financial Aid Available: No

PACIFIC PARADISE

THE PROGRAM

Description: A summer of travel with American Trails West is a broadening experience in discovering new places, and an opportunity to make friends with fellow travelers from across the United States, Canada, and Europe.

Specialty: All hotels and dorms; the best of the West and the Canadian Rockies, with NO one-night stops!

Program Type: Outdoors/adventure, travel/cultural

Classification: Coeducational, residential

Focus: Travel

Activities Center On: Travel and outdoors/adventure

Intensity Level: 1

Duration: 4–6 weeks

Program Offered: Summer

Location: Arizona, California, Montana, Nevada, Utah, Washington, Wyoming; Alberta and British Columbia, Canada

Accommodations: Dormitory, hotels

Years in Operation: 38

Religious Affiliation: Not relevant

STAFF

Student/Staff Ratio: 6:1

Staff Qualifications: College grads over 21 years of age; background and references are checked.

PARTICIPANTS

Average Number of Participants: 45

For Participants Aged: 14–18

Special Requirements for Participation: None.

COSTS

Average Cost: $7,895

Included in Cost: Includes three meals daily, all entertainment and recreation, all lodging, gratuities, and taxes. Round-trip airfare not included.

Financial Aid Available: No

SKYBLAZER

THE PROGRAM

Description: A summer of travel with American Trails West is a broadening experience in discovering new places, and an opportunity to make friends with fellow travelers from across the United States, Canada, and Europe.

Specialty: Summer snow skiing, water-skiing on Lake Tahoe, two raft trips, giant snowmobile tour, and NO one-night stops!

Program Type: Outdoors/adventure, travel/cultural

Classification: Coeducational, residential

Focus: Travel

Activities Center On: Travel, camping, and outdoors/adventure

Intensity Level: 1

Duration: 4–6 weeks

Program Offered: Summer

Location: Arizona, California, Colorado, Montan, Nevada, Oregon, South Dakota, Utah, Washington, Wyoming; Alberta and British Columbia, Canada

Accommodations: Dormitory, hotels, tent

Years in Operation: 38

Religious Affiliation: Not relevant

Staff

Student/Staff Ratio: 6:1

Staff Qualifications: College grads over 21 years of age; background and references aer checked.

Participants

Average Number of Participants: 45

For Participants Aged: 14–18

Special Requirements for Participation: None.

Costs

Average Cost: $6,995

Included in Cost: Includes three meals daily, all entertainment and recreation, all lodging, gratuities, and taxes. Round-trip airfare not included.

Financial Aid Available: No

Sunblazer

The Program

Description: A summer of travel with American Trails West is a broadening experience in discovering new places, and an opportunity to make friends with fellow travelers from across the United States, Canada, and Europe.

Specialty: California and Canyon Country action, with NO one-night stops!

Program Type: Outdoors/adventure, travel/cultural

Classification: Coeducational, residential

Focus: Travel

Activities Center On: Travel, camping, and outdoors/adventure

Intensity Level: 1

Duration: 2–4 weeks

Program Offered: Summer

Location: Arizona, California, Nevada, Utah

Accommodations: Dormitory, hotels, tent

Years in Operation: 38

Religious Affiliation: Not relevant

Staff

Student/Staff Ratio: 6:1

Staff Qualifications: College grads over 21 years of age; background and references are checked.

Participants

Average Number of Participants: 45

For Participants Aged: 14–18

Special Requirements for Participation: None.

Costs

Average Cost: $4,495

Included in Cost: Includes three meals daily, all entertainment and recreation, all lodging, gratuities, and taxes. Round-trip airfare not included.

Financial Aid Available: No

Wayfarer

The Program

Description: A summer of travel with American Trails West is a broadening experience in discovering new places, and an opportunity to make friends with fellow travelers from across the United States, Canada, and Europe.

Specialty: Coast-to-coast action; camping, hotels, and dorms; six weeks of action and excitement, and NO one-night stops!

Program Type: Outdoors/adventure, travel/cultural

Classification: Coeducational, residential

Focus: Travel

Activities Center On: Travel, outdoors/adventure, and camping

Intensity Level: 1

Duration: 4–6 weeks

Program Offered: Summer

Location: Arizona, California, Colorado, Illinois, Michigan, Minnesota, Nevada, New York, South Dakota, Utah, Wisconsin, Wyoming

Accommodations: Dormitory, hotels, tent

Years in Operation: 38

Religious Affiliation: Not relevant

Staff

Student/Staff Ratio: 6:1

Staff Qualifications: College grads over 21 yeasr of age; background and references are checked.

Participants

Average Number of Participants: 45

For Participants Aged: 14–18

Special Requirements for Participation: None.

Costs

Average Cost: $6,595

Included in Cost: Includes three meals daily, all entertainment and recreation, all lodging, gratuities, and taxes. Airfare not included.

Financial Aid Available: No

AMERICA'S ADVENTURE/ VENTURE EUROPE

Worldwide adventure travel tours for teenagers since 1976.

Years in Operation: 28

Religious Affiliation: Not relevant

Price Range of Programs: $1,988–$4,400

For More Information:
Contact: Abbott Wallis, Owner
2245 Stonecrop Way
Golden, CO 80401
Phone: 800-222-3595
Fax: 303-526-0885
Email: info@aave.com
Website: www.aave.com

AAVE—Australia

The Program

Description: Explore beauty and adventure Down Under.

Specialty: Small, cohesive groups face challenges and adventure.

Program Type: Outdoors/adventure

Classification: Coeducational, residential

Focus: Travel, leadership/teamwork, and cultural

Activities Center On: Outdoors/adventure, diving, and travel

Intensity Level: 3

Duration: 2–4 weeks

Program Offered: Summer

Location: Australia

Accommodations: Tent

Years in Operation: 28

Religious Affiliation: Not relevant

Staff

Student/Staff Ratio: 12:2

Staff Qualifications: College degree; Wilderness First Responder and lifeguard certification.

Participants

Average Number of Participants: 12

For Participants Aged: 14–18

The Ideal Candidate: Active, enthusiastic team player seeking adventure.

Special Requirements for Participation: None.

Costs

Average Cost: $3,500

Included in Cost: Everything is included except airfare.

Financial Aid Available: Yes

AAVE—Belize

The Program

Description: Outdoor adventure and ecology in Belize.

Specialty: Small, cohesive groups face challenges and learn leadership skills through adventure.

Program Type: Outdoors/adventure

Classification: Coeducational, residential

Goals: Ecology, culture, and adventure travel skills.

Focus: Academic/pre-college enrichment, travel, and leadership/teamwork

Activities Center On: Outdoors/adventure, science, and travel

Intensity Level: 3

Duration: 2–4 weeks

Program Offered: Summer

Location: Belize

Accommodations: Family-stay/host-family, tent, bunk/cabin, youth hostels

Years in Operation: 28

Religious Affiliation: Not relevant

Staff

Student/Staff Ratio: 12:2

Staff Qualifications: College degree; Wilderness First Responder and lifeguard certification.

Participants

Average Number of Participants: 13

For Participants Aged: 15–18

The Ideal Candidate: Adventurous, active team player seeking challenge and fun.

Special Requirements for Participation: None.

Costs

Average Cost: $3,500

Included in Cost: Everything is included except airfare.

Financial Aid Available: Yes

AAVE—Bold Europe

The Program

Description: Adventure and culture in France, Spain, and Italy.

Specialty: Small, cohesive groups face challenges and learn leadership skills through adventure activities.

Program Type: Outdoors/adventure

Classification: Coeducational, residential

Goals: Culture and adventure activities.

Focus: Travel, cultural, and leadership/teamwork

Activities Center On: Outdoors/adventure, travel, and cultural

Intensity Level: 3

Duration: 2–4 weeks

Program Offered: Summer

Location: France, Spain, and Italy

Accommodations: Tent, bunk/cabin, hotels, youth hostels

Years in Operation: 28

Religious Affiliation: Not relevant

STAFF

Student/Staff Ratio: 12:2

Staff Qualifications: College degree; Wilderness First Responder and lifeguard certification.

PARTICIPANTS

Average Number of Participants: 13

For Participants Aged: 14–18

The Ideal Candidate: Active, enthusiastic team player seeking adventure, challenge, and cultural exploration.

Special Requirements for Participation: None.

COSTS

Average Cost: $4,000

Included in Cost: Everything is included except airfare.

Financial Aid Available: Yes

AAVE—BOLD WEST

THE PROGRAM

Description: Exploration and adventure throughout America's West.

Specialty: Small, cohesive groups face challenges and learn leadership skills through adventure.

Program Type: Outdoors/adventure

Classification: Coeducational, residential

Goals: Leadership and outdoor skills.

Focus: Travel, leadership/teamwork, and skill-building

Activities Center On: Hiking, touring, and wilderness

Intensity Level: 3

Duration: 2–4 weeks

Program Offered: Summer

Location: Califonia, Nevada, and Utah

Accommodations: Tent, hotels, youth hostels

Years in Operation: 28

Religious Affiliation: Not relevant

STAFF

Student/Staff Ratio: 12:2

Staff Qualifications: College degree; and Wilderness First Responder and lifeguard certification.

PARTICIPANTS

Average Number of Participants: 13

For Participants Aged: 14–18

The Ideal Candidate: Active, enthusiastic team player seeking adventure.

Special Requirements for Participation: None.

COSTS

Average Cost: $3,500

Included in Cost: Everything included except airfare.

Financial Aid Available: Yes

AAVE—COSTA RICA

THE PROGRAM

Description: Spanish language, adventure, and community service in a beautiful, safe Central American country.

Specialty: Small, cohesive groups face challenges and learn leadership skills through adventure.

Program Type: Outdoors/adventure

Classification: Coeducational, residential

Goals: Spanish, outdoor activity, and leadership skills.

Focus: Academic/pre-college enrichment, community service, and cultural

Activities Center On: Academic, outdoors/adventure, and volunteer

Intensity Level: 3

Duration: 2–4 weeks

Program Offered: Summer

Location: Costa Rica

Accommodations: Family-stay/host-family, tent, bunk/cabin, youth hostels

Years in Operation: 28

Religious Affiliation: Not relevant

STAFF

Student/Staff Ratio: 12:2

Staff Qualifications: College degree; Wilderness First Responder and lifeguard certification.

PARTICIPANTS

Average Number of Participants: 13

For Participants Aged: 14–18

The Ideal Candidate: Enthusiastic, active team player seeking adventure.

Special Requirements for Participation: Minimum of one year of Spanish.

Costs

Average Cost: $3,500

Included in Cost: Everything except airfare is included.

Financial Aid Available: No

AAVE — Hawaii

The Program

Description: Adventure activities on the Big Island.

Specialty: Small, cohesive groups face challenges and adventure.

Program Type: Outdoors/adventure

Classification: Coeducational, residential

Focus: Travel, leadership/teamwork, and skill-building

Activities Center On: Outdoors/adventure, sailing, and backpacking

Intensity Level: 3

Duration: 2–4 weeks

Program Offered: Summer

Location: Hawaii

Accommodations: Tent

Years in Operation: 28

Religious Affiliation: Not relevant

Staff

Student/Staff Ratio: 12:2

Staff Qualifications: College degree; Wilderness First Responder and lifeguard certification.

Participants

Average Number of Participants: 13

For Participants Aged: 14–18

The Ideal Candidate: Enthusiastic, fun team player looking for active adventure experience.

Special Requirements for Participation: None.

Costs

Average Cost: $3,500

Included in Cost: Everything except airfare is included.

Financial Aid Available: Yes

AAVE — Leader's Pick

The Program

Description: Adventure activities in Colorado and Utah.

Specialty: Small, cohesive groups face challenges and enjoy adventure.

Program Type: Outdoors/adventure

Classification: Coeducational, residential

Goals: Rock climbing, backpacking, rafting, and mountain biking skills.

Focus: Skill-building, leadership/teamwork, and travel

Activities Center On: Outdoors/adventure, backpacking, and rafting

Intensity Level: 4

Duration: 2–4 weeks

Program Offered: Summer

Location: Colorado

Accommodations: Tent

Years in Operation: 28

Religious Affiliation: Not relevant

Staff

Student/Staff Ratio: 12:2

Staff Qualifications: College degree; Wilderness First Responder and lifeguard certification.

Participants

Average Number of Participants: 12

For Participants Aged: 14–18

The Ideal Candidate: Enthusiastic, active team player seeking adventure.

Special Requirements for Participation: None.

Costs

Average Cost: $3,500

Included in Cost: Everything except airfare is included.

Financial Aid Available: Yes

AAVE — New Zealand

The Program

Description: Wilderness exploration of New Zealand's beautiful landscapes.

Specialty: Teens are taught independence and leadership skills through rugged challenges. Small group sizes allow for personal growth and team dynamic.

Program Type: Outdoors/adventure

Classification: Coeducational, residential

Goals: Outdoor skills, teamwork and leadership skills, sea kayaking, backpacking, skiing, and cultural insights.

Focus: Travel, leadership/teamwork, and cultural

Activities Center On: Outdoors/adventure

Intensity Level: 3

Duration: 2–4 weeks

Program Offered: Summer

Location: New Zealand

Accommodations: Tent

Years in Operation: 28

Religious Affiliation: Not relevant

STAFF

Student/Staff Ratio: 12:2

Staff Qualifications: College degree; Wilderness First Responder, Professional Rescuer CPR, and lifeguard certification.

PARTICIPANTS

Average Number of Participants: 12

For Participants Aged: 15–18

The Ideal Candidate: Enthusiastic, active teenager seeking adventure and friendship as part of a team.

Special Requirements for Participation: None.

COSTS

Average Cost: $3,888

Included in Cost: Everything is included except for round-trip airfare to New Zealand.

Financial Aid Available: Yes

AAVE — THAILAND

THE PROGRAM

Description: Adventure and cultural exploration in Thailand.

Specialty: Small, cohesive groups face challenges and learn leadership skills through adventure.

Program Type: Outdoors/adventure

Classification: Coeducational, residential

Goals: Thai culture and cooking, adventure travel, and leadership skills.

Focus: Cultural, travel, and leadership/teamwork

Activities Center On: Outdoors/adventure, travel, and trekking

Intensity Level: 3

Duration: 2–4 weeks

Program Offered: Summer

Location: Thailand

Accommodations: Tent, bunk/cabin, youth hostels

Years in Operation: 28

Religious Affiliation: Not relevant

STAFF

Student/Staff Ratio: 12:2

Staff Qualifications: College degree; Wilderness First Responder and lifeguard certification.

PARTICIPANTS

Average Number of Participants: 12

For Participants Aged: 15–18

The Ideal Candidate: Adventurous, active team player seeking culture and fun.

Special Requirements for Participation: None.

COSTS

Average Cost: $3,500

Included in Cost: Everything except airfare is included.

Financial Aid Available: Yes

AAVE — VIVONS LE FRANÇAIS

THE PROGRAM

Description: French language program that combines academics with adventure.

Specialty: Small, cohesive groups face challenges and learn leadership skills through adventure.

Program Type: Travel/cultural

Classification: Coeducational, residential

Goals: French-speaking skills and outdoor adventure travel.

Focus: Travel, cultural, and academic/pre-college enrichment

Activities Center On: Travel, academic, and outdoors/adventure

Intensity Level: 3

Duration: 2–4 weeks

Program Offered: Summer

Location: France

Accommodations: Tent

Years in Operation: 28

Religious Affiliation: Not relevant

STAFF

Student/Staff Ratio: 12:2

Staff Qualifications: College degree; Wilderness First Responder and lifeguard certification.

PARTICIPANTS

Average Number of Participants: 13

For Participants Aged: 15–18

The Ideal Candidate: Adventurous, active team player seeking challenges and fun.

Special Requirements for Participation: One year of French.

COSTS

Average Cost: $4,000

Included in Cost: Everything except airfare is included.

Financial Aid Available: No

AAVE—WILD ISLES

THE PROGRAM

Description: Adventure in the British Isles.

Specialty: Small, cohesive groups face challenges and learn leadership skills through adventure.

Program Type: Outdoors/adventure

Classification: Coeducational, residential

Focus: Travel, cultural, and leadership/teamwork

Activities Center On: Outdoors/adventure, history, and travel

Intensity Level: 3

Duration: 2–4 weeks

Program Offered: Summer

Location: United Kingdom

Accommodations: Tent, bunk/cabin, youth hostels

Years in Operation: 28

Religious Affiliation: Not relevant

STAFF

Student/Staff Ratio: 12:2

Staff Qualifications: College degree; Wilderness First Responder and lifeguard certification.

PARTICIPANTS

Average Number of Participants: 13

For Participants Aged: 14–18

The Ideal Candidate: Adventurous, enthusiastic team player who seeks fun and culture.

Special Requirements for Participation: None.

COSTS

Average Cost: $3,500

Included in Cost: Everything except airfare is included.

Financial Aid Available: Yes

AAVE—ALASKA

THE PROGRAM

Specialty: Small groups face challenges and experience personal growth through adventure.

Program Type: Outdoors/adventure

Classification: Coeducational, residential

Focus: Travel, leadership/teamwork, and skill-building

Activities Center On: Outdoors/adventure, backpacking, and wilderness

Intensity Level: 4

Duration: 2–4 weeks

Program Offered: Summer

Location: Alaska

Accommodations: Tent

Years in Operation: 28

Religious Affiliation: Not relevant

STAFF

Student/Staff Ratio: 12:2

Staff Qualifications: College degree; Wilderness First Responder and lifeguard certification.

PARTICIPANTS

Average Number of Participants: 13

For Participants Aged: 14–18

The Ideal Candidate: Active, enthusiastic team player looking for adventure.

Special Requirements for Participation: None.

COSTS

Average Cost: $3,500

Included in Cost: Everything except airfare is included.

Financial Aid Available: Yes

AMIGOS DE LAS AMERICAS

Founded in 1965, Amigos is a youth-oriented and youth-led international, nonprofit organization that builds partnerships to empower young leaders, advance community development, and strengthen multicultural understanding in the Americas. Amigos trains and provides opportunities for a students to spend up to eight weeks in Latin America, volunteering in close collaboration with local agencies and host communities. Teams of two to three volunteers are assigned to live and work in host communities on health, education, and youth leadership projects.

Years in Operation: 39

Religious Affiliation: Not relevant

Price Range of Programs: $3,400–$3,600

For More Information:
Contact: Glenn Bayron, Director, Volunteer Administration
5618 Star Lane
Houston, TX 77057
Phone: 713-782-5290
Fax: 713-782-9267
Email: info@amigoslink.org
Website: www.amigoslink.org

LIDERAZGO Y COMUNIDAD

THE PROGRAM

Description: Volunteers promote skills in children and adolescents that will foster lifelong healthy habits, civic engagement, teamwork, and creative expression. Depending on the assigned country and local community priorities, volunteers are involved in a wide range of activities that promote disease prevention, social development, environmental conservation, and youth leadership.

Specialty: Latin American programs are managed by young adults who are former Amigos volunteers. Service projects address community priorities in sustainable and effective ways. Amigos has worked in most host countries for more than 20 years.

Program Type: Community service

Classification: Coeducational, residential

Goals: Communicating and working with people of diverse cultures; designing education programs and service projects; problem-solving skills; Spanish or Portuguese skills.

Focus: Community Service, leadership/teamwork, and cultural

Activities Center On: Volunteer

Intensity Level: 5

Duration: 6–8 weeks

Program Offered: Summer

Location: Brazil, Costa Rica, Dominican Republic, Honduras, Mexico, Nicaragua, Paraguay

Accommodations: Family-stay/host-family

Years in Operation: 39

Religious Affiliation: Not relevant

STAFF

Student/Staff Ratio: 10:1

Staff Qualifications: Project staff in Latin America are former Amigos volunteers who have demonstrated leadership and completed extensive training programs. The International Office in Houston maintains a high-level professional staff that are responsible for overall planning, management, and evaluation of programs.

PARTICIPANTS

Average Number of Participants: 700

For Participants Aged: 16–30

The Ideal Candidate: Students 16–21 years old who are inter-ested in and respectful of diverse cultures, have initiative, and good Spanish/Portuguese skills, and are willing to work hard on community projects in collaboration with others.

Special Requirements for Participation: Applicants must be at least 16 years of age, have completed sophomore year of high school, and have two years of high school Spanish or Portuguese, or an equivalent level of fluency.

COSTS

Average Cost: $3,600

Included in Cost: International airfare, food, lodging, transportion, medical insurance; training, project supplies, and supervision; emergency communications and professional support.

Financial Aid Available: Yes

APOGEE OUTDOOR ADVENTURES

Apogee offers summer bicycle touring and hiking adventures in New England and Canada to students ages 11 to 17.

Years in Operation: 3

Religious Affiliation: Not relevant

Price Range of Programs: $795–$1,995

For More Information:
Contact: Kevin Cashman, Director
40 Bowker Street
Brunswick, ME 04011
Phone: 207-725-7025
Fax: 509-693-8868
Email: info@apogeeadventures.com
Website: www.apogeeadventures.com

BURLINGTON TO BOSTON BICYCLE TOURING AND HIKING

THE PROGRAM

Description: On this moderate to challenging trip your group will bicycle tour through four spectacular New England states: Vermont, New Hampshire, Maine, and Massachusetts. This is a goal-oriented trip on which you will conquer the challenges and celebrate the rewards of adventure travel. By trip's end you will have ridden your bicycle from Burlington, Vermont, to Boston, Massachusetts, and hiked New England's tallest peak, Mount Washington—all on your own power.

Specialty: Small groups, strong leaders, trips with a goal, personal touch.

Program Type: Outdoors/adventure

Classification: Coeducational, residential

Goals: Apogee participants will develop a spirit of adventure; learn outdoor skills associated with bicycle touring, camping, and backpacking; and discover new traits and talents within themselves.

Focus: Leadership/teamwork, skill-building, and travel

Activities Center On: Touring, backpacking, and camping

Intensity Level: 3

Duration: 2–4 weeks

Program Offered: Summer

Location: Massachusetts (including Boston), Maine, New Hampshire, and Vermont (including Burlington)

Accommodations: Tent, youth hostels

Years in Operation: 3

Religious Affiliation: Not relevant

STAFF

Student/Staff Ratio: 5:1

Staff Qualifications: All leaders are at least 21 years of age and have completed their junior year in college. All are certified in first aid and CPR, and many have led for Apogee in the past.

PARTICIPANTS

Average Number of Participants: 10

For Participants Aged: 14–17

The Ideal Candidate: Apogee participants are cooperative, enthusiastic, open-minded, and determined.

Special Requirements for Participation: Participants need to be cooperative, enthusiastic, open-minded, and determined, and have some physical fitness.

COSTS

Average Cost: $2,395

Included in Cost: All food, accommodations, leaders, transport during the trip, group cooking gear, and tents are included in the cost. Personal clothing, bicycles, and gear is supplied by participants. Panniers (saddlebags) are available for rent.

Financial Aid Available: Yes

COAST TO QUÉBEC BICYCLE TOURING AND RAFTING

THE PROGRAM

Description: Imagine biking along the beautiful, craggy coast of Maine, rafting on the wild Kennebec River, moose spotting, stargazing, and having the opportunity to try out your French skills in a foreign city. You'll do all this and much more on our exciting Coast to Québec trip.

Specialty: Small groups, strong leaders, trips with a goal, personal touch.

Program Type: Outdoors/adventure

Classification: Coeducational, residential

Goals: Apogee participants will develop a spirit of adventure; learn outdoor skills associated with bicycle touring, camping, and rafting; and discover new traits and talents within themselves.

Focus: Travel, skill-building, and leadership/teamwork

Activities Center On: Outdoors/adventure, touring, and rafting

Intensity Level: 3

Duration: 2–4 weeks

Program Offered: Summer

Location: Maine; Québec, Canada

Accommodations: Tent

Years in Operation: 2

Religious Affiliation: Not relevant

STAFF

Student/Staff Ratio: 5:1

Staff Qualifications: All leaders are at least 21 years of age and have completed their junior year in college. All are certified in first aid and CPR, and many have led for Apogee in the past.

PARTICIPANTS

Average Number of Participants: 10

For Participants Aged: 14–17

The Ideal Candidate: Apogee participants are cooperative, enthusiastic, open-minded, and determined.

Special Requirements for Participation: Participants need to be cooperative, enthusiastic, open-minded, and determined, and have some physical fitness.

COSTS

Average Cost: $2,395

Included in Cost: All food, accommodations, leaders, transport during the trip, group cooking gear, and tents are included in the cost. Personal clothing, bicycles, and gear is supplied by participants. Panniers (saddlebags) are available for rent.

Financial Aid Available: Yes

ATELIER DES ARTS

Years in Operation: 8

Religious Affiliation: Not relevant

Price Range of Programs: $2,850

For More Information:
  Contact: Bruce Smith, Director
        55 Bethune Street, B645
        New York, NY 10014
  Phone: 212-727-1756
  Fax: 212-691-0631
  Email: info@atelierdesarts.org
  Website: www.atelierdesarts.org

ATELIER DES ARTS

THE PROGRAM

Description: Arts program.

Specialty: A lot of individual attention, a very warm and supportive environment.

Program Type: Music/arts

Classification: Coeducational, residential

Goals: Participants develop art and dance skills no matter what their starting level.

Activities Center On: Music/arts, dance, and travel

Intensity Level: 2

Duration: 2–4 weeks

Program Offered: Summer

Location: La Chaux-de-Fonds, Switzerland

Accommodations: Hotels

Years in Operation: 8

Religious Affiliation: Not relevant

STAFF

Student/Staff Ratio: 7:1

Staff Qualifications: Artists with art careers and many years of teaching experience.

PARTICIPANTS

Average Number of Participants: 19

For Participants Aged: 16+

The Ideal Candidate: Person with interest and focus in dance and arts.

Special Requirements for Participation: Some previous training in dance/art; all levels welcome.

COSTS

Average Cost: $2,350

Included in Cost: Included: courses, shared hotel room, pickup/return to Geneva Airport, daily buffet breakfast, five dinners a week, three day trips to interesting cities and historic and natural attractions. Not included: airfare, two dinners a week, lunches.

Financial Aid Available: Yes

AUBURN UNIVERSITY

For More Information:
Contact: Sam Burney, Director
Outreach Program Office
301 O.D. Smith Hall
171 S College St.
Auburn University, AL 36849
Phone: 334-844-5100
Fax: 334-844-3101

Email: opo@auburn.edu
Website: www.auburn.edu/outreach/opose

ARCHITECTURE SUMMER CAMP

THE PROGRAM

Description: A week long academic experience in which students work with Auburn University faculty in Dudley Hall, the home of the School of Architecture.

Specialty: Participants take Auburn University and architecture for a "test drive." Many college experiences are tried on for size: living in a campus dorm, eating meals on campus, meeting new people from a variety of places, and working hard.

Program Type: Academic/pre-college enrichment

Classification: Coeducational, residential

Goals: Students will be introduced to the challenge of being an architectural student. Experience will be gained in the studio and in the computer lab. A number of projects will be assigned during the week.

Focus: Academic/pre-college enrichment

Activities Center On: Architecture, drawing, and academic

Intensity Level: 3

Duration: 1–2 weeks

Program Offered: Summer

Location: Auburn University, Alabama

Accommodations: Dormitory

Years in Operation: 2

Religious Affiliation: Not relevant

STAFF

Student/Staff Ratio: 15:1

Staff Qualifications: Instructors are AU faculty members. Counselors are carefully selected AU students. Program developer is a continuing education professional from the AU staff.

PARTICIPANTS

Average Number of Participants: 20

For Participants Aged: 15–20

The Ideal Candidate: Highly motivated students with an artistic flair and a desire to experience being an architectural student.

Special Requirements for Participation: None.

COSTS

Average Cost: $495

Included in Cost: Instruction, materials, meals, room, and special social/recreational activities are included, as are a "Auburn Summer Experience" T-shirt and a group photo.

Financial Aid Available: No

Design Workshop

The Program

Description: A week-long academic camp in which students work in the facilities of the Industrial Design Department of the College of Architecture, Design, and Construction along side faculty members from the Design Department.

Specialty: Participants take Auburn University and industrial design for a "test drive." Students stay on campus in a dormitory, eat on campus, and enjoy special social/recreational activities.

Program Type: Academic/pre-college enrichment

Classification: Coeducational, residential

Goals: Students will split instruction time between the design studio, the computer lab, and the workshop. Various projects will be assigned in each lab. Skills learned range from basic drawing techniques to computer design to model making.

Focus: Academic/pre-college enrichment

Activities Center On: Academic, architecture, and drawing

Intensity Level: 3

Duration: 1–2 weeks

Program Offered: Summer

Location: Auburn University, Alabama

Accommodations: Dormitory

Years in Operation: 10

Religious Affiliation: Not relevant

Staff

Student/Staff Ratio: 15:1

Staff Qualifications: Instructors are AU faculty members. Counselors are carefully selected AU students. Program developer is continuing education professional from AU staff.

Participants

Average Number of Participants: 20

For Participants Aged: 15–20

The Ideal Candidate: Highly motivated students with a flair for artistic expression and an interest in design.

Special Requirements for Participation: None.

Costs

Average Cost: $495

Included in Cost: Instruction, materials, room, meals, and special social/recreational activities are included, as are a special "Auburn Summer Experience" T-shirt and a group photo.

Financial Aid Available: No

Josten Yearbook Summer Workshop

The Program

Description: This is a three-day workshop for the staff and sponsors of middle school, junior high, and high school yearbooks. Expert instruction, idea exchange, and hands-on design activities are included in the workshop.

Specialty: Staffs get a head start on the upcoming school year by identifying the new yearbook theme and design. All workshop activities and student housing take place in a first-class conference center and hotel on the AU campus.

Classification: Coeducational, residential

Goals: New ideas for upcoming yearbook, design techniques, and teamwork.

Focus: Skill-building and leadership/teamwork

Activities Center On: Graphic design, composing, and drawing

Intensity Level: 3

Duration: Less than 1 week

Program Offered: Summer

Location: Auburn University, Alabama

Accommodations: Hotels

Years in Operation: 10

Religious Affiliation: Not relevant

Staff

Student/Staff Ratio: 15:1

Staff Qualifications: Instructors are publishing professionals from Jostens Yearbook. Sponsors are teachers from the educational setting from which the students come. The program developer is a continuing education professional from the AU staff.

Participants

Average Number of Participants: 275

For Participants Aged: 14–18

The Ideal Candidate: A student already assigned to the yearbook staff who attends with the yearbook sponsor.

Special Requirements for Participation: None.

Costs

Average Cost: $195

Included in Cost: Two-night stay in hotel, meals in local fast food restaurants, materials and instruction, and special social/recreational events.

Financial Aid Available: No

BERKLEE COLLEGE OF MUSIC

Religious Affiliation: Not relevant

For More Information:
Contact: Office of Special Programs
1140 Boylston Street
MS-155 SP
Boston, MA 02215
Phone: 617-747-2245
Fax: 617-262-5419
Email: summer@berklee.edu
Website: www.berklee.edu

BUSINESS OF MUSIC PROGRAM

THE PROGRAM

Description: The Music Business/Management Department at Berklee College of Music presents a two-day workshop that focuses on music business for bands and artists, with particular emphasis on the recording industry and e-commerce.

Specialty: Web design, artist management, getting a record deal, copyright and legal issues, web marketing techniques, concert promotion, record contracts—deal points, web-commerce, and taxation in the music business.

Program Type: Music/arts

Classification: Coeducational, residential, day program

Goals: A series of seminars and workshops will cover strategies for getting a record deal; the business, legal, and taxation issues affecting record companies; music publishing; talent management; and concert promotion. The workshop will also cover website design and construction, name registration, links, chat lines, service providers, revenue generation, sound files, and marketing techniques.

Activities Center On: Music/arts

Intensity Level: 5

Duration: Less than 1 week

Program Offered: Summer

Location: Boston, Massachusetts

Accommodations: Dormitory

Years in Operation: 3

Religious Affiliation: Not relevant

STAFF

Student/Staff Ratio: 12:1

Staff Qualifications: Seminars and workshops will be conducted by Berklee's experienced and knowledgeable music business/management faculty as well as other industry professionals.

PARTICIPANTS

Average Number of Participants: 60

For Participants Aged: 15+

Special Requirements for Participation: None.

COSTS

Average Cost: $435

Included in Cost: Tuition, housing, and meals.

Financial Aid Available: No

BIRMINGHAM-SOUTHERN COLLEGE

Birmingham-Southern College is a four-year, liberal arts school affiliated with the United Methodist Church. It is located two miles west of downtown Birmingham with a current enrollment of about 1,300.

Religious Affiliation: Methodist

Price Range of Programs: $400–$1,200

For More Information:
Contact: David Driskill, Admission Counselor
BSC Box 549008
900 Arkadelphia Road
Birmingham, AL 35254
Phone: 800-523-5793
Fax: 205-226-3074
Email: dmdriski@bsc.edu
Website: www.bsc.edu

STUDENT LEADERS IN SERVICE PROGRAM

THE PROGRAM

Description: This program exposes high school students to leadership theories and provides opportunities to practice leadership through community service projects.

Specialty: A great combination of leadership and hands-on service opportunities.

Program Type: Community service

Classification: Coeducational, residential

Goals: Participants will learn different aspects of service and leadership. They will learn to recognize their own leadership skills and how to strengthen them.

Focus: Leadership/Teamwork and community service

Activities Center On: Volunteer

Intensity Level: 2

Duration: 1–2 weeks

Program Offered: Summer

Location: Birmingham, Alabama

Accommodations: Dormitory

Religious Affiliation: Methodist

STAFF

Student/Staff Ratio: 6:1

Staff Qualifications: An admission counselor will run the program along with other staff of the college. Current students will also assist.

PARTICIPANTS

Average Number of Participants: 20

For Participants Aged: 15–17

The Ideal Candidate: The ideal candidate is a rising junior or senior who is dedicated to service but wants to gain a more in-depth understanding of what it is and the many different ways to serve.

Special Requirements for Participation: None.

COSTS

Average Cost: $450

Included in Cost: Room and board, entertainment.

Financial Aid Available: No

SUMMER SCHOLAR PROGRAM

THE PROGRAM

Description: The Summer Scholar Program is a seven-week program in which rising seniors live on campus and take two college classes. Students also participate in extracurricular activities and service projects.

Specialty: It is a great combination of academics and extracurricular activities. The main focus is the two classes, but the program's extracurricular activites are designed to be enjoyable.

Program Type: Academic/pre-college enrichment, community service

Classification: Coeducational, residential, day program

Goals: Participants will take two college classes in a variety of fields. These classes are taught by college professors and are not modified in any way for the program. They are regular college classes.

Focus: Academic/pre-college enrichment, community service, and cultural

Activities Center On: Academic

Intensity Level: 2

Duration: 6–8 weeks

Program Offered: Summer

Location: Birmingham, Alabama

Accommodations: Dormitory

Religious Affiliation: Methodist

STAFF

Student/Staff Ratio: 15:1

Staff Qualifications: The director of the Summer Scholar Program is employed by the college as an admission counselor. Two current Birmingham-Southern students, one male and one female, will live in the dorms with the students and serve as assistants and resident advisors.

PARTICIPANTS

Average Number of Participants: 45

For Participants Aged: 16–17

The Ideal Candidate: The ideal candidate would be a rising senior who wants to get a feel for what college life is all about. They want to attain college credit, but that is not the main reason for their interest.

Special Requirements for Participation: None.

COSTS

Average Cost: $1,200

Included in Cost: Students living on campus will pay $1,200. Commuters will pay around $400. All students accepted to the program will receive the two classes as a scholarship.

Financial Aid Available: No

BOSTON UNIVERSITY SUMMER TERM

Boston University Summer Term sponsors three residential high school summer programs to academically challenge students while giving them an idea of what it is like to be a part of the Boston University community. Programs for rising seniors are six weeks in length, and programs for rising sophomores, juniors, and seniors are two weeks in length.

Years in Operation: 30

Religious Affiliation: Not relevant

Price Range of Programs: $4,100–$5,100

For More Information:
   Contact: Scott Alessandro, Director
             755 Commonwealth Avenue
             Room 105
             Boston, MA 02215
   Phone: 617-353-1378
   Fax: 617-353-5532
   Email: salessan@bu.edu
   Website: www.bu.edu/summer/programs

HIGH SCHOOL HONORS PROGRAM

THE PROGRAM

Description: High school students entering their senior year spend an academically challenging summer in this six-week residential program. Students register for two courses selected from all of Boston University's Summer Session 2 offerings.

Program Type: Academic/pre-college enrichment

Classification: Coeducational, residential

Focus: Academic/pre-college enrichment and educational exchange

Activities Center On: Academic

Intensity Level: 4

Duration: 4–6 weeks

Program Offered: Summer

Location: Boston, Massachusetts

Accommodations: Dormitory

Years in Operation: 26

Religious Affiliation: Not relevant

PARTICIPANTS

Average Number of Participants: 40

For Participants Aged: 16–19

Special Requirements for Participation: None.

COSTS

Average Cost: $5,100

Included in Cost: Tuition, room and board, and sponsored extracurricular activities and trips.

Financial Aid Available: Yes

SCIENCE RESEARCH INTERNSHIP

THE PROGRAM

Description: The program seeks highly talented and motivated rising high school seniors to participate in ongoing research under the direction of a faculty mentor.

Program Type: Academic/pre-college enrichment

Classification: Coeducational, residential

Focus: Internship and academic/pre-college enrichment

Activities Center On: Science

Intensity Level: 4

Duration: 4–6 weeks

Program Offered: Summer

Location: Boston, Massachusetts

Accommodations: Dormitory

Years in Operation: 26

Religious Affiliation: Not relevant

STAFF

Student/Staff Ratio: 1:1

PARTICIPANTS

Average Number of Participants: 15

For Participants Aged: 16–19

Special Requirements for Participation: None.

COSTS

Average Cost: $4,100

Included in Cost: Tuition, fees, room and board, and extracurricular trips and activities.

Financial Aid Available: Yes

SUMMER CHALLENGE

THE PROGRAM

Description: The Boston University Summer Challenge Program is a two-week college preparatory program for rising high school sophomores, juniors, and seniors. Students interact in a small, noncompetitive community and are encouraged to share their unique stories and abilities with their peers, counselors, and professors.

Program Type: Academic/pre-college enrichment

Classification: Coeducational, residential

Focus: Academic/pre-college enrichment

Activities Center On: Academic

Intensity Level: 3

Duration: 1–2 weeks

Program Offered: Summer

Location: Boston, Massachusetts

Accommodations: Dormitory

Years in Operation: 2

Religious Affiliation: Not relevant

PARTICIPANTS

Average Number of Participants: 40

For Participants Aged: 14–18

Special Requirements for Participation: None.

COSTS

Average Cost: $2,500

Included in Cost: Tuition, fees, room and board, and all extracurricular activities and trips.

Financial Aid Available: No

BRANDEIS UNIVERSITY

Years in Operation: 7

Religious Affiliation: Not relevant

Price Range of Programs: $4,250

For More Information:
  Contact: Bradley Solmsen, Director
        Genesis at Brandeis University
        415 South Street MS 085
        Waltham, MA 02454
  Phone: 781-736-8416
  Fax: 781-736-8122
  Email: genesis@brandeis.edu
  Website: www.brandeis.edu/genesis

GENESIS AT BRANDEIS UNIVERSITY

THE PROGRAM

Description: Genesis is an academic program, but it is much more than summer school. Teenagers with different beliefs and practices engage with an exceptional group of scholars, artists, activists, and experiential educators to participate in a dynamic Jewish living and learning experience.

Specialty: Throughout the summer, participants explore the Greater Boston area on major-course field trips, community service projects, or fun excursions such as going to the beach, Fenway Park, Harvard Square, or other such destinations.

Program Type: Academic/pre-college enrichment, community service, music/arts

Classification: Coeducational, residential

Goals: Courses offer in-depth, active exploration into one of five different fields: world religions; Israel and the Middle East; Judaism and the environment; law; and theater. The integration of Jewish studies into each course challenges students to find the connections between their field of interest and Judaism. Further, students choose an art workshop elective. Arts workshops are hands-on mini-courses focusing on personal exploration through the arts.

Focus: Academic/pre-college enrichment and leadership and teamwork

Activities Center On: Academic and cultural

Intensity Level: 4

Duration: 4–6 weeks

Program Offered: Summer

Location: Waltham, Massachusetts

Accommodations: Dormitory

Years in Operation: 7

Religious Affiliation: Not relevant

STAFF

Student/Staff Ratio: 6:1

Staff Qualifications: All staff are at the graduate-student level or the professional equivalent.

PARTICIPANTS

Average Number of Participants: 80

For Participants Aged: 16–18

Special Requirements for Participation: None.

COSTS

Average Cost: $4,250

Included in Cost: Tuition includes all academic programs, field trips, room and board, and all fees. Tuition does not include transportation to or from Brandeis University. Financial aid is available.

Financial Aid Available: Yes

BROADREACH SUMMER ADVENTURES FOR TEENAGERS

Summer adventures for teenagers including scuba, sailing, marine biology, and wilderness programs in Australia, the Caribbean, Costa Rica, Ecuador, Egypt, Fiji, the Galapagos Islands, Honduras, and Mexico. No experience is required for most trips. Small groups allow participants to do more, learn more, and have more fun! Adventures are hands-on, action-packed, and a blast. High school and college credit is available.

Years in Operation: 12

Religious Affiliation: Not relevant

Price Range of Programs: $3,000–$5,000

For More Information:
 Contact: Carlton Goldthwaite, Director
  PO Box 27076
  Raleigh, NC 27611
 Phone: 888-833-1907
 Fax: 919-833-2129
 Email: info@gobroadreach.com
 Website: www.gobroadreach.com

ADVENTURES DOWN UNDER

THE PROGRAM

Description: Discover the Land Down Under on this action-packed adventure to Australia! Trek and canoe through the Outback, kayak the coastline, hike in rainforests, and raft thrilling whitewater. Top it all off with a week-long scuba expedition to the Great Barrier Reef aboard a marine research vessel. No experience is necessary!

Specialty: Broadreach's program design, philosophy, and approach to experiential adventure are what make its trips so exceptional. Beyond having fun and making friends, participants in Broadreach programs have incredible opportunities for learning, discovery, and personal growth.

Program Type: Outdoors/adventure, travel/cultural

Classification: Coeducational, residential

Goals: Participants hone their skills in a variety of activities in a hands-on, learn-by-doing atmosphere including sea kayaking, rappelling, rafting, and scuba diving. They learn about the ecological and cultural diversity of Australia from the Outback to the Coral Sea. Living aboard a marine research vessel for a week, they study Minke whales and reef sharks while diving with marine scientists. They learn valuable lessons about teamwork, leadership, and openness to different beliefs and cultures.

Focus: Travel, skill-building, and cultural

Activities Center On: Outdoors/adventure, travel, and wilderness

Intensity Level: 3

Duration: 2–4 weeks

Program Offered: Summer

Location: Outback, Great Barrier Reef, coastal Australia

Accommodations: Tent, youth hostels

Years in Operation: 12

Religious Affiliation: Not relevant

STAFF

Student/Staff Ratio: 4:1

Staff Qualifications: Broadreach's diverse staff includes experiential education professionals, college professors, high school teachers, PADI scuba instructors, marine biologists, and Coast Guard–licensed sailing masters. All have a special understanding of group dynamics, teamwork, and leadership, and are motivated by a desire to work with teens and share their love of the outdoors. All lead instructors are certified as either Wilderness First Responders (WFR) or emergency medical technicians (EMT).

PARTICIPANTS

Average Number of Participants: 14

For Participants Aged: 15–19

The Ideal Candidate: Broadreach participants come from all 50 states and abroad, with a wide variety of backgrounds and experiences, but they all share a desire to have an exceptional summer by doing something different.

Special Requirements for Participation: Participants on this Broadreach trip are required to be certified in scuba diving before the program begins.

COSTS

Average Cost: $4,980

Included in Cost: Everything is included except airfare and personal spending money.

Financial Aid Available: No

AMAZON AND GALAPAGOS ENCOUNTER

THE PROGRAM

Description: Prepare for an action-packed eco-adventure! Trek snow-capped Andes Mountains and rare cloud forests. Raft, hike, and canoe through the mysterious Amazon Jungle. Top it all off with a week-long naturalist voyage through the incredible Galapagos Islands. World-class scuba diving and snorkeling is optional. Discover an abundance of wildlife both above and below the waterline in the world's most unique ecosystem.

Specialty: Broadreach's program design, philosophy, and approach to experiential adventure are what make its trips so exceptional. Beyond having fun and making friends, participants in Broadreach programs have incredible opportunities for learning, discovery, and personal growth.

Program Type: Outdoors/adventure, travel/cultural

Classification: Coeducational, residential

Goals: Participants on this eco-adventure will learn about and explore the culture and incredible ecological diversity of Ecuador, from the Andes Mountains to the Amazon Jungle to Darwin's Galapagos.

Focus: Travel, skill-building, and cultural

Activities Center On: Outdoors/adventure, wilderness, and cultural

Intensity Level: 3

Duration: 2–4 weeks

Program Offered: Summer

Location: Andes Mountains, the Amazon, Galapagos Islands, Netherland Antilles

Accommodations: Tent, youth hostels

Years in Operation: 12

Religious Affiliation: Not relevant

STAFF

Student/Staff Ratio: 4:1

Staff Qualifications: Broadreach's diverse staff includes PADI scuba instructors, experiential education professionals, college professors, high school teachers, marine biologists, and Coast Guard–licensed sailing masters. All have a special understanding of group dynamics, teamwork, and leadership, and are motivated by a desire to work with teens and share their love of the outdoors. All lead instructors are certified as either Wilderness First Responders (WFR) or emergency medical technicians (EMT).

PARTICIPANTS

Average Number of Participants: 12

For Participants Aged: 15–19

The Ideal Candidate: Broadreach participants come from all 50 states and abroad, with a wide variety of backgrounds and experiences, but they all share a desire to have an exceptional summer by doing something different.

Special Requirements for Participation: This trip is offered both with and without scuba in the Galapagos. Participants on the scuba voyage must be experienced certified divers.

COSTS

Average Cost: $4,880

Included in Cost: Most everything is included except airfare and personal spending money.

Financial Aid Available: No

ARC OF THE CARIBBEAN SAILING ADVENTURE

THE PROGRAM

Description: This once-in-a-lifetime sail-training adventure spans 600 miles across dozens of islands—Montserrat, Guadeloupe, Tobago, Statia. . . . Feel the freedom of life aboard a 50-foot yacht. Become an accomplished sailor and discover places few have been. What's next? Dominica's jungle? The Grenadine Passage? Bequia? Together we create the adventure! No experience is required.

Specialty: Broadreach's program design, philosophy, and approach to experiential adventure are what make its trips so exceptional. Beyond having fun and making friends, participants in Broadreach's programs enjoy incredible opportunities for learning, discovery, and personal growth.

Program Type: Outdoors/adventure, travel/cultural

Classification: Coeducational, residential

Goals: This comprehensive sail-training program is designed to train participants to be confident and competent sailors. No previous sailing experience is required. U.S. Sailing and ASA Sailing certifications are offered. Participants will also explore countless Caribbean Islands in a way ordinary tourists cannot.

Focus: Skill-building, leadership/teamwork, and travel

Activities Center On: Sailing, outdoors/adventure, and cultural

Intensity Level: 3

Duration: 4–6 weeks

Program Offered: Summer

Location: Leeward and Windward Islands, Trinidad and Tobago

Years in Operation: 12

Religious Affiliation: Not relevant

STAFF

Student/Staff Ratio: 5:1

Staff Qualifications: Broadreach's diverse staff includes Coast Guard–licensed sailing masters, PADI scuba instructors, experiential education professionals, college professors, high school teachers, and marine biologists. All have a special understanding of group dynamics, teamwork, and leadership, and are motivated by a desire to work with teens and share their love of the outdoors. All lead instructors are certified as either Wilderness First Responders (WFR) or emergency medical technicians (EMT).

PARTICIPANTS

Average Number of Participants: 10

For Participants Aged: 15–19

The Ideal Candidate: Broadreach participants come from all 50 states and abroad, with a wide variety of backgrounds and experiences, but they all share a desire to have an exceptional summer by doing something different.

Special Requirements for Participation: Come with a desire to try new things, work hard, learn a lot, make lifelong friends, and broaden your experiences.

COSTS

Average Cost: $4,990

Included in Cost: Most everything is included except airfare and personal spending money.

Financial Aid Available: No

BAJA EXTREME—SCUBA ADVENTURE

THE PROGRAM

Description: Experience spectacular blue-water diving on this scuba-intensive expedition to the Sea of Cortez. Encounter an extraordinary diversity of marine life—including 40-foot whale sharks, giant mantas, and playful sea lions—on over 25 dives. Sea kayak, hike in desert canyons, camp on pristine beaches, and try your hand at surfing. This is an adventure not to be missed for any scuba-certified teen!

Specialty: Broadreach's program design, philosophy, and approach to experiential adventure are what make its trips so exceptional. Beyond having fun and making friends, participants in Broadreach's programs enjoy incredible opportunities for learning, discovery, and personal growth.

Program Type: Outdoors/adventure, sports/athletic, travel/cultural

Classification: Coeducational, residential

Goals: Participants can earn several PADI scuba certifications while experiencing world-class diving in the Sea of Cortez. Discover an amazing underwater realm loaded with an incredible diversity of sea life, from huge whale sharks to tiny frogfish.

Focus: Skill-building, leadership/teamwork, and travel

Activities Center On: Diving, outdoors/adventure, and wilderness

Intensity Level: 3

Duration: 2–4 weeks

Program Offered: Summer

Location: Baja California Sur, Mexico

Accommodations: Tent, youth hostels

Years in Operation: 12

Religious Affiliation: Not relevant

STAFF

Student/Staff Ratio: 4:1

Staff Qualifications: Broadreach's diverse staff includes PADI scuba instructors, experiential education professionals, college professors, high school teachers, marine biologists, and Coast Guard–licensed sailing masters. All have a special understanding of group dynamics, teamwork, and leadership, and are motivated by a desire to work with teens and share their love of the outdoors. All lead instructors are certified as either Wilderness First Responders (WFR) or emergency medical technicians (EMT).

PARTICIPANTS

Average Number of Participants: 12

For Participants Aged: 15–19

The Ideal Candidate: Broadreach participants come from all 50 states and abroad, with a wide variety of backgrounds and experiences, but they all share a desire to have an exceptional summer by doing something different.

Special Requirements for Participation: Participants on this Broadreach trip must be scuba-certified before the start of the trip.

Costs

Average Cost: $4,180

Included in Cost: Most everything is included except airfare and personal spending money.

Financial Aid Available: No

COSTA RICA EXPERIENCE

THE PROGRAM

Description: Prepare for the ultimate eco-adventure. This program is action-packed with incredible wildlife encounters, intense whitewater rafting, surfing, sea kayaking, rainforest trekking, rappelling, remote-island camping, ecology studies, and more. No experience required!

Specialty: Broadreach's program design, philosophy, and approach to experiential adventure are what make its trips so exceptional. Beyond having fun and making friends, participants in Broadreach's programs enjoy incredible opportunities for learning, discovery, and personal growth.

Program Type: Outdoors/adventure, travel/cultural

Classification: Coeducational, residential

Goals: Learn about ecology and conservation as you explore dense jungles, raft world-class rapids, journey on horseback through cloud forest, sea kayak pristine coastline, and hike below howler monkeys playing in the trees.

Focus: Travel, leadership/teamwork, and skill-building

Activities Center On: Outdoors/adventure, wilderness, and hiking

Intensity Level: 3

Duration: 2–4 weeks

Program Offered: Summer

Location: Mostly backcountry locations in Costa Rica

Accommodations: Tent, youth hostels

Years in Operation: 12

Religious Affiliation: Not relevant

STAFF

Student/Staff Ratio: 4:1

Staff Qualifications: Broadreach's diverse staff includes experiential education professionals, college professors, high school teachers, PADI scuba instructors, marine biologists, and Coast Guard–licensed sailing masters. All have a special understanding of group dynamics, teamwork, and leadership, and are motivated by a desire to work with teens and share their love of the outdoors. All lead instructors are certified as either Wilderness First Responders (WFR) or emergency medical technicians (EMT).

PARTICIPANTS

Average Number of Participants: 12

For Participants Aged: 15–19

The Ideal Candidate: Broadreach participants come from all 50 states and abroad, with a wide variety of backgrounds and experiences, but they all share a desire to have an exceptional summer by doing something different.

Special Requirements for Participation: Come with a desire to try new things, learn new skills, explore amazing ecosystems, make great friends, and broaden your experiences.

COSTS

Average Cost: $3,960

Included in Cost: Most everything is included except airfare and personal spending money.

Financial Aid Available: No

FIJI VANUATU QUEST

THE PROGRAM

Description: Discover the wonders of the South Pacific on this scuba-diving adventure to Fiji, the Solomon Islands, and Vanuatu. The diving is outstanding, the people are incredibly friendly, and the mountainous islands are breathtaking. Dive WWII wrecks and visit an ancient headhunter shrine. Earn multiple PADI scuba certifications on over 24 dives.

Specialty: Broadreach's program design, philosophy, and approach to experiential adventure are what make its trips so exceptional. Beyond having fun and making friends, participants in Broadreach's programs enjoy incredible opportunities for learning, discovery, and personal growth.

Program Type: Outdoors/adventure, travel/cultural

Classification: Coeducational, residential

Goals: Participants should expect to discover the cultural, historical, and ecological wonders of the South Pacific—both above and below the waterline. Dive on WWII wrecks, breathtaking reefs, and pinnacles. Hike through lush rainforests, visit historical sites, and participate in village celebrations.

Focus: Skill-building, travel, and cultural

Activities Center On: Diving, outdoors/adventure, and cultural

Intensity Level: 3

Duration: 2–4 weeks

Program Offered: Summer

Location: Mostly remote villages in Fiji, Solomon Islands, and Vanuatu

Accommodations: Hotels, youth hostels

Years in Operation: 12

Religious Affiliation: Not relevant

STAFF

Student/Staff Ratio: 4:1

Staff Qualifications: Broadreach's diverse staff includes PADI scuba instructors, experiential education professionals, college professors, high school teachers, marine biologists, and Coast Guard–licensed sailing masters. All have a special understanding of group dynamics, teamwork, and leadership, and are motivated by a desire to work with teens and share their love of the outdoors. All lead instructors are certified as either Wilderness First Responders (WFR) or emergency medical technicians (EMT).

PARTICIPANTS

Average Number of Participants: 12

For Participants Aged: 15–19

The Ideal Candidate: Broadreach participants come from all 50 states and abroad, with a wide variety of backgrounds and experiences, but they all share a desire to have an exceptional summer by doing something different.

Special Requirements for Participation: Participants in this program must be scuba-certified prior to the trip. Come with a desire to try new things, learn new skills, explore amazing ecosystems, make great friends, and broaden your experiences.

COSTS

Average Cost: $4,190

Included in Cost: Most everything is included except airfare and personal spending money.

Financial Aid Available: No

GRENADINES VOYAGE—ADVANCED SCUBA

THE PROGRAM

Description: Set sail on a scuba-intensive voyage through the magical Windward Islands. Explore dense tropical jungles, majestic waterfalls, tiny villages, and remote islands you've never heard of before. Live aboard and learn to crew a 50-foot sailing yacht with 10 other teens your age. Earn multiple PADI scuba certifications on over 24 dives on pristine reefs, cool wrecks, and sheer-wall drop-offs. Join Broadreach for a summer experience you'll never forget.

Specialty: Broadreach's program design, philosophy, and approach to experiential adventure are what make its trips so exceptional. Beyond having fun and making friends, participants in Broadreach's programs enjoy incredible opportunities for learning, discovery, and personal growth.

Program Type: Outdoors/adventure, travel/cultural

Classification: Coeducational, residential

Goals: On this scuba-intensive sailing voyage participants can earn several PADI scuba certifications, including Rescue and Master Diver, as well as ASA or U.S. Sailing certifications. They will also learn a great deal about the underwater world, leadership, and teamwork.

Focus: Skill-building, travel, and leadership/teamwork

Activities Center On: Diving, sailing, and outdoors/adventure

Intensity Level: 3

Duration: 2–4 weeks

Program Offered: Summer

Location: Grenadines Islands, Grenada, Saint Lucia, Saint Vincent and the Grenadines, Trinidad and Tobago

Years in Operation: 12

Religious Affiliation: Not relevant

STAFF

Student/Staff Ratio: 5:1

Staff Qualifications: On this Broadreach program, at least one of the staff members is a PADI scuba instructor and another is a Coast Guard–licensed sailing master. All have a special understanding of group dynamics, teamwork, and leadership, and are motivated by a desire to work with teens and share their love of the outdoors. All lead instructors are certified as either Wilderness First Responders (WFR) or emergency medical technicians (EMT).

PARTICIPANTS

Average Number of Participants: 11

For Participants Aged: 14–19

The Ideal Candidate: Broadreach participants come from all 50 states and abroad, with a wide variety of backgrounds and experiences, but they all share a desire to have an exceptional summer by doing something different.

Special Requirements for Participation: Scuba certification prior to the start of trip.

COSTS

Average Cost: $4,300

Included in Cost: Most everything is included except airfare and personal spending money.

Financial Aid Available: No

HONDURAS ECO-ADVENTURE

THE PROGRAM

Description: Prepare for intense ecological adventure! Explore dense jungles with naturalists, raft thrilling whitewater, and visit dramatic Mayan ruins. Then scuba dive and study Roatan's thriving reef, and participate in dolphin research with marine mammal scientists. Earn several PADI scuba certifications on over 18 dives. No experience required!

Specialty: Broadreach's program design, philosophy, and approach to experiential adventure are what make its trips so exceptional. Beyond having fun and making friends, participants in Broadreach's programs enjoy incredible opportunities for learning, discovery, and personal growth.

Program Type: Outdoors/adventure, sports/athletic, travel/cultural

Classification: Coeducational, residential

Goals: Participants learn about both rainforest and marine ecology on an adventure that takes them from lush jungles to the world's second largest coral reef. Several PADI certifications are offered in addition to a dolphin studies certification.

Focus: Skill-building, travel, and cultural

Activities Center On: Diving, outdoors/adventure, and wilderness

Intensity Level: 3

Duration: 2–4 weeks

Program Offered: Summer

Location: Roatan and backcountry locations in Honduras

Accommodations: Tent, youth hostels

Years in Operation: 12

Religious Affiliation: Not relevant

STAFF

Student/Staff Ratio: 4:1

Staff Qualifications: Broadreach's diverse staff includes PADI scuba instructors, experiential education professionals, college professors, high school teachers, marine biologists, and Coast Guard–licensed sailing masters. All have a special understanding of group dynamics, teamwork and leadership, and are motivated by a desire to work with teens and share their love of the outdoors. All lead instructors are certified as either Wilderness First Responders (WFR) or emergency medical technicians (EMT).

PARTICIPANTS

Average Number of Participants: 12

For Participants Aged: 15–19

The Ideal Candidate: Broadreach participants come from all 50 states and abroad, with a wide variety of backgrounds and experiences, but they all share a desire to have an exceptional summer by doing something different.

Special Requirements for Participation: Non-scuba certified must complete a two-day course in their hometown to obtain a "PADI referral" before the program. All should come with a desire to try new things, learn new skills, explore amazing ecosystems, make great friends, and broaden their experiences.

COSTS

Average Cost: $3,980

Included in Cost: Most everything is included except airfare and personal spending money.

Financial Aid Available: No

MARINE BIOLOGY ACCREDITED

THE PROGRAM

Description: Unlock the secrets of the marine world on this intensive field-studies and diving program in the Bahamas. Learning is hands-on, and you'll dive with professional marine biologists with Eleuthera's thriving reefs as your class-

room. No experience is required! Earn PADI scuba certifications and high school and/or college academic credit.

Specialty: Broadreach's program design, philosophy, and approach to experiential adventure are what make its trips so exceptional. Beyond having fun and making friends, participants in Boradreach's programs enjoy incredible opportunities for learning, discovery, and personal growth.

Program Type: Academic/pre-college enrichment, outdoors/adventure

Classification: Coeducational, residential

Goals: Participants learn an incredible amount about the marine world with beautiful reefs and warm turquoise water as their classroom! Scuba training, field experiments, lectures, projects, and marine surveys qualify this course for high school/college credit.

Focus: Academic/pre-college enrichment, skill-building, and leadership/teamwork

Activities Center On: Science, diving, and outdoors/adventure

Intensity Level: 3

Duration: 2–4 weeks

Program Offered: Summer

Location: Cape Eleuthera, Bahamas

Accommodations: Dormitory

Years in Operation: 12

Religious Affiliation: Not relevant

STAFF

Student/Staff Ratio: 4:1

Staff Qualifications: Broadreach's diverse staff includes PADI scuba instructors, marine biologists, experiential education professionals, college professors, high school teachers, and Coast Guard–licensed sailing masters. All have a special understanding of group dynamics, teamwork, and leadership, and are motivated by a desire to work with teens and share their love of the outdoors. All lead instructors are certified as either Wilderness First Responders (WFR) or emergency medical technicians (EMT).

PARTICIPANTS

Average Number of Participants: 12

For Participants Aged: 15–19

The Ideal Candidate: Broadreach participants come from all 50 states and abroad, with a wide variety of backgrounds and experiences, but they all share a desire to have an exceptional summer by learning and doing something different.

Special Requirements for Participation: Come with a desire to learn new skills, explore amazing ecosystems, work hard, make great friends, and broaden your experiences.

COSTS

Average Cost: $4,080

Included in Cost: Most everything is included except for airfare and personal spending money.

Financial Aid Available: No

Red Sea Scuba Adventure

The Program

Description: The scuba diving in the Red Sea is simply outstanding—crystal clear waters; 3,000-foot drop-offs; amazing colors; and extraordinary marine life. Do tons of diving on the world's best reefs, swim with massive schools of fish, then camel-trek windswept deserts and experience Bedouin culture. Earn multiple PADI scuba certifications from Open Water Diver to Divemaster on over 30 dives. For anyone interested in scuba diving, this is a trip of a lifetime.

Specialty: Broadreach's program design, philosophy, and approach to experiential adventure are what make its trips so exceptional. Beyond having fun and making friends, participants in Broadreach's programs enjoy incredible opportunities for learning, discovery, and personal growth.

Program Type: Outdoors/adventure, travel/cultural

Classification: Coeducational, residential

Goals: Hone your scuba-diving skills and learn a ton about marine life on more than 30 dives in the world's most exotic underwater realm. PADI certifications are offered from Open Water Diver through Divemaster. Also learn about Bedouin culture and ancient history in the Sinai.

Focus: Skill-building, cultural, and travel

Activities Center On: Diving, outdoors/adventure, and cultural

Intensity Level: 3

Duration: 2–4 weeks

Program Offered: Summer

Location: Sharm El Sheikh and Na'ama Bay, Egypt

Accommodations: Youth hostels

Years in Operation: 12

Religious Affiliation: Not relevant

Staff

Student/Staff Ratio: 4:1

Staff Qualifications: Broadreach's diverse staff includes PADI scuba instructors, experiential education professionals, college professors, high school teachers, marine biologists, and Coast Guard–licensed sailing masters. All have a special understanding of group dynamics, teamwork, and leadership, and are motivated by a desire to work with teens and share their love of the outdoors. All lead instructors are certified as either Wilderness First Responders (WFR) or emergency medical technicians (EMT).

Participants

Average Number of Participants: 12

For Participants Aged: 15–19

The Ideal Candidate: Broadreach participants come from all 50 states and abroad, with a wide variety of backgrounds and experiences, but they all share a desire to have an exceptional summer by doing something different.

Special Requirements for Participation: Participants who are not scuba-certified must complete an easy two-day course to obtain a "PADI referral" before the program. Come with a desire to try new things, learn new skills, explore amazing ecosystems, make great friends, and broaden your experiences.

Costs

Average Cost: $4,280

Included in Cost: Most everything is included except airfare and personal spending money.

Financial Aid Available: No

CARLETON COLLEGE

Religious Affiliation: Not relevant

For More Information:
  Contact: Becky Fineran-Gardner, Coordinator of Summer
       Academic Programs
       1 North College Street
       Northfield, MN 55057
  Phone: 507-646-4038
  Fax: 507-646-4540
  Email: summer@carleton.edu
  Website: www.webapps.acs.carleton.edu/campus/SAP/writing

Summer Writing Program

The Program

Description: Every summer, 80 high school juniors gather on the Carleton College campus for three weeks of intensive writing instruction, activities, and friendship. Emphasizing a writing process approach, the program helps students learn to compose academic papers that are similar to those they will write in college.

Specialty: The program is primarily dedicated to helping students prepare for college-level writing; it offers a low staff/student ratio and individualized academic attention. Multiple components are designed to help the student prepare for the demands of college-level work.

Program Type: Academic/pre-college enrichment

Classification: Coeducational, residential

Goals: Students will learn to compose academic papers that are similar to those they will write in college.

Focus: Academic/pre-college enrichment

Activities Center On: Writing and ACT prep

Intensity Level: 2

Duration: 2–4 weeks

Program Offered: Summer

Location: Northfield, Minnesota

Accommodations: Dormitory

Years in Operation: 25

Religious Affiliation: Not relevant

STAFF

Student/Staff Ratio: 7:1

Staff Qualifications: College faculty and college students certifying in education and/or majoring in English.

PARTICIPANTS

Average Number of Participants: 80

For Participants Aged: 16–18

The Ideal Candidate: Candidates should currently be participating in upper-level academic courses at the high school level. Student must also exhibit strong writing skills.

Special Requirements for Participation: None.

COSTS

Average Cost: $1,950

Included in Cost: Tuition, college credit, books and class supplies, room and board, dinner and admission to a play or concert in the Twin Cities, activities, and a t-shirt.

Financial Aid Available: Yes

CARSON–NEWMAN COLLEGE

Years in Operation: 25

Religious Affiliation: Baptist

Price Range of Programs: $750–$1,400

For More Information:
Contact: Sheryl M. Gray, Director of Admissions
CNC Box 72025
Jefferson City, TN 37760
Phone: 865-471-3223
Fax: 865-471-3502
Email: sgray@cn.edu
Website: www.cn.edu

EXCEL PROGRAM

THE PROGRAM

Description: Excel is designated for students who have competed their junior year of high school and desire to begin their college career before high school graduation. Excel students may choose to enroll for one of two three-week summer terms or one six-week summer term. Courses will be available for selection from the Carson–Newman College summer curriculum.

Specialty: Students can earn up to 9 hours of college credit before their senior year of high school.

Program Type: Academic/pre-college enrichment

Classification: Coeducational, residential, day program

Goals: Participants may choose college coursework in the area of English, math, sociology, psychology, religion, history, and communication arts.

Focus: Academic/pre-college enrichment

Activities Center On: Academic

Intensity Level: 2

Duration: 2–4 weeks, 4–6 weeks

Program Offered: Summer

Location: Jefferson City, Tennessee

Accommodations: Dormitory

Years in Operation: 25

Religious Affiliation: Baptist

STAFF

Student/Staff Ratio: 15:1

Staff Qualifications: The sponsor is a full professor of education. The assistant is the director of admissions.

PARTICIPANTS

Average Number of Participants: 20

For Participants Aged: 16+

The Ideal Candidate: Participants must have a cumulative 3.0 grade point average or higher and strong recommendations from a high school teacher, principal, or guidance counselor.

Special Requirements for Participation: None.

COSTS

Average Cost: $741

Included in Cost: Tuition, room and board (15 meals), activity fees.

Financial Aid Available: No

THE CATHOLIC UNIVERSITY OF AMERICA

A friendly campus, small classes, and personal attention from accessible faculty members create a climate that stretches students' minds and broadens their horizons. CUA's commitment is to provide challenging opportunities that prepare students for an enriched academic life. The program emphasizes intellectual development, high ideals, and balance. CUA is distinguished as the national university of the Catholic Church; it was established by the U.S. Catholic Bishops in 1887.

Religious Affiliation: Roman Catholic

For More Information:
Contact: Jessica Madrigal, Director of Summer Sessions
330 Pangborn Hall
620 Michigan Ave, NE
Washington, DC 20064
Phone: 202-319-5257

Fax: 202-319-6725
Email: cua-summers@cua.edu
Website: summer.cua.edu

Capitol Classic Debate Institute

The Program

Description: The program offers concentrated instruction at the novice, junior varsity, and varsity level. Instruction consists of both lecture and hands-on experience. The Capitol Classic boasts one of the top faculties in the country.

Specialty: Students can stay to take multiple sessions.

Program Type: Academic/pre-college enrichment

Classification: Coeducational, day program

Goals: Debate theory such as counter plans, critiques, topicality, conditionality, and fiat. Lab groups focus on skill acquisition such as research, argument, and brief construction.

Focus: Academic/pre-college enrichment, skill-building, and leadership/teamwork

Intensity Level: 3

Duration: 4–6 weeks

Program Offered: Summer

Location: Washington, DC

Accommodations: Dormitory

Religious Affiliation: Roman Catholic

Staff

Staff Qualifications: The faculty includes college coaches who have led teams to the elimination rounds at the National Debate Tournament, college debaters who have cleared at most national level tournaments, and high school coaches with consistent national caliber teams.

Participants

Average Number of Participants: 50

For Participants Aged: 16–18

Special Requirements for Participation: None.

Costs

Average Cost: $2,229

Included in Cost: Tuition varies: Champion Series at $2,295; Senior Select at $2,795; and the Washington Group at $3,700.

Financial Aid Available? Yes

Eye on Engineering and Computer Science

The Program

Description: A week-long exploration of the fields of engineering: Learn what engineers do and how they are educated!

Specialty: This is a unique opportunity for interested students to get an overview of the field of engineering and a true taste of dorm life. Counselors are drawn from the current student body, and the faculty who lead the labs are the faculty of the school.

Program Type: Academic/pre-college enrichment

Classification: Coeducational, residential

Goals: The program provides an overview of the diverse fields of engineering. Students will learn the difference between a career in civil engineering and a career in biomedical engineering—or mechanical engineering or electrical engineering. They will participate in hands-on labs that help them to determine which field they might be interested in, and they will also meet with professionals who earn their living in those fields.

Focus: Academic/pre-college enrichment and skill-building

Activities Center On: Career Exploration, science, and academic

Intensity Level: 3

Duration: Less than 1 week

Program Offered: Summer

Location: Washington, DC

Accommodations: Dormitory

Years in Operation: 15

Religious Affiliation: Roman Catholic

Staff

Student/Staff Ratio: 10:1

Staff Qualifications: There are several types of program staff. An administrative staff organizes the program and supervises it. Students from the School of Engineering help to run the program and some of the labs. Faculty members teach the labs. Professional RAs and residence directors supervise the attendees in the evening.

Participants

Average Number of Participants: 100

For Participants Aged: 15–17

The Ideal Candidate: Our ideal candidate would be a rising senior, with a strong GPA, strong math test scores (PSAT or SAT), and good recommendations from math or science teachers. He or she would also work well in a team situation.

Special Requirements for Participation: Participants should complete the application, which can be found at http://engineering.cua.edu/activities/Engr2002/.
An official transcript and a letter of recommendation from a math or science teacher is also required.

Costs

Average Cost: $395

Included in Cost: The program fee includes the program and room and board. Only evening activities, which are optional, are not included in the program fee.

Financial Aid Available? Yes

OPERA INSTITUTE FOR YOUNG SINGERS

THE PROGRAM

Description: The Washington Opera with the Summer Opera Theater Company and the Benjamin T. Rome School of Music at Catholic University of America collaborate to provide a three-week program to encourage the development of young singers. Program culminates in a production.

Specialty: Institute participation may be taken for college credit.

Program Type: Music/arts

Classification: Coeducational, day program

Goals: Training in the essentials for well-educated singers, with a focus on art song literature, vocal couching, master classes, ear training, make-up, and more.

Focus: Skill-building

Activities Center On: Singing

Intensity Level: 4

Duration: 2–4 weeks

Program Offered: Summer

Location: Washington, DC

Accommodations: Dormitory

Religious Affiliation: Roman Catholic

STAFF

Staff Qualifications: Professional staff and artists from the Washington Opera engage students in workshops.

PARTICIPANTS

For Participants Aged: 15–18

The Ideal Candidate: Young singers interested in opera preparation for college and career.

Special Requirements for Participation: Auditions are held in February, and students must call ahead to schedule auditions at the Washington Opera.

COSTS

Average Cost: $1,200

Included in Cost: Cost does not include room and board. Students who take this program for credit are charged an additional $190 (summer 2003 fee).

Financial Aid Available? No

CENTER FOR CULTURAL INTERCHANGE

CCI is a nonprofit international student and adult exchange organization founded in 1985.

Years in Operation: 18

Religious Affiliation: Not relevant

Price Range of Programs: $700–$10,000

For More Information:
  Contact: Jacqui Metcalf, Outbound Programs Director
      17 North 2nd Avenue
      St. Charles, IL 60174
  Phone: 888-227-6231
  Fax: 630-377-2307
  Email: jacqui@cci-exchange.com
  Website: www.cci-exchange.com

ARGENTINA INDEPENDENT HOMESTAY

THE PROGRAM

Description: The Independent Homestay Program focuses exclusively on the short-term homestay experience and is perfect for teens and adults wanting complete immersion in a new culture.

Program Type: Travel/cultural

Classification: Coeducational, residential

Goals: Spanish Argentine culture and customs.

Focus: Cultural and travel

Activities Center On: Travel

Intensity Level: 4

Duration: 2–4 weeks

Program Offered: Fall, winter intersession/January term, spring, full academic year, summer

Location: Argentina

Accommodations: Family-stay/host-family

Years in Operation: 18

Religious Affiliation: Not relevant

PARTICIPANTS

For Participants Aged: 18+

The Ideal Candidate: Applicants should have an open mind, flexible attitude, good sense of humor, genuine interest in cultural exchange, and basic knowledge of Spanish.

Special Requirements for Participation: None.

COSTS

Average Cost: $1,000

Included in Cost: Program includes placement with a carefully selected host family, full board, medical insurance, and the support of a local counselor during the program.

Financial Aid Available: No

Australia High School Abroad

The Program

Description: CCI's High School Abroad Program offers the adventure of a lifetime! On this program, you will live with a host family, attend a local high school, and become a regular part of the community in your host country.

Program Type: Academic/pre-college enrichment, travel and cultural

Classification: Coeducational, residential

Goals: Culture and customs of Australia.

Focus: Cultural and academic/pre-college enrichment

Activities Center On: Cultural and academic

Intensity Level: 4

Duration: Over 8 weeks

Program Offered: Fall, spring, full academic year

Location: Australia

Accommodations: Family-stay/host-family

Years in Operation: 18

Religious Affiliation: Not relevant

Participants

For Participants Aged: 15–18

The Ideal Candidate: Applicants should have an open mind, flexible attitude, good sense of humor, above average grades, and genuine interest in cultural exchange.

Special Requirements for Participation: None.

Costs

Average Cost: $6,800

Included in Cost: Program includes placement with a carefully selected host family, enrollment in a high school and school fees, full board, medical insurance, and the support of a local counselor during the program.

Financial Aid Available: Yes

Brazil High School Abroad Program

The Program

Description: CCI's High School Abroad Program offers the adventure of a lifetime! On this program, you will live with a host family, attend a local high school, and become a regular part of the community in your host country.

Program Type: Academic/pre-college enrichment, travel and cultural

Classification: Coeducational, residential

Goals: Portuguese culture and customs of Brazil.

Focus: Cultural and academic/pre-college enrichment

Intensity Level: 4

Duration: Over 8 weeks

Program Offered: Fall, spring, full academic year

Location: Brazil

Accommodations: Family-stay/host-family

Years in Operation: 18

Religious Affiliation: Not relevant

Participants

For Participants Aged: 15–17

The Ideal Candidate: Applicants should have an open mind, flexible attitude, good sense of humor, above-average grades, and genuine interest in cultural exchange.

Special Requirements for Participation: None.

Costs

Average Cost: $4,450

Included in Cost: Program includes placement with a carefully selected host family, enrollment in a high school and school fees, full board, medical insurance, and the support of a local counselor during the program.

Financial Aid Available: Yes

Chile Independent Homestay

The Program

Description: The Independent Homestay Program focuses exclusively on the short-term homestay experience and is perfect for teens and adults wanting complete immersion in a new culture.

Program Type: Travel/cultural

Classification: Coeducational, residential

Goals: Spanish culture and customs of Chile.

Focus: Cultural

Intensity Level: 4

Duration: 2–4 weeks

Program Offered: Fall, winter intersession/January term, spring, full academic year, summer

Location: Chile

Accommodations: Family-stay/host-family

Years in Operation: 18

Religious Affiliation: Not relevant

Participants

For Participants Aged: 17+

The Ideal Candidate: Applicants should have an open mind, flexible attitude, good sense of humor, genuine interest in cultural exchange, and basic knowledge of Spanish.

Special Requirements for Participation: None.

Costs

Average Cost: $1,000

Included in Cost: Program includes placement with a carefully selected host family, full board, medical insurance, and the support of a local counselor during the program.

Financial Aid Available: No

ECUADOR INDEPENDENT HOMESTAY PROGRAM

THE PROGRAM

Description: The Independent Homestay Program focuses exclusively on the short-term homestay experience and is perfect for teens and adults wanting complete immersion in a new culture.

Program Type: Travel/cultural

Classification: Coeducational, residential

Goals: Spanish culture and customs of Ecuador.

Focus: Cultural

Intensity Level: 4

Duration: 2–4 weeks

Program Offered: Fall, winter intersession/January term, spring, full academic year, summer

Location: Ecuador

Accommodations: Family-stay/host-family

Years in Operation: 18

Religious Affiliation: Not relevant

PARTICIPANTS

For Participants Aged: 18+

The Ideal Candidate: Applicants should have basic knowledge of Spanish, an open mind, flexible attitude, good sense of humor, and genuine interest in cultural exchange.

Special Requirements for Participation: None.

COSTS

Average Cost: $800

Included in Cost: Program includes placement with a carefully selected host family, full board, medical insurance, and the support of a local counselor during the program.

Financial Aid Available: No

ECUADOR LANGUAGE SCHOOL PROGRAM

THE PROGRAM

Description: Participants in CCI's language school programs take intensive language classes with students from around the world for about four hours a day, participate in afternoon and weekend activities and excursions of local interest organized by the language school, and live with host families during the program for a comprehensive and enjoyable learning experience.

Program Type: Travel/cultural

Classification: Coeducational, residential

Goals: Spanish culture and customs of Ecuador.

Focus: Cultural

Intensity Level: 3

Duration: Varies

Program Offered: Fall, winter intersession/January term, spring, summer

Location: Quenca, Ecuador

Accommodations: Family-stay/host-family

Years in Operation: 18

Religious Affiliation: Not relevant

PARTICIPANTS

For Participants Aged: 18+

The Ideal Candidate: Applicants should have an open mind, flexible attitude, good sense of humor, above-average grades, and genuine interest in cultural exchange. No language experience is necessary.

Special Requirements for Participation: None.

COSTS

Average Cost: $1,600

Included in Cost: Program includes language courses, placement with a carefully selected host family, half board, medical insurance, and the support of a local counselor during the program.

Financial Aid Available: No

FRANCE HIGH SCHOOL ABROAD

THE PROGRAM

Description: CCI's High School Abroad Program offers the adventure of a lifetime! On this program, you will live with a host family, attend a local high school, and become a regular part of the community in your host country.

Program Type: Academic/pre-college enrichment, travel and cultural

Classification: Coeducational, residential

Goals: French culture and customs of France.

Focus: Cultural and academic/pre-college enrichment

Intensity Level: 4

Duration: Over 8 weeks

Program Offered: Fall, spring, full academic year

Location: France

Accommodations: Family-stay/host-family

Years in Operation: 18

Religious Affiliation: Not relevant

PARTICIPANTS

For Participants Aged: 15–18

The Ideal Candidate: Applicants should have taken at least two years of high school French and have an open mind, flexible attitude, good sense of humor, above-average grades, and genuine interest in cultural exchange.

Special Requirements for Participation: None.

COSTS

Average Cost: $5,150

Included in Cost: Program includes placement with a carefully selected host family, enrollment in a high school and school fees, full board, medical insurance, and the support of a local counselor during the program.

Financial Aid Available: Yes

FRANCE INDEPENDENT HOMESTAY

THE PROGRAM

Description: The Independent Homestay Program focuses exclusively on the short-term homestay experience and is perfect for teens and adults wanting complete immersion in a new culture.

Program Type: Travel/cultural

Classification: Coeducational, residential

Goals: French culture and customs of France.

Focus: Cultural

Intensity Level: 4

Duration: 2–4 weeks

Program Offered: Fall, winter intersession/January term, spring, full academic year, summer

Location: France

Accommodations: Family-stay/host-family

Years in Operation: 18

Religious Affiliation: Not relevant

PARTICIPANTS

For Participants Aged: 16+

The Ideal Candidate: Applicants should have an open mind, flexible attitude, good sense of humor, genuine interest in cultural exchange, and basic knowledge of French.

Special Requirements for Participation: None.

COSTS

Average Cost: $1,100

Included in Cost: Program includes placement with a carefully selected host family, full board, medical insurance, and the support of a local counselor during the program.

Financial Aid Available: No

FRANCE LANGUAGE SCHOOL PROGRAM

THE PROGRAM

Description: Participants in CCI's language school programs take intensive language classes with students from around the world for about four hours a day, participate in afternoon and weekend activities and excursions of local interest organized by the language school, and live with host families during the program for a comprehensive and enjoyable learning experience.

Program Type: Travel/cultural

Classification: Coeducational, residential

Goals: French culture and customs of France.

Focus: Cultural

Intensity Level: 3

Duration: Varies

Program Offered: Fall, winter intersession/January term, spring, summer

Location: Antibes and Paris, France

Accommodations: Family-stay/host-family

Religious Affiliation: Not relevant

PARTICIPANTS

For Participants Aged: 14+

The Ideal Candidate: Applicants should have an open mind, flexible attitude, good sense of humor, above-average grades, and genuine interest in cultural exchange. No language experience is necessary.

Special Requirements for Participation: None.

COSTS

Average Cost: $2,500

Included in Cost: Program includes language courses, placement with a carefully selected host family, half board, medical insurance, and the support of a local counselor during the program.

Financial Aid Available: No

GERMANY HIGH SCHOOL ABROAD

THE PROGRAM

Description: CCI's High School Abroad Program offers the adventure of a lifetime! On this program, you will live with a host family, attend a local high school, and become a regular part of the community in your host country.

Program Type: Academic/pre-college enrichment, travel and cultural

Classification: Coeducational, residential

Goals: German culture and customs of Germany.

Focus: Cultural and academic/pre-college enrichment

Intensity Level: 4

Duration: Over 8 weeks

Program Offered: Fall, spring, full academic year

Location: Germany

Accommodations: Family-stay/host-family

Years in Operation: 18

Religious Affiliation: Not relevant

PARTICIPANTS

For Participants Aged: 15–18

The Ideal Candidate: Applicants should have taken at least two years of high school German and have an open mind, flexible attitude, good sense of humor, above-average grades, and genuine interest in cultural exchange.

Special Requirements for Participation: None.

COSTS

Average Cost: $4,450

Included in Cost: Program includes placement with a carefully selected host family, enrollment in a high school and school fees, full board, medical insurance, and the support of a local counselor during the program.

Financial Aid Available: Yes

GERMANY INDEPENDENT HOMESTAY

THE PROGRAM

Description: The Independent Homestay Program focuses exclusively on the short-term homestay experience and is perfect for teens and adults wanting complete immersion in a new culture.

Program Type: Travel/cultural

Classification: Coeducational, residential

Goals: German culture and customs of Germany.

Focus: Cultural

Intensity Level: 4

Duration: 2–4 weeks

Program Offered: Fall, winter intersession/January term, spring, full academic year, summer

Location: Germany

Accommodations: Family-stay/host-family

Years in Operation: 18

Religious Affiliation: Not relevant

PARTICIPANTS

For Participants Aged: 16+

The Ideal Candidate: Applicants should have an open mind, flexible attitude, good sense of humor, genuine interest in cultural exchange, and basic knowledge of German.

Special Requirements for Participation: None.

COSTS

Average Cost: $1,200

Included in Cost: Program includes placement with a carefully selected host family, full board, medical insurance, and the support of a local counselor during the program.

Financial Aid Available: No

GERMANY LANGUAGE SCHOOL PROGRAM

THE PROGRAM

Description: Participants in CCI's language school programs take intensive language classes with students from around the world for about four hours a day, participate in afternoon and weekend activities and excursions of local interest organized by the language school, and live with host families during the program for a comprehensive and enjoyable learning experience.

Program Type: Travel/cultural

Classification: Coeducational, residential

Goals: German culture and customs of Germany.

Focus: Cultural

Intensity Level: 3

Duration: Varies

Program Offered: Fall, winter intersession/January term, spring, summer

Location: Munich and Berlin, Germany

Accommodations: Family-stay/host-family

Years in Operation: 18

Religious Affiliation: Not relevant

PARTICIPANTS

For Participants Aged: 17+

The Ideal Candidate: Applicants should have an open mind, flexible attitude, good sense of humor, above-average grades, and genuine interest in cultural exchange. No language experience is necessary.

Special Requirements for Participation: None.

COSTS

Average Cost: $2,200

Included in Cost: Program includes language courses, placement with a carefully selected host family, half board, medical insurance, and the support of a local counselor during the program.

Financial Aid Available: No

INDIA INDEPENDENT HOMESTAY PROGRAM

THE PROGRAM

Description: The Independent Homestay Program focuses exclusively on the short-term homestay experience and is perfect for teens and adults wanting complete immersion in a new culture.

Program Type: Travel/cultural

Classification: Coeducational, residential

Goals: Culture and customs of India.

Focus: Cultural

Intensity Level: 4

Duration: 2–4 weeks

Program Offered: Fall, winter intersession/January term, spring, full academic year, summer

Location: India

Accommodations: Family-stay/host-family

Years in Operation: 18

Religious Affiliation: Not relevant

PARTICIPANTS

For Participants Aged: 18+

The Ideal Candidate: Applicants should have an open mind, flexible attitude, good sense of humor, and genuine interest in cultural exchange.

Special Requirements for Participation: None.

COSTS

Average Cost: $1,300

Included in Cost: Program includes placement with a carefully selected host family, full board, medical insurance, and the support of a local counselor during the program.

Financial Aid Available: No

IRELAND COMMUNITY SERVICE PROGRAM

THE PROGRAM

Description: This program combines a family homestay with placement in a local organization as a volunteer. This combination offers participants the chance to experience several aspects of Irish life, meet new people, learn valuable work and life skills, become part of an Irish community, and contribute to a worthwhile cause.

Program Type: Community service, travel/cultural

Classification: Coeducational, residential

Goals: Culture and customs of Ireland, community service skills.

Focus: Community service and cultural

Activities Center On: Volunteer and cultural

Intensity Level: 3

Duration: 1–2 weeks, 2–4 weeks

Program Offered: Fall, winter intersession/January term, spring, summer

Location: Bray, Galway, Carrigaline, and County Kerry, Ireland

Accommodations: Family-stay/host-family

Years in Operation: 18

Religious Affiliation: Not relevant

PARTICIPANTS

For Participants Aged: 18+

The Ideal Candidate: Applicants should have an open mind, flexible attitude, good sense of humor, genuine interest in cultural exchange, and spirit for volunteerism.

Special Requirements for Participation: None.

COSTS

Average Cost: $1,400

Included in Cost: Program includes placement with a carefully selected host family, meals, placement with a local organization as a volunteer, medical insurance, and the support of a local counselor during the program.

Financial Aid Available: No

IRELAND HIGH SCHOOL ABROAD

THE PROGRAM

Description: CCI's High School Abroad Program offers the adventure of a lifetime! On this program, you will live with a host family, attend a local high school, and become a regular part of the community in your host country.

Program Type: Academic/pre-college enrichment, travel and cultural

Classification: Coeducational, residential

Goals: Culture and customs of Ireland.

Focus: Cultural and academic/pre-college enrichment

Intensity Level: 4

Duration: Over 8 weeks

Program Offered: Fall, spring, full academic year

Location: Ireland

Accommodations: Family-stay/host-family

Years in Operation: 18

Religious Affiliation: Not relevant

PARTICIPANTS

For Participants Aged: 15–18

The Ideal Candidate: Applicants should have an open mind, flexible attitude, good sense of humor, above-average grades, and genuine interest in cultural exchange.

Special Requirements for Participation: None.

Costs

Average Cost: $5,990

Included in Cost: Program includes placement with a carefully selected host family, enrollment in a high school and school fees, full board, medical insurance, and the support of a local counselor during the program.

Financial Aid Available: Yes

IRELAND INDEPENDENT HOMESTAY PROGRAM

THE PROGRAM

Description: The Independent Homestay Program focuses exclusively on the short-term homestay experience and is perfect for teens and adults wanting complete immersion in a new culture.

Program Type: Travel/cultural

Classification: Coeducational, residential

Goals: culture and customs of Ireland.

Focus: Cultural

Intensity Level: 4

Duration: 2–4 weeks

Program Offered: Fall, winter intersession/January term, spring, full academic year, summer

Location: Ireland

Accommodations: Family-stay/host-family

Years in Operation: 18

Religious Affiliation: Not relevant

PARTICIPANTS

For Participants Aged: 17+

The Ideal Candidate: Applicants should have an open mind, flexible attitude, good sense of humor, and genuine interest in cultural exchange.

Special Requirements for Participation: None.

COSTS

Average Cost: $1,300

Included in Cost: Program includes placement with a carefully selected host family, full board, medical insurance, and the support of a local counselor during the program.

Financial Aid Available: No

ITALY INDEPENDENT HOMESTAY PROGRAM

THE PROGRAM

Description: The Independent Homestay Program focuses exclusively on the short-term homestay experience and is perfect for teens and adults wanting complete immersion in a new culture.

Program Type: Travel/cultural

Classification: Coeducational, residential

Goals: Italian culture and customs of Italy.

Focus: Cultural

Intensity Level: 4

Duration: 2–4 weeks

Program Offered: Fall, winter intersession/January term, spring, full academic year, summer

Location: Italy

Accommodations: Family-stay/host-family

Years in Operation: 18

Religious Affiliation: Not relevant

PARTICIPANTS

For Participants Aged: 18+

The Ideal Candidate: Applicants should have basic knowledge of Italian, an open mind, flexible attitude, good sense of humor, and genuine interest in cultural exchange.

Special Requirements for Participation: None.

COSTS

Average Cost: $1,300

Included in Cost: Program includes placement with a carefully selected host family, full board, medical insurance, and the support of a local counselor during the program.

Financial Aid Available: No

ITALY LANGUAGE SCHOOL

THE PROGRAM

Description: Participants in CCI's language school programs take intensive language classes with students from around the world for about four hours a day, participate in afternoon and weekend activities and excursions of local interest organized by the language school, and live with host families during the program for a comprehensive and enjoyable learning experience.

Program Type: Travel/cultural

Classification: Coeducational, residential

Goals: Italian customs and culture of Italy.

Focus: Cultural

Intensity Level: 3

Duration: Varies

Program Offered: Fall, winter intersession/January term, spring, summer

Location: Florence, Italy

Accommodations: Family-stay/host-family

Years in Operation: 18

Religious Affiliation: Not relevant

PARTICIPANTS

For Participants Aged: 17+

The Ideal Candidate: Applicants should have an open mind, flexible attitude, good sense of humor, above-average grades, and genuine interest in cultural exchange. No language experience is necessary.

Special Requirements for Participation: None.

COSTS

Average Cost: $1,900

Included in Cost: Program includes language courses, placement with a carefully selected host family, half board, medical insurance, and the support of a local counselor during the program.

Financial Aid Available: No

JAPAN HIGH SCHOOL ABROAD PROGRAM

THE PROGRAM

Description: CCI's High School Abroad Program offers the adventure of a lifetime! On this program, you will live with a host family, attend a local high school, and become a regular part of the community in your host country.

Program Type: Academic/pre-college enrichment, travel and cultural

Classification: Coeducational, residential

Goals: Japanese culture and customs of Japan.

Focus: Cultural and academic/pre-college enrichment

Intensity Level: 4

Duration: Over 8 weeks

Program Offered: Fall, spring, full academic year

Location: Japan

Accommodations: Family-stay/host-family

Years in Operation: 18

Religious Affiliation: Not relevant

PARTICIPANTS

For Participants Aged: 15–18

The Ideal Candidate: Applicants should have taken at least one year of Japanese and have an open mind, flexible attitude, good sense of humor, above-average grades, and genuine interest in cultural exchange.

Special Requirements for Participation: None.

COSTS

Average Cost: $4,150

Included in Cost: Program includes placement with a carefully selected host family, enrollment in a high school and school fees, half board, medical insurance, and the support of a local counselor during the program.

Financial Aid Available: Yes

JAPAN INDEPENDENT HOMESTAY PROGRAM

THE PROGRAM

Description: The Independent Homestay Program focuses exclusively on the short-term homestay experience and is perfect for teens and adults wanting complete immersion in a new culture.

Program Type: Travel/cultural

Classification: Coeducational, residential

Goals: Japanese culture and customs of Japan.

Focus: Cultural

Intensity Level: 4

Duration: 2–4 weeks

Program Offered: Fall, winter intersession/January term, spring, full academic year, summer

Location: Japan

Accommodations: Family-stay/host-family

Years in Operation: 18

Religious Affiliation: Not relevant

PARTICIPANTS

For Participants Aged: 18–50

The Ideal Candidate: Applicants should have an open mind, flexible attitude, good sense of humor, and genuine interest in cultural exchange.

Special Requirements for Participation: None.

COSTS

Average Cost: $1,300

Included in Cost: Program includes placement with a carefully selected host family, full board, medical insurance, and the support of a local counselor during the program.

Financial Aid Available: No

JAPAN LANGUAGE SCHOOL PROGRAM

THE PROGRAM

Description: Participants in CCI's language school programs take intensive language classes with students from around the world for about four hours a day, participate in afternoon and weekend activities and excursions of local interest organized by the language school, and live with host families during the program for a comprehensive and enjoyable learning experience.

Program Type: Travel/cultural

Classification: Coeducational, residential

Goals: Japanese culture and customs of Japan.

Focus: Cultural

Intensity Level: 3

Duration: 2–4 weeks, 4–6 weeks

Program Offered: Fall, winter intersession/January term, spring, summer

Location: Tokyo, Japan

Accommodations: Family-stay/host-family

Years in Operation: 18

Religious Affiliation: Not relevant

PARTICIPANTS

For Participants Aged: 18–50

The Ideal Candidate: Applicants should have an open mind, flexible attitude, good sense of humor, above-average grades, and genuine interest in cultural exchange. Applicants must be able to write hiragana and katakana.

Special Requirements for Participation: None.

COSTS

Average Cost: $1,990

Included in Cost: Program includes language courses, placement with a carefully selected host family, half board, medical insurance, and the support of a local counselor during the program.

Financial Aid Available: No

MEXICO HIGH SCHOOL ABROAD PROGRAM

THE PROGRAM

Description: CCI's High School Abroad Program offers the adventure of a lifetime! On this program, you will live with a host family, attend a local high school, and become a regular part of the community in your host country.

Program Type: Academic/pre-college enrichment, travel and cultural

Classification: Coeducational, residential

Goals: Spanish culture and customs of Mexico.

Focus: Cultural and academic/pre-college enrichment

Intensity Level: 4

Duration: Over 8 weeks

Program Offered: Fall, spring, full academic year

Location: Mexico

Accommodations: Family-stay/host-family

Years in Operation: 18

Religious Affiliation: Not relevant

PARTICIPANTS

For Participants Aged: 14–17

The Ideal Candidate: Applicants should have taken at least two years of Spanish and have an open mind, flexible attitude, good sense of humor, above-average grades, and genuine interest in cultural exchange.

Special Requirements for Participation: None.

COSTS

Average Cost: $6,820

Included in Cost: Program includes placement with a carefully selected host family, enrollment in a high school and school fees, full board, medical insurance, and the support of a local counselor during the program.

Financial Aid Available: Yes

MEXICO INDEPENDENT HOMESTAY PROGRAM

THE PROGRAM

Description: The Independent Homestay Program focuses exclusively on the short-term homestay experience and is perfect for teens and adults wanting complete immersion in a new culture.

Program Type: Travel/cultural

Classification: Coeducational, residential

Goals: Spanish culture and customs of Mexico.

Focus: Cultural

Intensity Level: 4

Duration: 2–4 weeks

Program Offered: Fall, winter intersession/January term, spring, full academic year, summer

Location: Mexico

Accommodations: Family-stay/host-family

Years in Operation: 18

Religious Affiliation: Not relevant

PARTICIPANTS

For Participants Aged: 18+

The Ideal Candidate: Applicants should have basic knowledge of Spanish, an open mind, flexible attitude, good sense of humor, and genuine interest in cultural exchange.

Special Requirements for Participation: None.

COSTS

Average Cost: $1,000

Included in Cost: Program includes placement with a carefully selected host family, full board, medical insurance, and the support of a local counselor during the program.

Financial Aid Available: No

NETHERLANDS HIGH SCHOOL ABROAD

THE PROGRAM

Description: CCI's High School Abroad Program offers the adventure of a lifetime! On this program, you will live with a host family, attend a local high school, and become a regular part of the community in your host country.

Program Type: Academic/pre-college enrichment, travel and cultural

Classification: Coeducational, residential

Goals: Dutch culture and customs of the Netherlands.

Focus: Cultural and academic/pre-college enrichment

Intensity Level: 4

Duration: Over 8 weeks

Program Offered: Fall, spring, full academic year

Location: The Netherlands

Accommodations: Family-stay/host-family

Years in Operation: 18

Religious Affiliation: Not relevant

PARTICIPANTS

For Participants Aged: 15–18

The Ideal Candidate: Applicants should have an open mind, flexible attitude, good sense of humor, above-average grades, and genuine interest in cultural exchange.

Special Requirements for Participation: None.

COSTS

Average Cost: $5,120

Included in Cost: Program includes placement with a carefully selected host family, enrollment in a high school and school fees, full board, medical insurance, and the support of a local counselor during the program.

Financial Aid Available: Yes

NEW ZEALAND INDEPENDENT HOMESTAY PROGRAM

THE PROGRAM

Description: The Independent Homestay Program focuses exclusively on the short-term homestay experience and is perfect for teens and adults wanting complete immersion in a new culture.

Program Type: Travel/cultural

Classification: Coeducational, residential

Goals: Culture and customs of New Zealand.

Focus: Cultural

Intensity Level: 4

Duration: 2–4 weeks

Program Offered: Fall, winter intersession/January term, spring, full academic year, summer

Location: New Zealand

Accommodations: Family-stay/host-family

Years in Operation: 18

Religious Affiliation: Not relevant

PARTICIPANTS

For Participants Aged: 18+

The Ideal Candidate: Applicants should have an open mind, flexible attitude, good sense of humor, and genuine interest in cultural exchange.

Special Requirements for Participation: None.

COSTS

Average Cost: $590

Included in Cost: Program includes placement with a carefully selected host family, full board, medical insurance, and the support of a local counselor during the program.

Financial Aid Available: No

PERU LANGUAGE SCHOOL PROGRAM

THE PROGRAM

Description: Participants in CCI's language school programs take intensive language classes with students from around the world for about four hours a day, participate in afternoon and weekend activities and excursions of local interest organized by the language school, and live with host families during the program for a comprehensive and enjoyable learning experience.

Program Type: Travel/cultural

Classification: Coeducational, residential

Goals: Spanish culture and customs of Peru.

Focus: Cultural

Intensity Level: 3

Duration: Varies

Program Offered: Fall, winter intersession/January term, spring, summer

Location: Cusco, Peru

Accommodations: Family-stay/host-family

Years in Operation: 18

Religious Affiliation: Not relevant

PARTICIPANTS

For Participants Aged: 18+

The Ideal Candidate: Applicants should have an open mind, flexible attitude, good sense of humor, above-average grades and genuine interest in cultural exchange. No language experience necessary.

Special Requirements for Participation: None.

COSTS

Average Cost: $1,600

Included in Cost: Program includes language courses, placement with a carefully selected host family, half board, medical insurance and the support of a local counselor during the program.

Financial Aid Available? No

POLAND INDEPENDENT HOMESTAY PROGRAM

THE PROGRAM

Description: The Independent Homestay Program focuses exclusively on the short-term homestay experience and is perfect for teens and adults wanting complete immersion in a new culture.

Program Type: Travel/cultural

Classification: Coeducational, residential

Goals: Polish culture and customs of Poland.

Focus: Cultural

Intensity Level: 4

Duration: 2–4 weeks

Program Offered: Fall, winter intersession/January term, spring, full academic year, summer

Location: Poland

Accommodations: Family-stay/host-family

Years in Operation: 18

Religious Affiliation: Not relevant

PARTICIPANTS

For Participants Aged: 16+

The Ideal Candidate: Applicants should have an open mind, flexible attitude, good sense of humor, and genuine interest in cultural exchange.

Special Requirements for Participation: None.

COSTS

Average Cost: $1,000

Included in Cost: Program includes placement with a carefully selected host family, full board, medical insurance, and the support of a local counselor during the program.

Financial Aid Available? No

SOUTH AFRICA HIGH SCHOOL ABROAD PROGRAM

THE PROGRAM

Description: CCI's High School Abroad Program offers the adventure of a lifetime! On this program, you will live with a host family, attend a local high school, and become a regular part of the community in your host country.

Program Type: Academic/pre-college enrichment, travel/cultural

Classification: Coeducational, residential

Goals: Culture and customs of South Africa.

Focus: Cultural and academic/pre-college enrichment

Intensity Level: 4

Duration: Over 8 weeks

Program Offered: Fall, spring, full academic year

Location: South Africa

Accommodations: Family-stay/host-family

Years in Operation: 18

Religious Affiliation: Not relevant

PARTICIPANTS

For Participants Aged: 15–18

The Ideal Candidate: Applicants should have an open mind, flexible attitude, good sense of humor, above-average grades, and genuine interest in cultural exchange.

Special Requirements for Participation: None.

COSTS

Average Cost: $5,690

Included in Cost: Program includes placement with a carefully selected host family, enrollment in a high school and school fees, full board, medical insurance, and the support of a local counselor during the program.

Financial Aid Available? Yes

SPAIN HIGH SCHOOL ABROAD

THE PROGRAM

Description: CCI's High School Abroad Program offers the adventure of a lifetime! On this program, you will live with a host family, attend a local high school, and become a regular part of the community in your host country. a new culture.

Program Type: Academic/pre-college enrichment, travel/cultural

Classification: Coeducational, residential

Goals: Spanish culture and customs of Spain.

Focus: Cultural and academic/pre-college enrichment

Intensity Level: 4

Duration: Over 8 weeks

Program Offered: Fall, spring, full academic year

Location: Spain

Accommodations: Family-stay/host-family

Years in Operation: 18

Religious Affiliation: Not relevant

PARTICIPANTS

For Participants Aged: 15–18

The Ideal Candidate: Applicants should have taken at least two years of high school Spanish and have an open mind, flexible attitude, good sense of humor, above-average grades, and genuine interest in cultural exchange.

Special Requirements for Participation: None.

Costs

Average Cost: $5,650

Included in Cost: Program includes placement with a carefully selected host family, enrollment in a high school and school fees, full board, medical insurance, and the support of a local counselor during the program.

Financial Aid Available: Yes

Spain Independent Homestay Program

The Program

Description: The Independent Homestay Program focuses exclusively on the short-term homestay experience and is perfect for teens and adults wanting complete immersion in a new culture.

Program Type: Travel/cultural

Classification: Coeducational, residential

Goals: Spanish culture and customs of Spain.

Focus: Cultural

Intensity Level: 4

Duration: 2–4 weeks

Program Offered: Fall, winter intersession/January term, spring, full academic year, summer

Location: Spain

Accommodations: Family-stay/host-family

Religious Affiliation: Not relevant

Participants

For Participants Aged: 14+

The Ideal Candidate: Applicants should have basic knowledge of Spanish, an open mind, flexible attitude, good sense of humor, and genuine interest in cultural exchange.

Special Requirements for Participation: None.

Costs

Average Cost: $1,800

Included in Cost: Program includes placement with a carefully selected host family, full board, medical insurance, and the support of a local counselor during the program.

Financial Aid Available: No

Spain Language School Program

The Program

Description: Participants in CCI's language school programs take intensive language classes with students from around the world for about four hours a day, participate in afternoon and weekend activities and excursions of local interest organized by the language school, and live with host families during the program for a comprehensive and enjoyable learning experience.

Program Type: Travel/cultural

Classification: Coeducational, residential

Goals: Spanish culture and customs of Spain.

Focus: Cultural

Intensity Level: 3

Duration: Varies

Program Offered: Fall, winter intersession/January term, spring, summer

Location: Madrid, Salamanca, Granada, and other locations in Spain

Accommodations: Family-stay/host-family

Years in Operation: 18

Religious Affiliation: Not relevant

Participants

For Participants Aged: 14+

The Ideal Candidate: Applicants should have an open mind, flexible attitude, good sense of humor, above-average grades and genuine interest in cultural exchange. No language experience is necessary.

Special Requirements for Participation: None.

Costs

Average Cost: $2,000

Included in Cost: Program includes language courses, placement with a carefully selected host family, half board, medical insurance, and the support of a local counselor during the program.

Financial Aid Available: No

Switzerland Independent Homestay Program

The Program

Description: The Independent Homestay Program focuses exclusively on the short-term homestay experience and is perfect for teens and adults wanting complete immersion in a new culture.

Program Type: Travel/cultural

Classification: Coeducational, residential

Goals: Culture and customs of Switzerland.

Focus: Cultural

Intensity Level: 4

Duration: 2–4 weeks

Program Offered: Fall, winter intersession/January term, spring, full academic year, summer

Location: Switzerland

Accommodations: Family-stay/host-family

Years in Operation: 18

Religious Affiliation: Not relevant

PARTICIPANTS

For Participants Aged: 17+

The Ideal Candidate: Applicants should have either basic French or German language skills, as well as an open mind, flexible attitude, good sense of humor, and genuine interest in cultural exchange.

Special Requirements for Participation: None.

COSTS

Average Cost: $1,200

Included in Cost: Program includes placement with a carefully selected host family, full board, medical insurance, and the support of a local counselor during the program.

Financial Aid Available: No

THAILAND INDEPENDENT HOMESTAY PROGRAM

THE PROGRAM

Description: The Independent Homestay Program focuses exclusively on the short-term homestay experience and is perfect for teens and adults wanting complete immersion in a new culture.

Program Type: Travel/cultural

Classification: Coeducational, residential

Goals: Thai culture and customs of Thailand.

Focus: Cultural

Intensity Level: 4

Duration: 2–4 weeks

Program Offered: Fall, winter intersession/January term, spring, full academic year, summer

Location: Thailand

Accommodations: Family-stay/host-family

Years in Operation: 18

Religious Affiliation: Not relevant

PARTICIPANTS

For Participants Aged: 18+

The Ideal Candidate: Applicants should have a basic knowledge of the Thai language, an open mind, flexible attitude,

good sense of humor, and genuine interest in cultural exchange.

Special Requirements for Participation: None.

COSTS

Average Cost: $1,200

Included in Cost: Program includes placement with a carefully selected host family, full board, medical insurance, and the support of a local counselor during the program.

Financial Aid Available: No

TURKEY INDEPENDENT HOMESTAY PROGRAM

THE PROGRAM

Description: The Independent Homestay Program focuses exclusively on the short-term homestay experience and is perfect for teens and adults wanting complete immersion in a new culture.

Program Type: Travel/cultural

Classification: Coeducational, residential

Goals: Turkish culture and customs of Turkey.

Focus: Cultural

Intensity Level: 4

Duration: 2–4 weeks

Program Offered: Fall, winter intersession/January term, spring, full academic year, summer

Location: Turkey

Accommodations: Family-stay/host-family

Years in Operation: 18

Religious Affiliation: Not relevant

PARTICIPANTS

For Participants Aged: 18+

The Ideal Candidate: Applicants should have an open mind, flexible attitude, good sense of humor, and genuine interest in cultural exchange.

Special Requirements for Participation: None.

COSTS

Average Cost: $850

Included in Cost: Program includes placement with a carefully selected host family, full board, medical insurance, and the support of a local counselor during the program.

Financial Aid Available: No

UNITED KINGDOM INDEPENDENT HOMESTAY

THE PROGRAM

Description: The Independent Homestay Program focuses exclusively on the short-term homestay experience and is perfect for teens and adults wanting complete immersion in a new culture.

Program Type: Travel/cultural

Classification: Coeducational, residential

Goals: Culture and customs of the United Kingdom.

Focus: Cultural

Intensity Level: 4

Duration: 2–4 weeks

Program Offered: Fall, winter intersession/January term, spring, full academic year, summer

Location: United Kingdom

Accommodations: Family-stay/host-family

Years in Operation: 18

Religious Affiliation: Not relevant

PARTICIPANTS

For Participants Aged: 16+

The Ideal Candidate: Applicants should have an open mind, flexible attitude, good sense of humor, and genuine interest in cultural exchange.

Special Requirements for Participation: None.

COSTS

Average Cost: $1,300

Included in Cost: Program includes placement with a carefully selected host family, full board, medical insurance, and the support of a local counselor during the program.

Financial Aid Available: No

COLUMBIA COLLEGE CHICAGO

An early college program for students who've completed their sophomore, junior, or senior year of high school and who have not yet matriculated to college. It features more than 50 arts and communications classes.

Years in Operation: 19

Religious Affiliation: Not relevant

Price Range of Programs: $150 and up

For More Information:
Contact: Stephanie Strait, Coordinator, Undergraduate Admissions
600 South Michigan Avenue
Suite 301
Chicago, IL 60605
Phone: 312-344-7134
Fax: 312-344-8024
Email: sstrait@popmail.colum.edu
Website: www.colum.edu

HIGH SCHOOL SUMMER INSTITUTE

THE PROGRAM

Description: An early college program for students completing their sophomore, junior, or senior year of high school. It offers more than 50 classes in the arts and communications.

Specialty: Our facilities and faculty are second to none and specifically suited for students interested in studying arts and communications during their high school and/or college careers.

Program Type: Academic/pre-college enrichment

Classification: Coeducational, residential, day program

Goals: Participants will learn specific skills in one or more areas of the arts and communications, experience what it is like to study at an urban arts and communications college, and gain some idea of career paths in their chosen field.

Focus: Academic/pre-college enrichment and cultural

Activities Center On: Fine arts, performing arts, and writing

Intensity Level: 3

Duration: 4–6 weeks

Program Offered: Summer

Location: Chicago, Illinois

Accommodations: Dormitory

Years in Operation: 19

Religious Affiliation: Not relevant

STAFF

Student/Staff Ratio: 12:1

Staff Qualifications: Instructors are Columbia College Chicago faculty.

PARTICIPANTS

Average Number of Participants: 600

For Participants Aged: 14–18

The Ideal Candidate: A high school student who is college bound and interested in the arts and media.

Special Requirements for Participation: Students must have completed their sophomore, junior, or senior year of high school and not yet have matriculated to college.

COSTS

Average Cost: $600

Included in Cost: Tuition is $150 per hour of college credit. Housing is $1,400 for five weeks and includes out-of-class activities and the evening meal each day.

Financial Aid Available: Yes

COTTONWOOD GULCH FOUNDATION

Our wilderness expedition groups explore the historic, cultural, environmental, and natural wonders of the American Southwest. Programs are structured to emphasize outdoor living skills, scientific inquiry, wilderness camping, and fun and adventure within a framework of safety, health, and cooperative effort.

Years in Operation: 76

Religious Affiliation: Not relevant

Price Range of Programs: $1,225–$3,795

For More Information:
Contact: Seth Battis, Assistant Director
PO Box 3915
Albuquerque, NM 87190
Phone: 800-246-8735
Fax: 505-248-0563
Email: director@cottonwoodgulch.org
Website: www.cottonwoodgulch.org

PRAIRIE TREK EXPEDITION GROUP II

THE PROGRAM

Description: This wilderness expedition for young men and women takes the group through pristine backcountry areas and culturally important sites as they uncover the environmental science and cultures behind this amazing landscape.

Program Type: Academic/pre-college enrichment, outdoors/adventure, travel/cultural

Classification: Coeducational, residential

Focus: Leadership/teamwork and cultural

Activities Center On: Outdoors/adventure, wilderness, and cultural

Intensity Level: 4

Duration: 4–6 weeks

Program Offered: Summer

Location: Thoreau (Base Camp and Preserve), Arizona; Colorado, New Mexico, Utah

Accommodations: Tent

Years in Operation: 76

Religious Affiliation: Not relevant

STAFF

Student/Staff Ratio: 5:1

PARTICIPANTS

Average Number of Participants: 15

For Participants Aged: 15–18

Special Requirements for Participation: None.

COSTS

Average Cost: $3,795

Included in Cost: Small groups led by experienced, caring instructors. All group equipment is provided—tents, food, maps, hiking gear—as is full health care coverage. Not included are: travel to/from New Mexico and personal gear.

Financial Aid Available: Yes

DAVIDSON COLLEGE

Three-week summer academic program for rising high school seniors.

Years in Operation: 28

Religious Affiliation: Not relevant

Price Range of Programs: $2,100

For More Information:
Contact: Evelyn Gerdes, Director
PO Box 7151
Davidson, NC 28035
Phone: 704-894-2508
Fax: 704-894-2645
Email: julyexp@davidson.edu
Website: www.davidson.edu/academic/education/july-exp.html

DAVIDSON JULY EXPERIENCE

THE PROGRAM

Description: July Experience is a summer program for rising high school seniors. It provides the students with a unique educational and social three-week program on the campus of Davidson College. Students select two courses from several liberal arts disciplines for concentrated study during the program. Students will have a professionally directed recreational program and contact with a carefully selected group of college-student counselors.

Specialty: July Experience provides an experience that is both rigorous and humanizing, that helps the individual develop as a person—a whole person—with the resources for self-fulfillment and service to mankind.

Program Type: Academic/pre-college enrichment

Classification: Coeducational, residential

Focus: Academic/pre-college enrichment, educational exchange, and leadership/teamwork

Activities Center On: Academic, study skills, and career exploration

Intensity Level: 4

Duration: 2–4 weeks

Program Offered: Summer

Location: Davidson (Charlotte Area), North Carolina

Accommodations: Dormitory

Years in Operation: 28

Religious Affiliation: Not relevant

STAFF

Student/Staff Ratio: 10:1

Staff Qualifications: Upperclassmen chosen from the Davidson College student body on the basis of academic ability, sensitivity to people, maturity, specific skills, and experience. Often a counselor is a July Experience alumni.

PARTICIPANTS

Average Number of Participants: 75

For Participants Aged: 16–18

The Ideal Candidate: Young men and women who are highly motivated, academically oriented, and self-disciplined.

Special Requirements for Participation: Applicants are expected to have strong academic records and to be highly recommended by the principal and the counselor of the secondary school attended.

COSTS

Average Cost: $2,100

Included in Cost: Everything except textbooks and personal spending money.

Financial Aid Available: Yes

DICKINSON COLLEGE

Dickinson College offers five-week college-credit residential programs for high school students and recent graduates. In addition, we offer three-week noncredit research and writing workshops.

Religious Affiliation: Not relevant

Price Range of Programs: $2,600–$5,000

For More Information:
Contact: Diane Fleming, Director of Summer Programs
PO Box 1773
Carlisle, PA 17013
Phone: 717-245-8782
Fax: 717-245-1972
Email: summer@dickinson.edu
Website: www.dickinson.edu/summer

RESEARCH & WRITING WORKSHOP

THE PROGRAM

Description: This three-week residential program is project-oriented and provides and excellent opportunity for high school students working on senior projects, teacher-guided research, independent study capstone projects, and IB extended essay, for example. The broad goals of the program include enhancing skills of writing, argumentation, and research that will be invaluable to students in college and thereafter.

Specialty: Low student/faculty ratio of about 4:1, 24-hour availability of residential writing consultant.

Program Type: Academic/pre-college enrichment

Classification: Coeducational, residential

Goals: Writing, argumentation, and research skills to complete a project and prepare for college-level work.

Focus: Academic/pre-college enrichment

Activities Center On: Academic

Intensity Level: 4

Duration: 2–4 weeks

Program Offered: Summer

Location: Carlisle, Pennsylvania

Accommodations: Dormitory

Years in Operation: 3

Religious Affiliation: Not relevant

STAFF

Student/Staff Ratio: 5:1

Staff Qualifications: Trained Dickinson College residential advisors, Dickinson faculty, and full-time administrative staff.

PARTICIPANTS

Average Number of Participants: 8

For Participants Aged: 15–18

Special Requirements for Participation: None.

COSTS

Average Cost: $2,600

Included in Cost: Room and board, tuition, and social activities are included. Books and personal spending money are not included.

Financial Aid Available: Yes

SPANISH LANGUAGE AND CULTURAL IMMERSION PROGRAM

THE PROGRAM

Description: This five-week residential program includes travel to Queretaro, Mexico, to be hosted by the Universidad Autonoma de Queretaro for Spanish language and culture classes. In Mexico, you live with a carefully chosen family to round out your complete immersion into the Mexican culture. For the final week, you return to Dickinson for time to assimilate your experiences. Successful completion of the course and exam will lead to intermediate Spanish college credit.

Specialty: Full immersion in Spanish and culture (this is not simply a travel program); very low student/faculty ratio (8:1) plus assistant.

Program Type: Academic/pre-college enrichment

Classification: Coeducational, residential

Goals: Successful completion: mastering of Spanish at the intermediate college level and immersion in Mexican culture.

Focus: Academic/pre-college enrichment, travel, and cultural

Activities Center On: Language, academic, and travel

Intensity Level: 4

Duration: 4–6 weeks

Program Offered: Summer

Location: Carlisle, Pennsylvania; Queretaro, Mexico

Accommodations: Dormitory, family-stay/host-family

Years in Operation: 3

Religious Affiliation: Not relevant

Staff

Student/Staff Ratio: 8:1

Staff Qualifications: Trained Dickinson residential advisors, Dickinson faculty, and administrative staff.

Participants

Average Number of Participants: 8

For Participants Aged: 16–18

The Ideal Candidate: Successfully completed high school intermediate-level Spanish and has had some cross-cultural exposure.

Special Requirements for Participation: completed high school intermediate-level Spanish.

Costs

Average Cost: $4,900

Included in Cost: Full room and board both at Dickinson College and in Mexico, travel to and from Mexico, college tuition for intermediate Spanish, and social programming are all included. Books and personal spending money are not included.

Financial Aid Available: Yes

Summer College Program

The Program

Description: Our five-week program allows you to immerse yourself in topics you may only briefly encounter in high school while providing an opportunity to earn college credit. Courses range from astronomy to international business to photography and much more.

Specialty: Faculty-taught program; courses for college credit; college preparatory programs available, such as SAT prep, ESL, essay writing, mock interviews, etc.

Program Type: Academic/pre-college enrichment

Classification: Coeducational, residential

Goals: Upon successful completion earn college credit in chosen courses, prepare for college.

Focus: Academic/pre-college enrichment

Activities Center On: Academic

Intensity Level: 4

Duration: 4–6 weeks

Program Offered: Summer

Location: Carlisle, Pennsylvania

Accommodations: Dormitory

Years in Operation: 3

Religious Affiliation: Not relevant

Staff

Student/Staff Ratio: 8:1

Staff Qualifications: Trained Dickinson residential advisors, Dickinson faculty, full-time Dickinson staff.

Participants

Average Number of Participants: 35

For Participants Aged: 15–18

The Ideal Candidate: Strong academic program in high school, well-rounded, A/B student.

Special Requirements for Participation: None.

Costs

Average Cost: $4,400

Included in Cost: Room and board, tuition for two classes, and social programming are all included. Books and personal spending money are not included.

Financial Aid Available: No

EARTHWATCH INSTITUTE

Earthwatch supports scientific and environmental field research worldwide by engaging ordinary people of all ages in the expedition field tasks. Endangered species, marine ecology, archaeology—your help is needed on any of over 700 teams in 48 countries and 19 U.S. states. Give just one to two weeks, and join teachers, students, corporate employees—close to 4,000 others each year—in helping on the front lines of conservation.

Years in Operation: 33

Religious Affiliation: Not relevant

Price Range of Programs: $700–$3,000 donation

For More Information:
  Contact: Information Desk
      PO Box 75
      Maynard, MA 01754
  Phone: 800-776-0188
  Fax: 978-461-2332
  Email: info@earthwatch.org
  Website: www.earthwatch.org

ARCHAEOLOGY — ANCIENT NOMADS OF MONGOLIA

THE PROGRAM

Description: Modern Mongolian herdsmen follow many of the same migration patterns of their forbears and even appear to honor their favorite horses by placing their skulls near ancient burial mounds. Volunteers will survey and excavate ancient stone structures to reveal the origins of nomadic pastoralism.

Program Type: Community service, travel/cultural

Classification: Coeducational, residential

Intensity Level: 3

Duration: 2–4 weeks

Program Offered: Spring

Location: Khanuy River Valley, Central Mongolia

Accommodations: Tent

Religious Affiliation: Not relevant

PARTICIPANTS

Average Number of Participants: 12

For Participants Aged: 16+

Special Requirements for Participation: Volunteers will camp outside in tents in this remote but spectacular highland valley. With neither electricity nor running water, team members will use pit toilets with a view and bathe in a nearby river.

COSTS

Average Cost: $1,995

Included in Cost: Food and lodging. Volunteers must pay for their own airfare.

Financial Aid Available: No

ARCHAEOLOGY — ENGLAND'S HIDDEN KINGDOM

THE PROGRAM

Description: Never cut by the blade of a plow, Yorkshire sheep pastures have looked the same for centuries. This benign form of land management has left buried archaeological evidence—perhaps an entire kingdom—largely in place. Volunteers will lay the groundwork for excavating an area that may prove to be a previously unknown independent kingdom of early England.

Program Type: Community service, travel/cultural

Classification: Coeducational, residential

Intensity Level: 2

Duration: 2–4 weeks

Program Offered: Summer

Location: Yorkshire, United Kingdom

Religious Affiliation: Not relevant

STAFF

Staff Qualifications: Dr. Roger Martlew, University of Leeds.

PARTICIPANTS

Average Number of Participants: 12

For Participants Aged: 16+

Special Requirements for Participation: Volunteers will stay at Dale House, a large stone house in the village of Kettlewall with single or double bedrooms, and eat meals at the bistro next door.

COSTS

Average Cost: $1,895

Included in Cost: Food and lodging. Volunteers are responsible for their own airfare.

Financial Aid Available: No

ARCHAEOLOGY — FOOD & DRINK IN ANCIENT POMPEII

THE PROGRAM

Description: Volunteers will help conduct the first citywide study of comestibles in this fabled site to document how one Roman town fed its population. Investigate the culture and business of cooking and eating in the early Roman Empire.

Program Type: Community service and travel/cultural

Classification: Coeducational, residential

Intensity Level: 2

Duration: 2–4 weeks

Program Offered: Summer

Location: Pompeii, Italy

Accommodations: Hotels

Religious Affiliation: Not relevant

PARTICIPANTS

Average Number of Participants: 16

For Participants Aged: 16+

Special Requirements for Participation: Volunteers will share rooms with private baths and enjoy Italian cuisine and a pool at the Villa dei Misteri.

COSTS

Average Cost: $2,995

Included in Cost: Food and lodging. Airfare is not included.

Financial Aid Available: No

ARCHAEOLOGY—FRONTIER FORT IN VIRGINIA

THE PROGRAM

Description: A memorial stands at the site of Fort Christanna, near Williamsburg, Virginia, where early European colonists and Native Americans traded goods, cultural traditions, and diseases. Investigate how culturally different populations developed alliances over time.

Program Type: Community service, travel/cultural

Classification: Coeducational, residential

Intensity Level: 2

Duration: 2–4 weeks

Program Offered: Summer

Location: Fort Christanna, Lawrenceville, Virginia

Accommodations: Hotels

Religious Affiliation: Not relevant

PARTICIPANTS

Average Number of Participants: 10

For Participants Aged: 16+

Special Requirements for Participation: Based in an immaculate historic bed-and-breakfast near Lawrenceville, volunteers will enjoy cookouts and lectures at the staff house.

COSTS

Average Cost: $1,695

Included in Cost: Food and lodging. Airfare not included.

Financial Aid Available: No

ARCHAEOLOGY—JACKSON HOLE BISON DIG

THE PROGRAM

Description: If there is one symbol for the American West, it is the bison. With the Grand Tetons as backdrop, you'll investigate how important the American bison was in the local Native American economy. Volunteers will excavate a prehistoric site to determine the role of bison in Native American life.

Program Type: Community service, outdoors/adventure

Classification: Coeducational, residential

Intensity Level: 3

Duration: 2–4 weeks

Program Offered: Summer

Location: National Elk Refuge, Jackson Hole, Wyoming

Accommodations: Tent

Religious Affiliation: Not relevant

PARTICIPANTS

Average Number of Participants: 12

For Participants Aged: 16+

Special Requirements for Participation: None.

COSTS

Average Cost: $1,595

Included in Cost: Food and lodging. Airfare not included.

Financial Aid Available: No

ARCHAEOLOGY—MALLORCA'S COPPER AGE

THE PROGRAM

Description: Almost three decades of hard-working Earthwatch teams have helped Dr. Bill Waldren excavate the oldest ritual site yet discovered in the Mediterranean and, in the process, rewrite Mallorca's prehistory. Help sift through the prehistory of settlement and cultural evolution on Mallorca.

Program Type: Community service, travel/cultural

Classification: Coeducational, residential

Intensity Level: 2

Duration: 2–4 weeks

Program Offered: Fall, winter intersession/January term, summer

Location: Mallorca, Spain

Accommodations: Dormitory

Religious Affiliation: Not relevant

PARTICIPANTS

Average Number of Participants: 15

For Participants Aged: 16+

Special Requirements for Participation: Volunteers will stay in a unique stone house overlooking the classic, tile-roofed Mediterranean village of Deia and share dormitory rooms, showers, and toilets.

COSTS

Average Cost: $1,995

Included in Cost: Food and lodging. Airfare not included.

Financial Aid Available: No

ARCHAEOLOGY—MAMMOTH CAVE

THE PROGRAM

Description: Mammoth Cave has been used as everything from a saltpeter mine to a tuberculosis hospital. Volunteers can help explore its most intimate reaches for clues to 5,000 years of human history. Hike to the end of the world's longest cave system to reconstruct its entire human history.

Program Type: Community service

Classification: Coeducational, residential

Intensity Level: 3

Duration: 2–4 weeks

Program Offered: Fall, summer

Location: Mammoth Cave, Kentucky

Accommodations: Bunkhouse

Religious Affiliation: Not relevant

PARTICIPANTS

Average Number of Participants: 10

For Participants Aged: 16+

Special Requirements for Participation: Clambering over rocks and in-tight spaces at this site can be physically strenuous and requires a good level of fitness. Volunteers will stay at a comfortable bunkhouse with hot showers and bathrooms. Dinners are prepared by a local restaurant.

COSTS

Average Cost: $798

Financial Aid Available: No

ARCHAEOLOGY — NEW MEXICO'S SPANISH FRONTIER

THE PROGRAM

Description: Volunteers will help unearth the cultural identity of settlers of this historic boarder town of the Spanish Empire to reveal the interchange of Hispanic and Native American cultures.

Program Type: Community service

Classification: Coeducational, residential

Intensity Level: 2

Duration: 2–4 weeks

Program Offered: Summer

Location: San Jose de las Huertas, New Mexico

Accommodations: Apartment

Religious Affiliation: Not relevant

PARTICIPANTS

Average Number of Participants: 8

For Participants Aged: 16+

Special Requirements for Participation: After labors in the field, volunteers will return to Albuquerque, a 20-minute drive south, and stay in rented apartments or houses with all the amenities. A cook will prepare meals; food preparation and clean up is a group effort.

COSTS

Average Cost: $1,695

Included in Cost: Food and lodging. Airfare is not included.

Financial Aid Available: No

ARCHAEOLOGY — PREHISTORIC PUEBLOS OF THE AMERICAN SOUTHWEST

THE PROGRAM

Description: Earthwatch volunteers will screen for artifacts, among other duties, from ancient Pueblo settlements in the scenic Rio Alamosa Valley, the historic borderland between the Mogollon and Anasazi cultures. Volunteers will excavate settlements to discover the relationships between ancient Pueblo peoples.

Program Type: Community service, travel/cultural

Classification: Coeducational, residential

Intensity Level: 2

Duration: 2–4 weeks

Program Offered: Fall, summer

Location: Rio Alamosa, New Mexico

Accommodations: Tent

Religious Affiliation: Not relevant

PARTICIPANTS

Average Number of Participants: 6

For Participants Aged: 16+

Special Requirements for Participation: Volunteers will sleep in large field tents with light bed frames and mattresses. A cabin nearby with electricity features two full bathrooms, a two-hole privy, an outdoor shower, and a kitchen, where volunteers will prepare their own breakfasts and lunch.

COSTS

Average Cost: $1,515

Included in Cost: Food and lodging. Airfare not included.

Financial Aid Available: No

ARCHAEOLOGY — ROMAN FORT ON THE DANUBE

THE PROGRAM

Description: Two seasons ago, Earthwatch volunteers working at Halmyris (where the Danube forks and empties into the Black Sea) with Dr. Zahariade discovered a tomb of two early Christians martyred in 290 AD. Volunteers will unearth a major Roman fort and military supply depot to clarify the two-way street of acculturation.

Program Type: Community service, travel/cultural

Classification: Coeducational, residential

Intensity Level: 2

Duration: 2–4 weeks

Program Offered: Summer

Location: Halmyris, Tulcea, Romania

Accommodations: Motel

Religious Affiliation: Not relevant

PARTICIPANTS

Average Number of Participants: 8

For Participants Aged: 16+

Special Requirements for Participation: Volunteers will stay in a simple motel with single or double rooms, full plumbing, and the Danube Delta wildlife reserve nearby. Romanian cooks will prepare genuine Romanian food.

COSTS

Average Cost: $1,795

Financial Aid Available: No

BIODIVERSITY — CARING FOR CHIMPANZEES

THE PROGRAM

Description: If you ever doubted the intelligence and creativity of chimpanzees, working with them face to face will make you a believer. You can help discover how to provide the most stimulating environment for captive chimps.

Specialty: Volunteers will work directly with the chimpanzees, being taught by true leaders in the field of chimpanzee research, the Fouts.

Program Type: Academic/pre-college enrichment, community service

Classification: Coeducational, residential

Intensity Level: 2

Duration: 2–4 weeks

Program Offered: Fall, spring, summer

Location: Ellensburg, Washington

Accommodations: Dormitory

Religious Affiliation: Not relevant

STAFF

Staff Qualifications: Dr. Roger Fouts and his wife, Deborah, are world leaders in this field. They are widely known for their work with Washoe, the first chimp to learn American Sign Language.

PARTICIPANTS

Average Number of Participants: 12

For Participants Aged: 16+

Special Requirements for Participation: None.

COSTS

Average Cost: $1,695

Included in Cost: Housing and meals. Airfare is not included.

Financial Aid Available: Yes

BIODIVERSITY — CHEETAH

THE PROGRAM

Description: Cheetahs favor the same open savannah habitat preferred by ranchers in Africa. You can help conserve the largest remaining population of these important predators in Namibia's ranching heartland.

Program Type: Academic/pre-college enrichment, community service, outdoors/adventure, travel/cultural

Classification: Coeducational, residential

Intensity Level: 3

Duration: 2–4 weeks

Program Offered: Fall, winter intersession/January term, spring, summer

Location: North-central Namibia

Accommodations: Bungalow

Religious Affiliation: Not relevant

STAFF

Staff Qualifications: Dr. Laurie Marker is the cofounder of the Cheetah Conservation Fund and has spent her life dedicated to saving cheetahs.

PARTICIPANTS

Average Number of Participants: 4

For Participants Aged: 16+

Special Requirements for Participation: Volunteers will stay in a two-person bungalow equipped with sinks and beds equipped with mosquito nets. In separate bathhouses, volunteers will find showers and toilets with limited hot water. There is a cook on staff.

COSTS

Average Cost: $2,995

Included in Cost: Food and housing. Airfare is not included.

Financial Aid Available: No

BIODIVERSITY — KOALA ECOLOGY

THE PROGRAM

Description: You will explore the koala's world in this very hands-on expedition, which includes capturing, tagging, examining, releasing, and tracking koalas in an undisturbed habitat—all in the name of koala conservation.

Program Type: Academic/pre-college enrichment, community service, outdoors/adventure, travel/cultural

Classification: Coeducational, residential

Intensity Level: 3

Duration: 2–4 weeks

Program Offered: Fall, summer

Location: St. Bees Island, Queensland, Australia

Accommodations: Cottage

Religious Affiliation: Not relevant

PARTICIPANTS

Average Number of Participants: 13

For Participants Aged: 16+

Special Requirements for Participation: Volunteers will share rooms in a solar-powered cottage with hot showers and toilets. Volunteers will hike over steep and rocky terrain.

COSTS

Average Cost: $1,895

Included in Cost: Housing and meals. Airfare is not included.

Financial Aid Available: No

ENFOREX SPANISH IN THE SPANISH WORLD

At Enforex, we offer our students more than 20 courses in six centrally located schools throughout Spain (Madrid, Barcelona, Marbella, Salamanca, Granada, and Almuñecar) and Latin America (Argentina, Bolivia, Costa Rica, Ecuador, Guatemala, and Peru). Our schools are open year-round, and the average class has just five students (maximum of nine). Our multicultural student body, representing 48 nationalities, begins classes every Monday and may choose anything from a minimum one-week program in one location, to several months in up to three cities, paying a one-time application fee to really discover Spanish culture. Also, Summer Camp is available in Madrid, Marbella, and Salamanca for students ages 5 to 18 years. Of the camp students, 40 percent are international, 60 percent are Spanish.

Years in Operation: 14

Religious Affiliation: Not relevant

Price Range of Programs: 900 Euros for 4 weeks

For More Information:
Contact: Antonio Anadon, Promotion
Alberto Aguilera 26
Madrid, 28015
SPAIN
Phone: 011-34915943776
Fax: 011-34915945159
Email: info@enforex.es
Website: www.enforex.es

DELE EXAM PREPARATION — ENFOREX
BARCELONA

THE PROGRAM

Description: The DELE is the only official certificate of Spanish for foreign students recognized by the "Instituto Cervantes." In 1998, 1999, 2000, 2001, and 2002, all of our students passed the DELE exam.

Specialty: 100 percent success ratio; U.S. university credits system; flexibility, quality, and personal attention; wonderful school facilities; full program of activities and excursions; student services; possibility of combining the program in more than one location.

Program Type: Academic/pre-college enrichment

Classification: Coeducational, residential, day program

Goals: The diploma is especially useful for those students who desire to study at Spanish universities or who would like to work in a Spanish-speaking country. The specific aim of this course is to prepare students to pass the DELE exam at any of its three levels.

Focus: Skill-building, academic/pre-college enrichment, and cultural

Activities Center On: Language, academic, and career exploration

Intensity Level: 3

Duration: 4–6 weeks

Program Offered: Fall, spring

Location: Barcelona, Madrid, Marbella, and Salamanca, Spain

Accommodations: Dormitory, family-stay/host-family, apartment, hotels, youth hostels

Years in Operation: 5

Religious Affiliation: Not relevant

STAFF

Student/Staff Ratio: 5:2

Staff Qualifications: All staff have completed training courses or have master's degrees in the instruction of Spanish. They are a young and dynamic team with great experience, which has been recognized by several didactic publications in the research of this field.

PARTICIPANTS

Average Number of Participants: 200

For Participants Aged: 18+

The Ideal Candidate: Any student who wants to learn Spanish.

Special Requirements for Participation: None.

COSTS

Average Cost: $1,290

Included in Cost: Application fees, Enforex textbooks, Internet access, five-week course (20 hours per week of Spanish language lessons and 5 hours per week of Spanish cultural lessons), five weeks of shared apartment accommodation in double room.

Financial Aid Available: No

DELE Exam Preparation — ENFOREX Madrid

The Program

Description: The DELE is the only official certificate of Spanish for foreign students recognized by the "Instituto Cervantes." In 1998, 1999, 2000, 2001, and 2002, all of our students passed the DELE exam.

Specialty: 100 percent success ratio; U.S. university credits system; flexibility, quality, and personal attention; wonderful school facilities; full program of activities and excursions; student services; possibility of combining the program in more than one location.

Program Type: Academic/pre-college enrichment

Classification: Coeducational, residential

Goals: The diploma is especially useful for those students who desire to study at Spanish universities or who would like to work in a Spanish-speaking country. The specific aim of this course is to prepare students to pass the DELE exam at any of its three levels.

Focus: Academic/pre-college enrichment, educational exchange, and cultural

Activities Center On: Language and cultural

Intensity Level: 3

Duration: 4–6 weeks

Program Offered: Fall, spring, summer

Location: Barcelona, Madrid, Marbella, and Salamanca, Spain

Accommodations: Dormitory, family-stay/host-family, apartment, hotels

Years in Operation: 12

Religious Affiliation: Not relevant

Staff

Student/Staff Ratio: 5:1

Staff Qualifications: All staff have completed training courses or have master's degrees in the instruction of Spanish. They are a young and dynamic team with great experience, which has been recognized by several didactic publications in the research of this field.

Participants

Average Number of Participants: 200

For Participants Aged: 18+

The Ideal Candidate: Any student who wants to learn Spanish and receive the official certificate of his/her Spanish proficiency level.

Special Requirements for Participation: None.

Costs

Average Cost: $1,290

Included in Cost: Application fees, Enforex textbooks, Internet access, five-week course (20 hours per week of Spanish language lessons and 5 hours per week of Spanish cultural lessons), five weeks shared apartment accommodation in double room.

Financial Aid Available: No

DELE Exam Preparation — ENFOREX Marbella

The Program

Description: The DELE is the only official certificate of Spanish for foreign students recognized by the "Instituto Cervantes." In 1998, 1999, 2000, 2001, and 2002, all of our students passed the DELE exam.

Specialty: 100 percent success ratio; U.S. university credits system; flexibility, quality, and personal attention; wonderful school facilities; full program of activities and excursions; student services; possibility of combining the program in more than one location.

Program Type: Academic/pre-college enrichment

Classification: Coeducational, residential, day program

Goals: The diploma is especially useful for those students who desire to study at Spanish universities or who would like to work in a Spanish-speaking country. The specific aim of this course is to prepare students to pass the DELE exam at any of its three levels.

Focus: Academic/pre-college enrichment, educational exchange, and cultural

Activities Center On: Language and academic

Intensity Level: 3

Duration: 4–6 weeks

Program Offered: Fall, spring, summer

Location: Barcelona, Madrid, Marbella, and Salamancas, Spain

Accommodations: Dormitory, family-stay/host-family, apartment, hotels

Years in Operation: 12

Religious Affiliation: Not relevant

Staff

Student/Staff Ratio: 5:1

Staff Qualifications: All staff have completed training courses or have master's degrees in the instruction of Spanish. They are a young and dynamic team with great experience, which has been recognized by several didactic publications in the research of this field.

Participants

Average Number of Participants: 200

For Participants Aged: 18+

The Ideal Candidate: Any student who wants to learn Spanish and receive the official certificate of his/her Spanish proficiency level.

Special Requirements for Participation: None.

COSTS

Average Cost: $1,290

Included in Cost: Application fees, Enforex textbooks, Internet access, five-week course (20 hours per week of Spanish language lessons and 5 hours per week of Spanish cultural lessons), five weeks shared apartment accommodation in double room.

Financial Aid Available: No

DELE Exam Preparation — ENFOREX Salamanca

The Program

Description: The DELE is the only official certificate of Spanish for foreign students recognized by the "Instituto Cervantes." In 1998, 1999, 2000, 2001, and 2002 all of our students passed the DELE exam.

Specialty: 100 percent succesful ratio; U.S. university credits system; flexibility, quality, and personal attention; wonderful school facilities; full program of activities and excursions; student services; possibility of combining the program in more than one location.

Program Type: Academic/pre-college enrichment

Classification: Coeducational, residential, day program

Goals: The diploma is especially useful for those students who desire to study at Spanish universities or who would like to work in a Spanish-speaking country. The specific aim of this course is to prepare students to pass the DELE exam at any of its three levels.

Focus: Academic/pre-college enrichment, cultural, and skill-building

Activities Center On: Language and academic

Intensity Level: 3

Duration: 4–6 weeks

Program Offered: Fall, spring, summer

Location: Barcelona, Madrid, Marbella, and Salamanca, Spain

Accommodations: Dormitory, family-stay/host-family, apartment

Years in Operation: 12

Religious Affiliation: Not relevant

Staff

Student/Staff Ratio: 5:1

Staff Qualifications: All staff have completed training courses or have master's degrees in the instruction of Spanish. They are a young and dynamic team with great experience, which has been recognized by several didactic publications in the research of this field.

PARTICIPANTS

Average Number of Participants: 200

For Participants Aged: 18+

The Ideal Candidate: Any student who wants to learn Spanish and receive the official certificate of his/her Spanish proficiency level.

Special Requirements for Participation: None.

COSTS

Average Cost: $1,290

Included in Cost: Application fees, Enforex textbooks, Internet access, five-week course (20 hours per week of Spanish language lessons and 5 hours per week of Spanish cultural lessons), transcripts, five weeks shared apartment accommodation in double room.

Financial Aid Available: No

General Spanish — ENFOREX Almuñecar

The Program

Description: Spanish courses take place all year-round. Schools are always open. Minimum duration is one week. There is a maximum number of nine students per class; the average number per class is five. Oral and written placement test takes place on the first Monday. Methodology is based on acquiring the linguistic, pragmatic, and functional aspects of language learning along with the sociocultural elements of the Spanish way of life. Students are given 10 hours of language and 5 hours of cultural, 20 hours of language and 5 hours of cultural, or 30 hours of language and 5 hours of cultural lessons (55 minutes each per week). Every course features one hour per day of Spanish cultural lesson.

Specialty: U.S. university credits system; flexibility, quality, and personal attention; wonderful school facilities; full program of activities and excursions; conversation with Spanish students; student services, possibility of combining the program in more than one location.

Program Type: Academic/pre-college enrichment, middle school enrichment, outdoors/adventure, travel/cultural

Classification: Coeducational, residential, day program

Goals: In all our courses we try to instruct individually and then integrate the four language skills: reading, writing, speaking, and listening. In addition to these skills, we also emphasize grammatical structure so the student can eventually reach the threshold of communicative proficiency. In order to broaden the student's general perspective, we offer the possibility of studying many different aspects of the Spanish culture including history, art, civilization, literature, cinema, etc.

Focus: Academic/pre-college enrichment and travel

Activities Center On: Language

Intensity Level: 3

Duration: Varies

Program Offered: Summer

Location: Barcelona, Madrid, Marbella, and Salamanca, Spain

Accommodations: Dormitory, family-stay/host-family, apartment, youth hostels

Years in Operation: 12

Religious Affiliation: Not relevant

STAFF

Student/Staff Ratio: 5:1

Staff Qualifications: All staff have completed training courses or have master's degrees in the instruction of Spanish. They are a young and dynamic team with great experience, which has been recognized by several didactic publications in the research of this field.

PARTICIPANTS

Average Number of Participants: 80

For Participants Aged: 14+

The Ideal Candidate: Any student who wants to learn Spanish in one of the most prestigious Spanish language schools.

Special Requirements for Participation: None.

COSTS

Average Cost: $900

Included in Cost: Application fees, Enforex textbooks, Internet access, four-week intensive course (20 hours per week of Spanish language lessons and 5 hours per week of Spanish cultural lessons), transcripts, four weeks shared apartment accommodation in double room.

Financial Aid Available: No

GENERAL SPANISH—ENFOREX BARCELONA

THE PROGRAM

Description: Spanish courses take place all year-round. Schools are always open. Minimum duration is one week. There is a maximum number of nine students per class; the average number per class is five. Oral and written placement test takes place on the first Monday. Methodology is based on acquiring the linguistic, pragmatic, and functional aspects of language learning along with the sociocultural elements of the Spanish way of life. Students are given 10 hours of language and 5 hours of cultural, 20 hours of language and 5 hours of cultural, or 30 hours of language and 5 hours of cultural lessons (55 minutes each) per week. Every course features one hour per day of Spanish cultural lesson.

Specialty: U.S. university credits system; flexibility, quality, and personal attention; wonderful school facilities; full program of activities and excursions; conversation with Spanish students; student services; possibility of combining the program in more than one location.

Program Type: Academic/pre-college enrichment, middle school enrichment, travel/cultural

Classification: Coeducational, residential, day program

Goals: In all our courses we try to instruct individually and then integrate the four language skills: reading, writing, speaking, and listening. In addition to these skills, we also emphasize grammatical structure so the student can eventually reach the threshold of communicative proficiency. In order to broaden the student's general perspective, we offer the possibility of studying many different aspects of the Spanish culture including history, art, civilization, literature, cinema, etc.

Focus: Academic/pre-college enrichment, skill-building, and cultural

Activities Center On: Language, study skills, and travel

Intensity Level: 3

Duration: Varies

Program Offered: Fall, winter intersession/January term, spring, full academic year, summer

Location: Barcelona, Madrid, Marbella, and Salamanca, Spain

Accommodations: Dormitory, family-stay/host-family, apartment, hotels

Years in Operation: 14

Religious Affiliation: Not relevant

STAFF

Student/Staff Ratio: 5:1

Staff Qualifications: All staff have completed training courses or have master's degrees in the instruction of Spanish. They are a young and dynamic team with a great experience, which has been recognized by several didactic publications in the research of this field.

PARTICIPANTS

Average Number of Participants: 280

For Participants Aged: 14+

The Ideal Candidate: Any student who wants to learn Spanish.

Special Requirements for Participation: None.

COSTS

Average Cost: $900

Included in Cost: Application fees, Enforex textbooks, Internet access, four-week intensive course (20 hours per week of Spanish language lessons and 5 hours per week of Spanish cultural lessons), transcripts, four weeks shared apartment accommodation in double room.

Financial Aid Available: No

General Spanish—ENFOREX Granada

The Program

Description: Spanish courses take place all year-round. Schools are always open. Minimum duration is one week. There is a maximum number of nine students per class; the average number per class is five. Oral and written placement test takes place on the first Monday. Methodology is based on acquiring the linguistic, pragmatic, and functional aspects of language learning along with the sociocultural elements of the Spanish way of life. Students are given 10 hours of language and 5 hours of cultural, 20 hours of language and 5 hours of cultural, or 30 hours of language and 5 hours of cultural lessons (55 minutes each) per week. Every course features one hour per day of Spanish cultural lesson.

Specialty: U.S. university credits system; flexibility, quality, and personal attention; wonderful school facilities; full program of activities and excursions; conversation with Spanish students; student services; possibility of combining the program in more than one location.

Program Type: Academic/pre-college enrichment, middle school enrichment, travel/cultural

Classification: Coeducational, residential, day program

Goals: In all our courses we try to instruct individually and then integrate the four language skills: reading, writing, speaking, and listening. In addition to these skills, we also emphasize grammatical structure so the student can eventually reach the threshold of communicative proficiency. In order to broaden the student's general perspective, we offer the possibility of studying many different aspects of the Spanish culture including history, art, civilization, literature, cinema, etc.

Focus: Academic/pre-college enrichment, travel, and skill-building

Activities Center On: Language and academic

Intensity Level: 3

Duration: Varies

Program Offered: Fall, winter intersession/January term, spring, full academic year, summer

Location: Barcelona, Madrid, Marbella, and Granada, Spain

Accommodations: Dormitory, family-stay/host-family, apartment, hotels

Years in Operation: 14

Religious Affiliation: Not relevant

Staff

Student/Staff Ratio: 5:1

Staff Qualifications: All staff have completed training courses or have master's degrees in the instruction of Spanish. They are a young and dynamic team with a great experience, which has been recognized by several didactic publications in the research of this field.

Participants

Average Number of Participants: 120

For Participants Aged: 14+

The Ideal Candidate: Any student who wants to learn Spanish.

Special Requirements for Participation: None.

Costs

Average Cost: $900

Included in Cost: Application fees, Enforex textbooks, Internet access, four-week intensive course (20 hours per week of Spanish language lessons and 5 hours per week of Spanish cultural lessons), transcripts, four weeks shared apartment accommodation in double room.

Financial Aid Available: No

General Spanish—ENFOREX Madrid

The Program

Description: Spanish courses take place all year-round. Schools are always open. Minimum duration is one week. There is a maximum number of nine students per class; the average number per class is five. Oral and written placement test takes place on the first Monday. Methodology is based on acquiring the linguistic, pragmatic, and functional aspects of language learning along with the sociocultural elements of the Spanish way of life. Students are given 10 hours of language and 5 hours of cultural, 20 hours of language and 5 hours of cultural, or 30 hours of language and 5 hours of cultural lessons (55 minutes each) per week. Every course features one hour per day of Spanish cultural lesson.

Specialty: U.S. university credits system; flexibility, quality, and personal attention; wonderful school facilities; full program of activities and excursions; conversation with Spanish students; student services; possibility of combining the program in more than one location.

Program Type: Academic/pre-college enrichment, middle school enrichment, travel/cultural

Classification: Coeducational, residential, day program

Goals: In all our courses we try to instruct individually and then integrate the four language skills: reading, writing, speaking, and listening. In addition to these skills, we also emphasize grammatical structure so the student can eventually reach the threshold of communicative proficiency. In order to broaden the student's general perspective, we offer the possibility of studying many different aspects of the Spanish culture including history, art, civilization, literature, cinema, etc.

Focus: Academic/pre-college enrichment, skill-building, and cultural

Activities Center On: Language, academic, and travel

Intensity Level: 3

Duration: Varies

Program Offered: Fall, winter intersession/January term, spring, full academic year, summer

Location: Barcelona, Madrid, Marbella, and Salamanca, Spain

Accommodations: Dormitory, family-stay/host-family, apartment, hotels

Years in Operation: 14

Religious Affiliation: Not relevant

STAFF

Student/Staff Ratio: 5:1

Staff Qualifications: All staff have completed training courses or have master's degrees in the instruction of Spanish. They are a young and dynamic team with a great experience, which has been recognized by several didactic publications in the research of this field.

PARTICIPANTS

Average Number of Participants: 230

For Participants Aged: 18+

The Ideal Candidate: Any student who wants to learn Spanish.

Special Requirements for Participation: None.

COSTS

Average Cost: $900

Included in Cost: Application fees, Enforex textbooks, Internet access, four-week intensive course (20 hours per week of Spanish language lessons and 5 hours per week of Spanish cultural lessons), transcripts, four weeks shared apartment accommodation in double room.

Financial Aid Available: No

GENERAL SPANISH—ENFOREX MARBELLA

THE PROGRAM

Description: Spanish courses take place all year-round. Schools are always open. Minimum duration is one week. There is a maximum number of nine students per class; the average number per class is five. Oral and written placement test takes place on the first Monday. Methodology is based on acquiring the linguistic, pragmatic, and functional aspects of language learning along with the sociocultural elements of the Spanish way of life. Students are given 10 hours of language and 5 hours of cultural, 20 hours of language and 5 hours of cultural, or 30 hours of language and 5 hours of cultural lessons (55 minutes each) per week. Every course features one hour per day of Spanish cultural lesson.

Specialty: U.S. university credits system; flexibility, quality, and personal attention; wonderful school facilities; full program of activities and excursions; conversation with Spanish students; student services; possibility of combining the program in more than one location.

Program Type: Academic/pre-college enrichment

Classification: Coeducational, residential, day program

Goals: In all our courses we try to instruct individually and then integrate the four language skills: reading, writing, speaking, and listening. In addition to these skills, we also emphasize grammatical structure so the student can eventually reach the threshold of communicative proficiency. In order to broaden the student's general perspective, we offer the possibility of studying many different aspects of the Spanish culture including history, art, civilization, literature, cinema, etc.

Focus: Academic/pre-college enrichment, cultural, and travel

Activities Center On: Language, academic, and travel

Intensity Level: 3

Duration: Varies

Program Offered: Fall, winter intersession/January term, spring, full academic year, summer

Location: Barcelona, Madrid, Marbella, and Salamanca, Spain

Accommodations: Dormitory, family-stay/host-family, apartment, hotels

Years in Operation: 14

Religious Affiliation: Not relevant

STAFF

Student/Staff Ratio: 5:1

Staff Qualifications: All staff have completed training courses or have master's degrees in the instruction of Spanish. They are a young and dynamic team with a great experience, which has been recognized by several didactic publications in the research of this field.

PARTICIPANTS

Average Number of Participants: 130

For Participants Aged: 14+

The Ideal Candidate: Any student who wants to learn Spanish.

Special Requirements for Participation: None.

COSTS

Average Cost: $900

Included in Cost: Application fees, Enforex textbooks, Internet access, four-week intensive course (20 hours per week of Spanish language lessons and 5 hours per week of Spanish cultural lessons), transcripts, four weeks shared apartment accommodation in double room.

Financial Aid Available: No

GENERAL SPANISH—ENFOREX SALAMANCA

THE PROGRAM

Description: Spanish courses take place all year-round. Schools are always open. Minimum duration is one week. There is a maximum number of nine students per class; the average number per class is five. Oral and written placement test takes place on the first Monday. Methodology is based on acquiring the linguistic, pragmatic, and functional aspects of language learning along with the sociocultural elements of the Spanish way of life. Students are given 10 hours of language and 5 hours of cultural, 20 hours of language and 5 hours of cultural, or 30 hours of language and 5 hours of cultural lessons (55 minutes each) per week. Every course features one hour per day of Spanish cultural lesson.

Specialty: U.S. university credits system; flexibility, quality, and personal attention; wonderful school facilities; full program of activities and excursions; conversation with Spanish students; student services; possibility of combining the program in more than one location.

Program Type: Academic/pre-college enrichment, middle school enrichment, outdoors/adventure, sports/athletic, travel/cultural

Classification: Coeducational, residential, day program

Goals: In all our courses we try to instruct individually and then integrate the four language skills: reading, writing, speaking, and listening. In addition to these skills, we also emphasize grammatical structure so the student can eventually reach the threshold of communicative proficiency. In order to broaden the student's general perspective, we offer the possibility of studying many different aspects of the Spanish culture including history, art, civilization, literature, cinema, etc.

Focus: Academic/pre-college enrichment, travel, and skill-building

Activities Center On: Language, academic, and travel

Intensity Level: 3

Duration: Varies

Program Offered: Fall, winter intersession/January term, spring, full academic year, summer

Location: Barcelona, Madrid, Marbella, and Salamanca, Spain

Accommodations: Dormitory, family-stay/host-family, apartment, hotels

Years in Operation: 14

Religious Affiliation: Not relevant

STAFF

Student/Staff Ratio: 5:1

Staff Qualifications: All staff have completed training courses or have master's degrees in the instruction of Spanish. They are a young and dynamic team with a great experience, which has been recognized by several didactic publications in the research of this field.

PARTICIPANTS

Average Number of Participants: 150

For Participants Aged: 14+

The Ideal Candidate: Any student who wants to learn Spanish.

Special Requirements for Participation: None.

COSTS

Average Cost: $900

Included in Cost: Application fees, Enforex textbooks, Internet access, four-week intensive course (20 hours per week of Spanish language lessons and 5 hours per week of Spanish cultural lessons), transcripts, four weeks shared apartment accommodation in double room.

Financial Aid Available: No

HISPANIC CULTURE (HISTORY, ART, AND LITERATURE)—ENFOREX BARCELONA

THE PROGRAM

Description: We will trace the history of Spain from its very beginnings up to today. We will investigate the most representative literary trends of Spanish and Latin American literature, and we will study the history of architecture and Spanish painting and sculpture, and also focus on some of Spain's most important trends and artistic representations.

Specialty: U.S. university credits system; flexibility, quality, and personal attention; wonderful school facilities; full program of activities and excursions; conversation with Spanish students; student services; possibility of combining the program in more than one location.

Program Type: Academic/pre-college enrichment, middle school enrichment, music/arts, travel/cultural

Classification: Coeducational, residential, day program

Focus: Cultural, educational exchange, and travel

Activities Center On: Language, academic, and touring

Intensity Level: 3

Duration: 2–4 weeks

Program Offered: Fall, winter intersession/January term, spring, full academic year, summer

Location: Madrid, Barcelona, Salamanca, and Granada, Spain

Accommodations: Dormitory, family-stay/host-family, apartment, hotels

Years in Operation: 12

Religious Affiliation: Not relevant

STAFF

Student/Staff Ratio: 5:1

Staff Qualifications: All staff have completed training courses or have master's degrees in the instruction of Spanish. They are a young and dynamic team with a great experience, which has been recognized by several didactic publications in the research of this field.

PARTICIPANTS

Average Number of Participants: 35

For Participants Aged: 18+

The Ideal Candidate: Any student with an intermediate-level proficiency in Spanish who wants to focus deeply on some specific Spanish cultural subjects.

Special Requirements for Participation: An intermediate level of Spanish proficiency is requested.

COSTS

Average Cost: $1,265

Included in Cost: Application fees, Enforex textbooks, Internet access, four-week Hispanic culture course (20 hours per week of Spanish language lessons and 5 hours per week of Spanish cultural lessons), transcripts, four weeks shared apartment accommodation in double room.

Financial Aid Available: No

HISPANIC CULTURE (HISTORY, ART, AND LITERATURE) — ENFOREX GRANADA

THE PROGRAM

Description: We will trace the history of Spain from its very beginnings up to today. We will investigate the most representative literary trends of Spanish and Latin American literature, and we will study the history of architecture and Spanish painting and sculpture, and also focus on some of Spain's most important trends and artistic representations.

Specialty: U.S. university credits system; flexibility, quality, and personal attention; wonderful school facilities; full program of activities and excursions; conversation with Spanish students; student services; possibility of combining the program in more than one location.

Program Type: Academic/pre-college enrichment, middle school enrichment, music/arts, travel/cultural

Classification: Coeducational, residential, day program

Focus: Cultural, academic/pre-college enrichment, and travel

Activities Center On: Language, academic, and touring

Intensity Level: 3

Duration: 2–4 weeks

Program Offered: Fall, winter intersession/January term, spring, full academic year, summer

Location: Madrid, Barcelona, Salamanca, and Granada, Spain

Accommodations: Dormitory, family-stay/host-family, apartment, hotels

Years in Operation: 12

Religious Affiliation: Not relevant

STAFF

Student/Staff Ratio: 5:1

Staff Qualifications: All staff have completed training courses or have master's degrees in the instruction of Spanish. They are a young and dynamic team with a great experience, which has been recognized by several didactic publications in the research of this field.

PARTICIPANTS

Average Number of Participants: 14

For Participants Aged: 18+

The Ideal Candidate: Any student with an intermediate-level proficiency in Spanish who wants to focus deeply on some specific Spanish cultural subjects.

Special Requirements for Participation: An intermediate level of Spanish proficiency is requested.

COSTS

Average Cost: $1,265

Included in Cost: Application fees, Enforex textbooks, Internet access, four-week Hispanic culture course (20 hours per week of Spanish language lessons and 5 hours per week of Spanish cultural lessons), four weeks shared apartment accommodation in double room.

Financial Aid Available: No

HISPANIC CULTURE (HISTORY, ART & LITERATURE) — ENFOREX MADRID

THE PROGRAM

Description: We will trace the history of Spain from its very beginnings up to today. We will investigate the most representative literary trends of Spanish and Latin American literature, and we will study the history of architecture and Spanish painting and sculpture, and also focus on some of Spain's most important trends and artistic representations.

Specialty: U.S. university credits system; flexibility, quality, and personal attention; wonderful school facilities; full program of activities and excursions; conversation with Spanish students; student services; possibility of combining the program in more than one location.

Program Type: Academic/pre-college enrichment, middle school enrichment, music/arts, outdoors/adventure, travel/cultural

Classification: Coeducational, residential, day program

Focus: Cultural, travel, and educational exchange

Activities Center On: Language, academic, and touring

Intensity Level: 3

Duration: 2–4 weeks

Program Offered: Fall, winter intersession/January term, spring, full academic year, summer

Location: Madrid, Barcelona, Salamanca, and Granada, Spain

Accommodations: Dormitory, family-stay/host-family, apartment, hotels

Years in Operation: 12

Religious Affiliation: Not relevant

STAFF

Student/Staff Ratio: 5:1

Staff Qualifications: All staff have completed training courses or have master's degrees in the instruction of Spanish. They are a young and dynamic team with a great experience, which has been recognized by several didactic publications in the research of this field.

PARTICIPANTS

Average Number of Participants: 25

For Participants Aged: 18+

The Ideal Candidate: Any student with an intermediate-level proficiency in Spanish who wants to focus deeply on some specific Spanish cultural subjects.

Special Requirements for Participation: An intermediate level of Spanish proficiency is requested.

Costs

Average Cost: $1,265

Included in Cost: Application fees, Enforex textbooks, Internet access, four-week Hispanic culture course (20 hours per week of Spanish language lessons and 5 hours per week of Spanish cultural lessons), four weeks shared apartment accommodation in double room.

Financial Aid Available: No

Hispanic Culture (History, Art, and Literature) — ENFOREX Salamanca

The Program

Description: We will trace the history of Spain from its very beginnings up to today. We will investigate the most representative literary trends of Spanish and Latin American literature, and we will study the history of architecture and Spanish painting and sculpture, and also focus on some of Spain's most important trends and artistic representations.

Specialty: U.S. university credits system; flexibility, quality, and personal attention; wonderful school facilities; full program of activities and excursions; conversation with Spanish students; student services; possibility of combining the program in more than one location.

Program Type: Academic/pre-college enrichment, middle school enrichment, music/arts, travel/cultural

Classification: Coeducational, residential, day program

Focus: Cultural, travel, and academic/pre-college enrichment

Activities Center On: Language and touring

Intensity Level: 3

Duration: 2–4 weeks

Program Offered: Fall, winter intersession/January term, spring, full academic year, summer

Location: Madrid, Barcelona, Salamanca, and Granada, Spain

Accommodations: Dormitory, family-stay/host-family, apartment, hotels

Years in Operation: 12

Religious Affiliation: Not relevant

Staff

Student/Staff Ratio: 5:1

Staff Qualifications: All staff have completed training courses or have master's degrees in the instruction of Spanish. They are a young and dynamic team with a great experience, which has been recognized by several didactic publications in the research of this field.

Participants

Average Number of Participants: 20

For Participants Aged: 18+

The Ideal Candidate: Any student with an intermediate-level proficiency in Spanish who wants to focus deeply on some specific Spanish cultural subjects.

Special Requirements for Participation: An intermediate level of Spanish proficiency is requested.

Costs

Average Cost: $1,265

Included in Cost: Application fees, Enforex textbooks, Internet access, four-week Hispanic culture course (20 hours per week of Spanish language lessons and 5 hours per week of Spanish cultural lessons), four weeks shared apartment accommodation in double room.

Financial Aid Available: No

Intensive Spanish — ENFOREX La Antigua (Guatemala)

The Program

Description: 20/30 lessons per week; maximum class size: 5. The focus in class is mostly on grammar and conversation. Classes start Mondays year-round.

Specialty: U.S. university credits system; flexibility, quality, and personal attention; full program of activities and excursions; student services; possibility of combining the program in more than one location.

Program Type: Academic/pre-college enrichment, middle school enrichment, music/arts, outdoors/adventure, travel/cultural

Classification: Coeducational, residential, day program

Goals: Spanish in a Latin American country.

Focus: Cultural, travel, and other

Activities Center On: Language

Intensity Level: 3

Duration: Varies

Program Offered: Fall, winter intersession/January term, spring, full academic year, summer

Location: La Antigua, Guatemala

Accommodations: Family-stay/host-family

Years in Operation: 12

Religious Affiliation: Not relevant

Staff

Student/Staff Ratio: 3:1

Staff Qualifications: We have a wonderful teaching staff at ENFOREX. All teachers are university-educated native speakers and are rotated on a regular basis so that students can get used to hearing more than one voice. The teachers are all trained in the teaching methods of the school.

PARTICIPANTS

Average Number of Participants: 50

For Participants Aged: 18+

The Ideal Candidate: Any student who wants to learn Spanish in a Latin American country.

Special Requirements for Participation: None.

COSTS

Average Cost: $465

Included in Cost: Application fees, textbooks, four-week course (20 hours per week), transcripts, four-week homestay accommodation (single room), half board, airport pick-up.

Financial Aid Available: No

INTENSIVE SPANISH — ENFOREX
CORDOBA (ARGENTINA)

THE PROGRAM

Description: 20/30 lessons per week; maximum class size: 5. The focus in class is mostly on grammar and conversation. Classes start Mondays year-round.

Specialty: U.S. university credits system; flexibility, quality, and personal attention; full program of activities and excursions; student services; possibility of combining the program in more than one location.

Program Type: Academic/pre-college enrichment, middle school enrichment, music/arts, travel/cultural

Classification: Coeducational, residential, day program

Goals: Spanish in a Latin American country.

Focus: Cultural, skill-building, and travel

Activities Center On: Language

Intensity Level: 3

Duration: Varies

Program Offered: Fall, winter intersession/January term, spring, full academic year, summer

Location: Cordoba, Argentina

Accommodations: Family-stay/host-family

Years in Operation: 12

Religious Affiliation: Not relevant

STAFF

Student/Staff Ratio: 3:1

Staff Qualifications: We have a wonderful teaching staff at ENFOREX. All teachers are university-educated native speakers and are rotated on a regular basis so that students can get used to hearing more than one voice. The teachers are all trained in the teaching methods of the school.

PARTICIPANTS

Average Number of Participants: 25

For Participants Aged: 18+

The Ideal Candidate: Any student who wants to learn Spanish in a Latin American country.

Special Requirements for Participation: None.

COSTS

Average Cost: $625

Included in Cost: Application fees, textbooks, four-week course (20 hours per week), transcripts, four-week homestay accommodation (single room), half board, airport pick-up.

Financial Aid Available: No

INTENSIVE SPANISH — ENFOREX
CUSCO (PERU)

THE PROGRAM

Description: 20/30 lessons per week; maximum class size: 5. The focus in class is mostly on grammar and conversation. Classes start Mondays year-round.

Specialty: U.S. university credits system; flexibility, quality, and personal attention; full program of activities and excursions; student services; possibility of combining the program in more than one location.

Program Type: Academic/pre-college enrichment, middle school enrichment, music/arts, outdoors/adventure, travel/cultural

Classification: Coeducational, residential, day program

Goals: Spanish in a Latin American country.

Focus: Travel, cultural, and skill-building

Activities Center On: Language

Intensity Level: 3

Duration: Varies

Program Offered: Fall, winter intersession/January term, spring, full academic year, summer

Location: Cusco, Peru

Accommodations: Family-stay/host-family

Years in Operation: 12

Religious Affiliation: Not relevant

STAFF

Student/Staff Ratio: 3:1

Staff Qualifications: We have a wonderful teaching staff at ENFOREX. All teachers are university-educated native speakers and are rotated on a regular basis so that students can get used to hearing more than one voice. The teachers are all trained in the teaching methods of the school.

PARTICIPANTS

Average Number of Participants: 32

For Participants Aged: 18+

The Ideal Candidate: Any student who wants to learn Spanish in a Latin American country.

Special Requirements for Participation: None.

Costs

Average Cost: $665

Included in Cost: Application fees, textbooks, four-week course (20 hours per week), transcripts, four-week homestay accommodation (single room), half board, airport pick-up.

Financial Aid Available: No

Intensive Spanish — ENFOREX Flamingo Beach (Costa Rica)

The Program

Description: 20 lessons per week; maximum class size: 5. The focus in class is mostly on grammar and conversation. Classes start Mondays year-round.

Specialty: U.S. university credits system; flexibility, quality, and personal attention; full program of activities and excursions; student services; possibility of combining the program in more than one location.

Program Type: Academic/pre-college enrichment, middle school enrichment, outdoors/adventure, travel/cultural

Classification: Coeducational, residential, day program

Goals: Spanish in a Latin American country.

Focus: Cultural, educational exchange, and travel

Activities Center On: Language

Intensity Level: 3

Duration: Varies

Program Offered: Fall, winter intersession/January term, spring, full academic year, summer

Location: Flamingo Beach, Costa Rica

Accommodations: Family-stay/host-family

Years in Operation: 12

Religious Affiliation: Not relevant

Staff

Student/Staff Ratio: 3:1

Staff Qualifications: We have a wonderful teaching staff at ENFOREX. All teachers are university-educated native speakers and are rotated on a regular basis so that students can get used to hearing more than one voice. The teachers are all trained in the teaching methods of the school.

Participants

Average Number of Participants: 55

For Participants Aged: 18+

The Ideal Candidate: Any student who wants to learn Spanish in a Latin American country.

Special Requirements for Participation: None.

Costs

Average Cost: $865

Included in Cost: Application fees, textbooks, four-week course (20 hours per week), transcripts, four-week homestay accommodation (single room), half board.

Financial Aid Available: No

Intensive Spanish — ENFOREX Quito (Ecuador)

The Program

Description: 20/30 lessons per week; maximum class size: 5. The focus in class is mostly on grammar and conversation. Classes start Mondays year-round.

Specialty: U.S. university credits system; flexibility, quality, and personal attention; full program of activities and excursions; student services; possibility of combining the program in more than one location.

Program Type: Academic/pre-college enrichment, middle school enrichment, music/arts, outdoors/adventure, travel/cultural

Classification: Coeducational, residential, day program

Goals: Spanish (oral and written).

Focus: Cultural, educational exchange, and travel

Activities Center On: Language, wilderness, and travel

Intensity Level: 3

Duration: Varies

Program Offered: Fall, winter intersession/January term, spring, full academic year, summer

Location: Quito, Ecuador

Accommodations: Family-stay/host-family

Years in Operation: 12

Religious Affiliation: Not relevant

Staff

Student/Staff Ratio: 3:1

Staff Qualifications: We have a wonderful teaching staff at ENFOREX. All teachers are university-educated native speakers and are rotated on a regular basis so that students can get used to hearing more than one voice. The teachers are all trained in the teaching methods of the school.

Participants

Average Number of Participants: 40

For Participants Aged: 18+

The Ideal Candidate: Any student who wants to learn Spanish in a Latin American country.

Special Requirements for Participation: None.

COSTS

Average Cost: $665

Included in Cost: Application fees, textbooks, four-week course (20 hours per week), transcripts, four-week homestay accommodation (single room), half board, airport pick-up.

Financial Aid Available: No

INTENSIVE SPANISH—ENFOREX SUCRE (BOLIVIA)

THE PROGRAM

Description: 20/30 lessons per week; maximum class size: 5. The focus in class is mostly on grammar and conversation. Classes start Mondays year-round.

Specialty: U.S. university credits system; flexibility, quality, and personal attention; full program of activities and excursions; student services; possibility of combining the program in more than one location.

Program Type: Academic/pre-college enrichment, middle school enrichment, outdoors/adventure, travel/cultural

Classification: Coeducational, residential, day program

Goals: Spanish in a Latin American country.

Focus: Cultural, travel, and other

Activities Center On: Language

Intensity Level: 3

Duration: Varies

Program Offered: Fall, winter intersession/January term, spring, full academic year, summer

Location: Sucre, Bolivia

Accommodations: Family-stay/host-family

Years in Operation: 12

Religious Affiliation: Not relevant

STAFF

Student/Staff Ratio: 3:1

Staff Qualifications: We have a wonderful teaching staff at ENFOREX. All teachers are university-educated native speakers and are rotated on a regular basis so that students can get used to hearing more than one voice. The teachers are all trained in the teaching methods of the school.

PARTICIPANTS

Average Number of Participants: 45

For Participants Aged: 18+

The Ideal Candidate: Any student who wants to learn Spanish in a Latin American country.

Special Requirements for Participation: None.

COSTS

Average Cost: $665

Included in Cost: Application fees, textbooks, four-week course (20 hours per week), transcripts, four-week homestay accommodation (single room), half board, airport pick-up.

Financial Aid Available: No

ONE-TO-ONE PRIVATE LESSONS— ENFOREX ALMUÑECAR

THE PROGRAM

Description: The aim of this program is to offer a fully personalized method of teaching according to the student's specific needs and desires. Because classes are private, the student will be able to decide the schedule and content. The minimum duration of these courses is one hour per week.

Specialty: Flexibility, quality, and personal attention; wonderful school facilities; full program of activities and excursions; conversation with Spanish students; student services; possibility of combining the program in more than one location.

Program Type: Academic/pre-college enrichment, community service, middle school enrichment, music/arts, outdoors/adventure, sports/athletic, travel/cultural

Classification: Coeducational, residential, day program

Goals: The Spanish for Professionals course offers Intensive Business and Spanish for Specific Purposes options. Both programs offer individualized study in grammar, speaking, listening, reading, writing, and vocabulary. The student may also request to study any particular topic of interest, provided that he/she gives adequate notice before the classes actually begin.

Focus: Skill-building, cultural, and travel

Activities Center On: Language and academic

Intensity Level: 3

Duration: Less than 1 week

Program Offered: Summer

Location: Madrid, Barcelona, Marbella, and Salamanca, Spain

Accommodations: Family-stay/host-family, apartment

Years in Operation: 12

Religious Affiliation: Not relevant

STAFF

Student/Staff Ratio: 1:1

Staff Qualifications: All staff have completed training courses or have master's degrees in the instruction of Spanish. They are a young and dynamic team with great experience, which has been recognized by several didactic publications in the research of this field.

PARTICIPANTS

Average Number of Participants: 15

For Participants Aged: 14+

The Ideal Candidate: These courses are directed to those students who need an intensive Spanish course within a short period of time.

Special Requirements for Participation: None.

COSTS

Average Cost: $625

Included in Cost: Application fees, Enforex textbook, Internet access, one-week one-to-one course (10 hours per week), one-week shared apartment accommodation in individual room.

Financial Aid Available: No

ONE-TO-ONE PRIVATE LESSONS — ENFOREX BARCELONA

THE PROGRAM

Description: The aim of this program is to offer a fully personalized method of teaching according to the student's specific needs and desires. Becaue classes are private, the student will be able to decide the schedule and content. The minimum duration of these courses is one hour per week.

Specialty: Flexibility, quality, and personal attention; wonderful school facilities; full program of activities and excursions; conversation with Spanish students; student services; possibility of combining the program in more than one location.

Program Type: Academic/pre-college enrichment travel/cultural

Classification: Coeducational, residential, day program

Goals: The Spanish for Professionals course offers Intensive Business and Spanish for Specific Purposes options. Both programs offer individualized study in grammar, speaking, listening, reading, writing, and vocabulary. The student may also request to study any particular topic of interest, provided that he/she gives adequate notice before the classes actually begin.

Focus: Skill-building, leadership/teamwork, and travel

Activities Center On: Language and writing

Intensity Level: 3

Duration: 1–2 weeks

Program Offered: Fall, winter intersession/January term, spring, full academic year, summer

Location: Madrid, Barcelona, Marbella, Salamanca, and Granada

Accommodations: Dormitory, family-stay/host-family, apartment, hotels

Years in Operation: 12

Religious Affiliation: Not relevant

STAFF

Student/Staff Ratio: 1:1

Staff Qualifications: All staff have completed training courses or have master's degrees in the instruction of Spanish. They are a young and dynamic team with great experience, which has been recognized by several didactic publications in the research of this field.

PARTICIPANTS

Average Number of Participants: 60

For Participants Aged: 14+

The Ideal Candidate: These courses are directed to those students who need an intensive Spanish course within a short period of time.

Special Requirements for Participation: None.

COSTS

Average Cost: $625

Included in Cost: Application fees, Enforex textbook, Internet access, one-week one-to-one course (10 hours per week), one-week shared apartment accommodation in individual room.

Financial Aid Available: No

ONE-TO-ONE PRIVATE LESSONS — ENFOREX GRANADA

THE PROGRAM

Description: The aim of this program is to offer a fully personalized method of teaching according to the student's specific needs and desires. Because classes are private, the student will be able to decide the schedule and content. The minimum duration of these courses is one hour per week.

Specialty: Flexibility, quality, and personal attention; wonderful school facilities; full program of activities and excursions; conversation with Spanish students; student services; possibility of combining the program in more than one location.

Program Type: Academic/pre-college enrichment, community service, middle school enrichment, music/arts, outdoors/adventure, sports/athletic, travel/cultural

Classification: Coeducational, residential, day program

Goals: The Spanish for Professionals course offers Intensive Business and Spanish for Specific Purposes options. Both programs offer individualized study in grammar, speaking, listening, reading, writing, and vocabulary. The student may also request to study any particular topic of interest, provided that he/she gives adequate notice before the classes actually begin.

Focus: Educational exchange and academic/pre-college enrichment

Activities Center On: Language and cultural

Intensity Level: 3

Duration: Less than 1 week

Program Offered: Fall, winter intersession/January term, spring, full academic year, summer

Location: Madrid, Barcelona, Marbella, and Salamanca, Spain

Accommodations: Dormitory, family-stay/host-family, apartment, hotels

Years in Operation: 12

Religious Affiliation: Not relevant

STAFF

Student/Staff Ratio: 1:1

Staff Qualifications: All staff have completed training courses or have master's degrees in the instruction of Spanish. They are a young and dynamic team with great experience, which has been recognized by several didactic publications in the research of this field.

PARTICIPANTS

Average Number of Participants: 20

For Participants Aged: 14+

The Ideal Candidate: These courses are directed to those students who need an intensive Spanish course within a short period of time.

Special Requirements for Participation: None.

COSTS

Average Cost: $625

Included in Cost: Application fees, Enforex textbook, Internet access, one-week one-to-one course (10 hours per week), one-week shared apartment accommodation in individual room.

Financial Aid Available: No

ONE-TO-ONE PRIVATE LESSONS— ENFOREX MADRID

THE PROGRAM

Description: The aim of this program is to offer a fully personalized method of teaching according to the student's specific needs and desires. Because classes are private, the student will be able to decide the schedule and content. The minimum duration of these courses is one hour per week.

Specialty: Flexibility, quality, and personal attention; wonderful school facilities; full program of activities and excursions; conversation with Spanish students; student services; possibility of combining the program in more than one location.

Program Type: Academic/pre-college enrichment, middle school enrichment

Classification: Coeducational, residential, day program

Goals: The Spanish for Professionals course offers Intensive Business and Spanish for Specific Purposes options. Both programs offer individualized study in grammar, speaking, listening, reading, writing, and vocabulary. The student may also request to study any particular topic of interest, provided that he/she gives adequate notice before the classes actually begin.

Focus: Skill-building, cultural, and travel

Activities Center On: Language, and academic

Intensity Level: 3

Duration: Varies

Program Offered: Fall, winter intersession/January term, spring, full academic year, summer

Location: Madrid, Barcelona, Marbella, and Salamanca, Spain

Accommodations: Dormitory, family-stay/host-family, apartment, hotels

Years in Operation: 12

Religious Affiliation: Not relevant

STAFF

Student/Staff Ratio: 1:1

Staff Qualifications: All staff have completed training courses or have master's degrees in the instruction of Spanish. They are a young and dynamic team with great experience, which has been recognized by several didactic publications in the research of this field.

PARTICIPANTS

Average Number of Participants: 120

For Participants Aged: 14+

The Ideal Candidate: These courses are directed to those students who need an intensive Spanish course within a short period of time.

Special Requirements for Participation: None.

COSTS

Average Cost: $625

Included in Cost: Application fees, Enforex textbook, Internet access, one-week one-to-one course (10 hours per week), one-week shared apartment accommodation in individual room.

Financial Aid Available: No

ONE-TO-ONE PRIVATE LESSONS— ENFOREX MARBELLA

THE PROGRAM

Description: The aim of this program is to offer a fully personalized method of teaching according to the student's specific needs and desires. Because classes are private, the student will be able to decide the schedule and content. The minimum duration of these courses is one hour per week.

Specialty: Flexibility, quality, and personal attention; wonderful school facilities; full program of activities and excursions; conversation with Spanish students; student services; possibility of combining the program in more than one location.

Program Type: Academic/pre-college enrichment, middle school enrichment, outdoors/adventure, travel/cultural

Classification: Coeducational, residential, day program

Goals: The Spanish for Professionals course offers Intensive Business and Spanish for Specific Purposes options. Both programs offer individualized study in grammar, speaking, listening, reading, writing, and vocabulary. The student may also request to study any particular topic of interest, provided that he/she gives adequate notice before the classes actually begin.

Focus: Educational exchange, skill-building, and academic/pre-college enrichment

Activities Center On: Language, writing, and cultural

Intensity Level: 3

Duration: 1–2 weeks

Program Offered: Fall, winter intersession/January term, spring, full academic year, summer

Location: Madrid, Barcelona, Marbella, Salamanca, and Granada

Accommodations: Dormitory, family-stay/host-family, apartment, hotels

Years in Operation: 12

Religious Affiliation: Not relevant

STAFF

Student/Staff Ratio: 1:1

Staff Qualifications: All staff have completed training courses or have master's degrees in the instruction of Spanish. They are a young and dynamic team with a great experience, which has been recognized by several didactic publications in the research of this field.

PARTICIPANTS

Average Number of Participants: 40

For Participants Aged: 14+

The Ideal Candidate: These courses are directed to those students who need an intensive Spanish course within a short period of time.

Special Requirements for Participation: None.

COSTS

Average Cost: $625

Included in Cost: Application fees, Enforex textbook, Internet access, one-week one-to-one course (10 hours per week), one-week shared apartment accommodation in individual room.

Financial Aid Available: No

ONE-TO-ONE PRIVATE LESSONS — ENFOREX SALAMANCA

THE PROGRAM

Description: The aim of this program is to offer a fully personalized method of teaching according to the student's specific needs and desires. Because classes are private, the student will be able to decide the schedule and content. The minimum duration of these courses is one hour per week.

Specialty: Flexibility, quality, and personal attention; wonderful school facilities; full program of activities and excursions; conversation with Spanish students; student services; possibility of combining the program in more than one location.

Program Type: Academic/pre-college enrichment, community service, middle school enrichment, music/arts, outdoors/adventure, sports/athletic, travel/cultural

Classification: Coeducational, residential, day program

Goals: The Spanish for Professionals course offers Intensive Business and Spanish for Specific Purposes options. Both programs offer individualized study in grammar, speaking, listening, reading, writing, and vocabulary. The student may also request to study any particular topic of interest, provided that he/she gives adequate notice before the classes actually begin.

Focus: Cultural, skill-building, and leadership/teamwork

Activities Center On: Language, academic, and cultural

Intensity Level: 3

Duration: 1–2 weeks

Program Offered: Fall, winter intersession/January term, spring, full academic year, summer

Location: Madrid, Barcelona, Marbella, and Salamanca, Spain

Accommodations: Dormitory, family-stay/host-family, apartment, hotels

Years in Operation: 12

Religious Affiliation: Not relevant

STAFF

Student/Staff Ratio: 1:1

Staff Qualifications: All staff have completed training courses or have master's degrees in the instruction of Spanish. They are a young and dynamic team with great experience, which has been recognized by several didactic publications in the research of this field.

PARTICIPANTS

Average Number of Participants: 30

For Participants Aged: 14+

The Ideal Candidate: These courses are directed to those students who need an intensive Spanish course within a short period of time.

Special Requirements for Participation: None.

COSTS

Average Cost: $625

Included in Cost: Application fees, Enforex textbook, Internet access, one-week one-to-one course (10 hours per week), one-week shared apartment accommodation in individual room.

Financial Aid Available: No

SPANISH + FLAMENCO — ENFOREX GRANADA

THE PROGRAM

Description: This course of 20+8 lessons per week includes 20 Spanish lessons per week and 8 flamenco dance lessons during the afternoons/evenings at one of the best and oldest flamenco schools, very well known throughout Spain.

Specialty: Flexibility, quality, and personal attention; U.S. university credit system; wonderful school facilities; full program of activities and excursions; conversation with Spanish students; student services; possibility of combining the program in more than one location.

Program Type: Academic/pre-college enrichment, middle school enrichment, music/arts, travel/cultural

Classification: Coeducational, residential, day program

Goals: The students will share the stage with professional flamenco dancers and will learn how to improve technical and cultural aspects of this typical dance.

Focus: Educational exchange, travel, and cultural

Activities Center On: Language, dance, and other

Intensity Level: 3

Duration: 2–4 weeks

Program Offered: Fall, winter intersession/January term, spring, full academic year, summer

Location: Madrid, Marbella, and Granada, Spain

Accommodations: Dormitory, family-stay/host-family, apartment, hotels

Years in Operation: 12

Religious Affiliation: Not relevant

STAFF

Student/Staff Ratio: 5:1

Staff Qualifications: All staff have completed training courses or have master's degrees in the instruction of Spanish. They are a young and dynamic team with a great experience, which has been recognized by several didactic publications in the research of this field.

PARTICIPANTS

Average Number of Participants: 20

For Participants Aged: 18+

The Ideal Candidate: This program is designed for lovers of Spanish folklore and flamenco dance.

Special Requirements for Participation: None.

COSTS

Average Cost: $815

Included in Cost: Application fees, Enforex textbooks, Internet access, two-week course (20+8 hours per week), transcripts, two-week shared apartment accommodation in double room.

Financial Aid Available: No

SPANISH + FLAMENCO — ENFOREX MADRID

THE PROGRAM

Description: This course of 20+8 lessons per week includes 20 Spanish lessons per week and 8 flamenco dance lessons during the afternoons/evenings at one of the best and oldest flamenco schools, very well known throughout Spain.

Specialty: Flexibility, quality, and personal attention; U.S. university credit system; wonderful school facilities; full program

of activities and excursions; conversation with Spanish students; student services; possibility of combining the program in more than one location.

Program Type: Academic/pre-college enrichment, middle school enrichment, music/arts, travel/cultural

Classification: Coeducational, residential, day program

Goals: The students will share the stage with professional flamenco dancers and will learn how to improve technical and cultural aspects of this typical dance.

Focus: Cultural, educational exchange, and travel

Activities Center On: Language and dance

Intensity Level: 3

Duration: 2–4 weeks

Program Offered: Fall, winter intersession/January term, spring, full academic year, summer

Location: Madrid, Marbella, and Granada, Spain

Accommodations: Dormitory, family-stay/host-family, apartment, hotels

Years in Operation: 12

Religious Affiliation: Not relevant

STAFF

Student/Staff Ratio: 5:1

Staff Qualifications: All staff have completed training courses or have master's degrees in the instruction of Spanish. They are a young and dynamic team with a great experience, which has been recognized by several didactic publications in the research of this field.

PARTICIPANTS

Average Number of Participants: 30

For Participants Aged: 18+

The Ideal Candidate: This program is designed for lovers of Spanish folklore and flamenco dance.

Special Requirements for Participation: None.

COSTS

Average Cost: $815

Included in Cost: Application fees, Enforex textbooks, Internet access, two-week course (20+8 hours per week), transcripts, two-week shared apartment accommodation in double room.

Financial Aid Available: No

SPANISH + FLAMENCO — ENFOREX MARBELLA

THE PROGRAM

Description: This course of 20+8 lessons per week includes 20 Spanish lessons per week and 8 flamenco dance lessons during the afternoons/evenings at one of the best and oldest flamenco schools, very well known throughout Spain.

Specialty: Flexibility, quality, and personal attention; U.S. university credit system; wonderful school facilities; full program of activities and excursions; conversation with Spanish students; student services; possibility of combining the program in more than one location.

Program Type: Academic/pre-college enrichment, middle school enrichment, music/arts, travel/cultural

Classification: Coeducational, residential, day program

Goals: The students will share the stage with professional flamenco dancers and will learn how to improve technical and cultural aspects of this typical dance.

Focus: Cultural, educational exchange, and travel

Activities Center On: Language and dance

Intensity Level: 3

Duration: 2–4 weeks

Program Offered: Fall, winter intersession/January term, spring, full academic year, summer

Location: Madrid, Marbella, and Granada, Spain

Accommodations: Dormitory, family-stay/host-family, apartment, hotels

Years in Operation: 12

Religious Affiliation: Not relevant

STAFF

Student/Staff Ratio: 5:1

Staff Qualifications: All staff have completed training courses or have master's degrees in the instruction of Spanish. They are a young and dynamic team with a great experience, which has been recognized by several didactic publications in the research of this field.

PARTICIPANTS

Average Number of Participants: 15

For Participants Aged: 18+

The Ideal Candidate: This program is designed for lovers of Spanish folklore and flamenco dance.

Special Requirements for Participation: None.

COSTS

Average Cost: $815

Included in Cost: Application fees, Enforex textbooks, Internet access, two-week course (20+8 hours per week), transcripts, two-week shared apartment accommodation in double room.

Financial Aid Available: No

SPANISH + GOLF—ENFOREX MARBELLA

THE PROGRAM

Description: This course includes 20 Spanish lessons per week plus golf lessons in the afternoons/evenings at one of the best golf schools, very well known throughout the "Costa del Sol." If three or more students follow the same program on

the same dates, the course includes eight golf lessons per week; if fewer than three students follow the program on the same dates, the course includes four golf lessons and four hours of free practice per week.

Specialty: Flexibility, quality, and personal attention; U.S. university credits system; full program of activities and excursions; student services; possibility of combining the program in more than one location.

Program Type: Academic/pre-college enrichment, middle school enrichment, outdoors/adventure, sports/athletic, travel/cultural

Classification: Coeducational, residential, day program

Goals: This course is designed for those people who love golf and want to improve their golf skills while learning or improving their Spanish in one of the most selective, incredible, and sunny coasts in Europe. Marbella, on the southern coast of Spain in the province of Andalusia, is a luxurious summer resort village for Spaniards and foreign residents.

Focus: Travel, educational exchange, and cultural

Activities Center On: Golf, language, and sports/athletic

Intensity Level: 3

Duration: Varies

Program Offered: Fall

Location: Marbella, Spain

Accommodations: Dormitory, family-stay/host-family, apartment, hotels

Years in Operation: 12

Religious Affiliation: Not relevant

STAFF

Student/Staff Ratio: 5:1

Staff Qualifications: All staff have completed training courses or have master's degrees in the instruction of Spanish. They are a young and dynamic team with a great experience, which has been recognized by several didactic publications in the research of this field.

PARTICIPANTS

Average Number of Participants: 25

For Participants Aged: 18+

Special Requirements for Participation: None.

COSTS

Average Cost: $925

Included in Cost: Application fees, Enforex textbooks, Internet access, two-week course (20+8 hours per week), transcripts, two-week shared apartment accommodation in individual room.

Financial Aid Available: No

Spanish + Internship, Work Experience — ENFOREX Madrid

The Program

Description: This program consists of a combination of Spanish courses and work experience in a Spanish company. The minimum time needed for this program is 12 weeks, and it is possible to extend it an additional 8 weeks. There is a mandatory four-week Spanish language program (General Spanish or Business Spanish programs) before the work placement.

Specialty: Flexibility, quality, and personal attention; wonderful school facilities; full program of activities and excursions; conversation with Spanish students; student services; possibility of combining the program in more than one location.

Program Type: Community service, music/arts, travel/cultural

Classification: Coeducational, residential, day program

Goals: The professional internship is the most important link between the classroom and the professional world. An internship is always a valuable experience, and it is more beneficial if it is done in a foreign country with a foreign language.

Focus: Internship, educational exchange, and leadership and teamwork

Activities Center On: Language, career exploration, and cultural

Intensity Level: 3

Duration: 6–8 weeks

Program Offered: Fall, winter intersession/January term, spring, full academic year, summer

Location: Madrid, Spain

Accommodations: Dormitory, family-stay/host-family, apartment, hotels

Years in Operation: 12

Religious Affiliation: Not relevant

Staff

Student/Staff Ratio: 5:1

Staff Qualifications: All staff have completed training courses or have master's degrees in the instruction of Spanish. They are a young and dynamic team with a great experience, which has been recognized by several didactic publications in the research of this field.

Participants

Average Number of Participants: 50

For Participants Aged: 18–50

The Ideal Candidate: This program is designed for foreign university students with the appropriate skills, graduates and post-graduates, and professionals from all sectors.

Special Requirements for Participation: One of the most important requirements for the companies is that the applicant must speak an upper-intermediate level of Spanish by the time placement begins.

Costs

Average Cost: $2,865

Included in Cost: Application fees, Enforex textbooks, Internet access, 4-week intensive Spanish course (20 hours per week of Spanish language lessons and 5 hours per week of Spanish cultural lessons), training, evaluation, assessment and orientation, 8-week full-time internship, 12-week shared apartment accommodation (double room).

Financial Aid Available: No

Spanish + Tennis — ENFOREX Marbella

The Program

Description: This course includes 20 Spanish lessons per week plus tennis lessons in the afternoons/evenings at one of the best tennis schools, very well known throughout the "Costa del Sol." If three or more students follow the same program on the same dates, the course includes eight tennis lessons per week; if fewer than three students follow the program on the same dates, the course includes four tennis lessons and four hours of free practice.

Specialty: Flexibility, quality, and personal attention; U.S. university credits system; wonderful school facilities; full program of activities and excursions; conversation with Spanish students; student services; possibility of combining the program in more than one location.

Program Type: Academic/pre-college enrichment, middle school enrichment, outdoors/adventure, sports/athletic, travel/cultural

Classification: Coeducational, residential, day program

Goals: This course is designed for those people who love tennis and want to improve their tennis skills while learning or improving their Spanish in one of the most selective, incredible, and sunny coasts in Europe. Marbella, on the southern coast of Spain in the province of Andalusia, is a luxurious summer resort village for Spaniards and foreign residents.

Focus: Skill-building, educational exchange, and travel

Activities Center On: Tennis, language, and sailing

Intensity Level: 3

Duration: Varies

Program Offered: Fall, winter intersession/January term, spring, full academic year, summer

Location: Marbella, Spain

Accommodations: Dormitory, family-stay/host-family, apartment, hotels

Years in Operation: 12

Religious Affiliation: Not relevant

Staff

Student/Staff Ratio: 5:1

Staff Qualifications: All staff have completed training courses or have master's degrees in the instruction of Spanish. They are a young and dynamic team with a great experience, which has been recognized by several didactic publications in the research of this field.

PARTICIPANTS

Average Number of Participants: 23

For Participants Aged: 18+

Special Requirements for Participation: None.

COSTS

Average Cost: $925

Included in Cost: Application fees, Enforex textbooks, Internet access, two-week course (20+8 hours per week), transcripts, two-week shared apartment accommodation in single room.

Financial Aid Available: No

SPANISH FOR BUSINESS AND LAW— ENFOREX BARCELONA

THE PROGRAM

Description: The program consists of up to 25 lessons per week scheduled as follows: 10 Spanish lessons devoted to the general study of the Spanish language, 10 Spanish lessons related to the specific study of business and law in Spanish, and 5 cultural lessons.

Specialty: Flexibility, quality, personal attention; U.S. university credits system; wonderful school facilities; full program of activities and excursions; conversation with Spanish students; student services; possibility of combining the program in more than one location.

Program Type: Academic/pre-college enrichment, community service, middle school enrichment, travel/cultural

Classification: Coeducational, residential, day program

Goals: The objective is to achieve enough skills in the language to be able to communicate in business and legal situations. Commercial writing, presentations, and analysis of business newspapers (articles, vocabulary, and comprehension) are covered.

Focus: Educational exchange, skill-building, and leadership/teamwork

Activities Center On: Language, cultural, and career exploration

Intensity Level: 3

Duration: 2–4 weeks

Program Offered: Fall, winter intersession/January term, spring, full academic year, summer

Location: Madrid, Barcelona, Marbella, and Salamanca, Spain

Accommodations: Dormitory, family-stay/host-family, apartment, hotels

Years in Operation: 12

Religious Affiliation: Not relevant

STAFF

Student/Staff Ratio: 5:1

Staff Qualifications: All staff have completed training courses or have master's degrees in the instruction of Spanish. They are a young and dynamic team with a great experience, which has been recognized by several didactic publications in the research of this field.

PARTICIPANTS

Average Number of Participants: 50

For Participants Aged: 18+

The Ideal Candidate: This course is targeted at students and business professionals who want to improve their Spanish-language abilities with a focus on a particular business-related topic that interests them.

Special Requirements for Participation: This program is designed for students who have already reached an intermediate Spanish level (i.e., they can express themselves clearly and easily in everyday situations).

COSTS

Average Cost: $1,165

Included in Cost: Application fees, Enforex textbooks, Internet access, four-week course (20+5 hours per week), transcripts, four-week shared apartment accommodation in double room.

Financial Aid Available: No

SPANISH FOR BUSINESS AND LAW— ENFOREX GRANADA

THE PROGRAM

Description: The program is made up of 25 lessons per week scheduled as follows: 10 Spanish lessons devoted to the general study of the Spanish language, 10 Spanish lessons related to the specific study of business and law in Spanish, and 5 cultural lessons.

Specialty: Flexibility, quality, and personal attention; U.S. university credits system; wonderful school facilities; full program of activities and excursions; conversation with Spanish students; student services; possibility of combining the program in more than one location.

Program Type: Academic/pre-college enrichment, community service, middle school enrichment, travel/cultural

Classification: Coeducational, residential, day program

Goals: The objective is to achieve enough skills in the language to be able to communicate in business and legal situations. Commercial writing, presentations, analysis of business newspapers (articles, vocabulary, and comprehension) are covered.

Focus: Skill-building, academic/pre-college enrichment, and educational exchange

Activities Center On: Language and career exploration

Intensity Level: 3

Duration: 2–4 weeks

Program Offered: Fall, winter intersession/January term, spring, full academic year, summer

Location: Madrid, Barcelona, Marbella, and Granada, Spain

Accommodations: Dormitory, family-stay/host-family, apartment, hotels

Years in Operation: 12

Religious Affiliation: Not relevant

STAFF

Student/Staff Ratio: 5:1

Staff Qualifications: They have all done training courses or have a master degree in the tuition of Spanish. They all make a young and dynamic team with a great experience, which has been recognized by several didactic publications in the research of this field.

PARTICIPANTS

Average Number of Participants: 20

For Participants Aged: 18+

The Ideal Candidate: This course is targeted at students and business professionals who want to improve their Spanish-language abilities with a focus on a particular business-related topic that interests them.

Special Requirements for Participation: This program is designed for students who have already reached an intermediate Spanish level (i.e., they can express themselves clearly and easily in everyday situations).

COSTS

Average Cost: $1,165

Included in Cost: Application fees, Enforex textbooks, Internet access, four-week course (20+5 hours per week), transcripts, four-week shared apartment accommodation in double room.

Financial Aid Available: No

SPANISH FOR BUSINESS AND LAW — ENFOREX MADRID

THE PROGRAM

Description: The program is made up of 25 lessons per week scheduled as follows: 10 Spanish lessons devoted to the general study of the Spanish language, 10 Spanish lessons related to the specific study of business and law in Spanish, and 5 cultural lessons.

Specialty: Flexibility, quality, and personal attention; U.S. university credits system; wonderful school facilities; full program of activities and excursions; conversation with Spanish students; student services; possibility of combining the program in more than one location.

Program Type: Academic/pre-college enrichment, community service, travel/cultural

Classification: Coeducational, residential, day program

Goals: The objective is to achieve enough skills in the language to be able to communicate in business and legal situations. Commercial writing, presentations, analysis of business newspapers (articles, vocabulary, and comprehension) are covered.

Focus: Skill-building, academic/pre-college enrichment, and educational exchange

Activities Center On: Language and cultural

Intensity Level: 3

Duration: 2–4 weeks

Program Offered: Fall, winter intersession/January term, spring, full academic year, summer

Location: Madrid, Barcelona, Marbella, and Salamanca, Spain

Accommodations: Dormitory, family-stay/host-family, apartment, hotels

Years in Operation: 12

Religious Affiliation: Not relevant

STAFF

Student/Staff Ratio: 5:1

Staff Qualifications: All staff have completed training courses or have master's degrees in the instruction of Spanish. They are a young and dynamic team with a great experience, which has been recognized by several didactic publications in the research of this field.

PARTICIPANTS

Average Number of Participants: 45

For Participants Aged: 18+

The Ideal Candidate: This course is targeted at students and business professionals who want to improve their Spanish-language abilities with a focus on a particular business-related topic that interests them.

Special Requirements for Participation: This program is designed for students who have already reached an intermediate Spanish level (i.e., they can express themselves clearly and easily in everyday situations).

COSTS

Average Cost: $1,165

Included in Cost: Application fees, Enforex textbooks, Internet access, four-week course (20+5 hours per week), transcripts, four-week shared apartment accommodation in double room

Financial Aid Available: No

SPANISH FOR BUSINESS AND LAW— ENFOREX MARBELLA

THE PROGRAM

Description: The program consists of up to 25 lessons per week scheduled as follows: 10 Spanish lessons devoted to the general study of the Spanish language, 10 Spanish lessons related to the specific study of business and law in Spanish, and 5 cultural lessons.

Specialty: Flexibility, quality, personal attention; U.S. university credits system; wonderful school facilities; full program of activities and excursions; conversation with Spanish students; student services; possibility of combining the program in more than one location.

Program Type: Academic/pre-college enrichment, community service, middle school enrichment, travel/cultural

Classification: Coeducational, residential, day program

Goals: The objective is to achieve enough skills in the language to be able to communicate in business and legal situations. Commercial writing, presentations, and analysis of business newspapers (articles, vocabulary, and comprehension) are covered.

Focus: Educational exchange, skill-building, and cultural

Activities Center On: Language and travel

Intensity Level: 3

Duration: 2–4 weeks

Program Offered: Fall, winter intersession/January term, spring, full academic year, summer

Location: Madrid, Barcelona, Marbella, and Salamanca, Spain

Accommodations: Dormitory, family-stay/host-family, apartment, hotels

Years in Operation: 12

Religious Affiliation: Not relevant

STAFF

Student/Staff Ratio: 5:1

Staff Qualifications: All staff have completed training courses or have master's degrees in the instruction of Spanish. They are a young and dynamic team with a great experience, which has been recognized by several didactic publications in the research of this field.

PARTICIPANTS

Average Number of Participants: 20

For Participants Aged: 18+

The Ideal Candidate: This course is targeted at students and business professionals who want to improve their Spanish-language abilities with a focus on a particular business-related topic that interests them.

Special Requirements for Participation: This program is designed for students who have already reached an intermediate Spanish level (i.e., they can express themselves clearly and easily in everyday situations).

COSTS

Average Cost: $1,165

Included in Cost: Application fees, Enforex textbooks, Internet access, four-week course (20+5 hours per week), transcripts, four-week shared apartment accommodation in double room.

Financial Aid Available: No

SPANISH FOR BUSINESS AND LAW— ENFOREX SALAMANCA

THE PROGRAM

Description: The program consists of up to 25 lessons per week scheduled as follows: 10 Spanish lessons devoted to the general study of the Spanish language, 10 Spanish lessons related to the specific study of business and law in Spanish, and 5 cultural lessons.

Specialty: Flexibility, quality, personal attention; U.S. university credits system; wonderful school facilities; full program of activities and excursions; conversation with Spanish students; student services; possibility of combining the program in more than one location.

Program Type: Academic/pre-college enrichment, community service, middle school enrichment, travel/cultural

Classification: Coeducational, residential, day program

Goals: The objective is to achieve enough skills in the language to be able to communicate in business and legal situations. Commercial writing, presentations, and analysis of business newspapers (articles, vocabulary, and comprehension) are covered.

Focus: Educational exchange and academic/pre-college enrichment

Activities Center On: Language and cultural

Intensity Level: 3

Duration: 2–4 weeks

Program Offered: Fall, winter intersession/January term, spring, full academic year, summer

Location: Madrid, Barcelona, Marbella, and Salamanca, Spain

Accommodations: Dormitory, family-stay/host-family, apartment, hotels

Years in Operation: 12

Religious Affiliation: Not relevant

STAFF

Student/Staff Ratio: 5:1

Staff Qualifications: All staff have completed training courses or have master's degrees in the instruction of Spanish. They are a young and dynamic team with a great experience, which has been recognized by several didactic publications in the research of this field.

PARTICIPANTS

Average Number of Participants: 25

For Participants Aged: 18+

The Ideal Candidate: This course is targeted at students and business professionals who want to improve their Spanish-language abilities with a focus on a particular business-related topic that interests them.

Special Requirements for Participation: This program is designed for students who have already reached an intermediate Spanish level (i.e., they can express themselves clearly and easily in everyday situations).

COSTS

Average Cost: $1,165

Included in Cost: Application fees, Enforex textbooks, Internet access, four-week course (20+5 hours per week), transcripts, four-week shared apartment accommodation in double room.

Financial Aid Available: No

SPANISH TEACHER TRAINING COURSE–ENFOREX MADRID

THE PROGRAM

Description: This course is made up of two completely independent yet complementary programs (course 1 & course 2). Each program is two weeks long, and contains a minimum of 10 participants per class and a maximum of 25. The programs are based on 30 hours per week.

Specialty: Flexibility, quality, personal attention, wonderful schools facilities, full program of activities and excursions, conversation with Spanish students, students services, possibility of combining the program in more than one location.

Program Type: Special Interest/other, travel/cultural, other

Classification: Coeducational, residential, day program

Goals: ENFOREX has jointly designed this course with some of the most important and recognized universities. The principal objective of the program is to support teachers of Spanish by bringing them up to date and renewing their knowledge of our language.

Focus: Skill-building, cultural, and other

Activities Center On: Language, academic, and other

Intensity Level: 3

Duration: 2–4 weeks

Program Offered: Fall, winter intersession/January term, summer

Location: Madrid, Spain

Accommodations: Dormitory, family-stay/host-family, apartment, hotels

Years in Operation: 12

Religious Affiliation: Not relevant

STAFF

Student/Staff Ratio: 8:1

Staff Qualifications: Highly qualified university professors and doctors will give this postgraduate program, with many years of experience in this subject.

PARTICIPANTS

Average Number of Participants: 60

For Participants Aged: 18+

The Ideal Candidate: This extension course is especially designed for teachers of Spanish as a foreign language and for all those individuals who would like to extend and update their knowledge on foreign language teaching.

Special Requirements for Participation: High intermediate Spanish level is required.

COSTS

Average Cost: $1,165

Included in Cost: Application fees, Enforex textbook, Internet access, 2 week Spanish teacher training course (30 hours per week), 2 week shared apartment accommodation in individual room.

Financial Aid Available: No

EXPLORATION SCHOOL, INC.

Years in Operation: 26

Religious Affiliation: Not relevant

Price Range of Programs: $1,575–$3,395

For More Information:
  Contact: Becca Finer, Admissions Coordinator
        PO Box 368
        470 Washington Street
        Norwood, MA 02062
  Phone: 781-762-7400
  Fax: 781-762-7425
  Email: summer@explo.org
  Website: www.explo.org

EXPLORATION SENIOR PROGRAM (AT YALE UNIVERSITY)

THE PROGRAM

Description: Exploration combines the intellectual inquiry of school with the best aspects of camp: close friendships, activities, and adventure. Explo encourages students to celebrate the differences that make us individuals, and find the common ground that makes us a community. Supported by a passionate and nurturing faculty, our educational programs provide a safe structure in which students are encouraged to challenge themselves, discover new interests, and explore their relationships to the world.

Specialty: Exploration is fun, with an eye toward learning; we attempt to blur the distinction between learning and playing in the hopes of making education an experience that provides our students with lifelong enjoyment.

Program Type: Academic/pre-college enrichment, music/arts, sports/athletic, travel/cultural

Classification: Coeducational, residential, day program

Goals: Students at Exploration learn as much from their academic courses and mini-courses as they do from living in an international community of students who come to Explo from more than 40 states and 30 countries. Program participants should expect to learn more about themselves, their interests, and their relationship to the world.

Focus: Academic/pre-college enrichment, cultural, and educational exchange

Activities Center On: Academic

Intensity Level: 3

Duration: 2–4 weeks, 4–6 weeks

Program Offered: Summer

Location: New Haven, Connecticut

Accommodations: Dormitory

Years in Operation: 26

Religious Affiliation: Not relevant

STAFF

Student/Staff Ratio: 7:1

Staff Qualifications: Exploration faculty members are supportive teachers in the classroom, nurturing advisors in student life, and enthusiastic coaches in extracurricular activities and athletics. Comprised of undergraduate and graduate students from the nation's leading colleges and universities, our staff have a passion for teaching and a commitment to the safety of our students. During the summer, our staff are supported by a team of professional educators who work year-round planning and developing Exploration.

PARTICIPANTS

Average Number of Participants: 700

For Participants Aged: 15–17

The Ideal Candidate: Our ideal candidate is a student who is excited about spending the summer learning, trying new things, and discovering new interests and talents.

Special Requirements for Participation: None.

COSTS

Average Cost: $2,600

Financial Aid Available: Yes

GLS GERMAN LANGUAGE SCHOOL—BERLIN

GLS is located in the center of Berlin and offers German language courses all year-round for adults, and summer programs in Berlin, Potsdam, and Bavaria for kids and teens.

Years in Operation: 20

Religious Affiliation: Not relevant

Price Range of Programs: Starting at 500 Euros

For More Information:
  Contact: Barbara Jaeschke, Managing Director
             Kolonnenstrasse 26
             Berlin, 10829
             GERMANY
  Phone: 0049-30-7800890
  Fax: 49-30-787-4192
  Email: barbara.jaeschke@gls-berlin.com
  Website: www.german-courses.com

GLS BERLIN SUMMER SCHOOL

THE PROGRAM

Description: Students from up to 40 countries live and learn German in a beautiful villa in the center of Berlin. They enjoy sightseeing and social activities after class with German guides in Berlin and Potsdam.

Specialty: Location in the very center of Berlin, two daily activities, sightseeing outside Berlin, international ambience.

Program Type: Academic/pre-college enrichment, travel/cultural

Classification: Coeducational, residential

Goals: German.

Focus: Academic/pre-college enrichment, cultural, and travel

Activities Center On: Language, cultural, and travel

Intensity Level: 3

Duration: 2–4 weeks, 4–6 weeks, 6–8 weeks

Program Offered: Summer

Location: Berlin, Germany

Accommodations: Dormitory

Years in Operation: 5

Religious Affiliation: Not relevant

STAFF

Student/Staff Ratio: 1:10

Staff Qualifications: Qualified German teachers with university diplomas.

PARTICIPANTS

Average Number of Participants: 100

For Participants Aged: 16–19

The Ideal Candidate: Open, interested, and willing to communicate and learn.

Special Requirements for Participation: None.

Costs

Average Cost: $1,180

Included in Cost: 20 lessons weekly, residential accommodation, full board, activities.

Financial Aid Available: No

GLS German Language School

The Program

Description: GLS offers German language courses and internships all year-round to students from up to 60 nations. Highlights include location in the center of Berlin, accommodation service, and after-class social program.

Specialty: Good location, excellent teachers, extensive sightseeing and social activities, possibilty to acquire language certificates such as ZD and DHS.

Program Type: Academic/pre-college enrichment

Classification: Coeducational, residential, day program

Goals: German, more about Berlin and German culture.

Focus: Educational exchange, academic/pre-college enrichment, and travel

Activities Center On: Language, cultural, and travel

Intensity Level: 4

Duration: 1–2 weeks; 2–4 weeks; 4–6 weeks; 6–8 weeks; over 8 weeks

Program Offered: Full academic year

Location: Berlin, Germany

Accommodations: Family-stay/host-family, apartment, youth hostels

Years in Operation: 20

Religious Affiliation: Not relevant

Staff

Student/Staff Ratio: 12:1

Staff Qualifications: German teachers with university diplomas (MAs).

Participants

Average Number of Participants: 120

For Participants Aged: 16+

The Ideal Candidate: Open, communicative.

Special Requirements for Participation: None.

Costs

Average Cost: $400

Included in Cost: 20 weekly lessons, accommodations, activ-

ities, and excursions.

Financial Aid Available: No

GLS Potsdam Summer School

The Program

Description: Students learn German while living in the school right next to Albert Einstein's villa on a lake in Potsdam near Berlin. Classes are complemented by sightseeing and social activities.

Specialty: Beautiful location near a lake, possibility to explore both Potsdam and Berlin.

Program Type: Academic/pre-college enrichment, travel/cultural

Classification: Coeducational, residential

Goals: German, communicating in international groups.

Focus: Educational exchange, cultural, and travel

Activities Center On: Language, cultural, and travel

Intensity Level: 3

Duration: 2–4 weeks

Program Offered: Summer

Location: Potsdam, Germany

Accommodations: Dormitory

Years in Operation: 3

Religious Affiliation: Not relevant

Staff

Student/Staff Ratio: 10:1

Staff Qualifications: German teachers with university diplomas.

Participants

Average Number of Participants: 80

For Participants Aged: 14–17

The Ideal Candidate: Open, communicative.

Special Requirements for Participation: None.

Costs

Average Cost: $1,245

Included in Cost: 20 weekly lessons, accommodations, full board, activities.

Financial Aid Available: No

GRINNELL COLLEGE

Religious Affiliation: Not relevant

For More Information:
Contact: Jim Sumner, Dean of Admission/Financial Aid
Office of Admission
1103 Park St.
Grinnell, IA 50112
Phone: 800-247-0113
Fax: 641-269-4800
Email: sumnerj@grinnell.edu
Website: www.grinnell.edu

SUMMER INSTITUTE

THE PROGRAM

Description: The Grinnell College Summer Institute offers a valuable preview of college life through challenging academic programs, fun, and responsibility. All of the Summer Institute courses are taught by Grinnell College professors who are committed to helping students refine techniques in writing, researching, analyzing, and discussing. Outside of the classroom, much of the participants' recreational life revolves around friends from the institute and the numerous activities in which they choose to participate.

Program Type: Academic/pre-college enrichment

Classification: Coeducational, residential

Focus: Academic/pre-college enrichment

Intensity Level: 4

Duration: 2–4 weeks, 4–6 weeks

Program Offered: Summer

Location: Grinnell, Iowa

Accommodations: Dormitory

Religious Affiliation: Not relevant

PARTICIPANTS

Average Number of Participants: 20

For Participants Aged: 15–17

Special Requirements for Participation: None.

COSTS

Average Cost: $2,250

Financial Aid Available: No

HARVARD UNIVERSITY SUMMER SCHOOL

General College Program, Secondary School Program, English Language Programs, English Language for High School Students Program.

Years in Operation: 132

Religious Affiliation: Not relevant

Price Range of Programs: $2,000–$7,300

For More Information:
Contact: Karen Eichhorn, Advertising Assistant
51 Brattle Street
Cambridge, MA 02138
Phone: 617-495-2924
Fax: 617-496-2680
Email: summer@hudce.harvard.edu
Website: www.summer.harvard.edu

HARVARD SECONDARY SCHOOL PROGRAM

THE PROGRAM

Description: Highly qualified high school juniors and seniors take college-level courses. Program offers an introduction to college life and a college preparatory program that includes trips to New England colleges and workshops on topics such as writing college essays.

Specialty: Harvard facilities and faculty.

Program Type: Academic/pre-college enrichment

Classification: Coeducational, residential, day program

Goals: Exposure to life in a college environment; independence; subject matter of courses in which participants are enrolled.

Focus: Academic/pre-college enrichment

Activities Center On: Academic and liberal arts

Intensity Level: 4

Duration: 6–8 weeks

Program Offered: Summer

Location: Cambridge and Boston, Massachusetts

Accommodations: Dormitory

Years in Operation: 32

Religious Affiliation: Not relevant

STAFF

Student/Staff Ratio: 25:1

Staff Qualifications: AB, AM, PhD—varies.

PARTICIPANTS

Average Number of Participants: 1,000

For Participants Aged: 15–18

The Ideal Candidate: Academically talented, self-motivated high school junior or senior; some sophomores also admitted.

Special Requirements for Participation: Participants must have completed junior or senior year. Some academically talented sophomores are also admitted.

COSTS

Average Cost: $7,300

Included in Cost: Tuition and fees, room and board.

Financial Aid Available: Yes

SECONDARY SCHOOL ENGLISH LANGUAGE PROGRAM (SIEL)

THE PROGRAM

Description: Special four-week program open to international students aged 16 to 18 that combines advanced English language study with hands-on introduction to computer hardware, programming, and multimedia.

Specialty: Harvard facilities.

Classification: Coeducational, residential

Goals: English language, computers, American culture

Focus: Skill-building, academic/pre-college enrichment, and cultural

Activities Center On: English as a Second Language (ESL), and cultural

Intensity Level: 4

Duration: 4–6 weeks

Program Offered: Summer

Location: Cambridge and Boston, Massachusetts

Accommodations: Dormitory

Years in Operation: 3

Religious Affiliation: Not relevant

STAFF

Student/Staff Ratio: 10:1

Staff Qualifications: Varies

PARTICIPANTS

Average Number of Participants: 40

For Participants Aged: 16–18

The Ideal Candidate: Academically talented high school student.

Special Requirements for Participation: Participants must be 16–18.

COSTS

Average Cost: $7,050

Included in Cost: Tuition and fees, room and board.

Financial Aid Available: No

HIGH MOUNTAIN INSTITUTE

The High Mountain Institute is a nonprofit educational institution dedicated to nurturing personal and community growth through interaction with the natural world. The defining program of HMI is the Rocky Mountain Semester, a semester-long academic and wilderness program for high school juniors now in its fifth year. In addition, HMI offers a variety of short-term educational and leadership programs. HMI is accredited by the Association for Experiential Education (AEE).

Years in Operation: 8

Religious Affiliation: Not relevant

Price Range of Programs: $650–$2,600

For More Information:
  Contact: Kate Scanlon, Programs Manager
      PO Box 970
      Leadville, CO 80461
  Phone: 719-486-8200
  Fax: 719-486-8201
  Email: kscanlon@hminet.org
  Website: www.hminet.org

THE LEADING EDGE

THE PROGRAM

Description: The Leading Edge is an experiential, two-week leadership and wilderness adventure program at the High Mountain Institute that focuses on leadership development specifically for young adults. Using the wilderness and classroom environments, the program provides each student with a foundation for building leadership skills and a fantastic summer adventure in the Colorado mountains.

Specialty: We have a unique approach to leadership development for young adults. We focus on improving students' self-awareness and on helping them identify the ethical compass by which they will lead.

Program Type: Academic/pre-college enrichment, outdoors/adventure

Classification: Coeducational, residential

Goals: The Leading Edge is an intense introduction to leadership skills for young adults. As they embark on the development of their own leadership styles, we ask students to consider their roles as leaders within their communities and the ways in which they can be more effective.

Focus: Leadership/teamwork, skill-building, and travel

Activities Center On: Backpacking, outdoors/adventure, and academic

Intensity Level: 4

Duration: 2–4 weeks

Program Offered: Summer

Location: Leadville, Colorado

Accommodations: Tent, bunk/cabin

Years in Operation: 1

Religious Affiliation: Not relevant

STAFF

Student/Staff Ratio: 3:1

Staff Qualifications: Staffed by trained, professional outdoor educators. All wilderness staff have wilderness medical training and extensive experience leading youth in the backcountry. Adjunct Leading Edge faculty are leaders in the leadership development field.

PARTICIPANTS

Average Number of Participants: 10

For Participants Aged: 17–19

The Ideal Candidate: Anyone interested in developing their leadership skills; student government leaders; athletic team captains; student prefects, advisors, and peer counselors; leaders of student groups

Special Requirements for Participation: Application criteria: 17–19 years of age; completed junior or senior year of high school; ìBî average or better; excited about working hard to learn leadership skills

COSTS

Average Cost: $1,500

Included in Cost: Room and board, and transportation to and from Denver International Airport

Financial Aid Available: Yes

HUMANITIES SPRING IN ASSISI

HSIA is for students interested in poetry, art, ice cream, travel, and the Italian language and culture. At HSIA, students learn to connect individually to great works of art and literature, from classical to contemporary. Based in a turn-of-the-century schoolhouse in the hills outside Assisi, or on the road, students study and travel to see some of Italy's best works of art and architecture—in Florence, Venice, Rome, Pompeii, Ravenna, and more! Our method is interdisciplinary; students use a Robert Browning poem to help them understand Fra Lippo Lippi's joyful frescoes in Spoleto, or Greek mythology to explain a whimsical mosaic in a Roman bath. Students and staff tour, view art, converse, and learn together.

Years in Operation: 12

Religious Affiliation: Not relevant

Price Range of Programs: $3,200–$4,600

For More Information:
Contact: Jane Oliensis, Director
Santa Maria di Lignano, 2
Assisi, 06081
ITALY
Phone: 01139075-802400
Fax: 01139075-802400
Email: oliensij@libero.it
Website: www.humanitiesspring.com

HUMANITIES SPRING IN ASSISI

THE PROGRAM

Description: HSIA is for students interested in poetry, art, ice cream, travel, and Italian language and culture. Students read classical and Renaissance literature intensively and travel to see related amphitheaters, frescoes, castles, sculptures, festivals, and more! Assisi is home; students also travel widely in Italy, from Florence to Pompeii, from Rome to Ravenna to see some of the greatest art of all time. HSIA participants also attend operas, ballets, festivals, puppet shows, and concerts, from classical to jazz.

Specialty: Students learn to create individual, idiosyncratic dialogues with great works, and that art and literature can make their lives happier, more complete. Art, nature, and the Italian world view, its embracing and appreciation of beauty, become a part of their lives.

Program Type: Academic/pre-college enrichment, travel/cultural

Classification: Coeducational, residential

Goals: All learning at HSIA is experiential and first-hand. Students read poems, inscriptions, etc., in their original languages and travel to see art in situ. One student may discover the Renaissance through a sculpture in a Renaissance garden, another through a poem and its joyful personifications. Classes are in classical art, archaeology, poetry, prose, Renaissance everything, Italian language and literature, and art history. Afternoon activities include collage, gardening, bread-making, and writing poetry.

Focus: Cultural, travel, and academic/pre-college enrichment

Activities Center On: Humanities, fine arts, and writing

Intensity Level: 4

Duration: 2–4 weeks

Program Offered: Summer

Location: Assisi, Rome, Florence, Ravenna, and Amalfi Coast, Italy

Accommodations: Family-stay/host-family, bunk/cabin, hotels

Years in Operation: 12

Religious Affiliation: Not relevant

STAFF

Student/Staff Ratio: 3:1

Staff Qualifications: Staff includes art historians and painters, architects, archaeologists, poets, and classicists who have degrees from some of the best universities in the United States and Europe, from Harvard University to the Universita degli Studii in Perugia. Learning takes place inside the classroom and out—at meals, on trips, in a Roman amphitheater, at an old-fashioned Italian puppet show, at the beach. In a jokey atmosphere, there is constant conversation. At HSIA, we all learn together.

PARTICIPANTS

Average Number of Participants: 12

For Participants Aged: 15–20

The Ideal Candidate: Our ideal candidate loves to learn, is disciplined, and has intellectual and emotional courage.

Special Requirements for Participation: Enthusiasm and the desire to learn. We are happy if our students know some Latin or Greek, but this is not necessary. We do not assume (or require!) any background knowledge of Greek, Latin, Italian, art history, or anything else! Recent humanities—spring.

COSTS

Average Cost: $3,200

Included in Cost: This includes everything: tuition, room and board, museum fees, Spoleto Festival and Umbria Jazz tickets, airport pick-up and return, all traveling expenses within Italy—except the occasional meal out. Students pay their own airfare.

Financial Aid Available: Yes

HUMANITIES SPRING ON THE ROAD

THE PROGRAM

Description: HSOR is for students interested in poetry, art, ice-cream, adventure, and the Italian culture. Students spend a five-day orientation period in Assisi, then travel to see some of the best art and architecture, from Greek and Roman to Renaissanace to contemporary, in Italy. Students keep travel logs and/or sketch books. Our home bases for five days each are Rome, Florence, Ravenna (Venice), and the Amalfi Coast (Pompeii, Paestum). HSOT also attends operas, ballets, festivals, puppet shows, and concerts.

Specialty: Students learn that art and literature can make their lives happier, more complete. Renaissance gardens, Greek temples, Venetian peach-colored palazzi. The Italian world view, with its embracing/appreciation of beauty, becomes a part of their lives.

Program Type: Travel/cultural

Classification: Coeducational, residential

Goals: Students learn to use art and architecture as a spring-board for poems, sketches, prose, journal entries, etc., and their own individual development. Short trip-prep and where-we-are classes give students background knowledge and ways of thinking about the art we travel to see. Italian conversation classes (optional) help students communicate better on trips.

Focus: Travel, cultural, and academic/pre-college enrichment

Activities Center On: Touring, fine arts, and humanities

Intensity Level: 4

Duration: 2–4 weeks

Program Offered: Summer

Location: Florence, Ravenna/Venice, Rome, and the Amalfi Coast, Italy

Accommodations: Family-stay/host-family, apartment, hotels

Years in Operation: 2

Religious Affiliation: Not relevant

STAFF

Student/Staff Ratio: 4:1

Staff Qualifications: Staff and travel companions include art historians, painters, architects, archaeologists, poets, and classicists who have degrees from some of the best universities in the United States and Europe, from Harvard University to the Universita degli Studii, Perugia. Learning takes place everywhere: on a designer escalator in a medieval castle, at breakfast on a terrace near some Roman ruins, at an old-fashioned Italian puppet show in a Renaissance piazza, at the beach. At HSOR, we all learn together.

PARTICIPANTS

Average Number of Participants: 12

For Participants Aged: 14–19

The Ideal Candidate: Our ideal candidate loves to learn, is adventurous intellectually and emotionally, and is interested in engaging actively with art, literature, and the Italian culture, as well as with the rest of the HSOR group.

Special Requirements for Participation: Enthusiasm and the desire to learn. Students should be interested in the humanities and/or fine arts.

COSTS

Average Cost: $4,600

Included in Cost: This includes everything: room and board; museum fees; festival, ballet, and puppet show tickets; boat rides; airport pick-up and return, all traveling expenses within Italy—except the occasional meal out. Students pay their own airfare.

Financial Aid Available: Yes

THE INSPIREME CORPORATION

The InspireMe Corporation offers several programs for the advancement of young minds. Our company specializes in unique and inspirational education utilizing several institutions leading the industry in the field being taught.

Years in Operation: 4

Religious Affiliation: Not relevant

Price Range of Programs: $2,200

For More Information:
Contact: Nichelle Rodriguez, Director
    305 North 2nd Avenue
    #118
    Upland, CA 91786
Phone: 909-982-8059
Fax: 909-982-5328
Email: information@californiacampustours.com

CALIFORNIA CAMPUS TOURS

THE PROGRAM

Description: Tour the best universities throughout Calfiornia with experienced high school counselors. We will learn what questions to ask college staff and students. Not only will we learn how to apply, we will learn what makes and breaks an applicant. Study for the SAT on the beach.

Specialty: We are the only summer camp that specializes in the college entrance process and California schools. No other camp offers college tours along with in-depth entrance preparation and counseling.

Program Type: Academic/pre-college enrichment

Classification: Coeducational, residential

Goals: Learning how to choose a college, including what questions to ask of current students and staff; essay writing; and SAT test-taking skills.

Focus: Academic/pre-college enrichment, skill-building, and travel

Activities Center On: SAT prep, academic, and travel

Intensity Level: 2

Duration: 1–2 weeks

Program Offered: Summer

Location: Several cities in California

Accommodations: Dormitory, hotels

Years in Operation: 4

Religious Affiliation: Not relevant

STAFF

Student/Staff Ratio: 20:1

Staff Qualifications: Experienced high school and college counselors.

PARTICIPANTS

Average Number of Participants: 60

For Participants Aged: 15–20

The Ideal Candidate: High school junior and seniors who are college bound and who preferably have been pre-advised by high school counseling staff.

Special Requirements for Participation: Participants must be able walk long distances.

COSTS

Average Cost: $2,200

Included in Cost: Breakfast and lunch are included. Dinner is not included as this is down time in mostly tourist areas. All entrance fees, workshops, and couseling are included. Please see terms and conditions on our website for further details.

Financial Aid Available? Yes

INTERLOCKEN– CROSSROADS TRAVEL

Interlocken seeks to provide educational community-building experiences that can open minds, foster personal growth, and cultivate a spirit of proactive change, thus enabling students to respond to cultural, social, and environmental challenges as responsible citizens of the world.

Years in Operation: 43

Religious Affiliation: Not relevant

Price Range of Programs: $1,200–$5,000

For More Information:
Contact: David Love, Crossroads Director
19 Interlocken Way
Hillsboro, NH 03244
Phone: 603-478-3166
Fax: 603-478-5260
Email: mail@interlocken.org
Website: www.interlocken.org

ALASKA ODYSSEY

THE PROGRAM

Description: Venture deep into wild places, from stark tundra to glacier-cloaked peaks, from rainforests to the boundless coastline brimming with sea creatures. Descend on wild and woolly towns where arctic oil and salmon drive the economy. Converse with Alaskan native peoples, work with land preservationists, and debate with environmentalists. On foot, aboard boat, and on lonely highways, explore this grand land of the midnight sun on to the Kenai Peninsula.

Specialty: Interlocken's program holds true to combining service learning and cultural awareness with a solid outdoor travel experience.

Program Type: Community service, outdoors/adventure, travel/cultural

Classification: Coeducational, residential

Goals: Outdoor skills, including sea kayaking; Native Alaskan culture; fishing industry; artistic expression

Focus: Educational exchange, cultural, and travel

Activities Center On: Cultural, outdoors/adventure, and kayaking

Intensity Level: 2

Duration: 2–4 weeks

Program Offered: Summer

Location: Kenai Pennisula, Alaska

Accommodations: Family-stay/host-family, tent, youth hostels

Years in Operation: 5

Religious Affiliation: Not relevant

STAFF

Student/Staff Ratio: 6:1

Staff Qualifications: All our leaders are at least 24 years of age; have experience working with high school age students; and are certified in first aid, CPR and lifeguard training. In June, our leaders participate in an intensive training program that has been developed over our 42 years of experience.

PARTICIPANTS

Average Number of Participants: 13

For Participants Aged: 14–17

The Ideal Candidate: Good traveler willing to leave the comforts of home, good team player, respectful of other cultures.

Special Requirements for Participation: None.

COSTS

Average Cost: $3,995

Included in Cost: Everything is included except personal spending money and airfare to and from Anchorage.

Financial Aid Available: Yes

BONJOUR QUÉBEC

THE PROGRAM

Description: Discover a piece of Europe in North America. Explore rugged mountains and pristine lakes as you canoe, raft, bike, and hike the provincial parks. Enjoy a week-long homestay with a Québécois family and take part in an Interlocken mini-camp with local kids where games, historical explorations, and adventures in cultural discoveries will promote your opportunities to practice your French language skills. Camp with a Native Canadian family and share their way of life on the homestead.

Specialty: Interlocken programs not only create magnificent travel opportunities, but they also combine service learning and cultural awareness along the way.

Program Type: Community service, outdoors/adventure, travel/cultural

Classification: Coeducational, residential

Goals: French culture, wilderness skills, working with children, French language.

Focus: Cultural, community service, and travel

Activities Center On: Cultural, outdoors/adventure, and touring

Intensity Level: 2

Duration: 2–4 weeks

Program Offered: Summer

Location: Québec, Canada

Accommodations: Family-stay/host-family, tent, bunk/cabin, youth hostels

Years in Operation: 2

Religious Affiliation: Not relevant

STAFF

Student/Staff Ratio: 6:1

Staff Qualifications: All our leaders are at least 24 years of age; have experience working with high school age students; and are certified in first aid, CPR, and lifeguard training. In June, our leaders participate in an intensive training program that has been developed over our 42 years of experience.

PARTICIPANTS

Average Number of Participants: 13

For Participants Aged: 14–17

The Ideal Candidate: Willing to live away from the comforts of home, open to new people and new ideas, willing to accept new cultures.

Special Requirements for Participation: None.

COSTS

Average Cost: $3,195

Included in Cost: Everything is included except personal spending money and transportation to and from New Hampshire.

Financial Aid Available: Yes

BRIDGE SEMESTER PROGRAM

THE PROGRAM

Description: This is a 12-credit program offered through New England College in association with Interlocken. It provides academic enrichment and strengthens the life skills that will promote success at the college level.

Specialty: The program will allow successful participants to matriculate directly into New England College outside of the normal application process.

Program Type: Academic/pre-college enrichment, outdoors/adventure, travel/cultural

Classification: Coeducational, residential

Goals: Creative writing, outdoor leadership, science overviews, introduction to sociology.

Focus: Academic/pre-college enrichment, skill-building, and leadership/teamwork

Activities Center On: Academic, outdoors/adventure, and career exploration

Intensity Level: 2

Duration: Over 8 weeks

Program Offered: Fall

Location: Hillsborough, New Hampshire

Accommodations: Dormitory, tent

Years in Operation: 2

Religious Affiliation: Not relevant

STAFF

Student/Staff Ratio: 3:1

Staff Qualifications: All teaching is done through full-time professors or adjuct professors in the specific fields.

PARTICIPANTS

Average Number of Participants: 16

For Participants Aged: 17–22

The Ideal Candidate: The ideal candidate is the person who either is looking for something exciting and rewarding between high school and college, or needs some skill strengthening in both social and academic areas to be more succesful in college.

Special Requirements for Participation: High school graduate; SAT and/or ACTs are not required.

COSTS

Average Cost: $14,440

Included in Cost: All inclusive

Financial Aid Available: Yes

CALIFORNIA ADVENTURE

THE PROGRAM

Description: California has it all: Pacific surf, colossal redwoods, foaming whitewater, the beautiful valleys of Yosemite National Park, Latino culture, and vibrant San Francisco. Discover the Pacific Crest wilderness as you trek in the high country. California's diverse environment becomes your laboratory. Test your outdoor skills: minimum-impact camping, outdoor cooking, long-distance backpacking, and living lightly in a fragile ecosystem. Your adventure culminates in "the city by the bay."

Specialty: Interlocken takes pride in creating programs that combine outdoor living with service learning and cultural awareness components.

Program Type: Outdoors/adventure, travel/cultural

Classification: Coeducational, residential

Goals: Back-country skills, living with a group, cultural immersion.

Focus: Travel, cultural, and community service

Activities Center On: Outdoors/adventure, backpacking, and camping

Intensity Level: 2

Duration: 2–4 weeks

Program Offered: Summer

Location: San Francisco, California

Accommodations: Tent, youth hostels

Years in Operation: 5

Religious Affiliation: Not relevant

STAFF

Student/Staff Ratio: 6:1

Staff Qualifications: All our leaders are at least 24 years of age; have experience working with high school age students; and are certified in first aid, CPR, and lifeguard training. In June, our leaders participate in an intensive training program that has been developed over our 42 years of experience.

PARTICIPANTS

Average Number of Participants: 13

For Participants Aged: 14–17

The Ideal Candidate: The ideal candidate is capable of living without the comforts of home, and is a team player who yearns to learn about different cultures and who works well in a group.

Special Requirements for Participation: None.

COSTS

Average Cost: $3,595

Included in Cost: Everything is included except personal spending money and travel to and from San Francisco.

Financial Aid Available: Yes

CUBA FRIENDSHIP EXCHANGE

THE PROGRAM

Description: The program is designed to allow students from both Cuba and the United States to explore each other's culture, ideas, food, music, and more, and share in the warmth of new friendships forged for the first time in four decades. Interlocken has a long history of bringing young people together from distant countries and different cultures: China, Korea, the former Soviet Union, and the Middle East. Now we are extending a hand to a neighbor, Cuba.

Specialty: Interlocken's programs offer a long history of international friendship exchanges dating back over 30 years.

Program Type: Academic/pre-college enrichment, travel/cultural

Classification: Coeducational, residential

Goals: Spanish language, Cuban culture, governmental policies, and group skills.

Focus: Educational exchange, cultural, and academic/pre-college enrichment

Activities Center On: Cultural, language, and travel

Intensity Level: 2

Duration: 2–4 weeks

Program Offered: Summer

Location: Havana, Cuba

Accommodations: Family-stay/host-family, hotels, youth hostels

Years in Operation: 3

Religious Affiliation: Not relevant

STAFF

Student/Staff Ratio: 6:1

Staff Qualifications: All our leaders are at least 24 years of age; have experience working with high school age students; and are certified in first aid, CPR, and lifeguard training. In June, our leaders participate in an intensive training program that has been developed over our 42 years of experience.

PARTICIPANTS

Average Number of Participants: 25

For Participants Aged: 14–18

The Ideal Candidate: A person who can travel without the comforts of home and who can accept people and traditions from a culture different from his/her own.

Special Requirements for Participation: Must speak Spanish at an introductory level.

COSTS

Average Cost: $4,495

Included in Cost: Everything is included except personal spending money and airfare to and from Miami.

Financial Aid Available: Yes

EUROPEAN TRAVELING MINSTRELS

THE PROGRAM

Description: Commedia dell' Arte, the ancient art of physical theater, comes to life in your hands as you tour and perform for audiences in Italy, France, Spain, and Portugal. Create a touring show under the direction of world-renowned Commedia expert John Rudlin with such diverse elements as drama, physical theater, slapstick comedy, improvisation, and mask making. Perform for audiences of all ages in medieval villages, city plazas, beaches, and campgrounds.

Specialty: Interlocken's program has been the premier traveling troupe in Europe for over a generation. It combines exciting travel with cultural immersion and service learning.

Program Type: Music/arts, travel/cultural

Classification: Coeducational, residential

Goals: Performace skills; leadership skills; and language skills in French, Italian, Spanish, and Portugese.

Focus: Academic/pre-college enrichment, cultural, and travel

Activities Center On: Performing arts, drama, and language

Intensity Level: 2

Duration: 4–6 weeks

Program Offered: Summer

Location: Paris, France; Geneva, Italy; Lisbon, Portugal; Spain

Accommodations: Family-stay/host-family, youth hostels

Years in Operation: 25

Religious Affiliation: Not relevant

STAFF

Student/Staff Ratio: 6:1

Staff Qualifications: All our leaders are at least 24 years of age; have experience working with high school age students; and are certified in first aid, CPR and lifeguard training. In June, our leaders participate in an intensive training program that has been developed over our 42 years of experience.

PARTICIPANTS

Average Number of Participants: 13

For Participants Aged: 14–18

The Ideal Candidate: Experience in theater, able to work well within a diverse group, comfortable with travel away from home and within other cultures.

Special Requirements for Participation: Must audition with Interlocken.

COSTS

Average Cost: $4,795

Included in Cost: Everything except personal spending money and airfare to and from the gateway cities of Newark and Boston.

Financial Aid Available: Yes

HAWAIIAN OHANA

THE PROGRAM

Description: Visit with native Hawaiian Islanders whose unique culture is vibrant and healthy despite the pressures of the modern world. Explore the ocean teeming with life of the emerald islands: Maui, the "Big Island" (Hawaii), and Molokai. Explore Hawaiian ecology, so exotic and diverse, but which is under siege because of an invasion of non-native species introduced by humans. High above the clouds watch the sun rise over the endless Pacific Ocean and face the world's most active volcano.

Specialty: Interlocken strives to combine adventure travel with both cultural awareness and service learning opportunties.

Program Type: Community service, outdoors/adventure, travel/cultural

Classification: Coeducational, residential

Goals: Outdoor skills, Hawaiian culture, service learning opportunities, group skills.

Focus: Travel, cultural, and community service

Activities Center On: Outdoors/adventure, travel, and cultural

Intensity Level: 2

Duration: 2–4 weeks

Program Offered: Summer

Location: Kona, Kahuli, Kaunakakai, and Hilo, Hawaii

Accommodations: Tent, youth hostels

Years in Operation: 3

Religious Affiliation: Not relevant

STAFF

Student/Staff Ratio: 6:1

Staff Qualifications: All our leaders are at least 24 years of age; have experience working with high school age students; and are certified in first aid, CPR, and lifeguard training. In June, our leaders participate in an intensive training program that has been developed over our 42 years of experience.

PARTICIPANTS

Average Number of Participants: 13

For Participants Aged: 14–17

The Ideal Candidate: Travelers should be able to leave to leave the comforts of home, respectful of different cultures, and willing to try new things.

Special Requirements for Participation: None.

COSTS

Average Cost: $4,150

Included in Cost: Includes all expenses except airfare to Honolulu.

Financial Aid Available: Yes

LEADERS IN ACTION

THE PROGRAM

Description: The program offers high school students the opportunity to travel internationally with a group of student leaders to create a summer camp experience for children who would not be able to experience camp themselves.

Specialty: Interlocken combines travel with both service learning and cultural awareness that make a student grow.

Program Type: Academic/pre-college enrichment, community service

Classification: Coeducational, residential

Goals: Leadership skills, small group dynamics, and cultural awareness.

Focus: Leadership/teamwork, community service, and academic/pre-college enrichment

Activities Center On: Academic, career exploration, and volunteer

Intensity Level: 2

Duration: 2–4 weeks

Program Offered: Summer

Location: Jamaica

Accommodations: Family-stay/host-family, tent, youth hostels

Years in Operation: 10

Religious Affiliation: Not relevant

STAFF

Student/Staff Ratio: 6:1

Staff Qualifications: All our leaders are at least 24 years of age; have experience working with high school age students; and are certified in first aid, CPR, and lifeguard training. In June, our leaders participate in an intensive training program that has been developed over our 42 years of experience.

PARTICIPANTS

Average Number of Participants: 13

For Participants Aged: 14–16

The Ideal Candidate: Must have strong leadership potential and be a team player; must be able to work independently and travel without the comforts of home.

Special Requirements for Participation: None.

COSTS

Average Cost: $4,000

Included in Cost: Everything except personal spending money and travel expenses to and from the gateway city of New York.

Financial Aid Available: No

RANDOM ACTS OF KINDNESS

THE PROGRAM

Description: A community service adventure for students who want to help make the world a better place. You will venture throughout New England to volunteer on local service projects and to surprise and delight local communities as you practice "random acts of kindness." Take time to meet with local people to gain perspective on issues that affect their lives. As you practice random acts of kindness, you will build lasting friendships and make a contribution to the world around you.

Specialty: Our programs integrate the adventure travel with service learning and cultural immersion to make a well-rounded experience.

Program Type: Community service, travel/cultural

Classification: Coeducational, residential

Goals: Community service learning, group skills, cultural awareness, and personal growth.

Focus: Community service, travel, and leadership/teamwork

Intensity Level: 2

Duration: 2–4 weeks

Program Offered: Summer

Location: New England: Maine, Massachusetts, Vermont, and New Hampshire

Accommodations: Tent, bunk/cabin, hotels, youth hostels

Years in Operation: 5

Religious Affiliation: Not relevant

STAFF

Student/Staff Ratio: 6:1

Staff Qualifications: All our leaders are at least 24 years of age; have experience working with high school age students; and are certified in first aid, CPR, and lifeguard training. In June, our leaders participate in an intensive training program that has been developed over our 42 years of experience.

PARTICIPANTS

Average Number of Participants: 13

For Participants Aged: 14–17

The Ideal Candidate: Someone willing to live away from the comforts of home, open to diverse life styles and cultural differences, and wanting to make a difference.

Special Requirements for Participation: None.

COSTS

Average Cost: $3,395

Included in Cost: Everthing except personal spending money and travel to and from New Hampshire.

Financial Aid Available: Yes

SALSA AND SPANISH

THE PROGRAM

Description: S*S is an exciting adventure in Puerto Rico. Learn to dance Salsa, study Spanish, and explore Puerto Rican culture all while traveling the country dancing, performing, and observing local musical and dance styles. S*S is for all students who are interested in Latino culture, want to get involved and travel with local Puerto Rican youth, and want to focus on improving their Spanish skills.

Specialty: Interlocken combines adventure travel with cultural immersion and service learning options. We make travel fun, rewarding, and an educational experience.

Program Type: Academic/pre-college enrichment, travel/cultural

Classification: Coeducational, residential

Goals: Latin dance, Spanish language, cultural awareness, and group skills.

Focus: Educational exchange, cultural, and travel

Activities Center On: Dance, language, and music/arts

Intensity Level: 2

Duration: 2–4 weeks

Program Offered: Summer

Location: Puerto Rico

Accommodations: Family-stay/host-family

Years in Operation: 1

Religious Affiliation: Not relevant

STAFF

Student/Staff Ratio: 6:1

Staff Qualifications: All our leaders are at least 24 years of age; have experience working with high school age students; and are certified in first aid, CPR, and lifeguard training. In June, our leaders participate in an intensive training program that has been developed over our 42 years of experience.

PARTICIPANTS

Average Number of Participants: 15

For Participants Aged: 14–17

The Ideal Candidate: The ideal candidate is a traveler who can put behind their home and accept the lifestyle traditions and culture of a different land.

Special Requirements for Participation: None.

COSTS

Average Cost: $4,000

Included in Cost: Everything except personal spending money and the airfare to and from the gateway city of Miami.

Financial Aid Available: Yes

INTERN EXCHANGE INTERNATIONAL, LTD.

Intern Exchange International offers exciting summer internships in London for self-motivated high school students who want to gain hands-on experience in the profession of their choice.

Years in Operation: 17

Religious Affiliation: Not relevant

Price Range of Programs: $5,495 tuition for 2003

For More Information:
  Contact: Nina Miller Glickman, Director
      130 Harold Road
      Woodmere, NY 11598
  Phone: 516-374-3939
  Fax: 516-374-2104
  Email: info@internexchange.com
  Website: www.internexchange.com

FASHION AND DESIGN PLUS PROGRAM

THE PROGRAM

Description: Workshops will cover fashion theory, including trends, fashion drawing, and illustrating ideas using professional techniques. Create a fashion design project such as designing an accessory.

Specialty: Being able to learn a skill, create a portfolio, and spend the summer in London. Many of our students use their summer experience with us in the college application process.

Program Type: Academic/pre-college enrichment

Classification: Coeducational, residential

Goals: Learn the foundations of the fashion and design industry.

Focus: Skill-building and academic/pre-college enrichment

Intensity Level: 2

Duration: 4–6 weeks

Program Offered: Summer

Location: London, England

Accommodations: Dormitory

Years in Operation: 17

Religious Affiliation: Not relevant

PARTICIPANTS

For Participants Aged: 15–18

The Ideal Candidate: Self-motivated and independent with an interest in learning.

Special Requirements for Participation: Transcript, teacher recommendation, and completed application.

COSTS

Average Cost: $5,795

Included in Cost: Everything except airfare, lunches, and personal spending money.

Financial Aid Available: No

FINE ARTS PLUS PROGRAM

THE PROGRAM

Description: Instruction in art and art forms, creation of a professional-grade portfolio.

Specialty: A unique blend of instruction in the particular field, combined with travel and exploration throughout London, Stonehenge, Bath, Cambridge, etc.

Program Type: Music/arts

Classification: Coeducational, residential

Focus: Skill-building, internship, and travel

Activities Center On: Fine arts

Intensity Level: 3

Duration: 4–6 weeks

Program Offered: Summer

Location: London, England

Accommodations: Dormitory

Years in Operation: 17

Religious Affiliation: Not relevant

STAFF

Student/Staff Ratio: 12:1

Staff Qualifications: Professionals and graduate students in each specific field, many of whom have been interns with IEI in the past.

PARTICIPANTS

Average Number of Participants: 10

For Participants Aged: 15–18

The Ideal Candidate: Self-sufficient, independent student with a desire to learn about the particular field while enjoying the culture of London.

Special Requirements for Participation: High school transcript, teacher recommendation, written application.

COSTS

Average Cost: $5,495

Included in Cost: Included are room and board, tuition, trips, excursions, and events. Not included are personal spending, lunches, and airfare.

Financial Aid Available: No

IEI DIGITAL MEDIA PLUS PROGRAM

THE PROGRAM

Description: Our two programs allow you to get your hands on cutting-edge technology and build a portfolio of your work. The two areas include video production/TV graphics and website design.

Specialty: Being able to learn a skill, create a portfolio, and spend the summer in London. Many of our students use their summer experience with us in the college application process.

Program Type: Academic/pre-college enrichment

Classification: Coeducational, residential

Goals: To learn the basic skills required to produce a video and design a website as well as enhance and expand skills brought to the program.

Focus: Skill-building and academic/pre-college enrichment

Activities Center On: Graphic design and writing

Intensity Level: 2

Duration: 4–6 weeks

Program Offered: Summer

Location: London, England

Accommodations: Dormitory

Years in Operation: 17

Religious Affiliation: Not relevant

PARTICIPANTS

Average Number of Participants: 10

For Participants Aged: 15–18

The Ideal Candidate: Self-motivated and independent with an interest in learning.

Special Requirements for Participation: Transcript, teacher recommendation, and completed application.

COSTS

Average Cost: $5,495

Included in Cost: Everything except airfare, lunches, and personal spending money.

Financial Aid Available: No

IEI PHOTOGRAPHY PLUS PROGRAM

THE PROGRAM

Description: The program offers professionally tutored workshops in photography at different skill levels, from basic black-and-white through advanced digital work.

Specialty: IEI offers career internships and workshops combined with cultural activities, travel, etc. Many of our interns use their summer experience with us as part of the college application process.

Program Type: Academic/pre-college enrichment

Classification: Coeducational, residential

Goals: From basic to advanced skills in creative and technical photography

Focus: Academic/pre-college enrichment, skill-building, and travel

Intensity Level: 3

Duration: 4–6 weeks

Program Offered: Summer

Location: London, England

Accommodations: Dormitory

Years in Operation: 17

Religious Affiliation: Not relevant

STAFF

Staff Qualifications: Professional and technical staff are educators and professionals in their respective fields. Resident assistants are college seniors or above with a strong background in the fields to which they are assigned.

PARTICIPANTS

Average Number of Participants: 15

For Participants Aged: 15–18

The Ideal Candidate: Self-motivated and independent with an interest in learning.

Special Requirements for Participation: High school transcript, teacher recommendation, and completed application.

COSTS

Average Cost: $5,495

Included in Cost: Includes room and board, tuition, tube (train) pass, and theater and other outings and excursions. Does not include lunch, personal expenses, and airfare.

Financial Aid Available: No

PRINT AND BROADCAST JOURNALISM

THE PROGRAM

Description: This internship offers the skills for reporting, publishing, and printing the newspaper created each year by our interns.

Specialty: The people who supervise and the people who participate all join together in reaching a level of accomplishment, preparatory for college admission, while enjoying the sights and culture of London and the surrounding areas.

Program Type: Academic/pre-college enrichment

Classification: Coeducational, residential

Goals: To learn the skills required for finding and reporting an event, the way to write the story, the process by which a newspaper is prepared for printing, etc.

Focus: Academic/pre-college enrichment and skill-building

Intensity Level: 3

Duration: 4–6 weeks

Program Offered: Summer

Location: London, England

Accommodations: Dormitory

Years in Operation: 17

Religious Affiliation: Not relevant

STAFF

Staff Qualifications: Skilled professional staff and resident assitants with a strong background in the field.

PARTICIPANTS

Average Number of Participants: 10

For Participants Aged: 15–18

The Ideal Candidate: Self-motivated and independent, with an interest in learning.

Special Requirements for Participation: High school transcript, teacher recommendation, and completed application.

COSTS

Average Cost: $5,495

Included in Cost: Includes tuition, room and board, tube pass, excursions, etc. Does not include personal expenses, lunches, or airfare.

Financial Aid Available: No

STUDENT TRAVEL—INTERNSHIP PROGRAM IN LONDON

THE PROGRAM

Description: Program offers internships in law, business and finance, medicine, strategic studies, journalism, fine art, photography, theater, and others.

Specialty: We offer supervised internships in the career of your choice, allowing you to get a thorough grounding in that career while spending the summer enjoying the sights and culture of London and surrounding historical areas.

Program Type: Academic/pre-college enrichment

Classification: Coeducational, residential

Goals: To acquire the basic skills in the selected field of internship, as an insider completely involved in the work environment.

Focus: Academic/pre-college enrichment, skill-building, and travel

Activities Center On: Cultural and touring

Intensity Level: 3

Duration: 4–6 weeks

Program Offered: Summer

Location: London, England

Accommodations: Dormitory

Years in Operation: 17

Religious Affiliation: Not relevant

Staff

Staff Qualifications: Skilled professional staff includes educators and administrators. Student staff (resident assistants) are college seniors or higher with specific skills in the areas assigned.

Participants

Average Number of Participants: 125

For Participants Aged: 15–18

The Ideal Candidate: Self-motivated and independent with an interest in learning and advancement.

Special Requirements for Participation: High school transcript, teacher recommendation, and completed application.

Costs

Average Cost: $5,495

Included in Cost: Includes room and board, tuition, excursions, tube pass. Does not include personal expenses, lunch, or airfare.

Financial Aid Available: No

INTERNATIONAL BICYCLE FUND

In addition to promoting sustainable transport, IBF sponsors a series of cultural immersion bicycle programs in Africa, Asia, and the Americas that are designed to be fun and enriching, and give participants a better understanding of the world they live in.

Years in Operation: 20

Religious Affiliation: Not relevant

Price Range of Programs: $990–$1,490

For More Information:
  Contact: David Mozer, Director
         4887 Columbia Drive South
         Seattle, WA 98108
  Phone: 206-767-0848
  Fax: 206-767-0848
  Email: ibike@ibike.org
  Website: www.ibike.org/ibike

Bicycle Africa Tours

The Program

Description: A small-group, cultural-immersion, people-to-people bicycle program to explore the diversity, complexity, and beauty of all the different regions of Africa; for active people.

Specialty: Cultural immersion in small towns and villages.

Program Type: Academic/pre-college enrichment, outdoors/adventure, travel/cultural

Classification: Coeducational, residential

Goals: Participants will get an overview of the diversity and complexity of the area. Topics generally include history, politics, economics, culture, linguistics, religion, social programs, geography, botany, anthropology, and material culture.

Focus: Cultural, academic/pre-college enrichment, and skill-building

Activities Center On: Travel, outdoors/adventure, and social sciences

Intensity Level: 2

Duration: 2–4 weeks

Program Offered: Fall, spring, summer

Location: Benin, Cameroon, Eritrea, Ethiopia, The Gambia, Guinea, Kenya, Malawi, Mali, Senegal, Tanzania, Togo, Tunisia, Uganda, and Zimbabwe, Africa.

Accommodations: Dormitory, family-stay/host-family, hotels

Years in Operation: 20

Religious Affiliation: Not relevant

Staff

Student/Staff Ratio: 5:1

Staff Qualifications: Cultural specialist in the program area.

PARTICIPANTS

Average Number of Participants: 6

For Participants Aged: 15+

The Ideal Candidate: Someone who is excited about opportunities to encounter and learn from customs, cuisines, attitudes, accommodations, and living standards that may differ from his/her usual.

Special Requirements for Participation: Must be able to ride a bike at eight miles per hour for several hours over the course of a day.

COSTS

Average Cost: $1,190

Included in Cost: Included: accommodations, two meals a day, transfers, and activities that are part of the program. Not included: excess baggage charges, beverages, security and departure taxes, vaccination, drugs and medical expenses, insurance, personal items.

Financial Aid Available: No

BIKE TOURS

THE PROGRAM

Description: Small-group, cultural-immersion, people-to-people bicycle program to explore diversity, complexity, and beauty of the country and its people; for active people

Specialty: Cultural immersion in small towns and villages.

Program Type: Academic/pre-college enrichment, outdoors/adventure, travel/cultural

Classification: Coeducational, residential

Goals: Participants will get an overview of the diversity and complexity of the area. Topics generally include history, politics, economics, culture, linguistics, religion, social programs, geography, botany, anthropology, and material culture.

Focus: Cultural, academic/pre-college enrichment, and skill-building

Activities Center On: Touring, outdoors/adventure, and social sciences

Intensity Level: 2

Duration: 2–4 weeks

Program Offered: Fall, winter intersession/January term, spring, summer

Location: British Columbia, Canada; Ecuador; Nepal; Vietnam; Washington state

Accommodations: Dormitory, family-stay and host-family, hotels, youth hostels

Years in Operation: 20

Religious Affiliation: Not relevant

STAFF

Student/Staff Ratio: 5:1

Staff Qualifications: Cultural specialist in the program area.

PARTICIPANTS

Average Number of Participants: 6

For Participants Aged: 15+

The Ideal Candidate: Someone who is excited about opportunities to encounter and learn from customs, cuisines, attitudes, accommodations, and living standards that may differ from his/her usual.

Special Requirements for Participation: Must be able to ride a bike at eight miles per hour for several hours over the course of a day.

COSTS

Average Cost: $1,090

Included in Cost: Included: accommodations, two meals a day, transfers, and activities that are part of the program. Not included: excess baggage charges, beverages, security and departure taxes, vaccination, drugs and medical expenses, insurance, personal items.

Financial Aid Available: No

ROLLING THROUGH THE ISLANDS OF THE SALISH SEA (WASHINGTON/BRITISH COLUMBIA)

THE PROGRAM

Description: Small-group, cultural-immersion, people-to-people bicycle program to explore diversity, complexity, and beauty of the country and its people; for active people.

Specialty: Visiting small towns and meeting local people.

Program Type: Academic/pre-college enrichment, outdoors/adventure, travel/cultural

Classification: Coeducational, residential

Goals: Participants will get an overview of the diversity and complexity of the area. Topics generally include history, politics, economics, culture, linguistics, religion, social programs, geography, botany, anthropology, and material culture.

Focus: Cultural, academic/pre-college enrichment, and skill-building

Activities Center On: Outdoors/adventure, travel, and kayaking

Intensity Level: 2

Duration: 1–2 weeks

Program Offered: Summer

Location: Port Townsend and Seattle, Washington; Victoria, British Columbia, Canada

Accommodations: Dormitory, hotels, youth hostels

Years in Operation: 5

Religious Affiliation: Not relevant

STAFF

Student/Staff Ratio: 5:1

Staff Qualifications: Cultural specialist in the program area

PARTICIPANTS

Average Number of Participants: 6

For Participants Aged: 15+

The Ideal Candidate: Someone who is excited about opportunities to encounter and learn from customs, cuisines, attitudes, accommodations, and living standards that may differ from his/her usual.

Special Requirements for Participation: Must be able to ride a bike at eight miles per hour for several hours over the course of a day.

COSTS

Average Cost: $1,490

Included in Cost: Included: accommodations, two meals a day, transfers, and activities that are part of the program. Not included: excess baggage charges, beverages, security and departure taxes, vaccination, drugs and medical expenses, insurance, personal items.

Financial Aid Available: No

INTERNATIONAL CULTURAL ADVENTURES

ICA organizes extraordinary cultural, educational, and volunteer service experiences in Asia and South America. We create enriching and enlightening programs that provide participants with opportunities to acquire new perspectives on their lives and the world we live in. By combining elements of local culture with the special interests of our participants, we are able to customize unique cross-cultural experiences for individuals and groups. In addition to our custom programs, we offer several regularly scheduled summer and semester-length programs, called the Cultural Immersion Experience. We feel strongly that all of our programs provide numerous opportunities to enlighten the mind and enrich the spirit.

Years in Operation: 7

Religious Affiliation: Not relevant

Price Range of Programs: $2,200–$3,650

For More Information:
  Contact: David Pruskin, Program Director
        35 Suprenant Circle
        Brunswick, ME 04011
  Phone: 888-339-0460
  Email: info@ICAdventures.com
  Website: www.ICAdventures.com

THE NEPAL CULTURAL IMMERSION EXPERIENCE

THE PROGRAM

Description: Live with local families! Serve communities in need! Study the language and put it to use! Learn about the culture experientially through seminars and local exploration! A comprehensive orientation sets the stage for a deep and intimate cross-cultural experience. Make friends and make a contribution through this extraordinary immersion program in Nepal.

Specialty: Participants are immersed in the culture through a variety of engaging learning opportunities in a comprehensive Orientation & Education Phase that appropriately prepares participants to effectively serve in the volunteer project of their choice.

Program Type: Academic/pre-college enrichment, community service, outdoors/adventure, travel/cultural

Classification: Coeducational, residential

Goals: Participants should expect to gain a solid foundation of understanding about the cultures of Nepal by: living with a local family; studying the Nepali language; being exposed to life in rural and urban areas; learning about the local customs, geography, history, religions, and politics; and much more.

Focus: Cultural, community service, and educational exchange

Activities Center On: Volunteer, cultural, and language

Intensity Level: 4

Duration: 6–8 weeks

Program Offered: Fall, spring, summer

Location: Kathmandu, Nepal

Accommodations: Family-stay/host-family

Years in Operation: 7

Religious Affiliation: Not relevant

STAFF

Student/Staff Ratio: 6:1

Staff Qualifications: Many wonderful local people comprise the Nepal staff, including language instructors, cultural interpreters, guest speakers, and our in-country director, Rajesh Shrestha. Educated in law and political science, Rajesh has gained valuable experience training volunteers from various international organizations, including the U.S. Peace Corps, Canadian Crossroads International, and more. He truly exhibits the hospitality and grace of the Nepalese people, and we are proud to have him as our program director.

PARTICIPANTS

Average Number of Participants: 6

For Participants Aged: 16+

The Ideal Candidate: One who has a desire to gain an intimate understanding and appreciation of Nepalese cultures; and who is open-minded, respectful of local customs, and willing to engage with local communities through volunteer service

Special Requirements for Participation: There are no special requirements for participation on the program.

COSTS

Average Cost: $2,200

Included in Cost: All program activities, accommodations, and most meals are included. International airfare, insurance, visa fees, and personal expenses are not included.

Financial Aid Available: No

THE PERU CULTURAL IMMERSION EXPERIENCE

THE PROGRAM

Description: Live with local families! Serve communities in need! Study the language and put it to use! Learn about the culture experientially through seminars and local exploration! A comprehensive orientation sets the stage for a deep, intimate cross-cultural experience. Make friends and make a contribution through this extraordinary immersion program in Peru.

Specialty: Participants are immersed in the culture through a variety of engaging learning opportunities in a comprehensive Orientation & Education Phase that appropriately prepares participants to effectively serve in a volunteer project of their choice.

Program Type: Academic/pre-college enrichment, community service, outdoors/adventure, travel/cultural

Classification: Coeducational, residential

Goals: Participants should expect to gain a solid foundation of understanding about the cultures of Peru by: living with a local family; studying the Spanish language; being exposed to life in rural and urban areas; and learning about the local customs, geography, history, religions, the arts, and much more.

Focus: Cultural, community service, and educational exchange

Activities Center On: Volunteer, cultural, and language

Intensity Level: 4

Duration: 6–8 weeks

Program Offered: Fall, spring, summer

Location: Cusco, Peru

Accommodations: Family-stay/host-family, tent

Years in Operation: 3

Religious Affiliation: Not relevant

STAFF

Student/Staff Ratio: 6:1

Staff Qualifications: Silvia Uscamayta, our warm-hearted in-country program director, enthusiastically shares her culture with each participant in coordinating this enriching cultural experience. With a competent team of local personnel, such as cultural interpreters, host families, and language instructors who have among them years of experience in coordinating exchange programs in Peru, we are confident in providing participants with exceptional care and an authentic and unforgettable cultural learning experience.

PARTICIPANTS

Average Number of Participants: 6

For Participants Aged: 16+

The Ideal Candidate: One who has a desire to gain an intimate understanding and appreciation of the Andean cultures of Peru; and who is open-minded, respectful of local customs, and willing to engage with local communities through volunteer service.

Special Requirements for Participation: There are no special requirements for participation on the program. A working knowledge of the Spanish language is helpful but not necessary.

COSTS

Average Cost: $2,950

Included in Cost: All program activities, accommodations, and most meals are included. International airfare, insurance, and personal expenses are not included.

Financial Aid Available: No

INTERNATIONAL SEMINAR SERIES

For More Information:
Contact: John Nissen, Director
PO Box 297
North Barrington, VT 05254
Phone: 518-686-4350
Fax: 518-686-4350
Email: iss@study-serve.org
Website: www.study-serve.org

SERVICE-LEARNING IN PARIS

THE PROGRAM

Description: International Seminar Series' "Service-Learning in Paris" is a community service–based program. Based in the very French 15th arrondisement of Paris, participants take part in community service projects five days a week while also taking courses in either creative writing, French politics and history, or art and architecture. Programming includes French language instruction at all levels.

Specialty: Our program is one of the very few to actually "immerse" participants in the French culture. By doing so, students are able to learn about it much more rapidly than by, for example, taking classes.

Program Type: Community service, travel/cultural

Classification: Coeducational, residential

Goals: Participants should be fully prepared to learn much about the French culture, language, and way of life, as well as much about themselves.

Focus: Cultural, community service, and skill-building

Activities Center On: Cultural, volunteer, and language

Intensity Level: 4

Duration: 2–4 weeks

Program Offered: Summer

Location: Paris, France

Accommodations: Dormitory

Years in Operation: 5

Religious Affiliation: Not relevant

STAFF

Student/Staff Ratio: 3:1

Staff Qualifications: All program staff have a broad background in their field of interest. Nearly all work full time in their department of specialty or hold a degree.

PARTICIPANTS

Average Number of Participants: 32

For Participants Aged: 15–20

The Ideal Candidate: Because the program is community service–based, the ideal candidate should be ready to work with French people on a daily basis, sometimes with cultural barriers to overcome; these may obviously require some work as well.

Special Requirements for Participation: There are no special requirements for Service-Learning in Paris. Participants simply need an open mind.

COSTS

Average Cost: $7,000

Included in Cost: The program fee is $5,600 (including the $50 application fee, which is deducted from this total). All costs are included except for airfare (usually $800), a daily lunch (5 to 10 Euros), and any spending money.

Financial Aid Available: Yes

ITHACA COLLEGE

Religious Affiliation: Not relevant

For More Information:
Contact: E. Kimball Milling,
120 Towers Concourse
Ithaca, NY 14850
Phone: 607-274-3143
Fax: 607-274-1263
Email: cess@ithaca.edu
Website: www.ithaca.edu/summercollege

SUMMER COLLEGE FOR HIGH SCHOOL STUDENTS: SESSION I

THE PROGRAM

Description: Students in the three-week session enroll in one of eight courses for college credit. Courses are taught by Ithaca College faculty and are the same courses offered to first-year college students during the academic year. Students

live on campus and enjoy a full range of activities on and off campus.

Specialty: Excellent faculty and beautiful facilities on a great college campus in a beautiful college town

Program Type: Academic/pre-college enrichment

Classification: Coeducational, residential

Goals: Students have a college-level experience while in high school. In addition to learning discipline-based material in the academic course in which students enroll, students learn time managment skills, independence, and the ability to work with others.

Focus: Academic/pre-college enrichment and leadership and teamwork

Activities Center On: Academic and writing

Intensity Level: 3

Duration: 2–4 weeks

Program Offered: Summer

Location: Ithaca, New York

Accommodations: Dormitory

Years in Operation: 7

Religious Affiliation: Not relevant

STAFF

Student/Staff Ratio: 10:1

Staff Qualifications: Program staff are faculty and graduate and undergraduate students.

PARTICIPANTS

Average Number of Participants: 40

For Participants Aged: 15–18

The Ideal Candidate: The ideal candidate is a strong student academically, interested in meeting others, and able to be independent.

Special Requirements for Participation: Good academic preparation in high school.

COSTS

Average Cost: $3,000

Included in Cost: Cost includes room and board and tuition but not books or spending money.

Financial Aid Available: Yes

SUMMER COLLEGE FOR HIGH SCHOOL STUDENTS: SESSION II

THE PROGRAM

Description: In our five-week program students take two college courses and earn 6 to 8 credits. This program is primarily for students who will be seniors in the fall. Choose from 24 classes, many building upon Ithaca College's national reputation in communications, media arts, and culture.

Program Type: Academic/pre-college enrichment

Classification: Coeducational, residential

Focus: Academic/pre-college enrichment and leadership and teamwork

Activities Center On: Academic and liberal arts

Intensity Level: 4

Duration: 4–6 weeks

Program Offered: Summer

Location: Ithaca, New York

Accommodations: Dormitory

Years in Operation: 7

Religious Affiliation: Not relevant

STAFF

Student/Staff Ratio: 10:1

Staff Qualifications: The program director, Warren Schlesinger, is an associate professor in business accounting. The residential coordinator is a faculty or staff member. The residential assistants are college students who generally have experience as RAs or who have worked with high school students in other summer programs. Instructors for the classes are almost exclusively Ithaca College faculty.

PARTICIPANTS

Average Number of Participants: 40

For Participants Aged: 15–18

The Ideal Candidate: An "A" student who is active in his or her community and school, and who would enjoy an educational experience that is beyond what is offered in his/her high school.

Special Requirements for Participation: None.

COSTS

Average Cost: $5,000

Included in Cost: Room and board, tuition, and many activities are included. Text books, supplies, travel expenses to and from the program, and some activities are not included.

Financial Aid Available: Yes

LANDMARK VOLUNTEERS, INC.

Landmark programs provide an opportunity for high school students to perform community service at nonprofit organizations throughout the country.

Years in Operation: 12

Religious Affiliation: Not relevant

Price Range of Programs: $875

For More Information:
Contact: Ann Barrett, Executive Director
PO Box 455
Sheffield, MA 02157
Phone: 413-229-0255
Fax: 413-229-2050

Email: landmark@volunteers.com
Website: www.volunteers.com

LANDMARK VOLUNTEERS (CALIFORNIA)

THE PROGRAM

Description: Landmark programs provide an opportunity for high school students to perform community service at nonprofit organizations located throughout the United States. California sites: Golden Gate Recreation Area, Henry Coe Park.

Specialty: Volunteers experience after-hours activities the value of teamwork. They gain self-respect and pride in their work. Community service credit is awarded.

Program Type: Community service

Classification: Coeducational, residential

Goals: Familiarity with nonprofit and service organizations through volunteer work, exposure to career options, value of teamwork, and strong bonds of friendship.

Focus: Community service, leadership/teamwork, and skill-building

Activities Center On: Volunteer

Intensity Level: 3

Duration: 1–2 weeks

Program Offered: Summer

Location: California

Accommodations: Tent, bunk/cabin

Years in Operation: 12

Religious Affiliation: Not relevant

STAFF

Student/Staff Ratio: 13:1

Staff Qualifications: Team leaders are usually school teachers or outdoor educators who supervise the team members 24 hours a day and who are conscientious individuals and excellent role models.

PARTICIPANTS

Average Number of Participants: 13

For Participants Aged: 14–18

The Ideal Candidate: Diligent at work, supportive in team relationships, strong ability to work with others, dependable and reliable.

Special Requirements for Participation: None.

COSTS

Average Cost: $875

Included in Cost: Included are supervision in work projects, food, and accommodations. Travel arrangements and travel expenses are not included. We recommend bringing personal spending money for after-hours activities.

Financial Aid Available: Yes

Landmark Volunteers (Colorado)

The Program

Description: Landmark programs provide an opportunity for high school students to perform community service at non-profit organizations located throughout the United States. Colorado sites: Rocky Mountain Village, Colorado Trail, Windstar Foundation, Chico Basin Ranch.

Specialty: Volunteers experience after-hours activities the value of teamwork. They gain self-respect and pride in their work. Community service credit is awarded.

Program Type: Community service

Classification: Coeducational, residential

Goals: Familiarity with nonprofit and service organizations through volunteer work, exposure to career options, value of teamwork, and strong bonds of friendship.

Focus: Community service, leadership/teamwork, and skill-building

Activities Center On: Volunteer

Intensity Level: 3

Duration: 1–2 weeks

Program Offered: Summer

Location: Colorado

Accommodations: Tent, bunk/cabin

Years in Operation: 12

Religious Affiliation: Not relevant

Staff

Student/Staff Ratio: 13:1

Staff Qualifications: Team leaders are usually school teachers or outdoor educators who supervise the team members 24 hours a day and who are conscientious individuals and excellent role models.

Participants

Average Number of Participants: 13

For Participants Aged: 14–18

The Ideal Candidate: Diligent at work, supportive in team relationships, strong ability to work with others, dependable and reliable.

Special Requirements for Participation: None.

Costs

Average Cost: $875

Included in Cost: Included are supervision in work projects, food, and accommodations. Travel arrangements and travel expenses are not included. We recommend bringing personal spending money for after-hours activities.

Financial Aid Available: Yes

Landmark Volunteers (Connecticut)

The Program

Description: Landmark programs provide an opportunity for high school students to perform community service at non-profit organizations located throughout the United States. Connecticut sites: Hole in the Wall Camp, Sharon Audubon.

Specialty: Volunteers experience after-hours activities the value of teamwork. They gain self-respect and pride in their work. Community service credit is awarded.

Program Type: Community service

Classification: Coeducational, residential

Goals: Familiarity with nonprofit and service organizations through volunteer work, exposure to career options, value of teamwork, and strong bonds of friendship.

Focus: Community service, leadership/teamwork, and skill-building

Activities Center On: Volunteer

Intensity Level: 3

Duration: 1–2 weeks

Program Offered: Spring, summer

Location: Connecitcut

Accommodations: Bunk/cabin

Years in Operation: 12

Religious Affiliation: Not relevant

Staff

Student/Staff Ratio: 13:1

Staff Qualifications: Team leaders are usually school teachers or outdoor educators who supervise the team members 24 hours a day and who are conscientious individuals and excellent role models.

Participants

Average Number of Participants: 13

For Participants Aged: 14–18

The Ideal Candidate: Diligent at work, supportive in team relationships, strong ability to work with others, dependable and reliable.

Special Requirements for Participation: None.

Costs

Average Cost: $875

Included in Cost: Included are supervision in work projects, food, and accommodations. Travel arrangements and travel expenses are not included. We recommend bringing personal spending money for after-hours activities.

Financial Aid Available: Yes

Landmark Volunteers (Florida)

The Program

Description: Landmark programs provide an opportunity for high school students to perform community service at non-profit organizations located throughout the United States. Florida site: Blowing Rocks Preserve.

Specialty: Volunteers experience after-hours activities the value of teamwork. They gain self-respect and pride in their work. Community service credit is awarded.

Program Type: Community service

Classification: Coeducational, residential

Goals: Familiarity with nonprofit and service organizations through volunteer work, exposure to career options, value of teamwork, and strong bonds of friendship.

Focus: Community service, leadership/teamwork, and skill-building

Activities Center On: Volunteer

Intensity Level: 3

Duration: 1–2 weeks

Program Offered: Spring, summer

Location: Florida

Accommodations: Tent

Years in Operation: 12

Religious Affiliation: Not relevant

Staff

Student/Staff Ratio: 13:1

Staff Qualifications: Team leaders are usually school teachers or outdoor educators who supervise the team members 24 hours a day and who are conscientious individuals and excellent role models.

Participants

Average Number of Participants: 13

For Participants Aged: 14–18

The Ideal Candidate: Diligent at work, supportive in team relationships, strong ability to work with others, dependable and reliable.

Special Requirements for Participation: None.

Costs

Average Cost: $660

Included in Cost: Included are supervision in work projects, food, and accommodations. Travel arrangements and travel expenses are not included. We recommend bringing personal spending money for after-hours activities.

Financial Aid Available: Yes

Landmark Volunteers (Idaho)

The Program

Description: Landmark programs provide an opportunity for high school students to perform community service at non-profit organizations located throughout the United States. Idaho site: Sawtooth Recreation Area.

Specialty: Volunteers experience first-hand the value of team-work. They gain self-respect and pride in their work. Community service credit is awarded.

Program Type: Community service

Classification: Coeducational, residential

Goals: Familiarity with nonprofit and service organizations through volunteer work, exposure to career options, value of teamwork, and strong bonds of friendship.

Focus: Community service, leadership/teamwork, and skill-building

Activities Center On: Volunteer

Intensity Level: 3

Duration: 1–2 weeks

Program Offered: Summer

Location: Idaho

Accommodations: Bunk/cabin

Years in Operation: 12

Religious Affiliation: Not relevant

Staff

Student/Staff Ratio: 13:1

Staff Qualifications: Team leaders are usually school teachers or outdoor educators who supervise the team members 24 hours a day and who are conscientious individuals and excellent role models.

Participants

Average Number of Participants: 13

For Participants Aged: 14–18

The Ideal Candidate: Diligent at work, supportive in team relationships, strong ability to work with others, dependable and reliable.

Special Requirements for Participation: None.

Costs

Average Cost: $875

Included in Cost: Included are supervision in work projects, food, and accommodations. Travel arrangements and travel expenses are not included. We recommend bringing personal spending money for after-hours activities.

Financial Aid Available: Yes

Landmark Volunteers (Maine)

The Program

Description: Landmark programs provide an opportunity for high school students to perform community service at non-profit organizations located throughout the United States. Maine sites: Acadia National Park, Agassiz Village, Aldermere Farm, Blue Hill Heritage Trust, Kelmscott Farm, Kneisel Hall Music Festival, Camp Sunshine.

Specialty: Volunteers experience first-hand the value of team-work. They gain self-respect and pride in their work. Community service credit is awarded.

Program Type: Community service

Classification: Coeducational, residential

Goals: Familiarity with nonprofit and service organizations through volunteer work, exposure to career options, value of teamwork, and strong bonds of friendship.

Focus: Community service, leadership/teamwork, and skill-building

Activities Center On: Volunteer

Intensity Level: 3

Duration: 1–2 weeks

Program Offered: Summer

Location: Maine

Accommodations: Bunk/cabin

Years in Operation: 12

Religious Affiliation: Not relevant

Staff

Student/Staff Ratio: 13:1

Staff Qualifications: Team leaders are usually school teachers or outdoor educators who supervise the team members 24 hours a day and who are conscientious individuals and excellent role models.

Participants

Average Number of Participants: 13

For Participants Aged: 14–18

The Ideal Candidate: Diligent at work, supportive in team relationships, strong ability to work with others, dependable and reliable.

Special Requirements for Participation: None.

Costs

Average Cost: $875

Included in Cost: Included are supervision in work projects, food, and accommodations. Travel arrangements and travel expenses are not included. We recommend bringing personal spending money for after-hours activities.

Financial Aid Available: Yes

Landmark Volunteers (Massachusetts)

The Program

Description: Landmark programs provide an opportunity for high school students to perform community service at non-profit organizations located throughout the United States. Massachusetts sites: Appleton Farm, Boston Symphony Orchestra at Tanglewood, Gould Farm, Plimoth Plantation, Shakespeare and Co., Schenob Brook, Ventfort Hall.

Specialty: Volunteers experience first-hand the value of team-work. They gain self-respect and pride in their work. Community service credit is awarded.

Program Type: Community service

Classification: Coeducational, residential

Goals: Familiarity with nonprofit and service organizations through volunteer work, exposure to career options, value of teamwork, and strong bonds of friendship.

Focus: Community service, leadership/teamwork, and skill-building

Activities Center On: Volunteer

Intensity Level: 3

Duration: 1–2 weeks

Program Offered: Summer

Location: Massachusetts

Accommodations: Bunk/cabin

Years in Operation: 12

Religious Affiliation: Not relevant

Staff

Student/Staff Ratio: 13:1

Staff Qualifications: Team leaders are usually school teachers or outdoor educators who supervise the team members 24 hours a day and who are conscientious individuals and excellent role models.

Participants

Average Number of Participants: 13

For Participants Aged: 14–18

The Ideal Candidate: Diligent at work, supportive in team relationships, strong ability to work with others, dependable and reliable .

Special Requirements for Participation: None.

Costs

Average Cost: $875

Included in Cost: Included are supervision in work projects, food, and accommodations. Travel arrangements and travel expenses are not included. We recommend bringing personal spending money for after-hours activities.

Financial Aid Available: Yes

LANDMARK VOLUNTEERS (MICHIGAN)

THE PROGRAM

Description: Landmark programs provide an opportunity for high school students to perform community service at non-profit organizations located throughout the United States. Michigan site: Keweenaw Peninsula.

Specialty: Volunteers experience first-hand the value of teamwork. They gain self-respect and pride in their work. Community service credit is awarded.

Program Type: Community service

Classification: Coeducational, residential

Goals: Familiarity with nonprofit and service organizations through volunteer work, exposure to career options, value of teamwork, and strong bonds of friendship.

Focus: Community service, leadership/teamwork, and skill-building

Activities Center On: Volunteer

Intensity Level: 3

Duration: 1–2 weeks

Program Offered: Summer

Location: Michigan

Accommodations: Bunk/cabin

Years in Operation: 12

Religious Affiliation: Not relevant

STAFF

Student/Staff Ratio: 13:1

Staff Qualifications: Team leaders are usually school teachers or outdoor educators who supervise the team members 24 hours a day and who are conscientious individuals and excellent role models.

PARTICIPANTS

Average Number of Participants: 13

For Participants Aged: 14–18

The Ideal Candidate: Diligent at work, supportive in team relationships, strong ability to work with others, dependable and reliable.

Special Requirements for Participation: None.

COSTS

Average Cost: $875

Included in Cost: Included are supervision in work projects, food, and accommodations. Travel arrangements and travel expenses are not included. We recommend bringing personal spending money for after-hours activities.

Financial Aid Available: Yes

LANDMARK VOLUNTEERS (MINNESOTA)

THE PROGRAM

Description: Landmark programs provide an opportunity for high school students to perform community service at non-profit organizations located throughout the United States. Minnesota sites: Confidence Learning Center, Friendship Ventures.

Specialty: Volunteers experience first-hand the value of teamwork. They gain self-respect and pride in their work. Community service credit is awarded.

Program Type: Community service

Classification: Coeducational, residential

Goals: Familiarity with nonprofit and service organizations through volunteer work, exposure to career options, value of teamwork, and strong bonds of friendship.

Focus: Community service, leadership/teamwork, and skill-building

Activities Center On: Volunteer

Intensity Level: 3

Duration: 1–2 weeks

Program Offered: Summer

Location: Minnesota

Accommodations: Bunk/cabin

Years in Operation: 12

Religious Affiliation: Not relevant

STAFF

Student/Staff Ratio: 13:1

Staff Qualifications: Team leaders are usually school teachers or outdoor educators who supervise the team members 24 hours a day and who are conscientious individuals and excellent role models.

PARTICIPANTS

Average Number of Participants: 13

For Participants Aged: 14–18

The Ideal Candidate: Diligent at work, supportive in team relationships, strong ability to work with others, dependable and reliable.

Special Requirements for Participation: None.

COSTS

Average Cost: $875

Included in Cost: Included are supervision in work projects, food, and accommodations. Travel arrangements and travel expenses are not included. We recommend bringing personal spending money for after-hours activities.

Financial Aid Available: Yes

Landmark Volunteers (Montana)

The Program

Description: Landmark programs provide an opportunity for high school students to perform community service at non-profit organizations located throughout the United States. Montana site: Spotted Bear Ranger District.

Specialty: Volunteers experience first-hand the value of teamwork. They gain self-respect and pride in their work. Community service credit is awarded.

Program Type: Community service

Classification: Coeducational, residential

Goals: Familiarity with nonprofit and service organizations through volunteer work, exposure to career options, value of teamwork, and strong bonds of friendship.

Focus: Community service, leadership/teamwork, and skill-building

Activities Center On: Volunteer

Intensity Level: 3

Duration: 1–2 weeks

Program Offered: Summer

Location: Montana

Accommodations: Bunk/cabin

Years in Operation: 12

Religious Affiliation: Not relevant

Staff

Student/Staff Ratio: 13:1

Staff Qualifications: Team leaders are usually school teachers or outdoor educators who supervise the team members 24 hours a day and who are conscientious individuals and excellent role models.

Participants

Average Number of Participants: 13

For Participants Aged: 14–18

The Ideal Candidate: Diligent at work, supportive in team relationships, strong ability to work with others, dependable and reliable.

Special Requirements for Participation: None.

Costs

Average Cost: $875

Included in Cost: Included are supervision in work projects, food, and accommodations. Travel arrangements and travel expenses are not included. We recommend bringing personal spending money for after-hours activities.

Financial Aid Available: Yes

Landmark Volunteers (New Hampshire)

The Program

Description: Landmark programs provide an opportunity for high school students to perform community service at non-profit organizations located throughout the United States. New Hampshire site: Hidden Valley Easter Seal Camp.

Specialty: Volunteers experience first-hand the value of teamwork. They gain self-respect and pride in their work. Community service credit is awarded.

Program Type: Community service

Classification: Coeducational, residential

Goals: Familiarity with nonprofit and service organizations through volunteer work, exposure to career options, value of teamwork, and strong bonds of friendship.

Focus: Community service, leadership/teamwork, and skill-building

Activities Center On: Volunteer

Intensity Level: 3

Duration: 1–2 weeks

Program Offered: Summer

Location: New Hampshire

Accommodations: Bunk/cabin

Years in Operation: 12

Religious Affiliation: Not relevant

Staff

Student/Staff Ratio: 13:1

Staff Qualifications: Team leaders are usually school teachers or outdoor educators who supervise the team members 24 hours a day and who are conscientious individuals and excellent role models.

Participants

Average Number of Participants: 13

For Participants Aged: 14–18

The Ideal Candidate: Diligent at work, supportive in team relationships, strong ability to work with others, dependable and reliable.

Special Requirements for Participation: None.

Costs

Average Cost: $875

Included in Cost: Included are supervision in work projects, food, and accommodations. Travel arrangements and travel expenses are not included. We recommend bringing personal spending money for after-hours activities.

Financial Aid Available: Yes

LANDMARK VOLUNTEERS (NEW JERSEY)

THE PROGRAM

Description: Landmark programs provide an opportunity for high school students to perform community service at non-profit organizations located throughout the United States. New Jersey site: Camp Vacamas.

Specialty: Volunteers experience first-hand the value of teamwork. They gain self-respect and pride in their work. Community service credit is awarded.

Program Type: Community service

Classification: Coeducational, residential

Goals: Familiarity with nonprofit and service organizations through volunteer work, exposure to career options, value of teamwork, and strong bonds of friendship.

Focus: Community service, leadership/teamwork, and skill-building

Activities Center On: Volunteer

Intensity Level: 3

Duration: 1–2 weeks

Program Offered: Summer

Location: New Jersey

Accommodations: Bunk/cabin

Years in Operation: 12

Religious Affiliation: Not relevant

STAFF

Student/Staff Ratio: 13:1

Staff Qualifications: Team leaders are usually school teachers or outdoor educators who supervise the team members 24 hours a day and who are conscientious individuals and excellent role models.

PARTICIPANTS

Average Number of Participants: 13

For Participants Aged: 14–18

The Ideal Candidate: Diligent at work, supportive in team relationships, strong ability to work with others, dependable and reliable.

Special Requirements for Participation: None.

COSTS

Average Cost: $875

Included in Cost: Included are supervision in work projects, food, and accommodations. Travel arrangements and travel expenses are not included. We recommend bringing personal spending money for after-hours activities.

Financial Aid Available: Yes

LANDMARK VOLUNTEERS (NEW MEXICO)

THE PROGRAM

Description: Landmark programs provide an opportunity for high school students to perform community service at non-profit organizations located throughout the United States. New Mexico site: Bandelier National Monument.

Specialty: Volunteers experience first-hand the value of teamwork. They gain self-respect and pride in their work. Community service credit is awarded.

Program Type: Community service

Classification: Coeducational, residential

Goals: Familiarity with nonprofit and service organizations through volunteer work, exposure to career options, value of teamwork, and strong bonds of friendship.

Focus: Community service, leadership/teamwork, and skill-building

Activities Center On: Volunteer

Intensity Level: 3

Duration: 1–2 weeks

Program Offered: Summer

Location: New Mexico

Years in Operation: 12

Religious Affiliation: Not relevant

STAFF

Student/Staff Ratio: 13:1

Staff Qualifications: Team leaders are usually school teachers or outdoor educators who supervise the team members 24 hours a day and who are conscientious individuals and excellent role models.

PARTICIPANTS

Average Number of Participants: 13

For Participants Aged: 14–18

The Ideal Candidate: Diligent at work, supportive in team relationships, strong ability to work with others, dependable and reliable.

Special Requirements for Participation: None.

COSTS

Average Cost: $875

Included in Cost: Included are supervision in work projects, food, and accommodations. Travel arrangements and travel expenses are not included. We recommend bringing personal spending money for after-hours activities.

Financial Aid Available: Yes

LANDMARK VOLUNTEERS (NEW YORK)

THE PROGRAM

Description: Landmark program provide an opportunity for high school students to perform community service at nonprofit organizations located throughout the United States. New York sites: Adirondack Mountains Club, Boys & Girls Harbor, Clearpool Education Center, Double "H" Ranch, Glimmerglass Opera, Institute for Ecosystem Studies, Pathfinder Village, Paleontological Research Institute, Saratoga State Park, Snug Harbor Cultural Center, Wagon Road Camp.

Specialty: Volunteers experience first-hand the value of teamwork. They gain self-respect and pride in their work. Community service credit is awarded.

Program Type: Community service

Classification: Coeducational, residential

Goals: Familiarity with nonprofit and service organizations through volunteer work, exposure to career options, value of teamwork, and strong bonds of friendship.

Focus: Community service, leadership/teamwork, and skill-building

Activities Center On: Volunteer

Intensity Level: 3

Duration: 1–2 weeks

Program Offered: Summer

Location: New York

Accommodations: Tent, bunk/cabin

Years in Operation: 12

Religious Affiliation: Not relevant

STAFF

Student/Staff Ratio: 13:1

Staff Qualifications: Team leaders are usually school teachers or outdoor educators who supervise the team members 24 hours a day and who are conscientious individuals and excellent role models.

PARTICIPANTS

Average Number of Participants: 13

For Participants Aged: 14–18

The Ideal Candidate: Diligent at work, supportive in team relationships, strong ability to work with others, dependable and reliable.

Special Requirements for Participation: None.

COSTS

Average Cost: $875

Included in Cost: Included are supervision in work projects, food, and accommodations. Travel arrangements and travel expenses are not included. We recommend bringing personal spending money for after-hours activities.

Financial Aid Available: Yes

LANDMARK VOLUNTEERS (OHIO)

THE PROGRAM

Description: Landmark programs provide an opportunity for high school students to perform community service at nonprofit organizations located throughout the United States. Ohio site: Joy Outdoor Center.

Specialty: Volunteers experience first-hand the value of teamwork. They gain self-respect and pride in their work. Community service credit is awarded.

Program Type: Community service

Classification: Coeducational, residential

Goals: Familiarity with nonprofit and service organizations through volunteer work, exposure to career options, value of teamwork, and strong bonds of friendship.

Focus: Community service, leadership/teamwork, and skill-building

Activities Center On: Volunteer

Intensity Level: 3

Duration: 1–2 weeks

Program Offered: Summer

Location: Ohio

Accommodations: Bunk/cabin

Years in Operation: 12

Religious Affiliation: Not relevant

STAFF

Student/Staff Ratio: 13:1

Staff Qualifications: Team leaders are usually school teachers or outdoor educators who supervise the team members 24 hours a day and who are conscientious individuals and excellent role models.

PARTICIPANTS

Average Number of Participants: 13

For Participants Aged: 14–18

The Ideal Candidate: Diligent at work, supportive in team relationships, strong ability to work with others, dependable and reliable.

Special Requirements for Participation: None.

COSTS

Average Cost: $875

Included in Cost: Included are supervision in work projects, food, and accommodations. Travel arrangements and travel expenses are not included. We recommend bringing personal spending money for after-hours activities.

Financial Aid Available: Yes

LANDMARK VOLUNTEERS (RHODE ISLAND)

THE PROGRAM

Description: Landmark programs provide an opportunity for high school students to perform community service at non-profit organizations located throughout the United States. Rhode Island site: International Tennis Hall of Fame.

Specialty: Volunteers experience first-hand the value of teamwork. They gain self-respect and pride in their work. Community service credit is awarded.

Program Type: Community service

Classification: Coeducational, residential

Goals: Familiarity with nonprofit and service organizations through volunteer work, exposure to career options, value of teamwork, and strong bonds of friendship.

Focus: Community service, leadership/teamwork, and skill-building

Activities Center On: Volunteer

Intensity Level: 3

Duration: 1–2 weeks

Program Offered: Summer

Location: Rhode Island

Accommodations: Bunk/cabin

Years in Operation: 12

Religious Affiliation: Not relevant

STAFF

Student/Staff Ratio: 13:1

Staff Qualifications: Team leaders are usually school teachers or outdoor educators who supervise the team members 24 hours a day and who are conscientious individuals and excellent role models.

PARTICIPANTS

Average Number of Participants: 13

For Participants Aged: 14–18

The Ideal Candidate: Diligent at work, supportive in team relationships, strong ability to work with others, dependable and reliable.

Special Requirements for Participation: None.

COSTS

Average Cost: $875

Included in Cost: Included are supervision in work projects, food, and accommodations. Travel arrangements and travel expenses are not included. We recommend bringing personal spending money for after-hours activities.

Financial Aid Available: Yes

LANDMARK VOLUNTEERS (TENNESSEE)

THE PROGRAM

Description: Landmark programs provide an opportunity for high school students to perform community service at non-profit organizations located throughout the United States. Tennessee site: Cumberland Trail

Specialty: Volunteers experience first-hand the value of teamwork. They gain self-respect and pride in their work. Community service credit is awarded.

Program Type: Community service

Classification: Coeducational, residential

Goals: Familiarity with nonprofit and service organizations through volunteer work, exposure to career options, value of teamwork, and strong bonds of friendship.

Focus: Community service, leadership/teamwork, and skill-building

Activities Center On: Volunteer

Intensity Level: 3

Duration: 1–2 weeks

Program Offered: Summer

Location: Tennessee

Accommodations: Bunk/cabin

Years in Operation: 12

Religious Affiliation: Not relevant

STAFF

Student/Staff Ratio: 13:1

Staff Qualifications: Team leaders are usually school teachers or outdoor educators who supervise the team members 24 hours a day and who are conscientious individuals and excellent role models.

PARTICIPANTS

Average Number of Participants: 13

For Participants Aged: 14–18

The Ideal Candidate: Diligent at work, supportive in team relationships, strong ability to work with others, dependable and reliable.

Special Requirements for Participation: None.

COSTS

Average Cost: $875

Included in Cost: Included are supervision in work projects, food, and accommodations. Travel arrangements and travel expenses are not included. We recommend bringing personal spending money for after-hours activities.

Financial Aid Available: Yes

LANDMARK VOLUNTEERS (VERMONT)

THE PROGRAM

Description: Landmark programs provide an opportunity for high school students to perform community service at non-profit organizations located throughout the United States. Vermont sites: Calvin Coolidge Homestead, Marsh-Billings Rockefeller Historical Park, Morgan Horse Farm, Shelburne Museum.

Specialty: Volunteers experience first-hand the value of teamwork. They gain self-respect and pride in their work. Community service credit is awarded.

Program Type: Community service

Classification: Coeducational, residential

Goals: Familiarity with nonprofit and service organizations through volunteer work, exposure to career options, value of teamwork, and strong bonds of friendship.

Focus: Community service, leadership/teamwork, and skill-building

Activities Center On: Volunteer

Intensity Level: 3

Duration: 1–2 weeks

Program Offered: Summer

Location: Vermont

Years in Operation: 12

Religious Affiliation: Not relevant

STAFF

Student/Staff Ratio: 13:1

Staff Qualifications: Team leaders are usually school teachers or outdoor educators who supervise the team members 24 hours a day and who are conscientious individuals and excellent role models.

PARTICIPANTS

Average Number of Participants: 13

For Participants Aged: 14–18

The Ideal Candidate: Diligent at work, supportive in team relationships, strong ability to work with others, dependable and reliable.

Special Requirements for Participation: None.

COSTS

Average Cost: $875

Included in Cost: Included are supervision in work projects, food, and accommodations. Travel arrangements and travel expenses are not included. We recommend bringing personal spending money for after-hours activities.

Financial Aid Available: Yes

LANDMARK VOLUNTEERS (VIRGINIA)

THE PROGRAM

Description: Landmark programs provide an opportunity for high school students to perform community service at non-profit organizations located throughout the United States. Virginia sites: Claude Moore Colonial Farm, Colonial Williamsburg, Kerr Reservoir.

Specialty: Volunteers experience first-hand the value of teamwork. They gain self-respect and pride in their work. Community service credit is awarded.

Program Type: Community service

Classification: Coeducational, residential

Goals: Familiarity with nonprofit and service organizations through volunteer work, exposure to career options, value of teamwork, and strong bonds of friendship.

Focus: Community service, leadership/teamwork, and skill-building

Activities Center On: Volunteer

Intensity Level: 3

Duration: 1–2 weeks

Program Offered: Summer

Location: Virginia

Accommodations: Dormitory, bunk/cabin

Years in Operation: 12

Religious Affiliation: Not relevant

STAFF

Student/Staff Ratio: 13:1

Staff Qualifications: Team leaders are usually school teachers or outdoor educators who supervise the team members 24 hours a day and who are conscientious individuals and excellent role models.

PARTICIPANTS

Average Number of Participants: 13

For Participants Aged: 14–18

The Ideal Candidate: Diligent at work, supportive in team relationships, strong ability to work with others, dependable and reliable.

Special Requirements for Participation: None.

COSTS

Average Cost: $875

Included in Cost: Included are supervision in work projects, food, and accommodations. Travel arrangements and travel expenses are not included. We recommend bringing personal spending money for after-hours activities.

Financial Aid Available: Yes

Landmark Volunteers (Washington)

The Program

Description: Landmark programs provide an opportunity for high school students to perform community service at nonprofit organizations located throughout the United States. Washington sites: Olympic National Park, San Juan Island National Park, Washington State Park, Washington Trail Association.

Specialty: Volunteers experience first-hand the value of teamwork. They gain self-respect and pride in their work. Community service credit is awarded.

Program Type: Community service

Classification: Coeducational, residential

Goals: Familiarity with nonprofit and service organizations through volunteer work, exposure to career options, value of teamwork, and strong bonds of friendship.

Focus: Community service, leadership/teamwork, and skill-building

Activities Center On: Volunteer

Intensity Level: 3

Duration: 1–2 weeks

Program Offered: Summer

Location: Washington

Accommodations: Tent

Years in Operation: 12

Religious Affiliation: Not relevant

Staff

Student/Staff Ratio: 13:1

Staff Qualifications: Team leaders are usually school teachers or outdoor educators who supervise the team members 24 hours a day and who are conscientious individuals and excellent role models.

Participants

Average Number of Participants: 13

For Participants Aged: 14–18

The Ideal Candidate: Diligent at work, supportive in team relationships, strong ability to work with others, dependable and reliable.

Special Requirements for Participation: None.

Costs

Average Cost: $875

Included in Cost: Included are supervision in work projects, food, and accommodations. Travel arrangements and travel expenses are not included. We recommend bringing personal spending money for after-hours activities.

Financial Aid Available: Yes

Landmark Volunteers (Wyoming)

The Program

Description: Landmark programs provide an opportunity for high school students to perform community service at nonprofit organizations located throughout the United States. Wyoming sites: Grand Teton Music Festival, National Elk Refuge.

Specialty: Volunteers experience first-hand the value of teamwork. They gain self-respect and pride in their work. Community service credit is awarded.

Program Type: Community service

Classification: Coeducational, residential

Goals: Familiarity with nonprofit and service organizations through volunteer work, exposure to career options, value of teamwork, and strong bonds of friendship.

Focus: Community service, leadership/teamwork, and skill-building

Activities Center On: Volunteer

Intensity Level: 3

Duration: 1–2 weeks

Program Offered: Summer

Location: Wyoming

Accommodations: Bunk/cabin

Years in Operation: 12

Religious Affiliation: Not relevant

Staff

Student/Staff Ratio: 13:1

Staff Qualifications: Team leaders are usually school teachers or outdoor educators who supervise the team members 24 hours a day and who are conscientious individuals and excellent role models.

Participants

Average Number of Participants: 13

For Participants Aged: 14–18

The Ideal Candidate: Diligent at work, supportive in team relationships, strong ability to work with others, dependable and reliable.

Special Requirements for Participation: None.

Costs

Average Cost: $875

Included in Cost: Included are supervision in work projects, food, and accommodations. Travel arrangements and travel expenses are not included. We recommend bringing personal spending money for after-hours activities.

Financial Aid Available: Yes

LANGUAGE STUDIES ABROAD, INC.

Language Studies Abroad, Inc. offers affordable language immersion programs in more than 21 countries!

Years in Operation: 18

Religious Affiliation: Not relevant

Price Range of Programs: $200–$5,000+

For More Information:
Contact: Director
1801 Highway 50 East
Suite I
Carson City, NV 89701
Phone: 800-424-5522
Fax: 775-883-2266
Email: info@languagestudiesabroad.com
Website: www.languagestudiesabroad.com

ALICANTE, EL PUERTO DE SANTA MARIA, MADRID, AND SALAMANCA (SPAIN)

THE PROGRAM

Description: This program provides language instruction for all levels including cultural immersion in the location of the student's choice.

Specialty: Our programs give the students the opportunity to study abroad in a total immersion course. Lessons taught in our program could never be experienced in a classroom setting.

Program Type: Academic/pre-college enrichment, community service, travel/cultural

Classification: Coeducational, residential, day program

Goals: We offer programs that will enrich our students with the knowledge of a foreign language while teaching them valuable lessons about other cultures and their people.

Focus: Academic/pre-college enrichment, educational exchange, and cultural

Activities Center On: Language, cultural, and academic

Intensity Level: 2

Duration: Varies

Program Offered: Fall, spring, full academic year, summer

Location: Alicante, El Puerto, Madrid, and Salamanca, Spain

Accommodations: Family-stay/host-family, apartment, hotels

Years in Operation: 47

Religious Affiliation: Not relevant

STAFF

Student/Staff Ratio: 5:1

Staff Qualifications: We ensure the quality of our programs and service through our own internal monitoring and through external accreditation. National: In Spain, we have been inspected by CEELE (Certificate for the Quality of Teaching Spanish as a Foreign Language), and our program is "Qualified by the University of Alcal." We also have been accredited by the Cervantes Institute.

PARTICIPANTS

Average Number of Participants: 6,000 (in multiple cities)

For Participants Aged: 17+

The Ideal Candidate: Anyone interested in cultural exchange and education in a foreign language.

Special Requirements for Participation: The ability to travel and adapt to situations abroad.

COSTS

Average Cost: $650

Included in Cost: This cost includes two weeks of 20 group lessons per week and a homestay accommodation in a double room with two meals a day. This fee also includes some excursions and class materials.

Financial Aid Available: Yes

ALMUÑECAR, BARCELONA, GRANADA, MADRID, MARBELLA, AND SALAMANCA (SPAIN)

THE PROGRAM

Description: This program provides language instruction for all levels including cultural immersion in the location of the student's choice.

Specialty: Our programs give the students the opportunity to study abroad in a total immersion course. Lessons taught in our program could never be experienced in a classroom setting.

Program Type: Academic/pre-college enrichment, community service, travel/cultural

Classification: Coeducational, residential, day program

Goals: We offer programs that will enrich our students with the knowledge of a foreign language while teaching them valuable lessons about other cultures and their people.

Focus: Academic/pre-college enrichment, educational exchange, and cultural

Activities Center On: Language, cultural, and academic

Intensity Level: 2

Duration: Varies

Program Offered: Fall, winter intersession/January term, spring, full academic year, summer

Location: Almuñecar, Barcelona, Granada, Madrid, and Marbella, Spain

Accommodations: Dormitory, family-stay/host-family, apartment, hotels, youth hostels

Years in Operation: 8

Religious Affiliation: Not relevant

STAFF

Student/Staff Ratio: 8:1

Staff Qualifications: We are extremely proud of our Spanish teachers. All of them have a degree in Spanish philology and history and are specialized in teaching Spanish as a foreign language. They have all done training courses or have master's degrees in the instruction of Spanish. They make a young and dynamic team with a great experience, which has been recognized by several didactic publications in the research of this field.

PARTICIPANTS

Average Number of Participants: 9,800 (in multiple cities)

For Participants Aged: 15+

The Ideal Candidate: Anyone interested in cultural exchange and education in a foreign language.

Special Requirements for Participation: The ability to travel and adapt to situations abroad.

COSTS

Average Cost: $660

Included in Cost: 20 group lessons per week for two weeks, including a homestay in a double room with two meals a day; study materials; Internet access; and some cultural activities and excursions.

Financial Aid Available: Yes

AVILA (SPAIN)

THE PROGRAM

Description: This program provides language instruction for all levels including cultural immersion in the location of the student's choice.

Specialty: Our programs give the students the opportunity to study abroad in a total immersion course. Lessons taught in our program could never be experienced in a classroom setting.

Program Type: Academic/pre-college enrichment, community service, travel/cultural

Classification: Coeducational, residential, day program

Goals: We offer programs that will enrich our students with the knowledge of a foreign language while teaching them valuable lessons about other cultures and their people.

Focus: Academic/pre-college enrichment, educational exchange, and cultural

Activities Center On: Language, cultural, and academic

Intensity Level: 2

Duration: Varies

Program Offered: Fall, winter intersession/January term, spring, full academic year, summer

Location: Avila, Spain

Accommodations: Family-stay/host-family, hotels, youth hostels

Years in Operation: 14

Religious Affiliation: Not relevant

STAFF

Student/Staff Ratio: 4:1

Staff Qualifications: All teachers hold a university degree in teaching Spanish as a foreign language.

PARTICIPANTS

Average Number of Participants: 1,000 (in multiple cities)

For Participants Aged: 16+

The Ideal Candidate: Anyone interested in cultural exchange and education in a foreign language.

Special Requirements for Participation: The ability to travel and adapt to situations abroad.

COSTS

Average Cost: $550

Included in Cost: 20 group lessons per week for two weeks including a homestay in a double room and two meals a day.

Financial Aid Available: Yes

INTERNSHIP — MADRID (SPAIN)

THE PROGRAM

Description: This program combines four weeks of language program with an internship in a Spanish company. The student may pick the field of work. This program is unpaid.

Specialty: Our program provides the opportunity for young adults to work abroad and gain work experience for their goals here in the United States.

Program Type: Academic/pre-college enrichment, community service, middle school enrichment, music/arts, outdoors/adventure, sports/athletic, travel/cultural

Classification: Coeducational, residential, day program

Goals: Participants should expect to take a four-week Spanish language course (regardless of the level of Spanish at which the student is currently proficient). After the course, the student will be placed with a Spanish company.

Focus: Academic/pre-college enrichment, skill-building, and cultural

Activities Center On: Career exploration, language, and academic

Intensity Level: 3

Duration: Over 8 weeks

Program Offered: Fall, winter intersession/January term, spring, full academic year, summer

Location: Madrid, Spain

Accommodations: Dormitory, family-stay/host-family, apartment, hotels, youth hostels

Years in Operation: 8

Religious Affiliation: Not relevant

STAFF

Student/Staff Ratio: 4:1

Staff Qualifications: All teachers have university degrees in teaching Spanish as a foreign language.

PARTICIPANTS

Average Number of Participants: 100

For Participants Aged: 18+

The Ideal Candidate: Our ideal candidate must: be 18 or older; have finished high school with a degree; have at least an intermediate level of Spanish language ability; and be available to stay in Spain for a minimum of 12 weeks.

Special Requirements for Participation: Students must enroll two months before they would like to leave for Spain. They must purchase insurance to cover them globabally. All students must submit a resume. The minimum stay in Spain must be 12 weeks.

COSTS

Average Cost: $4,400

Included in Cost: 4 weeks of Spanish, 8 weeks of internship, and a 12-week homestay in a single room including two meals a day.

Financial Aid Available: Yes

MALAGA (SPAIN)

THE PROGRAM

Description: This program provides language instruction for all levels including cultural immersion in the location of the student's choice.

Specialty: Our programs give the students the opportunity to study abroad in a total immersion course. Lessons taught in our program could never be experienced in a classroom setting.

Program Type: Academic/pre-college enrichment, community service, travel/cultural

Classification: Coeducational, residential, day program

Goals: We offer programs that will enrich our students with the knowledge of a foreign language while time teaching them valuable lessons about other cultures and their people.

Focus: Academic/pre-college enrichment, educational exchange, and cultural

Activities Center On: Language, cultural, and academic

Intensity Level: 2

Duration: Varies

Program Offered: Fall, winter intersession/January term, spring, full academic year, summer

Location: Malaga, Spain

Accommodations: Dormitory, family-stay/host-family, apartment, hotels, youth hostels

Years in Operation: 32

Religious Affiliation: Not relevant

STAFF

Student/Staff Ratio: 5:1

Staff Qualifications: The quality of our teachers and the system of control and coordination we have developed is crucial in achieving the high scores we regularly gain in the independent inspections of institutions, such as the Instituto Cervantes and EAQUALS. The average length of service of our teachers is more than eight years, guaranteeing a high degree of professional experience and loyalty to the school and its students.

PARTICIPANTS

Average Number of Participants: 4,200 (in multiple cities)

For Participants Aged: 16+

The Ideal Candidate: Anyone interested in cultural exchange and education in a foreign language.

Special Requirements for Participation: The ability to travel and adapt to situations abroad.

COSTS

Average Cost: $760

Included in Cost: 20 group lessons per week for two weeks including a homestay in a double room with two meals a day, study materials, some cultural activities and excursions, Internet access.

Financial Aid Available: Yes

NERJA (SPAIN)

THE PROGRAM

Description: This program provides language instruction for all levels including cultural immersion in the location of the student's choice.

Specialty: Our programs give the students the opportunity to study abroad in a total immersion course. Lessons taught in our program could never be experienced in a classroom setting.

Program Type: Academic/pre-college enrichment, community service, travel/cultural

Classification: Coeducational, residential, day program

Goals: We offer programs that will enrich our students with the knowledge of a foreign language while teaching them valuable lessons about other cultures and their people.

Focus: Academic/pre-college enrichment, educational exchange, and cultural

Activities Center On: Language, cultural, and academic

Intensity Level: 2

Duration: Varies

Program Offered: Fall, winter intersession/January term, spring, full academic year, summer

Location: Nerja, Spain

Accommodations: Dormitory, family-stay/host-family, apartment, hotels, youth hostels

Years in Operation: 23

Religious Affiliation: Not relevant

STAFF

Student/Staff Ratio: 5:1

Staff Qualifications: Our teachers are philologists, specialists in the various courses we offer, who form an enthusiastic, well-coordinated team, qualified to help their students learn in the most effective manner possible.

PARTICIPANTS

Average Number of Participants: 1,400 (in multiple cities)

For Participants Aged: 16+

The Ideal Candidate: Anyone interested in cultural exchange and education in a foreign language.

Special Requirements for Participation: The ability to travel and adapt to situations abroad.

COSTS

Average Cost: $650

Included in Cost: 20 group lessons per week, homestay in a double room with two meals a day, study materials, some cultural activities and excursions, insurance, lectures, parties, and Internet access.

Financial Aid Available: Yes

SAN SEBASTIAN (SPAIN)

THE PROGRAM

Description: This program provides language instruction for all levels including cultural immersion in the location of the student's choice.

Specialty: Our programs give the students the opportunity to study abroad in a total immersion course. Lessons taught in our program could never be experienced in a classroom setting.

Program Type: Academic/pre-college enrichment, community service, travel/cultural

Classification: Coeducational, residential, day program

Goals: We offer programs that will enrich our students with the knowledge of a foreign language while teaching them valuable lessons about other cultures and their people.

Focus: Academic/pre-college enrichment, educational exchange, and cultural

Activities Center On: Language, cultural, and academic

Intensity Level: 2

Duration: Varies

Program Offered: Fall, winter intersession/January term, spring, full academic year, summer

Location: San Sebastian, Spain

Accommodations: Dormitory, family-stay/host-family, tent, apartment, hotels, youth hostels

Years in Operation: 14

Religious Affiliation: Not relevant

STAFF

Student/Staff Ratio: 3:1

Staff Qualifications: All our teachers have university degrees and have been specifically trained to teach Spanish to foreign students, following our methodology. They are great professionals who work as a team; they learn from each other and from their students. They regularly assist in intern training sessions, and we are also present at the important education fairs, to keep up to date.

PARTICIPANTS

Average Number of Participants: 2,000 (in multiple cities)

For Participants Aged: 17+

The Ideal Candidate: Anyone interested in cultural exchange and education in a foreign language.

Special Requirements for Participation: The ability to travel and adapt to situations abroad.

COSTS

Average Cost: $630

Included in Cost: 20 group lessons per week for two weeks, including a homestay in a double room with two meals per day; study materials.

Financial Aid Available: Yes

SEVILLA (SPAIN)

THE PROGRAM

Description: This program provides language instruction for all levels including cultural immersion in the location of the student's choice.

Specialty: Our programs give the students the opportunity to study abroad in a total immersion course. Lessons taught in our program could never be experienced in a classroom setting.

Program Type: Academic/pre-college enrichment, community service, travel/cultural

Classification: Coeducational, residential, day program

Goals: We offer programs that will enrich our students with the knowledge of a foreign language while teaching them valuable lessons about other cultures and their people.

Focus: Academic/pre-college enrichment, educational exchange, and cultural

Activities Center On: Language, cultural, and academic

Intensity Level: 2

Duration: Varies

Program Offered: Fall, winter intersession/January term, spring, full academic year, summer

Location: San Sebastian, Spain

Accommodations: Dormitory, family-stay/host-family, apartment

Years in Operation: 20

Religious Affiliation: Not relevant

STAFF

Student/Staff Ratio: 6:1

Staff Qualifications: More than 20 years experience teaching Spanish and training teachers

PARTICIPANTS

Average Number of Participants: 3,300 (in multiple cities)

For Participants Aged: 17+

The Ideal Candidate: Anyone interested in cultural exchange and education in a foreign language.

Special Requirements for Participation: The ability to travel and adapt to situations abroad.

COSTS

Average Cost: $580

Included in Cost: 20 group lessons plus 2 cultural lessons per week for two weeks, including a homestay in a single room with two meals per day; study materials; some cultural activities and excursions; Internet access.

Financial Aid Available: Yes

SEVILLA (SPAIN)

THE PROGRAM

Description: This program provides language instruction for all levels including cultural immersion in the location of the student's choice.

Specialty: Our programs give the students the opportunity to study abroad in a total immersion course. Lessons taught in our program could never be experienced in a classroom setting.

Program Type: Academic/pre-college enrichment, community service, travel/cultural

Classification: Coeducational, residential, day program

Goals: We offer programs that will enrich our students with the knowledge of a foreign language while teaching them valuable lessons about other cultures and their people.

Focus: Academic/pre-college enrichment, educational exchange, and cultural

Activities Center On: Language, cultural, and academic

Intensity Level: 2

Duration: Varies

Program Offered: Fall, winter intersession/January term, spring, full academic year, summer

Location: Sevilla, Spain

Accommodations: Family-stay/host-family, apartment, hotels, youth hostels

Years in Operation: 2

Religious Affiliation: Not relevant

STAFF

Student/Staff Ratio: 4:1

Staff Qualifications: All of our teachers hold degrees in teaching Spanish as a foreign language.

PARTICIPANTS

Average Number of Participants: 2,200 (in multiple cities)

For Participants Aged: 18+

The Ideal Candidate: Anyone interested in cultural exchange and education in a foreign language.

Special Requirements for Participation: The ability to travel and adapt to situations abroad.

COSTS

Average Cost: $715

Included in Cost: 20 group lessons plus 5 culture lessons per week for two weeks, including a homestay in a double room with two meals a day; study materials.

Financial Aid Available: Yes

VALENCIA (SPAIN)

THE PROGRAM

Description: This program provides language instruction for all levels including cultural immersion in the location of the student's choice.

Specialty: Our programs give the students the opportunity to study abroad in a total immersion course. Lessons taught in our program could never be experienced in a classroom setting.

Program Type: Academic/pre-college enrichment, community service, travel/cultural

Classification: Coeducational, residential, day program

Goals: We offer programs that will enrich our students with the knowledge of a foreign language while teaching them valuable lessons about other cultures and their people.

Focus: Academic/pre-college enrichment, educational exchange, and cultural

Activities Center On: Language, cultural, and academic

Intensity Level: 2

Duration: Varies

Program Offered: Fall, winter intersession/January term, spring, full academic year, summer

Location: Valencia, Spain

Accommodations: Dormitory, family-stay/host-family, apartment, hotels, youth hostels

Years in Operation: 2

Religious Affiliation: Not relevant

STAFF

Student/Staff Ratio: 4:1

Staff Qualifications: All teachers hold university degrees in teaching Spanish as a foreign language.

PARTICIPANTS

Average Number of Participants: 1,200 (in multiple cities)

For Participants Aged: 18+

The Ideal Candidate: Anyone interested in cultural exchange and education in a foreign language.

Special Requirements for Participation: The ability to travel and adapt to situations abroad.

COSTS

Average Cost: $740

Included in Cost: 20 group lessons per week for two weeks, including homestay in a double room with two meals a day; study materials.

Financial Aid Available: Yes

LAW PREVIEW

Law school preparatory program offered at law schools around the county. We provide entering students with the knowledge and skills they need to excel in law school.

Years in Operation: 6

Religious Affiliation: Not relevant

Price Range of Programs: $875–$1,275

For More Information:
Contact: Donald Macaulay, President & Founder
42 Tremont Street, Suite 11
Duxbury, NY 02332
Phone: 888-773-7968
Fax: 781-934-2320
Email: mac@lawpreview.com
Website: www.lawpreview.com

LAW PREVIEW LAW SCHOOL PREP COURSE

THE PROGRAM

Description: Law Preview's law school preparatory program provides entering law students with overviews of each of the first-year subjects taught by some of the country's best law school professors. Law Preview also teaches proven success tactics that help students conquer law school.

Specialty: Followup advice and support for particpants during their academic careers.

Program Type: Academic/pre-college enrichment

Classification: Coeducational; day program

Goals: Students learn the fundemental themes and doctrine studied in the first year of law school. Instructors also teach the study and exam-taking skills necessary for success in law school.

Focus: Academic/pre-college enrichment

Activities Center On: Academic, study skills, and other

Intensity Level: 4

Duration: 1–2 weeks

Program Offered: Summer

Location: California, Florida, Illinois, Massachusetts, New York, Pennsylvania, Texas, and Washington, D.C., United States

Accommodations: Hotels

Years in Operation: 6

Religious Affiliation: Not relevant

STAFF

Student/Staff Ratio: 50:1

Staff Qualifications: Practicing attorneys and accomplished law school professors.

PARTICIPANTS

Average Number of Participants: 100

The Ideal Candidate: Students who are entering or considering law school.

Special Requirements for Participation: None.

COSTS

Average Cost: $1,000

Included in Cost: 64 hours of classroom instruction and all course materials.

Financial Aid Available: Yes

LEADAMERICA

LeadAmerica's mission is to transform our world's next generation of young leaders by inspiring, educating, and instilling in them ethical and principled leadership values, attitudes, and skills. The question is not whether these students will lead, but how will they lead—what values and principles they will call upon to make important decisions and choices. LeadAmerica presents conferences for middle school and high school students. These conferences are presented by a distinguished faculty and combine challenging academics with hands-on experiential learning. Students learn to think on their feet, discuss and debate complex global issues and make critical split-second decisions.

Years in Operation: 15

Price Range of Programs: $1,095–$1,895

For More Information:
Contact: Program Director
7040 West Palmetto Park Road, #4-293
Boca Raton, FL 33433
Phone: 561-368-8085
Email: csalamone@lead-america.org
Website: www.lead-america.org

LeadAmerica

The Program

Description: LeadAmerica's mission is to transform our world's next generation of young leaders by inspiring and instilling in them ethical and principled leadership values, attitudes and skills. Conferences for high school (and middle school) students are on topics including legislative process, defense and intelligence, international diplomacy, law, medicine and business and entrepreneurship, are presented by a distinguished faculty and combine challenging academics with hands-on experiential learning.

Specialty: LeadAmerica's distinguished faculty combines challenging academics with hands-on experiential learning. Students learn to think on their feet, debate complex issues and make critical split-second decisions. Earn up to two hours of college credit.

Program Type: Academic/pre-college enrichment

Classification: Coeducational; residential

Goals: A LeadAmerica conference is a truly unique experience in leadership. Within the context of their chosen academic focus, students explore what leadership is all about and how being an effective leader will help them achieve their goals and dreams!

Focus: Special interest/other, academic/pre-college enrichment, and sports/athletic

Activities Center On: Academic/pre-college enrichment, career exploration, and other

Intensity Level: 4

Duration: Less than 1 week, 1–2 weeks

Program Offered: Spring, summer

Location: Washington, D.C.; Boston; Chicago; California, Illinois, Massachusetts, and Washington, D.C., United States

Accommodations: Dormitory, hotels

Years in Operation: 15

Staff

Student/Staff Ratio: 12:1

Staff Qualifications: The faculty of LeadAmerica conferences are university and graduate school professors and practicing professionals drawn from each field of study. They are carefully selected to ensure that our students receive the highest quality educational experience. Their role is to bring the core curriculum to life and stimulate thinking and discussion. Our faculty are involved in all aspects of the conference experience, giving students a chance to spend time with them outside the classroom.

Participants

Average Number of Participants: 160

For Participants Aged: 14–18

The Ideal Candidate: Admission to LeadAmerica conferences is open to students who have completed grades 9, 10, 11 or 12, who have demonstrated academic excellence and leadership potential. Students must have a minimum "B" average.

Costs

Average Cost: $1,495

Included in Cost: Tuition includes program fees, housing, on-campus meals, educational materials, activities and field trips.

Financial Aid Available? Yes

Congressional Student Leadership Conference

The Program

Description: CSLC's mission is to transform our world's next generation of young leaders by inspiring and instilling in them ethical and principled leadership values, attitudes and skills. Conferences for high school students are offered on topics including legislative process, defense and intelligence, international diplomacy, law, medicine and business and entrepreneurship.

Specialty: CSLC's distinguished faculty combines challenging academics with hands-on experiential learning. Students learn to think on their fee, debate complex issues and make critical split-second decisions.

Program Type: Academic/pre-college enrichment

Classification: Coeducational; Residential

Goals: The CSLC is a truly unique experience in leadership. Within the context of their chosen academic focus, students explore what leadership is all about and how being an effective leader will help them achieve their goals and dreams.

Focus: Special interest/other, academic/pre-college enrichment, and sports/athletic

Activities Center On: Academic/pre-college enrichment, career exploration, and other

Intensity Level: 4

Duration: Less than 1 week, 1–2 weeks

Program Offered: Spring, summer

Location: Washington, D.C.; Boston; Chicago; California, Illinois, Massachusetts, and Washington, D.C., United States

Accommodations: Dormitory, hotels

Years in Operation: 15

Staff

Student/Staff Ratio: 12:1

Staff Qualifications: The faculty of CSLC conferences are university and graduate school professors and practicing professionals drawn from each field of study. They are carefully selected to ensure that our students receive the highest quality educational experience.

Participants

Average Number of Participants: 160

For Participants Aged: 14–18

The Ideal Candidate: Admission to the CSLC is selective and is open to students who have a minimum B average, completed grades 9, 10, 11 or 12, and have demonstrated academic excellence and leadership potential. Community involvement.

COSTS

Average Cost: $1,495

Included in Cost: Tuition includes program fees, housing, on-campus meals, educational materials, activities and field trips.

Financial Aid Available? Yes

LEARNING PROGRAMS INTERNATIONAL

LPI provides academically challenging and culturally thorough four- and five-week study abroad programs for high school students. LPI works closely with fully accredited foreign universities and with LPI residential staff in each program location to provide tutoring services, intercambio opportunities, and numerous possibilities for improving class and language performance.

Years in Operation: 13

Religious Affiliation: Not relevant

Price Range of Programs: $2,500–$4,000

For More Information:
Contact: Michelle McRaney, Program Director
901 West 24th Street
Austin, TX 78705
Phone: 800-259-4439
Fax: 512-480-8866
Email: lpi@studiesabroad.com
Website: www.lpiabroad.com

LEARNING PROGRAMS INTERNATIONAL (COSTA RICA)

THE PROGRAM

Description: Each academic program is four weeks long. Students will earn college credit. Students are required to take a language placement exam upon arrival into the program city. Once the language level is determined, students will attend four hours of Spanish language instruction each day, Monday through Friday. The average class size is 15 students.

Specialty: We take each student's requests very seriously, and we are able to be flexible in order to meet the student's specific needs.

Program Type: Academic/pre-college enrichment, travel/cultural

Classification: Coeducational, residential

Goals: All LPI programs emphasize language acquisition and cultural immersion for students at various levels of proficiency.

Focus: Academic/pre-college enrichment, cultural, and skill-building

Activities Center On: Language, cultural, and travel

Intensity Level: 3

Duration: 2–4 weeks

Program Offered: Summer

Location: San José, Costa Rica

Accommodations: Family-stay/host-family

Years in Operation: 3

Religious Affiliation: Not relevant

STAFF

Student/Staff Ratio: 10:1

PARTICIPANTS

Average Number of Participants: 15

For Participants Aged: 16–18

Special Requirements for Participation: You must be 16 years of age by the program start date and have completed at least two years of high school Spanish or the equivalent. Students applying for the Guanajuato Program may be 15 years of age but must have completed at least one year of high school.

COSTS

Average Cost: $2,500

Included in Cost: Application fee, college credits, tuition, resident director, tutorial assistance, cultural excursions, overnight excursions, room and board, airport reception, medical insurance, entrance fees, Internet access.

Financial Aid Available: No

LEARNING PROGRAMS INTERNATIONAL (SPAIN)

THE PROGRAM

Description: Each academic program is four weeks long. Students will earn college credit. Students are required to take a language placement exam upon arrival into the program city. Once the language level is determined, students will attend four hours of Spanish language instruction each day, Monday through Friday. The average class size is 15 students.

Specialty: We take each student's requests very seriously, and we are able to be flexible in order to meet the student's specific needs.

Program Type: Academic/pre-college enrichment

Classification: Coeducational, residential

Goals: All LPI programs emphasize language acquisition and cultural immersion for students at various levels of proficiency.

Focus: Academic/pre-college enrichment, cultural, and skill-building

Activities Center On: Language, cultural, and travel

Intensity Level: 3

Duration: 2–4 weeks

Program Offered: Summer

Location: Salamanca or Santander, Spain

Accommodations: Family-stay/host-family

Years in Operation: 14

Religious Affiliation: Not relevant

STAFF

Student/Staff Ratio: 10:1

PARTICIPANTS

Average Number of Participants: 15

For Participants Aged: 16–18

Special Requirements for Participation: You must be 16 years of age by the program start date and have completed at least two years of high school Spanish or the equivalent. Students applying for the Guanajuato program may be 15 years of age but must have completed at least one year of high school.

COSTS

Average Cost: $2,500

Included in Cost: Application fee, college credits, tuition, resident director, tutorial assistance, cultural excursions, overnight excursions, room and board, airport reception, medical insurance, entrance fees, Internet access.

Financial Aid Available: No

LONGACRE EXPEDITIONS

Adventure travel for 11- to 19-year-olds in eastern and western North America, Hawaii, and the Virgin Islands. Longacre's challenging outdoor programs place equal emphasis on physical accomplishment and emotional growth. Each 14- to 28-day expedition is co-ed and grouped by age, and offers a different mix of activities. Kids backpack, bike, canoe, ice climb, kayak, mountain bike, mountaineer, rock climb, sail, sandboard, scuba dive, sea kayak, ski, snorkel, snowboard, surf, surf-kayak, whale watch, whitewater raft, and windsurf in world-class settings. They kayak amidst rumbling glaciers; get up close and personal with volcanoes; perform community service in tropical settings; and come face to face with moose, porpoise, or sea lions.

Years in Operation: 23

Religious Affiliation: Not relevant

Price Range of Programs: $2,000–$4,800

For More Information:
  Contact: Meredith Schuler, Director
         4030 Middle Range Road
         Newport, PA 17074
  Phone: 717-567-6790
  Fax: 717-567-3955
  Email: Merry@longacreexpeditions.com
  Website: www.longacreexpeditions.com

BELIZE

THE PROGRAM

Description: Adventure travel for teenagers in a developing country.

Specialty: As important as the physically challenging activities are our evening group meetings. Group exercises promote feelings-level communication, speaking and listening skills, increased trust, and significant bonds within the group.

Program Type: Community service, outdoors/adventure, travel/cultural

Classification: Coeducational, residential

Goals: Participants should expect to form significant friendships with their trip mates. Primitive settings, challenging activities, and group meetings that promote feelings-level communications foster amazing interpersonal bonds and individual growth. Kids learn a variety of outdoor and leadership skills, as well as how to function effectively in a group.

Focus: Leadership/teamwork, community service, and skill-building

Activities Center On: Diving, volunteer, and backpacking

Intensity Level: 4

Duration: 2–4 weeks

Program Offered: Summer

Location: Belize

Accommodations: Tent

Years in Operation: 14

Religious Affiliation: Not relevant

STAFF

Student/Staff Ratio: 12:2

Staff Qualifications: Staff are age 21 and over, and have experience working with teenagers and competence in a wide range of outdoor activities. In addition, they must hold current certifications in Wilderness First Responder, CPR, lifeguard training, and SCUBA; be in very good physical condition; and embrace our trip-leading philosophy and commitment to interpersonal communication.

PARTICIPANTS

Average Number of Participants: 12

For Participants Aged: 15–18

The Ideal Candidate: The ideal candidate brings an enthusiasm for the activities and a desire to work within the group; is in good physical condition; and has an openness to new people, places, and ideas. No experience in the activities is necessary.

Special Requirements for Participation: Any candidate who is physically capable of handling the rigors of the trip and emotionally comfortable with the challenge of group living may apply. Kids who are unable to enthusiastically engage in the activities and group responsibilities probably should not join.

COSTS

Average Cost: $3,900

Included in Cost: Tuition does not include airfare, personal equipment, tuition refund or medical insurance, or spending money.

Financial Aid Available: No

HAWAII

THE PROGRAM

Description: Adventure travel for teenagers on Kauai and the Big Island.

Specialty: As important as the physically challenging activities are our evening group meetings. Group exercises promote feelings-level communication, speaking and listening skills, increased trust, and significant bonds within the group.

Program Type: Community service, outdoors/adventure, travel/cultural

Classification: Coeducational, residential

Goals: Participants should expect to form significant friendships with their trip mates. Primitive settings, challenging activities, and group meetings that promote feelings-level communications foster amazing interpersonal bonds and individual growth. Kids learn a variety of outdoor and leadership skills, as well as how to function effectively in a group.

Focus: Leadership/teamwork, skill-building, and community service

Activities Center On: Diving, backpacking, and volunteer

Intensity Level: 3

Duration: 2–4 weeks

Program Offered: Summer

Location: Hawaii

Accommodations: Tent

Years in Operation: 6

Religious Affiliation: Not relevant

STAFF

Student/Staff Ratio: 12:2

Staff Qualifications: Staff are age 21 and over, and have experience working with teenagers and competence in a wide range of outdoor activities. In addition, they must hold current certifications in Wilderness First Responder, CPR, lifeguard training, and SCUBA; be in very good physical condition; and embrace our trip-leading philosophy and commitment to interpersonal communication.

PARTICIPANTS

Average Number of Participants: 12

For Participants Aged: 15–18

The Ideal Candidate: The ideal candidate brings an enthusiasm for the activities and a desire to work within the group; is in good physical condition; and has an openness to new people, places, and ideas. No experience in the activities is necessary.

Special Requirements for Participation: Any candidate who is physically capable of handling the rigors of the trip and emotionally comfortable with the challenge of group living may apply. Kids who are unable to enthusiastically engage in the activities and group responsibilities probably should not join.

COSTS

Average Cost: $4,500

Included in Cost: Tuition does not include airfare, personal equipment, tuition refund or medical insurance, or spending money.

Financial Aid Available: No

LEADERSHIP TRAINING

THE PROGRAM

Description: Leadership and adventure-based outdoor skills in spectacular Rocky Mountain settings.

Specialty: As important as the physically challenging activities are our evening group meetings. Group exercises promote feelings-level communication, speaking and listening skills, increased trust, and significant bonds within the group.

Program Type: Outdoors/adventure

Classification: Coeducational, residential

Goals: Participants should expect to form significant friendships with their trip mates. Primitive settings, challenging activities, and group meetings that promote feelings-level communications foster amazing interpersonal bonds and individual growth. Kids learn a variety of outdoor and leadership skills, as well as how to function effectively in a group.

Focus: Leadership/teamwork, skill-building, and travel

Activities Center On: Backpacking, kayaking, and wilderness

Intensity Level: 4

Duration: 2–4 weeks

Program Offered: Summer

Location: Colorado

Accommodations: Tent

Years in Operation: 15

Religious Affiliation: Not relevant

STAFF

Student/Staff Ratio: 12:3

Staff Qualifications: Staff are age 21 and over, and have experience working with teenagers and competence in a wide range of outdoor activities. In addition, they must hold current certifications in Wilderness First Responder, CPR, lifeguard training, and SCUBA; be in very good physical condition; and embrace our trip-leading philosophy and commitment to interpersonal communication.

PARTICIPANTS

Average Number of Participants: 12

For Participants Aged: 17–19

The Ideal Candidate: Extra application, essay, and references are necessary. Bring an enthusiasm for the activities, a desire to work within the group, and be in good physical condition. Previous wilderness experience is necessary.

Special Requirements for Participation: Candidates must have previous experience in wilderness settings, and be physically capable of handling the rigors of the trip and emotionally comfortable with the challenge of group living. Participants should bring a maturity and sense of responsibility to the equation.

COSTS

Average Cost: $4,200

Included in Cost: Tuition does not include airfare, personal equipment, tuition refund or medical insurance, or spending money.

Financial Aid Available: No

SEA TO SKY

THE PROGRAM

Description: Outdoor adventure in spectacular settings in Washington and British Columbia.

Specialty: As important as the physically challenging activities are our evening group meetings. Group exercises promote feelings-level communication, speaking and listening skills, increased trust, and significant bonds within the group.

Program Type: Outdoors/adventure, travel/cultural

Classification: Coeducational, residential

Goals: Participants should expect to form significant friendships with their trip mates. Primitive settings, challenging activities, and group meetings that promote feelings-level communications foster amazing interpersonal bonds and individual growth. Kids learn a variety of outdoor and leadership skills, as well as how to function effectively in a group.

Focus: Leadership/teamwork, skill-building, and travel

Activities Center On: Kayaking, rafting, and outdoors and adventure

Intensity Level: 4

Duration: 4–6 weeks

Program Offered: Summer

Location: Canada; Oregon; Washington

Accommodations: Tent

Years in Operation: 2

Religious Affiliation: Not relevant

STAFF

Student/Staff Ratio: 14:3

Staff Qualifications: Staff are age 21 and over, and have expe-

rience working with teenagers and competence in a wide range of outdoor activities. In addition, they must hold current certifications in Wilderness First Responder, CPR, lifeguard training, and SCUBA; be in very good physical condition; and embrace our trip-leading philosophy and commitment to interpersonal communication.

PARTICIPANTS

Average Number of Participants: 14

For Participants Aged: 14–17

The Ideal Candidate: The ideal candidate brings an enthusiasm for the activities and a desire to work within the group; is in good physical condition; and has an openness to new people, places, and ideas. No experience in the activities is necessary.

Special Requirements for Participation: Any candidate who is physically capable of handling the rigors of the trip and emotionally comfortable with the challenge of group living may apply. Kids who are unable to enthusiastically engage in the activities and group responsibilities should not join.

COSTS

Average Cost: $4,050

Included in Cost: Tuition does not include airfare, personal equipment, tuition refund or medical insurance, or spending money.

Financial Aid Available: No

MARBRIDGE FOUNDATION, INC.

Marbridge offers individualized residential care, education, and training to adults with various cognitive challenges. At Marbridge, residents enjoy a high quality of life in a safe, loving community where they may prosper, contribute, and reach their maximum potential.

Years in Operation: 50

Religious Affiliation: Not relevant

For More Information:
　　Contact: Will Hoermann, Director of Admissions
　　　　　　2310 Bliss Spillar Road
　　　　　　PO Box 2250
　　　　　　Manchaca, TX 78652
　　Phone: 512-282-1144
　　Fax: 512-282-3723
　　Email: wchoermann@marbridge.org
　　Website: www.marbridge.org

MARBRIDGE SUMMER CAMP

THE PROGRAM

Description: Marbridge reaches out to young adults with cognitive challenges who: are between the ages of 16 and 30 years old; want the excitement and fun of a camp in a safe, nurturing environment; need a helping hand when adapting to new tasks; and wish to begin the transition from home to a more independent lifestyle.

Specialty: Activities are adapted to meet the interests, skills, and ages of our campers. Our dedicated staff will positively reinforce the progress that each individual makes in independent living tasks.

Classification: Coeducational, residential

Goals: We hope that after our camp experience, young people will be better equipped to make successful transitions from high school or home settings to a more independent lifestyle.

Focus: Skill-building

Activities Center On: Academic, outdoors/adventure, and music/arts

Intensity Level: 1

Duration: Less than 1 week

Program Offered: Summer

Location: Manchaca, Texas

Accommodations: Bunk/cabin

Years in Operation: 4

Religious Affiliation: Not relevant

STAFF

Student/Staff Ratio: 8:3

Staff Qualifications: Camp counselors must have a high school diploma or GED. Some college credit is preferred, especially in a related field of study.

PARTICIPANTS

Average Number of Participants: 8

For Participants Aged: 16–30

The Ideal Candidate: 16–30 years of age; primary diagnosis of developmental disability or cognitive challenge; independent in activities of daily living and/or in need of verbal cueing; able to ambulate and transfer independently.

Special Requirements for Participation: None.

COSTS

Average Cost: $450

Included in Cost: $150 of the program cost is a nonrefundable reservation/application processing fee.

Financial Aid Available: No

MICHIGAN STATE UNIVERSITY

The High School Engineering Institute is a six-day summer residential program designed to encourage students to consider engineering as a career option. Students are exposed to eight disciplines within the field of engineering in order that they may better understand the many career pathways that are available. Participants delve into such areas as biosystems, civil, chemical, biomedical, mechanical, and electrical engineering; computer science; and materials science and mechan-

ics. Students with interests in science and math are especially encouraged to attend. The instructional staff is composed of faculty members and graduate assistants at Michigan State University.

Years in Operation: 41

Religious Affiliation: Not relevant

Price Range of Programs: $400–$450

For More Information:
Contact: Jennifer Hodges, Director
1410 Engineering Building
East Lansing, MI 48824
Phone: 517-355-6616
Fax: 517-432-1356
Email: egradv@egr.msu.edu
Website: www.egr.msu.edu/egr/programs/bachelors/hsei

HIGH SCHOOL ENGINEERING INSTITUTE

THE PROGRAM

Description: This is a six-day summer residential program designed to encourage students to consider engineering as a career option. Students are exposed to eight disciplines within the field of engineering so that they may better understand the many career pathways that are available. Participants delve into such areas as biosystems, civil, chemical, biomedical, mechanical, and electrical engineering; computer science; and materials science and mechanics.

Specialty: Overview of many areas of engineering in a variety of environments (classroom, lab, factory tours, etc.)

Program Type: Academic/pre-college enrichment

Classification: Coeducational, residential

Goals: Overview of eight different areas of engineering.

Focus: Academic/pre-college enrichment

Activities Center On: Career exploration and academic

Intensity Level: 3

Duration: Less than 1 week

Program Offered: Summer

Location: East Lansing, Michigan

Accommodations: Dormitory

Years in Operation: 41

Religious Affiliation: Not relevant

STAFF

Student/Staff Ratio: 4:1

Staff Qualifications: 8 full-time engineering faculty, 8–14 graduate assistants, 4–6 undergraduate assistants, 1 full-time student affairs staff member.

PARTICIPANTS

Average Number of Participants: 100

For Participants Aged: 15–18

The Ideal Candidate: Sophomore or junior in high school

with an interest in math, science, and/or engineering, and at least a 3.2 GPA.

Special Requirements for Participation: High school transcript and letter of recommendation.

COSTS

Average Cost: $435

Included in Cost: Housing, meals, educational materials, and transporation to institute events.

Financial Aid Available: Yes

MICHIGAN TECHNOLOGICAL UNIVERSITY

We offer educational excellence in beautiful Upper Michigan. We're famous for educating undergraduate and graduate engineers, scientists, business leaders, foresters, technologists, and communicators since 1885.

Years in Operation: 31

Religious Affiliation: Not relevant

Price Range of Programs: $0–$720

For More Information:
Contact: John Lehman, Youth Programs Coordinator
1400 Townsend Drive
Houghton, MI 49931
Phone: 906-487-2219
Fax: 906-487-3101
Email: yp@mtu.edu
Website: youthprograms.mtu.edu

EXPLORATIONS IN ENGINEERING

THE PROGRAM

Description: The Explorations in Engineering (EIE) Workshop provides young minority and/or economically disadvantaged men and women the opportunity to investigate careers in engineering and science. Through an intensive one-week residential workshop, the participants explore several areas of engineering and science. Each session includes a hands-on laboratory experience that demonstrates the kinds of information each engineering and science area uses.

Program Type: Academic/pre-college enrichment

Classification: Coeducational, residential

Goals: Academic and career exploration

Focus: Academic/pre-college enrichment

Activities Center On: Academic

Intensity Level: 4

Duration: 1–2 weeks

Program Offered: Summer

Location: Houghton, Michigan

Accommodations: Dormitory

Years in Operation: 12

Religious Affiliation: Not relevant

STAFF

Student/Staff Ratio: 10:1

Staff Qualifications: Sessions are led by practicing minority engineers, role-model speakers from industry, and university faculty.

PARTICIPANTS

Average Number of Participants: 120

For Participants Aged: 14–18

The Ideal Candidate: Academically talented students from educationally/economically disadvantaged backgrounds.

Special Requirements for Participation: None.

COSTS

Average Cost: $50

Included in Cost: $50 registration fee. Selected students receive a $650 scholarship covering the remaining tuition and fees.

Financial Aid Available: No

WOMEN IN ENGINEERING WORKSHOPS

THE PROGRAM

Description: The Women in Engineering Workshop provides young women the opportunity to investigate careers in engineering and science. Through an intensive one-week residential workshop, participants explore several areas of engineering and science.

Specialty: One of the most established pre-college programs in the country; hosted by a nationally recognized research university.

Program Type: Academic/pre-college enrichment

Classification: Single-sex, female; residential

Goals: Academic and career exploration. Practicing women engineers, role-model speakers, and university faculty lead labs and informational sessions. Each session includes a hands-on laboratory experience demonstrating information and equipment each engineering and science area uses. Throughout the week, students participate in a group engineering project.

Focus: Academic/pre-college enrichment

Activities Center On: Academic and career exploration

Intensity Level: 4

Duration: 1–2 weeks

Program Offered: Summer

Location: Houghton, Michigan

Accommodations: Dormitory

Years in Operation: 28

Religious Affiliation: Not relevant

STAFF

Student/Staff Ratio: 10:1

Staff Qualifications: Instructors are faculty members, graduate students, and community professionals. Undergraduate and graduate students serve as counselor/mentors.

PARTICIPANTS

Average Number of Participants: 120

For Participants Aged: 14–18

The Ideal Candidate: Talented and motivated high school female students.

Special Requirements for Participation: None.

COSTS

Average Cost: $50

Included in Cost: $50 application fee. Selected participants receive a $650 scholarship covering the rest of tuition and fees.

Financial Aid Available: No

MILLERSVILLE UNIVERSITY OF PENNSYLVANIA

Religious Affiliation: Not relevant

For More Information:
Contact: Celica Milovanovic, Chair, Department of Foreign Languages
PO Box 1002
Millersville, PA 17551
Phone: 717-872-3526
Fax: 717-871-2482
Email: camps@millersville.edu
Website: www.millersville.edu/~forlang

FOREIGN LANGUAGE SUMMER INSTITUTES AND WORKSHOPS

THE PROGRAM

Description: Graduate courses and workshops in French, German, and Spanish, based on total immersion (no English) principle, leading to an MA degree; can be taken for undergraduate credit too, or simply in order to improve one's language proficiency.

Specialty: The total immersion (no English) principle, as well as the social and cultural activities that are part of the program.

Program Type: Academic/pre-college enrichment

Classification: Coeducational, residential

Goals: To learn a great deal about the language, culture, history, literature, and art of the country/region being studied; a marked progress in their language proficiency.

Focus: Academic/pre-college enrichment and cultural

Activities Center On: Academic, cultural, and humanities

Intensity Level: 4

Duration: 4–6 weeks

Program Offered: Summer

Location: Millersville, Pennsylvania (near Lancaster)

Accommodations: Dormitory

Years in Operation: 36

Religious Affiliation: Not relevant

STAFF

Student/Staff Ratio: 10:1

Staff Qualifications: College teachers with PhD degrees; native speakers of French, German, or Spanish.

PARTICIPANTS

Average Number of Participants: 15

For Participants Aged: 18–65

The Ideal Candidate: A foreign language teacher (K–12) who wishes to earn an MA degree or continuing education credit, or simply to maintain language proficiency.

Special Requirements for Participation: Undergraduate degree, or substantial knowledge of the language in question.

COSTS

Average Cost: $876

Included in Cost: $876 is tuition only (for a 3-credit course); room and board is an additional $250.

Financial Aid Available: Yes

SUMMER LANGUAGE CAMPS FOR HIGH SCHOOL STUDENTS

THE PROGRAM

Description: High school students who are taking French, German, or Spanish can sharpen their language skills in a way that is both fun and educational, in a total language immersion program. The program consists of a week of classes, workshops, and recreational activities held at Millersville University, located in the center of the Lancaster County/Amish Country in Pennsylvania.

Specialty: The total immersion concept—that is, the "no-English-spoken-at-any-time" rule—applies to all participants.

Program Type: Academic/pre-college enrichment, middle school enrichment

Classification: Coeducational, residential

Goals: Increased ability to communicate in the target language (French, German, or Spanish).

Focus: Academic/pre-college enrichment and cultural

Activities Center On: Language and cultural

Intensity Level: 1

Duration: 1–2 weeks

Program Offered: Summer

Location: Millersville (near Lancaster), Pennsylvania

Accommodations: Dormitory

Years in Operation: 22

Religious Affiliation: Not relevant

STAFF

Student/Staff Ratio: 7:1

Staff Qualifications: Certified Pennsylvania teachers.

PARTICIPANTS

Average Number of Participants: 30

For Participants Aged: 15–18

The Ideal Candidate: A high school student who has had at least two years of language and is eager to improve his speaking ability.

Special Requirements for Participation: Recommendation from the high school teacher.

COSTS

Average Cost: $350

Included in Cost: Application fee, room and board, all activities.

Financial Aid Available: Yes

MISSISSIPPI UNIVERSITY FOR WOMEN

Four-year liberal arts university.

Years in Operation: 118

Religious Affiliation: Not relevant

Price Range of Programs: $0

For More Information:
  Contact: Robert W. Seney, Program Director
       PO Box W-129
       Columbus, MS 39701
  Phone: 601-329-7110
  Fax: 601-329-8515
  Email: bseney@muw.edu
  Website: www.muw.edu/govschool

MISSISSIPPI GOVERNOR'S SCHOOL

THE PROGRAM

Description: Three-week summer residential program open to academically gifted rising high school juniors and seniors who are residents of Mississippi; 3 hours of college credit if documented ACT of 25 or above.

Specialty: Full scholarship—tuition plus room and board—for those selected to attend; rigorous application process

Program Type: Academic/pre-college enrichment

Classification: Coeducational, residential

Goals: Academic challenge in selected courses with a focus on leadership, creativity, and community service.

Focus: Academic/pre-college enrichment, leadership/teamwork, and community service

Activities Center On: Academic and humanities

Intensity Level: 4

Duration: 2–4 weeks

Program Offered: Summer

Location: Columbus, Mississippi

Accommodations: Dormitory

Years in Operation: 23

Religious Affiliation: Not relevant

STAFF

Student/Staff Ratio: 12:1

Staff Qualifications: Instructors must have a master's degree or above. Most are college professors.

PARTICIPANTS

Average Number of Participants: 130

For Participants Aged: 15–20

The Ideal Candidate: Academically gifted rising junior or senior with a minimum ACT score of 25.

Special Requirements for Participation: Resident of Mississippi.

COSTS

Average Cost: $0

Included in Cost: Full scholarship for students who are selected to attend.

Financial Aid Available: No

NATIONAL OUTDOOR LEADERSHIP SCHOOL (NOLS)

The National Outdoor Leadership School, a nonprofit organization, is the leader in wilderness education and offers courses in the world's most spectacular classrooms. From two weeks to three months, NOLS offers over 65 different course types in skill areas including backpacking, mountaineering, sea kayaking, canoeing, skiing, caving, horsepacking, and rock climbing. Skills, leadership, and the environment: Become an outdoor leader at NOLS.

Years in Operation: 38

Religious Affiliation: Not relevant

Price Range of Programs: $2,500–$10,000

For More Information:
  Contact: Bruce Palmer, Director of Admission
             284 Lincoln Street
             Lander, WY 82520
  Phone: 800-710-6657
  Fax: 307-332-1220
  Email: admissions@nols.edu
  Website: www.nols.edu

12-Day Whitewater River Expedition

The Program

Description: The 12-day course staged out of NOLS' river base in Vernal, Utah, offers a thorough introduction to river travel skills. Students learn to kayak, captain a paddle raft, and row an oar rig as they negotiate the breathtaking canyons of the West's wild Green River. With a student/instructor ratio of 4:1, the learning will come fast with a lot of opportunity for personal attention. The 12-day course is a fast-paced program in Utah's Desolation Canyon.

Specialty: NOLS is the only school that focuses exclusively on leadership, wilderness skills, and the environment. The experience and training of our instructors leads the outdoor education industry.

Program Type: Outdoors/adventure

Classification: Coeducational, residential

Goals: Students should expect to learn wilderness skills—navigation, leave-no-trace outdoor ethics, and first aid. They will develop leadership by actually leading in the backcountry. Students will also learn about the environments in which they are traveling—flora, fauna, geology, and weather.

Focus: Leadership/teamwork, skill-building, and travel

Activities Center On: Boating, kayaking, and rafting

Intensity Level: 4

Duration: 1–2 weeks

Program Offered: Summer

Location: Vernal, Utah

Accommodations: Tent

Religious Affiliation: Not relevant

Staff

Student/Staff Ratio: 4:1

Staff Qualifications: All NOLS instructors complete the 35-day NOLS instructor course. All possess a minimum of Wilderness First Responder certification. Average age is 31. Typical NOLS instructor has worked for the school five years.

Participants

For Participants Aged: 16–70

The Ideal Candidate: NOLS students are motivated to learn. They are adventurous and in good physical condition. NOLS students are successful individuals who come to NOLS for our unique hands-on approach to education.

Special Requirements for Participation: Good physical condition.

Costs

Average Cost: $2,050

Included in Cost: The tuition covers instruction, group gear, food, and lodging. Additional expenses will include transportation to Lander, Wyoming, and personal gear. NOLS rents personal gear.

Financial Aid Available: Yes

16-Day Whitewater River Expedition

The Program

Description: The 16-day course staged out of NOLS' river base in Vernal, Utah, offers a thorough introduction to river travel skills. Students learn to kayak, captain a paddle raft, and row an oar rig as they negotiate the breathtaking canyons of the West's wild Green River. With a student/instructor ratio of 4:1, the learning comes quickly. The 16-day course allows additonal time to build proficiency and takes place in both Utah's Desolation Canyon and Colorado's Lodore Canyon.

Specialty: NOLS is the only school that focuses exclusively on leadership, wilderness skills, and the environment. The experience and training of our instructors leads the outdoor education industry.

Program Type: Outdoors/adventure

Classification: Coeducational, residential

Goals: Students should expect to learn wilderness skills—navigation, leave-no-trace outdoor ethics, and first aid. They will develop leadership by actually leading in the backcountry. Students will also learn about the environments in which they are traveling—flora, fauna, geology, and weather.

Focus: Leadership/teamwork, skill-building, and travel

Activities Center On: Boating, kayaking, and rafting

Intensity Level: 4

Duration: 1–2 weeks

Program Offered: Summer

Location: Vernal, Utah

Accommodations: Tent

Religious Affiliation: Not relevant

Staff

Student/Staff Ratio: 4:1

Staff Qualifications: All NOLS instructors complete the 35-

day NOLS instructor course. All possess a minimum of Wilderness First Responder certification. Average age is 31. Typical NOLS instructor has worked for the school five years.

PARTICIPANTS

For Participants Aged: 16–70

The Ideal Candidate: NOLS students are motivated to learn. They are adventurous and in good physical condition. NOLS students are successful individuals who come to NOLS for our unique hands-on approach to education.

Special Requirements for Participation: Good physical condition.

COSTS

Average Cost: $2,650

Included in Cost: The tuition covers instruction, group gear, food, and lodging. Additional expenses will include transportation to Lander, Wyoming, and personal gear. NOLS rents personal gear.

Financial Aid Available: Yes

ABSAROKA BACKPACKING

THE PROGRAM

Description: This 30-day course, offered in Wyoming's Absaroka (Ab-sor-ka) Range, focuses on outdoor skills, leadership, and environmental studies. This course features traveling through broad river valleys surrounded by cliffs of volcanic rock, hiking through alpine plateaus, and learning to fly fish.

Specialty: NOLS is the only school that focuses exclusively on leadership, wildernes skills, and the environment. The experience and training of our instructors leads the outdoor education industry.

Program Type: Outdoors/adventure

Classification: Coeducational, residential

Goals: Students should expect to learn wilderness skills—navigation, leave-no-trace outdoor ethics, and first aid. They will develop leadership by actually leading in the backcountry. Students will also learn about the environments in which they are traveling—flora, fauna, geology, and weather.

Focus: Leadership/teamwork, skill-building, and travel

Activities Center On: Backpacking and wilderness

Intensity Level: 4

Duration: 4–6 weeks

Program Offered: Summer

Location: Lander, Wyoming

Accommodations: Tent

Years in Operation: 38

Religious Affiliation: Not relevant

STAFF

Student/Staff Ratio: 6:1

Staff Qualifications: All NOLS instructors complete the 35-day NOLS instructor course. All possess a minimum of Wilderness First Responder certification. Average age is 31. Typical NOLS instructor has worked for the school five years.

PARTICIPANTS

Average Number of Participants: 300

For Participants Aged: 16–70

The Ideal Candidate: NOLS students are motivated to learn. They are adventurous and in good physical condition. NOLS students are successful individuals who come to NOLS for our unique hands-on approach to education.

Special Requirements for Participation: Good physical condition.

COSTS

Average Cost: $2,975

Included in Cost: The tuition covers instruction, group gear, food, and lodging. Additional expenses will include transportation to Lander, Wyoming, and personal gear. NOLS rents personal gear.

Financial Aid Available: Yes

ALASKA BACKPACKING

THE PROGRAM

Description: An Alaska backpacking course is a wilderness expedition in every sense! Students travel in the Talkeetna Mountains or the Alaska Range. Some courses begin their route by traveling by bush plane, and all courses recieve food every 7 to 10 days by plane. However students get there, the skills learned in the Alaska backcountry stay with them for life!

Specialty: NOLS is the only school that focuses exclusively on leadership, wilderness skills, and the environment. The experience and training of our instructors leads the outdoor education industry.

Program Type: Outdoors/adventure

Classification: Coeducational, residential

Goals: Students should expect to learn wilderness skills—navigation, leave-no-trace outdoor ethics, and first aid. They will develop leadership by actually leading in the backcountry. Students will also learn about the environments in which they are traveling—flora, fauna, geology, and weather.

Focus: Leadership/teamwork and skill-building

Activities Center On: Backpacking, wilderness, and travel

Intensity Level: 4

Duration: 2–4 weeks

Program Offered: Summer

Location: Palmer, Alaska

Accommodations: Tent

Religious Affiliation: Not relevant

STAFF

Student/Staff Ratio: 4:1

Staff Qualifications: All NOLS instructors complete the 35-day NOLS instructor course. All possess a minimum of Wilderness First Responder certification. Average age is 31. Typical NOLS instructor has worked for the school five years.

PARTICIPANTS

For Participants Aged: 16–70

The Ideal Candidate: NOLS students are motivated to learn. They are adventurous and in good physical condition. NOLS students are successful individuals who come to NOLS for our unique hands-on approach to education.

Special Requirements for Participation: Good physical condition.

COSTS

Average Cost: $3,070

Included in Cost: The tuition covers instruction, group gear, food, and lodging. Additional expenses will include transportation to Lander, Wyoming, and personal gear. NOLS rents personal gear.

Financial Aid Available: Yes

ALASKA MOUNTAINEERING

THE PROGRAM

Description: This course takes students to a place in southern Alaska to explore either the Chugach Range, the Interior Range, or the Wrangell Range. The route for each course is season-dependent with early season expeditions climbing mostly above snowline to access terrain via huge snowfields, and later season courses completing technical glacier routes on ice and rock. All routes are ideal training grounds for learning to live and travel safely in challenging mountain terrain.

Specialty: NOLS is the only school that focuses exclusively on leadership, wilderness skills, and the environment. The experience and training of our instructors leads the outdoor education industry.

Program Type: Outdoors/adventure

Classification: Coeducational, residential

Goals: Students should expect to learn wilderness skills—navigation, leave-no-trace outdoor ethics, and first aid. They will develop leadership by actually leading in the backcountry. Students will also learn about the environments in which they are traveling—flora, fauna, geology, and weather.

Focus: Leadership/teamwork and skill-building

Activities Center On: Backpacking

Intensity Level: 4

Duration: 2–4 weeks

Program Offered: Summer

Location: Palmer, Alaska

Accommodations: Tent

Religious Affiliation: Not relevant

STAFF

Student/Staff Ratio: 4:1

Staff Qualifications: All NOLS instructors complete the 35-day NOLS instructor course. All possess a minimum of Wilderness First Responder certification. Average age is 31. Typical NOLS instructor has worked for the school five years.

PARTICIPANTS

For Participants Aged: 17–70

The Ideal Candidate: NOLS students are motivated to learn. They are adventurous and in good physical condition. NOLS students are successful individuals who come to NOLS for our unique hands-on approach to education.

Special Requirements for Participation: Good physical condition.

COSTS

Average Cost: $3,925

Included in Cost: The tuition covers instruction, group gear, food, and lodging. Additional expenses will include transportation to Lander, Wyoming, and personal gear. NOLS rents personal gear.

Financial Aid Available: Yes

ALASKA OUTDOOR EDUCATOR BACKPACKING

THE PROGRAM

Description: This backpacking course takes students into Alaska's sweeping tundra and steep mountain passes for a 24-day immersion into how to lead and teach in the wilderness. Students learn effective teaching techniques and get a chance to implement those techniques. The lessons learned here in the open tundra travel home with each student, and for challenging, wild terrain and opportunities to see bear, caribou, and wolves, this course has no equal.

Specialty: NOLS is the only school that focuses exclusively on leadership, wilderness skills, and the environment. The experience and training of our instructors leads the outdoor education industry.

Program Type: Outdoors/adventure

Classification: Coeducational, residential

Goals: Students should expect to learn wilderness skills—navigation, leave-no-trace outdoor ethics, and first aid. They will develop leadership by actually leading in the backcountry. Students will also learn about the environments in which they are traveling—flora, fauna, geology, and weather.

Focus: Leadership/teamwork and skill-building

Activities Center On: Backpacking, wilderness, and travel

Intensity Level: 4

Duration: 2–4 weeks

Program Offered: Summer

Location: Palmer, Alaska

Accommodations: Tent

Religious Affiliation: Not relevant

STAFF

Student/Staff Ratio: 4:1

Staff Qualifications: All NOLS instructors complete the 35-day NOLS instructor course. All possess a minimum of Wilderness First Responder certification. Average age is 31. Typical NOLS instructor has worked for the school five years.

PARTICIPANTS

For Participants Aged: 18–70

The Ideal Candidate: NOLS students are motivated to learn. They are adventurous and in good physical condition. NOLS students are successful individuals who come to NOLS for our unique hands-on approach to education.

Special Requirements for Participation: Good physical condition.

COSTS

Average Cost: $2,490

Included in Cost: The tuition covers instruction, group gear, food, and lodging. Additional expenses will include transportation to Lander, Wyoming, and personal gear. NOLS rents personal gear.

Financial Aid Available: Yes

ALASKA SEA KAYAKING

THE PROGRAM

Description: Since 1971, NOLS students have been exploring and experiencing the wilds of Alaska via sea kayak. The Alaska sea kayaking course brings students to an amazing place and provides a wide variety of learning experiences.

Specialty: NOLS is the only school that focuses exclusively on leadership, wilderness skills, and the environment. The experience and training of our instructors leads the outdoor education industry.

Program Type: Outdoors/adventure

Classification: Coeducational, residential

Goals: Students should expect to learn wilderness skills—navigation, leave-no-trace outdoor ethics, and first aid. They will develop leadership by actually leading in the backcountry. Students will also learn about the environments in which they are traveling—flora, fauna, geology, and weather.

Focus: Leadership/teamwork and skill-building

Activities Center On: Kayaking and wilderness

Intensity Level: 4

Duration: 2–4 weeks

Program Offered: Summer

Location: Palmer, Alaska

Accommodations: Tent

Religious Affiliation: Not relevant

STAFF

Student/Staff Ratio: 4:1

Staff Qualifications: All NOLS instructors complete the 35-day NOLS instructor course. All possess a minimum of Wilderness First Responder certification. Average age is 31. Typical NOLS instructor has worked for the school five years.

PARTICIPANTS

For Participants Aged: 16–70

The Ideal Candidate: NOLS students are motivated to learn. They are adventurous and in good physical condition. NOLS students are successful individuals who come to NOLS for our unique hands-on approach to education.

Special Requirements for Participation: Good physical condition.

COSTS

Average Cost: $3,075

Included in Cost: The tuition covers instruction, group gear, food, and lodging. Additional expenses will include transportation to course start location and personal gear. NOLS rents personal gear.

Financial Aid Available: Yes

AUSTRALIA BACKPACKING

THE PROGRAM

Description: Australia has a rich cultural history, semi-tropical habitats, and ancient land formations ideal for an educational expedition. Students travel in four-wheel drive vehicles, light planes, or boats to a remote area of the Kimberley, where they will backpack through tight canyons, past secluded waterfalls, and over dry plateaus.

Specialty: NOLS is the only school that focuses exclusively on leadership, wilderness skills, and the environment. The experience and training of our instructors leads the outdoor education industry.

Program Type: Outdoors/adventure

Classification: Coeducational, residential

Goals: Students should expect to learn wilderness skills—navigation, leave-no-trace outdoor ethics, and first aid. They will develop leadership by actually leading in the backcountry. Students will also learn about the environments in which they are traveling—flora, fauna, geology, and weather.

Focus: Leadership/teamwork, skill-building, and cultural

Activities Center On: Backpacking and wilderness

Intensity Level: 4

Duration: 4–6 weeks

Program Offered: Spring, summer

Location: Broome, Australia

Accommodations: Tent

Religious Affiliation: Not relevant

STAFF

Student/Staff Ratio: 4:1

Staff Qualifications: All NOLS instructors complete the rigorous 35-day NOLS instructor course. All possess a minimum of Wilderness First Responder certification. Average age is 31. Typical NOLS instructor has worked for the school five years.

PARTICIPANTS

For Participants Aged: 18–70

The Ideal Candidate: NOLS students are motivated to learn. They are adventurous and in good physical condition. NOLS students are successful individuals who come to NOLS for our unique hands-on approach to education.

Special Requirements for Participation: Good physical condition.

COSTS

Average Cost: $4,435 cluded in Cost: The tuition covers instruction, group gear, food, and lodging. Additional expenses will include transportation to course start location and personal gear. NOLS rents personal gear.

Financial Aid Available: Yes

AUSTRALIA BACKPACKING AND SEA KAYAKING

THE PROGRAM

Description: Australia has a rich cultural history, semi-tropical habitats, and ancient land formations ideal for an educational expedition. Students travel to a remote area of the Kimberley, where they will backpack through tight canyons, past secluded waterfalls, and over dry plateaus. Students will sea kayak the waters around the Dampier Archipelago—a group of 42 rocky islands and an excellent location to develop sea kayaking skills and marine ecology knowledge.

Specialty: NOLS is the only school that focuses exclusively on leadership, wilderness skills, and the environment. The experience and training of our instructors leads the outdoor education industry.

Program Type: Outdoors/adventure

Classification: Coeducational, residential

Goals: Students should expect to learn wilderness skills—navigation, leave-no-trace outdoor ethics, and first aid. They will develop leadership by actually leading in the backcountry. Students will also learn about the environments in which they are traveling—flora, fauna, geology, and weather.

Focus: Leadership/teamwork, skill-building, and cultural

Activities Center On: Backpacking, kayaking, and wilderness

Intensity Level: 4

Duration: 4–6 weeks

Program Offered: Spring, summer

Location: Broome, Australia

Accommodations: Tent

Religious Affiliation: Not relevant

STAFF

Student/Staff Ratio: 4:1

Staff Qualifications: All NOLS instructors complete the rigorous 35-day NOLS instructor course. All possess a minimum of Wilderness First Responder certification. Average age is 31. Typical NOLS instructor has worked for the school five years.

PARTICIPANTS

For Participants Aged: 18–70

The Ideal Candidate: NOLS students are motivated to learn. They are adventurous and in good physical condition. NOLS students are successful individuals who come to NOLS for our unique hands-on approach to education.

Special Requirements for Participation: Good physical condition.

COSTS

Average Cost: $5,400

Included in Cost: The tuition covers instruction, group gear, food, and lodging. Additional expenses will include transportation to course start location and personal gear. NOLS rents personal gear.

Financial Aid Available: Yes

BAJA BACKPACKING

THE PROGRAM

Description: The Sierra Guadalupe, renowned for its spectacular views, historic ranchero homesteads, and cave paintings, is a rugged, volcanic range carved by water and wind erosion. For 14 days students backpack through these mountains studying natural history, environmental issues, and archaeology. Pack animals will lighten the load of backs and provide the opportunity to learn the art of traveling with stock.

Specialty: NOLS is the only school that focuses exclusively on leadership, wilderness skills, and the environment. The experience and training of our instructors leads the outdoor education industry.

Program Type: Outdoors/adventure

Classification: Coeducational, residential

Goals: Students should expect to learn wilderness skills—navigation, leave-no-trace outdoor ethics, and first aid. They will develop leadership by actually leading in the backcountry. Students will also learn about the environments in which they are traveling—flora, fauna, geology, and weather.

Focus: Leadership/teamwork, skill-building, and travel

Activities Center On: Backpacking and wilderness

Intensity Level: 4

Duration: 2–4 weeks

Program Offered: Spring

Location: Mulege, Mexico

Accommodations: Tent

Religious Affiliation: Not relevant

STAFF

Student/Staff Ratio: 4:1

Staff Qualifications: All NOLS instructors complete the rigorous 35-day NOLS instructor course. All possess a minimum of Wilderness First Responder certification. Average age is 31. Typical NOLS instructor has worked for the school five years.

PARTICIPANTS

For Participants Aged: 17–70

The Ideal Candidate: NOLS students are motivated to learn. They are adventurous and in good physical condition. NOLS students are successful individuals who come to NOLS for our unique hands-on approach to education.

Special Requirements for Participation: Good physical condition.

COSTS

Average Cost: $2,430

Included in Cost: The tuition covers instruction, group gear, food, and lodging. Additional expenses will include transportation to course start location and personal gear. NOLS rents personal gear.

Financial Aid Available: Yes

BAJA COASTAL SAILING

THE PROGRAM

Description: A NOLS sailing course prepares students for sailing expeditions of their own. NOLS uses a unique boat called a Crascombe Longboat, a light, maneuverable craft that operates on the same principles as larger boats but can explore shallow coves or be hauled onto a desert beach. On the boat, students explore a sea rich with marine life.

Specialty: NOLS is the only school that focuses exclusively on leadership, wilderness skills, and the environment. The experience and training of our instructors leads the outdoor education industry.

Program Type: Outdoors/adventure

Classification: Coeducational, residential

Goals: Students should expect to learn wilderness skills—navigation, leave-no-trace outdoor ethics, and first aid. They will develop leadership by actually leading in the backcountry. Students will also learn about the environments in which they are traveling—flora, fauna, geology, and weather.

Focus: Leadership/teamwork, skill-building, and travel

Activities Center On: Boating and wilderness

Intensity Level: 4

Duration: 2–4 weeks

Program Offered: Fall, spring

Location: Mulege, Mexico

Accommodations: Tent

Religious Affiliation: Not relevant

STAFF

Student/Staff Ratio: 4:1

Staff Qualifications: All NOLS instructors complete the rigorous 35-day NOLS instructor course. All possess a minimum of Wilderness First Responder certification. Average age is 31. Typical NOLS instructor has worked for the school five years.

PARTICIPANTS

For Participants Aged: 16–70

The Ideal Candidate: NOLS students are motivated to learn. They are adventurous and in good physical condition. NOLS students are successful individuals who come to NOLS for our unique hands-on approach to education.

Special Requirements for Participation: Good physical condition.

COSTS

Average Cost: $2,725

Included in Cost: The tuition covers instruction, group gear, food, and lodging. Additional expenses will include transportation to course start location and personal gear. NOLS rents personal gear.

Financial Aid Available: Yes

BAJA SEA KAYAKING

THE PROGRAM

Description: A Baja sea-kayaking expedition is an immersion in culture, land, water, and sky. This course provides students with the opportunity for learning in a setting unmatched by anything in the world. The Baja California penisula and the Sea of Cortez are beautifully dramatic environments. Students learn all the skills to travel safely by sea kayak in and explore the rich natural history of the region by kayak, snorkel, and foot.

Specialty: NOLS is the only school that focuses exclusively on leadership, wilderness skills, and the environment. The experience and training of our instructors leads the outdoor education industry.

Program Type: Outdoors/adventure

Classification: Coeducational, residential

Goals: Students should expect to learn wilderness skills—navigation, leave-no-trace outdoor ethics, and first aid. They will develop leadership by actually leading in the backcountry. Students will also learn about the environments in which they are traveling—flora, fauna, geology, and weather.

Focus: Leadership/teamwork, skill-building, and travel

Activities Center On: Kayaking and wilderness

Intensity Level: 4

Duration: 2–4 weeks

Program Offered: Fall, spring

Location: Loreto, Mexico

Accommodations: Tent

Religious Affiliation: Not relevant

STAFF

Student/Staff Ratio: 4:1

Staff Qualifications: All NOLS instructors complete the rigorous 35-day NOLS instructor course. All possess a minimum of Wilderness First Responder certification. Average age is 31. Typical NOLS instructor has worked for the school five years.

PARTICIPANTS

Average Number of Participants: 0

For Participants Aged: 16–70

The Ideal Candidate: NOLS students are motivated to learn. They are adventurous and in good physical condition. NOLS students are successful individuals who come to NOLS for our unique hands-on approach to education.

Special Requirements for Participation: Good physical condition.

COSTS

Average Cost: $2,725

Included in Cost: The tuition covers instruction, group gear, food, and lodging. Additional expenses will include transportation to course start location and personal gear. NOLS rents personal gear.

Financial Aid Available: Yes

BROOKS RANGE BACKPACKING AND RIVER

THE PROGRAM

Description: Students spend the first 10 days of this extended arctic expedition on foot moving across the tundra and up braided river channels. A bush plane will fly in and swap backpacks for folding canoes and touring kayaks for a three-week trip down an arctic river—either the Sheenjek or Noatak Rivers.

Specialty: NOLS is the only school that focuses exclusively on leadership, wilderness skills, and the environment. The experience and training of our instructors leads the outdoor education industry.

Program Type: Outdoors/adventure

Classification: Coeducational, residential

Goals: Students should expect to learn wilderness skills—navigation, leave-no-trace outdoor ethics, and first aid. They will develop leadership by actually leading in the backcountry. Students will also learn about the environments in which they are traveling—flora, fauna, geology, and weather.

Focus: Leadership/teamwork and skill-building

Activities Center On: Backpacking and boating

Intensity Level: 4

Duration: 4–6 weeks

Program Offered: Summer

Location: Palmer, Alaska

Accommodations: Tent

Religious Affiliation: Not relevant

STAFF

Student/Staff Ratio: 4:1

Staff Qualifications: All NOLS instructors complete the 35-day NOLS instructor course. All possess a minimum of Wilderness First Responder certification. Average age is 31. Typical NOLS instructor has worked for the school five years.

PARTICIPANTS

For Participants Aged: 18–70

The Ideal Candidate: NOLS students are motivated to learn. They are adventurous and in good physical condition. NOLS students are successful individuals who come to NOLS for our unique hands-on approach to education.

Special Requirements for Participation: Good physical condition.

COSTS

Average Cost: $3,075

Included in Cost: The tuition covers instruction, group gear, food, and lodging. Additional expenses will include transportation to course start location and personal gear. NOLS rents personal gear.

Financial Aid Available: Yes

DENALI MOUNTAINEERING

THE PROGRAM

Description: This course is offered for qualified NOLS graduates only and takes students to the highest peak in North America.

Specialty: NOLS is the only school that focuses exclusively on leadership, wilderness skills, and the environment. The experience and training of our instructors leads the outdoor education industry.

Program Type: Outdoors/adventure

Classification: Coeducational, residential

Goals: Students should expect to learn wilderness skills—navigation, leave-no-trace outdoor ethics, and first aid. They will develop leadership by actually leading in the backcountry. Students will also learn about the environments in which they are traveling—flora, fauna, geology, and weather.

Focus: Leadership/teamwork and skill-building

Activities Center On: Wilderness

Intensity Level: 5

Duration: 4–6 weeks

Program Offered: Summer

Location: Palmer, Alaska

Accommodations: Tent

Religious Affiliation: Not relevant

Staff

Student/Staff Ratio: 4:1

Staff Qualifications: All NOLS instructors complete the 35-day NOLS instructor course. All possess a minimum of Wilderness First Responder certification. Average age is 31. Typical NOLS instructor has worked for the school five years.

Participants

For Participants Aged: 17–70

The Ideal Candidate: NOLS students are motivated to learn. They are adventurous and in good physical condition. NOLS students are successful individuals who come to NOLS for our unique hands-on approach to education.

Special Requirements for Participation: Good physical condition.

Costs

Average Cost: $5,700

Included in Cost: The tuition covers instruction, group gear, food, and lodging. Additional expenses will include transportation to course start location and personal gear. NOLS rents personal gear.

Financial Aid Available: Yes

Fall Semester in the Rockies

The Program

Description: This is the original semester in wilderness education. A semester in the Rockies allows students to gain a complete set of skills to lead and teach in the backcountry. Semester in the Rockies grads can paddle down a canoe in Class II rapids, navigate networks of underground caves, make quick medical decisions miles from the nearest roadhead, and lead a 5.7 climb.

Specialty: NOLS is the only school that focuses exclusively on leadership, wilderness skills, and the environment. The experience and training of our instructors leads the outdoor education industry.

Program Type: Outdoors/adventure

Classification: Coeducational, residential

Goals: Students should expect to learn wilderness skills—navigation, leave-no-trace outdoor ethics, and first aid. They will develop leadership by actually leading in the backcountry. Students will also learn about the environments in which they are traveling—flora, fauna, geology, and weather.

Focus: Leadership/teamwork, skill-building, and travel

Activities Center On: Backpacking, outdoors/adventure, and wilderness

Intensity Level: 4

Duration: Over 8 weeks

Program Offered: Fall

Location: Lander, Wyoming

Accommodations: Tent

Years in Operation: 38

Religious Affiliation: Not relevant

Staff

Student/Staff Ratio: 6:1

Staff Qualifications: All NOLS instructors complete the 35-day NOLS instructor course. All possess a minimum of Wilderness First Responder certification. Average age is 31. Typical NOLS instructor has worked for the school five years.

Participants

Average Number of Participants: 300

For Participants Aged: 17–70

The Ideal Candidate: NOLS students are motivated to learn. They are adventurous and in good physical condition. NOLS students are successful individuals who come to NOLS for our unique hands-on approach to education.

Special Requirements for Participation: Good physical condition.

Costs

Average Cost: $8,510

Included in Cost: The tuition covers instruction, group gear, food, and lodging. Additional expenses will include transportation to Lander, Wyoming, and personal gear. NOLS rents personal gear.

Financial Aid Available: Yes

Fall Semester in the Sonoran Desert

The Program

Description: The Sonoran Desert spans 120,000 sqare miles from the American Southwest all the way to the tip of Baja California, Mexico. This mixture of land and water gives students the opportunities to learn sea kayaking, rock climbing, and hiking skills in one of the world's most unique ecosystems.

Specialty: NOLS is the only school that focuses exclusively on leadership, wilderness skills, and the environment. The experience and training of our instructors leads the outdoor education industry.

Program Type: Outdoors/adventure

Classification: Coeducational, residential

Goals: Students should expect to learn wilderness skills—navigation, leave-no-trace outdoor ethics, and first aid. They will develop leadership by actually leading in the backcountry. Students will also learn about the environments in which they are traveling—flora, fauna, geology, and weather.

Focus: Leadership/teamwork, skill-building, and travel

Activities Center On: Backpacking, kayaking, and wilderness

Intensity Level: 4

Duration: Over 8 weeks

Program Offered: Fall

Location: Tucson, Arizona

Accommodations: Tent

Religious Affiliation: Not relevant

STAFF

Student/Staff Ratio: 4:1

Staff Qualifications: All NOLS instructors complete the 35-day NOLS instructor course. All possess a minimum of Wilderness First Responder certification. Average age is 31. Typical NOLS instructor has worked for the school five years.

PARTICIPANTS

For Participants Aged: 17–70

The Ideal Candidate: NOLS students are motivated to learn. They are adventurous and in good physical condition. NOLS students are successful individuals who come to NOLS for our unique hands-on approach to education.

Special Requirements for Participation: Good physical condition.

COSTS

Average Cost: $8,800

Included in Cost: The tuition covers instruction, group gear, food, and lodging. Additional expenses will include transportation to Lander, Wyoming, and personal gear. NOLS rents personal gear.

Financial Aid Available: Yes

GANNETT PEAK MOUNTAINEERING

THE PROGRAM

Description: This course is designed for NOLS alumni only. Hidden deep in the Wind River Range, Gannet Peak is Wyoming's highest peak. Reaching this remote 13,804-foot summit requires an approach of several days, followed by the climb itself. This expedition is the perfect opportunity to put the camping and travel skills you learned on your NOLS course back to work!

Specialty: NOLS is the only school that focuses exclusively on leadership, wilderness skills, and the environment. The experience and training of our instructors leads the outdoor education industry.

Program Type: Outdoors/adventure

Classification: Coeducational, residential

Goals: Students should expect to learn wilderness skills—navigation, leave-no-trace outdoor ethics, and first aid. They

will develop leadership by actually leading in the backcountry. Students will also learn about the environments in which they are traveling—flora, fauna, geology, and weather.

Focus: Leadership/teamwork, skill-building, and travel

Intensity Level: 4

Duration: 1–2 weeks

Program Offered: Spring, summer

Location: Lander, Wyoming

Accommodations: Tent

Religious Affiliation: Not relevant

STAFF

Student/Staff Ratio: 6:1

Staff Qualifications: All NOLS instructors complete the 35-day NOLS instructor course. All possess a minimum of Wilderness First Responder certification. Average age is 31. Typical NOLS instructor has worked for the school five years.

PARTICIPANTS

For Participants Aged: 16–70

The Ideal Candidate: NOLS students are motivated to learn. They are adventurous and are in good physical condition. NOLS students are successful individuals who come to NOLS for our unique hands-on approach to education.

Special Requirements for Participation: Good physical condition.

COSTS

Average Cost: $1,890

Included in Cost: The tuition covers instruction, group gear, food, and lodging. Additional expenses will include transportation to Lander, Wyoming, and personal gear. NOLS rents personal gear.

Financial Aid Available: Yes

GILA RANGE BACKPACKING

THE PROGRAM

Description: New Mexico's Gila Range is the birthplace of the American concept of wilderness. For 30 days students hike and travel through pinyon pine forests, deep canyons, and snow-covered peaks. Students travel through canyons inhabited 900 years ago by the Mibres culture, and 100 years ago by the Apache.

Specialty: NOLS is the only school that focuses exclusively on leadership, wilderness skills, and the environment. The experience and training of our instructors leads the outdoor education industry.

Program Type: Outdoors/adventure

Classification: Coeducational, residential

Goals: Students should expect to learn wilderness skills—navigation, leave-no-trace outdoor ethics, and first aid. They will develop leadership by actually leading in the backcountry. Students will also learn about the environments in which they are traveling—flora, fauna, geology, and weather.

Focus: Leadership/teamwork, skill-building, and travel

Activities Center On: Backpacking and wilderness

Intensity Level: 4

Duration: 2–4 weeks

Program Offered: Spring

Location: Tucson, Arizona

Accommodations: Tent

Religious Affiliation: Not relevant

STAFF

Student/Staff Ratio: 4:1

Staff Qualifications: All NOLS instructors complete the 35-day NOLS instructor course. All possess a minimum of Wilderness First Responder certification. Average age is 31. Typical NOLS instructor has worked for the school five years.

PARTICIPANTS

For Participants Aged: 16–70

The Ideal Candidate: NOLS students are motivated to learn. They are adventurous and in good physical condition. NOLS students are successful individuals who come to NOLS for our unique hands-on approach to education.

Special Requirements for Participation: Good physical condition.

COSTS

Average Cost: $3,035

Included in Cost: The tuition covers instruction, group gear, food, and lodging. Additional expenses will include transportation to Lander, Wyoming, and personal gear. NOLS rents personal gear.

Financial Aid Available: Yes

try. Students will also learn about the environments in which they are traveling—flora, fauna, geology, and weather.

Focus: Leadership/teamwork, skill-building, and cultural

Activities Center On: Backpacking and wilderness

Intensity Level: 4

Duration: 6–8 weeks

Program Offered: Fall, spring

Location: Conway, Washington

Accommodations: Tent

Religious Affiliation: Not relevant

STAFF

Student/Staff Ratio: 4:1

Staff Qualifications: All NOLS instructors complete the rigorous 35-day NOLS instructor course. All possess a minimum of Wilderness First Responder certification. Average age is 31. Typical NOLS instructor has worked for the school five years.

PARTICIPANTS

For Participants Aged: 18–70

The Ideal Candidate: NOLS students are motivated to learn. They are adventurous and are in good physical condition. NOLS students are successful individuals who come to NOLS for our unique hands-on approach to education.

Special Requirements for Participation: Good physical condition.

COSTS

Average Cost: $4,515

Included in Cost: The tuition covers instruction, group gear, food, and lodging. Additional expenses will include transportation to course start location and personal gear. NOLS rents personal gear.

Financial Aid Available: Yes

HIMALAYA BACKPACKING

THE PROGRAM

Description: On this course, students learn basic backcountry skills but also learn cultural skills and basic Hindi as students interact with local villagers. Students will make their way up high mountain passes, some reaching 15,000 feet above sea leve, and travel through river valleys lush with foilage.

Specialty: NOLS is the only school that focuses exclusively on leadership, wilderness skills, and the environment. The experience and training of our instructors leads the outdoor education industry.

Program Type: Outdoors/adventure

Classification: Coeducational, residential

Goals: Students should expect to learn wilderness skills—navigation, leave-no-trace outdoor ethics, and first aid. They will develop leadership by actually leading in the backcoun-

HIMALAYA MOUNTAINEERING

THE PROGRAM

Description: The remote and spectacular Kumaon region of Northern India is the setting for this high-altitude mountaineering expedition. In these surroundings, students learn how to plan and carry out an international expedition, focusing on topics such as expedition planning, cultural awareness, altitude physiology, and mountaineering skills.

Specialty: NOLS is the only school that focuses exclusively on leadership, wilderness skills, and the environment. The experience and training of our instructors leads the outdoor education industry.

Program Type: Outdoors/adventure

Classification: Coeducational, residential

Goals: Students should expect to learn wilderness skills—navigation, leave-no-trace outdoor ethics, and first aid. They will develop leadership by actually leading in the backcountry. Students will also learn about the environments in which they are traveling—flora, fauna, geology, and weather.

Focus: Leadership/teamwork, skill-building, and cultural

Activities Center On: Backpacking and outdoors/adventure

Intensity Level: 4

Duration: 6–8 weeks

Program Offered: Fall, spring

Location: Conway, Washington

Accommodations: Tent

Religious Affiliation: Not relevant

STAFF

Student/Staff Ratio: 4:1

Staff Qualifications: All NOLS instructors complete the rigorous 35-day NOLS instructor course. All possess a minimum of Wilderness First Responder certification. Average age is 31. Typical NOLS instructor has worked for the school five years.

PARTICIPANTS

For Participants Aged: 18–70

The Ideal Candidate: NOLS students are motivated to learn. They are adventurous and are in good physical condition. NOLS students are successful individuals who come to NOLS for our unique hands-on approach to education.

Special Requirements for Participation: Good physical condition.

COSTS

Average Cost: $5,100

Included in Cost: The tuition covers instruction, group gear, food, and lodging. Additional expenses will include transportation to course start location and personal gear. NOLS rents personal gear.

Financial Aid Available: Yes

IDAHO ADVENTURE FOR 14- AND 15-YEAR-OLDS

THE PROGRAM

Description: Independence, responsiblity, achievemnet, fun: These qualities and more are the essence of this course. Students learn skills in a classroom unlike any ever experienced. Skills learned include backpacking, fly fishing, camping, communication, and leadership. Adventure courses are not "kid" versions of other NOLS courses. Students get the famous NOLS curriculum taught by the same high-quality instructors.

Specialty: NOLS is the only school that focuses exclusively on leadership, wilderness skills, and the environment. The experience and training of our instructors leads the outdoor education industry.

Program Type: Outdoors/adventure

Classification: Coeducational, residential

Goals: Students should expect to learn wilderness skills—navigation, leave-no-trace outdoor ethics, and first aid. They will develop leadership by actually leading in the backcountry. Students will also learn about the environments in which they are traveling—flora, fauna, geology, and weather.

Focus: Leadership/teamwork and skill-building

Activities Center On: Backpacking and wilderness

Intensity Level: 3

Duration: 1–2 weeks

Program Offered: Summer

Location: Driggs, Idaho

Accommodations: Tent

Religious Affiliation: Not relevant

STAFF

Student/Staff Ratio: 4:1

Staff Qualifications: All NOLS instructors complete the rigorous 35-day NOLS instructor course. All possess a minimum of Wilderness First Responder certification. Average age is 31. Typical NOLS instructor has worked for the school five years.

PARTICIPANTS

For Participants Aged: 14–15

The Ideal Candidate: NOLS students are motivated to learn. They are adventurous and are in good physical condition. NOLS students are successful individuals who come to NOLS for our unique hands-on approach to education.

Special Requirements for Participation: Good physical condition.

COSTS

Average Cost: $2,100

Included in Cost: The tuition covers instruction, group gear, food, and lodging. Additional expenses include travel to course starting location and personal gear. NOLS rents personal gear.

Financial Aid Available: Yes

NORTHERN ROCKIES BACKPACKING AND RIVER

THE PROGRAM

Description: This course combines wilderness and whitewater for an exciting 30-day backcountry adventure. The backpacking section takes place in either the Beaverheads or Lemhi Ranges in Idaho or the Eagle Cap wilderness area in Oregon. For the remaining 10 days students swap backpacks for boats and hit the wild waters of the famous Salmon River.

Specialty: NOLS is the only school that focuses exclusively on leadership, wilderness skills, and the environment. The experience and training of our instructors leads the outdoor education industry.

Program Type: Outdoors/adventure

Classification: Coeducational, residential

Goals: Students should expect to learn wilderness skills—navigation, leave-no-trace outdoor ethics, and first aid. They will develop leadership by actually leading in the backcountry. Students will also learn about the environments in which they are traveling—flora, fauna, geology, and weather.

Focus: Leadership/teamwork and skill-building

Activities Center On: Backpacking and boating

Intensity Level: 4

Duration: 2–4 weeks

Program Offered: Summer

Location: Salmon or Boise, Idaho

Accommodations: Tent

Religious Affiliation: Not relevant

STAFF

Student/Staff Ratio: 4:1

Staff Qualifications: All NOLS instructors complete the 35-day NOLS instructor course. All possess a minimum of Wilderness First Responder certification. Average age is 31. Typical NOLS instructor has worked for the school five years.

PARTICIPANTS

For Participants Aged: 18–70

The Ideal Candidate: NOLS students are motivated to learn. They are adventurous and are in good physical condition. NOLS students are successful individuals who come to NOLS for our unique hands-on approach to education.

Special Requirements for Participation: Good physical condition.

COSTS

Average Cost: $4,025

Included in Cost: The tuition covers instruction, group gear, food, and lodging. Additional expenses include travel to course starting location and personal gear. NOLS rents personal gear.

Financial Aid Available: Yes

OWYHEE BACKPACKING AND RIVER

THE PROGRAM

Description: This is one of the few unique combination courses in which students run rivers and explore a canyon all on one course. The first 12 days are spent canoeing through deeply incised, volcanic canyons of the Owyhee River. This desert river winds through a labyrinth of massive cliffs and canyons. Students learn basic canoe strokes, river reading, and hazard evaluation to name a few. For the last two weeks, students switch to backpacks and learn "canyoneering"

through the Owyhee's canyons.

Specialty: NOLS is the only school that focuses exclusively on leadership, wilderness skills, and the environment. The experience and training of our instructors leads the outdoor education industry.

Program Type: Outdoors/adventure

Classification: Coeducational, residential

Goals: Students should expect to learn wilderness skills—navigation, leave-no-trace outdoor ethics, and first aid. They will develop leadership by actually leading in the backcountry. Students will also learn about the environments in which they are traveling—flora, fauna, geology, and weather.

Focus: Leadership/teamwork, skill-building, and travel

Activities Center On: Boating and backpacking

Intensity Level: 4

Duration: 2–4 weeks

Program Offered: Summer

Location: Boise, Idaho

Accommodations: Tent

Religious Affiliation: Not relevant

STAFF

Student/Staff Ratio: 4:1

Staff Qualifications: All NOLS instructors complete the 35-day NOLS instructor course. All possess a minimum of Wilderness First Responder certification. Average age is 31. Typical NOLS instructor has worked for the school five years.

PARTICIPANTS

For Participants Aged: 18–70

The Ideal Candidate: NOLS students are motivated to learn. They are adventurous and are in good physical condition. NOLS students are successful individuals who come to NOLS for our unique hands-on approach to education.

Special Requirements for Participation: Good physical condition.

COSTS

Average Cost: $4,025

Included in Cost: The tuition covers instruction, group gear, food, and lodging. Additional expenses include travel to course starting location and personal gear. NOLS rents personal gear.

Financial Aid Available: Yes

PACIFIC NORTHWEST BACKPACKING

THE PROGRAM

Description: The Pacific Northwest is a richly diverse wilderness classroom, ranging from jagged, glacier-carved mountains and valleys, to old growth forests and stands of lodgepole pine. These courses have two options for travel—the Pasayten Wilderness in north central Washington or

Olympic National Park on the Olympic Peninsula. Students will learn to live and lead comfortably in remote wilderness settings.

Specialty: NOLS is the only school that focuses exclusively on leadership, wilderness skills, and the environment. The experience and training of our instructors leads the outdoor education industry.

Program Type: Outdoors/adventure

Classification: Coeducational, residential

Goals: Students should expect to learn wilderness skills—navigation, leave-no-trace outdoor ethics, and first aid. They will develop leadership by actually leading in the backcountry. Students will also learn about the environments in which they are traveling—flora, fauna, geology, and weather.

Focus: Leadership/teamwork, skill-building, and travel

Activities Center On: Backpacking and wilderness

Intensity Level: 4

Duration: 2–4 weeks

Program Offered: Spring, summer

Location: Conway, Washington

Accommodations: Tent

Religious Affiliation: Not relevant

STAFF

Student/Staff Ratio: 4:1

Staff Qualifications: All NOLS instructors complete the rigorous 35-day NOLS instructor course. All possess a minimum of Wilderness First Responder certification. Average age is 31. Typical NOLS instructor has worked for the school five years.

PARTICIPANTS

For Participants Aged: 16–70

The Ideal Candidate: NOLS students are motivated to learn. They are adventurous and are in good physical condition. NOLS students are successful individuals who come to NOLS for our unique hands-on approach to education.

Special Requirements for Participation: Good physical condition.

COSTS

Average Cost: $2,960

Included in Cost: The tuition covers instruction, group gear, food, and lodging. Additional expenses will include transportation to course start location and personal gear. NOLS rents personal gear.

Financial Aid Available: Yes

PACIFIC NORTHWEST OUTDOOR EDUCATOR SEA KAYAKING

THE PROGRAM

Description: This course takes place in the forested Discovery Coast Islands off the central coast of British Columbia. Teaching others how to sea kayak is the focus of this course. Students will be guided in developing classes and lesson plans and then have the opportunity to present those lessons to fellow students and instructors. The course emphasizes not only technical skills, but also leadership, expedition planning, and decision-making.

Specialty: NOLS is the only school that focuses exclusively on leadership, wilderness skills, and the environment. The experience and training of our instructors leads the outdoor education industry.

Program Type: Outdoors/adventure

Classification: Coeducational, residential

Goals: Students should expect to learn wilderness skills—navigation, leave-no-trace outdoor ethics, and first aid. They will develop leadership by actually leading in the backcountry. Students will also learn about the environments in which they are traveling—flora, fauna, geology, and weather.

Focus: Leadership/teamwork, skill-building, and travel

Activities Center On: Kayaking and wilderness

Intensity Level: 4

Duration: 2–4 weeks

Program Offered: Summer

Location: Conway, Washington

Accommodations: Tent

Religious Affiliation: Not relevant

STAFF

Student/Staff Ratio: 4:1

Staff Qualifications: All NOLS instructors complete the rigorous 35-day NOLS instructor course. All possess a minimum of Wilderness First Responder certification. Average age is 31. Typical NOLS instructor has worked for the school five years.

PARTICIPANTS

For Participants Aged: 18–70

The Ideal Candidate: NOLS students are motivated to learn. They are adventurous and are in good physical condition. NOLS students are successful individuals who come to NOLS for our unique hands-on approach to education.

Special Requirements for Participation: Good physical condition.

COSTS

Average Cost: $2,990

Included in Cost: The tuition covers instruction, group gear, food, and lodging. Additional expenses will include transportation to course start location and personal gear. NOLS rents personal gear.

Financial Aid Available: Yes

PACIFIC NORTHWEST TRIP LEADER

THE PROGRAM

Description: This course is designed for practicing outdoor leaders and educators who do not have a lot of time and a huge budget but are motivated to learn the ABC's of taking out groups. Washington's Pasayten Wilderness and Mount Rainier National Park are ideal training grounds for learning how to lead backpacking trips.

Specialty: NOLS is the only school that focuses exclusively on leadership, wilderness skills, and the environment. The experience and training of our instructors leads the outdoor education industry.

Program Type: Outdoors/adventure

Classification: Coeducational, residential

Goals: Students should expect to learn wilderness skills—navigation, leave-no-trace outdoor ethics, and first aid. They will develop leadership by actually leading in the backcountry. Students will also learn about the environments in which they are traveling—flora, fauna, geology, and weather.

Focus: Leadership/teamwork, skill-building, and travel

Activities Center On: Backpacking and wilderness

Intensity Level: 4

Duration: 1–2 weeks

Program Offered: Summer

Location: Seattle, Washington

Accommodations: Tent

Religious Affiliation: Not relevant

STAFF

Student/Staff Ratio: 4:1

Staff Qualifications: All NOLS instructors complete the rigorous 35-day NOLS instructor course. All possess a minimum of Wilderness First Responder certification. Average age is 31. Typical NOLS instructor has worked for the school five years.

PARTICIPANTS

For Participants Aged: 18–70

The Ideal Candidate: NOLS students are motivated to learn. They are adventurous and are in good physical condition. NOLS students are successful individuals who come to NOLS for our unique hands-on approach to education.

Special Requirements for Participation: Good physical condition.

COSTS

Average Cost: $795

Included in Cost: The tuition covers instruction, group gear, food, and lodging. Additional expenses will include trans-

---

portation to course start location and personal gear. NOLS rents personal gear.

Financial Aid Available: Yes

PATAGONIA MOUNTAINEERING

THE PROGRAM

Description: Patagonia's northern and southern icefields extend for hundreds of kilometers along the spine of the Patagonian Andes. They are the largest continuous icefields outside of Antartica and Greenland. Students will learn all the skills needed to carry out remote expeditions. In addition to mountaineering skills, students will also work on teamwork and communication as they are critical components for mountaineering.

Specialty: NOLS is the only school that focuses exclusively on leadership, wilderness skills, and the environment. The experience and training of our instructors leads the outdoor education industry.

Program Type: Outdoors/adventure

Classification: Coeducational, residential

Goals: Students should expect to learn wilderness skills—navigation, leave-no-trace outdoor ethics, and first aid. They will develop leadership by actually leading in the backcountry. Students will also learn about the environments in which they are traveling—flora, fauna, geology, and weather.

Focus: Leadership/teamwork, skill-building, and travel

Activities Center On: Backpacking and wilderness

Intensity Level: 4

Duration: 4–6 weeks

Program Offered: Winter intersession/January term, spring

Location: Coyhaique, Chile

Accommodations: Tent

Religious Affiliation: Not relevant

STAFF

Student/Staff Ratio: 4:1

Staff Qualifications: All NOLS instructors complete the rigorous 35-day NOLS instructor course. All possess a minimum of Wilderness First Responder certification. Average age is 31. Typical NOLS instructor has worked for the school five years.

PARTICIPANTS

For Participants Aged: 17–70

The Ideal Candidate: NOLS students are motivated to learn. They are adventurous and are in good physical condition. NOLS students are successful individuals who come to NOLS for our unique hands-on approach to education.

Special Requirements for Participation: Good physical condition.

COSTS

Average Cost: $4,445

Included in Cost: The tuition covers instruction, group gear, food, and lodging. Additional expenses will include transportation to course start location and personal gear. NOLS rents personal gear.

Financial Aid Available: Yes

RIVER GUIDES

THE PROGRAM

Description: For 21 days, students learn the essentials of whitewater guiding. The River Guides course is designed to give you the skills you need to become a raft guide throughout the United States. Students will be on two different sections of Utah's Green River learning to read rapids, rig boats, captain paddle rafts, row oar rigs, and gain a solid foundation in NOLS' core curriculum.

Specialty: NOLS is the only school that focuses exclusively on leadership, wilderness skills, and the environment. The experience and training of our instructors leads the outdoor education industry.

Program Type: Outdoors/adventure

Classification: Coeducational, residential

Goals: Students should expect to learn wilderness skills—navigation, leave-no-trace outdoor ethics, and first aid. They will develop leadership by actually leading in the backcountry. Students will also learn about the environments in which they are traveling—flora, fauna, geology, and weather.

Focus: Leadership/teamwork and skill-building

Activities Center On: Boating and rafting

Intensity Level: 4

Duration: 2–4 weeks

Program Offered: Summer

Location: Vernal, Utah

Accommodations: Tent

Religious Affiliation: Not relevant

STAFF

Student/Staff Ratio: 4:1

Staff Qualifications: All NOLS instructors complete the rigorous 35-day NOLS instructor course. All possess a minimum of Wilderness First Responder certification. Average age is 31. Typical NOLS instructor has worked for the school five years.

PARTICIPANTS

For Participants Aged: 18–70

The Ideal Candidate: NOLS students are motivated to learn. They are adventurous and are in good physical condition. NOLS students are successful individuals who come to NOLS for our unique hands-on approach to education.

Special Requirements for Participation: Good physical condition.

COSTS

Average Cost: $3,550

Included in Cost: The tuition covers instruction, group gear, food, and lodging. Additional expenses will include transportation to course start location and personal gear. NOLS rents personal gear.

Financial Aid Available: Yes

ROCK AND RIVER

THE PROGRAM

Description: This course combines rock climbing and river travel to give students a solid base of skills to use on other rivers and crags long after the course ends.

Specialty: NOLS is the only school that focuses exclusively on leadership, wilderness skills, and the environment. The experience and training of our instructors leads the outdoor education industry.

Program Type: Outdoors/adventure

Classification: Coeducational, residential

Goals: Students should expect to learn wilderness skills—navigation, leave-no-trace outdoor ethics, and first aid. They will develop leadership by actually leading in the backcountry. Students will also learn about the environments in which they are traveling—flora, fauna, geology, and weather.

Focus: Leadership/teamwork, skill-building, and travel

Activities Center On: Wilderness and kayaking

Intensity Level: 4

Duration: 2–4 weeks

Program Offered: Summer

Location: Lander, Wyoming

Accommodations: Tent

Religious Affiliation: Not relevant

STAFF

Student/Staff Ratio: 6:1

Staff Qualifications: All NOLS instructors complete the 35-day NOLS instructor course. All possess a minimum of Wilderness First Responder certification. Average age is 31. Typical NOLS instructor has worked for the school five years.

PARTICIPANTS

For Participants Aged: 17–70

The Ideal Candidate: NOLS students are motivated to learn. They are adventurous and are in good physical condition. NOLS students are successful individuals who come to NOLS for our unique hands-on approach to education.

Special Requirements for Participation: Good physical condition.

COSTS

Average Cost: $4,025

Included in Cost: The tuition covers instruction, group gear, food, and lodging. Additional expenses will include transportation to Lander, Wyoming. and personal gear. NOLS rents personal gear.

Financial Aid Available: Yes

ROCK CLIMBING

THE PROGRAM

Description: This course is a comprehensive immersion in the fast-growing sport of traditional rock climbing. NOLS has been teaching rock climbing for nearly 40 years, and students in this course benefit from that knowledge and experience. Students have ample time to practice their climbing skills while also developing a strong foundation in wilderness ethics and experience in extended backcountry living.

Specialty: NOLS is the only school that focuses exclusively on leadership, wilderness skills, and the environment. The experience and training of our instructors leads the outdoor education industry.

Program Type: Outdoors/adventure

Classification: Coeducational, residential

Goals: Students should expect to learn wilderness skills—navigation, leave-no-trace outdoor ethics, and first aid. They will develop leadership by actually leading in the backcountry. Students will also learn about the environments in which they are traveling—flora, fauna, geology, and weather.

Focus: Leadership/teamwork, skill-building, and travel

Activities Center On: Wilderness

Intensity Level: 4

Duration: 2–4 weeks

Program Offered: Summer

Location: Lander, Wyoming

Accommodations: Tent

Religious Affiliation: Not relevant

STAFF

Student/Staff Ratio: 4:1

Staff Qualifications: All NOLS instructors complete the 35-day NOLS instructor course. All possess a minimum of Wilderness First Responder certification. Average age is 31. Typical NOLS instructor has worked for the school five years.

PARTICIPANTS

For Participants Aged: 17–70

The Ideal Candidate: NOLS students are motivated to learn. They are adventurous and are in good physical condition. NOLS students are successful individuals who come to NOLS for our unique hands-on approach to education.

Special Requirements for Participation: Good physical condition.

COSTS

Average Cost: $3,100

Included in Cost: The tuition covers instruction, group gear, food and lodging. Additional expenses will include transportation to Lander, Wyoming, and personal gear. NOLS rents personal gear.

Financial Aid Available: Yes

ROCKY MOUNTAIN OUTDOOR EDUCATOR BACKPACKING

THE PROGRAM

Description: On this 23-day course, students learn the latest in outdoor education skills and techniques alongside other individuals for whom teaching is a passion. This course includes a 17-day backpacking session and a 4-day rock climbing camp.

Specialty: NOLS is the only school that focuses exclusively on leadership, wilderness skills, and the environment. The experience and training of our instructors leads the outdoor education industry.

Program Type: Outdoors/adventure

Classification: Coeducational, residential

Goals: Students should expect to learn wilderness skills—navigation, leave-no-trace outdoor ethics, and first aid. They will develop leadership by actually leading in the backcountry. Students will also learn about the environments in which they are traveling—flora, fauna, geology, and weather.

Focus: Leadership/teamwork, skill-building, and travel

Activities Center On: Backpacking and wilderness

Intensity Level: 4

Duration: 2–4 weeks

Program Offered: Summer

Location: Lander, Wyoming

Accommodations: Tent

Religious Affiliation: Not relevant

STAFF

Student/Staff Ratio: 6:1

Staff Qualifications: All NOLS instructors complete the 35-day NOLS instructor course. All possess a minimum of Wilderness First Responder certification. Average age is 31. Typical NOLS instructor has worked for the school five years.

PARTICIPANTS

For Participants Aged: 18–70

The Ideal Candidate: NOLS students are motivated to learn. They are adventurous and are in good physical condition. NOLS students are successful individuals who come to NOLS for our unique hands-on approach to education.

Special Requirements for Participation: Good physical condition.

COSTS

Average Cost: $2,490

Included in Cost: The tuition covers instruction, group gear, food, and lodging. Additional expense will include transportation to Lander, Wyoming, and personal gear. NOLS rents personal gear.

Financial Aid Available: Yes

SEMESTER IN ALASKA

THE PROGRAM

Description: The semester in Alaska includes everyting from the forested coastlines to the snow of the high mountain peaks and the tundra, rivers, and forests in between. With the long days of the northern summer, students have plenty of time to practice skills including sea kayaking, backpacking, river travel, and glacier mountaineering. A semester in Alaska will include an extensive environmental studies curriculum, giving students a unique perspective into some of the world's most stunning wilderness.

Specialty: NOLS is the only school that focuses exclusively on leadership, wilderness skills, and the environment. The experience and training of our instructors leads the outdoor education industry.

Program Type: Outdoors/adventure

Classification: Coeducational, residential

Goals: Students should expect to learn wilderness skills—navigation, leave-no-trace outdoor ethics, and first aid. They will develop leadership by actually leading in the backcountry. Students will also learn about the environments in which they are traveling—flora, fauna, geology, and weather.

Focus: Leadership/teamwork and skill-building

Activities Center On: Backpacking and kayaking

Intensity Level: 4

Duration: Over 8 weeks

Program Offered: Summer

Location: Palmer, Alaska

Accommodations: Tent

Religious Affiliation: Not relevant

STAFF

Student/Staff Ratio: 4:1

Staff Qualifications: All NOLS instructors complete the 35-day NOLS instructor course. All possess a minimum of Wilderness First Responder certification. Average age is 31. Typical NOLS instructor has worked for the school five years.

PARTICIPANTS

For Participants Aged: 17–70

The Ideal Candidate: NOLS students are motivated to learn. They are adventurous and are in good physical condition. NOLS students are successful individuals who come to NOLS for our unique hands-on approach to education.

Special Requirements for Participation: Good physical condition.

COSTS

Average Cost: $7,875

Included in Cost: The tuition covers instruction, group gear, food, and lodging. Additional expense will include transportation to course start location and personal gear. NOLS rents personal gear.

Financial Aid Available: Yes

SEMESTER IN AUSTRALIA

THE PROGRAM

Description: Semester students will have the opportunity to explore one of the most remote regions in the world. For 75 days students tavel as a group through northwestern Australia's Kimberly region. The semester will begin on the Drysdale River for 42 days. Following the canoe section, students backpack for 18 days through escarpment lands. The remaining week is spent living on Sunday Island to learn about Bardi aboriginal culture.

Specialty: NOLS is the only school that focuses exclusively on leadership, wilderness skills, and the environment. The experience and training of our instructors leads the outdoor education industry.

Program Type: Outdoors/adventure

Classification: Coeducational, residential

Goals: Students should expect to learn wilderness skills—navigation, leave-no-trace outdoor ethics, and first aid. They will develop leadership by actually leading in the backcountry. Students will also learn about the environments in which they are traveling—flora, fauna, geology, and weather.

Focus: Leadership/teamwork, skill-building, and cultural

Activities Center On: Boating, backpacking, and wilderness

Intensity Level: 4

Duration: Over 8 weeks

Program Offered: Spring

Location: Broome, Australia

Accommodations: Tent

Religious Affiliation: Not relevant

STAFF

Student/Staff Ratio: 4:1

Staff Qualifications: All NOLS instructors complete the rigorous 35-day NOLS instructor course. All possess a minimum of Wilderness First Responder certification. Average age is 31. Typical NOLS instructor has worked for the school five years.

PARTICIPANTS

For Participants Aged: 18–70

The Ideal Candidate: NOLS students are motivated to learn. They are adventurous and are in good physical condition.

NOLS students are successful individuals who come to NOLS for our unique hands-on approach to education.

Special Requirements for Participation: Good physical condition.

COSTS

Average Cost: $9,925

Included in Cost: The tuition covers instruction, group gear, food, and lodging. Additional expenses will include transportation to course start location and personal gear. NOLS rents personal gear.

Financial Aid Available: Yes

SEMESTER IN BAJA (FALL AND SPRING)

THE PROGRAM

Description: Flanked on the west by the Pacific Ocean and on the east by the Sea of Cortez, the Baja California peninsula is a land of extremes and contrasts. For three months, students explore these contrasting environments on foot, in sea kayak and on a sailboat while learning the skills needed in order to visit these ecosystems comfortably and responsibly in the future.

Specialty: NOLS is the only school that focuses exclusively on leadership, wilderness skills, and the environment. The experience and training of our instructors leads the outdoor education industry.

Program Type: Outdoors/adventure

Classification: Coeducational, residential

Goals: Students should expect to learn wilderness skills—navigation, leave-no-trace outdoor ethics, and first aid. They will develop leadership by actually leading in the backcountry. Students will also learn about the environments in which they are traveling—flora, fauna, geology, and weather.

Focus: Leadership/teamwork, skill-building, and travel

Activities Center On: Backpacking, kayaking, and boating

Intensity Level: 4

Duration: Over 8 weeks

Program Offered: Fall, spring

Location: Mulege, Mexico

Accommodations: Tent

Religious Affiliation: Not relevant

STAFF

Student/Staff Ratio: 4:1

Staff Qualifications: All NOLS instructors complete the rigorous 35-day NOLS instructor course. All possess a minimum of Wilderness First Responder certification. Average age is 31. Typical NOLS instructor has worked for the school five years.

PARTICIPANTS

For Participants Aged: 17–70

The Ideal Candidate: NOLS students are motivated to learn. They are adventurous and are in good physical condition.

NOLS students are successful individuals who come to NOLS for our unique hands-on approach to education.

Special Requirements for Participation: Good physical condition.

COSTS

Average Cost: $8,700

Included in Cost: The tuition covers instruction, group gear, food, and lodging. Additional expenses will include transportation to course start location and personal gear. NOLS rents personal gear.

Financial Aid Available: Yes

SEMESTER IN PATAGONIA (FALL OR SPRING)

THE PROGRAM

Description: For the duration of this semester, students will be in the wilderness. This is a "continuos expedition" with a rendezvous when students meet another semester group to trade mountaineering gear for sea-kayaking gear. Students camp and travel in Patagonia's valleys, travel in the mountains, and sea kayak in breathtaking fjords. Leadership outcomes are strong on the Semester in Patagonia due to the remote nature of the travel.

Specialty: NOLS is the only school that focuses exclusively on leadership, wilderness skills, and the environment. The experience and training of our instructors leads the outdoor education industry.

Program Type: Outdoors/adventure

Classification: Coeducational, residential

Goals: Students should expect to learn wilderness skills—navigation, leave-no-trace outdoor ethics, and first aid. They will develop leadership by actually leading in the backcountry. Students will also learn about the environments in which they are traveling—flora, fauna, geology, and weather.

Focus: Leadership/teamwork, skill-building, and travel

Activities Center On: Backpacking, kayaking, and wilderness

Intensity Level: 4

Duration: Over 8 weeks

Program Offered: Fall, spring

Location: Coyhaique, Chile

Accommodations: Tent

Religious Affiliation: Not relevant

STAFF

Student/Staff Ratio: 4:1

Staff Qualifications: All NOLS instructors complete the rigorous 35-day NOLS instructor course. All possess a minimum of Wilderness First Responder certification. Average age is 31. Typical NOLS instructor has worked for the school five years.

PARTICIPANTS

For Participants Aged: 17–70

The Ideal Candidate: NOLS students are motivated to learn.

They are adventurous and are in good physical condition. NOLS students are successful individuals who come to NOLS for our unique hands-on approach to education.

Special Requirements for Participation: Good physical condition.

COSTS

Average Cost: $10,030

Included in Cost: The tuition covers instruction, group gear, food, and lodging. Additional expenses will include transportation to course start location and personal gear. NOLS rents personal gear.

Financial Aid Available: Yes

SEMESTER IN THE SOUTHWEST (FALL AND SPRING)

THE PROGRAM

Description: Fall and Spring Semesters in the Southwest give students a unique glimpse into the American Southwest's living desert. With rich natural history to explore, students also learn the skills including backpacking, caving, climbing, and canoeing.

Specialty: NOLS is the only school that focuses exclusively on leadership, wilderness skills, and the environment. The experience and training of our instructors leads the outdoor education industry.

Program Type: Outdoors/adventure

Classification: Coeducational, residential

Goals: Students should expect to learn wilderness skills—navigation, leave-no-trace outdoor ethics, and first aid. They will develop leadership by actually leading in the backcountry. Students will also learn about the environments in which they are traveling—flora, fauna, geology, and weather.

Focus: Leadership/teamwork, skill-building, and travel

Activities Center On: Backpacking, boating, and wilderness

Intensity Level: 4

Duration: Over 8 weeks

Program Offered: Fall, summer

Location: Tucson, Arizona

Accommodations: Tent

Religious Affiliation: Not relevant

STAFF

Student/Staff Ratio: 4:1

Staff Qualifications: All NOLS instructors complete the 35-day NOLS instructor course. All possess a minimum of Wilderness First Responder certification. Average age is 31. Typical NOLS instructor has worked for the school five years.

PARTICIPANTS

For Participants Aged: 17–70

The Ideal Candidate: NOLS students are motivated to learn. They are adventurous and are in good physical condition. NOLS students are successful individuals who come to NOLS for our unique hands-on approach to education.

Special Requirements for Participation: Good physical condition.

COSTS

Average Cost: $8,930

Included in Cost: The tuition covers instruction, group gear, food, and lodging. Additional expenses will include transportation to Lander, Wyoming, and personal gear. NOLS rents personal gear.

Financial Aid Available: Yes

SEMESTER IN THE YUKON (SUMMER)

THE PROGRAM

Description: This 75-day expedition explores the the wilds of the Yukon Territory with a backpack, canoe, and mountaineering gear. Students gain skills to be safe and comfortable in remote wilderness areas.

Specialty: NOLS is the only school that focuses exclusively on leadership, wilderness skills, and the environment. The experience and training of our instructors leads the outdoor education industry.

Program Type: Outdoors/adventure

Classification: Coeducational, residential

Goals: Students should expect to learn wilderness skills—navigation, leave-no-trace outdoor ethics, and first aid. They will develop leadership by actually leading in the backcountry. Students will also learn about the environments in which they are traveling—flora, fauna, geology, and weather.

Focus: Leadership/teamwork, skill-building, and travel

Activities Center On: Backpacking, boating, and wilderness

Intensity Level: 3

Duration: Over 8 weeks

Program Offered: Summer

Location: Whitehorse, Yukon Territory, Canada

Accommodations: Tent

Religious Affiliation: Not relevant

STAFF

Student/Staff Ratio: 4:1

Staff Qualifications: All NOLS instructors complete the rigorous 35-day NOLS instructor course. All possess a minimum of Wilderness First Responder certification. Average age is 31. Typical NOLS instructor has worked for the school five years.

PARTICIPANTS

For Participants Aged: 17–70

The Ideal Candidate: NOLS students are motivated to learn. They are adventurous and are in good physical condition.

NOLS students are successful individuals who come to NOLS for our unique hands-on approach to education.

Special Requirements for Participation: Good physical condition.

COSTS

Average Cost: $7,665

Included in Cost: The tuition covers instruction, group gear, food, and lodging. Additional expenses include travel to course starting location and personal gear. NOLS rents personal gear.

Financial Aid Available: Yes

SKIING

THE PROGRAM

Description: This course combines backcountry travel with experience at a commercial ski area to develop skilled and responsible winter wilderness travelers. Ski instruction begins with two days at Grand Targhee Ski Resort where students learn basic cross-country techniques and the telemark turn. Students then head into the backcountry for a nine-day expedition.

Specialty: NOLS is the only school that focuses exclusively on leadership, wilderness skills, and the environment. The experience and training of our instructors leads the outdoor education industry.

Program Type: Outdoors/adventure

Classification: Coeducational, residential

Goals: Students should expect to learn wilderness skills—navigation, leave-no-trace outdoor ethics, and first aid. They will develop leadership by actually leading in the backcountry. Students will also learn about the environments in which they are traveling—flora, fauna, geology, and weather.

Focus: Leadership/teamwork and skill-building

Activities Center On: Skiing and wilderness

Intensity Level: 4

Duration: 1–2 weeks

Program Offered: Winter intersession/January term

Location: Driggs, Idaho

Accommodations: Tent

Religious Affiliation: Not relevant

STAFF

Student/Staff Ratio: 4:1

Staff Qualifications: All NOLS instructors complete the rigorous 35-day NOLS instructor course. All possess a minimum of Wilderness First Responder certification. Average age is 31. Typical NOLS instructor has worked for the school five years.

PARTICIPANTS

For Participants Aged: 17–70

The Ideal Candidate: NOLS students are motivated to learn.

They are adventurous and are in good physical condition. NOLS students are successful individuals who come to NOLS for our unique hands-on approach to education.

Special Requirements for Participation: Good physical condition.

COSTS

Average Cost: $1,385

Included in Cost: The tuition covers instruction, group gear, food, and lodging. Additional expenses include travel to course starting location and personal gear. NOLS rents personal gear.

Financial Aid Available: Yes

SNOWBOARDING

THE PROGRAM

Description: A NOLS snowboarding course begins with learning basic skills needed for safe winter travel in the backcountry—everything from lighting stoves and lanterns to dressing for the field and knowing what to do in an avalanche. After learning snowboarding techniques at the Gran Targhee Ski Resort, students head out into either the Snake River Range, Bighole Range, or the Tetons.

Specialty: NOLS is the only school that focuses exclusively on leadership, wilderness skills, and the environment. The experience and training of our instructors leads the outdoor education industry.

Program Type: Outdoors/adventure

Classification: Coeducational, residential

Goals: Students should expect to learn wilderness skills—navigation, leave-no-trace outdoor ethics, and first aid. They will develop leadership by actually leading in the backcountry. Students will also learn about the environments in which they are traveling—flora, fauna, geology, and weather.

Focus: Leadership/teamwork and skill-building

Activities Center On: Wilderness

Intensity Level: 4

Duration: 1–2 weeks

Program Offered: Winter intersession/January term

Location: Driggs, Idaho

Accommodations: Tent

Religious Affiliation: Not relevant

STAFF

Student/Staff Ratio: 4:1

Staff Qualifications: All NOLS instructors complete the rigorous 35-day NOLS instructor course. All possess a minimum of Wilderness First Responder certification. Average age is 31. Typical NOLS instructor has worked for the school five years.

PARTICIPANTS

For Participants Aged: 17–70

The Ideal Candidate: NOLS students are motivated to learn. They are adventurous and are in good physical condition. NOLS students are successful individuals who come to NOLS for our unique hands-on approach to education.

Special Requirements for Participation: Good physical condition.

COSTS

Average Cost: $1,675

Included in Cost: The tuition covers instruction, group gear, food, and lodging. Additional expenses include travel to course starting location and personal gear. NOLS rents personal gear.

Financial Aid Available: Yes

SONORAN NATURAL HISTORY

THE PROGRAM

Description: This unique NOLS course combines 2 days of formal natural history training with 18 days of wilderness living and travel for a further study of the desert ecosystem.

Specialty: NOLS is the only school that focuses exclusively on leadership, wilderness skills, and the environment. The experience and training of our instructors leads the outdoor education industry.

Program Type: Outdoors/adventure

Classification: Coeducational, residential

Goals: Students should expect to learn wilderness skills—navigation, leave-no-trace outdoor ethics, and first aid. They will develop leadership by actually leading in the backcountry. Students will also learn about the environments in which they are traveling—flora, fauna, geology, and weather.

Focus: Leadership/teamwork, skill-building, and travel

Activities Center On: Backpacking and wilderness

Intensity Level: 4

Duration: 2–4 weeks

Program Offered: Spring

Location: Tucson, Arizona

Accommodations: Tent

Religious Affiliation: Not relevant

STAFF

Student/Staff Ratio: 4:1

Staff Qualifications: All NOLS instructors complete the rigorous 35-day NOLS instructor course. All possess a minimum of Wilderness First Responder certification. Average age is 31. Typical NOLS instructor has worked for the school five years.

PARTICIPANTS

For Participants Aged: 18–70

The Ideal Candidate: NOLS students are motivated to learn. They are adventurous and are in good physical condition. NOLS students are successful individuals who come to NOLS

for our unique hands-on approach to education.

Special Requirements for Participation: Good physical condition.

COSTS

Average Cost: $2,585

Included in Cost: The tuition covers instruction, group gear, food, and lodging. Additional expenses will include transportation to course start location and personal gear. NOLS rents personal gear.

Financial Aid Available: Yes

SOUTHWEST OUTDOOR EDUCATOR BACKPACKING

THE PROGRAM

Description: This 31-day course begins with a 19-day backpacking expedition in the remote Kofa National Wildlife Refuge in southwestern Arizona. Ten days are spent at a backcountry base camp learning rock climbing skills. This course is designed for active and aspiring outdoor educators and teachers looking for the opportunity to develop the knowledge for teaching field-based wilderness education programs.

Specialty: NOLS is the only school that focuses exclusively on leadership, wilderness skills, and the environment. The experience and training of our instructors leads the outdoor education industry.

Program Type: Outdoors/adventure

Classification: Coeducational, residential

Goals: Students should expect to learn wilderness skills—navigation, leave-no-trace outdoor ethics, and first aid. They will develop leadership by actually leading in the backcountry. Students will also learn about the environments in which they are traveling—flora, fauna, geology, and weather.

Focus: Leadership/teamwork, skill-building, and travel

Activities Center On: Backpacking, outdoors/adventure, and wilderness

Intensity Level: 4

Duration: 2–4 weeks

Program Offered: Spring

Location: Tucson, Arizona

Accommodations: Tent

Religious Affiliation: Not relevant

STAFF

Student/Staff Ratio: 4:1

Staff Qualifications: All NOLS instructors complete the 35-day NOLS instructor course. All possess a minimum of Wilderness First Responder certification. Average age is 31. Typical NOLS instructor has worked for the school five years.

PARTICIPANTS

For Participants Aged: 18–70

The Ideal Candidate: NOLS students are motivated to learn.

They are adventurous and are in good physical condition. NOLS students are successful individuals who come to NOLS for our unique hands-on approach to education.

Special Requirements for Participation: Good physical condition.

Costs

Average Cost: $3,165

Included in Cost: The tuition covers instruction, group gear, food, and lodging. Additional expenses will include transportation to Lander, Wyoming, and personal gear. NOLS rents personal gear.

Financial Aid Available: Yes

Southwest Rock Climbing

The Program

Description: This course is for students interested in learning comprehensive rock climbing and desert travel skills.

Specialty: NOLS is the only school that focuses exclusively on leadership, wilderness skills, and the environment. The experience and training of our instructors leads the outdoor education industry.

Program Type: Outdoors/adventure

Classification: Coeducational, residential

Goals: Students should expect to learn wilderness skills—navigation, leave-no-trace outdoor ethics, and first aid. They will develop leadership by actually leading in the backcountry. Students will also learn about the environments in which they are traveling—flora, fauna, geology, and weather.

Focus: Leadership/teamwork and skill-building

Intensity Level: 4

Duration: 2–4 weeks

Program Offered: Spring

Location: Tucson, Arizona

Accommodations: Tent

Religious Affiliation: Not relevant

Staff

Student/Staff Ratio: 4:1

Staff Qualifications: All NOLS instructors complete the 35-day NOLS instructor course. All possess a minimum of Wilderness First Responder certification. Average age is 31. Typical NOLS instructor has worked for the school five years.

Participants

For Participants Aged: 17–70

The Ideal Candidate: NOLS students are motivated to learn. They are adventurous and are in good physical condition. NOLS students are successful individuals who come to NOLS for our unique hands-on approach to education.

Special Requirements for Participation: Good physical condition.

Costs

Average Cost: $3,050

Included in Cost: The tuition covers instruction, group gear, food, and lodging. Additional expenses will include transportation to Lander, Wyoming, and personal gear. NOLS rents personal gear.

Financial Aid Available: Yes

Spring Semester in the Rockies

The Program

Description: This 70-day semester is the original semester in wilderness education. A spring semester may include river travel, caving, winter camping and skiing, horsepacking, and rock climbing. Students leave with a complete set of skills to lead and teach in the backcountry, whether in the field of outdoor education or with family and friends.

Specialty: NOLS is the only school that focuses exclusively on leadership, wilderness skills, and the environment. The experience and training of our instructors leads the outdoor education industry.

Program Type: Outdoors/adventure

Classification: Coeducational, residential

Goals: Students should expect to learn wilderness skills—navigation, leave-no-trace outdoor ethics, and first aid. They will develop leadership by actually leading in the backcountry. Students will also learn about the environments in which they are traveling—flora, fauna, geology, and weather.

Focus: Leadership/teamwork, skill-building, and travel

Activities Center On: Backpacking and outdoors/adventure

Intensity Level: 4

Duration: Over 8 weeks

Program Offered: Spring

Location: Lander, Wyoming

Accommodations: Tent

Religious Affiliation: Not relevant

Staff

Student/Staff Ratio: 4:1

Staff Qualifications: All NOLS instructors complete the 35-day NOLS instructor course. All possess a minimum of Wilderness First Responder certification. Average age is 31. Typical NOLS instructor has worked for the school five years.

Participants

For Participants Aged: 17–70

The Ideal Candidate: NOLS students are motivated to learn. They are adventurous and are in good physical condition. NOLS students are successful individuals who come to NOLS for our unique hands-on approach to education.

Special Requirements for Participation: Good physical condition.

Costs

Average Cost: $7,825

Included in Cost: The tuition covers instruction, group gear, food, and lodging. Additional expenses will include transportation to Lander, Wyoming, and personal gear. NOLS rents personal gear.

Financial Aid Available: Yes

SUMMER SEMESTER IN THE ROCKIES

THE PROGRAM

Description: This 70-day semester is the original semester in wilderness education. With three sections—including backpacking, rock climbing, and river travel—students leave with a complete set of skills to lead and teach in the backcountry, whether in the field of outdoor education or with family and friends.

Specialty: NOLS is the only school that focuses exclusively on leadership, wilderness skills, and the environment. The experience and training of our instructors leads the outdoor education industry.

Program Type: Outdoors/adventure

Classification: Coeducational, residential

Goals: Students should expect to learn wilderness skills—navigation, leave-no-trace outdoor ethics, and first aid. They will develop leadership by actually leading in the backcountry. Students will also learn about the environments in which they are traveling—flora, fauna, geology, and weather.

Focus: Leadership/teamwork, skill-building, and travel

Activities Center On: Backpacking, outdoors/adventure, and boating

Intensity Level: 4

Duration: Over 8 weeks

Program Offered: Summer

Location: Lander, Wyoming

Accommodations: Tent

Religious Affiliation: Not relevant

STAFF

Student/Staff Ratio: 4:1

Staff Qualifications: All NOLS instructors complete the 35-day NOLS instructor course. All possess a minimum of Wilderness First Responder certification. Average age is 31. Typical NOLS instructor has worked for the school five years.

PARTICIPANTS

For Participants Aged: 17–70

The Ideal Candidate: NOLS students are motivated to learn. They are adventurous and are in good physical condition. NOLS students are successful individuals who come to NOLS for our unique hands-on approach to education.

Special Requirements for Participation: Good physical condition.

Costs

Average Cost: $7,825

Included in Cost: The tuition covers instruction, group gear, food, and lodging. Additional expenses will include transportation to Lander, Wyoming, and personal gear. NOLS rents personal gear.

Financial Aid Available: Yes

TETON VALLEY SEMESTER (SUMMER OR FALL)

THE PROGRAM

Description: Semester students in the Teton Valley will cover a variety of skills and topics to give students the ability and confidence to travel comfortably and safely in the wilderness. Summer semester sections include backpacking, river travel, and rock climbing. Fall semester sections include backpacking, river travel, winter camping and skiing, rock climbing, canyon travel, and Wilderness First Responder.

Specialty: NOLS is the only school that focuses exclusively on leadership, wilderness skills, and the environment. The experience and training of our instructors leads the outdoor education industry.

Program Type: Outdoors/adventure

Classification: Coeducational, residential

Goals: Students should expect to learn wilderness skills—navigation, leave-no-trace outdoor ethics, and first aid. They will develop leadership by actually leading in the backcountry. Students will also learn about the environments in which they are traveling—flora, fauna, geology, and weather.

Focus: Leadership/teamwork, skill-building, and travel

Activities Center On: Backpacking, boating, and wilderness

Intensity Level: 4

Duration: Over 8 weeks

Program Offered: Fall, summer

Location: Driggs, Idaho

Accommodations: Tent

Religious Affiliation: Not relevant

STAFF

Student/Staff Ratio: 4:1

Staff Qualifications: All NOLS instructors complete the rigorous 35-day NOLS instructor course. All possess a minimum of Wilderness First Responder certification. Average age is 31. Typical NOLS instructor has worked for the school five years.

PARTICIPANTS

For Participants Aged: 17–70

The Ideal Candidate: NOLS students are motivated to learn. They are adventurous and are in good physical condition. NOLS students are successful individuals who come to NOLS for our unique hands-on approach to education.

Special Requirements for Participation: Good physical condition.

COSTS

Average Cost: $7,850

Included in Cost: The tuition covers instruction, group gear, food, and lodging. Additional expenses include travel to course starting location and personal gear. NOLS rents personal gear.

Financial Aid Available: Yes

TETON VALLEY WINTER OUTDOOR EDUCATOR

THE PROGRAM

Description: This course, designed for practicing or aspiring winter educators, will give students the skills they need to teach in any winter wilderness. This course provides some of the best expedition training at the school and is the longest of our winter course offerings. NOLS asks that students bring some skiing ability to this course. Students also receive instruction in telemark skiing, avalanche clinic, and camping comfortably in snow caves and igloos.

Specialty: NOLS is the only school that focuses exclusively on leadership, wilderness skills, and the environment. The experience and training of our instructors leads the outdoor education industry.

Program Type: Outdoors/adventure

Classification: Coeducational, residential

Goals: Students should expect to learn wilderness skills—navigation, leave-no-trace outdoor ethics, and first aid. They will develop leadership by actually leading in the backcountry. Students will also learn about the environments in which they are traveling—flora, fauna, geology, and weather.

Focus: Leadership/teamwork and skill-building

Activities Center On: Skiing, backpacking, and travel

Intensity Level: 4

Duration: 2–4 weeks

Program Offered: Winter intersession/January term

Location: Driggs, Idaho

Accommodations: Tent

Religious Affiliation: Not relevant

STAFF

Student/Staff Ratio: 4:1

Staff Qualifications: All NOLS instructors complete the rigorous 35-day NOLS instructor course. All possess a minimum of Wilderness First Responder certification. Average age is 31. Typical NOLS instructor has worked for the school five years.

PARTICIPANTS

For Participants Aged: 18–70

The Ideal Candidate: NOLS students are motivated to learn. They are adventurous and are in good physical condition. NOLS students are successful individuals who come to NOLS for our unique hands-on approach to education.

Special Requirements for Participation: Good physical condition.

COSTS

Average Cost: $1,775

Included in Cost: The tuition covers instruction, group gear, food, and lodging. Additional expenses include travel to course starting location and personal gear. NOLS rents personal gear.

Financial Aid Available: Yes

WILDERNESS HORSEPACKING

THE PROGRAM

Description: This three-week backcountry horsepacking expedition will take you from the NOLS-owned and -operated Three Peaks Ranch into the wilderness of Wyoming. On this course students learn the basics of western horsemanship—care and feeding, horse behavior, tack, saddling, and riding. Additionally students learn the unique skills of packing and traveling with horses.

Specialty: NOLS is the only school that focuses exclusively on leadership, wilderness skills, and the environment. The experience and training of our instructors leads the outdoor education industry.

Program Type: Outdoors/adventure

Classification: Coeducational, residential

Goals: Students should expect to learn wilderness skills—navigation, leave-no-trace outdoor ethics, and first aid. They will develop leadership by actually leading in the backcountry. Students will also learn about the environments in which they are traveling—flora, fauna, geology, and weather.

Focus: Leadership/teamwork, skill-building, and travel

Activities Center On: Wilderness and outdoors/adventure

Intensity Level: 3

Duration: 2–4 weeks

Program Offered: Summer

Location: Boulder, Wyoming

Accommodations: Tent

Religious Affiliation: Not relevant

STAFF

Student/Staff Ratio: 6:1

Staff Qualifications: All NOLS instructors complete the 35-day NOLS instructor course. All possess a minimum of Wilderness First Responder certification. Average age is 31. Typical NOLS instructor has worked for the school five years.

PARTICIPANTS

For Participants Aged: 16–70

The Ideal Candidate: NOLS students are motivated to learn. They are adventurous and are in good physical condition. NOLS students are successful individuals who come to NOLS for our unique hands-on approach to education.

Special Requirements for Participation: Good physical condition.

Costs

Average Cost: $3,530

Included in Cost: The tuition covers instruction, group gear, food, and lodging. Additional expense will include transportation to Lander, Wyoming, and personal gear. NOLS rents personal gear.

Financial Aid Available: Yes

Wilderness Natural History

The Program

Description: NOLS offers one course with a curriculum focused on natural history. Students travel across rugged mountain terrain, learn to camp in grizzly bear country, and cross rivers. This course is for students with a background in biology who want a nontraditional approach to biology, ecology, zoology, and natural history while learning to live and travel in the wilderness.

Specialty: NOLS is the only school that focuses exclusively on leadership, wilderness skills, and the environment. The experience and training of our instructors leads the outdoor education industry.

Program Type: Outdoors/adventure

Classification: Coeducational, residential

Goals: Students should expect to learn wilderness skills—navigation, leave-no-trace outdoor ethics, and first aid. They will develop leadership by actually leading in the backcountry. Students will also learn about the environments in which they are traveling—flora, fauna, geology, and weather.

Focus: Academic/pre-college enrichment, leadership/teamwork, and travel

Activities Center On: Backpacking

Intensity Level: 4

Duration: 2–4 weeks

Program Offered: Summer

Location: Lander, Wyoming

Accommodations: Tent

Religious Affiliation: Not relevant

Staff

Student/Staff Ratio: 4:1

Staff Qualifications: All NOLS instructors complete the 35-day NOLS instructor course. All possess a minimum of Wilderness First Responder certification. Average age is 31. Typical NOLS instructor has worked for the school five years.

Participants

For Participants Aged: 16–70

The Ideal Candidate: NOLS students are motivated to learn. They are adventurous and are in good physical condition. NOLS students are successful individuals who come to NOLS

for our unique hands-on approach to education.

Special Requirements for Participation: Good physical condition.

Costs

Average Cost: $3,150

Included in Cost: The tuition covers instruction, group gear, food, and lodging. Additional expense will include transportation to Lander, Wyoming, and personal gear. NOLS rents personal gear.

Financial Aid Available: Yes

Wind River Mountaineering

The Program

Description: The rugged glacier-carved Wind River Range is famous for its sheer granite headwalls, spires, and towering 13,000-foot summits covered with rock and ice. NOLS students learn real mountaineering skills such as belaying, rappelling, climbing techniques, and anchor placement—all while traveling over, around, and through the rocky steep terrain of the Wind Rivers. The route may allow students to learn snow and ice climbing techniques as well.

Specialty: NOLS is the only school that focuses exclusively on leadership, wilderness skills, and the environment. The experience and training of our instructors leads the outdoor education industry.

Program Type: Outdoors/adventure

Classification: Coeducational, residential

Goals: Students should expect to learn wilderness skills—navigation, leave-no-trace outdoor ethics, and first aid. They will develop leadership by actually leading in the backcountry. Students will also learn about the environments in which they are traveling—flora, fauna, geology, and weather.

Focus: Leadership/teamwork, skill-building, and travel

Activities Center On: Wilderness and outdoors/adventure

Intensity Level: 4

Duration: 2–4 weeks

Program Offered: Summer

Location: Lander, Wyoming

Accommodations: Tent

Religious Affiliation: Not relevant

Staff

Student/Staff Ratio: 4:1

Staff Qualifications: All NOLS instructors complete the 35-day NOLS instructor course. All possess a minimum of Wilderness First Responder certification. Average age is 31. Typical NOLS instructor has worked for the school five years.

Participants

For Participants Aged: 17–70

The Ideal Candidate: NOLS students are motivated to learn. They are adventurous and are in good physical condition.

NOLS students are successful individuals who come to NOLS for our unique hands-on approach to education.

Special Requirements for Participation: Good physical condition.

Costs

Average Cost: $3,240

Included in Cost: The tuition covers instruction, group gear, food, and lodging. Additional expenses will include transportation to Lander, Wyoming, and personal gear. NOLS rents personal gear.

Financial Aid Available: Yes

Wind River Wilderness

The Program

Description: This 30-day backpacking course, offered in Wyoming's Wind River Range, focuses on outdoor skills, leadership, and environmental studies. This course features some rock climbing and fly fishing.

Specialty: NOLS is the only school that focuses exclusively on leadership, wilderness, and the environment. The experience and the training of our instructors leads the outdoor education industry.

Program Type: Outdoors/adventure

Classification: Coeducational, residential

Goals: Students should expect to learn wilderness skills—navigation, leave-no-trace camping, and first aid. They will develop leadership by actually leading in the backcountry. They will also learn abou the environments in which they are traveling—flora, fauna, geology, meteorology, etc.

Focus: Leadership/teamwork, skill-building, and travel

Activities Center On: Backpacking and wilderness

Intensity Level: 4

Duration: 4–6 weeks

Program Offered: Summer

Location: Lander, Wyoming

Accommodations: Tent

Years in Operation: 38

Religious Affiliation: Not relevant

Staff

Student/Staff Ratio: 6:1

Staff Qualifications: All NOLS instructors complete the 35-day NOLS instructors course. All posess minimum of Wilderness First Responder certification. Average age is 31. Typical NOLS instructor has worked for the school five years.

Participants

Average Number of Participants: 300

For Participants Aged: 16–70

The Ideal Candidate: NOLS students are motivated to learn.

They are adventurous and are in good physical condition. They are successful individuals who come to NOLS for our unique hands-on approach to education.

Special Requirements for Participation: Good physical condition.

Costs

Average Cost: $3,070

Included in Cost: The tuition covers instruction, group gear, food, and lodging. Additional expenses will include transportation to Lander, Wyoming, and personal gear. NOLS rents personal gear.

Financial Aid Available: Yes

Wyoming Adventure

The Program

Description: This 30-day course, offered in Wyoming's Wind River Range, focuses on outdoor skills, leadership, and environmental studies. This course features traveling camp to camp, rock climbing, fly fishing, exploring, and achieving.

Specialty: NOLS is the only school that focuses exclusively on leadership, wilderness skills, and the environment. The experience and training of our instructors leads the outdoor education industry.

Program Type: Outdoors/adventure

Classification: Coeducational, residential

Goals: Students should expect to learn wilderness skills—navigation, leave-no-trace outdoor ethics, and first aid. They will develop leadership by actually leading in the backcountry. Students will also learn about the environments in which they are traveling—flora, fauna, geology, and weather.

Focus: Leadership/teamwork, skill-building, and travel

Activities Center On: Backpacking and wilderness

Intensity Level: 3

Duration: 4–6 weeks

Program Offered: Summer

Location: Lander, Wyoming

Accommodations: Tent

Years in Operation: 38

Religious Affiliation: Not relevant

Staff

Student/Staff Ratio: 6:1

Staff Qualifications: All NOLS instructors complete the 35-day NOLS instructor course. All possess a minimum of Wilderness First Responder certification. Average age is 31. Typical NOLS instructor has worked for the school five years.

Participants

Average Number of Participants: 300

For Participants Aged: 14–15

The Ideal Candidate: NOLS students are motivated to learn. They are adventurous and are in good physical condition. NOLS students are successful individuals who come to NOLS for our unique hands-on approach to education.

Special Requirements for Participation: Good physical condition.

Costs

Average Cost: $3,575

Included in Cost: The tuition covers instruction, group gear, food, and lodging. Additional expene will include transportation to Lander, Wyoming, and personal gear. NOLS rents personal gear.

Financial Aid Available: Yes

Yukon Backpacking

The Program

Description: The Yukon Territory is a wild and trail-less wilderness of thick bush and stunning open mountain travel. Students explore and learn in one of the following remote Yukon ranges: the Ogilvie, Pelly, Ruby, Coast, Cassiar, or Selwyn Mountains. Students learn to cross rivers, cook, travel in bear country, and explore areas visited by only a few people.

Specialty: NOLS is the only school that focuses exclusively on leadership, wilderness skills, and the environment. The experience and training of our instructors leads the outdoor education industry.

Program Type: Outdoors/adventure

Classification: Coeducational, residential

Goals: Students should expect to learn wilderness skills—navigation, leave-no-trace outdoor ethics, and first aid. They will develop leadership by actually leading in the backcountry. Students will also learn about the environments in which they are traveling—flora, fauna, geology, and weather.

Focus: Leadership/teamwork and skill-building

Activities Center On: Backpacking and wilderness

Intensity Level: 4

Duration: 2–4 weeks

Program Offered: Summer

Location: Whitehorse, Yukon Territory, Canada

Accommodations: Tent

Religious Affiliation: Not relevant

Staff

Student/Staff Ratio: 4:1

Staff Qualifications: All NOLS instructors complete the rigorous 35-day NOLS instructor course. All possess a minimum of Wilderness First Responder certification. Average age is 31. Typical NOLS instructor has worked for the school five years.

Participants

For Participants Aged: 16–70

The Ideal Candidate: NOLS students are motivated to learn. They are adventurous and are in good physical condition. NOLS students are successful individuals who come to NOLS for our unique hands-on approach to education.

Special Requirements for Participation: Good physical condition

Costs

Average Cost: $2,850

Included in Cost: The tuition covers instruction, group gear, food, and lodging. Additional expenses include travel to course starting location and personal gear. NOLS rents personal gear.

Financial Aid Available: Yes

Yukon Backpacking and River

The Program

Description: This 45-day summer expedition begins with backpacking in the alpine region of the Pelly or Cassiar Mountains of the Yukon Territory. After two or three weeks, students trade in boots for boats. The students travel on the Hess or South MacMillan River in tandem canoes learning the art of wilderness canoe expeditions.

Specialty: NOLS is the only school that focuses exclusively on leadership, wilderness skills, and the environment. The experience and training of our instructors leads the outdoor education industry.

Program Type: Outdoors/adventure

Classification: Coeducational, residential

Goals: Students should expect to learn wilderness skills—navigation, leave-no-trace outdoor ethics, and first aid. They will develop leadership by actually leading in the backcountry. Students will also learn about the environments in which they are traveling—flora, fauna, geology, and weather.

Focus: Leadership/teamwork and skill-building

Activities Center On: Boating, backpacking, and wilderness

Intensity Level: 4

Duration: 4–6 weeks

Program Offered: Summer

Location: Whitehorse, Yukon Territory, Canada

Accommodations: Tent

Religious Affiliation: Not relevant

STAFF

Student/Staff Ratio: 4:1

Staff Qualifications: All NOLS instructors complete the rigorous 35-day NOLS instructor course. All possess a minimum of Wilderness First Responder certification. Average age is 31. Typical NOLS instructor has worked for the school five years.

PARTICIPANTS

For Participants Aged: 17+

The Ideal Candidate: NOLS students are motivated to learn. They are adventurous and are in good physical condition. NOLS students are successful individuals who come to NOLS for our unique hands-on approach to education.

Special Requirements for Participation: Good physical condition.

COSTS

Average Cost: $5,355

Included in Cost: The tuition covers instruction, group gear, food, and lodging. Additional expenses include travel to course starting location and personal gear. NOLS rents personal gear.

Financial Aid Available? Yes

YUKON CANOEING 32-DAY EXPEDITION

THE PROGRAM

Description: This 32-day canoe expedition travels the Hart or Hess River in the Yukon Territory of northern Canada. Both rivers are preeminent examples of remote, challenging wilderness canoeing. In addition to learning paddling skills, students also learn to camp and be comfortable with a group in the outdoors in all weather.

Specialty: NOLS is the only school that focuses exclusively on leadership, wilderness skills, and the environment. The experience and training of our instructors leads the outdoor education industry.

Program Type: Outdoors/adventure

Classification: Coeducational, residential

Goals: Students should expect to learn wilderness skills—navigation, leave-no-trace outdoor ethics, and first aid. They will develop leadership by actually leading in the backcountry. Students will also learn about the environments in which they are traveling—flora, fauna, geology, and weather.

Focus: Leadership/teamwork and skill-building

Activities Center On: Boating and wilderness

Intensity Level: 4

Duration: 4–6 weeks

Program Offered: Summer

Location: Whitehorse, Yukon Territory, Canada

Accommodations: Tent

Religious Affiliation: Not relevant

STAFF

Student/Staff Ratio: 4:1

Staff Qualifications: All NOLS instructors complete the rigorous 35-day NOLS instructor course. All possess a minimum of Wilderness First Responder certification. Average age is 31. Typical NOLS instructor has worked for the school five years.

PARTICIPANTS

For Participants Aged: 17–70

The Ideal Candidate: NOLS students are motivated to learn. They are adventurous and are in good physical condition. NOLS students are successful individuals who come to NOLS for our unique hands-on approach to education.

Special Requirements for Participation: Good physical condition.

COSTS

Average Cost: $3,340

Included in Cost: The tuition covers instruction, group gear, food, and lodging. Additional expenses include travel to course starting location and personal gear. NOLS rents personal gear.

Financial Aid Available: Yes

YUKON CANOEING 55-DAY EXPEDITION

THE PROGRAM

Description: This 55-day expedition explores an entire watershed in the Yukon and Northwest Territories of northern Canada. The course begins by exploring the threads and twists of a creek at the Continental Divide that flows down to become a mountain whitewater river, the Keele, which eventually spills into the Mackenzie River—one of the largest rivers in North America. The land here is accessible only by boat or plane, and tandem canoes serve as both home and vehicle!

Specialty: NOLS is the only school that focuses exclusively on leadership, wilderness skills, and the environment. The experience and training of our instructors leads the outdoor education industry.

Program Type: Outdoors/adventure

Classification: Coeducational, residential

Goals: Students should expect to learn wilderness skills—navigation, leave-no-trace outdoor ethics, and first aid. They will develop leadership by actually leading in the backcountry. Students will also learn about the environments in which they are traveling—flora, fauna, geology, and weather.

Focus: Leadership/teamwork and skill-building

Activities Center On: Boating and wilderness

Intensity Level: 4

Duration: 4–6 weeks

Program Offered: Summer

Location: Whitehorse, Yukon Territory, Canada

Accommodations: Tent

Religious Affiliation: Not relevant

STAFF

Student/Staff Ratio: 4:1

Staff Qualifications: All NOLS instructors complete the rigorous 35-day NOLS instructor course. All possess a minimum of Wilderness First Responder certification. Average age is 31. Typical NOLS instructor has worked for the school five years.

PARTICIPANTS

For Participants Aged: 17–70

The Ideal Candidate: NOLS students are motivated to learn. They are adventurous and are in good physical condition. NOLS students are successful individuals who come to NOLS for our unique hands-on approach to education.

Special Requirements for Participation: Good physical condition.

COSTS

Average Cost: $5,980

Included in Cost: The tuition covers instruction, group gear, food, and lodging. Additional expenses include travel to course starting location and personal gear. NOLS rents personal gear.

Financial Aid Available: Yes

YUKON OUTDOOR EDUCATOR BACKPACKING AND RIVER

THE PROGRAM

Description: This expedition for practicing and aspiring outdoor educators combines the skill of wilderness backpacking with an introduction to northern river canoeing in Canada's Yukon Territory. Throughout the 24-day course, students observe and discuss different teaching techniques.

Specialty: NOLS is the only school that focuses exclusively on leadership, wilderness skills, and the environment. The experience and training of our instructors leads the outdoor education industry.

Program Type: Outdoors/adventure

Classification: Coeducational, residential

Goals: Students should expect to learn wilderness skills—navigation, leave-no-trace outdoor ethics, and first aid. They will develop leadership by actually leading in the backcountry. Students will also learn about the environments in which they are traveling—flora, fauna, geology, and weather.

Focus: Leadership/teamwork and skill-building

Activities Center On: Backpacking, boating, and wilderness

Intensity Level: 4

Duration: 2–4 weeks

Program Offered: Summer

Location: Whitehorse, Yukon Territory, Canada

Accommodations: Tent

Religious Affiliation: Not relevant

STAFF

Student/Staff Ratio: 4:1

Staff Qualifications: All NOLS instructors complete the rigorous 35-day NOLS instructor course. All possess a minimum of Wilderness First Responder certification. Average age is 31. Typical NOLS instructor has worked for the school five years.

PARTICIPANTS

For Participants Aged: 18–70

The Ideal Candidate: NOLS students are motivated to learn. They are adventurous and are in good physical condition. NOLS students are successful individuals who come to NOLS for our unique hands-on approach to education.

Special Requirements for Participation: Good physical condition.

COSTS

Average Cost: $2,490

Included in Cost: The tuition covers instruction, group gear, food, and lodging. Additional expenses include travel to course starting location and personal gear. NOLS rents personal gear.

Financial Aid Available: Yes

NATIONAL STUDENT LEADERSHIP CONFERENCE

Religious Affiliation: Not relevant

For More Information:
  Contact: Paul Lisnek, Executive Director
       4800 North Federal Highway
       Suite 302A
       Boca Raton, FL 33431
  Phone: 561-362-8585
  Fax: 561-362-8383
  Email: information@nslcleaders.org
  Website: www.nslcleaders.org

BUSINESS AND TECHNOLOGY

THE PROGRAM

Description: A comprehensive program of seminars, interactive business simulations, and debate that shows students the different angles of the business world.

Specialty: Focus on academic and leadership skills to simulate the realities of working in the business world.

Program Type: Academic/pre-college enrichment

Classification: Coeducational, residential

Goals: Realistic view of the way the business world operates—from profits to ethics.

Focus: Academic/pre-college enrichment, leadership/teamwork, and educational exchange

Activities Center On: Academic

Intensity Level: 4

Duration: 1–2 weeks

Program Offered: Summer

Location: Washington, DC

Accommodations: Dormitory

Years in Operation: 14

Religious Affiliation: Not relevant

STAFF

Student/Staff Ratio: 12:1

Staff Qualifications: Speakers and professors of varied professional backgrounds; additional staffing: college and graduate students, almost all of which are alumni of past NSLC programs.

PARTICIPANTS

Average Number of Participants: 200

For Participants Aged: 14–18

The Ideal Candidate: Strong students who want to be involved in projects that simulate the business experience.

Special Requirements for Participation: None.

COSTS

Average Cost: $1,799

Included in Cost: Food, housing, field trips, and course materials.

Financial Aid Available: Yes

INTERNATIONAL DIPLOMACY

THE PROGRAM

Description: Students learn about Diplomacy and world issues through lectures, guest speakers, and a UN Security Council simulation.

Specialty: Great guest speakers; professors who imbue the students with the knowledge to debate issues in the context of the UN; students who push the envelope of debate.

Program Type: Academic/pre-college enrichment

Classification: Coeducational, residential

Goals: Students will learn about the pressing issues on the international agenda as they confront them through the UN Security Council.

Focus: Academic/pre-college enrichment, leadership/teamwork, and educational exchange

Activities Center On: Academic

Intensity Level: 4

Duration: 1–2 weeks

Program Offered: Summer

Location: Washinton, DC

Accommodations: Dormitory

Years in Operation: 14

Religious Affiliation: Not relevant

STAFF

Student/Staff Ratio: 12:1

Staff Qualifications: Speakers and professors from universities, nongovernmental organizations, and government agencies; additional staffing: college and graduate-level students who are alumni of NSLC programs.

PARTICIPANTS

Average Number of Participants: 200

For Participants Aged: 14–18

The Ideal Candidate: Strong students who are interested in learning about the give and take of diplomatic relations between nations.

Special Requirements for Participation: None.

COSTS

Average Cost: $1,799

Included in Cost: Room and board is included, as well as all field trips and course materials.

Financial Aid Available: No

LAW AND ADVOCACY

THE PROGRAM

Description: Students learn about the trial process from a faculty of lawyers and law school professors. The course culminates in a mock trial at a real courthouse.

Specialty: Experienced trial lawyers guiding the students through the legal process, and the exchange of ideas and information among students from different backgrounds.

Program Type: Academic/pre-college enrichment

Classification: Coeducational, residential

Goals: Students will learn about the trial process and the role of leadership in application to legal issues.

Focus: Academic/pre-college enrichment, leadership/teamwork, and educational exchange

Intensity Level: 4

Duration: 1–2 weeks

Program Offered: Summer

Location: Washington, DC

Accommodations: Dormitory

Years in Operation: 14

Religious Affiliation: Not relevant

STAFF

Student/Staff Ratio: 12:1

Staff Qualifications: Faculty consists of practicing lawyers and law school professors; additional staff includes college and graduate students, most of them alumni of NSLC programs.

PARTICIPANTS

Average Number of Participants: 200

For Participants Aged: 14–18

The Ideal Candidate: Strong students who are interested in learning what it takes to become a lawyer and what it takes to navigate the American legal system.

Special Requirements for Participation: None.

COSTS

Average Cost: $1,799

Included in Cost: Room and board, and all field trips and class materials.

Financial Aid Available: No

MASTERING LEADERSHIP

THE PROGRAM

Description: Leadership skills program that explores principles and qualities of world leaders, with additional focus on personal communication skills and conflict resolution.

Specialty: Interaction of students, staff, and leadership facilitators. Students are advanced, staff are mostly alumni, and leadership facilitators are among the best in the country.

Program Type: Academic/pre-college enrichment

Classification: Coeducational, residential

Goals: Communications, public speaking, conflict resolution, and team-building.

Focus: Leadership/teamwork and academic/pre-college enrichment

Activities Center On: Academic

Intensity Level: 4

Duration: Less than 1 week

Program Offered: Fall, spring, summer

Location: Washington, DC

Accommodations: Dormitory, hotels

Years in Operation: 14

Religious Affiliation: Not relevant

STAFF

Student/Staff Ratio: 12:1

PARTICIPANTS

Average Number of Participants: 150

For Participants Aged: 14–18

The Ideal Candidate: Academically motivated students looking for an experience beyond what they've seen in high school.

Special Requirements for Participation: Minimum GPA: B.

COSTS

Average Cost: $1,099

Included in Cost: Room and board, all field trips, all course materials.

Financial Aid Available: Yes

MEDICINE AND HEALTH CARE

THE PROGRAM

Description: Leadership-based medical program exploring modern medical issues, including ethics, research, and genetic engineering.

Specialty: The incorporation of leadership into the medical field—using it to enhance patient communication and care and to work with a board of directors, and applying it to research and ethical matters.

Program Type: Academic/pre-college enrichment

Classification: Coeducational, residential

Goals: Overall view of the health care industry—from doctors in the emergency room to researchers in the lab to administrators on medical boards.

Focus: Academic/pre-college enrichment, leadership/teamwork, and educational exchange

Activities Center On: Academic

Intensity Level: 4

Duration: 1–2 weeks

Program Offered: Summer

Location: College Park, Maryland; San Diego, California

Accommodations: Dormitory

Years in Operation: 14

Religious Affiliation: Not relevant

STAFF

Student/Staff Ratio: 12:1

Staff Qualifications: Instructors are practicing doctors and medical school professors. The staff are mostly former students.

PARTICIPANTS

Average Number of Participants: 200

For Participants Aged: 14–18

The Ideal Candidate: Academically motivated students

searching for a pre-med type experience who want to learn from physicians and professors.

Special Requirements for Participation: Minimum GPA: B.

COSTS

Average Cost: $1,799

Included in Cost: Room and board, all field trips, all course materials.

Financial Aid Available: Yes

NORTH CAROLINA STATE UNIVERSITY, NUCLEAR ENGINEERING DEPARTMENT

Are you interested in the role that nuclear energy and other nuclear engineering techniques play in solving our everyday problems? Then join the Department of Nuclear Engineering this July! Through a combination of projects, labs, lectures/guest speakers, and field trips, you will answer such questions as: How can we develop energy sources for deep space missions? How can we detect very low concentrations of pollutants in the environment? How are nuclear methods revolutionizing medical diasgnostics and treatment? You will work with our nuclear reactor and other facilities. Our three-week residential program is open to rising high school juniors and seniors as well as graduating seniors.

Years in Operation: 15

Religious Affiliation: Not relevant

Price Range of Programs: $900 for 3 weeks

For More Information:
Contact: Lisa Marshall, Director of Outreach Programs
Department of Nuclear Engineering
PO Box 7909
Raleigh, NC 27695
Phone: 919-515-5876
Fax: 919-515-5115
Email: lisa.marshall@ncsu.edu
Website: www.ne.ncsu.edu

YOUNG INVESTIGATORS' SUMMER PROGRAM IN NUCLEAR SCIENCE AND TECHNOLOGY

THE PROGRAM

Description: Interested in the role nuclear energy and other nuclear techniques play in solving our everyday problems? Then join the Department of Nuclear Engineering in July! There will be a combination of projects, labs, lectures/guest speakers, and field trips. You will work with our nuclear reactor and other facilities. Our three-week residential program is open to rising high school juniors and seniors and graduating seniors.

Specialty: There are 3.5 job offers for every graduate within the United States. In addition, nuclear engineering is in the Top 3 of the engineering fields. This program provides a glimpse into nuclear fission, fusion, and radiation applications.

Program Type: Academic/pre-college enrichment

Classification: Coeducational, residential

Goals: The applications of nuclear engineering in various industries; academic preparedness for an engineering program; scientific research procedure at the university level.

Focus: Academic/pre-college enrichment and skill-building

Activities Center On: Academic and career exploration

Intensity Level: 3

Duration: 2–4 weeks

Program Offered: Summer

Location: Raleigh, North Carolina

Accommodations: Dormitory

Years in Operation: 15

Religious Affiliation: Not relevant

STAFF

Student/Staff Ratio: 10:1

Staff Qualifications: Staff are undergraduate and graduate students in our Department of Nuclear Engineering, and some are graduates of the Summer Program.

PARTICIPANTS

Average Number of Participants: 30

For Participants Aged: 15–19

The Ideal Candidate: A personable student who wants to explore engineering technology and its application to solve everyday issues in society, and who is curious and serious about scientific research.

Special Requirements for Participation: None.

COSTS

Average Cost: $900

Included in Cost: It is an all inclusive three-week program: accommodations, meals, field trips, and planned weekend activities are covered.

Financial Aid Available: Yes

NORTHLAND COLLEGE

Northland College was founded in 1892. It is a four-year, private, environmental liberal arts college with about 750 students. Northland students come from 45 U.S. states and 13 other countries. The student/faculty ratio is 13:1. Northland College is located one mile from Lake Superior on Chequamegon Bay in the city of Ashland, Wisconsin—home to 8,300 people. With its Main Street shops and theater marquis, Ashland has a great small-town feel. The area is surrounded by nearly a million acres of the Chequamegon

National Forest.

Years in Operation: 111

Religious Affiliation: Congregational (United Church of Christ)

Price Range of Programs: $50–$2,000

For More Information:
  Contact: Nicole Wilde, Director, Wild Careers
                1411 Ellis Avenue
                Ashland, WI 54806
  Phone: 715-682-1260
  Fax: 715-682-1691
  Email: wilde@northland.edu
  Website: www.northland.edu

WILD CAREERS

THE PROGRAM

Description: High school students explore fields and careers in science, outdoor education, natural resources, biology, meteorology, leadership, writing, or environmental education with Northland faculty and students at this week-long residential program. Extracurricular activities include kayaking, fishing, mountain biking, canoeing, camping, and backpacking. College credit is available.

Specialty: Faculty, location, setting, and content. Imaging learning about wildlife in Wisconsin's North Woods one day and kayaking on Lake Superior the next.

Program Type: Academic/pre-college enrichment, outdoors/adventure

Classification: Coeducational, residential

Goals: Varies by program. Students will work in the field with professionals and Northland faculty members. Hands-on activities that introduce students to various academic fields and careers are a major component of the programs. Also, students will learn a new adventure activity skill when not in class.

Focus: Academic/pre-college enrichment and leadership and teamwork

Activities Center On: Academic and wilderness

Intensity Level: 2

Duration: 1–2 weeks

Program Offered: Summer

Location: Ashland, Wisconsin

Accommodations: Dormitory

Years in Operation: 8

Religious Affiliation: Congregational (United Church of Christ)

STAFF

Student/Staff Ratio: 4:1

Staff Qualifications: All prgrams are led by Northland faculty members, and Northland College students. Faculty members hold PhDs.

PARTICIPANTS

Average Number of Participants: 16

For Participants Aged: 15–18

The Ideal Candidate: Any student who is interested in learning more about a specific career field and who enjoys the outdoors.

Special Requirements for Participation: None.

COSTS

Average Cost: $600

Included in Cost: Everything is included except transportation to and from Northland College, and spending money for shopping. Students can earn college credit.

Financial Aid Available: Yes

ONSHORE OFFSHORE EXPEDITIONS

OOE offers wilderness adventure, service learning, and cultural/language immersion programs for students and adults.

Years in Operation: 15

Religious Affiliation: Not relevant

Price Range of Programs: $1,500–$3,500

For More Information:
  Contact: Audrey Spindle, Director
                PO Box 4480
                Durango, CO 81302
  Phone: 800-947-4673
  Fax: 970-247-0494
  Email: ooe@frontier.net
  Website: www.ooeadventures.com

ONSHORE OFFSHORE EXPEDITIONS (COSTA RICA)

THE PROGRAM

Description: Participants backpack in Chirripo National Park, experience the warmth and hospitality of a small Tico village, perform service work in local schools, go whitewater rafting, and kayak off the coast.

Specialty: OOE has deep friendships with the people of Costa Rica—they know we are not there to be tourists, but rather to live, learn, work, and play with them side by side. This relationship is expanded through having a Tico instructor on every course.

Program Type: Community service, outdoors/adventure, travel/cultural

Classification: Coeducational, residential

Goals: Participants will concentrate on improving Spanish skills, learning about the culture and history of Costa Rica, and exploring the natural environment of the country.

Focus: Cultural, community service, and educational exchange

Activities Center On: Cultural, volunteer, and backpacking

Intensity Level: 3

Duration: 2–4 weeks

Program Offered: Full academic year

Location: San Gerardo, Orosi, and Quepos, Costa Rica

Accommodations: Family-stay/host-family, tent

Years in Operation: 10

Religious Affiliation: Not relevant

STAFF

Student/Staff Ratio: 4:1

Staff Qualifications: Instructors must be at least 23 years of age, fluent in Spanish, and certified as a Wilderness First Responder. All instructors have first participated as assistants or apprentices before becoming full instructors.

PARTICIPANTS

Average Number of Participants: 12

For Participants Aged: 14–19

The Ideal Candidate: The ideal OOE participant is curious about and engaged with the larger world—eager to step outside his or her comfort zone and gain a broader perspective on both the Tico culture and their own.

Special Requirements for Participation: None.

COSTS

Average Cost: $3,500

Included in Cost: The tuition includes all meals, activities, group equipment (i.e., tents) and 24-hour staff. It does not include airfare or personal equipment (i.e., sleeping bags).

Financial Aid Available: Yes

ONSHORE OFFSHORE EXPEDITIONS (DOMINICAN REPUBLIC)

THE PROGRAM

Description: Participants climb the highest peak in the Caribbean, are welcomed by host families in a small mountain village, and learn about the Dominican Republic's natural beauty while spending time on the coast.

Specialty: We travel to the rural and agricultural areas of the Dominican Republic, avoiding tourist traps in favor of seeking out real places inhabited by real people who lead rich lives that they desire to share with teenagers from other countries.

Program Type: Community service, outdoors/adventure, travel/cultural

Classification: Coeducational, residential

Goals: Participants should expect to hone Spanish skills, learn about the Dominican Republic's rich history and traditions, and study the natural environment.

Focus: Cultural, community service, and educational exchange

Activities Center On: Cultural, volunteer, and backpacking

Intensity Level: 3

Duration: 2–4 weeks

Program Offered: Full academic year

Location: Angostura, Jarabacoa, and Pinar Quemado, Dominican Republic

Accommodations: Family-stay/host-family, tent

Years in Operation: 10

Religious Affiliation: Not relevant

STAFF

Student/Staff Ratio: 4:1

Staff Qualifications: Instructors must be at least 23 years of age, fluent in Spanish, and certified as a Wilderness First Responder. Instructors must first serve as assistants or apprentices before becoming full instructors.

PARTICIPANTS

Average Number of Participants: 12

For Participants Aged: 14–19

The Ideal Candidate: The ideal OOE participant wishes to be challenged physically and mentally—to step outside his or her comfort zone and see the world from a different perspective.

Special Requirements for Participation: A minimum of one year of high school Spanish is required.

COSTS

Average Cost: $3,300

Included in Cost: All meals, activities, and group equipment (i.e., tents) are included as well as 24-hour staffing. Airfare and personal equipment (i.e., backpacks) are not included.

Financial Aid Available: Yes

ONSHORE OFFSHORE EXPEDITIONS (NAVAJO NATION)

THE PROGRAM

Description: Participants backpack in the stunning San Juan Mountains, experience the rich traditions and warm hospitality of the Navajo (Dine) people, and whitewater raft in the most beautiful redrock canyons of the Southwest.

Specialty: OOE began in the Southwest, and it is here that we still hold our most trusted relationships with the Native Americans who have welcomed us into their lives.

Program Type: Community service, outdoors/adventure

Classification: Coeducational, residential

Goals: Students should expect to learn about the natural environment of the Southwest and the ways in which it has affected the development of Navajo (Dine) culture over the last thousand years.

Focus: Cultural, community service, and educational exchange

Activities Center On: Cultural, volunteer, and outdoors and adventure

Intensity Level: 3

Duration: 2–4 weeks

Program Offered: Full academic year

Location: Lukachukai and Tsaile, Arizona; Durango, Colorado; Utah

Accommodations: Family-stay/host-family, tent

Years in Operation: 15

Religious Affiliation: Not relevant

STAFF

Student/Staff Ratio: 6:1

Staff Qualifications: All instructors must be at least 23 years of age, skilled in group dynamics and outdoor activities, and certified as Wilderness First Responders.

PARTICIPANTS

Average Number of Participants: 12

For Participants Aged: 14–19

The Ideal Candidate: The ideal OOE participant is curious about the world and has a desire to learn more by doing rather than by reading or listening.

Special Requirements for Participation: None.

COSTS

Average Cost: $3,000

Included in Cost: All meals, activities, and group equipment (i.e., tents) are included. Airfare and personal equipment (i.e., sleeping bags) are not included.

Financial Aid Available: Yes

ONTARIO PIONEER CAMP

Pioneer Camp, with almost 1,000 beds, is one of Canada's premier Christian camp experiences. We have many challenging opportunities in all four seasons, and an opportunity awaits you! Great staff, great stuff, great seasons!

Years in Operation: 75

Religious Affiliation: Interdominational Christian

Price Range of Programs: $90–$600

For More Information:
Contact: Calvin Bennett, Director
942 Clearwater Lake Road
RR #1
Port Sydney, Ontario
P0B 1L0, CANADA
Phone: 800-361-2267
Fax: 705-385-3649

Email: summer@pioneercamp.com
Website: www.pioneercamp.ca

OUTDOOR EDUCATION PROGRAM

THE PROGRAM

Description: Outdoor Education is a 10-month program to learn how to train for and lead outdoor education courses, and programs for school groups and guests.

Specialty: It is one of the longest programs for leadership and skill development; the program allows students to actively work in the field while taking the course.

Program Type: Academic/pre-college enrichment

Classification: Coeducational, residential

Goals: Skill development, team work, internship, and personal leadership development.

Focus: Academic/pre-college enrichment, internship, and skill-building

Activities Center On: Academic, camping, and career exploration

Intensity Level: 3

Duration: Over 8 weeks

Program Offered: Fall, winter intersession/January term, spring

Location: Toronto Area, Canada

Accommodations: Dormitory

Years in Operation: 75

Religious Affiliation: Interdominational Christian

STAFF

Student/Staff Ratio: 5:1

Staff Qualifications: Experienced teachers and outdoor education enthuiasists.

PARTICIPANTS

Average Number of Participants: 15

For Participants Aged: 18–50

The Ideal Candidate: High school or college graduate. (This is a great program to fill the gap between high school and university.)

Special Requirements for Participation: Interview, application, police check.

COSTS

Average Cost: $400

Included in Cost: All included.

Financial Aid Available: Yes

OPERAFESTIVAL DI ROMA

Seeks to provide a performing and training experience in Italian opera.

Years in Operation: 10

Religious Affiliation: Not relevant

Price Range of Programs: $5,000–$6,000

For More Information:
Contact: Louisa Panou, Artistic Director
1445 Willow Lake Drive
Charlottesville, VA 22902
Phone: 804-984-4945
Fax: 804-984-5220
Email: operafest@aol.com
Website: www.operafest.com

OPERAFESTIVAL DI ROMA

THE PROGRAM

Description: An educational program seeking to provide performing experience and training in Italian opera.

Specialty: The only program of its kind in the world that offers both musical training and a performing opportunity in a fully produced full-length opera.

Program Type: Music/arts, travel/cultural

Classification: Coeducational, residential

Goals: Vocal and performance skills

Focus: Skill-building and cultural

Activities Center On: Music/arts, singing, and performing arts

Intensity Level: 4

Duration: 4–6 weeks

Program Offered: Summer

Location: Rome, Italy

Accommodations: Hotels

Years in Operation: 10

Religious Affiliation: Not relevant

STAFF

Student/Staff Ratio: 2:1

Staff Qualifications: University teacher, performing experience, interest in helping students.

PARTICIPANTS

Average Number of Participants: 50

For Participants Aged: 16+

The Ideal Candidate: Good voice, some musical and/or theatrical experience, hard worker, interest in challenging experience.

Special Requirements for Participation: None.

COSTS

Average Cost: $5,500

Included in Cost: Voice lessons, masterclasses, opera scenes program, recital performing experience, and opera performing experience; housing in air-conditioned room with private bath; breakfast and lunch daily.

Financial Aid Available: No

OUTPOST WILDERNESS ADVENTURE

We offer teen adventure programming, with specialty in guiding rock climbing, mountain biking, alpine climbing, and international trips.

Years in Operation: 25

Religious Affiliation: Not relevant

Price Range of Programs: $800–$900 per week

For More Information:
Contact: Quentin Keith, Director
2107 Shovel Mountain Road
Cypress Mill, TX 78654
Phone: 830-825-3015
Fax: 830-825-3116
Email: q@owa.com
Website: www.owa.com

ULTIMATE COPPER CANYON

THE PROGRAM

Description: Guided adventure in Mexico's Copper Canyon area. Participants mountain bike, rock climb, and hike, and provide up to 60 hours of community service teaching local children to rock climb and helping with "La Onza," a local mountain bike race.

Specialty: OWA specializes in small group adventure programming where participants learn the "real thing." OWA guides are highly skilled and trained and consider themselves "adventure lifestyle specialists."

Program Type: Community service, outdoors/adventure, travel/cultural

Classification: Coeducational, residential

Goals: Learn about the Tarahumara Indians of Copper Canyon and other cultures of Mexico. Provide community service. Ride, climb, and hike all around the biggest canyons in North America.

Focus: Community service, leadership/teamwork, and skill-building

Activities Center On: Outdoors/adventure, wilderness, and touring

Intensity Level: 4

Duration: 2–4 weeks

Program Offered: Summer

Location: Creel and Chihuahau, Mexico

Accommodations: Bunk/cabin

Years in Operation: 5

Religious Affiliation: Not relevant

STAFF

Student/Staff Ratio: 3:1

Staff Qualifications: Guides are: 21 years or older; have a minimum of two years prior experience; are in college or college-educated; and are specialists in rock climbing, mountain biking, and/or mountaineering.

PARTICIPANTS

Average Number of Participants: 15

For Participants Aged: 14–18

The Ideal Candidate: Motivated, smart people interested in learning about other cultures and willing to help.

Special Requirements for Participation: Willing and ready to have fun, try new things, and help people.

COSTS

Average Cost: $2,600

Included in Cost: Travel from El Paso, Texas, and all lodging, food, transportation, and guided adventure.

Financial Aid Available: No

OUTWARD BOUND WEST

To enhance individual character, promote self-discovery, and challenge students to cultivate self-reliance, leadership, fitness, compassion, and service through exceptional wilderness education.

Years in Operation: 42

Religious Affiliation: Not relevant

Price Range of Programs: $600–$8,595

For More Information:
Contact: Carrie Fox, Recruiting/Marketing Department
910 Jackson St.
Golden, CO 80401
Phone: 800-547-3312
Fax: 720-497-2421
Email: info@obwest.org
Website: www.outwardboundwest.org

BACKPACKING

THE PROGRAM

Description: Backpacking through the wilderness terrain. Come see where your legs can take you.

Specialty: Programs since 1942.

Program Type: Outdoors/adventure

Classification: Coeducational, residential

Goals: Map and compass navigation, route planning, on- and off-trail hiking, stream crossing, peak ascents, gear and pack organization, self arrest and ice axe use (when possible), geology, mountain ecology, natural history.

Focus: Leadership/teamwork, skill-building, and travel

Activities Center On: Backpacking, camping, and outdoors/adventure

Intensity Level: 4

Duration: 1–2 weeks, 2–4 weeks, 4–6 weeks, 6–8 weeks,

Program Offered: Fall, winter intersession/January term, spring, full academic year

Location: Multiple locations: California, Colorado, Oregon, Utah, Washington

Accommodations: Tent

Years in Operation: 42

Religious Affiliation: Not relevant

STAFF

Student/Staff Ratio: 5:1

Staff Qualifications: Certified in Wilderness First Responder and in technical outdoor skills, and trained in experiential education and counseling.

PARTICIPANTS

Average Number of Participants: 15

For Participants Aged: 14–80

The Ideal Candidate: Willing to travel in remote wilderness areas, work as a team, develop wilderness skills, and become more self-aware.

Special Requirements for Participation: Physical and mentally prepared for an Outward Bound West course.

COSTS

Average Cost: $2,000

Included in Cost: Travel, personal clothing, and boots are not included.

Financial Aid Available: Yes

DESERT BACKPACKING

THE PROGRAM

Description: Explore, live, and learn in rugged primitive desert environments. Backpack, rappel, and discover natural wonders in beautiful desert wilderness areas.

Specialty: Programs since 1942, certified instructors, quality experiential education.

Program Type: Outdoors/adventure

Classification: Coeducational, residential

Goals: Backpacking skills, rapelling, desert travel, self-confidence, and personal strength.

Focus: Leadership/teamwork, skill-building, and travel

Activities Center On: Backpacking, camping, and wilderness

Intensity Level: 4

Duration: 1–2 weeks

Program Offered: Fall, winter intersession/January term, spring

Location: California, Utah

Accommodations: Tent

Years in Operation: 42

Religious Affiliation: Not relevant

STAFF

Student/Staff Ratio: 7:1

Staff Qualifications: Wilderness First Responder certification, advanced technical skills, advanced experiential education/counseling skills.

PARTICIPANTS

Average Number of Participants: 15

For Participants Aged: 18–80

The Ideal Candidate: Adventurous spirit, willingness to go further, physically and mentally prepared for an Outward Bound West course.

Special Requirements for Participation: Physically and mentally prepared for an Outward Bound West course.

COSTS

Average Cost: $1,000

Included in Cost: Travel and personal gear are not included.

Financial Aid Available: Yes

MOUNTAINEERING

THE PROGRAM

Description: Come climb snow-capped peaks and cross glaciers and crevasses on remote peaks. Discover mountain ecology while you learn fixed-line use, self and team arrest, snow and glacier travel, ice-axe use, and rock and ice climbing, as well as how to travel in a rope team, step-kick, and ascend peaks.

Specialty: Programs since 1942

Program Type: Outdoors/adventure

Classification: Coeducational, residential

Goals: Fixed-line use, self and team arrest, snow and glacier travel, ice-axe use, and peak ascents; travelling in a rope team, step-kicking, and rock and ice climbing; teamwork, communication skills, self-confidence

Focus: Skill-building, leadership/teamwork, and travel

Activities Center On: Wilderness and backpacking

Intensity Level: 5

Duration: 1–2 weeks, 2–4 weeks, 4–6 weeks

Program Offered: Fall, spring, summer

Location: Alaska, California, Colorado, Oregon, Washington

Accommodations: Tent

Years in Operation: 42

Religious Affiliation: Not relevant

STAFF

Student/Staff Ratio: 5:1

Staff Qualifications: Wilderness First Responder and technical mountaineering certifications, experiential education and counseling training.

PARTICIPANTS

Average Number of Participants: 15

For Participants Aged: 14–80

The Ideal Candidate: Adventurous spirit, physically and mentally prepared.

Special Requirements for Participation: Physically and mentally prepared for an Outward Bound West course.

COSTS

Average Cost: $2,000

Included in Cost: Travel, personal clothing, and boots are not included.

Financial Aid Available: Yes

MULTI-ELEMENT COURSES

THE PROGRAM

Description: Two or three elements on each course. Choose from backpacking and rafting, rock climbing and whitewater, mountaineering and whitewater, sailing and mountaineering, sea kayaking and mountaineering, sailing and sea kayaking, canoeing and hiking, and rafting and desert backpacking.

Specialty: Programs for 42 years.

Program Type: Outdoors/adventure

Classification: Coeducational, residential

Goals: Multi-element skills

Focus: Travel

Activities Center On: Wilderness

Intensity Level: 4

Duration: 1–2 weeks, 2–4 weeks

Program Offered: Fall, spring, summer

Location: California, Colorado, Oregon, Utah, Washington

Years in Operation: 42

Religious Affiliation: Not relevant

STAFF

Student/Staff Ratio: 5:1

PARTICIPANTS

Average Number of Participants: 15

For Participants Aged: 14–80

The Ideal Candidate: Physically and mentally prepared for an Outward Bound course.

Special Requirements for Participation: Physically and mentally prepared for an Outward Bound course.

COSTS

Average Cost: $2,000

Included in Cost: Travel and personal clothes are not included.

Financial Aid Available: Yes

MYSTERY COURSE

THE PROGRAM

Description: It's a mystery.

Specialty: It's a mystery.

Program Type: Outdoors/adventure

Classification: Coeducational, residential

Goals: Expeditionary learning.

Intensity Level: 3

Duration: 1–2 weeks

Program Offered: Summer

Location: Utah

Accommodations: Tent

Years in Operation: 42

Religious Affiliation: Not relevant

STAFF

Student/Staff Ratio: 5:1

PARTICIPANTS

Average Number of Participants: 15

For Participants Aged: 16–80

The Ideal Candidate: Adventurous spirit.

Special Requirements for Participation: Physically and mentally prepared for an Outward Bound West course.

COSTS

Average Cost: $1,595

Included in Cost: Travel and personal clothing are not included.

Financial Aid Available: Yes

ROCK CLIMBING

THE PROGRAM

Description: A challenge of balance and strength

Specialty: Experiential education since 1942

Program Type: Outdoors/adventure

Classification: Coeducational, residential

Goals: Challenge of the mind and body through group dynamics and technical rock climbing skills. Learn climbing techniques, route-selection, bouldering problems, rappelling skills, and anchor placement.

Focus: Skill-building and leadership/teamwork

Activities Center On: Outdoors/adventure and wilderness

Intensity Level: 4

Duration: 1–2 weeks

Program Offered: Fall, spring, full academic year, summer

Location: Multiple locations: California, Colorado, Utah, Wyoming

Accommodations: Tent

Years in Operation: 42

Religious Affiliation: Not relevant

STAFF

Student/Staff Ratio: 5:1

Staff Qualifications: Wilderness First Resonder and technical rock climbing certifications, educational and counseling training.

PARTICIPANTS

Average Number of Participants: 15

For Participants Aged: 14–80

The Ideal Candidate: Willing to face fears and overcome obstacles in a wilderness setting, willing to learn and make lasting relationships.

Special Requirements for Participation: Physically and mentally prepared for an Outward Bound West course.

COSTS

Average Cost: $1,295

Included in Cost: Travel and personal clothing are not included.

Financial Aid Available: Yes

SAILING

THE PROGRAM

Description: The ultimate team experience sailing, navigating, and captaining your high-sea adventure.

Specialty: Programs for 42 years, outstanding instructors

Program Type: Outdoors/adventure

Classification: Coeducational, residential

Goals: Seamanship and navigation; sail handling, rowing and boat handling, ocean expedition planning, anchoring, chart reading, and knot tying; island ecology and oceanography.

Focus: Leadership/teamwork, skill-building, and travel

Activities Center On: Sailing and outdoors/adventure

Intensity Level: 3

Duration: 1–2 weeks, 2–4 weeks

Program Offered: Spring, summer

Location: Washington

Years in Operation: 42

Religious Affiliation: Not relevant

STAFF

Student/Staff Ratio: 5:1

Staff Qualifications: Certified in Wilderness First Responder, trained in all aspects of sailing and experiential education

PARTICIPANTS

Average Number of Participants: 15

For Participants Aged: 14–80

The Ideal Candidate: Adventurous spirit, prepared physically and mentally.

Special Requirements for Participation: Prepared physically and mentally for an Outward Bound West course.

COSTS

Average Cost: $2,000

Included in Cost: Travel and personal clothing are not included.

Financial Aid Available: Yes

SEA KAYAKING

THE PROGRAM

Description: Lessons of the ocean: Travel into waters too shallow for most boats as you explore the Sea of Cortez in Baja, San Juan Islands in Washington, or Kenai Fjords in Alaska.

Specialty: Programs for 42 years

Program Type: Outdoors/adventure

Classification: Coeducational, residential

Goals: Paddling techniques, wet exit, self and group rescue, water safety, and first aid; compass and chart reading, nautical expedition planning/navigation, and weather monitoring and forecasting; wind and wave theory, natural history, and island ecology.

Focus: Leadership/teamwork, skill-building, and travel

Activities Center On: Boating, camping, and wilderness

Intensity Level: 3

Duration: 1–2 weeks

Program Offered: Winter intersession/January term, spring, summer

Location: Alaska, California, Washington; Mexico

Years in Operation: 42

Religious Affiliation: Not relevant

STAFF

Student/Staff Ratio: 5:1

Staff Qualifications: Wilderness First Responder certification and all qualifications for sea kayaking and water safety.

PARTICIPANTS

Average Number of Participants: 15

For Participants Aged: 18–80

The Ideal Candidate: Passionate about adventure and learning.

Special Requirements for Participation: Physically and mentally prepared for an Outward Bound West course.

COSTS

Average Cost: $2,000

Included in Cost: Travel and personal clothing are not included.

Financial Aid Available: Yes

SEMESTER

THE PROGRAM

Description: Let the wilderness be your classroom.

Specialty: Experiential education since 1941, expert staff, quality wilderness education.

Program Type: Outdoors/adventure

Classification: Coeducational, residential

Goals: Leadeship skills, technical outdoor skills, cultural and natural history of different areas, decision-making skills, self-discovery.

Focus: Leadership/teamwork, skill-building, and travel

Activities Center On: Outdoors/adventure and wilderness

Intensity Level: 5

Duration: Over 8 weeks

Program Offered: Fall, winter Intersession/January term, spring, full academic year, summer

Location: Multiple locations: Alaska, California, Colorado, Idaho, Oregon, Utah, Washington

Accommodations: Tent

Years in Operation: 42

Religious Affiliation: Not relevant

STAFF

Student/Staff Ratio: 10:1

Staff Qualifications: Certification in Wilderness First Responder Certified, technical skills in specific areas, training in leadership, communication, and counseling.

PARTICIPANTS

Average Number of Participants: 15

For Participants Aged: 18–80

The Ideal Candidate: Willing to test your limits, live bigger, try new things, develop life-lasting friendships, learn wilderness and leadership skills, travel to remote places, and have an experience of a lifetime.

Special Requirements for Participation: Physically and mentally prepared for an Outward Bound West course.

COSTS

Average Cost: $7,000

Included in Cost: Travel and personal clothing are not included. Scholarships are available!

Financial Aid Available: Yes

SKIING/SNOWBOARDING

THE PROGRAM

Description: Cut fresh tracks: You'll come to know the joy of carving fresh tracks in the pristine snow and exploring the backcountry.

Specialty: Programs for 42 years

Program Type: Outdoors/adventure

Classification: Coeducational, residential

Goals: Backcountry snow skills, skiing and snowboarding techniques.

Focus: Leadership/teamwork and skill-building

Activities Center On: Skiing and wilderness

Intensity Level: 4

Duration: 1–2 weeks

Program Offered: Winter intersession/January term

Location: Colorado

Accommodations: Tent

Years in Operation: 42

Religious Affiliation: Not relevant

STAFF

Student/Staff Ratio: 5:1

PARTICIPANTS

Average Number of Participants: 15

For Participants Aged: 16–80

The Ideal Candidate: Prepared for backcountry snow travel, adventurous spirit.

Special Requirements for Participation: Experience with snow sports (intermediate level).

COSTS

Average Cost: $1,295

Included in Cost: Travel and personal clothing are not included.

Financial Aid Available: Yes

WHITEWATER

THE PROGRAM

Description: Read and master the river: Grab a paddle and feel the rush.

Specialty: Programs for 42 years

Program Type: Outdoors/adventure

Classification: Coeducational, residential

Goals: Maneuvering techniques for one-, two-, and/or multi-person craft; basic and advanced paddling strokes; river reading and rapid navigation; scouting, staging, and portaging rapids; river safety and whitewater risk management; paddle signals; swiftwater rescue.

Focus: Leadership/teamwork and skill-building

Activities Center On: Rafting, kayaking, and boating

Intensity Level: 3

Duration: 1–2 weeks, 2–4 weeks

Program Offered: Spring, summer

Location: Colorado, Oregon, Utah

Years in Operation: 42

Religious Affiliation: Not relevant

STAFF

Student/Staff Ratio: 5:1

Staff Qualifications: Wilderness First Responder certification.

PARTICIPANTS

Average Number of Participants: 15

For Participants Aged: 14–80

The Ideal Candidate: Passionate about adventure and learning.

Special Requirements for Participation: Physically and mentally prepared for an Outward Bound West course.

COSTS

Average Cost: $1,500

Included in Cost: Travel and personal clothing are not included.

Financial Aid Available: Yes

OXBRIDGE ACADEMIC PROGRAMS

Oxbridge Academic Programs sponsors intensive academic summer programs at Oxford and Cambridge Universities, as well as in Paris.

Years in Operation: 19

Religious Affiliation: Not relevant

Price Range of Programs: $4,595–$5,195

For More Information:
Contact: Claire le Comte du Nouy, Head of Admissions
601 West 110th Street
Suite 7-R
New York, NY 10025
Phone: 800-828-8349
Fax: 212-663-8169
Email: info@oxbridgeprograms.com
Website: www.oxbridgeprograms.com

ACADÉMIE DE PARIS

THE PROGRAM

Description: L'Académie de Paris is an intensive pre-college academic summer program set in the heart of the French capital. Students study among peers from all over the United States and the world, taking courses in the humanities, arts, or sciences in English or French.

Specialty: The unique blend of independence and organized academic and cultural activities gives our students the ability to explore the wonders of the City of Lights with the comfort that staff are always close by and on call.

Program Type: Academic/pre-college enrichment

Classification: Coeducational, residential

Goals: Participants should expect to learn in depth about their major class subject and related material, and should also expect a broad overview of their minor class. The comprehensive activities schedule gives students the opportunity to explore different historic neighborhoods and museums with expert guides from our faculty.

Focus: Academic/pre-college enrichment and cultural

Activities Center On: Academic and cultural

Intensity Level: 4

Duration: 4–6 weeks

Program Offered: Summer

Location: Paris, France

Accommodations: Dormitory

Years in Operation: 13

Religious Affiliation: Not relevant

STAFF

Student/Staff Ratio: 7:1

Staff Qualifications: All faculty either have advanced degrees or are established professionals in their field. Most of the faculty and staff live in Paris throughout the year and have extensive knowledge about and experience with neighborhoods and places of interest. Administrators usually come from top secondary boarding and day schools from all over the United States and have many years of experience with this particular age group.

PARTICIPANTS

Average Number of Participants: 155

For Participants Aged: 15–18

The Ideal Candidate: The ideal Académie de Paris student is motivated and passionate about learning while being independent, curious, and willing to explore new cultures.

Special Requirements for Participation: There are no special requirements other than the usual admissions process that incudes an essay and a transcript.

COSTS

Average Cost: $5,195

Included in Cost: This fee includes all tuition and instruction, accommodation in a college room, breakfast and dinner daily, all course materials, and all scheduled activities. It does not include airfare, lunch daily, or snacks, laundry, souvenirs, and so forth.

Financial Aid Available: Yes

CAMBRIDGE PREP EXPERIENCE

THE PROGRAM

Description: The Cambridge Prep Experience offers highly talented and motivated students finishing eighth and ninth grade the opportunity to study at Cambridge University during the month of July.

Specialty: The combination of supervised activities and class field trips along with some independent time to explore Cambridge gives students the opportunity to feel safe and secure while exploring their own interests.

Program Type: Academic/pre-college enrichment

Classification: Coeducational, residential

Goals: Participants will learn about their major course extensively while also being introduced to their minor course. Through coursework, field trips, and organized activities, students receive a complete academic and cultural immersion into Cambridge and British life.

Focus: Academic/pre-college enrichment, cultural, and travel

Activities Center On: Academic, cultural, and sports/athletic

Intensity Level: 4

Duration: 2–4 weeks

Program Offered: Summer

Location: Cambridge, United Kingdom

Accommodations: Dormitory

Years in Operation: 9

Religious Affiliation: Not relevant

STAFF

Student/Staff Ratio: 10:1

Staff Qualifications: Most faculty have advanced degrees from Cambridge or Oxford Universities or are professionals in their fields. Deans and pastoral care are provided by experienced middle and high school administrators and teachers from all over the United States.

PARTICIPANTS

Average Number of Participants: 160

For Participants Aged: 14–15

The Ideal Candidate: Our ideal candidate is a highly motivated student who is looking for a meaningful and enriching way to spend part of his or her summer.

Special Requirements for Participation: There are no special requirements other than the requested information such as a transcript and personal statement.

COSTS

Average Cost: $4,595

Included in Cost: This fee includes: all tuition and instruction, accommodation in a college room, breakfast and dinner daily, all course materials, and all scheduled activities. It does not include airfare, lunch daily, or snacks, laundry, souvenirs, and so forth.

Financial Aid Available: Yes

CAMBRIDGE TRADITION

THE PROGRAM

Description: The Cambridge Tradition is a summer program based at Cambridge University for bright and enthusiastic students completing grades 10–12. Participants study two courses for four weeks in July and are taught by leading scholars and professionals.

Specialty: The combination of activities and class field trips along with independent time to explore Cambridge gives students the opportunity to explore their own interests while having a selection of organized activities to choose from.

Program Type: Academic/pre-college enrichment

Classification: Coeducational, residential

Goals: Participants will learn about their major course extensively while also being introduced to their minor course. Through coursework, field trips, and organized activities, students receive a complete academic and cultural immersion into Cambridge and British life.

Focus: Academic/pre-college enrichment and cultural

Activities Center On: Academic and cultural

Intensity Level: 4

Duration: 4–6 weeks

Program Offered: Summer

Location: Cambridge, United Kingdom

Accommodations: Dormitory

Years in Operation: 5

Religious Affiliation: Not relevant

STAFF

Student/Staff Ratio: 6:1

Staff Qualifications: Most faculty have advanced degrees from Cambridge or Oxford Universities or are professionals in their fields. Deans and pastoral care are provided by experienced middle and high school administrators and teachers from all over the United States.

PARTICIPANTS

Average Number of Participants: 196

For Participants Aged: 15–18

The Ideal Candidate: Our ideal candidate is a highly motivated student who is looking for a meaningful and enriching way to spend part of his or her summer.

Special Requirements for Participation: There are no special requirements other than the requested information such as a transcript and personal statement.

COSTS

Average Cost: $5,195

Included in Cost: This fee includes all tuition and instruction, accommodation in a college room, breakfast and dinner daily, all course materials, and all scheduled activities. It does not include airfare, lunch daily, or snacks, laundry, souvenirs, and so forth.

Financial Aid Available: Yes

OXFORD TRADITION

THE PROGRAM

Description: The Oxford Tradition is a summer program based at Oxford University for bright and enthusiastic students completing grades 10–12. Participants study two courses for four weeks in July and are taught by leading scholars and professionals.

Specialty: The combination of activities and class field trips along with independent time to explore Oxford gives students the opportunity to explore their own interests while having a selection of organized activities to choose from.

Program Type: Academic/pre-college enrichment

Classification: Coeducational, residential

Goals: Each participant will learn about his or her major course extensively while also being introduced to a minor course. Through coursework, field trips, and organized activities, students receive a complete academic and cultural immersion into Oxford and British life.

Focus: Academic/pre-college enrichment and cultural

Activities Center On: Academic and cultural

Intensity Level: 4

Duration: 4–6 weeks

Program Offered: Summer

Location: Oxford, United Kingdom

Accommodations: Dormitory

Years in Operation: 19

Religious Affiliation: Not relevant

STAFF

Student/Staff Ratio: 8:1

Staff Qualifications: Most faculty have advanced degrees from Cambridge or Oxford Universities or are professionals in their fields. Deans and pastoral care are provided by experienced middle and high school administrators and teachers from all over the United States.

PARTICIPANTS

Average Number of Participants: 370

For Participants Aged: 15–18

The Ideal Candidate: Our ideal candidate is a highly motivated student who is looking for a meaningful and enriching way to spend part of his or her summer.

Special Requirements for Participation: There are no special requirements other than the requested information such as a transcript and personal statement.

COSTS

Average Cost: $5,195

Included in Cost: This fee includes all tuition and instruction, accommodation in a college room, breakfast and dinner daily, all course materials, and all scheduled activities. It does not include airfare, lunch daily, or snacks, laundry, souvenirs, and so forth.

Financial Aid Available: Yes

OXFORD ADVANCED STUDIES PROGRAM

This unique academic and cultural experience takes place each summer in Oxford, home of England's oldest and most celebrated university. The setting is Magdalen College, one of the most beautiful and magnificent colleges of the university. Academically talented high school students take two or three stimulating courses and are taught in the Oxbridge one-on-one mode. Academic work is complemented by a superb program of visits, activities, and sports, giving a wonderful taste of England's history, culture, and traditions. Participants frequently describe the experience as one of the most wonderful and rewarding of their lives.

Years in Operation: 21

Religious Affiliation: Not relevant

Price Range of Programs: $4,900–$5,800

For More Information:
Contact: Joel Roderick, Academic Registrar
12 King Edward Street
Oxford, OX1 4HT
UNITED KINGDOM
Phone: 203-966-2886
Fax: 44-1865-793233
Email: joel.roderick@oasp.ac.uk
Website: www.oasp.ac.uk

OXFORD ADVANCED STUDIES PROGRAM

THE PROGRAM

Description: This unique academic and cultural experience takes place each summer in Oxford, home of England's oldest and most celebrated university. The setting is Magdalen College, one of the most beautiful and magnificent colleges of the university. Academically talented high school students take two or three stimulating courses and are taught in the Oxbridge one-on-one mode. Academic work is complemented by a superb program of visits, activities, and sports.

Specialty: The chance to stay and study in a medieval Oxford college and study in the Oxbridge tutorial mode.

Program Type: Academic/pre-college enrichment, music and arts, travel/cultural

Classification: Coeducational, residential

Goals: Students expand their academic horizons in their chosen field under the close guidance of expert tutors.

Focus: Academic/pre-college enrichment, cultural, and travel

Activities Center On: Academic, travel, and writing

Intensity Level: 3

Duration: 2–4 weeks

Program Offered: Summer

Location: Oxford, United Kingdom

Years in Operation: 21

Religious Affiliation: Not relevant

STAFF

Student/Staff Ratio: 3:1

Staff Qualifications: Mainly Oxbridge graduates.

PARTICIPANTS

Average Number of Participants: 90

For Participants Aged: 15–22

The Ideal Candidate: Bright, dedicated, hard-working, mature with a curious mind.

Special Requirements for Participation: None.

COSTS

Average Cost: $5,000

Included in Cost: Fully inclusive.

Financial Aid Available: No

PENN STATE—UNIVERSITY PARK

Women in the Sciences and Engineering Camp—Career Exploration Summer Program.

Years in Operation: 8

Religious Affiliation: Not relevant

Price Range of Programs: $350–$400

For More Information:
Contact: Katie Rung, Assistant Director
111G Kern Building
University Park, PA 16802
Phone: 814-865-3342
Fax: 814-863-0085
Email: cxg1@psu.edu
Website: www.psu.edu/dept/wise

WOMEN IN THE SCIENCES AND ENGINEERING CAMP

THE PROGRAM

Description: One-week career exploration residential program for young women entering 11th or 12th grades who are interested in math and science.

Specialty: Broad base of lab experiences in science and engineering.

Program Type: Academic/pre-college enrichment

Classification: Single-sex, female; residential

Goals: Broad base of hands-on experiences in science and engineering labs, and experience of college campus life.

Focus: Academic/pre-college enrichment and leadership and teamwork

Activities Center On: Career exploration, science, and academic

Intensity Level: 4

Duration: 1–2 weeks

Program Offered: Summer

Location: University Park, Pennsylvania

Accommodations: Dormitory

Years in Operation: 9

Religious Affiliation: Not relevant

STAFF

Student/Staff Ratio: 12:1

Staff Qualifications: Undergraduate or graduate women students in science or engineering fields; camp counselor experience preferred but not required.

PARTICIPANTS

Average Number of Participants: 36

For Participants Aged: 15–17

The Ideal Candidate: Female student with average to above-average grades in science/math courses and a high interest in learning more about fields in science, math, engineering, and technology.

Special Requirements for Participation: Minimum math: Algebra II. Application requires transcript, test scores, recommendation letter, and student essay.

COSTS

Average Cost: $350

Included in Cost: Includes room, meals, and all materials for program. Does not include transportation to and from the program site.

Financial Aid Available: Yes

PROGRAMS ABROAD TRAVEL ALTERNATIVES

Designed to boost student fluency in a short period of time, PATA programs attract serious students who pledge to use only their language of study during their study abroad. Because PATA on-site directors are teachers of French, German, Italian, Russian, and/or Spanish, the entire program is conducted in the language of study. Programs are offered in Costa Rica, France, Germany, Guatemala, Italy, Mexico, Russia, and Spain.

Years in Operation: 7

Religious Affiliation: Not relevant

Price Range of Programs: $1,000–$4,500

For More Information:
Contact: Rose Potter, Founder/CEO
6200 Adel Cove
Austin, TX 78749
Phone: 888-777-7282
Fax: 512-282-7076
Email: immerse@gopata.com
Website: www.gopata.com

PROGRAMS ABROAD TRAVEL ALTERNATIVES (COSTA RICA)

THE PROGRAM

Description: This unique PATA program is designed to expand interest in the language and culture of Costa Rica and to create an awareness of environmental concerns affecting the entire planet, specifically the conservation of the Costa Rican rainforests and endangered species.

Specialty: Students receive 32 contact hours on a language institute transcript, which, when presented to their receiving university with a portfolio of their coursework, may be used to petition for up to 2 hours of college credit.

Program Type: Academic/pre-college enrichment

Classification: Coeducational, residential

Goals: Students participate in Spanish classes Monday through Thursday each week of the program, four hours per day.

Focus: Academic/pre-college enrichment, cultural, and travel

Activities Center On: Language, outdoors/adventure, and travel

Intensity Level: 3

Duration: 2–4 weeks

Program Offered: Summer

Location: Costa Rica

Accommodations: Family-stay/host-family

Years in Operation: 7

Religious Affiliation: Not relevant

STAFF

Student/Staff Ratio: 10:1

Staff Qualifications: All directors are certified foreign language teachers.

PARTICIPANTS

Average Number of Participants: 25

For Participants Aged: 15–19

The Ideal Candidate: Students must be 15 years old by the departure date, have completed their freshman year, and have a teacher recommendation. Novice Spanish speakers are encouraged to particpate.

Special Requirements for Participation: None.

COSTS

Average Cost: $3,500

Included in Cost: Round-trip airfare from Houston, all ground transportation, program costs (classes and homestay), meals (excluding the meals during excursions), admission fees on excursions, transcript service, medical insurance, and orientation materials.

Financial Aid Available: No

PROGRAMS ABROAD TRAVEL ALTERNATIVES (FRANCE)

THE PROGRAM

Description: Designed to boost student fluency in a short

period of time, PATA programs attract serious students who pledge to use only their language of study during their study abroad. Because PATA on-site directors are teachers of French, German, Italian, Russian, and/or Spanish, the entire program is conducted in the language of study.

Program Type: Academic/pre-college enrichment

Classification: Coeducational, residential

Goals: Students receive 40 contact hours on an Azurlingua and an Institut Parisien transcript (80 hours total), which, when presented to their receiving university with a portfolio of their coursework, may be used to petition for up to 5 hours of college credit.

Focus: Academic/pre-college enrichment, cultural, and travel

Activities Center On: Language, academic, and travel

Intensity Level: 3

Duration: 2–4 weeks

Program Offered: Summer

Location: France

Accommodations: Family-stay/host-family

Years in Operation: 7

Religious Affiliation: Not relevant

STAFF

Student/Staff Ratio: 10:1

Staff Qualifications: All directors are certified foreign language teachers.

PARTICIPANTS

Average Number of Participants: 25

For Participants Aged: 16–19

The Ideal Candidate: Students must be 16 years old by the departure date and have completed the equivalent of two years of high school French or be 15 and have completed the equivalent of three years of high school French.

Special Requirements for Participation: None.

COSTS

Average Cost: $4,500

Included in Cost: Round-trip airfare from Houston, all ground transportation, all program costs (including homestay and classes), meals with the homestay family, orientation information, entrance fees.

Financial Aid Available: No

PROGRAMS ABROAD TRAVEL ALTERNATIVES (GERMANY)

THE PROGRAM

Description: Designed to boost student fluency in a short period of time, PATA programs attract serious students who pledge to use only their language of study during their study abroad. Because PATA on-site directors are teachers of French,

German, Italian, Russian, and/or Spanish, the entire program is conducted in the language of study.

Specialty: Students may choose their city of study: Freiburg or Jena.

Program Type: Academic/pre-college enrichment

Classification: Coeducational, residential

Goals: Students participating in the Freiburg program study at the International House, from which they receive 80 contact hours reflected on a transcript. Students studying in Jena study at Jena Kollege, from which they also receive 80 hours reflected on a transcript.

Focus: Academic/pre-college enrichment, cultural, and travel

Activities Center On: Language, academic, and travel

Intensity Level: 3

Duration: 2–4 weeks

Program Offered: Summer

Location: Germany

Accommodations: Family-stay/host-family

Years in Operation: 7

Religious Affiliation: Not relevant

STAFF

Student/Staff Ratio: 10:1

Staff Qualifications: All directors are certified foreign language teachers.

PARTICIPANTS

Average Number of Participants: 25

For Participants Aged: 15–19

The Ideal Candidate: Students must be 15 years old by the departure date and have completed their freshman year, and must submit a teacher recommendation.

Special Requirements for Participation: None.

COSTS

Average Cost: $4,000

Included in Cost: Round-trip airfare from Houston, classes and host family, meals with host family, ground transportation, entrance fees on excursions, medical insurance, orientation materials.

Financial Aid Available: No

PROGRAMS ABROAD TRAVEL ALTERNATIVES (GUATEMALA)

THE PROGRAM

Description: Designed to boost student fluency in a short period of time, PATA programs attract serious students who pledge to use only their language of study during their study abroad. Because PATA on-site directors are teachers of French, German, Italian, Russian, and/or Spanish, the entire program

is conducted in the language of study.

Specialty: Students participate in language classes in the mornings and then explore the culture of Guatemala during afternoon and weekend excursions.

Program Type: Academic/pre-college enrichment

Classification: Coeducational, day program

Goals: Students study at CSA and receive 80 contact hours on a transcript, which, when presented to their receiving university with a portfolio of their coursework, may be used to petition for up to 5 hours of college credit.

Focus: Academic/pre-college enrichment, cultural, and travel

Activities Center On: Academic, language, and cultural

Intensity Level: 3

Duration: 2–4 weeks

Program Offered: Summer

Location: Guatemala

Accommodations: Family-stay/host-family

Years in Operation: 7

Religious Affiliation: Not relevant

STAFF

Student/Staff Ratio: 10:1

Staff Qualifications: All directors are certified foreign language teachers.

PARTICIPANTS

Average Number of Participants: 25

For Participants Aged: 15–19

The Ideal Candidate: Students must be 16 years old by the departure date and have completed the equivalent of two years of high school Spanish, or be 15 and have completed the equivalent of three years of high school Spanish.

Special Requirements for Participation: None.

COSTS

Average Cost: $3,700

Included in Cost: Round-trip airfare from Houston; program costs including homestay arrangements and classes, meals with family, entrance fees, medical insurance, ground transportation, and orientation materials.

Financial Aid Available: No

PROGRAMS ABROAD TRAVEL ALTERNATIVES (ITALY)

THE PROGRAM

Description: Designed to boost student fluency in a short period of time, PATA programs attract serious students who pledge to use only their language of study during their study abroad. Because PATA on-site directors are teachers of French, German, Italian, Russian, and/or Spanish, the entire program is conducted in the language of study.

Program Type: Academic/pre-college enrichment

Classification: Coeducational, residential

Goals: Students receive 40 contact hours on a Dilit International House transcript, which, when presented to their receiving university with a portfolio of their coursework, maybe used to petition for up to 2 hours of college credit.

Focus: Academic/pre-college enrichment, cultural, and travel

Activities Center On: Academic, language, and travel

Intensity Level: 3

Duration: 2–4 weeks

Program Offered: Summer

Location: Germany

Accommodations: Family-stay/host-family

Years in Operation: 7

Religious Affiliation: Not relevant

STAFF

Student/Staff Ratio: 10:1

Staff Qualifications: All directors are certified foreign language teachers.

PARTICIPANTS

Average Number of Participants: 25

For Participants Aged: 15–19

The Ideal Candidate: Students must be 15 years old by the departure date and have completed their freshman year, and must submit a teacher recommendation. Novice language learners are accepted.

Special Requirements for Participation: None.

COSTS

Average Cost: $4,000

Included in Cost: Round-trip airfare from Houston, homestay, meals with family, classes, medical insurance, orientation materials, entrance fees on all excursions.

Financial Aid Available: No

PROGRAMS ABROAD TRAVEL ALTERNATIVES (MEXICO)

THE PROGRAM

Description: Designed to boost student fluency in a short period of time, PATA programs attract serious students who pledge to use only their language of study during their study abroad. Because PATA on-site directors are teachers of French, German, Italian, Russian, and/or Spanish, the entire program is conducted in the language of study.

Specialty: Students spend two weeks in the cultural city of Oaxaca, Mexico, and then spend the last week of the program in Playa del Carmen, Mexico, while continuing with language classes.

Program Type: Academic/pre-college enrichment

Classification: Coeducational, residential

Goals: Students receive 80 hours of contact hours on a Solexico transcript, which, when presented to their receiving university with a portfolio of their coursework, may be used to petition for up to 5 hours of college credit.

Focus: Academic/pre-college enrichment, cultural, and travel

Activities Center On: Language, academic, and travel

Intensity Level: 3

Duration: 2–4 weeks

Program Offered: Summer

Location: Mexico

Accommodations: Family-stay/host-family

Years in Operation: 7

Religious Affiliation: Not relevant

STAFF

Student/Staff Ratio: 10:1

Staff Qualifications: All staff are certified foreign language teachers.

PARTICIPANTS

Average Number of Participants: 25

For Participants Aged: 16–19

The Ideal Candidate: Students must be 16 years old by the departure date and have completed the equivalent of two years of high school Spanish, or be 15 and have completed the equivalent of three years of high school Spanish.

Special Requirements for Participation: None.

COSTS

Average Cost: $3,500

Included in Cost: Round-trip airfare from San Antonio, Texas; all ground transportation, all program costs (including classes and homestay family), meals with family, orientation materials, medical insurance.

Financial Aid Available: No

PROGRAMS ABROAD TRAVEL ALTERNATIVES (RUSSIA)

THE PROGRAM

Description: Designed to boost student fluency in a short period of time, PATA programs attract serious students who pledge to use only their language of study during their study abroad. Because PATA on-site directors are teachers of French, German, Italian, Russian, and/or Spanish, the entire program is conducted in the language of study.

Program Type: Academic/pre-college enrichment

Classification: Coeducational, residential

Goals: Students receive 80 contact hours on a university transcript, which represents 4–5 hours of college credit.

Focus: Academic/pre-college enrichment, cultural, and travel

Activities Center On: Language, academic, and travel

Intensity Level: 3

Duration: 2–4 weeks

Program Offered: Summer

Location: Russia

Accommodations: Family-stay/host-family

Years in Operation: 7

Religious Affiliation: Not relevant

STAFF

Student/Staff Ratio: 10:1

Staff Qualifications: All directors are certified foreign language teachers.

PARTICIPANTS

Average Number of Participants: 25

For Participants Aged: 15–19

The Ideal Candidate: Students must be 15 by the departure date and submit a teacher recommendation. Novice language learners are accepted. PATA encourages all students who have studied other languages to consider immersion in Russian.

Special Requirements for Participation: None.

COSTS

Average Cost: $4,000

Included in Cost: Round-trip airfare from Houston, all ground transportation, classes, homestay arrangements and meals with the family, medical insurance, and orientation materials.

Financial Aid Available: No

PROGRAMS ABROAD TRAVEL ALTERNATIVES (SPAIN)

THE PROGRAM

Description: Designed to boost student fluency in a short period of time, PATA programs attract serious students who pledge to use only their language of study during their study abroad. Because PATA on-site directors are teachers of French, German, Italian, Russian, and/or Spanish, the entire program is conducted in the language of study.

Specialty: Students can choose from programs in Barcelona, Santander, or Cadiz.

Program Type: Academic/pre-college enrichment

Classification: Coeducational, residential

Goals: Participants receive 60 contact hours on a university transcript, which represents 4 hours of college credit.

Focus: Academic/pre-college enrichment, cultural, and travel

Activities Center On: Academic, language, and travel

Intensity Level: 3

Duration: 2–4 weeks

Program Offered: Summer

Location: Spain

Accommodations: Family-stay/host-family

Years in Operation: 7

Religious Affiliation: Not relevant

STAFF

Student/Staff Ratio: 10:1

Staff Qualifications: All directors are certified Spanish teachers at the secondary level.

PARTICIPANTS

Average Number of Participants: 25

For Participants Aged: 15–19

The Ideal Candidate: Students must be 16 years old by the departure date and have completed two years of high school Spanish, or be 15 and completed the equivalent of three years of high school Spanish.

Special Requirements for Participation: None.

COSTS

Average Cost: $4,000

Included in Cost: Round-trip airfare from Houston, classes, homestay, meals with homestay family, orientation materials, medical insurance, all ground transportation, fees on all excursion sites.

Financial Aid Available: No

PROWORLD SERVICE CORPS

The ProWorld Service Corps offers profound 2- to 26-week cultural, service, and academic experiences in the Caribbean Coast of Belize and the Sacred Valley of the Incas in Peru.

Years in Operation: 5

Religious Affiliation: Not relevant

Price Range of Programs: $1,250–$8,750

For More Information:
Contact: Richard Webb, Executive Director
262 East 10th Street
New York, NY 10009
Phone: 877-733-7378
Fax: 406-252-3973
Email: info@properu.org
Website: www.properu.org

NGO Internship in Belize

The Program

Description: Intern with a local Belizean development agency while learning about the Garifuna culture and exploring Belize. Set along the picturesque Caribbean Coast, this immersive program provides unforgettable internship experiences. You will work with one of our affiliated nongovernmental organizations (NGOs) on a development project in the areas of health care, education, micro business, youth sports, or environment. The focus of your development project is determined by your specific interests and the needs of the local community.

Specialty: Watch the moon rise over the the Caribbean, swim off your front porch, explore Mayan ruins, and see monkeys in the secluded jungle. These and other adventures combine with productive volunteer work to form a comprehensive volunteer experience.

Program Type: Academic/pre-college enrichment, community service, outdoors/adventure, travel/cultural

Classification: Coeducational, residential

Goals: Participants will learn about intercultural interaction, the Garifuna culture, Mayan history, self sufficiency, courage, integrity, and community service.

Focus: Internship, academic/pre-college enrichment, and community service

Activities Center On: Academic, cultural, and outdoors/adventure

Intensity Level: 3

Duration: 4–6 weeks, 6–8 weeks, over 8 weeks

Program Offered: Fall, winter Intersession/January term, spring, summer

Location: Caribbean Coast of Belize and Hopkins, Belize

Accommodations: Dormitory, family-stay/host-family

Years in Operation: 5

Religious Affiliation: Not relevant

Staff

Student/Staff Ratio: 6:1

Staff Qualifications: ProWorld staff are confident, able, and dedicated individuals who are veteran travelers and community leaders. Program staff members are bilingual and spend a minimum of one year on site in Peru. For every seven program participants there is at least one in-country ProPeru staff member. CPR and first aid training are basic requirements of all staff members. ProPeru staff are part of every aspect of the program experience, often becoming friends as well as guides for the participant's journey.

Participants

Average Number of Participants: 12

For Participants Aged: 18–90

The Ideal Candidate: Participants must have an adventurous spirit, an open mind, and a true desire to help others.

Special Requirements for Participation: None.

Costs

Average Cost: $1,900

Included in Cost: Program fees help support ongoing development projects in Belize and include: full room and board, domestic transportation, 24-hour safety and medical services, funding of development projects and internships, and weekly adventures.

Financial Aid Available: Yes

NGO Internship in Peru

The Program

Description: Intern with a local Peruvian development agency while learning Spanish and exploring Peru. Set in a picturesque valley lined with snow-capped Andean peaks, this is an immersive and rewarding program. In addition to private Spanish classes and numerous adventures, you will work with one of our 20 affiliated nongovernmental organizations (NGOs) on a focused development project. The focus of your development project is determined by your specific skills and interests, and the needs of the local community.

Specialty: Hike the Inca Trail, watch the sun rise over Machu Picchu, see the sun temple of Pisaq, and explore the Amazon Jungle. These and other adventures combine with classes and productive volunteer work to form a comprehensive educational experience.

Program Type: Academic/pre-college enrichment, community service, outdoors/adventure, travel/cultural

Classification: Coeducational, residential

Goals: Participants will learn about: intercultural interaction, the Spanish language, Incan history, self sufficiency, courage, integrity, and community service.

Focus: Internship, community service, and academic/pre-college enrichment

Activities Center On: Volunteer, academic, and outdoors and adventure

Intensity Level: 4

Duration: 4–6 weeks, 6–8 weeks, over 8 weeks

Program Offered: Fall, winter Intersession/January term, spring, summer

Location: Sacred Valley of the Incas, Peru

Accommodations: Dormitory, family-stay/host-family

Years in Operation: 5

Religious Affiliation: Not relevant

Staff

Student/Staff Ratio: 6:1

Staff Qualifications: ProPeru staff are confident, able, and dedicated individuals who are veteran travelers and community leaders. Program staff members are bilingual and spend a minimum of one year on site in Peru. For every seven program participants there is at least one in-country ProPeru staff member. CPR and first aid training are basic requirements of all staff members. ProPeru staff are part of every aspect of the program experience, often becoming friends as well as guides for the participant's journey.

PARTICIPANTS

Average Number of Participants: 12

For Participants Aged: 18–90

The Ideal Candidate: ProWorld volunteers are adventurous, caring, passionate, and curious individuals with a true desire to explore while improving themselves and the world in which they live.

Special Requirements for Participation: Participants must have an adventurous spirit, an open mind, and a true desire to help others.

COSTS

Average Cost: $1,900

Included in Cost: Program fees help support ongoing development projects in Peru and include: full room and board, domestic transportation, 24-hour safety and medical services, full funding of development projects and internships, and weekly adventures.

Financial Aid Available: Yes

SEMESTER IN PERU

THE PROGRAM

Description: Watch the sun rise over Machu Picchu, walk the Inca Trail, see the sun temple of Ollantaytambo, and explore the mystical city of Cusco—this is your class schedule. Experiential learning combines with weekly adventures and productive volunteer work to form a comprehensive and unforgettable educational experience.

Program Type: Academic/pre-college enrichment, community service, outdoors/adventure, travel/cultural

Classification: Coeducational, residential

Goals: Participants will learn about anthropology, development work, intercultural interaction, the Spanish language, Incan history, self sufficiency, courage, integrity, and community service.

Focus: Academic/pre-college enrichment, community service, and cultural

Activities Center On: Cultural, outdoors/adventure, and volunteer

Intensity Level: 4

Duration: Over 8 weeks

Program Offered: Fall, spring, full academic year

Location: Sacred Valley of the Incas, Peru

Accommodations: Dormitory, family-stay/host-family

Years in Operation: 5

Religious Affiliation: Not relevant

STAFF

Student/Staff Ratio: 4:1

Staff Qualifications: ProWorld staff are confident, able, and dedicated individuals who are veteran travelers and community leaders. Program staff members are bilingual and spend a minimum of one year on site in Peru. For every seven program participants there is at least one in-country ProPeru staff member. CPR and first aid training are basic requirements of all staff members. ProPeru staff are part of every aspect of the program experience, often becoming friends as well as guides for the participant's journey.

PARTICIPANTS

Average Number of Participants: 12

For Participants Aged: 18–90

The Ideal Candidate: Participants must have an adventurous spirit, an open mind, and a true desire to help others.

Special Requirements for Participation: None.

COSTS

Average Cost: $8,750

Included in Cost: Program fees help support ongoing development projects in Peru and include: full room and board, domestic airfare and transportation, 24-hour safety and medical services, funding of development projects and internships, and weekly adventures.

Financial Aid Available: Yes

TEACH ENGLISH OR MATH IN BELIZE

THE PROGRAM

Description: Teach English or math and work with one of our local schools on a focused literacy, math, science, or other educational project. The focus of your teaching project is determined by your specific skills and the needs of the local children. Set along the picturesque Caribbean Coast, this immersive program provides unforgettable internship experiences. In addition to hands-on teaching experience, you will take part in weekly adventures and cultural activities in the peaceful village of Hopkins.

Specialty: Watch the moon rise over the Caribbean, swim off your front porch, explore Mayan ruins, and see monkeys in the secluded jungle. These and other adventures combine with productive volunteer work to form a comprehensive volunteer experience.

Program Type: Academic/pre-college enrichment, community service, outdoors/adventure, travel/cultural

Classification: Coeducational, residential

Goals: Participants will learn about intercultural interaction, the Garifuna culture, Mayan history, self sufficiency, courage, integrity, and community service.

Focus: Community service, leadership/teamwork, and internship

Activities Center On: Outdoors/adventure, travel, and academic

Intensity Level: 3

Duration: 4–6 weeks, 6–8 weeks, over 8 weeks

Program Offered: Fall, winter Intersession/January term, spring, summer

Location: Caribbean Coast of Belize; Hopkins, Belize

Accommodations: Family-stay/host-family, bunk/cabin

Years in Operation: 5

Religious Affiliation: Not relevant

STAFF

Student/Staff Ratio: 6:1

Staff Qualifications: ProWorld staff are confident, able, and dedicated individuals who are veteran travelers and community leaders. Program staff members are bilingual and spend a minimum of one year on site in Peru. For every seven program participants there is at least one in-country ProPeru staff member. CPR and first aid training are basic requirements of all staff members. ProPeru staff are part of every aspect of the program experience, often becoming friends as well as guides for the participant's journey.

PARTICIPANTS

Average Number of Participants: 12

For Participants Aged: 18–90

The Ideal Candidate: Participants must have an adventurous spirit, an open mind, and a true desire to help others.

Special Requirements for Participation: None.

COSTS

Average Cost: $1,900

Included in Cost: Program fees help support ongoing development projects in Belize and include: full room and board, domestic transportation, 24-hour safety and medical services, funding of development projects and internships, and weekly adventures.

Financial Aid Available: Yes

RHODES COLLEGE

Rhodes is a Top-50 liberal arts college in midtown Memphis, Tennessee.

Religious Affiliation: Not relevant

Price Range of Programs: $1,275

For More Information:
  Contact: Rebecca Finlayson, Director
       2000 North Parkway
       Memphis, TN 38112
  Phone: 901-843-3794
  Fax: 901-843-3728
  Email: finlayson@rhodes.edu
  Website: www.rhodes.edu

RHODES SUMMER WRITING INSTITUTE

THE PROGRAM

Description: The Writing Institute is a two-week, writing-intensive residential program for college-bound high school students (rising juniors and seniors). Participants select one course from offerings in creative writing, literature, psychology, history, political science, and even mathematics. Course selection varies each year. Classes are small (between 8–12 students), taught by Rhodes professors, and worth 2 college credits, transferable to any college or university as general credits.

Specialty: The program offers students intensive writing instruction; the classes are small, allowing students to receive personal attention. Evening seminars offer students the opportunity to explore and write about other disciplines.

Program Type: Academic/pre-college enrichment

Classification: Coeducational, residential

Goals: Participants who successfully complete the program will have learned college-level writing skills and received college-level instruction in a variety of fields.

Focus: Academic/pre-college enrichment

Activities Center On: Academic and writing

Intensity Level: 4

Duration: 1–2 weeks

Program Offered: Summer

Location: Memphis, Tennessee

Accommodations: Dormitory

Years in Operation: 10

Religious Affiliation: Not relevant

STAFF

Student/Staff Ratio: 8:1

Staff Qualifications: Faculty: Rhodes professors with PhDs; resident assistants: Rhodes undergraduates; director: Rhodes professor with PhD and also Director of Writing Center.

PARTICIPANTS

Average Number of Participants: 60

For Participants Aged: 15–19

The Ideal Candidate: Rising high school junior or senior with an A/B average who has an interest in writing.

Special Requirements for Participation: Applications must include the following: personal statement, transcript, and teacher or counselor recommendation.

COSTS

Average Cost: $1,275

Included in Cost: Everything is included: room and board (meals), books, course tuition, evening seminars, and extracurricular and social events.

Financial Aid Available: Yes

THE ROAD LESS TRAVELED

Wilderness expeditions, community service adventures, coast-to-coast adventure challenges, cultural experiences, and leadership courses. Participants: coeducational and international; ages 13–19 and families with children ages 10 and up, grouped according to age. Enrollment: 10–15 participants per program. Program dates: 15- to 39-day programs, June through August.

Years in Operation: 12

Religious Affiliation: Not relevant

For More Information:
Contact: Jim Stein, Owner/Director
2331 North Elston Avenue
Chicago, IL 60614
Phone: 800-939-9839
Fax: 773-342-5703
Email: jim@theroadlesstraveled.com
Website: www.theroadlesstraveled.com

AUSTRALIAN WALKABOUT (AUSTRALIA)

THE PROGRAM

Description: This 27-day expedition begins with a 4-day hike through North Queensland's magnificent rainforests. The group spends 3 days kayaking the Barnard Islands. For the next 5 days, participants hike through the wilderness and immerse themselves in Australia's indigenous culture. The expedition continues with a 3-day backpack along Queensland's beaches, then journeys along the Great Barrier Reef for 3 days, and concludes with another aquatic adventure—2 days of rafting on the North Johnstone River.

Program Type: Outdoors/adventure, travel/cultural

Classification: Coeducational, residential

Focus: Skill-building, travel, and leadership/teamwork

Activities Center On: Outdoors/adventure, backpacking, and rafting

Intensity Level: 3

Duration: 2–4 weeks

Program Offered: Summer

Location: Australia

Accommodations: Tent

Years in Operation: 12

Religious Affiliation: Not relevant

STAFF

Student/Staff Ratio: 6:1

Staff Qualifications: Our staff are genuine, spirited, friendly, athletic, well-educated, well-traveled experts in wilderness adventure who are selected for their ability to prevent and solve problems. All leaders are certified Wilderness Emergency Medical Tecnicians (WEMT), Emergency Medical Technicians (EMT), or Wilderness First Responders (WFR).

PARTICIPANTS

Average Number of Participants: 13

For Participants Aged: 15–18

Special Requirements for Participation: None.

COSTS

Average Cost: $5,050

Included in Cost: Everything is included except airfare.

Financial Aid Available: Yes

CRESTS AND CANYONS

THE PROGRAM

Description: This 24-day expedition begins in the Great Sand Dunes in Colorado, then travels to New Mexico for a 4-day backpacking adventure in the Latir Peaks Wilderness. Participants then travel to Colorado's Arkansas River for 3 days of whitewater rafting. The group takes 3 days to paddle the waters of Lake Powell in Arizona. After a visit with the Navajo in Utah, the group heads up to the San Juan Mountains in Colorado for 3 days of rock climbing.

Program Type: Outdoors/adventure, travel/cultural

Classification: Coeducational, residential

Focus: Skill-building, travel, and cultural

Activities Center On: Outdoors/adventure, backpacking, and rafting

Intensity Level: 3

Duration: 2–4 weeks

Program Offered: Summer

Location: Arizona, Colorado, New Mexico, Utah

Accommodations: Tent

Years in Operation: 12

Religious Affiliation: Not relevant

STAFF

Student/Staff Ratio: 6:1

Staff Qualifications: Our staff are genuine, spirited, friendly, athletic, well-educated, well-traveled experts in wilderness adventure who are selected for their ability to prevent and solve problems. All leaders are certified as Wilderness Emergency Medical Tecnicians (WEMT), Emergency Medical Technicians (EMT), or Wilderness First Responders (WFR).

PARTICIPANTS

Average Number of Participants: 13

For Participants Aged: 14–18

Special Requirements for Participation: None.

COSTS

Average Cost: $3,780

Included in Cost: Everything is included except airfare.

Financial Aid Available: Yes

El Sendero—Costa Rica
Community Service

The Program

Description: This 18-day Spanish-immersion community service adventure begins in San Jose, Costa Rica. For 2 days, the group explores the cloud forest preserve. Next, the group moves to the small riverside village of Bajo Tigre, where the next 9 days are spent working with the villagers on various community projects. After completing their service project, participants raft the Rio Pacuare before concluding with 2 days of sea kayaking the canals of Tortuguero.

Program Type: Community service, outdoors/adventure

Classification: Coeducational, residential

Focus: Community service, cultural, and leadership/teamwork

Activities Center On: Volunteer, outdoors/adventure, and cultural

Intensity Level: 3

Duration: 2–4 weeks

Program Offered: Summer

Location: Costa Rica

Accommodations: Tent, bunk/cabin

Years in Operation: 12

Religious Affiliation: Not relevant

Staff

Student/Staff Ratio: 5:1

Staff Qualifications: Our staff are genuine, spirited, friendly, athletic, well-educated, well-traveled experts in wilderness adventure who are selected for their ability to prevent and solve problems. All leaders are certified Wilderness Emergency Medical Tecnicians (WEMT), Emergency Medical Technicians (EMT), or Wilderness First Responders (WFR).

Participants

Average Number of Participants: 15

For Participants Aged: 14–18

Special Requirements for Participation: None.

Costs

Average Cost: $3,150

Included in Cost: Everything is included except airfare.

Financial Aid Available: Yes

Fire and Sky

The Program

Description: This 33-day journey begins with a 4-day backpack through Rocky Mountain National Park. From there, the group enters Dark Canyon Primitive Area for a 3-day desert hike. Next, participants head toward the Green River to spend 5 days whitewater rafting and kayaking in hard-shell and inflatable kayaks. Then participants travel north to Montana for a 6-day hike through the Pioneer Mountains. The journey ends in Jackson, Wyoming, with 2 exhilarating days of rock climbing.

Program Type: Outdoors/adventure, travel/cultural

Classification: Coeducational, residential

Focus: Skill-building, travel, and cultural

Activities Center On: Outdoors/adventure, backpacking, and rafting

Intensity Level: 3

Duration: 4–6 weeks

Program Offered: Summer

Location: Colorado, Montana, Utah, Wyoming

Accommodations: Tent

Years in Operation: 12

Religious Affiliation: Not relevant

Staff

Student/Staff Ratio: 6:1

Staff Qualifications: Our staff are genuine, spirited, friendly, athletic, well-educated, well-traveled experts in wilderness adventure who are selected for their ability to prevent and solve problems. All leaders are certified Wilderness Emergency Medical Tecnicians (WEMT), Emergency Medical Technicians (EMT), or Wilderness First Responders (WFR).

Participants

Average Number of Participants: 13

For Participants Aged: 14–18

Special Requirements for Participation: None.

Costs

Average Cost: $4,750

Included in Cost: Everything is included except airfare.

Financial Aid Available: Yes

Leadership Challenge

The Program

Description: This is a leadership course offered to former Road Less Traveled participants and new students with comparable backcountry experience. On this 26-day course, participants sea kayak in the San Juan Islands for 5 days, summit Mount Shuksan during a 5-day technical ice-climbing seminar, and hike for 10 days through British Columbia's Manning Provincial Park. Personal responsibility and individual challenge are at the heart of this experience.

Program Type: Outdoors/adventure, travel/cultural

Classification: Coeducational, residential

Focus: Leadership/teamwork, skill-building, and travel

Activities Center On: Outdoors/adventure, backpacking, and rafting

Intensity Level: 4

Duration: 2–4 weeks

Program Offered: Summer

Location: British Columbia, Canada; Washington

Accommodations: Tent

Years in Operation: 12

Religious Affiliation: Not relevant

STAFF

Student/Staff Ratio: 5:1

Staff Qualifications: Our staff are genuine, spirited, friendly, athletic, well-educated, well-traveled experts in wilderness adventure who are selected for their ability to prevent and solve problems. All leaders are certified Wilderness Emergency Medical Tecnicians (WEMT), Emergency Medical Technicians (EMT), or Wilderness First Responders (WFR).

PARTICIPANTS

Average Number of Participants: 13

For Participants Aged: 16–19

Special Requirements for Participation: None.

COSTS

Average Cost: $3,995

Included in Cost: Everything is included except airfare.

Financial Aid Available: Yes

MIDNIGHT SUN—ALASKA

THE PROGRAM

Description: This 39-day adventure begins with a five-day backpack through Wrangell–St. Elias National Park, then moves to Prince William Sound for 4 days of sea kayaking along the coastline. The next 19 days are spent in the Talkeetna Mountains, where participants backpack for 10 days, learn technical ice-climbing skills, travel across glaciers, summit an unnamed peak, and descend to the Talkeetna River for a thrilling 4-day whitewater rafting adventure.

Program Type: Outdoors/adventure, travel/cultural

Classification: Coeducational, residential

Focus: Skill-building, Travel, and leadership/teamwork

Activities Center On: Outdoors/adventure, backpacking, and rafting

Intensity Level: 4

Duration: 4–6 weeks

Program Offered: Summer

Location: Alaska

Accommodations: Tent

Years in Operation: 12

Religious Affiliation: Not relevant

STAFF

Student/Staff Ratio: 6:1

Staff Qualifications: Our staff are genuine, spirited, friendly, athletic, well-educated, well-traveled experts in wilderness adventure who are selected for their ability to prevent and solve problems. All leaders are certified Wilderness Emergency Medical Tecnicians (WEMT), Emergency Medical Technicians (EMT), or Wilderness First Responders (WFR).

PARTICIPANTS

Average Number of Participants: 13

For Participants Aged: 16–19

Special Requirements for Participation: None.

COSTS

Average Cost: $4,995

Included in Cost: Everything is included except airfare.

Financial Aid Available: Yes

NORTHERN EXPOSURE—NOVA SCOTIA COMMUNITY SERVICE

THE PROGRAM

Description: This 18-day French language–exposure community service program takes place in the scenic beauty of Canada's east coast. Participants explore the stunning natural beauty of the area before spending 9 days in a local village, working with the community on various service projects. Following the completion of our service project, participants spend 3 days sea kayaking in coastal waters and 2 days hiking through craggy highlands.

Program Type: Community service, outdoors/adventure

Classification: Coeducational, residential

Focus: Community service, cultural, and leadership/teamwork

Activities Center On: Volunteer, cultural, and kayaking

Intensity Level: 3

Duration: 2–4 weeks

Program Offered: Summer

Location: Nova Scotia, Canada

Accommodations: Tent

Years in Operation: 12

Religious Affiliation: Not relevant

STAFF

Student/Staff Ratio: 5:1

Staff Qualifications: Our staff are genuine, spirited, friendly, athletic, well-educated, well-traveled experts in wilderness adventure who are selected for their ability to prevent and solve problems. All leaders are certified Wilderness Emergency Medical Tecnicians (WEMT), Emergency Medical Technicians (EMT), or Wilderness First Responders (WFR).

PARTICIPANTS

Average Number of Participants: 15

For Participants Aged: 14–18

Special Requirements for Participation: None.

COSTS

Average Cost: $3,150

Included in Cost: Everything is included except airfare.

Financial Aid Available: Yes

PEAKS AND VALLEYS

THE PROGRAM

Description: This 28-day exploration begins in Wyoming's Bridger-Teton National Forest with a 5-day backpacking trip. Next, the group follows the bends of Idaho's Salmon River for 4 days of thrilling whitewater rafting and kayaking, then backpacks for 6 days through Idaho's Selway Bitterroot Wilderness. Returning to Wyoming, participants spend 4 days learning the essentials of multipitch rock climbing, as preparation for the final and ultimate challenge—an ascent of the 13,766-foot Grand Teton.

Program Type: Outdoors/adventure, travel/cultural

Classification: Coeducational, residential

Focus: Skill-building, travel, and leadership/teamwork

Activities Center On: Outdoors/adventure, backpacking, and rafting

Intensity Level: 3

Duration: 2–4 weeks

Program Offered: Summer

Location: Idaho, Montana, Wyoming

Accommodations: Tent

Years in Operation: 12

Religious Affiliation: Not relevant

STAFF

Student/Staff Ratio: 6:1

Staff Qualifications: Our staff are genuine, spirited, friendly, athletic, well-educated, well-traveled experts in wilderness adventure who are selected for their ability to prevent and solve problems. All leaders are certified Wilderness Emergency Medical Tecnicians (WEMT), Emergency Medical Technicians (EMT), or Wilderness First Responders (WFR).

PARTICIPANTS

Average Number of Participants: 13

For Participants Aged: 14–18

Special Requirements for Participation: None.

COSTS

Average Cost: $4,550

Included in Cost: Everything is included except airfare.

Financial Aid Available: Yes

PURA VIDA—COSTA RICA

THE PROGRAM

Description: This 22-day expedition begins with 2 days of exploration through a private cloud forest preserve. From there, the group moves to Parque Nacional Chirripo for 5 days, hiking to Costa Rica's highest peak. Enjoy 4 spectacular days of sea kayaking before heading to Parque Nacional Corcovado for 4 more days of backpacking. Spend 2 days exploring in both Parque Nacional Manuel Antonio and Parque Nacional Arenal before concluding with a 4-day rafting adventure on the Rio Pacuare.

Program Type: Outdoors/adventure, travel/cultural

Classification: Coeducational, residential

Focus: Skill-building, travel, and leadership/teamwork

Activities Center On: Backpacking, rafting, and kayaking

Intensity Level: 3

Duration: 2–4 weeks

Program Offered: Summer

Location: Costa Rica

Accommodations: Tent

Years in Operation: 12

Religious Affiliation: Not relevant

STAFF

Student/Staff Ratio: 6:1

Staff Qualifications: Our staff are genuine, spirited, friendly, athletic, well-educated, well-traveled experts in wilderness adventure who are selected for their ability to prevent and solve problems. All leaders are certified Wilderness Emergency Medical Tecnicians (WEMT), Emergency Medical Technicians (EMT), or Wilderness First Responders (WFR).

PARTICIPANTS

Average Number of Participants: 15

For Participants Aged: 15–18

Special Requirements for Participation: None.

COSTS

Average Cost: $3,950

Included in Cost: Everything is included except airfare.

Financial Aid Available: Yes

RIDGES AND RAPIDS

THE PROGRAM

Description: The Flattops Wilderness, nestled in the heart of the White River National Forest, is where this 17-day expedition begins with 4 days of backpacking. The group then moves to the Green River in Utah for 5 days of whitewater rafting and kayaking in both hard-shell and inflatable kayaks. The journey concludes with 2 days of rock climbing near Rocky Mountain National Park.

Program Type: Outdoors/adventure, travel/cultural

Classification: Coeducational, residential

Focus: Skill-building, travel, and leadership/teamwork

Activities Center On: Outdoors/adventure, rafting, and backpacking

Intensity Level: 3

Duration: 2–4 weeks

Program Offered: Summer

Location: Colorado, Wyoming

Accommodations: Tent

Years in Operation: 12

Religious Affiliation: Not relevant

STAFF

Student/Staff Ratio: 6:1

Staff Qualifications: Our staff are genuine, spirited, friendly, athletic, well-educated, well-traveled experts in wilderness adventure who are selected for their ability to prevent and solve problems. All leaders are certified Wilderness Emergency Medical Tecnicians (WEMT), Emergency Medical Technicians (EMT), or Wilderness First Responders (WFR).

PARTICIPANTS

Average Number of Participants: 13

For Participants Aged: 14–18

Special Requirements for Participation: None.

COSTS

Average Cost: $2,995

Included in Cost: Everything is included except airfare.

Financial Aid Available: Yes

THE GREAT DIVIDE

THE PROGRAM

Description: This 15-day adventure begins amid the splendor of the Grand Tetons. The group travels to Bridger-Teton National Forest for a 4-day backpack. Then it's back north to Yellowstone National Park for a 3-day sea kayaking adventure and a half-day of whitewater rafting the Snake River. The journey ends in Jackson, Wyoming, with a 2-day climb in the Tetons.

Program Type: Outdoors/adventure, travel/cultural

Classification: Coeducational, residential

Focus: Skill-building, travel, and leadership/teamwork

Activities Center On: Outdoors/adventure, rafting, and kayaking

Intensity Level: 3

Duration: 2–4 weeks

Program Offered: Summer

Location: Montana, Wyoming

Accommodations: Tent

Years in Operation: 12

Religious Affiliation: Not relevant

STAFF

Student/Staff Ratio: 6:1

Staff Qualifications: Our staff are genuine, spirited, friendly, athletic, well-educated, well-traveled experts in wilderness adventure who are selected for their ability to prevent and solve problems. All leaders are certified Wilderness Emergency Medical Tecnicians (WEMT), Emergency Medical Technicians (EMT), or Wilderness First Responders (WFR).

PARTICIPANTS

Average Number of Participants: 13

For Participants Aged: 14–18

Special Requirements for Participation: None.

COSTS

Average Cost: $2,875

Included in Cost: Everything is included except airfare.

Financial Aid Available: Yes

WATER AND ROCKS

THE PROGRAM

Description: This 34-day journey begins with a 6-day backpack through the Italian Peaks. Participants then spend 5 days hiking and exploring the beaches of the Pacific Ocean in Olympic National Park. Then it's off to summit Mount Rainier. Before the climb, participants are trained by the world-class climbers of Rainier Mountaineering, Inc. Two days of rock climbing in the San Juan Islands are followed by 4 days of whitewater rafting and kayaking on Idaho's Salmon River.

Program Type: Outdoors/adventure, travel/cultural

Classification: Coeducational, residential

Focus: Skill-building, travel, and leadership/teamwork

Activities Center On: Outdoors/adventure, backpacking, and rafting

Intensity Level: 3

Duration: 4–6 weeks

Program Offered: Summer

Location: Idaho, Montana, Utah, Washington

Accommodations: Tent

Years in Operation: 12

Religious Affiliation: Not relevant

STAFF

Student/Staff Ratio: 6:1

Staff Qualifications: Our staff are genuine, spirited, friendly, athletic, well-educated, well-traveled experts in wilderness adventure who are selected for their ability to prevent and solve problems. All leaders are certified Wilderness Emergency Medical Tecnicians (WEMT), Emergency Medical Technicians (EMT), or Wilderness First Responders (WFR).

PARTICIPANTS

Average Number of Participants: 13

For Participants Aged: 14–18

Special Requirements for Participation: None.

COSTS

Average Cost: $4,890

Included in Cost: Everything is included except airfare.

Financial Aid Available: Yes

SAVANNAH SCIENCE MUSEUM

Religious Affiliation: Not relevant

For More Information:
    Contact: Kris Williams, Project Director
             PO Box 9841
             Savannah, GA 31412
    Phone: 912-355-6705
    Fax: 912-447-8656
    Email: wassawcrp@aol.com
    Website: members.aol.com/wassawCRP/index.html

CARETTA RESEARCH PROJECT

THE PROGRAM

Description: The Caretta Research Project is a hands-on research, conservation, and education program that protects the threatened loggerhead sea turtles that nest on Wassaw National Wildlife Refuge, Georgia.

Specialty: Participants get a hands-on experience in collecting data and protecting nests. When they leave the island, they feel as if they have truly made a difference.

Program Type: Outdoors/adventure

Classification: Coeducational, residential

Goals: Participants will help collect data on loggerhead sea turtles and will learn about choices and conflicts involved in protecting a threatened species.

Activities Center On: Science and outdoors/adventure

Intensity Level: 2

Duration: 1–2 weeks

Program Offered: Summer

Location: Savannah, Georgia

Accommodations: Bunk/cabin

Years in Operation: 30

Religious Affiliation: Not relevant

STAFF

Student/Staff Ratio: 3:2

Staff Qualifications: The three full-time staff members have been working with sea turtles for over 10 years each; the two interns have worked with sea turtles for at least 6 years each.

PARTICIPANTS

Average Number of Participants: 96

For Participants Aged: 15–70

The Ideal Candidate: All participants should be in good shape (there may be plenty of walking at night) and have a good, cheerful attitude. The conditions are rustic (no electricity or hot water and very buggy) so they must prepare accordingly.

Special Requirements for Participation: None.

COSTS

Average Cost: $550

Included in Cost: Transportation to and from Wassaw Island, accommodations, and food.

Financial Aid Available: No

THE SCHOOL FOR FIELD STUDIES

SFS is a not-for-profit university-level academic institution providing both semester and summer fully accredited undergraduate programs for American students in community-based environmental science through its five international field stations, located in Australia, Costa Rica, British West Indies, Kenya, and Mexico.

Years in Operation: 23

Religious Affiliation: Not relevant

Price Range of Programs: $3,180–$13,950

For More Information:
    Contact: Paul Houlihan, President
             10 Federal Street
             Salem, MA 01970
    Phone: 978-741-3544
    Fax: 978-741-3551
    Email: phoulihan@fieldstudies.org
    Website: www.fieldstudies.org

SFS, CENTER FOR COASTAL STUDIES

THE PROGRAM

Description: Hands-on field work experience with a focus on sea turtle and gray whale ecology/conservation, and on sustainable harvest and management of important commercial marine resources.

Specialty: Oldest study abroad organization; program well-respected in the science community; chance to get hands-on experience in the environmental field; community service; amazing location.

Program Type: Academic/pre-college enrichment, community service, outdoors/adventure, travel/cultural

Classification: Coeducational, residential

Goals: Introduction to field work for summer: learn plant and animal identification; study resource management, coastal ecology, and socio-economic policy; monitor human impact on turtles and whales; participate in directed research.

Focus: Academic/pre-college enrichment, skill-building, and community service

Activities Center On: Academic, science, and cultural

Intensity Level: 4

Duration: 2–4 weeks, over 8 weeks

Program Offered: Fall, spring, summer

Location: Magdalena Bay, Mexico

Accommodations: Bunk/cabin

Years in Operation: 13

Religious Affiliation: Not relevant

STAFF

Student/Staff Ratio: 3:1

Staff Qualifications: Faculty members are selected based on their teaching and research qualifications, leadership skills, and commitment to field research and community-based environmental work. Most are native to the country in which they teach.

PARTICIPANTS

Average Number of Participants: 20

For Participants Aged: 16+

The Ideal Candidate: Flexible, mature, driven team player with an interest in and awareness of environmental and cross-cultural issues; minimum GPA of 2.5 for college students, 3.6 for high school students.

Special Requirements for Participation: Send in the completed application form with two references, transcript, essays, and $45 application fee in order to be considered. Spanish language ability is preferred. For the semester program, the minimum age is 18, and applicant must have completed one semester of college-level ecology/biology with lab. For the summer program, the minimum age is 16, and applicant must have completed junior year.

COSTS

Average Cost: $8,150

Included in Cost: Tuition, room and board, and fees are included. Travel costs, personal expenses, and books are not included. Summer average cost: $3,200; semester average cost: $13,100.

Financial Aid Available: Yes

SFS, CENTER FOR MARINE RESOURCE STUDIES

THE PROGRAM

Description: Hands-on field research and classroom time devoted to conserving critical marine and terrestrial habitats; snorkeling and scuba diving to identify marine organisms and habitats.

Specialty: Oldest study abroad organization; program well-respected in the science community; chance to get hands-on experience in the environmental field; community service; amazing location.

Program Type: Academic/pre-college enrichment, community service, outdoors/adventure, travel/cultural

Classification: Coeducational, residential

Goals: Introduction to field work for summer: learn about coral reef and fish identification; study resource management, marine ecology, socio-economic policy, and dynamics of marine protected areas; participate in directed research.

Focus: Academic/pre-college enrichment, skill-building, and community service

Activities Center On: Academic, science, and career exploration

Intensity Level: 4

Duration: 2–4 weeks, over 8 weeks

Program Offered: Fall, spring, summer

Location: South Caicos Island

Accommodations: Dormitory

Years in Operation: 13

Religious Affiliation: Not relevant

STAFF

Student/Staff Ratio: 3:1

Staff Qualifications: Faculty members are selected based on their teaching and research qualifications, leadership skills, and commitment to field research and community-based environmental work. Most are native to the country in which they teach.

PARTICIPANTS

Average Number of Participants: 20

For Participants Aged: 16+

The Ideal Candidate: Flexible, mature, driven team player with an interest in and awareness of environmental and cross-cultural issues; minimum GPA of 2.5 for college students, 3.6 for high school students.

Special Requirements for Participation: Send in the completed application form with two references, transcript, essays, and $45 application fee in order to be considered. Spanish language ability is preferred. For the semester program, the minimum age is 18, and applicant must have completed one semester of college-level ecology/biology with lab. For the summer program, the minimum age is 16, and applicant must have completed junior year.

Costs

Average Cost: $8,300

Included in Cost: Tuition, room and board, and fees are included. Travel costs, personal expenses, and books are not included. Summer average cost: $3,500; semester average cost: $13,100.

Financial Aid Available: Yes

SFS, Center for Rainforest Studies

The Program

Description: Hands-on field-research experience and classroom study with a focus on rainforest management and restoration strategies and practices; work with local landholders.

Specialty: Oldest study abroad organization; program well-respected in the science community; chance to get hands-on experience in the environmental field; community service; amazing location.

Program Type: Academic/pre-college enrichment, community service, outdoors/adventure, travel/cultural

Classification: Coeducational, residential

Goals: Study rainforest ecology, resource management, socio-economic policy, and plant and animal identification; learn tree planting skills; gain tree nursery experience; participate in directed research.

Focus: Academic/pre-college enrichment, skill-building, and community service

Activities Center On: Academic, science, and career exploration

Intensity Level: 4

Duration: 2–4 weeks, over 8 weeks

Program Offered: Fall, spring, summer

Location: Northeastern Queensland, Australia

Accommodations: Bunk/cabin

Years in Operation: 16

Religious Affiliation: Not relevant

Staff

Student/Staff Ratio: 3:1

Staff Qualifications: Faculty are chosen based on their teaching and research qualifications, leadership skills, and commitment to field research and community-based environmental work.

Participants

Average Number of Participants: 20

For Participants Aged: 16+

The Ideal Candidate: Flexible, mature, driven team player with an interest in and awareness of environmental and cross-cultural issues; minimum GPA of 2.5 for college students, 3.6 for high school students.

Special Requirements for Participation: Send in the completed application form with two references, transcript, essays, and $45 application fee in order to be considered. Spanish language ability is preferred. For the semester program, the minimum age is 18, and applicant must have completed one semester of college-level ecology/biology with lab. For the summer program, the minimum age is 16, and applicant must have completed junior year.

Costs

Average Cost: $8,700

Included in Cost: Tuition, room and board, and fees are included. Travel costs, personal expenses, and books are not included. Summer average cost: $3,800; semester average cost: $13,600.

Financial Aid Available: Yes

SFS, Center for Sustainable Development Studies

The Program

Description: Hands-on field research experience with a focus on the transition to sustainable agricultural practices, ways to enhance biodiversity through protected areas, and the study of eco-tourism.

Specialty: Oldest study abroad organization; program well-respected in the science community; chance to get hands-on experience in the environmental field; community service; amazing location.

Program Type: Academic/pre-college enrichment, community service, outdoors/adventure, travel/cultural

Classification: Coeducational, residential

Goals: Introduction to field work for summer: learn plant and animal identification; study resource management, tropical ecology, socio-economic policy, sustainable development, organic farming practices, and the Spanish language; participate in directed research.

Focus: Academic/pre-college enrichment, skill-building, and cultural

Activities Center On: Academic, science, and cultural

Intensity Level: 4

Duration: 2–4 weeks, over 8 weeks

Program Offered: Fall, spring, summer

Location: Atenas, Costa Rica

Accommodations: Dormitory, family-stay/host-family

Years in Operation: 12

Religious Affiliation: Not relevant

STAFF

Student/Staff Ratio: 3:1

Staff Qualifications: Faculty members are selected based on their teaching and research qualifications, leadership skills, and commitment to field research and community-based environmental work. Most are native to the country in which they teach.

PARTICIPANTS

Average Number of Participants: 20

For Participants Aged: 16+

The Ideal Candidate: Flexible, mature, driven team player with an interest in and awareness of environmental and cross-cultural issues; minimum GPA of 2.5 for college students, 3.6 for high school students.

Special Requirements for Participation: Send in the completed application form with two references, transcript, essays, and $45 application fee in order to be considered. Spanish language ability is preferred. For the semester program, the minimum age is 18, and applicant must have completed one semester of college-level ecology/biology with lab. For the summer program, the minimum age is 16, and applicant must have completed junior year.

COSTS

Average Cost: $8,300

Included in Cost: Tuition, room and board, and fees are included. Travel costs, personal expenses, and books are not included. Summer average cost: $3,400; semester average cost: $13,200.

Financial Aid Available: Yes

SFS, CENTER FOR WILDLIFE MANAGEMENT STUDIES

THE PROGRAM

Description: Hands-on field work experience with a focus on management strategies for Nairobi National Park, including reasearching the human-wildlife conflict in migration corridors near Mount Kilimanjaro.

Specialty: Oldest study abroad organization; program well-respected in the science community; chance to get hands-on experience in the environmental field; community service; amazing location.

Program Type: Academic/pre-college enrichment, community service, outdoors/adventure, travel/cultural

Classification: Coeducational, residential

Goals: Introduction to field work for summer: learn plant and animal identification; study resource management, wildlife ecology, socio-economic policy, informal Swahili, and the Maasai culture; participate in directed research.

Focus: Academic/pre-college enrichment, skill-building, and cultural

Activities Center On: Academic, science, and cultural

Intensity Level: 4

Duration: 2–4 weeks, over 8 weeks

Program Offered: Fall, spring, summer

Location: Kimana, Kenya

Accommodations: Bunk/cabin

Years in Operation: 18

Religious Affiliation: Not relevant

STAFF

Student/Staff Ratio: 3:1

Staff Qualifications: Faculty members are selected based on their teaching and research qualifications, leadership skills, and commitment to field research and community-based environmental work. Most are native to the country in which they teach.

PARTICIPANTS

Average Number of Participants: 27

For Participants Aged: 16+

The Ideal Candidate: Flexible, mature, driven team player with an interest in and awareness of environmental and cross-cultural issues; minimum GPA of 2.5 for college students, 3.6 for high school students.

Special Requirements for Participation: Send in the completed application form with two references, transcript, essays, and $45 application fee in order to be considered. Spanish language ability is preferred. For the semester program, the minimum age is 18, and applicant must have completed one semester of college-level ecology/biology with lab. For the summer program, the minimum age is 16, and applicant must have completed junior year.

COSTS

Average Cost: $9,000

Included in Cost: Tuition, room and board, and fees are included. Travel costs, personal expenses, and books are not included. Summer average cost: $4,000; semester average cost: $14,000.

Financial Aid Available: Yes

SKIDMORE COLLEGE

A selective liberal arts college with a lively and varied set of summer programs, sponsored by the Office of the Dean of Special Programs.

Years in Operation: 100

Religious Affiliation: Not relevant

Price Range of Programs: Varies

For More Information:
    Contact: James Chansky, Director, Summer Sessions

Skidmore College
Office of the Dean of Special Programs
815 North Broadway
Saratoga Springs, NY 12866
Phone: 518-580-5590
Fax: 518-580-5548
Email: jchansky@skidmore.edu
Website: www.skidmore.edu/summer

AP/ART (ACCELERATION PROGRAM IN ART)

THE PROGRAM

Description: A pre-collegiate program focusing on the studio arts, offering college credit–bearing courses and noncredit workshops in the full range of the studio arts.

Specialty: In addition to courses offering college credit, Skidmore in the summer offers experiences for pre-collegiate students rarely found at other college campuses in the summer.

Program Type: Music/arts

Classification: Coeducational, residential, day program

Goals: Develop and expand skills and abilities in the studio arts.

Focus: Academic/pre-college enrichment, skill-building, and cultural

Activities Center On: Fine arts, music/arts, and liberal arts

Intensity Level: 4

Duration: 4–6 weeks

Program Offered: Summer

Location: Saratoga Springs, New York

Accommodations: Dormitory

Years in Operation: 30

Religious Affiliation: Not relevant

STAFF

Student/Staff Ratio: 12:1

Staff Qualifications: Courses are taught by Skidmore College faculty; residence hall is supervised by staff of trained college students and adult hall director.

PARTICIPANTS

Average Number of Participants: 65

For Participants Aged: 15–18

The Ideal Candidate: Students serious about their art work and interested in learning new things.

Special Requirements for Participation: Serious art students

COSTS

Average Cost: $4,300

Included in Cost: Tuition for two credit-bearing courses (program cost will be less for noncredit workshops), room and board, and activities.

Financial Aid Available: Yes

PRE-COLLEGE PROGRAM IN THE LIBERAL ARTS FOR HIGH SCHOOL STUDENTS

THE PROGRAM

Description: Offers mature high school students the opportunity to attend regular college credit–bearing courses in the humanities, and the social and natural sciences. Enables students to get started on their college careers early, explore interests not available at their high schools, strengthen their skills, and experience college life and learning. Numerous social and cultural activities on Skidmore's lively summer campus and in historic Saratoga Springs supplement the program.

Specialty: In addition to courses offering college credit, Skidmore in the summer offers a unique array of cultural opportunities not found on comparable small college campuses.

Program Type: Academic/pre-college enrichment

Classification: Coeducational, residential, day program

Goals: In addition to mastering the subject matter of two courses of their choice, students will experience college life and learning on a small liberal arts college campus.

Focus: Academic/pre-college enrichment, cultural, and skill-building

Activities Center On: Academic, liberal arts, and cultural

Intensity Level: 4

Duration: 4–6 weeks

Program Offered: Summer

Location: Saratoga Springs, New York

Accommodations: Dormitory

Years in Operation: 25

Religious Affiliation: Not relevant

STAFF

Student/Staff Ratio: 10:1

Staff Qualifications: Courses are taught by Skidmore College Faculty; residence hall is supervised by trained residential life staff of college students and adult supervisor.

PARTICIPANTS

Average Number of Participants: 45

For Participants Aged: 15–18

The Ideal Candidate: One who is prepared for college-level study and wants to experience the combination of independence and responsibility that comes from residence-hall living on a college campus.

Special Requirements for Participation: The desire to work hard and learn, and experience new things.

COSTS

Average Cost: $4,300

Included in Cost: Tuition for two courses, room and all meals, all activities.

Financial Aid Available: Yes

SOUTHERN METHODIST UNIVERSITY

SMU offers excellent undergraduate and graduate programs through Dedman College of Humanities and Sciences, Cox School of Business, Meadows School of the Arts, and the School of Engineering. It offers professional studies through Dedman School of Law and Perkins School of Theology. In addition, the Division of Education and Lifelong Learning provides credit and noncredit programs for students of all ages. SMU offers a total collegiate experience that includes opportunities for interaction with outstanding faculty in small classes, internships, community service, hands-on research, and leadership development. More than 500 cultural and artistic events, lectures, and a world-renowned museum make SMU a rich resource for the community.

Years in Operation: 25

Religious Affiliation: Not relevant

Price Range of Programs: $2,300–$3,000

For More Information:
Contact: Marilyn Swanson, Assistant Director of Pre-College Programs
PO Box 750383
Dallas, TX 75275
Phone: 214-768-0123
Fax: 214-768-3147
Email: gifted@smu.edu
Website: www.smu.edu/tag

COLLEGE EXPERIENCE

THE PROGRAM

Description: Academically talented high school students can get a head start on college and a taste of campus life during this exciting five-week summer program at SMU. The selection of college-credit subjects for morning classes includes philosophy, English, math, psychology, history, and government. In the afternoon, all College Experience students will participate in a "core" class or humanities overview class for 3 hours of college credit.

Specialty: College Experience students can earn up to 6 college credits per summer.

Program Type: Academic/pre-college enrichment

Classification: Coeducational, residential, day program

Goals: College Experience participants study a variety of topics from the SMU summer course offerings as well as participate in a humanities seminar. Students who elect to live in the CE residence hall will participate in special cultural, educational, and recreational activities.

Focus: Academic/pre-college enrichment

Activities Center On: Academic

Intensity Level: 3

Duration: 4–6 weeks

Program Offered: Summer

Location: Dallas, Texas

Accommodations: Dormitory

Years in Operation: 25

Religious Affiliation: Not relevant

STAFF

Student/Staff Ratio: 7:1

PARTICIPANTS

Average Number of Participants: 40

For Participants Aged: 15–18

The Ideal Candidate: Students that are serious about the academic careers and are interested in getting a head start on college will enjoy SMU's College Experience.

Special Requirements for Participation: None.

COSTS

Average Cost: $3,000

Included in Cost: Estimated tuition: $1,710; estimated room and board: $1,250. Books are not included in the cost.

Financial Aid Available: Yes

SOUTHERN UTAH UNIVERSITY

Professional theater in a lovely outdoor setting.

Years in Operation: 15

Religious Affiliation: Not relevant

Price Range of Programs: $750–$960

For More Information:
Contact: Michael Flachmann, Program Director
CSUB
9001 Stockdale Highway
Bakersfield, CA 93311
Phone: 661-664-2121
Email: mflachmann@csub.edu
Website: www.csub.edu/campshakespeare

CAMP SHAKESPEARE

THE PROGRAM

Description: Students get down-center tickets to see all six professional productions at the Tony Award–winning Utah Shakespearean Festival, plus room and board and college credit.

Specialty: Down-center seats, Tony Award–winning theater, room and board, chance to meet the actors, college credit.

Program Type: Travel/cultural

Classification: Coeducational, residential

Goals: To love and appreciate Shakespeare's plays; insight into the lives of actors.

Focus: Academic/pre-college enrichment, and cultural

Activities Center On: Drama, academic, and fine arts

Intensity Level: 3

Duration: Less than 1 week

Program Offered: Summer

Location: Cedar City, Utah

Accommodations: Hotels

Years in Operation: 15

Religious Affiliation: Not relevant

STAFF

Student/Staff Ratio: 10:1

Staff Qualifications: PhD in English literature, company dramaturg for the Utah Shakespearean Festival, friendly and helpful.

PARTICIPANTS

Average Number of Participants: 80

For Participants Aged: 16+

The Ideal Candidate: Enthusiastic, willing to travel.

Special Requirements for Participation: Love of theater.

COSTS

Average Cost: $960

Included in Cost: Down-center tickets to all six professional productions, room and board, college credit. The only item not included is transportation to and from Cedar City, Utah.

Financial Aid Available: No

MINI CAMP SHAKESPEARE

THE PROGRAM

Description: Attend six professional productions at the Tony Award–winning Utah Shakespearean Festival; panel discussions with the actors, backstage tours, parties, and room and board are included.

Specialty: Great plays, Tony Award–winning theater, intimate outdoor setting, chance to really get to know the plays and the actors, a gorgeous mountain location, clean air, friendly fellow participants.

Program Type: Travel/cultural

Classification: Coeducational, residential

Goals: A love and appreciation for Shakespeare's plays in performance.

Focus: Cultural and academic/pre-college enrichment

Activities Center On: Drama, music/arts, and cultural

Intensity Level: 3

Duration: Less than 1 week

Program Offered: Summer

Location: Cedar City, Utah

Accommodations: Hotels

Years in Operation: 1

Religious Affiliation: Not relevant

STAFF

Student/Staff Ratio: 10:1

Staff Qualifications: PhD in English literature, company dramaturg at Utah Shakespearean Festival.

PARTICIPANTS

Average Number of Participants: 60

For Participants Aged: 16+

The Ideal Candidate: Someone who loves to watch live theater, is adventurous, and enjoys being around actors and other theater people.

Special Requirements for Participation: Enthusiasm for theater.

COSTS

Average Cost: $750

Included in Cost: Six down-center theater tickets, room and board, college credit. Everything is included except for transportation to and from Cedar City, Utah.

Financial Aid Available: No

SPELMAN COLLEGE

Mission Statement: An outstanding historically Black college for women, Spelman promotes academic excellence in the liberal arts and develops the intellectual, ethical, and leadership potential of its students. Spelman seeks to empower the total person, who appreciates the many cultures of the world and commits to positive social change.

Years in Operation: 122

Religious Affiliation: Not relevant

For More Information:
   Contact: Pauline E. Drake, Dean of Continuing Education
         350 Spelman Lane, SW
         Campus Box 849
         Atlanta, GA 30314
   Phone: 404-223-1460
   Fax: 404-215-7768
   Email: pdrake@spelman.edu
   Website: www.spelman.edu/academic/continuing/summer

EARLY COLLEGE SUMMER PROGRAM

THE PROGRAM

Description: The purpose is to prepare rising high school seniors and college freshmen for college studies. Students take the English and mathematics courses that they would take as first-year college students. Upon successful completion (grades of A, B, or C) of each college-level course, students will earn college credit. If students' placement test scores indicate that they need more assistance in English or mathematics, they will be assigned to noncredit, developmental courses.

Program Type: Academic/pre-college enrichment

Classification: Single-sex, female; residential

Focus: Academic/pre-college enrichment, leadership/teamwork, and cultural

Activities Center On: Academic and cultural

Intensity Level: 4

Duration: 4–6 weeks

Program Offered: Summer

Location: Atlanta, Georgia

Accommodations: Dormitory

Years in Operation: 17

Religious Affiliation: Not relevant

STAFF

Student/Staff Ratio: 15:1

PARTICIPANTS

Average Number of Participants: 38

For Participants Aged: 15–18

Special Requirements for Participation: Applicants must be juniors or seniors in high school when they apply; submit the application form and college entrance examination scores (SAT or ACT or PSAT); have completed at least three years of English and mathematics through algebra; have at least a 2.5 grade point average in academic courses, and obtain a recommendation from a teacher.

COSTS

Average Cost: $3,200

Included in Cost: The cost includes registration, tuition, fees, room and board, and planned activities. The cost does not include textbooks.

Financial Aid Available: No

SPOLETO STUDY ABROAD

A four-week summer study abroad program in Spoleto, Italy, for students ages 15–19 interested in visual arts, music (voice and instrumental), drama, creative writing, and photography.

Years in Operation: 7

Religious Affiliation: Not relevant

Price Range of Programs: $5,300

For More Information:
Contact: Debbie Schofield, Marketing and Program Director
PO Box 99147
Raleigh, NC 27624
Phone: 919-384-0031
Fax: 919-846-2371
Email: spoleto@mindspring.com
Website: www.spoletostudyabroad.com

SPOLETO STUDY ABROAD

THE PROGRAM

Description: Spoleto Study Abroad is a four-week summer study abroad program in Spoleto, Italy focusing on the fine arts and the humanities for students ages 15–19 interested in music (vocal and instrumental), drama, visual arts, photography, and creative writing.

Specialty: Students have the opportunity to explore their academic and artistic interests through exposure to an integrated style of learning in a unique European setting and through our twice-a-week excursions to Rome, Florence, Siena, and Assisi, to name a few.

Program Type: Music/arts, travel/cultural

Classification: Coeducational, residential

Goals: Students should expect to grow artistically, intellectually, and personally while being surrounded by talented, experienced, and motivated faculty.

Focus: Academic/pre-college enrichment, cultural, and travel

Activities Center On: Fine arts, music/arts, and photography

Intensity Level: 4

Duration: 4–6 weeks

Program Offered: Summer

Location: Spoleto, Italy

Years in Operation: 7

Religious Affiliation: Not relevant

STAFF

Student/Staff Ratio: 4:1

Staff Qualifications: Spoleto Study Abroad faculty are among the finest in their fields. They are chosen for their extensive knowledge, experience, and enthusiasm; their dynamic teaching methods; and their willingness and ability to work closely with students.

PARTICIPANTS

Average Number of Participants: 60

For Participants Aged: 15–19

The Ideal Candidate: Our ideal candidate is a student interested in the fine arts and the humanities, as well as in immersing themselves in the vibrant and diverse culture that Spoleto, Italy, has to offer.

Special Requirements for Participation: Students must have finished the ninth grade and be between the ages of 15 and 19; and have demonstrated marked proficiency in either instrumental or vocal music through an audition process, artistic skills through submission of a slide portfolio, and acting skills through a video tape audition.

COSTS

Average Cost: $5,300

Included in Cost: The $5,300 fee includes tuition, all meals, lodging, books, activity fees, and transportation in Italy. The fee does not include round-trip airfare to Rome, passport fees, personal expenses, tuition insurance, and spending money.

Financial Aid Available: No

SPRINGFIELD COLLEGE

Years in Operation: 118

Religious Affiliation: Not relevant

Price Range of Programs: $550–$650

For More Information:
   Contact: Gina Ricciardi, Administrative Secretary
          Office of Special Programs
          263 Alden Street
          Springfield, MA 01109
   Phone: 413-748-5287
   Fax: 413-748-3534
   Email: gricciardi@spfldcol.edu
   Website: www.springfieldcollege.edu

ALLIED HEALTH CAREER EXPLORATION PROGRAM

THE PROGRAM

Description: This workshop has been designed to guide and support your exploration of the current and forecasted professional opportunities in the growing field of allied health. You will have the chance to attend lectures to learn about educational requirements, skills, employment opportunities, and certification and licensing guidelines for the following areas: athletic training and sports medicine, emergency medical services, health fitness promotion, registered nurse, physical therapy, and physician assistant.

Program Type: Academic/pre-college enrichment

Classification: Coeducational, residential

Focus: Academic/pre-college enrichment, skill-building, and leadership/teamwork

Activities Center On: Career Exploration

Intensity Level: 1

Duration: Less than 1 week

Program Offered: Summer

Location: Springfield, Massachusetts

Accommodations: Dormitory

Years in Operation: 5

Religious Affiliation: Not relevant

STAFF

Student/Staff Ratio: 2:1

Staff Qualifications: Lectures and clinical activities are taught by Springfield College faculty members from the Departments of Physical Therapy, Health Fitness, Occupational Therapy, Physician Assistant, Athletic Training, and Emergency Medical Services, in addition to allied health professionals from the greater Springfield area.

PARTICIPANTS

Average Number of Participants: 25

For Participants Aged: 15–18

Special Requirements for Participation: None.

COSTS

Average Cost: $525

Financial Aid Available: No

ATHLETIC TRAINER WORKSHOP

THE PROGRAM

Description: This workshop is intended for high school students interested in careers in athletic training and sports medicine. It offers lectures, demonstrations, and practice sessions on athletic injury prevention and care, as well as presentations on career options and profesional preparation.

Program Type: Academic/pre-college enrichment

Classification: Coeducational, residential

Goals: Injury prevention and evaluation, management of athletic injuries, lectures and demonstrations, reconditioning, sports safety training and CPR certification, education, use of college recreational facilities, professional preparation and career training.

Focus: Academic/pre-college enrichment, and skill-building, and leadership/teamwork

Activities Center On: Career exploration

Intensity Level: 2

Duration: Less than 1 week

Program Offered: Summer

Location: Springfield, Massachusetts

Accommodations: Dormitory

Years in Operation: 10

Religious Affiliation: Not relevant

STAFF

Student/Staff Ratio: 2:1

Staff Qualifications: Staff are NATA-certified and Springfield College faculty.

PARTICIPANTS

Average Number of Participants: 50

For Participants Aged: 15–18

Special Requirements for Participation: None.

COSTS

Average Cost: $577

Financial Aid Available: No

SPORTS MANAGEMENT CAREER EXPLORATION PROGRAM

THE PROGRAM

Description: This workshop is designed to guide and support your exploration of the current and forecasted professional opportunities in the growing field of sport managment. You will attend seminars with sport managment faculty, travel to sport venues for a behind-the-scenes look at event managment, and participate in your own sport management venture.

Program Type: Academic/pre-college enrichment

Classification: Coeducational, residential

Focus: Academic/pre-college enrichment, skill-building, and leadership/teamwork

Activities Center On: Career exploration

Intensity Level: 2

Duration: Less than 1 week

Program Offered: Summer

Location: Springfield, Massachusetts

Accommodations: Dormitory

Years in Operation: 5

Religious Affiliation: Not relevant

STAFF

Student/Staff Ratio: 2:1

PARTICIPANTS

Average Number of Participants: 50

For Participants Aged: 15–18

Special Requirements for Participation: None.

COSTS

Average Cost: $650

Financial Aid Available: No d.

Financial Aid Available: No

STUDENT CONSERVATION ASSOCIATION

Years in Operation: 46

Religious Affiliation: Not relevant

Price Range of Programs: $20 application fee

For More Information:
   Contact: Shaundrea Kenyon, Operations Director, Recruitment
       PO Box 550
       Charlestown, NH 03603
   Phone: 603-543-1700

Fax: 603-543-1828
Email: crews@thesca.org
Website: www.thesca.org

CONSERVATION CREW PROGRAM (ALASKA)

THE PROGRAM

Description: The Student Conservation Association (SCA) offers 15- to 19-year-old high school students the opportunity to serve on conservation crews of six to eight members with one to two trained adult crew leaders for three to five weeks during the summer months. They most often build or repair hiking trails, restore threatened habitats, and remove invasive plants. They learn to live outdoors as part of a cooperating team and participate in many outdoor activities, including a three- to five-day recreation trip. Crew sites vary year to year.

Specialty: High school students are offered a no- to low-cost option to participate in a team-based program that allows them to give back to communities by volunteer service to nature. Also, academic credit may be available.

Program Type: Community service and outdoors/adventure

Classification: Coeducational, residential

Goals: Participants should expect to learn improved leadership skills, enhanced problem-solving abilities, greater confidence and self-esteem, as well as some hand tools skills.

Focus: Community service, leadership/teamwork, and skill-building

Activities Center On: Volunteer and camping

Intensity Level: 3

Duration: 4–6 weeks

Program Offered: Summer

Location: All 50 states

Accommodations: Tent

Years in Operation: 46

Religious Affiliation: Not relevant

STAFF

Student/Staff Ratio: 3:1

Staff Qualifications: Crew leaders are required to be at least 21 years old and possess proven youth leadership skills, camping/backpacking experience, and Wilderness First Aid (WFA) certification (Wilderness First Responder [WFR] certification is preferred). Trail construction skills and environmental education experience are highly desirable.

PARTICIPANTS

Average Number of Participants: 750

For Participants Aged: 15–19

The Ideal Candidate: No experience is necessary—just ample supplies of enthusiasm, a positive attitude, and a commitment to give it everything you've got!

Special Requirements for Participation: There must be a particular "comfort level" related to issues such as doing hard physical labor, sleeping in a tent, interacting with wildlife, or in some cases, making do without regular hot showers. Also needed is a physician's approval provided by completing our standard medical form.

COSTS

Average Cost: $0

Included in Cost: Serving in SCA is tuition-free; however, applicants pay a $20 application fee (fee waiver available). Participant costs include round-trip travel from home to service site and any personal gear needed. Financial aid available upon acceptance to a crew.

Financial Aid Available: Yes

CONSERVATION CREW PROGRAM (ARIZONA)

THE PROGRAM

Description: The Student Conservation Association (SCA) offers 15- to 19-year-old high school students the opportunity to serve on conservation crews of six to eight members with one to two trained adult crew leaders for three to five weeks during the summer months. They most often build or repair hiking trails, restore threatened habitats, and remove invasive plants. They learn to live outdoors as part of a cooperating team and participate in many outdoor activities, including a three- to five-day recreation trip. Crew sites vary year to year.

Specialty: High school students are offered a no- to low-cost option to participate in a team-based program that allows them to give back to communities by volunteer service to nature. Also, academic credit may be available.

Program Type: Community service, outdoors/adventure

Classification: Coeducational, residential

Goals: Participants should expect to learn improved leadership skills, enhanced problem-solving abilities, greater confidence and self-esteem, as well as some hand tools skills.

Focus: Community service, leadership/teamwork, and skill-building

Activities Center On: Volunteer and camping

Intensity Level: 3

Duration: 4–6 weeks

Program Offered: Summer

Location: All 50 states

Accommodations: Tent

Years in Operation: 46

Religious Affiliation: Not relevant

STAFF

Student/Staff Ratio: 3:1

Staff Qualifications: Crew Leaders are required to be at least 21 years old and possess proven youth leadership skills, camping/backpacking experience, and Wilderness First Aid (WFA) certification (Wilderness First Responder [WFR] certification is preferred). Trail construction skills and environmental education experience are highly desirable.

PARTICIPANTS

Average Number of Participants: 750

For Participants Aged: 15–19

The Ideal Candidate: No experience is necessary—just ample supplies of enthusiasm, a positive attitude, and a commitment to give it everything you've got!

Special Requirements for Participation: There must be a particular "comfort level" related to issues such as doing hard physical labor, sleeping in a tent, interacting with wildlife, or in some cases, making do without regular hot showers. Also needed is a physician's approval provided by completing our standard medical form.

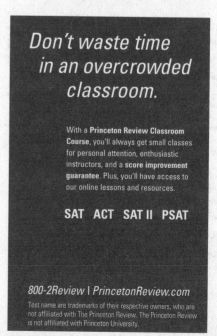

COSTS

Average Cost: $0

Included in Cost: Serving in SCA is tuition-free; however, applicants pay a $20 application fee (fee waiver available). Participant costs include round-trip travel from home to service site and any personal gear needed. Financial aid available upon acceptance to a crew.

Financial Aid Available: Yes

CONSERVATION CREW PROGRAM (ARKANSAS)

THE PROGRAM

Description: The Student Conservation Association (SCA) offers 15- to 19-year-old high school students the opportunity to serve on conservation crews of six to eight members with one to two trained adult crew leaders for three to five weeks during the summer months. They most often build or repair hiking trails, restore threatened habitats, and remove invasive plants. They learn to live outdoors as part of a cooperating team and participate in many outdoor activities, including a three- to five-day recreation trip. Crew sites vary year to year.

Specialty: High school students are offered a no- to low-cost option to participate in a team-based program that allows them to give back to communities by volunteer service to nature. Also, academic credit may be available.

Program Type: Community service, outdoors/adventure

Classification: Coeducational, residential

Goals: Participants should expect to learn improved leadership skills, enhanced problem-solving abilities, greater confidence and self-esteem, as well as some hand tools skills.

Focus: Community Service, leadership/teamwork, and skill-building

Activities Center On: Volunteer and camping

Intensity Level: 3

Duration: 4–6 weeks

Program Offered: Summer

Location: All 50 states

Accommodations: Tent

Years in Operation: 46

Religious Affiliation: Not relevant

STAFF

Student/Staff Ratio: 3:1

Staff Qualifications: Crew Leaders are required to be at least 21 years old and possess proven youth leadership skills, camping/backpacking experience, and Wilderness First Aid (WFA) certification (Wilderness First Responder [WFR] certification is preferred). Trail construction skills and environmental education experience are highly desirable.

PARTICIPANTS

Average Number of Participants: 750

For Participants Aged: 15–19

The Ideal Candidate: No experience is necessary—just ample supplies of enthusiasm, a positive attitude, and a commitment to give it everything you've got!

Special Requirements for Participation: There must be a particular "comfort level" related to issues such as doing hard physical labor, sleeping in a tent, interacting with wildlife, or in some cases, making do without regular hot showers. Also needed is a physician's approval provided by completing our standard medical form.

COSTS

Average Cost: $0

Included in Cost: Serving in SCA is tuition-free; however, applicants pay a $20 application fee (fee waiver available). Participant costs include round-trip travel from home to service site and any personal gear needed. Financial aid available upon acceptance to a crew.

Financial Aid Available: Yes

CONSERVATION CREW PROGRAM (CALIFORNIA)

THE PROGRAM

Description: The Student Conservation Association (SCA) offers 15- to 19-year-old high school students the opportunity to serve on conservation crews of six to eight members with one to two trained adult crew leaders for three to five weeks during the summer months. They most often build or repair hiking trails, restore threatened habitats, and remove invasive plants. They learn to live outdoors as part of a cooperating team and participate in many outdoor activities, including a three- to five-day recreation trip. Crew sites vary year to year.

Specialty: High school students are offered a no- to low-cost option to participate in a team-based program that allows them to give back to communities by volunteer service to nature. Also, academic credit may be available.

Program Type: Community service and outdoors/adventure

Classification: Coeducational, residential

Goals: Participants should expect to learn improved leadership skills, enhanced problem-solving abilities, greater confidence and self-esteem, as well as some hand tools skills.

Focus: Community service, leadership/teamwork, and skill-building

Activities Center On: Volunteer and camping

Intensity Level: 3

Duration: 4–6 weeks

Program Offered: Summer

Location: All 50 states

Accommodations: Tent

Years in Operation: 46

Religious Affiliation: Not relevant

STAFF

Student/Staff Ratio: 3:1

Staff Qualifications: Crew Leaders are required to be at least 21 years old and possess proven youth leadership skills, camping/backpacking experience, and Wilderness First Aid (WFA) certification (Wilderness First Responder [WFR] certification is preferred). Trail construction skills and environmental education experience are highly desirable.

PARTICIPANTS

Average Number of Participants: 750

For Participants Aged: 15–19

The Ideal Candidate: No experience is necessary—just ample supplies of enthusiasm, a positive attitude, and a commitment to give it everything you've got!

Special Requirements for Participation: There must be a particular "comfort level" related to issues such as doing hard physical labor, sleeping in a tent, interacting with wildlife, or in some cases, making do without regular hot showers. Also needed is a physician's approval provided by completing our standard medical form.

COSTS

Average Cost: $0

Included in Cost: Serving in SCA is tuition-free; however, applicants pay a $20 application fee (fee waiver available). Participant costs include round-trip travel from home to service site and any personal gear needed. Financial aid available upon acceptance to a crew.

Financial Aid Available: Yes

CONSERVATION CREW PROGRAM (COLORADO)

THE PROGRAM

Description: The Student Conservation Association (SCA) offers 15- to 19-year-old high school students the opportunity to serve on conservation crews of six to eight members with one to two trained adult crew leaders for three to five weeks during the summer months. They most often build or repair hiking trails, restore threatened habitats, and remove invasive plants. They learn to live outdoors as part of a cooperating team and participate in many outdoor activities, including a three- to five-day recreation trip. Crew sites vary year to year.

Specialty: High school students are offered a no- to low-cost option to participate in a team-based program that allows them to give back to communities by volunteer service to nature. Also, academic credit may be available.

Program Type: Community service and outdoors/adventure

Classification: Coeducational, residential

Goals: Participants should expect to learn improved leadership skills, enhanced problem-solving abilities, greater confidence and self-esteem, as well as some hand tools skills.

Focus: Community service, leadership/teamwork, and skill-building

Activities Center On: Volunteer and camping

Intensity Level: 3

Duration: 4–6 weeks

Program Offered: Summer

Location: All 50 states

Accommodations: Tent

Years in Operation: 46

Religious Affiliation: Not relevant

STAFF

Student/Staff Ratio: 3:1

Staff Qualifications: Crew leaders are required to be at least 21 years old and possess proven youth leadership skills, camping/backpacking experience, and Wilderness First Aid (WFA) certification (Wilderness First Responder [WFR] certification is preferred). Trail construction skills and environmental education experience are highly desirable.

PARTICIPANTS

Average Number of Participants: 750

For Participants Aged: 15–19

The Ideal Candidate: No experience is necessary—just ample supplies of enthusiasm, a positive attitude, and a commitment to give it everything you've got!

Special Requirements for Participation: There must be a particular "comfort level" related to issues such as doing hard physical labor, sleeping in a tent, interacting with wildlife, or in some cases, making do without regular hot showers. Also needed is a physician's approval provided by completing our standard medical form.

COSTS

Average Cost: $0

Included in Cost: Serving in SCA is tuition-free; however, applicants pay a $20 application fee (fee waiver available). Participant costs include round-trip travel from home to service site and any personal gear needed. Financial aid available upon acceptance to a crew.

Financial Aid Available: Yes

CONSERVATION CREW PROGRAM (CONNECTICUT)

THE PROGRAM

Description: The Student Conservation Association (SCA) offers 15- to 19-year-old high school students the opportunity to serve on conservation crews of six to eight members with one to two trained adult crew leaders for three to five weeks during the summer months. They most often build or repair hiking trails, restore threatened habitats, and remove invasive plants. They learn to live outdoors as part of a cooperating team and participate in many outdoor activities, including a three- to five-day recreation trip. Crew sites vary year to year.

Specialty: High school students are offered a no- to low-cost option to participate in a team-based program that allows them to give back to communities by volunteer service to nature. Also, academic credit may be available.

Program Type: Community service, outdoors/adventure

Classification: Coeducational, residential

Goals: Participants should expect to learn improved leadership skills, enhanced problem-solving abilities, greater confidence and self-esteem, as well as some hand tools skills.

Focus: Community service, leadership/teamwork, and skill-building

Activities Center On: Volunteer and camping

Intensity Level: 3

Duration: 4–6 weeks

Program Offered: Summer

Location: All 50 states

Accommodations: Tent

Years in Operation: 46

Religious Affiliation: Not relevant

STAFF

Student/Staff Ratio: 3:1

Staff Qualifications: Crew leaders are required to be at least 21 years old and possess proven youth leadership skills, camping/backpacking experience, and Wilderness First Aid (WFA) certification (Wilderness First Responder [WFR] certification is preferred). Trail construction skills and environmental education experience are highly desirable.

PARTICIPANTS

Average Number of Participants: 750

For Participants Aged: 15–19

The Ideal Candidate: No experience is necessary—just ample supplies of enthusiasm, a positive attitude, and a commitment to give it everything you've got!

Special Requirements for Participation: There must be a particular "comfort level" related to issues such as doing hard physical labor, sleeping in a tent, interacting with wildlife, or in some cases, making do without regular hot showers. Also needed is a physician's approval provided by completing our standard medical form.

COSTS

Average Cost: $0

Included in Cost: Serving in SCA is tuition-free; however, applicants pay a $20 application fee (fee waiver available). Participant costs include round-trip travel from home to service site and any personal gear needed. Financial aid available upon acceptance to a crew.

Financial Aid Available: Yes

CONSERVATION CREW PROGRAM (DELAWARE)

THE PROGRAM

Description: The Student Conservation Association (SCA) offers 15- to 19-year-old high school students the opportunity to serve on conservation crews of six to eight members with one to two trained adult crew leaders for three to five weeks during the summer months. They most often build or repair hiking trails, restore threatened habitats, and remove invasive plants. They learn to live outdoors as part of a cooperating team and participate in many outdoor activities, including a three- to five-day recreation trip. Crew sites vary year to year.

Specialty: High school students are offered a no- to low-cost option to participate in a team-based program that allows them to give back to communities by volunteer service to nature. Also, academic credit may be available.

Program Type: Community service, outdoors/adventure

Classification: Coeducational, residential

Goals: Participants should expect to learn improved leadership skills, enhanced problem-solving abilities, greater confidence and self-esteem, as well as some hand tools skills.

Focus: Community service, leadership/teamwork, and skill-building

Activities Center On: Volunteer and camping

Intensity Level: 3

Duration: 4–6 weeks

Program Offered: Summer

Location: All 50 states

Accommodations: Tent

Years in Operation: 46

Religious Affiliation: Not relevant

STAFF

Student/Staff Ratio: 3:1

Staff Qualifications: Crew leaders are required to be at least 21 years old and possess proven youth leadership skills, camping/backpacking experience, and Wilderness First Aid (WFA) certification (Wilderness First Responder [WFR] certification is preferred). Trail construction skills and environmental education experience are highly desirable.

PARTICIPANTS

Average Number of Participants: 750

For Participants Aged: 15–19

The Ideal Candidate: No experience is necessary—just ample supplies of enthusiasm, a positive attitude, and a commitment to give it everything you've got!

Special Requirements for Participation: There must be a particular "comfort level" related to issues such as doing hard physical labor, sleeping in a tent, interacting with wildlife, or in some cases, making do without regular hot showers. Also needed is a physician's approval provided by completing our standard medical form.

Costs

Average Cost: $0

Included in Cost: Serving in SCA is tuition-free; however, applicants pay a $20 application fee (fee waiver available). Participant costs include round-trip travel from home to service site and any personal gear needed. Financial aid available upon acceptance to a crew.

Financial Aid Available: Yes

CONSERVATION CREW PROGRAM (FLORIDA)

THE PROGRAM

Description: The Student Conservation Association (SCA) offers 15- to 19-year-old high school students the opportunity to serve on conservation crews of six to eight members with one to two trained adult crew leaders for three to five weeks during the summer months. They most often build or repair hiking trails, restore threatened habitats, and remove invasive plants. They learn to live outdoors as part of a cooperating team and participate in many outdoor activities, including a three- to five-day recreation trip. Crew sites vary year to year.

Specialty: High school students are offered a no- to low-cost option to participate in a team-based program that allows them to give back to communities by volunteer service to nature. Also, academic credit may be available.

Program Type: Community service, outdoors/adventure

Classification: Coeducational, residential

Goals: Participants should expect to learn improved leadership skills, enhanced problem-solving abilities, greater confidence and self-esteem, as well as some hand tools skills.

Focus: Community service, leadership/teamwork, and skill-building

Activities Center On: Volunteer and camping

Intensity Level: 3

Duration: 4–6 weeks

Program Offered: Summer

Location: All 50 states

Accommodations: Tent

Years in Operation: 46

Religious Affiliation: Not relevant

STAFF

Student/Staff Ratio: 3:1

Staff Qualifications: Crew leaders are required to be at least 21 years old and possess proven youth leadership skills, camping/backpacking experience, and Wilderness First Aid (WFA) certification (Wilderness First Responder [WFR] certification is preferred). Trail construction skills and environmental education experience are highly desirable.

PARTICIPANTS

Average Number of Participants: 750

For Participants Aged: 15–19

The Ideal Candidate: No experience is necessary—just ample supplies of enthusiasm, a positive attitude, and a commitment to give it everything you've got!

Special Requirements for Participation: There must be a particular "comfort level" related to issues such as doing hard physical labor, sleeping in a tent, interacting with wildlife, or in some cases, making do without regular hot showers. Also needed is a physician's approval provided by completing our standard medical form.

Costs

Average Cost: $0

Included in Cost: Serving in SCA is tuition-free; however, applicants pay a $20 application fee (fee waiver available). Participant costs include round-trip travel from home to service site and any personal gear needed. Financial aid available upon acceptance to a crew.

Financial Aid Available: Yes

CONSERVATION CREW PROGRAM (GEORGIA)

THE PROGRAM

Description: The Student Conservation Association (SCA) offers 15- to 19-year-old high school students the opportunity to serve on conservation crews of six to eight members with one to two trained adult crew leaders for three to five weeks during the summer months. They most often build or repair hiking trails, restore threatened habitats, and remove invasive plants. They learn to live outdoors as part of a cooperating team and participate in many outdoor activities, including a three- to five-day recreation trip. Crew sites vary year to year.

Specialty: High school students are offered a no- to low-cost option to participate in a team-based program that allows them to give back to communities by volunteer service to nature. Also, academic credit may be available.

Program Type: Community service, outdoors/adventure

Classification: Coeducational, residential

Goals: Participants should expect to learn improved leadership skills, enhanced problem-solving abilities, greater confidence and self-esteem, as well as some hand tools skills.

Focus: Community Service, leadership/teamwork, and Skill-building

Activities Center On: Volunteer and camping

Intensity Level: 3

Duration: 4–6 weeks

Program Offered: Summer

Location: All 50 states

Accommodations: Tent

Years in Operation: 46

Religious Affiliation: Not relevant

STAFF

Student/Staff Ratio: 3:1

Staff Qualifications: Crew leaders are required to be at least 21 years old and possess proven youth leadership skills, camping/backpacking experience, and Wilderness First Aid (WFA) certification (Wilderness First Responder [WFR] certification is preferred). Trail construction skills and environmental education experience are highly desirable.

PARTICIPANTS

Average Number of Participants: 750

For Participants Aged: 15–19

The Ideal Candidate: No experience is necessary—just ample supplies of enthusiasm, a positive attitude, and a commitment to give it everything you've got!

Special Requirements for Participation: There must be a particular "comfort level" related to issues such as doing hard physical labor, sleeping in a tent, interacting with wildlife, or in some cases, making do without regular hot showers. Also needed is a physician's approval provided by completing our standard medical form.

COSTS

Average Cost: $0

Included in Cost: Serving in SCA is tuition-free; however, applicants pay a $20 application fee (fee waiver available). Participant costs include round-trip travel from home to service site and any personal gear needed. Financial aid available upon acceptance to a crew.

Financial Aid Available: Yes

CONSERVATION CREW PROGRAM (HAWAII)

THE PROGRAM

Description: The Student Conservation Association (SCA) offers 15- to 19-year-old high school students the opportunity to serve on conservation crews of six to eight members with one to two trained adult crew leaders for three to five weeks during the summer months. They most often build or repair hiking trails, restore threatened habitats, and remove invasive plants. They learn to live outdoors as part of a cooperating team and participate in many outdoor activities, including a three- to five-day recreation trip. Crew sites vary year to year.

Specialty: High school students are offered a no- to low-cost option to participate in a team-based program that allows them to give back to communities by volunteer service to nature. Also, academic credit may be available.

Program Type: Community service, outdoors/adventure

Classification: Coeducational, residential

Goals: Participants should expect to learn improved leadership skills, enhanced problem-solving abilities, greater confidence and self-esteem, as well as some hand tools skills.

Focus: Community Service, leadership/teamwork, and skill-building

Activities Center On: Volunteer and camping

Intensity Level: 3

Duration: 4–6 weeks

Program Offered: Summer

Location: All 50 states

Accommodations: Tent

Years in Operation: 46

Religious Affiliation: Not relevant

STAFF

Student/Staff Ratio: 3:1

Staff Qualifications: Crew leaders are required to be at least 21 years old and possess proven youth leadership skills, camping/backpacking experience, and Wilderness First Aid (WFA) certification (Wilderness First Responder [WFR] certification is preferred). Trail construction skills and environmental education experience are highly desirable.

PARTICIPANTS

Average Number of Participants: 750

For Participants Aged: 15–19

The Ideal Candidate: No experience is necessary—just ample supplies of enthusiasm, a positive attitude, and a commitment to give it everything you've got!

Special Requirements for Participation: There must be a particular "comfort level" related to issues such as doing hard physical labor, sleeping in a tent, interacting with wildlife, or in some cases, making do without regular hot showers. Also needed is a physician's approval provided by completing our standard medical form.

COSTS

Average Cost: $0

Included in Cost: Serving in SCA is tuition-free; however, applicants pay a $20 application fee (fee waiver available). Participant costs include round-trip travel from home to service site and any personal gear needed. Financial aid available upon acceptance to a crew.

Financial Aid Available: Yes

CONSERVATION CREW PROGRAM (IDAHO)

THE PROGRAM

Description: The Student Conservation Association (SCA) offers 15- to 19-year-old high school students the opportunity to serve on conservation crews of six to eight members with one to two trained adult crew leaders for three to five weeks during the summer months. They most often build or repair hiking trails, restore threatened habitats, and remove invasive plants. They learn to live outdoors as part of a cooperating team and participate in many outdoor activities, including a three- to five-day recreation trip. Crew sites vary year to year.

Specialty: High school students are offered a no- to low-cost option to participate in a team-based program that allows them to give back to communities by volunteer service to nature. Also, academic credit may be available.

Program Type: Community service, outdoors/adventure

Classification: Coeducational, residential

Goals: Participants should expect to learn improved leadership skills, enhanced problem-solving abilities, greater confidence and self-esteem, as well as some hand tools skills.

Focus: Community service, leadership/teamwork, and skill-building

Activities Center On: Volunteer and camping

Intensity Level: 3

Duration: 4–6 weeks

Program Offered: Summer

Location: All 50 states

Accommodations: Tent

Years in Operation: 46

Religious Affiliation: Not relevant

STAFF

Student/Staff Ratio: 3:1

Staff Qualifications: Crew leaders are required to be at least 21 years old and possess proven youth leadership skills, camping/backpacking experience, and Wilderness First Aid (WFA) certification (Wilderness First Responder [WFR] certification is preferred). Trail construction skills and environmental education experience are highly desirable.

PARTICIPANTS

Average Number of Participants: 750

For Participants Aged: 15–19

The Ideal Candidate: No experience is necessary—just ample supplies of enthusiasm, a positive attitude, and a commitment to give it everything you've got!

Special Requirements for Participation: There must be a particular "comfort level" related to issues such as doing hard physical labor, sleeping in a tent, interacting with wildlife, or in some cases, making do without regular hot showers. Also needed is a physician's approval provided by completing our standard medical form.

COSTS

Average Cost: $0

Included in Cost: Serving in SCA is tuition-free; however, applicants pay a $20 application fee (fee waiver available). Participant costs include round-trip travel from home to service site and any personal gear needed. Financial aid available upon acceptance to a crew.

Financial Aid Available: Yes

CONSERVATION CREW PROGRAM (ILLINOIS)

THE PROGRAM

Description: The Student Conservation Association (SCA) offers 15- to 19-year-old high school students the opportunity to serve on conservation crews of six to eight members with one to two trained adult crew leaders for three to five weeks during the summer months. They most often build or repair hiking trails, restore threatened habitats, and remove invasive plants. They learn to live outdoors as part of a cooperating team and participate in many outdoor activities, including a three- to five-day recreation trip. Crew sites vary year to year.

Specialty: High school students are offered a no- to low-cost option to participate in a team-based program that allows them to give back to communities by volunteer service to nature. Also, academic credit may be available.

Program Type: Community service, outdoors/adventure

Classification: Coeducational, residential

Goals: Participants should expect to learn improved leadership skills, enhanced problem-solving abilities, greater confidence and self-esteem, as well as some hand tools skills.

Focus: Community service, leadership/teamwork, and skill-building

Activities Center On: Volunteer and camping

Intensity Level: 3

Duration: 4–6 weeks

Program Offered: Summer

Location: All 50 states

Accommodations: Tent

Years in Operation: 46

Religious Affiliation: Not relevant

STAFF

Student/Staff Ratio: 3:1

Staff Qualifications: Crew leaders are required to be at least 21 years old and possess proven youth leadership skills, camping/backpacking experience, and Wilderness First Aid (WFA) certification (Wilderness First Responder [WFR] certification is preferred). Trail construction skills and environmental education experience are highly desirable.

PARTICIPANTS

Average Number of Participants: 750

For Participants Aged: 15–19

The Ideal Candidate: No experience is necessary—just ample supplies of enthusiasm, a positive attitude, and a commitment to give it everything you've got!

Special Requirements for Participation: There must be a particular "comfort level" related to issues such as doing hard physical labor, sleeping in a tent, interacting with wildlife, or in some cases, making do without regular hot showers. Also needed is a physician's approval provided by completing our standard medical form.

Costs

Average Cost: $0

Included in Cost: Serving in SCA is tuition-free; however, applicants pay a $20 application fee (fee waiver available). Participant costs include round-trip travel from home to service site and any personal gear needed. Financial aid available upon acceptance to a crew.

Financial Aid Available: Yes

Conservation Crew Program (Indiana)

The Program

Description: The Student Conservation Association (SCA) offers 15- to 19-year-old high school students the opportunity to serve on conservation crews of six to eight members with one to two trained adult crew leaders for three to five weeks during the summer months. They most often build or repair hiking trails, restore threatened habitats, and remove invasive plants. They learn to live outdoors as part of a cooperating team and participate in many outdoor activities, including a three- to five-day recreation trip. Crew sites vary year to year.

Specialty: High school students are offered a no- to low-cost option to participate in a team-based program that allows them to give back to communities by volunteer service to nature. Also, academic credit may be available.

Program Type: Community Service, outdoors/adventure

Classification: Coeducational, residential

Goals: Improved leadership skills, enhanced problem-solving abilities, greater confidence and self-esteem, as well as some hand tools skills

Focus: Community service, leadership/teamwork, and skill-building

Activities Center On: Volunteer and camping

Intensity Level: 3

Duration: 4–6 weeks

Program Offered: Summer

Location: All 50 states

Accommodations: Tent

Years in Operation: 46

Religious Affiliation: Not relevant

Staff

Student/Staff Ratio: 3:1

Staff Qualifications: Crew leaders are required to be at least 21 years old and possess proven youth leadership skills, camping/backpacking experience, and Wilderness First Aid (WFA) certification (Wilderness First Responder [WFR] certification is preferred). Trail construction skills and environmental education experience are highly desirable.

Participants

Average Number of Participants: 750

For Participants Aged: 15–19

The Ideal Candidate: No experience is necessary—just ample supplies of enthusiasm, a positive attitude, and a commitment to give it everything you've got!

Special Requirements for Participation: There must be a particular "comfort level" related to issues such as doing hard physical labor, sleeping in a tent, interacting with wildlife, or in some cases, making do without regular hot showers. Also needed is a physician's approval provided by completing our standard medical form.

Costs

Average Cost: $0

Included in Cost: Serving in SCA is tuition-free; however, applicants pay a $20 application fee (fee waiver available). Participant costs include round-trip travel from home to service site and any personal gear needed.

Financial Aid Available: Yes

Conservation Crew Program (Iowa)

The Program

Description: The Student Conservation Association (SCA) offers 15- to 19-year-old high school students the opportunity to serve on conservation crews of six to eight members with one to two trained adult crew leaders for three to five weeks during the summer months. They most often build or repair hiking trails, restore threatened habitats, and remove invasive plants. They learn to live outdoors as part of a cooperating team and participate in many outdoor activities, including a three- to five-day recreation trip. Crew sites vary year to year.

Specialty: High school students are offered a no- to low-cost option to participate in a team-based program that allows them to give back to communities by volunteer service to nature. Also, academic credit may be available.

Program Type: Community service, outdoors/adventure

Classification: Coeducational, residential

Goals: Participants should expect to learn improved leadership skills, enhanced problem-solving abilities, greater confidence and self-esteem, as well as some hand tools skills.

Focus: Community Service, leadership/teamwork, and skill-building

Activities Center On: Volunteer and camping

Intensity Level: 3

Duration: 4–6 weeks

Program Offered: Summer

Location: All 50 states

Accommodations: Tent

Years in Operation: 46

Religious Affiliation: Not relevant

Staff

Student/Staff Ratio: 3:1

Staff Qualifications: Crew leaders are required to be at least 21 years old and possess proven youth leadership skills, camping/backpacking experience, and Wilderness First Aid (WFA) certification (Wilderness First Responder [WFR] certification is preferred). Trail construction skills and environmental education experience are highly desirable.

PARTICIPANTS

Average Number of Participants: 750

For Participants Aged: 15–19

The Ideal Candidate: No experience is necessary—just ample supplies of enthusiasm, a positive attitude, and a commitment to give it everything you've got!

Special Requirements for Participation: There must be a particular "comfort level" related to issues such as doing hard physical labor, sleeping in a tent, interacting with wildlife, or in some cases, making do without regular hot showers. Also needed is a physician's approval provided by completing our standard medical form.

COSTS

Average Cost: $0

Included in Cost: Serving in SCA is tuition-free; however, applicants pay a $20 application fee (fee waiver available). Participant costs include round-trip travel from home to service site and any personal gear needed.

Financial Aid Available: Yes

CONSERVATION CREW PROGRAM (KANSAS)

THE PROGRAM

Description: The Student Conservation Association (SCA) offers 15- to 19-year-old high school students the opportunity to serve on conservation crews of six to eight members with one to two trained adult crew leaders for three to five weeks during the summer months. They most often build or repair hiking trails, restore threatened habitats, and remove invasive plants. They learn to live outdoors as part of a cooperating team and participate in many outdoor activities, including a three- to five-day recreation trip. Crew sites vary year to year.

Specialty: High school students are offered a no- to low-cost option to participate in a team-based program that allows them to give back to communities by volunteer service to nature. Also, academic credit may be available.

Program Type: Community service, outdoors/adventure

Classification: Coeducational, residential

Goals: Participants should expect to learn improved leadership skills, enhanced problem-solving abilities, greater confidence and self-esteem, as well as some hand tools skills.

Focus: Community service, leadership/teamwork, and skill-building

Activities Center On: Volunteer and camping

Intensity Level: 3

Duration: 4–6 weeks

Program Offered: Summer

Location: All 50 states

Accommodations: Tent

Years in Operation: 46

Religious Affiliation: Not relevant

STAFF

Student/Staff Ratio: 3:1

Staff Qualifications: Crew leaders are required to be at least 21 years old and possess proven youth leadership skills, camping/backpacking experience, and Wilderness First Aid (WFA) certification (Wilderness First Responder [WFR] certification is preferred). Trail construction skills and environmental education experience are highly desirable.

PARTICIPANTS

Average Number of Participants: 750

For Participants Aged: 15–19

The Ideal Candidate: No experience is necessary—just ample supplies of enthusiasm, a positive attitude, and a commitment to give it everything you've got!

Special Requirements for Participation: There must be a particular "comfort level" related to issues such as doing hard physical labor, sleeping in a tent, interacting with wildlife, or in some cases, making do without regular hot showers. Also needed is a physician's approval provided by completing our standard medical form.

COSTS

Average Cost: $0

Included in Cost: Serving in SCA is tuition-free; however, applicants pay a $20 application fee (fee waiver available). Participant costs include round-trip travel from home to service site and any personal gear needed. Financial aid available upon acceptance to a crew.

Financial Aid Available: Yes

CONSERVATION CREW PROGRAM (KENTUCKY)

THE PROGRAM

Description: The Student Conservation Association (SCA) offers 15- to 19-year-old high school students the opportunity to serve on conservation crews of six to eight members with one to two trained adult crew leaders for three to five weeks during the summer months. They most often build or repair hiking trails, restore threatened habitats, and remove invasive plants. They learn to live outdoors as part of a cooperating team and participate in many outdoor activities, including a three- to five-day recreation trip. Crew sites vary year to year.

Specialty: High school students are offered a no- to low-cost option to participate in a team-based program that allows them to give back to communities by volunteer service to nature. Also, academic credit may be available.

Program Type: Community service, outdoors/adventure

Classification: Coeducational, residential

Goals: Participants should expect to learn improved leadership skills, enhanced problem-solving abilities, greater confidence and self-esteem, as well as some hand tools skills.

Focus: Community service, leadership/teamwork, and skill-building

Activities Center On: Volunteer and camping

Intensity Level: 3

Duration: 4–6 weeks

Program Offered: Summer

Location: All 50 states

Accommodations: Tent

Years in Operation: 46

Religious Affiliation: Not relevant

STAFF

Student/Staff Ratio: 3:1

Staff Qualifications: Crew leaders are required to be at least 21 years old and possess proven youth leadership skills, camping/backpacking experience, and Wilderness First Aid (WFA) certification (Wilderness First Responder [WFR] certification is preferred). Trail construction skills and environmental education experience are highly desirable.

PARTICIPANTS

Average Number of Participants: 75

For Participants Aged: 15–19

The Ideal Candidate: No experience is necessary—just ample supplies of enthusiasm, a positive attitude, and a commitment to give it everything you've got!

Special Requirements for Participation: There must be a particular "comfort level" related to issues such as doing hard physical labor, sleeping in a tent, interacting with wildlife, or in some cases, making do without regular hot showers. Also needed is a physician's approval provided by completing our standard medical form.

COSTS

Average Cost: $0

Included in Cost: Serving in SCA is tuition-free; however, applicants pay a $20 application fee (fee waiver available). Participant costs include round-trip travel from home to service site and any personal gear needed.

Financial Aid Available: Yes

CONSERVATION CREW PROGRAM (LOUISIANA)

THE PROGRAM

Description: The Student Conservation Association (SCA) offers 15- to 19-year-old high school students the opportunity to serve on conservation crews of six to eight members with one to two trained adult crew leaders for three to five weeks during the summer months. They most often build or repair hiking trails, restore threatened habitats, and remove invasive plants. They learn to live outdoors as part of a cooperating team and participate in many outdoor activities, including a three- to five-day recreation trip. Crew sites vary year to year.

Specialty: High school students are offered a no- to low-cost option to participate in a team-based program that allows them to give back to communities by volunteer service to nature. Also, academic credit may be available.

Program Type: Community service, outdoors/adventure

Classification: Coeducational, residential

Goals: Participants should expect to learn improved leadership skills, enhanced problem-solving abilities, greater confidence and self-esteem, as well as some hand tools skills.

Focus: Community service, leadership/teamwork, and skill-building

Activities Center On: Volunteer and camping

Intensity Level: 3

Duration: 4–6 weeks

Program Offered: Summer

Location: All 50 states

Accommodations: Tent

Years in Operation: 46

Religious Affiliation: Not relevant

STAFF

Student/Staff Ratio: 3:1

Staff Qualifications: Crew leaders are required to be at least 21 years old and possess proven youth leadership skills, camping/backpacking experience, and Wilderness First Aid (WFA) certification (Wilderness First Responder [WFR] certification is preferred). Trail construction skills and environmental education experience are highly desirable.

PARTICIPANTS

Average Number of Participants: 760

For Participants Aged: 15–19

The Ideal Candidate: No experience is necessary—just ample supplies of enthusiasm, a positive attitude, and a commitment to give it everything you've got!

Special Requirements for Participation: There must be a particular "comfort level" related to issues such as doing hard physical labor, sleeping in a tent, interacting with wildlife, or in some cases, making do without regular hot showers. Also needed is a physician's approval provided by completing our standard medical form.

COSTS

Average Cost: $0

Included in Cost: Serving in SCA is tuition-free; however, applicants pay a $20 application fee (fee waiver available). Participant costs include round-trip travel from home to service site and any personal gear needed. Financial aid available upon acceptance to a crew.

Financial Aid Available: Yes

CONSERVATION CREW PROGRAM (MAINE)

THE PROGRAM

Description: The Student Conservation Association (SCA) offers 15- to 19-year-old high school students the opportunity to serve on conservation crews of six to eight members with one to two trained adult crew leaders for three to five weeks during the summer months. They most often build or repair hiking trails, restore threatened habitats, and remove invasive plants. They learn to live outdoors as part of a cooperating team and participate in many outdoor activities, including a three- to five-day recreation trip. Crew sites vary year to year.

Specialty: High school students are offered a no- to low-cost option to participate in a team-based program that allows them to give back to communities by volunteer service to nature. Also, academic credit may be available.

Program Type: Community service, outdoors/adventure

Classification: Coeducational, residential

Goals: Participants should expect to learn improved leadership skills, enhanced problem-solving abilities, greater confidence and self-esteem, as well as some hand tools skills.

Focus: Community service, leadership/teamwork, and skill-building

Activities Center On: Volunteer and camping

Intensity Level: 3

Duration: 4–6 weeks

Program Offered: Summer

Location: All 50 states

Accommodations: Tent

Years in Operation: 46

Religious Affiliation: Not relevant

STAFF

Student/Staff Ratio: 3:1

Staff Qualifications: Crew leaders are required to be at least 21 years old and possess proven youth leadership skills, camping/backpacking experience, and Wilderness First Aid (WFA) certification (Wilderness First Responder [WFR] certification is preferred). Trail construction skills and environmental education experience are highly desirable.

PARTICIPANTS

Average Number of Participants: 760

For Participants Aged: 15–19

The Ideal Candidate: No experience is necessary—just ample supplies of enthusiasm, a positive attitude, and a commitment to give it everything you've got!

Special Requirements for Participation: There must be a particular "comfort level" related to issues such as doing hard physical labor, sleeping in a tent, interacting with wildlife, or in some cases, making do without regular hot showers. Also needed is a physician's approval provided by completing our standard medical form.

COSTS

Average Cost: $0

Included in Cost: Serving in SCA is tuition-free; however, applicants pay a $20 application fee (fee waiver available). Participant costs include round-trip travel from home to service site and any personal gear needed. Financial aid available upon acceptance to a crew.

Financial Aid Available: Yes

CONSERVATION CREW PROGRAM (MARYLAND)

THE PROGRAM

Description: The Student Conservation Association (SCA) offers 15- to 19-year-old high school students the opportunity to serve on conservation crews of six to eight members with one to two trained adult crew leaders for three to five weeks during the summer months. They most often build or repair hiking trails, restore threatened habitats, and remove invasive plants. They learn to live outdoors as part of a cooperating team and participate in many outdoor activities, including a three- to five-day recreation trip. Crew sites vary year to year.

Specialty: High school students are offered a no- to low-cost option to participate in a team-based program that allows them to give back to communities by volunteer service to nature. Also, academic credit may be available.

Program Type: Community service, outdoors/adventure

Classification: Coeducational, residential

Goals: Participants should expect to learn improved leadership skills, enhanced problem-solving abilities, greater confidence and self-esteem, as well as some hand tools skills.

Focus: Community service, leadership/teamwork, and skill-building

Activities Center On: Volunteer and camping

Intensity Level: 3

Duration: 4–6 weeks

Program Offered: Summer

Location: All 50 states

Accommodations: Tent

Years in Operation: 46

Religious Affiliation: Not relevant

STAFF

Student/Staff Ratio: 3:1

Staff Qualifications: Crew leaders are required to be at least 21 years old and possess proven youth leadership skills, camping/backpacking experience, and Wilderness First Aid (WFA) certification (Wilderness First Responder [WFR] certification is preferred). Trail construction skills and environmental education experience are highly desirable.

PARTICIPANTS

Average Number of Participants: 760

For Participants Aged: 15–19

The Ideal Candidate: No experience is necessary—just ample supplies of enthusiasm, a positive attitude, and a commitment to give it everything you've got!

Special Requirements for Participation: There must be a particular "comfort level" related to issues such as doing hard physical labor, sleeping in a tent, interacting with wildlife, or in some cases, making do without regular hot showers. Also needed is a physician's approval provided by completing our standard medical form.

COSTS

Average Cost: $0

Included in Cost: Serving in SCA is tuition-free; however, applicants pay a $20 application fee (fee waiver available). Participant costs include round-trip travel from home to service site and any personal gear needed.

Financial Aid Available: Yes

CONSERVATION CREW PROGRAM (MASSACHUSETTS)

THE PROGRAM

Description: The Student Conservation Association (SCA) offers 15- to 19-year-old high school students the opportunity to serve on conservation crews of six to eight members with one to two trained adult crew leaders for three to five weeks during the summer months. They most often build or repair hiking trails, restore threatened habitats, and remove invasive plants. They learn to live outdoors as part of a cooperating team and participate in many outdoor activities, including a three- to five-day recreation trip. Crew sites vary year to year.

Specialty: High school students are offered a no- to low-cost option to participate in a team-based program that allows them to give back to communities by volunteer service to nature. Also, academic credit may be available.

Program Type: Community service, outdoors/adventure

Classification: Coeducational, residential

Goals: Participants should expect to learn improved leadership skills, enhanced problem-solving abilities, greater confidence and self-esteem, as well as some hand tools skills.

Focus: Community service, leadership/teamwork, and skill-building

Activities Center On: Volunteer and camping

Intensity Level: 3

Duration: 4–6 weeks

Program Offered: Summer

Location: All 50 states

Accommodations: Tent

Years in Operation: 46

Religious Affiliation: Not relevant

STAFF

Student/Staff Ratio: 3:1

Staff Qualifications: Crew leaders are required to be at least 21 years old and possess proven youth leadership skills, camping/backpacking experience, and Wilderness First Aid (WFA) certification (Wilderness First Responder [WFR] certification is preferred). Trail construction skills and environmental education experience are highly desirable.

PARTICIPANTS

Average Number of Participants: 760

For Participants Aged: 15–19

The Ideal Candidate: No experience is necessary—just ample supplies of enthusiasm, a positive attitude, and a commitment to give it everything you've got!

Special Requirements for Participation: There must be a particular "comfort level" related to issues such as doing hard physical labor, sleeping in a tent, interacting with wildlife, or in some cases, making do without regular hot showers. Also needed is a physician's approval provided by completing our standard medical form.

COSTS

Average Cost: $0

Included in Cost: Serving in SCA is tuition-free; however, applicants pay a $20 application fee (fee waiver available). Participant costs include round-trip travel from home to service site and any personal gear needed.

Financial Aid Available: Yes

CONSERVATION CREW PROGRAM (MICHIGAN)

THE PROGRAM

Description: The Student Conservation Association (SCA) offers 15- to 19-year-old high school students the opportunity to serve on conservation crews of six to eight members with one to two trained adult crew leaders for three to five weeks during the summer months. They most often build or repair hiking trails, restore threatened habitats, and remove invasive plants. They learn to live outdoors as part of a cooperating team and participate in many outdoor activities, including a three- to five-day recreation trip. Crew sites vary year to year.

Specialty: High school students are offered a no- to low-cost option to participate in a team-based program that allows them to give back to communities by volunteer service to nature. Also, academic credit may be available.

Program Type: Community service, outdoors/adventure

Classification: Coeducational, residential

Goals: Participants should expect to learn improved leadership skills, enhanced problem-solving abilities, greater confidence and self-esteem, as well as some hand tools skills.

Focus: Community service, leadership/teamwork, and skill-building

Activities Center On: Volunteer and camping

Intensity Level: 3

Duration: 4–6 weeks

Program Offered: Summer

Location: All 50 states

Accommodations: Tent

Years in Operation: 46

Religious Affiliation: Not relevant

STAFF

Student/Staff Ratio: 3:1

Staff Qualifications: Crew leaders are required to be at least 21 years old and possess proven youth leadership skills, camping/backpacking experience, and Wilderness First Aid (WFA) certification (Wilderness First Responder [WFR] certification is preferred). Trail construction skills and environmental education experience are highly desirable.

PARTICIPANTS

Average Number of Participants: 760

For Participants Aged: 15–19

The Ideal Candidate: No experience is necessary—just ample supplies of enthusiasm, a positive attitude, and a commitment to give it everything you've got!

Special Requirements for Participation: There must be a particular "comfort level" related to issues such as doing hard physical labor, sleeping in a tent, interacting with wildlife, or in some cases, making do without regular hot showers. Also needed is a physician's approval provided by completing our standard medical form.

COSTS

Average Cost: $0

Included in Cost: Serving in SCA is tuition-free; however, applicants pay a $20 application fee (fee waiver available). Participant costs include round-trip travel from home to service site and any personal gear needed.

Financial Aid Available: Yes

CONSERVATION CREW PROGRAM (MINNESOTA)

THE PROGRAM

Description: The Student Conservation Association (SCA) offers 15- to 19-year-old high school students the opportunity to serve on conservation crews of six to eight members with one to two trained adult crew leaders for three to five weeks during the summer months. They most often build or repair hiking trails, restore threatened habitats, and remove invasive plants. They learn to live outdoors as part of a cooperating team and participate in many outdoor activities, including a three- to five-day recreation trip. Crew sites vary year to year.

Specialty: High school students are offered a no- to low-cost option to participate in a team-based program that allows them to give back to communities by volunteer service to nature. Also, academic credit may be available.

Program Type: Community service, outdoors/adventure

Classification: Coeducational, residential

Goals: Participants should expect to learn improved leadership skills, enhanced problem-solving abilities, greater confidence and self-esteem, as well as some hand tools skills.

Focus: Community service, leadership/teamwork, and skill-building

Activities Center On: Volunteer and camping

Intensity Level: 3

Duration: 4–6 weeks

Program Offered: Summer

Location: All 50 states

Accommodations: Tent

Years in Operation: 46

Religious Affiliation: Not relevant

STAFF

Student/Staff Ratio: 3:1

Staff Qualifications: Crew leaders are required to be at least 21 years old and possess proven youth leadership skills, camping/backpacking experience, and Wilderness First Aid (WFA) certification (Wilderness First Responder [WFR] certification is preferred). Trail construction skills and environmental education experience are highly desirable.

PARTICIPANTS

Average Number of Participants: 760

For Participants Aged: 15–19

The Ideal Candidate: No experience is necessary—just ample supplies of enthusiasm, a positive attitude, and a commitment to give it everything you've got!

Special Requirements for Participation: There must be a particular "comfort level" related to issues such as doing hard physical labor, sleeping in a tent, interacting with wildlife, or in some cases, making do without regular hot showers. Also needed is a physician's approval provided by completing our standard medical form.

COSTS

Average Cost: $0

Included in Cost: Serving in SCA is tuition-free; however, applicants pay a $20 application fee (fee waiver available). Participant costs include round-trip travel from home to service site and any personal gear needed. Financial aid available upon acceptance to a crew.

Financial Aid Available: Yes

CONSERVATION CREW PROGRAM (MISSISSIPPI)

THE PROGRAM

Description: The Student Conservation Association (SCA) offers 15- to 19-year-old high school students the opportunity to serve on conservation crews of six to eight members with one to two trained adult crew leaders for three to five weeks during the summer months. They most often build or repair hiking trails, restore threatened habitats, and remove invasive plants. They learn to live outdoors as part of a cooperating team and participate in many outdoor activities, including a three- to five-day recreation trip. Crew sites vary year to year.

Specialty: High school students are offered a no- to low-cost option to participate in a team-based program that allows them to give back to communities by volunteer service to nature. Also, academic credit may be available.

Program Type: Community service, outdoors/adventure

Classification: Coeducational, residential

Goals: Participants should expect to learn improved leadership skills, enhanced problem-solving abilities, greater confidence and self-esteem, as well as some hand tools skills.

Focus: Community service, leadership/teamwork, and skill-building

Activities Center On: Volunteer and camping

Intensity Level: 3

Duration: 4–6 weeks

Program Offered: Summer

Location: All 50 states

Accommodations: Tent

Years in Operation: 46

Religious Affiliation: Not relevant

STAFF

Student/Staff Ratio: 3:1

Staff Qualifications: Crew leaders are required to be at least 21 years old and possess proven youth leadership skills, camping/backpacking experience, and Wilderness First Aid (WFA) certification (Wilderness First Responder [WFR] certification is preferred). Trail construction skills and environmental education experience are highly desirable.

PARTICIPANTS

Average Number of Participants: 760

For Participants Aged: 15–19

The Ideal Candidate: No experience is necessary—just ample supplies of enthusiasm, a positive attitude, and a commitment to give it everything you've got!

Special Requirements for Participation: There must be a particular "comfort level" related to issues such as doing hard physical labor, sleeping in a tent, interacting with wildlife, or in some cases, making do without regular hot showers. Also needed is a physician's approval provided by completing our standard medical form.

COSTS

Average Cost: $0

Included in Cost: Serving in SCA is tuition-free; however, applicants pay a $20 application fee (fee waiver available). Participant costs include round-trip travel from home to service site and any personal gear needed.

Financial Aid Available: Yes

CONSERVATION CREW PROGRAM (MISSOURI)

THE PROGRAM

Description: The Student Conservation Association (SCA) offers 15- to 19-year-old high school students the opportunity to serve on conservation crews of six to eight members with one to two trained adult crew leaders for three to five weeks during the summer months. They most often build or repair hiking trails, restore threatened habitats, and remove invasive plants. They learn to live outdoors as part of a cooperating team and participate in many outdoor activities, including a three- to five-day recreation trip. Crew sites vary year to year.

Specialty: High school students are offered a no- to low-cost option to participate in a team-based program that allows them to give back to communities by volunteer service to nature. Also, academic credit may be available.

Program Type: Community service, outdoors/adventure

Classification: Coeducational, residential

Goals: Participants should expect to learn improved leadership skills, enhanced problem-solving abilities, greater confidence and self-esteem, as well as some hand tools skills.

Focus: Community service, leadership/teamwork, and skill-building

Activities Center On: Volunteer and camping

Intensity Level: 3

Duration: 4–6 weeks

Program Offered: Summer

Location: All 50 states

Accommodations: Tent

Years in Operation: 46

Religious Affiliation: Not relevant

STAFF

Student/Staff Ratio: 3:1

Staff Qualifications: Crew leaders are required to be at least 21 years old and possess proven youth leadership skills, camping/backpacking experience, and Wilderness First Aid (WFA) certification (Wilderness First Responder [WFR] certification is preferred). Trail construction skills and environmental education experience are highly desirable.

PARTICIPANTS

Average Number of Participants: 760

For Participants Aged: 15–19

The Ideal Candidate: No experience is necessary—just ample supplies of enthusiasm, a positive attitude, and a commitment to give it everything you've got!

Special Requirements for Participation: There must be a particular "comfort level" related to issues such as doing hard physical labor, sleeping in a tent, interacting with wildlife, or in some cases, making do without regular hot showers. Also needed is a physician's approval provided by completing our standard medical form.

COSTS

Average Cost: $0

Included in Cost: Serving in SCA is tuition-free; however, applicants pay a $20 application fee (fee waiver available). Participant costs include round-trip travel from home to service site and any personal gear needed. Financial aid available upon acceptance to a crew.

Financial Aid Available: Yes

CONSERVATION CREW PROGRAM (MONTANA)

THE PROGRAM

Description: The Student Conservation Association (SCA) offers 15- to 19-year-old high school students the opportunity to serve on conservation crews of six to eight members with one to two trained adult crew leaders for three to five weeks during the summer months. They most often build or repair hiking trails, restore threatened habitats, and remove invasive plants. They learn to live outdoors as part of a cooperating team and participate in many outdoor activities, including a three- to five-day recreation trip. Crew sites vary year to year.

Specialty: High school students are offered a no- to low-cost option to participate in a team-based program that allows them to give back to communities by volunteer service to nature. Also, academic credit may be available.

Program Type: Community service, outdoors/adventure

Classification: Coeducational, residential

Goals: Participants should expect to learn improved leadership skills, enhanced problem-solving abilities, greater confidence and self-esteem, as well as some hand tools skills.

Focus: Community service, leadership/teamwork, and skill-building

Activities Center On: Volunteer and camping

Intensity Level: 3

Duration: 4–6 weeks

Program Offered: Summer

Location: All 50 states

Accommodations: Tent

Years in Operation: 46

Religious Affiliation: Not relevant

STAFF

Student/Staff Ratio: 3:1

Staff Qualifications: Crew leaders are required to be at least 21 years old and possess proven youth leadership skills, camping/backpacking experience, and Wilderness First Aid (WFA) certification (Wilderness First Responder [WFR] certification is preferred). Trail construction skills and environmental education experience are highly desirable.

PARTICIPANTS

Average Number of Participants: 760

For Participants Aged: 15–19

The Ideal Candidate: No experience is necessary—just ample supplies of enthusiasm, a positive attitude, and a commitment to give it everything you've got!

Special Requirements for Participation: There must be a particular "comfort level" related to issues such as doing hard physical labor, sleeping in a tent, interacting with wildlife, or in some cases, making do without regular hot showers. Also needed is a physician's approval provided by completing our standard medical form.

COSTS

Average Cost: $0

Included in Cost: Serving in SCA is tuition-free; however, applicants pay a $20 application fee (fee waiver available). Participant costs include round-trip travel from home to service site and any personal gear needed.

Financial Aid Available: Yes

CONSERVATION CREW PROGRAM (NEBRASKA)

THE PROGRAM

Description: The Student Conservation Association (SCA) offers 15- to 19-year-old high school students the opportunity to serve on conservation crews of six to eight members with one to two trained adult crew leaders for three to five weeks during the summer months. They most often build or repair hiking trails, restore threatened habitats, and remove invasive plants. They learn to live outdoors as part of a cooperating team and participate in many outdoor activities, including a three- to five-day recreation trip. Crew sites vary year to year.

Specialty: High school students are offered a no- to low-cost option to participate in a team-based program that allows them to give back to communities by volunteer service to nature. Also, academic credit may be available.

Program Type: Community service, outdoors/adventure

Classification: Coeducational, residential

Goals: Participants should expect to learn improved leadership skills, enhanced problem-solving abilities, greater confidence and self-esteem, as well as some hand tools skills.

Focus: Community service, leadership/teamwork, and skill-building

Activities Center On: Volunteer and camping

Intensity Level: 3

Duration: 4–6 weeks

Program Offered: Summer

Location: All 50 states

Accommodations: Tent

Years in Operation: 46

Religious Affiliation: Not relevant

STAFF

Student/Staff Ratio: 3:1

Staff Qualifications: Crew Leaders are required to be at least 21 years old and possess proven youth leadership skills, camping/backpacking experience, and Wilderness First Aid (WFA) certification (Wilderness First Responder [WFR] certification is preferred). Trail construction skills and environmental education experience are highly desirable.

PARTICIPANTS

Average Number of Participants: 760

For Participants Aged: 15–19

The Ideal Candidate: No experience is necessary—just ample supplies of enthusiasm, a positive attitude, and a commitment to give it everything you've got!

Special Requirements for Participation: There must be a particular "comfort level" related to issues such as doing hard physical labor, sleeping in a tent, interacting with wildlife, or in some cases, making do without regular hot showers. Also needed is a physician's approval provided by completing our standard medical form.

COSTS

Average Cost: $0

Included in Cost: Serving in SCA is tuition-free; however, applicants pay a $20 application fee (fee waiver available). Participant costs include round-trip travel from home to service site and any personal gear needed. Financial aid available upon acceptance to a crew.

Financial Aid Available: Yes

CONSERVATION CREW PROGRAM (NEVADA)

THE PROGRAM

Description: The Student Conservation Association (SCA) offers 15- to 19-year-old high school students the opportunity to serve on conservation crews of six to eight members with one to two trained adult crew leaders for three to five weeks during the summer months. They most often build or repair hiking trails, restore threatened habitats, and remove invasive plants. They learn to live outdoors as part of a cooperating team and participate in many outdoor activities, including a three- to five-day recreation trip. Crew sites vary year to year.

Specialty: High school students are offered a no- to low-cost option to participate in a team-based program that allows them to give back to communities by volunteer service to nature. Also, academic credit may be available.

Program Type: Community service, outdoors/adventure

Classification: Coeducational, residential

Goals: Participants should expect to learn improved leadership skills, enhanced problem-solving abilities, greater confidence and self-esteem, as well as some hand tools skills.

Focus: Community service, leadership/teamwork, and skill-building

Activities Center On: Volunteer and camping

Intensity Level: 3

Duration: 4–6 weeks

Program Offered: Summer

Location: All 50 states

Accommodations: Tent

Years in Operation: 46

Religious Affiliation: Not relevant

STAFF

Student/Staff Ratio: 3:1

Staff Qualifications: Crew Leaders are required to be at least 21 years old and possess proven youth leadership skills, camping/backpacking experience, and Wilderness First Aid (WFA) certification (Wilderness First Responder [WFR] certification is preferred). Trail construction skills and environmental education experience are highly desirable.

PARTICIPANTS

Average Number of Participants: 760

For Participants Aged: 15–19

The Ideal Candidate: No experience is necessary—just ample supplies of enthusiasm, a positive attitude, and a commitment to give it everything you've got!

Special Requirements for Participation: There must be a particular "comfort level" related to issues such as doing hard physical labor, sleeping in a tent, interacting with wildlife, or in some cases, making do without regular hot showers. Also needed is a physician's approval provided by completing our standard medical form.

COSTS

Average Cost: $0

Included in Cost: Serving in SCA is tuition-free; however, applicants pay a $20 application fee (fee waiver available). Participant costs include round-trip travel from home to service site and any personal gear needed.

Financial Aid Available: Yes

CONSERVATION CREW PROGRAM (NEW HAMPSHIRE)

THE PROGRAM

Description: The Student Conservation Association (SCA) offers 15- to 19-year-old high school students the opportunity to serve on conservation crews of six to eight members with one to two trained adult crew leaders for three to five weeks during the summer months. They most often build or repair hiking trails, restore threatened habitats, and remove invasive plants. They learn to live outdoors as part of a cooperating team and participate in many outdoor activities, including a three- to five-day recreation trip. Crew sites vary year to year.

Specialty: High school students are offered a no- to low-cost option to participate in a team-based program that allows them to give back to communities by volunteer service to nature. Also, academic credit may be available.

Program Type: Community service, outdoors/adventure

Classification: Coeducational, residential

Goals: Participants should expect to learn improved leadership skills, enhanced problem-solving abilities, greater confidence and self-esteem, as well as some hand tools skills.

Focus: Community service, leadership/teamwork, and skill-building

Activities Center On: Volunteer and camping

Intensity Level: 3

Duration: 4–6 weeks

Program Offered: Summer

Location: All 50 states

Accommodations: Tent

Years in Operation: 46

Religious Affiliation: Not relevant

STAFF

Student/Staff Ratio: 3:1

Staff Qualifications: Crew Leaders are required to be at least 21 years old and possess proven youth leadership skills, camping/backpacking experience, and Wilderness First Aid (WFA) certification (Wilderness First Responder [WFR] certification is preferred). Trail construction skills and environmental education experience are highly desirable.

PARTICIPANTS

Average Number of Participants: 760

For Participants Aged: 15–19

The Ideal Candidate: No experience is necessary—just ample supplies of enthusiasm, a positive attitude, and a commitment to give it everything you've got!

Special Requirements for Participation: There must be a particular "comfort level" related to issues such as doing hard physical labor, sleeping in a tent, interacting with wildlife, or in some cases, making do without regular hot showers. Also needed is a physician's approval provided by completing our standard medical form.

COSTS

Average Cost: $0

Included in Cost: Serving in SCA is tuition-free; however, applicants pay a $20 application fee (fee waiver available). Participant costs include round-trip travel from home to service site and any personal gear needed. Financial aid available upon acceptance to a crew.

Financial Aid Available: Yes

CONSERVATION CREW PROGRAM (NEW JERSEY)

THE PROGRAM

Description: The Student Conservation Association (SCA) offers 15- to 19-year-old high school students the opportunity to serve on conservation crews of six to eight members with one to two trained adult crew leaders for three to five weeks during the summer months. They most often build or repair hiking trails, restore threatened habitats, and remove invasive plants. They learn to live outdoors as part of a cooperating team and participate in many outdoor activities, including a three- to five-day recreation trip. Crew sites vary year to year.

Specialty: High school students are offered a no- to low-cost option to participate in a team-based program that allows them to give back to communities by volunteer service to nature. Also, academic credit may be available.

Program Type: Community service, outdoors/adventure

Classification: Coeducational, residential

Goals: Participants should expect to learn improved leadership skills, enhanced problem-solving abilities, greater confidence and self-esteem, as well as some hand tools skills.

Focus: Community service, leadership/teamwork, and skill-building

Activities Center On: Volunteer and camping

Intensity Level: 3

Duration: 4–6 weeks

Program Offered: Summer

Location: All 50 states

Accommodations: Tent

Years in Operation: 46

Religious Affiliation: Not relevant

STAFF

Student/Staff Ratio: 3:1

Staff Qualifications: Crew Leaders are required to be at least 21 years old and possess proven youth leadership skills, camping/backpacking experience, and Wilderness First Aid (WFA) certification (Wilderness First Responder [WFR] certification is preferred). Trail construction skills and environmental education experience are highly desirable.

PARTICIPANTS

Average Number of Participants: 760

For Participants Aged: 15–19

The Ideal Candidate: No experience is necessary—just ample supplies of enthusiasm, a positive attitude, and a commitment to give it everything you've got!

Special Requirements for Participation: There must be a particular "comfort level" related to issues such as doing hard physical labor, sleeping in a tent, interacting with wildlife, or in some cases, making do without regular hot showers. Also needed is a physician's approval provided by completing our standard medical form.

COSTS

Average Cost: $0

Included in Cost: Serving in SCA is tuition-free; however, applicants pay a $20 application fee (fee waiver available). Participant costs include round-trip travel from home to service site and any personal gear needed.

Financial Aid Available: Yes

CONSERVATION CREW PROGRAM (NEW MEXICO)

THE PROGRAM

Description: The Student Conservation Association (SCA) offers 15- to 19-year-old high school students the opportunity to serve on conservation crews of six to eight members with one to two trained adult crew leaders for three to five weeks during the summer months. They most often build or repair hiking trails, restore threatened habitats, and remove invasive plants. They learn to live outdoors as part of a cooperating team and participate in many outdoor activities, including a three- to five-day recreation trip. Crew sites vary year to year.

Specialty: High school students are offered a no- to low-cost option to participate in a team-based program that allows them to give back to communities by volunteer service to nature. Also, academic credit may be available.

Program Type: Community service, outdoors/adventure

Classification: Coeducational, residential

Goals: Participants should expect to learn improved leadership skills, enhanced problem-solving abilities, greater confidence and self-esteem, as well as some hand tools skills.

Focus: Community service, leadership/teamwork, and skill-building

Activities Center On: Volunteer and camping

Intensity Level: 3

Duration: 4–6 weeks

Program Offered: Summer

Location: All 50 states

Accommodations: Tent

Years in Operation: 46

Religious Affiliation: Not relevant

STAFF

Student/Staff Ratio: 3:1

Staff Qualifications: Crew Leaders are required to be at least 21 years old and possess proven youth leadership skills, camping/backpacking experience, and Wilderness First Aid (WFA) certification (Wilderness First Responder [WFR] certification is preferred). Trail construction skills and environmental education experience are highly desirable.

PARTICIPANTS

Average Number of Participants: 760

For Participants Aged: 15–19

The Ideal Candidate: No experience is necessary—just ample supplies of enthusiasm, a positive attitude, and a commitment to give it everything you've got!

Special Requirements for Participation: There must be a particular "comfort level" related to issues such as doing hard physical labor, sleeping in a tent, interacting with wildlife, or in some cases, making do without regular hot showers. Also needed is a physician's approval provided by completing our standard medical form.

COSTS

Average Cost: $0

Included in Cost: Serving in SCA is tuition-free; however, applicants pay a $20 application fee (fee waiver available). Participant costs include round-trip travel from home to service site and any personal gear needed.

Financial Aid Available: Yes

CONSERVATION CREW PROGRAM (NEW YORK)

THE PROGRAM

Description: The Student Conservation Association (SCA) offers 15- to 19-year-old high school students the opportunity to serve on conservation crews of six to eight members with one to two trained adult crew leaders for three to five weeks during the summer months. They most often build or repair hiking trails, restore threatened habitats, and remove invasive plants. They learn to live outdoors as part of a cooperating team and participate in many outdoor activities, including a three- to five-day recreation trip. Crew sites vary year to year.

Specialty: High school students are offered a no- to low-cost option to participate in a team-based program that allows them to give back to communities by volunteer service to nature. Also, academic credit may be available.

Program Type: Community service, outdoors/adventure

Classification: Coeducational, residential

Goals: Participants should expect to learn improved leadership skills, enhanced problem-solving abilities, greater confidence and self-esteem, as well as some hand tools skills.

Focus: Community service, leadership/teamwork, and skill-building

Activities Center On: Volunteer and camping

Intensity Level: 3

Duration: 4–6 weeks

Program Offered: Summer

Location: All 50 states

Accommodations: Tent

Years in Operation: 46

Religious Affiliation: Not relevant

STAFF

Student/Staff Ratio: 3:1

Staff Qualifications: Crew Leaders are required to be at least 21 years old and possess proven youth leadership skills, camping/backpacking experience, and Wilderness First Aid (WFA) certification (Wilderness First Responder [WFR] certification is preferred). Trail construction skills and environmental education experience are highly desirable.

PARTICIPANTS

Average Number of Participants: 760

For Participants Aged: 15–19

The Ideal Candidate: No experience is necessary—just ample supplies of enthusiasm, a positive attitude, and a commitment to give it everything you've got!

Special Requirements for Participation: There must be a particular "comfort level" related to issues such as doing hard physical labor, sleeping in a tent, interacting with wildlife, or in some cases, making do without regular hot showers. Also needed is a physician's approval provided by completing our standard medical form.

COSTS

Average Cost: $0

Included in Cost: Serving in SCA is tuition-free; however, applicants pay a $20 application fee (fee waiver available). Participant costs include round-trip travel from home to service site and any personal gear needed.

Financial Aid Available: Yes

CONSERVATION CREW PROGRAM
(NORTH CAROLINA)

THE PROGRAM

Description: The Student Conservation Association (SCA) offers 15- to 19-year-old high school students the opportunity to serve on conservation crews of six to eight members with one to two trained adult crew leaders for three to five weeks during the summer months. They most often build or repair hiking trails, restore threatened habitats, and remove invasive plants. They learn to live outdoors as part of a cooperating team and participate in many outdoor activities, including a three- to five-day recreation trip. Crew sites vary year to year.

Specialty: High school students are offered a no- to low-cost option to participate in a team-based program that allows them to give back to communities by volunteer service to nature. Also, academic credit may be available.

Program Type: Community service, outdoors/adventure

Classification: Coeducational, residential

Goals: Participants should expect to learn improved leadership skills, enhanced problem-solving abilities, greater confidence and self-esteem, as well as some hand tools skills.

Focus: Community service, leadership/teamwork, and skill-building

Activities Center On: Volunteer and camping

Intensity Level: 3

Duration: 4–6 weeks

Program Offered: Summer

Location: All 50 states

Accommodations: Tent

Years in Operation: 46

Religious Affiliation: Not relevant

STAFF

Student/Staff Ratio: 3:1

Staff Qualifications: Crew Leaders are required to be at least 21 years old and possess proven youth leadership skills, camping/backpacking experience, and Wilderness First Aid (WFA) certification (Wilderness First Responder [WFR] certification is preferred). Trail construction skills and environmental education experience are highly desirable.

PARTICIPANTS

Average Number of Participants: 760

For Participants Aged: 15–19

The Ideal Candidate: No experience is necessary—just ample supplies of enthusiasm, a positive attitude, and a commitment to give it everything you've got!

Special Requirements for Participation: There must be a particular "comfort level" related to issues such as doing hard physical labor, sleeping in a tent, interacting with wildlife, or in some cases, making do without regular hot showers. Also needed is a physician's approval provided by completing our standard medical form.

COSTS

Average Cost: $0

Included in Cost: Serving in SCA is tuition-free; however, applicants pay a $20 application fee (fee waiver available). Participant costs include round-trip travel from home to service site and any personal gear needed.

Financial Aid Available: Yes

CONSERVATION CREW PROGRAM
(NORTH DAKOTA)

THE PROGRAM

Description: The Student Conservation Association (SCA) offers 15- to 19-year-old high school students the opportunity to serve on conservation crews of six to eight members with one to two trained adult crew leaders for three to five weeks during the summer months. They most often build or repair hiking trails, restore threatened habitats, and remove invasive plants. They learn to live outdoors as part of a cooperating team and participate in many outdoor activities, including a three- to five-day recreation trip. Crew sites vary year to year.

Specialty: High school students are offered a no- to low-cost option to participate in a team-based program that allows them to give back to communities by volunteer service to nature. Also, academic credit may be available.

Program Type: Community service, outdoors/adventure

Classification: Coeducational, residential

Goals: Participants should expect to learn improved leadership skills, enhanced problem-solving abilities, greater confidence and self-esteem, as well as some hand tools skills.

Focus: Community service, leadership/teamwork, and skill-building

Activities Center On: Volunteer and camping

Intensity Level: 3

Duration: 4–6 weeks

Program Offered: Summer

Location: All 50 states

Accommodations: Tent

Years in Operation: 46

Religious Affiliation: Not relevant

STAFF

Student/Staff Ratio: 3:1

Staff Qualifications: Crew Leaders are required to be at least 21 years old and possess proven youth leadership skills, camping/backpacking experience, and Wilderness First Aid (WFA) certification (Wilderness First Responder [WFR] certification is preferred). Trail construction skills and environmental education experience are highly desirable.

PARTICIPANTS

Average Number of Participants: 760

For Participants Aged: 15–19

The Ideal Candidate: No experience is necessary—just ample supplies of enthusiasm, a positive attitude, and a commitment to give it everything you've got!

Special Requirements for Participation: There must be a particular "comfort level" related to issues such as doing hard physical labor, sleeping in a tent, interacting with wildlife, or in some cases, making do without regular hot showers. Also needed is a physician's approval provided by completing our standard medical form.

COSTS

Average Cost: $0

Included in Cost: Serving in SCA is tuition-free; however, applicants pay a $20 application fee (fee waiver available). Participant costs include round-trip travel from home to service site and any personal gear needed.

Financial Aid Available: Yes

CONSERVATION CREW PROGRAM (OHIO)

THE PROGRAM

Description: The Student Conservation Association (SCA) offers 15- to 19-year-old high school students the opportunity to serve on conservation crews of six to eight members with one to two trained adult crew leaders for three to five weeks during the summer months. They most often build or repair hiking trails, restore threatened habitats, and remove invasive plants. They learn to live outdoors as part of a cooperating team and participate in many outdoor activities, including a three- to five-day recreation trip. Crew sites vary year to year.

Specialty: High school students are offered a no- to low-cost option to participate in a team-based program that allows them to give back to communities by volunteer service to nature. Also, academic credit may be available.

Program Type: Community service, outdoors/adventure

Classification: Coeducational, residential

Goals: Participants should expect to learn improved leadership skills, enhanced problem-solving abilities, greater confidence and self-esteem, as well as some hand tools skills.

Focus: Community service, leadership/teamwork, and skill-building

Activities Center On: Volunteer and camping

Intensity Level: 3

Duration: 4–6 weeks

Program Offered: Summer

Location: All 50 states

Accommodations: Tent

Years in Operation: 46

Religious Affiliation: Not relevant

STAFF

Student/Staff Ratio: 3:1

Staff Qualifications: Crew Leaders are required to be at least 21 years old and possess proven youth leadership skills, camping/backpacking experience, and Wilderness First Aid (WFA) certification (Wilderness First Responder [WFR] certification is preferred). Trail construction skills and environmental education experience are highly desirable.

PARTICIPANTS

Average Number of Participants: 760

For Participants Aged: 15–19

The Ideal Candidate: No experience is necessary—just ample supplies of enthusiasm, a positive attitude, and a commitment to give it everything you've got!

Special Requirements for Participation: There must be a particular "comfort level" related to issues such as doing hard physical labor, sleeping in a tent, interacting with wildlife, or in some cases, making do without regular hot showers. Also needed is a physician's approval provided by completing our standard medical form.

COSTS

Average Cost: $0

Included in Cost: Serving in SCA is tuition-free; however, applicants pay a $20 application fee (fee waiver available). Participant costs include round-trip travel from home to service site and any personal gear needed.

Financial Aid Available: No

CONSERVATION CREW PROGRAM (OKLAHOMA)

THE PROGRAM

Description: The Student Conservation Association (SCA) offers 15- to 19-year-old high school students the opportunity to serve on conservation crews of six to eight members with one to two trained adult crew leaders for three to five weeks during the summer months. They most often build or repair hiking trails, restore threatened habitats, and remove invasive plants. They learn to live outdoors as part of a cooperating team and participate in many outdoor activities, including a three- to five-day recreation trip. Crew sites vary year to year.

Specialty: High school students are offered a no- to low-cost option to participate in a team-based program that allows them to give back to communities by volunteer service to nature. Also, academic credit may be available.

Program Type: Community service, outdoors/adventure

Classification: Coeducational, residential

Goals: Participants should expect to learn improved leadership skills, enhanced problem-solving abilities, greater confidence and self-esteem, as well as some hand tools skills.

Focus: Community service, leadership/teamwork, and skill-building

Activities Center On: Volunteer and camping

Intensity Level: 3

Duration: 4–6 weeks

Program Offered: Summer

Location: All 50 states

Accommodations: Tent

Years in Operation: 46

Religious Affiliation: Not relevant

STAFF

Student/Staff Ratio: 3:1

Staff Qualifications: Crew Leaders are required to be at least 21 years old and possess proven youth leadership skills, camping/backpacking experience, and Wilderness First Aid (WFA) certification (Wilderness First Responder [WFR] certification is preferred). Trail construction skills and environmental education experience are highly desirable.

PARTICIPANTS

Average Number of Participants: 760

For Participants Aged: 15–19

The Ideal Candidate: No experience is necessary—just ample supplies of enthusiasm, a positive attitude, and a commitment to give it everything you've got!

Special Requirements for Participation: There must be a particular "comfort level" related to issues such as doing hard physical labor, sleeping in a tent, interacting with wildlife, or in some cases, making do without regular hot showers. Also needed is a physician's approval provided by completing our standard medical form.

COSTS

Average Cost: $0

Included in Cost: Serving in SCA is tuition-free; however, applicants pay a $20 application fee (fee waiver available). Participant costs include round-trip travel from home to service site and any personal gear needed.

Financial Aid Available: Yes

CONSERVATION CREW PROGRAM (OREGON)

THE PROGRAM

Description: The Student Conservation Association (SCA) offers 15- to 19-year-old high school students the opportunity to serve on conservation crews of six to eight members with one to two trained adult crew leaders for three to five weeks during the summer months. They most often build or repair hiking trails, restore threatened habitats, and remove invasive plants. They learn to live outdoors as part of a cooperating team and participate in many outdoor activities, including a three- to five-day recreation trip. Crew sites vary year to year.

Specialty: High school students are offered a no- to low-cost option to participate in a team-based program that allows them to give back to communities by volunteer service to nature. Also, academic credit may be available.

Program Type: Community service, outdoors/adventure

Classification: Coeducational, residential

Goals: Participants should expect to learn improved leadership skills, enhanced problem-solving abilities, greater confidence and self-esteem, as well as some hand tools skills.

Focus: Community service, leadership/teamwork, and skill-building

Activities Center On: Volunteer and camping

Intensity Level: 3

Duration: 4–6 weeks

Program Offered: Summer

Location: All 50 states

Accommodations: Tent

Years in Operation: 46

Religious Affiliation: Not relevant

STAFF

Student/Staff Ratio: 3:1

Staff Qualifications: Crew Leaders are required to be at least 21 years old and possess proven youth leadership skills, camping/backpacking experience, and Wilderness First Aid (WFA) certification (Wilderness First Responder [WFR] certification is preferred). Trail construction skills and environmental education experience are highly desirable.

PARTICIPANTS

Average Number of Participants: 760

For Participants Aged: 15–19

The Ideal Candidate: No experience is necessary—just ample supplies of enthusiasm, a positive attitude, and a commitment to give it everything you've got!

Special Requirements for Participation: There must be a particular "comfort level" related to issues such as doing hard physical labor, sleeping in a tent, interacting with wildlife, or in some cases, making do without regular hot showers. Also needed is a physician's approval provided by completing our standard medical form.

Costs

Average Cost: $0

Included in Cost: Serving in SCA is tuition-free; however, applicants pay a $20 application fee (fee waiver available). Participant costs include round-trip travel from home to service site and any personal gear needed.

Financial Aid Available: Yes

Conservation Crew Program (Pennsylvania)

The Program

Description: The Student Conservation Association (SCA) offers 15- to 19-year-old high school students the opportunity to serve on conservation crews of six to eight members with one to two trained adult crew leaders for three to five weeks during the summer months. They most often build or repair hiking trails, restore threatened habitats, and remove invasive plants. They learn to live outdoors as part of a cooperating team and participate in many outdoor activities, including a three- to five-day recreation trip. Crew sites vary year to year.

Specialty: High school students are offered a no- to low-cost option to participate in a team-based program that allows them to give back to communities by volunteer service to nature. Also, academic credit may be available.

Program Type: Community service, outdoors/adventure

Classification: Coeducational, residential

Goals: Participants should expect to learn improved leadership skills, enhanced problem-solving abilities, greater confidence and self-esteem, as well as some hand tools skills.

Focus: Community service, leadership/teamwork, and skill-building

Activities Center On: Volunteer and camping

Intensity Level: 3

Duration: 4–6 weeks

Program Offered: Summer

Location: All 50 states

Accommodations: Tent

Years in Operation: 46

Religious Affiliation: Not relevant

Staff

Student/Staff Ratio: 3:1

Staff Qualifications: Crew Leaders are required to be at least 21 years old and possess proven youth leadership skills, camping/backpacking experience, and Wilderness First Aid (WFA) certification (Wilderness First Responder [WFR] certification is preferred). Trail construction skills and environmental education experience are highly desirable.

Participants

Average Number of Participants: 760

For Participants Aged: 15–19

The Ideal Candidate: No experience is necessary—just ample supplies of enthusiasm, a positive attitude, and a commitment to give it everything you've got!

Special Requirements for Participation: There must be a particular "comfort level" related to issues such as doing hard physical labor, sleeping in a tent, interacting with wildlife, or in some cases, making do without regular hot showers. Also needed is a physician's approval provided by completing our standard medical form.

Costs ·

Average Cost: $0

Included in Cost: Serving in SCA is tuition-free; however, applicants pay a $20 application fee (fee waiver available). Participant costs include round-trip travel from home to service site and any personal gear needed.

Financial Aid Available: Yes

Conservation Crew Program (Rhode Island)

The Program

Description: The Student Conservation Association (SCA) offers 15- to 19-year-old high school students the opportunity to serve on conservation crews of six to eight members with one to two trained adult crew leaders for three to five weeks during the summer months. They most often build or repair hiking trails, restore threatened habitats, and remove invasive plants. They learn to live outdoors as part of a cooperating team and participate in many outdoor activities, including a three- to five-day recreation trip. Crew sites vary year to year.

Specialty: High school students are offered a no- to low-cost option to participate in a team-based program that allows them to give back to communities by volunteer service to nature. Also, academic credit may be available.

Program Type: Community service, outdoors/adventure

Classification: Coeducational, residential

Goals: Participants should expect to learn improved leadership skills, enhanced problem-solving abilities, greater confidence and self-esteem, as well as some hand tools skills.

Focus: Community service, leadership/teamwork, and skill-building

Activities Center On: Volunteer and camping

Intensity Level: 3

Duration: 4–6 weeks

Program Offered: Summer

Location: All 50 states

Accommodations: Tent

Years in Operation: 46

Religious Affiliation: Not relevant

STAFF

Student/Staff Ratio: 3:1

Staff Qualifications: Crew Leaders are required to be at least 21 years old and possess proven youth leadership skills, camping/backpacking experience, and Wilderness First Aid (WFA) certification (Wilderness First Responder [WFR] certification is preferred). Trail construction skills and environmental education experience are highly desirable.

PARTICIPANTS

Average Number of Participants: 760

For Participants Aged: 15–19

The Ideal Candidate: No experience is necessary—just ample supplies of enthusiasm, a positive attitude, and a commitment to give it everything you've got!

Special Requirements for Participation: There must be a particular "comfort level" related to issues such as doing hard physical labor, sleeping in a tent, interacting with wildlife, or in some cases, making do without regular hot showers. Also needed is a physician's approval provided by completing our standard medical form.

COSTS

Average Cost: $0

Included in Cost: Serving in SCA is tuition-free; however, applicants pay a $20 application fee (fee waiver available). Participant costs include round-trip travel from home to service site and any personal gear needed.

Financial Aid Available: Yes

CONSERVATION CREW PROGRAM (SOUTH CAROLINA)

THE PROGRAM

Description: The Student Conservation Association (SCA) offers 15- to 19-year-old high school students the opportunity to serve on conservation crews of six to eight members with one to two trained adult crew leaders for three to five weeks during the summer months. They most often build or repair hiking trails, restore threatened habitats, and remove invasive plants. They learn to live outdoors as part of a cooperating team and participate in many outdoor activities, including a three- to five-day recreation trip. Crew sites vary year to year.

Specialty: High school students are offered a no- to low-cost option to participate in a team-based program that allows them to give back to communities by volunteer service to nature. Also, academic credit may be available.

Program Type: Community service, outdoors/adventure

Classification: Coeducational, residential

Goals: Participants should expect to learn improved leadership skills, enhanced problem-solving abilities, greater confidence and self-esteem, as well as some hand tools skills.

Focus: Community service, leadership/teamwork, and skill-building

Activities Center On: Volunteer and camping

Intensity Level: 3

Duration: 4–6 weeks

Program Offered: Summer

Location: All 50 states

Accommodations: Tent

Years in Operation: 46

Religious Affiliation: Not relevant

STAFF

Student/Staff Ratio: 3:1

Staff Qualifications: Crew Leaders are required to be at least 21 years old and possess proven youth leadership skills, camping/backpacking experience, and Wilderness First Aid (WFA) certification (Wilderness First Responder [WFR] certification is preferred). Trail construction skills and environmental education experience are highly desirable.

PARTICIPANTS

Average Number of Participants: 760

For Participants Aged: 15–19

The Ideal Candidate: No experience is necessary—just ample supplies of enthusiasm, a positive attitude, and a commitment to give it everything you've got!

Special Requirements for Participation: There must be a particular "comfort level" related to issues such as doing hard physical labor, sleeping in a tent, interacting with wildlife, or in some cases, making do without regular hot showers. Also needed is a physician's approval provided by completing our standard medical form.

COSTS

Average Cost: $0

Included in Cost: Serving in SCA is tuition-free; however, applicants pay a $20 application fee (fee waiver available). Participant costs include round-trip travel from home to service site and any personal gear needed.

Financial Aid Available: Yes

CONSERVATION CREW PROGRAM (SOUTH DAKOTA)

THE PROGRAM

Description: The Student Conservation Association (SCA) offers 15- to 19-year-old high school students the opportunity to serve on conservation crews of six to eight members with one to two trained adult crew leaders for three to five weeks during the summer months. They most often build or repair hiking trails, restore threatened habitats, and remove invasive plants. They learn to live outdoors as part of a cooperating team and participate in many outdoor activities, including a three- to five-day recreation trip. Crew sites vary year to year.

Specialty: High school students are offered a no- to low-cost option to participate in a team-based program that allows them to give back to communities by volunteer service to nature. Also, academic credit may be available.

Program Type: Community service, outdoors/adventure

Classification: Coeducational, residential

Goals: Participants should expect to learn improved leadership skills, enhanced problem-solving abilities, greater confidence and self-esteem, as well as some hand tools skills.

Focus: Community service, leadership/teamwork, and skill-building

Activities Center On: Volunteer and camping

Intensity Level: 3

Duration: 4–6 weeks

Program Offered: Summer

Location: All 50 states

Accommodations: Tent

Years in Operation: 46

Religious Affiliation: Not relevant

STAFF

Student/Staff Ratio: 3:1

Staff Qualifications: Crew Leaders are required to be at least 21 years old and possess proven youth leadership skills, camping/backpacking experience, and Wilderness First Aid (WFA) certification (Wilderness First Responder [WFR] certification is preferred). Trail construction skills and environmental education experience are highly desirable.

PARTICIPANTS

Average Number of Participants: 760

For Participants Aged: 15–19

The Ideal Candidate: No experience is necessary—just ample supplies of enthusiasm, a positive attitude, and a commitment to give it everything you've got!

Special Requirements for Participation: There must be a particular "comfort level" related to issues such as doing hard physical labor, sleeping in a tent, interacting with wildlife, or in some cases, making do without regular hot showers. Also needed is a physician's approval provided by completing our standard medical form.

COSTS

Average Cost: $0

Included in Cost: Serving in SCA is tuition-free; however, applicants pay a $20 application fee (fee waiver available). Participant costs include round-trip travel from home to service site and any personal gear needed.

Financial Aid Available: Yes

CONSERVATION CREW PROGRAM (TENNESSEE)

THE PROGRAM

Description: The Student Conservation Association (SCA) offers 15- to 19-year-old high school students the opportunity to serve on conservation crews of six to eight members with one to two trained adult crew leaders for three to five weeks during the summer months. They most often build or repair hiking trails, restore threatened habitats, and remove invasive plants. They learn to live outdoors as part of a cooperating team and participate in many outdoor activities, including a three- to five-day recreation trip. Crew sites vary year to year.

Specialty: High school students are offered a no- to low-cost option to participate in a team-based program that allows them to give back to communities by volunteer service to nature. Also, academic credit may be available.

Program Type: Community service, outdoors/adventure

Classification: Coeducational, residential

Goals: Participants should expect to learn improved leadership skills, enhanced problem-solving abilities, greater confidence and self-esteem, as well as some hand tools skills.

Focus: Community service, leadership/teamwork, and skill-building

Activities Center On: Volunteer and camping

Intensity Level: 3

Duration: 4–6 weeks

Program Offered: Summer

Location: All 50 states

Accommodations: Tent

Years in Operation: 46

Religious Affiliation: Not relevant

STAFF

Student/Staff Ratio: 3:1

Staff Qualifications: Crew Leaders are required to be at least 21 years old and possess proven youth leadership skills, camping/backpacking experience, and Wilderness First Aid (WFA) certification (Wilderness First Responder [WFR] certification is preferred). Trail construction skills and environmental education experience are highly desirable.

PARTICIPANTS

Average Number of Participants: 760

For Participants Aged: 15–19

The Ideal Candidate: No experience is necessary—just ample supplies of enthusiasm, a positive attitude, and a commitment to give it everything you've got!

Special Requirements for Participation: There must be a particular "comfort level" related to issues such as doing hard physical labor, sleeping in a tent, interacting with wildlife, or in some cases, making do without regular hot showers. Also needed is a physician's approval provided by completing our standard medical form.

COSTS

Average Cost: $0

Included in Cost: Serving in SCA is tuition-free; however, applicants pay a $20 application fee (fee waiver available). Participant costs include round-trip travel from home to service site and any personal gear needed.

Financial Aid Available: Yes

CONSERVATION CREW PROGRAM (TEXAS)

THE PROGRAM

Description: The Student Conservation Association (SCA) offers 15- to 19-year-old high school students the opportunity to serve on conservation crews of six to eight members with one to two trained adult crew leaders for three to five weeks during the summer months. They most often build or repair hiking trails, restore threatened habitats, and remove invasive plants. They learn to live outdoors as part of a cooperating team and participate in many outdoor activities, including a three- to five-day recreation trip. Sites vary from year to year.

Specialty: High school students are offered a no- to low-cost option to participate in a team-based program that allows them to give back to communities by volunteer service to nature. Also, academic credit may be available.

Program Type: Community service, outdoors/adventure

Classification: Coeducational, residential

Goals: Participants should expect to learn improved leadership skills, enhanced problem-solving abilities, greater confidence and self-esteem, as well as some hand tools skills.

Focus: Community service, leadership/teamwork, and skill-building

Activities Center On: Volunteer and camping

Intensity Level: 3

Duration: 4–6 weeks

Program Offered: Summer

Location: All 50 states

Accommodations: Tent

Years in Operation: 46

Religious Affiliation: Not relevant

STAFF

Student/Staff Ratio: 3:1

Staff Qualifications: Crew leaders are required to be at least 21 years old and possess proven youth leadership skills, camping/backpacking experience, and Wilderness First Aid (WFA) certification (Wilderness First Responder [WFR] certification is preferred). Trail construction skills and environmental education experience are highly desirable.

PARTICIPANTS

Average Number of Participants: 760

For Participants Aged: 15–19

The Ideal Candidate: No experience is necessary—just ample supplies of enthusiasm, a positive attitude, and a commitment to give it everything you've got!

Special Requirements for Participation: There must be a particular "comfort level" related to issues such as doing hard physical labor, sleeping in a tent, interacting with wildlife, or in some cases, making do without regular hot showers. Also needed is a physician's approval provided by completing our standard medical form.

COSTS

Average Cost: $0

Included in Cost: Serving in SCA is tuition-free; however, applicants pay a $20 application fee (fee waiver available). Participant costs include roundtrip travel from home to service site and any personal gear needed.

Financial Aid Available: Yes

CONSERVATION CREW PROGRAM (UTAH)

THE PROGRAM

Description: The Student Conservation Association (SCA) offers 15- to 19-year-old high school students the opportunity to serve on conservation crews of six to eight members with one to two trained adult crew leaders for three to five weeks during the summer months. They most often build or repair hiking trails, restore threatened habitats, and remove invasive plants. They learn to live outdoors as part of a cooperating team and participate in many outdoor activities, including a three- to five-day recreation trip. Sites vary from year to year.

Specialty: High school students are offered a no- to low-cost option to participate in a team-based program that allows them to give back to communities by volunteer service to nature. Also, academic credit may be available.

Program Type: Community service, outdoors/adventure

Classification: Coeducational, residential

Goals: Participants should expect to learn improved leadership skills, enhanced problem-solving abilities, greater confidence and self-esteem, as well as some hand tools skills.

Focus: Community service, leadership/teamwork, and skill-building

Activities Center On: Volunteer and camping

Intensity Level: 3

Duration: 4–6 weeks

Program Offered: Summer

Location: All 50 states

Accommodations: Tent

Years in Operation: 46

Religious Affiliation: Not relevant

STAFF

Student/Staff Ratio: 3:1

Staff Qualifications: Crew leaders are required to be at least

21 years old and possess proven youth leadership skills, camping/backpacking experience, and Wilderness First Aid (WFA) certification (Wilderness First Responder [WFR] certification is preferred). Trail construction skills and environmental education experience are highly desirable.

PARTICIPANTS

Average Number of Participants: 760

For Participants Aged: 15–19

The Ideal Candidate: No experience is necessary—just ample supplies of enthusiasm, a positive attitude, and a commitment to give it everything you've got!

Special Requirements for Participation: There must be a particular "comfort level" related to issues such as doing hard physical labor, sleeping in a tent, interacting with wildlife, or in some cases, making do without regular hot showers. Also needed is a physician's approval provided by completing our standard medical form.

COSTS

Average Cost: $0

Included in Cost: Serving in SCA is tuition-free; however, applicants pay a $20 application fee (fee waiver available). Participant costs include round-trip travel from home to service site and any personal gear needed.

Financial Aid Available: Yes

CONSERVATION CREW PROGRAM (VERMONT)

THE PROGRAM

Description: The Student Conservation Association (SCA) offers 15- to 19-year-old high school students the opportunity to serve on conservation crews of six to eight members with one to two trained adult crew leaders for three to five weeks during the summer months. They most often build or repair hiking trails, restore threatened habitats, and remove invasive plants. They learn to live outdoors as part of a cooperating team and participate in many outdoor activities, including a three- to five-day recreation trip. Sites vary from year to year.

Specialty: High school students are offered a no- to low-cost option to participate in a team-based program that allows them to give back to communities by volunteer service to nature. Also, academic credit may be available.

Program Type: Community service, outdoors/adventure

Classification: Coeducational, residential

Goals: Participants should expect to learn improved leadership skills, enhanced problem-solving abilities, greater confidence, and self-esteem, as well as some hand tools skills.

Focus: Community service, leadership/teamwork, and skill-building

Activities Center On: Volunteer and camping

Intensity Level: 3

Duration: 4–6 weeks

Program Offered: Summer

Location: All 50 states

Accommodations: Tent

Years in Operation: 46

Religious Affiliation: Not relevant

STAFF

Student/Staff Ratio: 3:1

Staff Qualifications: Crew leaders are required to be at least 21 years old and possess proven youth leadership skills, camping/backpacking experience, and Wilderness First Aid (WFA) certification (Wilderness First Responder [WFR] certification is preferred). Trail construction skills and environmental education experience are highly desirable.

PARTICIPANTS

Average Number of Participants: 760

For Participants Aged: 15–19

The Ideal Candidate: No experience is necessary—just ample supplies of enthusiasm, a positive attitude, and a commitment to give it everything you've got!

Special Requirements for Participation: There must be a particular "comfort level" related to issues such as doing hard physical labor, sleeping in a tent, interacting with wildlife, or in some cases, making do without regular hot showers. Also needed is a physician's approval provided by completing our standard medical form.

COSTS

Average Cost: $0

Included in Cost: Serving in SCA is tuition-free; however, applicants pay a $20 application fee (fee waiver available). Participant costs include roundtrip travel from home to service site and any personal gear needed.

Financial Aid Available: Yes

CONSERVATION CREW PROGRAM (VIRGINIA)

THE PROGRAM

Description: The Student Conservation Association (SCA) offers 15- to 19-year-old high school students the opportunity to serve on conservation crews of six to eight members with one to two trained adult crew leaders for three to five weeks during the summer months. They most often build or repair hiking trails, restore threatened habitats, and remove invasive plants. They learn to live outdoors as part of a cooperating team and participate in many outdoor activities, including a three- to five-day recreation trip. Sites vary from year to year.

Specialty: High school students are offered a no- to low-cost option to participate in a team-based program that allows them to give back to communities by volunteer service to nature. Also, academic credit may be available.

Program Type: Community service, outdoors/adventure

Classification: Coeducational, residential

Goals: Participants should expect to learn improved leadership skills, enhanced problem-solving abilities, greater confidence and self-esteem, as well as some hand tools skills.

Focus: Community service, leadership/teamwork, and skill-building

Activities Center On: Volunteer and camping

Intensity Level: 3

Duration: 4–6 weeks

Program Offered: Summer

Location: All 50 states

Accommodations: Tent

Years in Operation: 46

Religious Affiliation: Not relevant

STAFF

Student/Staff Ratio: 3:1

Staff Qualifications: Crew leaders are required to be at least 21 years old and possess proven youth leadership skills, camping/backpacking experience, and Wilderness First Aid (WFA) certification (Wilderness First Responder [WFR] certification is preferred). Trail construction skills and environmental education experience are highly desirable.

PARTICIPANTS

Average Number of Participants: 760

For Participants Aged: 15–19

The Ideal Candidate: No experience is necessary—just ample supplies of enthusiasm, a positive attitude, and a commitment to give it everything you've got!

Special Requirements for Participation: There must be a particular "comfort level" related to issues such as doing hard physical labor, sleeping in a tent, interacting with wildlife, or in some cases, making do without regular hot showers. Also needed is a physician's approval provided by completing our standard medical form.

COSTS

Average Cost: $0

Included in Cost: Serving in SCA is tuition-free; however, applicants pay a $20 application fee (fee waiver available). Participant costs include round-trip travel from home to service site and any personal gear needed.

Financial Aid Available: Yes

CONSERVATION CREW PROGRAM (WASHINGTON)

THE PROGRAM

Description: The Student Conservation Association (SCA) offers 15- to 19-year-old high school students the opportunity to serve on conservation crews of six to eight members with one to two trained adult crew leaders for three to five weeks during the summer months. They most often build or repair

hiking trails, restore threatened habitats, and remove invasive plants. They learn to live outdoors as part of a cooperating team and participate in many outdoor activities, including a three- to five-day recreation trip. Sites vary from year to year.

Specialty: High school students are offered a no- to low-cost option to participate in a team-based program that allows them to give back to communities by volunteer service to nature. Also, academic credit may be available.

Program Type: Community service, outdoors/adventure

Classification: Coeducational, residential

Goals: Participants should expect to learn improved leadership skills, enhanced problem-solving abilities, greater confidence and self-esteem, as well as some hand tools skills.

Focus: Community service, leadership/teamwork, and skill-building

Activities Center On: Volunteer and camping

Intensity Level: 3

Duration: 4–6 weeks

Program Offered: Summer

Location: All 50 states

Accommodations: Tent

Years in Operation: 46

Religious Affiliation: Not relevant

STAFF

Student/Staff Ratio: 3:1

Staff Qualifications: Crew leaders are required to be at least 21 years old and possess proven youth leadership skills, camping/backpacking experience, and Wilderness First Aid (WFA) certification (Wilderness First Responder [WFR] certification is preferred). Trail construction skills and environmental education experience are highly desirable.

PARTICIPANTS

Average Number of Participants: 760

For Participants Aged: 15–19

The Ideal Candidate: No experience is necessary—just ample supplies of enthusiasm, a positive attitude, and a commitment to give it everything you've got!

Special Requirements for Participation: There must be a particular "comfort level" related to issues such as doing hard physical labor, sleeping in a tent, interacting with wildlife, or in some cases, making do without regular hot showers. Also needed is a physician's approval provided by completing our standard medical form.

COSTS

Average Cost: $0

Included in Cost: Serving in SCA is tuition-free; however, applicants pay a $20 application fee (fee waiver available). Participant costs include round-trip travel from home to service site and any personal gear needed.

Financial Aid Available: Yes

Conservation Crew Program (West Virginia)

The Program

Description: The Student Conservation Association (SCA) offers 15- to 19-year-old high school students the opportunity to serve on conservation crews of six to eight members with one to two trained adult crew leaders for three to five weeks during the summer months. They most often build or repair hiking trails, restore threatened habitats, and remove invasive plants. They learn to live outdoors as part of a cooperating team and participate in many outdoor activities, including a three- to five-day recreation trip. Sites vary from year to year.

Specialty: High school students are offered a no- to low-cost option to participate in a team-based program that allows them to give back to communities by volunteer service to nature. Also, academic credit may be available.

Program Type: Community service, outdoors/adventure

Classification: Coeducational, residential

Goals: Participants should expect to learn improved leadership skills, enhanced problem-solving abilities, greater confidence and self-esteem, as well as some hand tools skills.

Focus: Community service, leadership/teamwork, and skill-building

Activities Center On: Volunteer and camping

Intensity Level: 3

Duration: 4–6 weeks

Program Offered: Summer

Location: All 50 states

Accommodations: Tent

Years in Operation: 46

Religious Affiliation: Not relevant

Staff

Student/Staff Ratio: 3:1

Staff Qualifications: Crew leaders are required to be at least 21 years old and possess proven youth leadership skills, camping/backpacking experience, and Wilderness First Aid (WFA) certification (Wilderness First Responder [WFR] certification is preferred). Trail construction skills and environmental education experience are highly desirable.

Participants

Average Number of Participants: 760

For Participants Aged: 15–19

The Ideal Candidate: No experience is necessary—just ample supplies of enthusiasm, a positive attitude, and a commitment to give it everything you've got!

Special Requirements for Participation: There must be a particular "comfort level" related to issues such as doing hard physical labor, sleeping in a tent, interacting with wildlife, or in some cases, making do without regular hot showers. Also needed is a physician's approval provided by completing our standard medical form.

Costs

Average Cost: $0

Included in Cost: Serving in SCA is tuition-free; however, applicants pay a $20 application fee (fee waiver available). Participant costs include round-trip travel from home to service site and any personal gear needed.

Financial Aid Available: Yes

Conservation Crew Program (Wisconsin)

The Program

Description: The Student Conservation Association (SCA) offers 15- to 19-year-old high school students the opportunity to serve on conservation crews of six to eight members with one to two trained adult crew leaders for three to five weeks during the summer months. They most often build or repair hiking trails, restore threatened habitats, and remove invasive plants. They learn to live outdoors as part of a cooperating team and participate in many outdoor activities, including a three- to five-day recreation trip. Sites vary from year to year.

Specialty: High school students are offered a no- to low-cost option to participate in a team-based program that allows them to give back to communities by volunteer service to nature. Also, academic credit may be available.

Program Type: Community service, outdoors/adventure

Classification: Coeducational, residential

Goals: Participants should expect to learn improved leadership skills, enhanced problem-solving abilities, greater confidence and self-esteem, as well as some hand tools skills.

Focus: Community service, leadership/teamwork, and skill-building

Activities Center On: Volunteer and camping

Intensity Level: 3

Duration: 4–6 weeks

Program Offered: Summer

Location: All 50 states

Accommodations: Tent

Years in Operation: 46

Religious Affiliation: Not relevant

Staff

Student/Staff Ratio: 3:1

Staff Qualifications: Crew leaders are required to be at least 21 years old and possess proven youth leadership skills, camping/backpacking experience, and Wilderness First Aid (WFA) certification (Wilderness First Responder [WFR] certification is preferred). Trail construction skills and environmental education experience are highly desirable.

Participants

Average Number of Participants: 760

For Participants Aged: 15–19

The Ideal Candidate: No experience is necessary—just ample supplies of enthusiasm, a positive attitude, and a commitment to give it everything you've got!

Special Requirements for Participation: There must be a particular "comfort level" related to issues such as doing hard physical labor, sleeping in a tent, interacting with wildlife, or in some cases, making do without regular hot showers. Also needed is a physician's approval provided by completing our standard medical form.

Costs

Average Cost: $0

Included in Cost: Serving in SCA is tuition-free; however, applicants pay a $20 application fee (fee waiver available). Participant costs include round-trip travel from home to service site and any personal gear needed.

Financial Aid Available: Yes

Conservation Crew Program (Wyoming)

The Program

Description: The Student Conservation Association (SCA) offers 15- to 19-year-old high school students the opportunity to serve on conservation crews of six to eight members with one to two trained adult crew leaders for three to five weeks during the summer months. They most often build or repair hiking trails, restore threatened habitats, and remove invasive plants. They learn to live outdoors as part of a cooperating team and participate in many outdoor activities, including a three- to five-day recreation trip. Sites vary from year to year.

Specialty: High school students are offered a no- to low-cost option to participate in a team-based program that allows them to give back to communities by volunteer service to nature. Also, academic credit may be available.

Program Type: Community service, outdoors/adventure

Classification: Coeducational, residential

Goals: Participants should expect to learn improved leadership skills, enhanced problem-solving abilities, greater confidence and self-esteem, as well as some hand tools skills.

Focus: Community service, leadership/teamwork, and skill-building

Activities Center On: Volunteer and camping

Intensity Level: 3

Duration: 4–6 weeks

Program Offered: Summer

Location: All 50 states

Accommodations: Tent

Years in Operation: 46

Religious Affiliation: Not relevant

Staff

Student/Staff Ratio: 3:1

Staff Qualifications: Crew leaders are required to be at least 21 years old and possess proven youth leadership skills, camping/backpacking experience, and Wilderness First Aid (WFA) certification (Wilderness First Responder [WFR] certification is preferred). Trail construction skills and environmental education experience are highly desirable.

Participants

Average Number of Participants: 760

For Participants Aged: 15–19

The Ideal Candidate: No experience is necessary—just ample supplies of enthusiasm, a positive attitude, and a commitment to give it everything you've got!

Special Requirements for Participation: There must be a particular "comfort level" related to issues such as doing hard physical labor, sleeping in a tent, interacting with wildlife, or in some cases, making do without regular hot showers. Also needed is a physician's approval provided by completing our standard medical form.

Costs

Average Cost: $0

Included in Cost: Serving in SCA is tuition-free; however, applicants pay a $20 application fee (fee waiver available). Participant costs include round-trip travel from home to service site and any personal gear needed.

Financial Aid Available: Yes

STUDENT HOSTELING PROGRAM

The Student Hosteling Program offers one- to eight-week teenage bicycle touring and off-road trips through the countrysides and cultural centers of the United States, Canada, and Europe. Small co-ed groups of 8–12 students and 2 leaders are grouped in very compatible grade groupings. Easy, moderate, and challenging trips available.

Years in Operation: 34

Religious Affiliation: Not relevant

Price Range of Programs: $900–$1,500

For More Information:
Contact: Ted Lefkowitz, Director
1356 Ashfield Road
PO Box 419
Conway, MA 01341
Phone: 800-343-6132
Fax: 413-369-4257
Email: shpbike@aol.com
Website: www.bicycletrips.com

Student Hosteling Program — A Thousand Miles: Massachusetts to Nova Scotia

The Program

Description: Travel 1,000 miles through Massachusetts, Vermont, New Hampshire, Maine, and Nova Scotia! This is a challenging 25-day bicycle touring trip.

Program Type: Outdoors/adventure, sports/athletic, travel/cultural

Classification: Coeducational, residential

Focus: Travel

Activities Center On: Touring

Intensity Level: 4

Duration: 2–4 weeks

Program Offered: Summer

Location: Conway, Massachusetts; Maine; New Hampshire; Vermont; Nova Scotia, Canada

Accommodations: Tent

Years in Operation: 34

Religious Affiliation: Not relevant

Staff

Student/Staff Ratio: 11:2

Staff Qualifications: Senior leaders are at least 21 and hold Red Cross first aid certification. Assistant leaders are at least 18 and have completed one year of college.

Participants

Average Number of Participants: 10

For Participants Aged: 15–18

Special Requirements for Participation: None.

Costs

Average Cost: $2,625

Included in Cost: Includes rental equipment package and transportation from Boston or New York. Participants should provide their own bicycles and helmets.

Financial Aid Available: No

SUMMER DISCOVERY

SUMMER DISCOVERY offers 3- to 6-week pre-college enrichment programs for high school students at UCLA, UC-Santa Barbara, UC-San Diego, Georgetown University, University of Vermont, University of Michigan, Cambridge University (UK), and the University of Sydney, Australia. Students can take classes for college credit, gain academic enrichment through study skills workshops, and have access to The Princeton Review SAT preparation, TOEFL/ESL preparation, community service, academic counseling, sports instruction and intramurals, evening programs, weekend excursions, concerts, plays, major league baseball games, museums, and other area attractions. Visits to several college campuses are also provided.

Years in Operation: 37

Religious Affiliation: Not relevant

Price Range of Programs: $3,600–$6,900

For More Information:
   Contact: Musiker and Waldman Family, Owner/Directors
           1326 Old Northern Boulevard
           Roslyn Village, NY 11576
   Phone: 888-878-6637
   Fax: 516-625-3438
   Email: discovery@summerfun.comdiscovery@summerfun.com
   Website: www.summerfun.com

Jr. Discovery (Michigan)

Description: Famous for its unparalleled cultural and learning environment, incredible school spirit, and athletic success, the University of Michigan is consistently ranked as one of America's top universities. The University of Michigan has more living alumni than any other university in the world, including one U.S. president, three supreme court justices, six Nobel prize winners, seven astronauts, academy award winners, Olympic gold medalists, and who knows, maybe you someday!

Specialty: SUMMER DISCOVERY and JR. DISCOVERY offer the world's most popular 3- to 6-week pre-college enrichment programs for high school students at 8 distinct college campuses.

Program Type: Middle school enrichment

Classification: Coeducational; residential

Goals: Enjoy an intellectually-stimulating, cultural, and social experience with the respect you deserve, while increasing your self-esteem, confidence, and independence.

Focus: Skill-building, cultural, and travel

Activities Center On: Academic

Intensity Level: 3

Duration: 2–4 weeks

Program Offered: Summer

Location: Ann Arbor, MI

Accommodations: Dormitory

Years in Operation: 55

Religious Affiliation: Not relevant

STAFF

Student/Staff Ratio: 7:1

Staff Qualifications: All staff must be 21 or over and have a valid driver's license, DMV clearance, reference, and security check.

PARTICIPANTS

Average Number of Participants: 45

For Participants Aged: 12–14

The Ideal Candidate: Enthusiastic and eager to learn.

Special Requirements for Participation: Application and recommendation.

COSTS

Average Cost: $3,599

Included in Cost: Includes term fees, use of facilities, housing, breakfast, and dinner while on campus, plus trips and excursions per catalog. Not included: transportation to and from your home city, or transfers to and from the airport.

Financial Aid Available: No

JR. DISCOVERY (UCLA)

THE PROGRAM

Description: The beautiful communities of Beverly Hills, Bel-Air, Westwood, and Santa Monica surround UCLA's magnificent suburban campus. The diverse cultural and learning environment of UCLA provides opportunities to make friends from all over the world. This welcoming environment, combined with UCLA's remarkable educational resources, reputation for academic distinction, athletic excellence, spirited student body, and superb location create an ideal setting for JR. DISCOVERY.

Specialty: SUMMER DISCOVERY and JR. DISCOVERY offer the world's most popular 3- to 6-week pre-college enrichment programs for high school students at 8 distinct college campuses.

Program Type: Middle school enrichment

Classification: Coeducational; residential

Goals: Enjoy an intellectually-stimulating, cultural, and social experience with the respect you deserve, while increasing self-esteem, confidence, and independence.

Focus: Skill-building, cultural, and travel

Activities Center On: Academic

Intensity Level: 3

Duration: 2–4 weeks

Program Offered: Summer

Location: Los Angeles, CA

Accommodations: Dormitory

Years in Operation: 55

Religious Affiliation: Not relevant

STAFF

Student/Staff Ratio: 7:1

Staff Qualifications: All staff must be 21 or over and have a valid driver's license, DMV clearance, reference, and security check.

PARTICIPANTS

Average Number of Participants: 100

For Participants Aged: 12–14

The Ideal Candidate: Enthusiastic and eager to learn.

Special Requirements for Participation: Application and recommendation.

COSTS

Average Cost: $4,599

Included in Cost: Includes term fees, use of facilities, housing, breakfast, and dinner while on campus, and trips and excursions per catalog. Not included: transportation to and from your home city, or transfers to and from the airport.

Financial Aid Available: No

JR. DISCOVERY (VERMONT)

THE PROGRAM

Description: Founded more than 200 years ago, UVM remains one of the most popular and competitive universities in the northeast. On JR. DISCOVERY, you'll get to enjoy all that the school has to offer without having to worry about "getting in." Indoors or out, you'll enjoy phenomenal academics, arts, athletics, recreation, clean mountain air, and friends everywhere.

Specialty: SUMMER DISCOVERY and JR. DISCOVERY offer the world's most popular 3- to 6-week pre-college enrichment programs for high school students at 8 distinct college campuses.

Program Type: Middle school enrichment

Classification: Coeducational, residential

Goals: Enjoy an intellectually-stimulating, cultural, and social experience with the respect you deserve, while increasing self-esteem, confidence, and independence.

Focus: Skill-building, cultural, and travel

Activities Center On: Academic

Intensity Level: 3

Duration: 2–4 weeks

Program Offered: Summer

Location: Burlington, VT

Accommodations: Dormitory

Years in Operation: 44

Religious Affiliation: Not relevant

STAFF

Student/Staff Ratio: 7:1

Staff Qualifications: All staff must be 21 or over and have a valid driver's license, DMV clearance, reference, and security check.

PARTICIPANTS

Average Number of Participants: 50

For Participants Aged: 12–14

The Ideal Candidate: Enthusiastic and eager to learn.

Special Requirements for Participation: Application and recommendation.

COSTS

Average Cost: $4,299

Included in Cost: Includes term fees, use of facilities, housing, breakfast, and dinner while on campus, and trips and excursions per catalog. Not included: transportation to and from your home city, or transfers to and from the airport.

Financial Aid Available: No

MUSIKER ACTIVE TEEN TOURS

THE PROGRAM

Description: The best in active student tours for teenagers. Travel throughout USA, Canada, or Europe. Specialty program in golf.

Specialty: MUSIKER TOURS invites students grades 7 to 12 (in compatible age groups) to experience a fantastic summer traveling across the USA, Canada, and Europe. We offer the finest 3- to six-week activity-oriented, quality teen tour programs.

Program Type: Outdoors/adventure, sports/athletic, travel/cultural

Classification: Coeducational, residential

Goals: As the innovative leader in active student travel, each program is action-packed with a great variety and choice of activities. If you are not familiar with an activity, don't worry, we'll show you how. Every tour is equipped with a full set of athletic gear.

Focus: Travel, cultural, and leadership/teamwork

Activities Center On: Other

Intensity Level: 1

Duration: 2–4 weeks, 4–6 weeks

Program Offered: Summer

Location: AK, AZ, CA, DC, FL, HI, IL, MA, MD, MI, MT, NV, UT, United States

United States; France, Italy, Switzerland, and United Kingdom

Accommodations: Dormitory, hotels, tent, other

Years in Operation: 38

Religious Affiliation: Not relevant

STAFF

Student/Staff Ratio: 8:1

Staff Qualifications: All staff must be 21 or over and have a valid driver's license, DMV clearance, reference, and security check.

PARTICIPANTS

Average Number of Participants: 50

For Participants Aged: 12–17

The Ideal Candidate: Enthusiastic and eager to have fun.

COSTS

Average Cost: $5,500

Included in Cost: Includes all fees, use of facilities, housing, 3 meals daily, trips, and excursions per catalog. Not included: transportation to and from your home city, or transfers to and from the airport.

Financial Aid Available: No

THE PRINCETON REVIEW COLLEGE DISCOVERY EXPERIENCE

THE PROGRAM

Description: A unique two-week summer program designed to help improve your PSAT and SAT scores, while preparing you for college admissions and the demanding application process.

Specialty: SUMMER DISCOVERY offers the world's most popular pre-college enrichment programs for high school students.

Program Type: Academic/pre-college enrichment

Classification: Coeducational, residential

Goals: Improve your PSAT/SAT scores, tour college campuses, meet college admissions officers, get the best expert guidance on how to pick the right college, learn how to write a great essay, and experience campus life at one of two prestigious universities.

Focus: Academic/pre-college enrichment, cultural, and skill-building

Activities Center On: SAT prep, academic, and writing

Intensity Level: 2

Duration: 2–4 weeks

Program Offered: Summer

Location: Washington, D.C.; Boston

Accommodations: Dormitory

Religious Affiliation: Not relevant

STAFF

Student/Staff Ratio: 10:1

Staff Qualifications: All staff must be 21 or over and have a valid driver's license, DMV clearance, reference, and security check.

PARTICIPANTS

Average Number of Participants: 100

For Participants Aged: 14–17

The Ideal Candidate: Anyone who wants to get a leg up on preparing for the PSAT/SAT and the college admissions process.

Special Requirements for Participation: College-bound students.

COSTS

Average Cost: $2,899

Included in Cost: Includes term fees, use of facilities, housing, breakfast, and dinner while on campus, and trips and excursions to colleges. Not included: transportation to and from your home city, or transfers to and from the airport.

Financial Aid Available: No

SUMMER DISCOVERY (AUSTRALIA)

THE PROGRAM

Description: SUMMER DISCOVERY students live in the Camperdown/Darlington campus, the main campus of the University of Sydney. This 180-acre site, located only minutes from central Sydney, features landscaped grounds, sports ovals, museums, galleries, two major complexes devoted to student recreation, the famous Quadrangle-the university's original building-and many other beautiful modern and historic buildings.

Specialty: SUMMER DISCOVERY offers the world's most popular 3- to 6-week pre-college enrichment programs for high school students at 8 distinct college campuses.

Program Type: Academic/pre-college enrichment

Classification: Coeducational, residential

Goals: Enjoy an intellectually-stimulating, cultural, and social experience with the respect you deserve, while increasing self-esteem, confidence, and independence.

Focus: Academic/pre-college enrichment, cultural, and travel

Activities Center On: Academic

Intensity Level: 3

Duration: 4–6 weeks

Program Offered: Summer

Location: Sydney, Australia

Accommodations: Dormitory, hotels, tent

Religious Affiliation: Not relevant

STAFF

Student/Staff Ratio: 10:1

Staff Qualifications: All staff must be 21 or over and have a valid driver's license, DMV clearance, reference, and security check.

PARTICIPANTS

Average Number of Participants: 100

For Participants Aged: 14–17

The Ideal Candidate: College-bound students eager to experience a pre-college experience.

Special Requirements for Participation: Application, recommendation, and transcript.

COSTS

Average Cost: $6,999

Included in Cost: Includes term fees, use of facilities, housing, breakfast, and dinner while on campus, and trips and excursions per catalog. Not included: transportation to and from your home city, or transfers to and from the airport.

Financial Aid Available: No

SUMMER DISCOVERY (CAMBRIDGE)

THE PROGRAM

Description: Cambridge is one of the world's great academic and cultural centers. Cambridge University is comprised of 31 separate colleges distinguished by a wealth of architectural styles, grand bridges over the River Cam, meticulously manicured courtyards, beautiful gardens, and green open spaces.

Specialty: SUMMER DISCOVERY offers the world's most popular 3- to 6-week pre-college enrichment programs for high school students at 8 distinct college campuses.

Program Type: Academic/pre-college enrichment

Classification: Coeducational, residential

Goals: Enjoy an intellectually-stimulating, cultural, and social experience with the respect you deserve, while increasing self-esteem, confidence, and independence.

Focus: Academic/pre-college enrichment, cultural, and travel

Activities Center On: Academic

Intensity Level: 3

Duration: 2–4 weeks

Program Offered: Summer

Location: Cambridge, England

Accommodations: Dormitory

Years in Operation: 14

Religious Affiliation: Not relevant

STAFF

Student/Staff Ratio: 10:1

Staff Qualifications: All staff must be 21 or over and have a valid driver's license, DMV clearance, reference, and security check.

PARTICIPANTS

Average Number of Participants: 200

For Participants Aged: 15–18

The Ideal Candidate: College-bound students eager to experience a pre-college experience.

Special Requirements for Participation: Application, recommendation, and transcript.

COSTS

Average Cost: $5,899

Included in Cost: Includes term fees, use of facilities, housing, breakfast, and dinner while on campus, and trips and excursions per catalog. Not included: transportation to and from your home city, or transfers to and from the airport.

Financial Aid Available: No

SUMMER DISCOVERY DISCOVERYWORKS

THE PROGRAM

Description: Community service, conservation, exploration, adventure, and fun!

Specialty: SUMMER DISCOVERY, JR. DISCOVERY and DISCOVERYWORKS offer the world's most popular community service program.

Program Type: Community service

Classification: Coeducational, residential

Goals: Enjoy an intellectually-stimulating, cultural, and social experience with the respect you deserve, while increasing self-esteem, confidence, and independence with community service.

Focus: Community service

Intensity Level: 3

Duration: 2-4 weeks

Program Offered: Summer

Location: ME, MA, NH, United States

Accommodations: Dormitory, bunk/cabin, hotels

Religious Affiliation: Not relevant

STAFF

Student/Staff Ratio: 10:1

Staff Qualifications: All staff must be 21 or over and have a valid driver's license, DMV clearance, reference, and security check

PARTICIPANTS

Average Number of Participants: 50

For Participants Aged: 13–15

The Ideal Candidate: Enthusiastic and eager to learn.

COSTS

Average Cost: $4,299

Included in Cost: Includes term fees, use of facilities, housing, breakfast, dinner, and trips and excursions per catalog. Not included: transportation to and from your home city, or transfers to and from the airport.

Financial Aid Available: No

SUMMER DISCOVERY (GEORGETOWN)

THE PROGRAM

Description: Georgetown University was founded in 1789, the same year George Washington became the first U.S. president. Georgetown's hilltop campus commands the same panoramic views of the Potomac River that it did over 200 years ago.

Specialty: SUMMER DISCOVERY offers the world's most popular 3- to 6-week pre-college enrichment programs for high school students at 8 distinct college campuses.

Program Type: Academic/pre-college enrichment

Classification: Coeducational, residential

Goals: Enjoy an intellectually-stimulating, cultural, and social experience with the respect you deserve, while increasing self-esteem, confidence, and independence.

Focus: Academic/pre-college enrichment, cultural, and travel

Activities Center On: Academic

Intensity Level: 3

Duration: 4–6 weeks

Program Offered: Summer

Location: Washington, D.C.

Accommodations: Dormitory

Years in Operation: 10

Religious Affiliation: Not relevant

STAFF

Student/Staff Ratio: 10:1

Staff Qualifications: All staff must be 21 or over and have a valid driver's license, DMV clearance, reference, and security check.

PARTICIPANTS

Average Number of Participants: 200

For Participants Aged: 14–17

The Ideal Candidate: College-bound students eager to experience a pre-college experience.

Special Requirements for Participation: Application, recommendation, and transcript.

COSTS

Average Cost: $5,599

Included in Cost: Includes term fees, use of facilities, housing, breakfast, and dinner while on campus, and trips and excursions per catalog. Not included: transportation to and from your home city, or transfers to and from the airport.

Financial Aid Available: No

Summer Discovery (Michigan)

The Program

Description: Renowned for its unparalleled cultural and academic environment, fervent school spirit, and athletic success, the University of Michigan is consistently ranked as one of America's top ten universities. The largest pre-med and pre-law university in the country, UM excels in the classroom, the laboratory and beyond.

Specialty: SUMMER DISCOVERY offers the world's most popular 3- to 6-week pre-college enrichment programs for high school students at 8 distinct college campuses.

Program Type: Academic/pre-college enrichment

Classification: Coeducational, residential

Goals: Enjoy an intellectually-stimulating, cultural, and social experience with the respect you deserve, while increasing self-esteem, confidence, and independence.

Focus: Academic/pre-college enrichment, cultural, and travel

Activities Center On: Academic

Intensity Level: 3

Duration: 4–6 weeks

Program Offered: Summer

Location: Ann Arbor, MI

Accommodations: Dormitory

Years in Operation: 15

Religious Affiliation: Not relevant

Staff

Student/Staff Ratio: 10:1

Staff Qualifications: All staff must be 21 or over and have a valid driver's license, DMV clearance, reference, and security check.

Participants

Average Number of Participants: 450

For Participants Aged: 14–17

The Ideal Candidate: College-bound students eager to experience a pre-college experience.

Special Requirements for Participation: Application, recommendation, and transcript.

Costs

Average Cost: $5,899

Included in Cost: Includes term fees, use of facilities, housing, breakfast, and dinner while on campus, and trips and excursions per catalog. Not included: transportation to and from your home city, or transfers to and from the airport.

Financial Aid Available: No

Summer Discovery (UCLA)

The Program

Description: UCLA is one of the world's best-known and well-respected universities. The largest of the nine University of California campuses, UCLA is internationally-recognized for its innovative curricula and commitment to community service.

Specialty: SUMMER DISCOVERY offers the world's most popular 3- to 6-week pre-college enrichment programs for high school students at 8 distinct college campuses.

Program Type: Academic/pre-college enrichment

Classification: Coeducational, residential

Goals: Enjoy an intellectually-stimulating, cultural, and social experience with the respect you deserve, while increasing self-esteem, confidence, and independence.

Focus: Academic/pre-college enrichment, cultural, and travel

Activities Center On: Academic

Intensity Level: 3

Duration: 4–6 weeks

Program Offered: Summer

Location: Los Angeles, CA

Accommodations: Dormitory

Years in Operation: 20

Religious Affiliation: Not relevant

Staff

Student/Staff Ratio: 10:1

Staff Qualifications: All staff must be 21 or over and have a valid driver's license, DMV clearance, reference, and security check.

Participants

Average Number of Participants: 450

For Participants Aged: 14–18

The Ideal Candidate: College-bound students eager to experience a pre-college experience.

Special Requirements for Participation: Application, recommendation, and transcript.

Costs

Average Cost: $6,699

Included in Cost: Includes term fees, use of facilities, housing, breakfast, and dinner while on campus, and trips and excursions per catalog. Not included: transportation to and from your home city, or transfers to and from the airport.

Financial Aid Available: No

SUMMER DISCOVERY (UC—SAN DIEGO)

THE PROGRAM

Description: The University of California—San Diego is a world-class university, with state-of-the-art facilities and a breathtaking view of the Pacific Ocean. UCSD is one of America's premier research universities, boasting an outstanding faculty and a big, beautiful campus with a friendly, small campus environment-perfect for a summer of discovery.

Specialty: SUMMER DISCOVERY offers the world's most popular 3- to 6-week pre-college enrichment programs for high school students at 8 distinct college campuses.

Program Type: Academic/pre-college enrichment

Classification: Coeducational, residential

Goals: Enjoy an intellectually-stimulating, cultural, and social experience with the respect you deserve, while increasing self-esteem, confidence, and independence.

Focus: Academic/pre-college enrichment, cultural, and travel

Activities Center On: Academic

Intensity Level: 3

Duration: 4–6 weeks

Program Offered: Summer

Location: San Diego, CA

Accommodations: Dormitory

Years in Operation: 55

Religious Affiliation: Not relevant

STAFF

Student/Staff Ratio: 10:1

Staff Qualifications: All staff must be 21 or over and have a valid driver's license, DMV clearance, reference, and security check.

PARTICIPANTS

Average Number of Participants: 100

For Participants Aged: 14–17

The Ideal Candidate: College-bound students eager to experience a pre-college experience.

Special Requirements for Participation: Application, recommendation, and transcript.

COSTS

Average Cost: $5,599

Included in Cost: Includes term fees, use of facilities, housing, breakfast, and dinner while on campus, and trips and excursions per catalog. Not included: transportation to and from your home city, or transfers to and from the airport.

Financial Aid Available: No

SUMMER DISCOVERY (UC—SANTA BARBARA)

THE PROGRAM

Description: UCSB has a breathtaking 989-acre campus located approximately 100 miles north of Los Angeles, bordered by the Pacific Ocean and the Santa Ynez Mountains. UCSB offers three different college credit programs. The Early Start and 1+1 Programs feature approximately 100 classes in over 35 different fields. Also available is an intensive Research Mentorship Program.

Specialty: SUMMER DISCOVERY offers the world's most popular 3- to 6-week pre-college enrichment programs for high school students at 8 distinct college campuses.

Program Type: Academic/pre-college enrichment

Classification: Coeducational, residential

Goals: Enjoy an intellectually-stimulating, cultural, and social experience with the respect you deserve, while increasing self-esteem, confidence, and independence.

Focus: Academic/pre-college enrichment, cultural, and internship

Activities Center On: Academic

Intensity Level: 3

Duration: 4–6 weeks

Program Offered: Summer

Location: Santa Barbara, CA

Accommodations: Dormitory

Years in Operation: 33

Religious Affiliation: Not relevant

STAFF

Student/Staff Ratio: 10:1

Staff Qualifications: All staff must be 21 or over and have a valid driver's license, DMV clearance, reference, and security check.

PARTICIPANTS

Average Number of Participants: 150

For Participants Aged: 15–18

The Ideal Candidate: College-bound students eager to experience a pre-college experience.

Special Requirements for Participation: Application, recommendation, and transcript.

COSTS

Average Cost: $5,599

Included in Cost: Includes term fees, use of facilities, housing, breakfast, and dinner while on campus, and trips and excursions per catalog. Not included: transportation to and from your home city, or transfers to and from the airport.

Financial Aid Available: No

SUMMER DISCOVERY (UVM)

THE PROGRAM

Description: Founded 1791, the University boasts many notable achievements including: Vermont's largest library (1,000,000 volumes); the first university to admit students regardless of religion; the university first in New England to admit women; the twentieth college to be founded in the USA; and the greatest participation by students in community service activities in the nation.

Specialty: SUMMER DISCOVERY offers the world's most popular 3- to 6-week pre-college enrichment programs for high school students at 8 distinct college campuses.

Program Type: Academic/pre-college enrichment

Classification: Coeducational, residential

Goals: Enjoy an intellectually-stimulating, cultural, and social experience with the respect you deserve, while increasing self-esteem, confidence, and independence.

Focus: Academic/pre-college enrichment, cultural, and travel

Activities Center On: Academic

Intensity Level: 3

Duration: 4–6 weeks

Program Offered: Summer

Location: Burlington, VT

Accommodations: Dormitory

Years in Operation: 15

Religious Affiliation: Not relevant

STAFF

Student/Staff Ratio: 10:1

Staff Qualifications: All staff must be 21 or over and have a valid driver's license, DMV clearance, reference, and security check.

PARTICIPANTS

Average Number of Participants: 175

For Participants Aged: 14–17

The Ideal Candidate: College-bound students eager to experience a pre-college experience.

Special Requirements for Participation: Application, recommendation, and transcript.

COSTS

Average Cost: $5,599

Included in Cost: Includes term fees, use of facilities, housing, breakfast, and dinner while on campus, and trips and excursions per catalog. Not included: transportation to and from your home city, or transfers to and from the airport.

Financial Aid Available: No

SUMMER SCIENCE PROGRAM, INC.

An independent 501(c)(3) nonprofit corporation formed for the purpose of operating the Summer Science Program at one or more sites

Years in Operation: 44

Religious Affiliation: Not relevant

Price Range of Programs: $2,950

For More Information:
  Contact: Richard Bowdon, Executive Director
        108 Whiteberry Drive
        Cary, NC 27519
  Phone: 866-728-0999
  Fax: 419-735-2251
  Email: info@summerscience.org
  Website: www.summerscience.org

SUMMER SCIENCE PROGRAM—OJAI CAMPUS

THE PROGRAM

Description: SSP students do hands-on research that is supported by instruction in astronomy, physics, and math, and supplemented by guest lectures and field trips. Working in small teams, students determine the orbit of an asteroid using their own measurements and software. This intense experience inspires students both intellectually and socially, immersing them in a "community of scholars."

Specialty: Many alumni cite SSP as a life-changing experience, even decades later. That's why it's the only summer enrichment program now operated and funded by its own alumni.

Program Type: Academic/pre-college enrichment

Classification: Coeducational, residential

Goals: Astronomy, differential and integral calculus, spherical trigonometry, mechanics, electromagnetic theory, programming, photographic and darkroom techniques, teamwork, collaboration.

Focus: Academic/pre-college enrichment, leadership/teamwork, and skill-building

Activities Center On: Science, math, and career exploration

Intensity Level: 5

Duration: 4–6 weeks

Program Offered: Summer

Location: Ojai, California

Accommodations: Dormitory

Years in Operation: 44

Religious Affiliation: Not relevant

STAFF

Student/Staff Ratio: 5:1

Staff Qualifications: Working scientists, science and math teachers, graduate students studying physical science, and upperclassmen majoring in physical science.

PARTICIPANTS

Average Number of Participants: 34

For Participants Aged: 15–18

The Ideal Candidate: A junior or outstanding sophomore who are near the top of the class, taking the most advanced math and science classes offered and earning top grades, and who have an interest in astronomy.

Special Requirements for Participation: None.

COSTS

Average Cost: $2,950

Included in Cost: All inclusive: tuition, room and board, supplies, local transportation.

Financial Aid Available: Yes

SUMMER SCIENCE PROGRAM — SOCORRO CAMPUS

THE PROGRAM

Description: SSP students do hands-on research that is supported by instruction in astronomy, physics, and math, and supplemented by guest lectures and field trips. Working in small teams, students determine the orbit of an asteroid using their own measurements and software. This intense experience inspires students both intellectually and socially, immersing them in a "community of scholars."

Specialty: Many alumni cite SSP as a life-changing experience, even decades later. That's why it's the only summer enrichment program now operated and funded by its own alumni.

Program Type: Academic/pre-college enrichment

Classification: Coeducational, residential

Goals: Astronomy, differential and integral calculus, spherical trigonometry, mechanics, electromagnetic theory, programming, photographic and darkroom techniques, teamwork, collaboration.

Focus: Academic/pre-college enrichment, leadership/teamwork, and skill-building

Activities Center On: Science, math, and career exploration

Intensity Level: 5

Duration: 4–6 weeks

Program Offered: Summer

Location: Socorro, New Mexico

Accommodations: Dormitory

Years in Operation: 1

Religious Affiliation: Not relevant

STAFF

Student/Staff Ratio: 5:1

Staff Qualifications: Working scientists, science and math teachers, graduate students studying physical science, and upperclassmen majoring in physical science.

PARTICIPANTS

Average Number of Participants: 36

For Participants Aged: 15–18

The Ideal Candidate: A junior or outstanding sophomore who is near the top of the class, taking the most advanced math and science classes offered and earning top grades, and who has an interest in astronomy.

Special Requirements for Participation: None.

COSTS

Average Cost: $2,950

Included in Cost: All inclusive: tuition, room and board, supplies, local transportation.

Financial Aid Available: Yes

SUSQUEHANNA UNIVERSITY

The Writers' Institute oversees an undergraduate creative writing major staffed by three full-time, nationally recognized writers and enriched by a visiting writers series, four student-operated magazines, and a variety of internship and practicum opportunities.

Years in Operation: 16

Religious Affiliation: Not relevant

Price Range of Programs: $525

For More Information:
Contact: Gary Fincke, Workshop Director
The Writers' Institute
Susquehanna University
Selinsgrove, PA 17870
Phone: 570-372-4164
Fax: 570-372-2774
Email: gfincke@susqu.edu
Website: www.susqu.edu/writers

ADVANCED WRITERS WORKSHOP FOR HIGH SCHOOL STUDENTS

THE PROGRAM

Description: This is a one-week workshop experience in fiction, poetry, or creative nonfiction for rising high school juniors and seniors. Admission is competitive and requires a portfolio.

Specialty: The program is selective, and it is taught by widely published writers with national reputations and enriched by visits from additional guest writers.

Program Type: Academic/pre-college enrichment, music and arts

Classification: Coeducational, residential

Goals: Participants are immersed in the writing and workshopping of their creative work in fiction, poetry, or creative nonfiction.

Focus: Academic/pre-college enrichment and skill-building

Activities Center On: Writing and academic

Intensity Level: 4

Duration: 1–2 weeks

Program Offered: Summer

Location: Selinsgrove, Pennsylvania

Accommodations: Dormitory

Years in Operation: 16

Religious Affiliation: Not relevant

STAFF

Student/Staff Ratio: 7:1

Staff Qualifications: The faculty are published writers and professors; the resident assistants are current undergraduate writing majors.

PARTICIPANTS

Average Number of Participants: 42

For Participants Aged: 16–18

The Ideal Candidate: A student with experience in and enthusiasm for creative writing, preferably about to enter his or her senior year in high school.

Special Requirements for Participation: A six- to eight-page writing portfolio is required with the application.

COSTS

Average Cost: $520

Included in Cost: Everything is included: room and board, etc.

Financial Aid Available: Yes

TALISMAN SUMMER PROGRAMS

Wilderness adventure camp for children and teens with ADHD, LD, and high-functioning autism and Aspergers.

Years in Operation: 23

Religious Affiliation: Not relevant

Price Range of Programs: $2,600–$2,800

For More Information:
  Contact: Linda Tatsapaugh, Talisman Director
        126 Camp Elliott Road
        Black Mountain, NC 28711
  Phone: 828-669-8639
  Fax: 828-669-2521
  Email: summer@stonemountainschool.com
  Website: www.talismansummercamp.com

TALISMAN OPEN BOAT ADVENTURES (TOBA)

THE PROGRAM

Program Type: Outdoors/adventure

Classification: Coeducational, residential

Focus: Leadership/teamwork and skill-building

Activities Center On: Boating, camping, and outdoors and adventure

Intensity Level: 3

Duration: 2–4 weeks

Program Offered: Winter intersession/January term, summer

Location: NC, United States

Accommodations: Tent, bunk/cabin

Religious Affiliation: Not relevant

STAFF

Student/Staff Ratio: 3:1

PARTICIPANTS

For Participants Aged: 14–17

Special Requirements for Participation: None.

COSTS

Average Cost: $2,800

Financial Aid Available: No

TRAILS WILDERNESS SCHOOL

Wilderness skills camp based in Jackson Hole, Wyoming, offering trips throughout the western United States, Alaska, Canada, Mexico, and Europe.

Years in Operation: 10

Religious Affiliation: Not relevant

Price Range of Programs: $600–$4,500

For More Information:
  Contact: Whig Mullins, Director/Owner
        5 Whitegate Lane
        St. Louis, MO 63124
  Phone: 800-869-8228
  Fax: 413-723-8255
  Email: info@trailsws.com
  Website: www.trailsws.com

ALASKA LEADERSHIP

THE PROGRAM

Description: Heading into the Chugach Range for a backpacking expedition, we are surrounded by tundra, glaciers, and peaks. Teamwork and our new skills combine as we cross the four-glacier traverse. This gives us time to explore this sea of glaciers and jutting peaks. Sea kayaking, we explore the heart of Prince William Sound; we see whales, walrus, and calving blue glaciers. Next, we head to Denali National Park to backpack. Teamwork, self-reliance, and wilderness skills combine to take us across the "Last Frontier."

Specialty: Our community focus and backcountry teamwork come together to form a unique program with individual focus and challenge.

Program Type: Outdoors/adventure

Classification: Coeducational, residential

Goals: A community focus, teamwork, leadership skills, backpacking, sea kayaking, glacier travel, respect for the wilderness and each other.

Focus: Leadership/teamwork, skill-building, and travel

Activities Center On: Backpacking, kayaking, and camping

Intensity Level: 4

Duration: 2–4 weeks

Program Offered: Summer

Location: Anchorage, Alaska

Accommodations: Tent

Years in Operation: 9

Religious Affiliation: Not relevant

STAFF

Student/Staff Ratio: 1:4

Staff Qualifications: Our staff have prior wilderness experience in the area they are leading, prior experience leading high school or junior high school kids, and Wilderness First Responder and CPR certification. The average age is 30, with most having a bachelor's degree, and 50 percent having an advanced degree. We receive 1,300 applications for an average of four openings per year. We have an 85 percent staff-return rate yearly. These are professionals who enjoy working with teens in the wilderness.

PARTICIPANTS

Average Number of Participants: 10

For Participants Aged: 15–18

The Ideal Candidate: A mid-teen who is motivated to be in the outdoors and live in a group setting, and who is constantly seeking new challenges and adventure.

Special Requirements for Participation: None.

COSTS

Average Cost: $4,395

Included in Cost: All activity equipment, such as sleeping bag, backpack, kayaks, lifejackets, and climbing; food; travel to and from Anchorage International Airport; specialty activity gear, etc. Please call for more information.

Financial Aid Available: Yes

ALPINE COURSE 2

THE PROGRAM

Description: We explore some of the world's most beautiful natural environments. This is a land inhabited by eagles, moose, and big horn sheep. Our journey may take us glissading on a snowy peak, swimming in alpine lakes, or exploring high mountain meadows. Next, the group attends climbing school to learning climbing technique and safety. No previous experience is necessary. Climbing instruction builds to a summit attempt of the Grand Teton. We enjoy a final banquet to watch one last sunset over the Tetons.

Specialty: Our community focus and backcountry teamwork come together to form a unique program with individual focus and challenge.

Program Type: Outdoors/adventure

Classification: Coeducational, residential

Goals: A community focus, teamwork, leadership skills, backpacking, rock climbing, and respect for the wilderness and each other.

Focus: Leadership/teamwork, travel, and skill-building

Activities Center On: Outdoors/adventure, backpacking, and camping

Intensity Level: 3

Duration: 1–2 weeks, 2–4 weeks

Program Offered: Summer

Location: Jackson Hole, Wyoming

Accommodations: Tent

Years in Operation: 9

Religious Affiliation: Not relevant

STAFF

Student/Staff Ratio: 4:1

Staff Qualifications: Our staff have prior wilderness experience in the area they are leading, prior experience leading high school or junior high school kids, and Wilderness First Responder and CPR certification. The average age is 30, with most having a bachelor's degrees, and 50 percent having an advanced degree. We receive 1,300 applications for an average of four openings per year. We have an 85 percent staff-return rate yearly. These are professionals who enjoy working with teens in the wilderness.

PARTICIPANTS

Average Number of Participants: 10

For Participants Aged: 14–18

The Ideal Candidate: A teen who is motivated to live outdoors in a group setting, and who is constantly seeking new challenges and adventure.

Special Requirements for Participation: None.

COSTS

Average Cost: $2,195

Included in Cost: All activity equipment, such as sleeping bag, backpack, kayaks, lifejackets, and climbing gear; food; travel to and from Jackson Hole International Airport; specialty activity gear, etc. Please call for more information.

Financial Aid Available: Yes

ALPS ADVENTURE

THE PROGRAM

Description: Join us to see the highlights as we make our way across the top of the Alps! We meet in Paris. From there we tour the sights of Paris. Next we hike along the Austro-Italian border. Evening hut life finds us talking with locals and soaking up traditional Tirolean mountain culture. Making our way to Chamonix, France, we hike the world famous Haute Route through green valleys and over mountain passes along the Swiss-Italian border. Experiencing French/Swiss culture and language is our focus.

Specialty: Our community focus and backcountry teamwork come together to form a unique program with individual focus and challenge.

Program Type: Outdoors/adventure

Classification: Coeducational, residential

Goals: Students should expect to learn about French, Swiss, and Austrian culture; some German and French; and Alps etiquette; as well as a community focus, teamwork, leadership skills, and respect for the wilderness and each other.

Focus: Cultural and travel

Activities Center On: Cultural, hiking, and outdoors/adventure

Intensity Level: 2

Duration: 2–4 weeks, 4–6 weeks

Program Offered: Summer

Location: Innsbruck, Austria; Chamonix and Paris, France; Geneva, Switzerland; Germany

Accommodations: Hotels

Years in Operation: 2

Religious Affiliation: Not relevant

STAFF

Student/Staff Ratio: 4:1

Staff Qualifications: Our staff have prior wilderness experience in the area they are leading, prior experience leading high school or junior high school kids, and Wilderness First Responder and CPR certification. The average age is 30, with most having a bachelor's degree, and 50 percent having an advanced degree. We receive 1,300 applications for an average of four openings per year. We have an 85 percent staff-return rate yearly. These are professionals who enjoy working with teens in the wilderness.

PARTICIPANTS

Average Number of Participants: 10

For Participants Aged: 15–18

The Ideal Candidate: A teen who is motivated to be in the outdoors and live in a group setting, and who is constantly seeking new challenges and adventure.

Special Requirements for Participation: None.

COSTS

Average Cost: $4,345

Included in Cost: All activity equipment, such as sleeping bag and backpack; food; travel to and from an international airport; specialty activity gear, etc. Please call for more information.

Financial Aid Available: Yes

INSTRUCTOR'S COURSE

THE PROGRAM

Description: The challenges of the 30-day Instructor Course are specifically designed to develop outdoor leaders. This fast-paced program focuses on hands-on learning. The curriculum develops the skills for a well-rounded outdoor leader and instructor. We begin with the fundamentals for a successful expedition: trip planning, logistics, and outfitting. While backpacking, we expand upon leadership and decision-making with a strong emphasis on safety, group dynamics, and creating outstanding programs.

Specialty: Our community focus and backcountry teamwork come together to form a unique program with individual focus and challenge.

Program Type: Outdoors/adventure

Classification: Coeducational, residential

Goals: This fast-paced program focuses on hands-on learning. The curriculum develops the skills for a well-rounded outdoor leader and instructor. We begin with the fundamentals for a successful expedition: trip planning, logistics, and outfitting. While backpacking, we expand upon leadership and decision-making with a strong emphasis on safety, group dynamics, and creating outstanding programs. We cover snow travel, hazard evaluation, rescue procedures, teaching techniques, and much more.

Focus: Leadership/teamwork, skill-building, and travel

Activities Center On: Backpacking, camping, and outdoors/adventure

Intensity Level: 4

Duration: 4–6 weeks, 6–8 weeks

Program Offered: Summer

Location: Jackson Hole, Wyoming

Accommodations: Tent

Years in Operation: 5

Religious Affiliation: Not relevant

STAFF

Student/Staff Ratio: 4:1

Staff Qualifications: Our staff have prior wilderness experience in the area they are leading, prior experience leading high school or junior high school kids, and Wilderness First Responder and CPR certification. The average age is 30, with most having a bachelor's, and 50 percent having an advanced degree. We receive 1,300 applications for an average of four openings per year. We have an 85 percent staff-return rate yearly. These are professionals who enjoy working with teens in the wilderness.

PARTICIPANTS

Average Number of Participants: 8

For Participants Aged: 17–25

The Ideal Candidate: A young teen who is motivated to be in the outdoors and live in a group setting, and who is constantly seeking new challenges and adventure.

Special Requirements for Participation: None.

COSTS

Average Cost: $2,695

Included in Cost: All activity equipment, such as sleeping bag, backpack, kayaks, lifejackets, and climbing gear; food; travel to and from Jackson Hole International Airport; specialty activity gear, etc. Please call for more information.

Financial Aid Available: No

SKIING AND SNOWBOARDING COURSE

THE PROGRAM

Description: With expert instruction from professional guides, this course launches us onto the slopes of the Tetons. We explore special snow and terrain assessment techniques in backcountry conditions. This is the program for you if you are an experienced rider or skier with skills at the intermediate level or above. Come carve turns in the Tetons! This is some of the finest backcountry skiing and snowboarding available.

Specialty: Our community focus and backcountry teamwork come together to form a unique program with individual focus and challenge.

Program Type: Outdoors/adventure

Classification: Coeducational, residential

Goals: A community focus; teamwork; leadership skills; wilderness travel skills; local culture and language, where applicable; respect for the wilderness and each other.

Focus: Leadership/teamwork, skill-building, and travel

Activities Center On: Skiing, skiing, and backpacking

Intensity Level: 4

Duration: 1–2 weeks, 2–4 weeks

Program Offered: Summer

Location: Jackson Hole, Wyoming

Accommodations: Tent

Years in Operation: 6

Religious Affiliation: Not relevant

STAFF

Student/Staff Ratio: 2:1

Staff Qualifications: Our staff have prior wilderness experience in the area they are leading, prior experience leading high school or junior high school kids, and Wilderness First Responder and CPR certification. The average age is 30, with most having a bachelor's, and 50 percent having an advanced degree. We receive 1,300 applications for an average of four openings per year. We have an 85 percent staff-return rate yearly. These are professionals who enjoy working with teens in the wilderness.

PARTICIPANTS

Average Number of Participants: 8

For Participants Aged: 14–18

The Ideal Candidate: A young teen who is motivated to be in the outdoors and live in a group setting, who is constantly seeking new challenges and adventure.

Special Requirements for Participation: None.

COSTS

Average Cost: $2,295

Included in Cost: All activity equipment, such as sleeping bag, backpack, and climbing gear; food; all ground transportation; specialty activity gear, etc. The cost does not include skiis, snowboard, or ski poles. Please call for more information.

Financial Aid Available: Yes

WILDERNESS COURSE

THE PROGRAM

Description: Beginning with an extended backpacking expedition we explore towering peaks and serene alpine lakes of northwest Wyoming. Teamwork and personal initiative get us to our destination and beyond. Base camped in Jackson Hole, we spend the following days enjoying the graceful freedom of whitewater kayaking with professional guides. Next, we are off to climbing school, learning the fundamentals of climbing technique and safety, then attempt to climb the Grand Teton with guides.

Specialty: Our community focus and backcountry teamwork come together to form a unique program with individual focus and challenge.

Program Type: Outdoors/adventure

Classification: Coeducational, residential

Goals: A community focus; teamwork; leadership skills; wilderness travel skills; local culture and language, where applicable; and respect for the wilderness and each other. Participants will learn specific skills in backpacking, rock climbing, and whitewater kayaking.

Focus: Leadership/teamwork, skill-building, and travel

Activities Center On: Backpacking and kayaking

Intensity Level: 3

Duration: 2–4 weeks, 4–6 weeks

Program Offered: Summer

Location: Jackson Hole, Wyoming

Accommodations: Tent

Years in Operation: 9

Religious Affiliation: Not relevant

STAFF

Student/Staff Ratio: 4:1

Staff Qualifications: Our staff have prior wilderness experience in the area they are leading, prior experience leading high school or junior high school kids, and Wilderness First Responder and CPR certification. The average age is 30, with most having a bachelor's degrees, and 50 percent having an advanced degree. We receive 1,300 applications for an average of four openings per year. We have an 85 percent staff-return rate yearly. These are professionals who enjoy working with teens in the wilderness.

PARTICIPANTS

Average Number of Participants: 12

For Participants Aged: 14–18

The Ideal Candidate: A teen who is motivated to be in the outdoors and live in a group setting, and who is constantly seeking new challenges and adventure.

Special Requirements for Participation: None.

COSTS

Average Cost: $3,495

Included in Cost: All activity equipment, such as sleeping bag, backpack, kayaks, lifejackets, climbing gear; food; all ground transportation; specialty activity gear, etc. Please call for more information.

Financial Aid Available: Yes

TUFTS UNIVERSITY

Religious Affiliation: Not relevant

For More Information:
  Contact: Sean Recroft, Manager
        108 Packard Avenue
        Medford, MA 02155
  Phone: 617-627-3454
  Fax: 617-627-3295
  Email: highschool@tufts.edu
  Website: ase.tufts.edu/summer

TUFTS SUMMIT

THE PROGRAM

Program Type: Academic/pre-college enrichment

Classification: Coeducational, residential

Focus: Educational exchange and cultural

Activities Center On: Academic, language, and hiking

Intensity Level: 3

Duration: 2–4 weeks

Program Offered: Summer

Location: Talloires, France

Accommodations: Family-stay/host-family

Religious Affiliation: Not relevant

PARTICIPANTS

Average Number of Participants: 25

For Participants Aged: 16–19

Special Requirements for Participation: None.

COSTS

Average Cost: $4,550

Financial Aid Available: Yes

UNITED STATES COAST GUARD ACADEMY

Religious Affiliation: Not relevant

For More Information:
  Contact: Lt.Commander Pat Knowles, AIM Project Officer
        31 Mohegan Avenue
        New London, CT 06320
  Phone: 860-701-6780
  Fax: 860-701-6700
  Email: admissions@cga.uscg.mil
  Website: www.cga.edu/admiss

ACADEMY INTRODUCTION MISSION

THE PROGRAM

Description: AIM is a one-week summer program for rising high school seniors. AIM serves to introduce students to cadet life and the possibilities of becoming a Coast Guard officer.

Specialty: AIM is a unique program that serves as a great tool for students to experience what it would be like to be a cadet at the Coast Guard Academy and the possibilities that are available to them as officers in the Coast Guard.

Program Type: Academic/pre-college enrichment, outdoors/adventure, sports/athletic

Classification: Coeducational, residential

Goals: An introduction to the Coast Guard Academy, military bearing, teamwork, followership, and the Coast Guard.

Focus: Leadership/teamwork and academic/pre-college enrichment

Activities Center On: Military, sports/athletic, and academic

Intensity Level: 4

Duration: 1–2 weeks

Program Offered: Summer

Location: New London, Connecticut

Accommodations: Dormitory

Years in Operation: 54

Religious Affiliation: Not relevant

PARTICIPANTS

Average Number of Participants: 230

For Participants Aged: 15–18

The Ideal Candidate: An ideal candidate would be a college-bound junior entering his/her senior year who is interested in a tuition-free, four-year undergraduate program in which they would graduate with a BS and a commission in the U.S. Coast Guard.

Special Requirements for Participation: None.

COSTS

Average Cost: $150

Included in Cost: The student and family is responsible for $150 plus the transportation to and from the academy. Lodging and food will be provided at no additional cost.

Financial Aid Available: Yes

MITE

THE PROGRAM

Description: MITE is a one-week program for college-bound students entering their senior year. The program is designed to introduce students to the technical majors offered at the Coast Guard Academy, as well as give them a taste of the cadet life.

Program Type: Academic/pre-college enrichment and sports/athletic

Classification: Coeducational, residential

Goals: Students should expect to learn about the technical majors offered at the Coast Guard Academy, and about life as a cadet with regards to military bearing, athleticism, teamwork, and followership.

Focus: Academic/pre-college enrichment and leadership/teamwork

Activities Center On: Academic, military, and sports/athletic

Intensity Level: 3

Duration: 1–2 weeks

Program Offered: Summer

Location: New London, Connecticut

Accommodations: Dormitory

Religious Affiliation: Not relevant

PARTICIPANTS

Average Number of Participants: 90

For Participants Aged: 15–18

The Ideal Candidate: Students must be interested in engineering, demonstrate excellence in math and science, have completed their junior year in high school, be U.S. citizens, and be physically fit.

Special Requirements for Participation: None.

COSTS

Average Cost: $0

Included in Cost: MITE is an all-paid summer program—including transportation to and from the academy, lodging, and food—for students who are selected.

Financial Aid Available: Yes

UNIVERSITY OF CALIFORNIA— SAN DIEGO

Academic Connections is a University of California—San Diego initiative designed to provide students access to the resources of a research university. This program gives motivated students the opportunity to explore different fields of study, pursue their interest, and better prepare for a university experience. A combination of summer residential programs, year-around academies, and distance education courses will extend the reach of the university to better serve the San Diego community and beyond.

Years in Operation: 3

Religious Affiliation: Not relevant

Price Range of Programs: $550–$2,650

For More Information:
  Contact: Becky Arce, Assistant Director
        9500 Gilman Drive
        La Jolla, CA 92093
  Phone: 858-534-0804
  Fax: 858-534-8271
  Email: barce@ucsd.edu
  Website: www.academicconnections.ucsd.edu

ACADEMIC CONNECTIONS AT UCSD

THE PROGRAM

Description: Academic Connections is an opportunity for young students (grades 9–12) to explore the best the University of California—San Diego has to offer. Our goal is to help young people touch the future by exposing them to some of the most exciting fields of research. Subjects include biomedical sciences, physics, engineering, marine science, humanities/arts, social sciences, communications, and more.

Specialty: This is an intense immersion program. All courses are challenging and emphasize active learning and putting knowledge to use in independent and creative ways.

Program Type: Academic/pre-college enrichment

Classification: Coeducational, residential, day program

Goals: In-depth knowledge of a selected course of study.

Focus: Academic/pre-college enrichment

Activities Center On: Academic

Intensity Level: 5

Duration: 2–4 weeks

Program Offered: Summer

Location: La Jolla, California

Accommodations: Dormitory

Years in Operation: 3

Religious Affiliation: Not relevant

STAFF

Student/Staff Ratio: 10:1

Staff Qualifications: Current student at UCSD.

PARTICIPANTS

Average Number of Participants: 200

For Participants Aged: 14–18

The Ideal Candidate: Students must have a mimimum 3.3 GPA, be in grades 9–12, and be committed to taking charge of their educational progress.

Special Requirements for Participation: None.

COSTS

Average Cost: $2,650

Included in Cost: Room and board, activities, field trips, and class materials.

Financial Aid Available: No

CRAFT OF WRITING

THE PROGRAM

Description: The Craft of Writing is an on-line course offered by Academic Connections at the University of California—San Diego (UCSD). The course content is modeled on the successful "Writers' Workshop" popular in many writing programs across the country. Course materials for The Craft of Writing focus on the basics of writing and are derived from the live class lectures so that the curriculum maintains the same high quality as in traditional educational programs.

Program Type: Academic/pre-college enrichment

Classification: Coeducational, residential, day program

Goals: Students interact with instructors and classmates in a "real" classroom setting through online workshops and writing exercises. In 10 short weeks, students can expect to learn effective grammar and style, sharpen editing skills, and discover creative writing techniques.

Focus: Academic/pre-college enrichment

Activities Center On: Writing

Intensity Level: 3

Duration: Over 8 weeks

Program Offered: Full academic year, summer

Location: Distance education program, all 50 of the United States, American Samoa, British Columbia, Northern Mariana Islands, Guam, Manitoba, New Brunswick, Nova Scotia, Northwest Territory, Newfoundland, Ontario, Puerto Rico, Prince Edward Island, Quebec, Saskatchewan, U.S. Virgin Islands, Yukon Territory

Years in Operation:

Religious Affiliation: Not relevant

STAFF

Student/Staff Ratio: 10:1

Staff Qualifications: University writing instructors

PARTICIPANTS

Average Number of Participants: 20

For Participants Aged: 15–18

The Ideal Candidate: While the course will benefit almost any writer, it is specifically designed to prepare high school students for the demands of college-level writing.

Special Requirements for Participation: None.

COSTS

Average Cost: $550

Included in Cost: Access to on-line course and access to instructor.

Financial Aid Available: No

UNIVERSITY OF DALLAS

The University of Dallas offers a variety of summer programs abroad, allowing high school students to enjoy the unique mix of study and travel for college credit.

Years in Operation: 50

Religious Affiliation: Roman Catholic

Price Range of Programs: $3,650 plus airfare

For More Information:
   Contact: Ryan Chism, Summer Programs Coordinator
             1845 East Northgate Drive
             Irving, TX 75062
   Phone: 972-721-5181
   Fax: 972-721-5283
   Email: dsummer@udallas.edu
   Website: www.udallas.edu/udtravel

LATIN IN ROME

THE PROGRAM

Description: High school students who attend the program travel to our campus just outside of Rome, Italy. Both on campus and at ancient sites in and around Rome and the Bay of Naples, students study Latin texts of Virgil, Livy, Cicero, and Horace with faculty of the University of Dallas Classics Department. The three-week program earns the students 3 credits of intermediate college Latin.

Specialty: The unique combination of study and travel coupled with the unparalleled experience of studying texts at their original sites.

Program Type: Academic/pre-college enrichment, travel/cultural

Classification: Coeducational, residential

Goals: Students participating in Latin in Rome will gain experience in sight reading and translation of great Latin texts. In addition, students will visit the sights about which they may have only read.

Focus: Academic/pre-college enrichment and travel

Activities Center On: Academic, travel, and language

Intensity Level: 3

Duration: 2–4 weeks

Program Offered: Summer

Location: Rome, Italy

Accommodations: Dormitory

Years in Operation: 8

Religious Affiliation: Roman Catholic

STAFF

Student/Staff Ratio: 6:1

Staff Qualifications: The program director is a UD faculty member who has previous experience teaching abroad. The rest of the staff is made up of undergraduate and graduate students in related fields who have prior experience working with UD summer programs abroad.

PARTICIPANTS

Average Number of Participants: 30

For Participants Aged: 16+

The Ideal Candidate: Students are expected to be rising juniors or seniors.

Special Requirements for Participation: Students are required to have completed three years of high school Latin before attending the course.

COSTS

Average Cost: $3,600

Included in Cost: The cost of the program includes room and board, travel fees, and course materials. It does not include airfare.

Financial Aid Available: Yes

SHAKESPEARE IN ITALY

THE PROGRAM

Description: Students study Shakespeare's Julius Caesar and The Tempest at the University of Dallas campus in Rome, Italy. In addition, students explore Italian and Reniassance culture in the historic cities of Rome, Venice, Urbino, and Albano, earning 3 college credits.

Specialty: The unique combination of study and travel, as well as the unparalleled experience of visiting the sites about which most students only read.

Program Type: Academic/pre-college enrichment, travel/cultural

Classification: Coeducational, residential

Goals: The participant should expect to come away from the program with greater understanding and appreciation of Shakespeare and the Italian Rennaissance as well as their place in the literary and cultural tradition of the West.

Focus: Academic/pre-college enrichment, travel, and cultural

Activities Center On: Academic, travel, and liberal arts

Intensity Level: 4

Duration: 2–4 weeks

Program Offered: Summer

Location: Rome, Italy

Accommodations: Dormitory

Years in Operation: 9

Religious Affiliation: Roman Catholic

STAFF

Student/Staff Ratio: 6:1

Staff Qualifications: The program director is a faculty member of the University of Dallas English Department with prior experience teaching abroad. The rest of the staff consist of graduate and undergraduate students who have previously studied abroad.

PARTICIPANTS

Average Number of Participants: 30

For Participants Aged: 15+

The Ideal Candidate: Participating students should be thoughtful, academically serious, and prepared for an intensive study of the texts.

Special Requirements for Participation: Participating students should be rising juniors or seniors in high school.

COSTS

Average Cost: $3,600

Included in Cost: The cost of the program includes room and board, travel fees, and course materials. The price does not include airfare.

Financial Aid Available: Yes

THOMAS MORE IN ENGLAND

THE PROGRAM

Description: Students travel to England with faculty and staff of the University of Dallas to study the life and works of Thomas More in and around the sites of London, Oxford, Canturbury, and Stratford-on-Avon. Text's include Robert Bolt's A Man for All Seasons, Shakespeare's Richard III, and More's own Utopia. Students who complete the course earn 3 college credits.

Specialty: The unique combination of study and travel, as well as the unparalleled experience of visiting the sites about which most students only read.

Program Type: Academic/pre-college enrichment, travel/cultural

Classification: Coeducational, residential

Goals: Students should expect to come away from the program with a greater appreciation for Thomas More's contributions to the intellectual tradition of the West.

Focus: Academic/pre-college enrichment, travel, and cultural

Activities Center On: Academic, travel, and liberal arts

Intensity Level: 4

Duration: 2–4 weeks

Program Offered: Summer

Location: Berkshire, United Kingdom

Accommodations: Dormitory

Years in Operation: 5

Religious Affiliation: Roman Catholic

STAFF

Student/Staff Ratio: 5:1

Staff Qualifications: The program director is a faculty member of the University of Dallas English Department with prior experience teaching abroad. The rest of the staff consist of graduate and undergraduate students who have previously studied abroad.

PARTICIPANTS

Average Number of Participants: 30

For Participants Aged: 16+

The Ideal Candidate: Students who participate should be thoughtful, academically serious, and prepared for an intensive and rewarding study of the texts.

Special Requirements for Participation: Students should be rising juniors or seniors in high school.

COSTS

Average Cost: $3,600

Included in Cost: The cost of the program includes room and board, travel fees, and course materials. The price does not include airfare.

Financial Aid Available: Yes

WINSTON CHURCHILL IN ENGLAND

THE PROGRAM

Description: High school students travel to England with University of Dallas faculty and staff to study the life and works of Winston Churchill. Sites include Parliament, the Imerial War Museum, the Cabinet War Room, and Blenheim Palace. Texts include Churchill's My Early Life, The Second World War, and The History of English-Speaking Peoples. Students who complete the course will earn 3 college credits.

Specialty: The unique combination of study and travel combined with the unparalleled experience of visiting the sites about which most students only read.

Program Type: Academic/pre-college enrichment, travel/cultural

Classification: Coeducational, residential

Goals: Students should expect to come away from the program with a greater appreciation for Winston Churchill's dynamic role in the history of the twentieth century.

Focus: Academic/pre-college enrichment, travel, and cultural

Activities Center On: Academic, travel, and history

Intensity Level: 4

Duration: 2–4 weeks

Program Offered: Summer

Location: Berkshire, United Kingdom

Accommodations: Dormitory

Years in Operation: 5

Religious Affiliation: Roman Catholic

STAFF

Student/Staff Ratio: 5:1

PARTICIPANTS

Average Number of Participants: 30

For Participants Aged: 16+

The Ideal Candidate: Students should be thoughtful, academically serious, and prepared for and intensive and rewarding study of the subject.

Special Requirements for Participation: Students should be rising juniors or seniors in high school.

COSTS

Average Cost: $3,600

Included in Cost: The cost of the program includes room and board, travel fees, and course materials. The price does not include airfare.

Financial Aid Available: Yes

UNIVERSITY OF DELAWARE

Years in Operation: 20

Religious Affiliation: Not relevant

For More Information:
Contact: Elizabeth B. Reynolds, Coordinator
206 Elliott Hall
Newark, DE 19716
Phone: 302-831-6560
Fax: 302-831-4339
Email: summercollege@udel.edu
Website: www.udel.edu/summercollege

UNIVERSITY OF DELAWARE SUMMER COLLEGE PROGRAM

THE PROGRAM

Description: A five-week pre-college program for rising high school seniors in which they take two courses for credit, live in dorms, enjoy many activities, and prepare for college.

Specialty: Affordability; location in a quiet college town but near cities; small enough for personal attention but large enough to make many new friends.

Program Type: Academic/pre-college enrichment

Classification: Coeducational, residential

Goals: Adaptation to dormitory life, time management, intellectual stimulation, increased maturity.

Focus: Academic/pre-college enrichment

Activities Center On: Academic

Intensity Level: 3

Duration: 4–6 weeks

Program Offered: Summer

Location: Newark, Delaware

Accommodations: Dormitory

Years in Operation: 20

Religious Affiliation: Not relevant

STAFF

Student/Staff Ratio: 12:1

Staff Qualifications: The staff is selected from UD undergraduates.

PARTICIPANTS

Average Number of Participants: 130

For Participants Aged: 16–18

The Ideal Candidate: 3.0 or higher in rigorous high school courses, PSAT of 1000 or higher, emotional maturity, intellectual curiosity.

Special Requirements for Participation: None.

COSTS

Average Cost: $3,700

Included in Cost: $3,650 in 2003. The cost includes room and board, tuition, tickets and transportation for day trips, and cultural events. Textbooks and spending money are not included.

Financial Aid Available: Yes

UNIVERSITY OF MIAMI

Religious Affiliation: Not relevant

For More Information:
Contact: Brian Blythe, Director of High School Programs
Allen Hall 111
PO Box 248005
Coral Gables, FL 33124
Phone: 305-284-6107
Fax: 305-284-2620
Email: ssp.cstudies@miami.edu
Website: www.summerscholar.miami.edu

SUMMER SCHOLAR PROGRAMS

THE PROGRAM

Description: The University of Miami Summer Scholar Programs offer three-week intensive programs in areas such as broadcast journalism, filmmaking, health and medicine, marine science, and sports management. Students experience college life at a major research university while taking a customized program of study that includes lectures, laboratories, and field trips.

Specialty: SSP gives students a chance to see what college life in general and the University of Miami in particular is like while exploring an area of interest and earning college credit, all in the subtropics of south Florida.

Program Type: Academic/pre-college enrichment

Classification: Coeducational, residential

Goals: Summer Scholar Programs (SSP) provides participants hands-on and theoretical classroom experiences.

Focus: Academic/pre-college enrichment

Activities Center On: Academic, career exploration, and camping

Intensity Level: 4

Duration: 2–4 weeks

Program Offered: Summer

Location: Coral Gables, Florida

Accommodations: Dormitory

Years in Operation: 12

Religious Affiliation: Not relevant

STAFF

Student/Staff Ratio: 14:1

Staff Qualifications: Scholars are taught by University of Miami faculty. Resident assistants (UM resident assistants and/or former SSP participants currently attending UM) live on the floors of the residential hall with the scholars.

PARTICIPANTS

Average Number of Participants: 115

For Participants Aged: 16–17

The Ideal Candidate: Students should have high academic standards and a desire to explore new career opportunities.

Special Requirements for Participation: All applicants must submit an application, a letter of introduction, a recommendation, and an official high school transcript. Students interested in health and medicine must have Bs in two science courses, one of which must be biology.

COSTS

Average Cost: $3,900

Included in Cost: The fees include tuition, housing, meals, lab fees, field/fun trips, etc. Students should bring extra spending money for free time.

Financial Aid Available: Yes

UNIVERSITY OF PENNSYLVANIA

Summer at Penn is a rich experience intellectually, socially, and culturally. Study in the nation's largest open-stack library, visit world-renowned museums, take advantage of our state-of-the-art laboratories and facilities, and enjoy the innumerable resources of a premier university in one of the nation's greatest cities. The largest university research complex in the Mid-Atlantic, the University of Pennsylvania is one of the world's leading educational, research, and health services institutions. A private university and member of the Ivy League, Penn has a reputation for academic excellence that draw tens of thousands of students, researchers, entrepreneurs, and visitors to the region each year.

Religious Affiliation: Not relevant

For More Information:
   Contact: Emma Foley, Assistant Director of Summer
           Sessions
           3440 Market Street
           Suite 100
           Philadelphia, PA 19104
   Phone: 215-898-5716
   Fax: 215-573-2053
   Email: summer@sas.upenn.edu
   Website: www.upenn.edu/summer

PRECOLLEGE PROGRAM

THE PROGRAM

Description: The Precollege Program at Penn permits qualified participants to take classes with regular undergraduates in Penn courses. Students who successfully complete these courses receive college credit from Penn and an official transcript from the university. These credits will apply toward a Penn degree and are also generally easy to transfer to other universities. (It's always best to check with the particular university beforehand if credit transferability is a concern.)

Program Type: Academic/pre-college enrichment, music and arts

Classification: Coeducational, residential, day program

Focus: Academic/pre-college enrichment

Activities Center On: Academic

Intensity Level: 5

Duration: 6–8 weeks

Program Offered: Summer

Location: Philadelphia, Pennsylvania

Accommodations: Dormitory

Religious Affiliation: Not relevant

PARTICIPANTS

Average Number of Participants: 300

For Participants Aged: 15–18

Special Requirements for Participation: None.

COSTS

Average Cost: $4,500

Included in Cost: These figures include room, dining service (three meals per day, Monday through Friday), workshops, and most activities. One course (1 credit unit): $4,300; two courses (2 credit units): $6,200.

Financial Aid Available: Yes

UNIVERSITY OF SOUTHERN CALIFORNIA, SCHOOL OF ARCHITECTURE

Religious Affiliation: Not relevant

For More Information:
   Contact: Jennifer Park, Undergraduate Admission
           Watt Hall 204
           Los Angeles, CA 90089
   Phone: 213-740-2420
   Fax: 213-740-8884
   Email: jenpark@usc.edu
   Website: www.usc.edu/dept/architechture/explor/

Exploration of Architecture

The Program

Description: Students who are considering a career in architecture, landscape architecture, engineering, or urban planning have the chance to explore interests in a studio setting at one of the top architecture schools in the country. This summer program lasts either one, two, or three weeks, depending upon the student's level of interest.

Specialty: As it is interest based, no transcripts or test scores are required.

Program Type: Academic/pre-college enrichment

Classification: Coeducational, residential

Focus: Academic/pre-college enrichment

Intensity Level: 4

Duration: 1–2 weeks, 2–4 weeks

Program Offered: Summer

Location: Los Angeles, California

Accommodations: Dormitory

Religious Affiliation: Not relevant

Participants

Average Number of Participants: 100

For Participants Aged: 15–18

The Ideal Candidate: Any student interested in learning about architecture.

Special Requirements for Participation: None.

Costs

Average Cost: $1,850

Included in Cost: 1 week: $1,075; 2 weeks: $1,850; 3 weeks: $2,450. (Transportation to Los Angeles and supplies are included.)

Financial Aid Available: Yes

VISIONS SERVICE ADVENTURES

Visions Service Adventures offers summer experiences for teenagers that blend construction-based and other service work, intercultural learning, and outdoor exploration. Some programs offer Spanish or French language immersion. A maximum of 25 students and 6 experienced leaders live in the heart of host communities where the projects accomplished add to and improve local resources. Beginning with a small group committed to a common goal, Visions is a journey of discovery and shared accomplishment. Visions has program sites in Alaska and Montana native communities, South Carolina Sea Islands, Australia, Peru, British Virgin Islands, Trinidad, Dominica, Dominican Republic, Guadeloupe.

Years in Operation: 15

Religious Affiliation: Not relevant

Price Range of Programs: $2,600–$3,950

For More Information:

Contact: Joanne Pinaire, Director
PO Box 220
110 North 2nd Street
Newport, PA 17074
Phone: 717-567-7313
Fax: 717-567-7853
Email: visions@pa.net
Website: www.VisionsServiceAdventures.com

Visions Alaska

The Program

Description: Participants will live and work about five hours northeast of Anchorage in native Ahtna villages near Wrangell-St. Elias National Preserve. Construction projects have included finish work to log milling, bridges, playgrounds, community buildings, and basketball courts. Hike, backpack, and ice climb in Wrangell Mountains. Play basketball with local kids. Spend time with village elders. Learn beadwork while listening to stories of Alaska life. Ladle water onto the hot rocks in an Athabaskan steambath.

Specialty: Deep ties and exposure to host communities; careful planning and preparation ahead of participants' arrival; technical skills applied to projects that benefit the community; deliberate communication process and team-building; high caliber, committed staff.

Program Type: Community service, outdoors/adventure, travel/cultural

Classification: Coeducational, residential

Goals: Hard technical skills—both building/construction skills and outdoor skills; new perspective on lives very different from one's own; Athabascan native culture, history, and traditions, as well as present-day life in Athabascan village; increased self-confidence; community-living skills.

Focus: Community service, cultural, and leadership/teamwork

Activities Center On: Cultural and wilderness

Intensity Level: 3

Duration: 2–4 weeks

Program Offered: Summer

Location: Tanacross, Alaska

Years in Operation: 8

Religious Affiliation: Not relevant

Staff

Student/Staff Ratio: 4:1

Staff Qualifications: Minimum age 22; average age mid- to late 20s; first aid, CPR, WFA, or WFR certified; experience working with teens and living in other than mainstream U.S. culture; enthusiasm for and proven commitment to Visions' mission of cross-cultural community service and cross-cultural learning.

PARTICIPANTS

Average Number of Participants: 23

For Participants Aged: 14–18

The Ideal Candidate: Motivated, curious, and open-minded; willing to push personal comfort zone; team player; does not come with a friend.

Special Requirements for Participation: None.

COSTS

Average Cost: $3,100

Included in Cost: Cost includes everything except airfare.

Financial Aid Available: Yes

VISIONS AUSTRALIA

THE PROGRAM

Description: Visions' is at the southern tip of the Great Barrier Reef in the coastal town of Hervey Bay where about 1,000 Aboriginals live. Our home base is Scrub Hill Farm, which is 10 minutes from town. The 70-acre organic farm, an Aboriginal initiative, is an education/training/employment center. Collaborative projects add to the farm's resources and facilities. Work with and learn from elders, craftspersons, storytellers. Swim with dolphins. Watch wildlife in the wild. Explore extraordinary Fraser Island.

Specialty: Deep ties and exposure to host communities; careful planning and preparation ahead of participants' arrival; technical skills applied to projects that benefit community; multi-faceted; deliberate communication process; high caliber, committed staff.

Program Type: Community service, outdoors/adventure, travel/cultural

Classification: Coeducational, residential

Goals: Technical skills, including building/construction skills; new perspective on lives very different from one's own; Aboriginal culture, history, traditions, and challenges of present-day life; Australia flora and fauna; increased self-confidence; community-living skills.

Focus: Community service, cultural, and leadership/teamwork

Activities Center On: Cultural and outdoors/adventure

Intensity Level: 3

Duration: 2–4 weeks

Program Offered: Summer

Location: Hervey Bay, Australia

Years in Operation: 3

Religious Affiliation: Not relevant

STAFF

Student/Staff Ratio: 4:1

Staff Qualifications: Minimum age 22; average age mid- to late 20s; first aid, CPR, WFA, or WFR certified; experience working with teens and living in other than mainstream U.S. culture; enthusiasm for and proven commitment to Visions' mission of cross-cultural community service and cross-cultural learning.

PARTICIPANTS

Average Number of Participants: 23

For Participants Aged: 14–18

The Ideal Candidate: Motivated, curious, and open-minded; willing to push personal comfort zone; team player; does not come with a friend.

Special Requirements for Participation: None.

COSTS

Average Cost: $3,900

Included in Cost: Cost does not include airfare.

Financial Aid Available: Yes

VISIONS BRITISH VIRGIN ISLANDS

THE PROGRAM

Description: The British Virgin Islands are classic Caribbean. White sand beaches, turquoise waters, shimmering green mountains. Unlike the U.S. Virgins, Tortola and Virgin Gorda are mostly undeveloped. Participants have built houses, playgrounds, public shelters, and park structures, and have renovated public schools and hurricane shelters. VISIONS volunteers assist in summer school programs and help harvest farmers' crops for market. Swim, snorkel, dive, dance, play basketball with local teens, listen to steel drums, explore.

Specialty: Deep ties and exposure to host communities; careful planning and preparation ahead of participants' arrival; technical skills applied to projects that benefit the community; deliberate communication process and team-building; high caliber, committed staff.

Program Type: Community service, outdoors/adventure, travel/cultural

Classification: Coeducational, residential

Goals: Hard technical skills, including building/construction skills; new perspective on lives very different from one's own; Caribbean culture, history, and traditions, as well as present-day life; increased self-confidence; community-living skills.

Focus: Community service, cultural, and leadership/teamwork

Activities Center On: Cultural and outdoors/adventure

Intensity Level: 3

Duration: 2–4 weeks

Program Offered: Summer

Location: Road Town, British Virgin Islands

Years in Operation: 12

Religious Affiliation: Not relevant

STAFF

Student/Staff Ratio: 4:1

Staff Qualifications: Minimum age 22; average age mid- to late 20s; first aid, CPR, WFA, or WFR certified; experience working with teens and living in other than mainstream U.S. culture; enthusiasm for and proven commitment to Visions' mission of cross-cultural community service and cross-cultural learning.

PARTICIPANTS

Average Number of Participants: 23

For Participants Aged: 14–18

The Ideal Candidate: Motivated, curious, and open-minded; willing to push personal comfort zone; team player; does not come with a friend.

Special Requirements for Participation: None.

COSTS

Average Cost: $3,100

Included in Cost: Cost does not include airfare.

Financial Aid Available: Yes

VISIONS DOMINICA

THE PROGRAM

Description: The Caribbean's Nature Island. 365 rivers and streams. Most of Dominica is a rainforest mountain range teeming with birds and fragrant flowers. Visions lives in Carib Indian Territory off the northeast coast, where resources are few and primitive. Some past projects include constructing a pre-school building, bus shelter, library, road, and community garage. Work with Carib children. Swim or snorkel coral reefs off isolated beaches. Tour Roseau and Marigot. Hike to Victoria and Trafalgar Falls.

Specialty: Deep ties and exposure to host communities; careful planning and preparation ahead of participants' arrival; technical skills applied to projects that benefit community; multi-faceted; deliberate communication process; high caliber, committed staff.

Program Type: Community service, outdoors/adventure, travel/cultural

Classification: Coeducational, residential

Goals: Technical skills, including building/construction; new perspective on lives very different from one's own;culture, history, and tradition of the Carib people; new flora and fauna; increased self-confidence; community-living skills.

Focus: Community service, cultural, and leadership/teamwork

Activities Center On: Cultural and outdoors/adventure

Intensity Level: 3

Duration: 2–4 weeks

Program Offered: Summer

Location: Roseau, Dominica

Years in Operation: 8

Religious Affiliation: Not relevant

STAFF

Student/Staff Ratio: 4:1

Staff Qualifications: Minimum age 22; average age mid- to late 20s; first aid, CPR, WFA, or WFR certified; experience working with teens and living in other than mainstream U.S. culture; enthusiasm for and proven commitment to Visions' mission of cross-cultural community service and cross-cultural learning.

PARTICIPANTS

Average Number of Participants: 23

For Participants Aged: 14–18

The Ideal Candidate: Motivated, curious, and open-minded; willing to push personal comfort zone; team player; does not come with a friend.

Special Requirements for Participation: None.

COSTS

Average Cost: $3,650

Included in Cost: Cost does not include airfare.

Financial Aid Available: Yes

VISIONS DOMINICAN REPUBLIC

THE PROGRAM

Description: A buoyant, welcoming nation and people. Visions collaborates with local service organizations and many old friends. We work and recreate with Dominican teens. With maestros assistance, we build homes, schools, parks. Participants also operate Campamento de Juveniles every summer for young children. Visit markets, Santo Domingo's historic colonial section, and sugar cane plantations. Dance to merengue. Swim off white sand beaches in clear blue waters. Hike the Dominican Alps. Homestay component two to four days.

Specialty: Deep ties and exposure to host community; careful planning and preparation ahead of participants' arrival; technical skills applied to projects that benefit the community.

Program Type: Community service, outdoors/adventure, travel/cultural

Classification: Coeducational, residential

Goals: Improved Spanish; hard technical skills, including building/construction skills; new perspective on lives very different from one's own; Dominican culture, history, and the conditions and challenges of modern life in the Dominican Republic; increased self-confidence; community-living skills.

Focus: Community service, cultural, and leadership/teamwork

Activities Center On: Cultural and outdoors/adventure

Intensity Level: 3

Duration: 2–4 weeks

Program Offered: Summer

Location: Santo Domingo and San Pedro de Marcoris, Dominican Republic

Accommodations: Other

Years in Operation: 13

Religious Affiliation: Not relevant

STAFF

Student/Staff Ratio: 4:1

Staff Qualifications: Minimum age 22; average age mid- to late 20s; first aid, CPR, WFA, or WFR certified; experience working with teens and living in other than mainstream U.S. culture; enthusiasm for and proven commitment to Visions' mission of cross-cultural community service and cross-cultural learning.

PARTICIPANTS

Average Number of Participants: 23

For Participants Aged: 14–18

The Ideal Candidate: Motivated, curious, and open-minded; willing to push personal comfort zone; team player; does not come with a friend.

Special Requirements for Participation: Minimum of two years high school Spanish or equivalent fluency.

COSTS

Average Cost: $3,175

Included in Cost: Cost does not include airfare.

Financial Aid Available: Yes

VISIONS GUADELOUPE

THE PROGRAM

Description: Visions collaborates with Guadeloupe's Department of Youth and Culture. Participants work with local teens on projects such as building community parks and playgrounds, renovating schools, designing murals, and assisting in summer school programs. Experience Guadeloupe's culture: Beguine dancing, Zouk music, Gwoka drumming, exotic marketplaces, prehistoric pictographs. Hike in the national park, to waterfalls, rain forests, and La Soufriere volcano. Swim and snorkel in turquoise waters. Scuba dive in one of Jaques Cousteau's favorite lagoons.

Specialty: Deep ties and exposure to host community; careful planning and preparation ahead of participants' arrival; technical skills applied to projects that benefit the community; multi-faceted; deliberate communication process; high caliber, committed staff.

Program Type: Community service, travel/cultural

Classification: Coeducational, residential

Goals: Hard technical skills, including building/construction skills; new perspective on lives very different from one's own; improved French language skills; French Caribbean culture, history, traditions, and present-day life in Caribbean;

increased self-confidence; community-living skills.

Focus: Cultural, community service, and leadership/teamwork

Activities Center On: Cultural and outdoors/adventure

Intensity Level: 2

Duration: 2–4 weeks

Program Offered: Summer

Location: Basse Terre

Years in Operation: 8

Religious Affiliation: Not relevant

STAFF

Student/Staff Ratio: 4:1

Staff Qualifications: Minimum age 22; average age mid- to late 20s; first aid, CPR, WFA, or WFR certified; experience working with teens and living in other than mainstream U.S. culture; enthusiasm for and proven commitment to Visions' mission of cross-cultural community service and cross-cultural learning.

PARTICIPANTS

Average Number of Participants: 23

For Participants Aged: 14–18

The Ideal Candidate: Motivated, curious, open-minded; willing to push personal comfort zone; team player who wants to improve French language skills; does not come with a friend.

Special Requirements for Participation: Minimum two years high school French or equivalent fluency.

COSTS

Average Cost: $3,750

Included in Cost: Cost does not include airfare.

Financial Aid Available: Yes

VISIONS MONTANA

THE PROGRAM

Description: Participants discover Native American culture while living in a Plains Indian Reservation community. Service has included building playgrounds, softball fields, dugouts, basketball courts, picnic pavilions, additions to community buildings, elders' homes, and ceremonial structures. Meet tribal historians, storytellers, and spiritual leaders. Enter a sweat lodge. Learn beading. Attend a pow wow. Rock climb, raft, hike, and backpack in the Beartooth Mountains, Rocky Mountains, or Glacier Park.

Specialty: Deep ties and exposure to host community; careful planning and preparation ahead of participants' arrival; technical skills applied to projects that benefit the community; deliberate communication process and team-building; high caliber, committed staff.

Program Type: Community service, outdoors/adventure, travel/cultural

Classification: Coeducational, residential

Goals: Technical skills—both construction and outdoor skills; new perspectives on lives very different from one's own; Plains Indian culture and traditions as well as present-day life on a reservation; increased self-confidence; community-living skills.

Focus: Community service, cultural, and leadership/teamwork

Activities Center On: Cultural and wilderness

Intensity Level: 3

Duration: 2–4 weeks

Program Offered: Summer

Location: Browning and Lame Deer, Montana

Accommodations: Other

Years in Operation: 13

Religious Affiliation: Not relevant

STAFF

Student/Staff Ratio: 4:1

Staff Qualifications: Minimum age 22; average age mid- to late 20s; first aid, CPR, WFA, or WFR certified; experience working with teens and living in other than mainstream U.S. culture; enthusiasm for and proven commitment to Visions' mission of cross-cultural community service and cross-cultural learning.

PARTICIPANTS

Average Number of Participants: 23

For Participants Aged: 14–18

The Ideal Candidate: Motivated, curious, and open-minded; willing to push personal comfort zone; team player; does not come with a friend.

Special Requirements for Participation: None.

COSTS

Average Cost: $3,100

Included in Cost: Cost includes everything except airfare.

Financial Aid Available: Yes

VISIONS PERU

THE PROGRAM

Description: We live in Urubamba in the Andean highlands one hour from Cusco. Assist in adobe construction of community buildings, volunteer in schools, or participate in internships with small businesses. Meet artisans, farmers, teachers, officials, and musicians. Hike the Inca trail tp Machu Picchu. Tour ancient markets. Travel to Cusco, the oldest continually inhabited city in the Americas, with gilded artwork in Spanish cathedrals, the historic Plaza de Armas, and the fortress of Saqsaywaman, whose walls boast 125-ton stones.

Specialty: Deep ties and exposure to host community; careful planning and preparation ahead of participants' arrival; tech-

nical skills applied to projects that benefit the community; multi-faceted; deliberate communication process; high caliber, committed staff.

Program Type: Community service, outdoors/adventure, travel/cultural

Classification: Coeducational, residential

Goals: Technical skills, including building/construction skills; new perspective on lives very different from one's own; Peru and Inca culture, history, traditions as well as present-day life in Peru; improved Spanish language skills; increased self-confidence; community-living skills.

Focus: Community service, cultural, and leadership/teamwork

Activities Center On: Cultural and outdoors/adventure

Intensity Level: 3

Duration: 2–4 weeks

Program Offered: Summer

Location: Urubamba and Cusco, Peru

Accommodations: Dormitory

Years in Operation: 5

Religious Affiliation: Not relevant

STAFF

Student/Staff Ratio: 4:1

Staff Qualifications: Minimum age 22; average age mid- to late 20s; first aid, CPR, WFA, or WFR certified; experience working with teens and living in other than mainstream U.S. culture; enthusiasm for and proven commitment to Visions' mission of cross-cultural community service and cross-cultural learning.

PARTICIPANTS

Average Number of Participants: 23

For Participants Aged: 14–18

The Ideal Candidate: Motivated, curious, open-minded; willing to push personal comfort zone; team player who wants to improve French language skills; does not come with a friend.

Special Requirements for Participation: Minimum two years of high school Spanish or equivalent fluency.

COSTS

Average Cost: $3,400

Included in Cost: Cost does not include airfare.

Financial Aid Available: Yes

VISIONS SOUTH CAROLINA

THE PROGRAM

Description: Visions' site on St. Helena Island, South Carolina, is a part of the United States that is visually stunning and historically intriguing. We work on a sea island, one among hundreds that stretch down the coast to northern

Florida. The people of these communities are mostly descendents of slaves that worked plantations centuries ago. The islands' isolation influenced a unique language and culture called Gullah. Gullah is a Creolized composite of words from English and several African tongues.

Specialty: Deep ties and exposure to host community; careful planning and preparation ahead of participants' arrival; technical skills applied to projects that benefit the community; multi-faceted; deliberate communication process; high caliber, committed staff.

Program Type: Community service, outdoors/adventure, travel/cultural

Classification: Coeducational, residential

Goals: Technical skills—both construction and outdoor skills; new perspectives on lives very different from one's own; Gullah culture and traditions as well as present-day life; increased self-confidence; community-living skills.

Focus: Community service, cultural, and leadership/teamwork

Activities Center On: Cultural and outdoors/adventure

Intensity Level: 2

Duration: 2–4 weeks

Program Offered: Summer

Location: St. Helena Island, South Carolina

Accommodations: Dormitory

Years in Operation: 7

Religious Affiliation: Not relevant

STAFF

Student/Staff Ratio: 4:1

Staff Qualifications: Minimum age 22; average age mid- to late 20s; first aid, CPR, WFA, or WFR certified; experience working with teens and living in other than mainstream U.S. culture; enthusiasm for and proven commitment to Visions' mission of cross-cultural community service and cross-cultural learning.

PARTICIPANTS

Average Number of Participants: 23

For Participants Aged: 14–18

The Ideal Candidate: Motivated, curious, open-minded; willing to push personal comfort zone; team player; does not come with a friend.

Special Requirements for Participation: None.

COSTS

Average Cost: $3,400

Included in Cost: Cost includes everything but airfare.

Financial Aid Available: Yes

VOLUNTEERS FOR PEACE INTERNATIONAL WORK CAMPS

VFP offers more than 2,400 affordable international voluntary service projects worldwide. Since 1982, we have exchanged over 20,000 volunteers with our partners in more than 90 countries. These programs are an affordable way to complete meaningful community service while living and interacting in an international environment. VFP has opportunities throughout Africa, Asia, Australia, Europe, Latin America, and Russia.

Years in Operation: 23

Religious Affiliation: Not relevant

Price Range of Programs: $200–$400

For More Information:
Contact: Peter Coldwell, Director
1034 Tiffany Road
Belmont, VT 05730
Phone: 802-259-2759
Fax: 802-259-2922
Email: vfp@vfp.org
Website: www.vfp.org

VOLUNTEERS FOR PEACE INTERNATIONAL WORK CAMP

THE PROGRAM

Description: VFP offers more than 2,400 affordable international voluntary service projects in more than 90 countries. Since 1982, we have exchanged over 21,000 volunteers.

Specialty: Volunteers from more than four countries live and work together while focusing on a meaningful community service project.

Program Type: Community service, travel/cultural

Classification: Coeducational, residential

Goals: Participants live and work with an international group from four or more countries for two to three weeks, providing a diverse cultural exchange with the other volunteers as well as the local hosts. Twenty-five percent of VFP volunteers participate in multiple camps in the same or different countries. Volunteers will learn to relate to other volunteers and the hosting community.

Focus: Community service, leadership/teamwork, and travel

Activities Center On: Cultural, volunteer, and travel

Intensity Level: 3

Duration: 2–4 weeks, 6–8 weeks, over 8 weeks

Program Offered: Fall, winter intersession/January term, spring, full academic year, summer

Location: Various: Alaska; Arkansas; California; Florida; Hawaii; Iowa; Illinois; Indiana; Kansas; Massachusetts; Maine; Michigan; Montana; Missouri; Missippi; New Hampshire; New Jersey; New York; Ohio; Oregon; Pennsylvania; Rhode Island; South Dakota; Tennessee; Texas;

Virginia; Vermont; Washington; Washington, DC; Wisconsin; West Virginia; British Columbia, Nova Scotia, and Quebec, Canada; over 90 countries

Accommodations: Dormitory, tent, bunk/cabin, youth hostels

Years in Operation: 21

Religious Affiliation: Not relevant

STAFF

Student/Staff Ratio: 12:1

Staff Qualifications: Previous international work-camp experience.

PARTICIPANTS

Average Number of Participants: 800

For Participants Aged: 15+

The Ideal Candidate: Motivated person with a strong interest in other cultures.

Special Requirements for Participation: Strong motivation.

COSTS

Average Cost: $200

Included in Cost: The standard VFP fee of $200 covers full room and board for the duration of the program.

Financial Aid Available: No

WASHINGTON AND LEE UNIVERSITY

Years in Operation: 23

Religious Affiliation: Not relevant

Price Range of Programs: $2,200

For More Information:
  Contact: Mimi Milner Elrod, Director
        Hill House
        218 West Washington Street
        Lexington, VA 24450
  Phone: 540-458-8727
  Fax: 540-458-8113
  Email: summerscholars@wlu.edu
  Website: summerscholars.wlu.edu

SUMMER SCHOLARS

THE PROGRAM

Description: This program gives college-bound students the opportunity to experience college life. Participants choose an area of study from: American politics, business and economics, brain and behavioral sciences, environmental studies, humanities, journalism, law and society, and pre-medical studies. Students may participate in a chorus, art classes, a

writing lab, intramural athletics, and field trips to local attractions.

Specialty: Self-contained; designed with rising senior in mind.

Program Type: Academic/pre-college enrichment

Classification: Coeducational, residential

Goals: Learning the content of courses; discovering about self; getting along with a wide variety of people.

Focus: Academic/pre-college enrichment

Activities Center On: Academic

Intensity Level: 3

Duration: 2–4 weeks

Program Offered: Summer

Location: Lexington, Virginia

Accommodations: Dormitory

Years in Operation: 23

Religious Affiliation: Not relevant

STAFF

Student/Staff Ratio: 15:1

Staff Qualifications: Must be excellent in area of study.

PARTICIPANTS

Average Number of Participants: 150

For Participants Aged: 17+

The Ideal Candidate: Strong academic credentials.

Special Requirements for Participation: None.

COSTS

Average Cost: $2,200

Financial Aid Available: Yes

WASHINGTON UNIVERSITY IN ST. LOUIS

Religious Affiliation: Not relevant

For More Information:
  Contact: Marsha Hussung
        1 Brookings Drive
        St. Louis, MO 63130
  Phone: 866-209-0691
  Website: wustl.edu

HIGH SCHOOL SUMMER SCHOLARS PROGRAM

THE PROGRAM

Description: Residential academic summer program for rising high school seniors, awarding up to 7 units of Washington University college credit; two five-week sessions available.

Specialty: Scholars earn up to 7 units of college credit that will transfer to most accredited colleges and universities, giving them a head start toward their college career.

Program Type: Academic/pre-college enrichment

Classification: Coeducational, residential

Goals: High School Summer Scholars develop academic and social skills that will give them a tremendous advantage when they leave for college.

Focus: Academic/pre-college enrichment

Activities Center On: Academic and career exploration

Intensity Level: 3

Duration: 4–6 weeks

Program Offered: Summer

Location: St. Louis, Missouri

Accommodations: Dormitory

Years in Operation: 15

Religious Affiliation: Not relevant

STAFF

Student/Staff Ratio: 10:1

Staff Qualifications: Resident advisors are current Washington University students or recent graduates who have undergone specialized training in counseling and emergency response.

PARTICIPANTS

Average Number of Participants: 70

For Participants Aged: 16–18

The Ideal Candidate: Academic averages of B+ or better; combined SAT scores of at least 1200, combined math and verbal PSAT scores of at least 120, or an ACT or PLAN composite score of at least 25.

Special Requirements for Participation: Students must be at least 16 years of age and just have completed the junior year of high school.

COSTS

Average Cost: $4,400

Included in Cost: Program fee of $4,400 covers tuition, housing and meals, and participation in social activities. It does not include books and supplies, travel, or personal and incidental expenses.

Financial Aid Available: Yes

WESTCOAST CONNECTION TEEN TRAVEL EXPERIENCES

Westcoast Connection programs give students the opportunity to discover new and exciting places and, in turn, develop self-reliance and become an integral member of a close group. No experience is necessary, just a willingness and a desire to participate. Programs explore regions of the United States, Canada, Europe, and Australia, and run for three to six weeks. Four distinct types of travel are offered: Outdoor Adventures, which are more challenging; Active Touring programs, which are more recreational in focus; Sports and Touring programs, which combine the excitement of travel with focused instruction in either golfing or skiing/snowboarding; and Community Service, in which students travel while participating in various community projects.

Years in Operation: 21

Religious Affiliation: Not relevant

Price Range of Programs: $2,499–$7,499

For More Information:
  Contact: Mark Segal, Director
         154 East Boston Post Road
         Mamaroneck, NY 10543
  Phone: 800-767-0227
  Fax: 914-835-0798
  Email: usa@westcoastconnection.com
  Website: www.westcoastconnection.com

AUSTRALIAN OUTBACK + HAWAII

THE PROGRAM

Description: Active touring around Australia and Hawaii including scuba diving, sea kayaking, snorkeling, surfing, hiking, mountain biking, whitewater rafting, and more.

Specialty: The hallmark of a summer with Westcoast Connection is a special individual attention and extraordinary care devoted to each tour member. Under the direction of responsible, caring leaders, Westcoast offers the best itineraries in teen travel.

Program Type: Outdoors/adventure, travel/cultural

Classification: Coeducational, residential

Goals: While traveling, participants will learn about all the places they visit and the people they meet, and more about themselves in the process.

Focus: Travel, cultural, and leadership/teamwork

Activities Center On: Touring and outdoors/adventure

Intensity Level: 3

Duration: 4–6 weeks

Program Offered: Summer

Location: Hawaii, Australia

Accommodations: Hotels

Years in Operation: 21

Religious Affiliation: Not relevant

STAFF

Student/Staff Ratio: 7:1

Staff Qualifications: All staff must be at least 21 and are non-smokers. Staff are certified in CPR and first aid, and have an extensive background in working with young people. Staff are energetic, creative, and responsible.

PARTICIPANTS

Average Number of Participants: 35

For Participants Aged: 14–18

The Ideal Candidate: No prior experience is necessary, just a desire and willingness to participate.

Special Requirements for Participation: None.

COSTS

Average Cost: $6,699

Included in Cost: Tuition includes all activities, accommodations, meals, gratuities, and taxes. Personal spending money is recommended for souvenirs and personal items. Airfare to and from the trip is not included.

Financial Aid Available: No

EUROPEAN DISCOVERY

THE PROGRAM

Description: A six-country tour balancing big city highlights and nightlife with adventure in the French and Swiss Alps and recreation on the French and Adriatic Riviera.

Specialty: The hallmark of a summer with Westcoast Connection is a special individual attention and extraordinary care devoted to each tour member. Under the direction of responsible, caring leaders, Westcoast offers the best itineraries in teen travel.

Program Type: Outdoors/adventure, travel/cultural

Classification: Coeducational, residential

Goals: While traveling, participants will learn about all the places they visit and the people they meet, and more about themselves in the process.

Focus: Travel

Activities Center On: Touring and cultural

Intensity Level: 3

Duration: 4–6 weeks

Program Offered: Summer

Location: Belgium, France, Italy, the Netherlands, Switzerland, United Kingdom

Accommodations: Hotels

Years in Operation: 21

Religious Affiliation: Not relevant

STAFF

Student/Staff Ratio: 7:1

Staff Qualifications: All staff must be at least 21 and are non-smokers. Staff are certified in CPR and first aid, and have an extensive background in working with young people. Staff are energetic, creative, and responsible.

PARTICIPANTS

Average Number of Participants: 40

For Participants Aged: 14–17

The Ideal Candidate: No prior experience is necessary, just a desire and willingness to participate.

Special Requirements for Participation: None.

COSTS

Average Cost: $7,299

Included in Cost: Tuition includes all activities, accommodations, meals, gratuities, and taxes. Personal spending money is recommended for souvenirs and personal items. Airfare to and from the trip is not included.

Financial Aid Available: No

EUROPEAN ESCAPE

THE PROGRAM

Description: A four-country tour balancing big city highlights and nightlife with adventure in the French and Swiss Alps and recreation on the French and Adriatic Riviera.

Specialty: The hallmark of a summer with Westcoast Connection is a special individual attention and extraordinary care devoted to each tour member. Under the direction of responsible, caring leaders, Westcoast offers the best itineraries in teen travel.

Program Type: Outdoors/adventure, travel/cultural

Classification: Coeducational, residential

Goals: While traveling, participants will learn about all the places they visit and the people they meet, and more about themselves in the process.

Focus: Travel and leadership/teamwork

Activities Center On: Touring, cultural, and outdoors/adventure

Intensity Level: 3

Duration: 2–4 weeks

Program Offered: Summer

Location: Paris, France; Rome, Florence, and Venice, Italy; Geneva, Switzerland; United Kingdom

Accommodations: Hotels

Years in Operation: 21

Religious Affiliation: Not relevant

STAFF

Student/Staff Ratio: 7:1

Staff Qualifications: All staff must be at least 21 and are non-smokers. Staff are certified in CPR and first aid, and have an extensive background in working with young people. Staff are energetic, creative, and responsible.

PARTICIPANTS

Average Number of Participants: 25

For Participants Aged: 14–17

The Ideal Candidate: No prior experience is necessary, just a desire and willingness to participate.

Special Requirements for Participation: None.

COSTS

Average Cost: $6,299

Included in Cost: Tuition includes all activities, accommodations, meals, gratuities, and taxes. Personal spending money is recommended for souvenirs and personal items. Airfare to and from the trip is not included.

Financial Aid Available: No

HAWAIIAN SPIRIT

THE PROGRAM

Description: Balancing the exciting cities and great outdoors of the Pacific Northwest with the beauty of the Hawaiian Islands.

Specialty: The hallmark of a summer with Westcoast Connection is a special individual attention and extraordinary care devoted to each tour member. Under the direction of responsible, caring leaders, Westcoast offers the best itineraries in teen travel.

Program Type: Outdoors/adventure, travel/cultural

Classification: Coeducational, residential

Goals: While traveling, participants will learn about all the places they visit and the people they meet, and more about themselves in the process.

Focus: Travel and leadership/teamwork

Activities Center On: Touring and outdoors/adventure

Intensity Level: 2

Duration: 2–4 weeks

Program Offered: Summer

Location: San Francisco, California; Honolulu, Hawaii; Seattle, Washington; Oregon

Accommodations: Dormitory, hotels

Years in Operation: 21

Religious Affiliation: Not relevant

STAFF

Student/Staff Ratio: 7:1

Staff Qualifications: All staff must be at least 21 and are non-smokers. Staff are certified in CPR and first aid, and have an extensive background in working with young people. Staff are energetic, creative, and responsible.

PARTICIPANTS

Average Number of Participants: 35

For Participants Aged: 14–17

The Ideal Candidate: No prior experience is necessary, just a desire and willingness to participate.

Special Requirements for Participation: None.

COSTS

Average Cost: $5,699

Included in Cost: Tuition includes all activities, accommodations, meals, gratuities, and taxes. Personal spending money is recommended for souvenirs and personal items. Airfare to and from the trip is not included.

Financial Aid Available: No

ON TOUR CANADIAN MOUNTAIN MAGIC

THE PROGRAM

Description: This program is designed for greater independence for ages 17–19. It's an outdoor adventure in Whistler and the Canadian Rockies with a visit to Vancouver.

Specialty: The hallmark of a summer with Westcoast Connection is a special individual attention and extraordinary care devoted to each tour member. Under the direction of responsible, caring leaders, Westcoast offers the best itineraries in teen travel.

Program Type: Community service, outdoors/adventure, travel/cultural

Classification: Coeducational, residential

Goals: Participants will mature as individuals; they will leave the trip having developed team, social, and outdoor skills.

Focus: Leadership/teamwork, travel, and community service

Activities Center On: Travel, outdoors/adventure, and camping

Intensity Level: 3

Duration: 2–4 weeks

Program Offered: Summer

Location: Canada: Banff and Jasper, Alberta; Vancouver and Whistler, British Columbia

Accommodations: Dormitory, tent

Years in Operation: 21

Religious Affiliation: Not relevant

STAFF

Student/Staff Ratio: 6:1

Staff Qualifications: All staff must be at least 22 and are non-smokers. Staff are certified in CPR and first aid, and have an extensive background in working with young people. Staff are energetic, creative, and responsible.

PARTICIPANTS

Average Number of Participants: 15

For Participants Aged: 17–19

The Ideal Candidate: No prior experience is necessary, just a desire and willingness to participate.

Special Requirements for Participation: None.

COSTS

Average Cost: $3,699

Included in Cost: Tuition includes all activities, accommodations, meals, gratuities, and taxes. Personal spending money is recommended for souvenirs and personal items. Airfare to and from the trip is not included.

Financial Aid Available: No

ON TOUR EUROPEAN EXPERIENCE

THE PROGRAM

Description: This program is designed for greater independence for ages 17–19. A three- or four-country tour balancing big city highlights and nightlife with adventure on the French and Swiss Alps, and recreation on the French and Adriatic Rivieras.

Specialty: The hallmark of a summer with Westcoast Connection is a special individual attention and extraordinary care devoted to each tour member. Under the direction of responsible, caring leaders, Westcoast offers the best itineraries in teen travel.

Program Type: Travel/cultural

Classification: Coeducational, residential

Goals: While traveling, participants will learn about all the places they visit and the people they meet, and more about themselves in the process.

Focus: Travel and cultural

Activities Center On: Touring and cultural

Intensity Level: 3

Duration: 2–4 weeks

Program Offered: Summer

Location: Paris, France; Venice, Italy; Monaco; Geneva and Zermatt, Switzerland; London, United Kingdon

Accommodations: Hotels

Years in Operation: 21

Religious Affiliation: Not relevant

STAFF

Student/Staff Ratio: 7:1

Staff Qualifications: All staff must be at least 22 and are non-smokers. Staff are certified in CPR and first aid, and have an extensive background in working with young people. Staff are energetic, creative, and responsible.

PARTICIPANTS

Average Number of Participants: 45

For Participants Aged: 17–19

The Ideal Candidate: No prior experience is necessary, just a desire and willingness to participate.

Special Requirements for Participation: None.

COSTS

Average Cost: $5,999

Included in Cost: Tuition includes all activities, accommodations, breakfasts and dinners, gratuities, and taxes. Personal spending money is recommended for souvenirs and personal items. Airfare to and from the trip is not included.

Financial Aid Available: No

ON TOUR NORTHWESTERN ODYSSEY

THE PROGRAM

Description: A balanced variety of daytime activities, the sights and sounds of cities, exciting nightly entertainment, and the natural wonders of the great outdoors.

Specialty: The hallmark of a summer with Westcoast Connection is a special individual attention and extraordinary care devoted to each tour member. Under the direction of responsible, caring leaders, Westcoast offers the best itineraries in teen travel.

Program Type: Outdoors/adventure, travel/cultural

Classification: Coeducational, residential

Goals: While traveling, participants will learn about all the places they visit and the people they meet, and more about themselves in the process.

Focus: Travel and leadership/teamwork

Activities Center On: Touring and outdoors/adventure

Intensity Level: 3

Duration: 2–4 weeks

Program Offered: Summer

Location: Montana; Oregon; Salt Lake City, Utah; Seattle, Washington; Wyoming; Vancouver, British Columbia, and Alberta, Canada

Accommodations: Dormitory, tent, hotels

Years in Operation: 21

Religious Affiliation: Not relevant

STAFF

Student/Staff Ratio: 10:1

Staff Qualifications: All staff must be at least 22 and are non-smokers. Staff are certified in CPR and first aid, and have an extensive background in working with young people. Staff are energetic, creative, and responsible.

PARTICIPANTS

Average Number of Participants: 30

For Participants Aged: 17–19

The Ideal Candidate: No prior experience is necessary, just a desire and willingness to participate.

Special Requirements for Participation: None.

COSTS

Average Cost: $4,199

Included in Cost: Tuition includes all activities, accommodations, meals, gratuities, and taxes. Personal spending money is recommended for souvenirs and personal items. Airfare to and from the trip is not included.

Financial Aid Available: No

WASHINGTON STATE COMMUNITY SERVICE

THE PROGRAM

Description: Students will participate in various community service projects around the Pacific Northwest, including Habitat for Humanity, Easter Seals Camp, and the Washington Trails Association. Days of service are interspersed with activities such as whitewater rafting, hiking, and mountain biking.

Specialty: The hallmark of a summer with Westcoast Connection is a special individual attention and extraordinary care devoted to each tour member. Under the direction of responsible, caring leaders, Westcoast offers the best itineraries in teen travel.

Program Type: Community service, outdoors/adventure, travel/cultural

Classification: Coeducational, residential

Goals: Students will mature as individuals while learning the value of teamwork and helping others. While traveling, they will learn about all the places they visit and the people they meet, and more about themselves in the process.

Focus: Community service, leadership/teamwork, and travel

Activities Center On: Volunteer and travel

Intensity Level: 3

Duration: 2–4 weeks

Program Offered: Summer

Location: Washington

Accommodations: Dormitory, bunk/cabin

Years in Operation: 21

Religious Affiliation: Not relevant

STAFF

Student/Staff Ratio: 6:1

Staff Qualifications: All staff must be at least 22 and are non-smokers. Staff are certified in CPR and first aid, and have an extensive background in working with young people. Staff are energetic, creative, and responsible.

PARTICIPANTS

Average Number of Participants: 13

For Participants Aged: 16–19

The Ideal Candidate: No prior experience is necessary, just a desire and willingness to participate.

Special Requirements for Participation: None.

COSTS

Average Cost: $2,999

Included in Cost: Tuition includes all activities, accommodations, meals, gratuities, and taxes. Personal spending money is recommended for personal items and souvenirs. Airfare to and from the trip is not included.

Financial Aid Available: No

WESTERN WASHINGTON UNIVERSITY

Academic youth programs offered to students entering grades 3 through 12.

Years in Operation: 21

Religious Affiliation: Not relevant

Price Range of Programs: $250–$750

For More Information:
    Contact: Debbie Gibbons, Program Manager
              Extended Education and Summer Programs, MS 5293
              516 High Street
              Bellingham, WA 98225
    Phone: 360-650-6820
    Fax: 360-650-6858
    Email: adventures@wwu.edu
    Website: www.wwu.edu/~adventur

COLLEGE QUEST

THE PROGRAM

Description: Students entering grades 10 through 12 will get a taste of real college life at Western Washington University's campus in Bellingham, Washington. Live in a college dorm, take a short college course, earn college credit, and explore what it's like to be a college student.

Specialty: Academic focus and college life experience

Program Type: Academic/pre-college enrichment

Classification: Coeducational, residential

Goals: A 1-credit course in environmental studies is offered as part of the program. Participants will experience college living, and will learn about university admissions and application processes.

Focus: Academic/pre-college enrichment

Activities Center On: Academic

Intensity Level: 3

Duration: 1–2 weeks

Program Offered: Summer

Location: Bellingham, Washington

Accommodations: Dormitory

Years in Operation: 3

Religious Affiliation: Not relevant

STAFF

Student/Staff Ratio: 10:1

Staff Qualifications: Trained and experienced residence advisers; university instructor from Huxley College of the Environment.

PARTICIPANTS

Average Number of Participants: 10

For Participants Aged: 15–18

The Ideal Candidate: High school students interested in attending college.

Special Requirements for Participation: Students must submit personal essay, letter of recommendation, and school transcript.

COSTS

Average Cost: $700

Included in Cost: College course, residential dorm, food.

Financial Aid Available: No

WILDERNESS VENTURES

As the worldwide leader in student outdoor adventures, we have been providing students with life-changing, multi-adventure experiences for over 31 years. We offer backpacking, bike touring, sea kayaking, whitewater kayaking, rock climbing, sailing, scuba diving, snorkeling, mountain biking, ice climbing, and mountaineering in the finest wilderness areas in the western United States and six foreign countries.

Years in Operation: 31

Religious Affiliation: Not relevant

Price Range of Programs: $2,490–$6,290

For More Information:
  Contact: Mike Cottingham, Director
       PO Box 2768
       Jackson Hole, WY 83001
  Phone: 800-533-2281
  Fax: 307-739-1934
  Email: info@wildernessventures.com
  Website: www.wildernessventures.com

ALASKA COLLEGE LEADERSHIP

THE PROGRAM

Description: An advanced leadership program for college-age students, this trek combines backpacking and sea kayak trips to the Talkeetna Mountains and Prince William Sound. This program is an ideal sequel to our other offerings and an excellent beginning experience for older students interested in pursuing outdoor leadership positions.

Specialty: We are special because of our experience, our low student/staff ratios, the comparable ages of our groups, our unmatched safety record, our personal attention, the enthusiasm of our participants, and the special places where we expedition.

Program Type: Outdoors/adventure

Classification: Coeducational, residential

Focus: Leadership/teamwork

Activities Center On: Outdoors/adventure

Intensity Level: 3

Duration: 2–4 weeks

Program Offered: Summer

Location: Alaska

Accommodations: Tent

Years in Operation: 20

Religious Affiliation: Not relevant

STAFF

Student/Staff Ratio: 6:1

Staff Qualifications: Staff members average 27 years of age with a minimum age of 21 and are selected from hundreds of applicants based upon their proven outdoor skills and leadership backgrounds. While most have completed their undergraduate degrees, many are graduate students, full-time outdoor educators, secondary teachers, or college professors. They are excellent role models who exhibit positive life direction and who share a burning desire to have fun while teaching and facilitating groups of young adults.

PARTICIPANTS

Average Number of Participants: 12

For Participants Aged: 18–21

The Ideal Candidate: The ideal candidate for this expedition is a student who has a strong desire to participate in the activity offered. Students need not be super athletes—average physical condition and a positive attitude are all that are required!

Special Requirements for Participation: None.

COSTS

Average Cost: $3,790

Included in Cost: All food, lodging, activities, and group gear are included. The cost of airfare and personal gear is not included.

Financial Aid Available: Yes

ALASKA EXPEDITION

THE PROGRAM

Description: This wonderful 39-day expedition has been one of our most popular and challenging programs since 1976. Backpack through the remote Talkeetna Mountains, then raft out of the wilderness for 3 days. Glacial trek and ice climb in the spectacular Wrangell-St. Elias Range. Conclude your adventure with a sea kayaking journey into breathtakingly beautiful Prince William Sound.

Specialty: We are special because of our experience, our low student/staff ratios, the comparable ages of our groups, our unmatched safety record, our personal attention, the enthusiasm of our participants, and the special places where we expedition.

Program Type: Outdoors/adventure

Classification: Coeducational, residential

Focus: Leadership/teamwork

Activities Center On: Outdoors/adventure

Intensity Level: 3

Duration: 4–6 weeks

Program Offered: Summer

Location: Alaska

Accommodations: Tent

Years in Operation: 20

Religious Affiliation: Not relevant

STAFF

Student/Staff Ratio: 6:1

Staff Qualifications: Staff members average 27 years of age with a minimum age of 21 and are selected from hundreds of applicants based upon their proven outdoor skills and leadership backgrounds. While most have completed their undergraduate degrees, many are graduate students, full-time outdoor educators, secondary teachers, or college professors. They are excellent role models who exhibit positive life direction and who share a burning desire to have fun while teaching and facilitating groups of young adults.

PARTICIPANTS

Average Number of Participants: 12

For Participants Aged: 15–18

The Ideal Candidate: The ideal candidate for this expedition is a student who has a strong desire to participate in the activity offered. Students need not be super athletes—average physical condition and a positive attitude are all that are required!

Special Requirements for Participation: None.

COSTS

Average Cost: $4,890

Included in Cost: All food, lodging, activities, and group gear are included. The cost of airfare and personal gear is not included.

Financial Aid Available: Yes

ALASKA SERVICE

THE PROGRAM

Description: Our Southeast Alaska Service Adventure combines nine days (60 hours) of community service and cultural immersion with backpacking, sea kayaking, and whitewater rafting in one of the most beautiful environments in the world.

Specialty: We are special because of our experience, our low student/staff ratios, the comparable ages of our groups, our unmatched safety record, our personal attention, the enthusiasm of our participants, and the special places where we expedition.

Program Type: Outdoors/adventure

Classification: Coeducational, residential

Focus: Leadership/teamwork and community service

Activities Center On: Outdoors/adventure and cultural

Intensity Level: 3

Duration: 2–4 weeks

Program Offered: Summer

Location: Alaska

Accommodations: Tent

Religious Affiliation: Not relevant

STAFF

Student/Staff Ratio: 5:1

Staff Qualifications: Staff members average 27 years of age with a minimum age of 21 and are selected from hundreds of applicants based upon their proven outdoor skills and leadership backgrounds. While most have completed their undergraduate degrees, many are graduate students, full-time outdoor educators, secondary teachers, or college professors. They are excellent role models who exhibit positive life direction and who share a burning desire to have fun while teaching and facilitating groups of young adults.

PARTICIPANTS

Average Number of Participants: 10

For Participants Aged: 15–18

The Ideal Candidate: The ideal candidate for this expedition is a student who has a strong desire to participate in the activity offered. Students need not be super athletes—average physical condition and a positive attitude are all that are required!

Special Requirements for Participation: None.

COSTS

Average Cost: $3,890

Included in Cost: All food, lodging, activities, and group gear are included. The cost of airfare and personal gear is not included.

Financial Aid Available: Yes

Alaska South Central

The Program

Description: Our three-week Alaska South Central adventure is filled with challenge, beauty, and excitement. Spend five days backpacking among glaciers in the Chugach Range, four days paddling the glacier-filled fjords of Prince William Sound, five days backpacking over tundra in the shadow of Mount McKinley, and conclude with an exciting whitewater raft trip down the Matanuska River.

Specialty: We are special because of our experience, our low student/staff ratios, the comparable ages of our groups, our unmatched safety record, our personal attention, the enthusiasm of our participants, and the special places where we expedition.

Program Type: Outdoors/adventure

Classification: Coeducational, residential

Focus: Leadership/teamwork

Activities Center On: Outdoors/adventure

Intensity Level: 3

Duration: 2–4 weeks

Program Offered: Summer

Location: Alaska

Accommodations: Tent

Years in Operation: 10

Religious Affiliation: Not relevant

Staff

Student/Staff Ratio: 6:1

Staff Qualifications: Staff members average 27 years of age with a minimum age of 21 and are selected from hundreds of applicants based upon their proven outdoor skills and leadership backgrounds. While most have completed their undergraduate degrees, many are graduate students, full-time outdoor educators, secondary teachers, or college professors. They are excellent role models who exhibit positive life direction and who share a burning desire to have fun while teaching and facilitating groups of young adults.

Participants

Average Number of Participants: 12

For Participants Aged: 15–18

The Ideal Candidate: The ideal candidate for this expedition is a student who has a strong desire to participate in the activity offered. Students need not be super athletes—average physical condition and a positive attitude are all that are required!

Special Requirements for Participation: None.

Costs

Average Cost: $3,390

Included in Cost: All food, lodging, activities, and group gear are included. The cost of airfare and personal gear is not included.

Financial Aid Available: Yes

Alaska Southeast

The Program

Description: Join our three-week Southeast Alaska adventure. View humpback whales from your sea kayak in the Northern Hemisphere's finest waters; backpack over the historic Chilkoot Trail into the Yukon; raft the Blanchard River; and learn ice climbing skills in some of the finest glacial terrain Alaska has to offer.

Specialty: We are special because of our experience, our low student/staff ratios, the comparable ages of our groups, our unmatched safety record, our personal attention, the enthusiasm of our participants, and the special places where we expedition.

Program Type: Outdoors/adventure

Classification: Coeducational, residential

Focus: Leadership/teamwork

Activities Center On: Outdoors/adventure

Intensity Level: 3

Duration: 2–4 weeks

Program Offered: Summer

Location: Alaska

Accommodations: Tent

Religious Affiliation: Not relevant

Staff

Student/Staff Ratio: 6:1

Staff Qualifications: Staff members average 27 years of age with a minimum age of 21 and are selected from hundreds of applicants based upon their proven outdoor skills and leadership backgrounds. While most have completed their undergraduate degrees, many are graduate students, full-time outdoor educators, secondary teachers, or college professors. They are excellent role models who exhibit positive life direction and who share a burning desire to have fun while teaching and facilitating groups of young adults.

Participants

Average Number of Participants: 12

For Participants Aged: 15–18

The Ideal Candidate: The ideal candidate for this expedition is a student who has a strong desire to participate in the activity offered. Students need not be super athletes—average physical condition and a positive attitude are all that are required!

Special Requirements for Participation: None.

Costs

Average Cost: $3,890

Included in Cost: All food, lodging, activities, and group gear are included. The cost of airfare and personal gear is not included.

Financial Aid Available: Yes

Alpine Leadership

The Program

Description: This fabulous advanced leadership program traverses the North Cascade Range. It is designed for those who wish to further develop and refine their outdoor, interpersonal, and leadership skills.

Specialty: We are special because of our experience, our low student/staff ratios, the comparable ages of our groups, our unmatched safety record, our personal attention, the enthusiasm of our participants, and the special places where we expedition.

Program Type: Outdoors/adventure

Classification: Coeducational, residential

Focus: Leadership/teamwork

Activities Center On: Outdoors/adventure

Intensity Level: 3

Duration: 2–4 weeks

Program Offered: Summer

Location: Washington

Accommodations: Tent

Years in Operation: 20

Religious Affiliation: Not relevant

Staff

Student/Staff Ratio: 5:1

Staff Qualifications: Staff members average 27 years of age with a minimum age of 21 and are selected from hundreds of applicants based upon their proven outdoor skills and leadership backgrounds. While most have completed their undergraduate degrees, many are graduate students, full-time outdoor educators, secondary teachers, or college professors. They are excellent role models who exhibit positive life direction and who share a burning desire to have fun while teaching and facilitating groups of young adults.

Participants

Average Number of Participants: 10

For Participants Aged: 16–18

The Ideal Candidate: The ideal candidate for this expedition is a student who has a strong desire to participate in the activity offered. Students need not be super athletes—average physical condition and a positive attitude are all that are required!

Special Requirements for Participation: None.

Costs

Average Cost: $3,390

Included in Cost: All food, lodging, activities, and group gear are included. The cost of airfare and personal gear is not included.

Financial Aid Available: Yes

Australia

The Program

Description: Join us in the Land Down Under. From Nitmiluk and Kakadu National Parks, we backpack the eco-diverse Australian Outback, paddle the Katherine River, then visit an aboriginal village as honored guests. We'll raft the North Johnstone, one of the world's finest whitewater jungle rivers, and scuba dive the incomparable Great Barrier Reef.

Specialty: We are special because of our experience, our low student/staff ratios, the comparable ages of our groups, our unmatched safety record, our personal attention, the enthusiasm of our participants, and the special places where we expedition.

Program Type: Outdoors/adventure

Classification: Coeducational, residential

Focus: Leadership/teamwork and cultural

Activities Center On: Outdoors/adventure

Intensity Level: 3

Duration: 2–4 weeks

Program Offered: Summer

Location: Australia

Accommodations: Tent

Years in Operation: 4

Religious Affiliation: Not relevant

Staff

Student/Staff Ratio: 7:1

Staff Qualifications: Staff members average 27 years of age with a minimum age of 21 and are selected from hundreds of applicants based upon their proven outdoor skills and leadership backgrounds. While most have completed their undergraduate degrees, many are graduate students, full-time outdoor educators, secondary teachers, or college professors. They are excellent role models who exhibit positive life direction and who share a burning desire to have fun while teaching and facilitating groups of young adults.

Participants

Average Number of Participants: 14

For Participants Aged: 15–18

The Ideal Candidate: The ideal candidate for this expedition is a student who has a strong desire to participate in the activity offered. Students need not be super athletes—average physical condition and a positive attitude are all that are required!

Special Requirements for Participation: None.

Costs

Average Cost: $6,290

Included in Cost: Price includes all food, lodging, activities, and group gear as well as round-trip airfare from Los Angeles to Sydney. It does not include the cost of your airfare to and from Los Angeles or personal gear.

Financial Aid Available: Yes

CALIFORNIA

THE PROGRAM

Description: Enroll in this California adventure for three weeks of amazing wilderness variety. Backpack the lofty peaks of the Sierra Nevada; raft thrilling Class III whitewater; trek along a wilderness coastline; and hike among towering redwoods.

Specialty: We are special because of our experience, our low student/staff ratios, the comparable ages of our groups, our unmatched safety record, our personal attention, the enthusiasm of our participants, and the special places where we expedition.

Program Type: Outdoors/adventure

Classification: Coeducational, residential

Focus: Leadership/teamwork

Activities Center On: Outdoors/adventure

Intensity Level: 3

Duration: 2–4 weeks

Program Offered: Summer

Location: California

Accommodations: Tent

Religious Affiliation: Not relevant

STAFF

Student/Staff Ratio: 6:1

Staff Qualifications: Staff members average 27 years of age with a minimum age of 21 and are selected from hundreds of applicants based upon their proven outdoor skills and leadership backgrounds. While most have completed their undergraduate degrees, many are graduate students, full-time outdoor educators, secondary teachers, or college professors. They are excellent role models who exhibit positive life direction and who share a burning desire to have fun while teaching and facilitating groups of young adults.

PARTICIPANTS

Average Number of Participants: 12

For Participants Aged: 14–18

The Ideal Candidate: The ideal candidate for this expedition is a student who has a strong desire to participate in the activity offered. Students need not be super athletes—average physical condition and a positive attitude are all that are required!

Special Requirements for Participation: None.

COSTS

Average Cost: $3,190

Included in Cost: All food, lodging, activities, and group gear are included. The cost of airfare or personal gear is not included.

Financial Aid Available: Yes

CASCADE/OLYMPIC

THE PROGRAM

Description: Explore the finest wilderness in Washington. Backpack pristine beaches on the Olympic Peninsula and in the North Cascades; sea kayak Puget Sound; and raft the scenic Sauk River. Top your adventure with a climb of snow clad Mount Rainier.

Specialty: We are special because of our experience, our low student/staff ratios, the comparable ages of our groups, our unmatched safety record, our personal attention, the enthusiasm of our participants, and the special places where we expedition.

Program Type: Outdoors/adventure

Classification: Coeducational, residential

Focus: Leadership/teamwork

Activities Center On: Outdoors/adventure

Intensity Level: 3

Duration: 2–4 weeks

Program Offered: Summer

Location: Washington

Accommodations: Tent

Years in Operation: 25

Religious Affiliation: Not relevant

STAFF

Student/Staff Ratio: 5:1

Staff Qualifications: Staff members average 27 years of age with a minimum age of 21 and are selected from hundreds of applicants based upon their proven outdoor skills and leadership backgrounds. While most have completed their undergraduate degrees, many are graduate students, full-time outdoor educators, secondary teachers, or college professors. They are excellent role models who exhibit positive life direction and who share a burning desire to have fun while teaching and facilitating groups of young adults.

PARTICIPANTS

Average Number of Participants: 10

For Participants Aged: 15–18

The Ideal Candidate: The ideal candidate for this expedition is a student who has a strong desire to participate in the activity offered. Students need not be super athletes—average physical condition and a positive attitude are all that are required!

Special Requirements for Participation: None.

COSTS

Average Cost: $3,690

Included in Cost: All food, lodging, activities, and group gear are included. The cost of airfare and personal gear is not included.

Financial Aid Available: Yes

CASCADE/SAN JUAN

THE PROGRAM

Description: This wonderful three-week advanced outdoor leadership program combines extensive wilderness skill training in two dramatic locations: the rugged and beautiful North Cascades and Washington's scenic San Juan Islands. This challenging program is open to both returning Wilderness Ventures participants and to students without previous experience.

Specialty: We are special because of our experience, our low student/staff ratios, the comparable ages of our groups, our unmatched safety record, our personal attention, the enthusiasm of our participants, and the special places where we expedition.

Program Type: Outdoors/adventure

Classification: Coeducational, residential

Focus: Leadership/teamwork

Activities Center On: Outdoors/adventure

Intensity Level: 3

Duration: 2–4 weeks

Program Offered: Summer

Location: Washington

Accommodations: Tent

Religious Affiliation: Not relevant

STAFF

Student/Staff Ratio: 5:1

Staff Qualifications: Staff members average 27 years of age with a minimum age of 21 and are selected from hundreds of applicants based upon their proven outdoor skills and leadership backgrounds. While most have completed their undergraduate degrees, many are graduate students, full-time outdoor educators, secondary teachers, or college professors. They are excellent role models who exhibit positive life direction and who share a burning desire to have fun while teaching and facilitating groups of young adults.

PARTICIPANTS

Average Number of Participants: 10

For Participants Aged: 14–18

The Ideal Candidate: The ideal candidate for this expedition is a student who has a strong desire to participate in the activity offered. Students need not be super athletes—average physical condition and a positive attitude are all that are required!

Special Requirements for Participation: None.

COSTS

Average Cost: $3,090

Financial Aid Available: Yes

COSTA RICA

THE PROGRAM

Description: Our Costa Rican exploration is an exciting combination of diverse wilderness travel and stimulating cultural immersion in an unspoiled tropical paradise. From sea kayaking along the Pacific Coast, to rafting jungle river, to backpacking amidst exotic birds and wildlife in lofty cloud forests, this 21-day expedition not only offers high adventure but also the cross-cultural education of a lifetime.

Specialty: We are special because of our experience, our low student/staff ratios, the comparable ages of our groups, our unmatched safety record, our personal attention, the enthusiasm of our participants, and the special places where we expedition.

Program Type: Outdoors/adventure

Classification: Coeducational, residential

Focus: Leadership/teamwork and cultural

Activities Center On: Outdoors/adventure

Intensity Level: 3

Duration: 2–4 weeks

Program Offered: Summer

Location: Costa Rica

Accommodations: Tent

Years in Operation: 5

Religious Affiliation: Not relevant

STAFF

Student/Staff Ratio: 7:1

Staff Qualifications: Staff members average 27 years of age with a minimum age of 21 and are selected from hundreds of applicants based upon their proven outdoor skills and leadership backgrounds. While most have completed their undergraduate degrees, many are graduate students, full-time outdoor educators, secondary teachers, or college professors. They are excellent role models who exhibit positive life direction and who share a burning desire to have fun while teaching and facilitating groups of young adults.

PARTICIPANTS

Average Number of Participants: 14

For Participants Aged: 15–18

The Ideal Candidate: The ideal candidate for this expedition is a student who has a strong desire to participate in the activity offered. Students need not be super athletes—average physical condition and a positive attitude are all that are required!

Special Requirements for Participation: None.

COSTS

Average Cost: $3,890

Included in Cost: All food, lodging, activities, and group gear are included. The cost of airfare and personal gear is not included.

Financial Aid Available: Yes

ECUADOR AND GALAPAGOS

THE PROGRAM

Description: This incredible expedition takes us backpacking in the Andes, whitewater rafting on the Rio Toachi and Rio Blanco, canoeing into the Amazon, and sailing in the Galapagos.

Specialty: We are special because of our experience, our low student/staff ratios, the comparable ages of our groups, our unmatched safety record, our personal attention, the enthusiasm of our participants, and the special places where we expedition.

Program Type: Outdoors/adventure

Classification: Coeducational, residential

Focus: Leadership/teamwork and cultural

Activities Center On: Outdoors/adventure

Intensity Level: 3

Duration: 2–4 weeks

Program Offered: Summer

Location: Ecuador

Accommodations: Tent

Religious Affiliation: Not relevant

STAFF

Student/Staff Ratio: 7:1

Staff Qualifications: Staff members average 27 years of age with a minimum age of 21 and are selected from hundreds of applicants based upon their proven outdoor skills and leadership backgrounds. While most have completed their undergraduate degrees, many are graduate students, full-time outdoor educators, secondary teachers, or college professors. They are excellent role models who exhibit positive life direction and who share a burning desire to have fun while teaching and facilitating groups of young adults.

PARTICIPANTS

Average Number of Participants: 14

For Participants Aged: 15–18

The Ideal Candidate: The ideal candidate for this expedition is a student who has a strong desire to participate in the activity offered. Students need not be super athletes—average physical condition and a positive attitude are all that are required!

Special Requirements for Participation: None.

COSTS

Average Cost: $4,990

Included in Cost: All food, lodging, activities, and group gear are included. The cost of airfare and personal gear is not included.

Financial Aid Available: Yes

EUROPEAN ALPS

THE PROGRAM

Description: Our European Alps trek combines spectacular backpacking over two of Europe's most famous routes with visits to charming villages in France, Switzerland, and Italy. The trip culminates with a glacier hike up the Briethorn at 13,450 feet, followed by three days in Paris.

Specialty: We are special because of our experience, our low student/staff ratios, the comparable ages of our groups, our unmatched safety record, our personal attention, the enthusiasm of our participants, and the special places where we expedition.

Program Type: Outdoors/adventure

Classification: Coeducational, residential

Focus: Leadership/teamwork, cultural, and travel

Activities Center On: Outdoors/adventure

Intensity Level: 3

Duration: 2–4 weeks

Program Offered: Summer

Location: France, Italy, Switzerland

Religious Affiliation: Not relevant

STAFF

Student/Staff Ratio: 6:1

Staff Qualifications: Staff members average 27 years of age with a minimum age of 21 and are selected from hundreds of applicants based upon their proven outdoor skills and leadership backgrounds. While most have completed their undergraduate degrees, many are graduate students, full-time outdoor educators, secondary teachers, or college professors. They are excellent role models who exhibit positive life direction and who share a burning desire to have fun while teaching and facilitating groups of young adults.

PARTICIPANTS

Average Number of Participants: 12

For Participants Aged: 15–18

The Ideal Candidate: The ideal candidate for this expedition is a student who has a strong desire to participate in the activity offered. Students need not be super athletes—average physical condition and a positive attitude are all that are required!

Special Requirements for Participation: None.

COSTS

Average Cost: $4,590

Included in Cost: All food, lodging, activities, and group gear are included. The cost of airfare and personal gear is not included.

Financial Aid Available: Yes

GRAND TETON

THE PROGRAM

Description: Explore the most amazing wilderness in the lower 48 states. Backpack through the magnificent Wind River Range; raft the wild Snake River; canoe through the geologic wonder that is Yellowstone; backpack along the Continental Divide in the Teton Wilderness; and climb the 13,771-foot Grand Teton.

Specialty: We are special because of our experience, our low student/staff ratios, the comparable ages of our groups, our unmatched safety record, our personal attention, the enthusiasm of our participants, and the special places where we expedition.

Program Type: Outdoors/adventure

Classification: Coeducational, residential

Focus: Leadership/teamwork

Activities Center On: Outdoors/adventure

Intensity Level: 3

Duration: 2–4 weeks

Program Offered: Summer

Location: Wyoming

Accommodations: Tent

Years in Operation: 25

Religious Affiliation: Not relevant

STAFF

Student/Staff Ratio: 6:1

Staff Qualifications: Staff members average 27 years of age with a minimum age of 21 and are selected from hundreds of applicants based upon their proven outdoor skills and leadership backgrounds. While most have completed their undergraduate degrees, many are graduate students, full-time outdoor educators, secondary teachers, or college professors. They are excellent role models who exhibit positive life direction and who share a burning desire to have fun while teaching and facilitating groups of young adults.

PARTICIPANTS

Average Number of Participants: 12

For Participants Aged: 15–18

The Ideal Candidate: The ideal candidate for this expedition is a student who has a strong desire to participate in the activity offered. Students need not be super athletes—average physical condition and a positive attitude are all that are required!

Special Requirements for Participation: None.

COSTS

Average Cost: $3,490

Included in Cost: All food, lodging, activities, and group gear are included. The cost of airfare and personal gear is not included.

Financial Aid Available: Yes

GREAT DIVIDE

THE PROGRAM

Description: This exceptional expedition combines all of the activities of our popular Grand Teton and Rocky Mountain programs, creating a wonderful and extensive backpacking, canoeing, whitewater rafting, and rock climbing adventure in the northern Rockies.

Specialty: We are special because of our experience, our low student/staff ratios, the comparable ages of our groups, our unmatched safety record, our personal attention, the enthusiasm of our participants, and the special places where we expedition.

Program Type: Outdoors/adventure

Classification: Coeducational, residential

Focus: Leadership/teamwork

Activities Center On: Outdoors/adventure

Intensity Level: 3

Duration: 2–4 weeks

Program Offered: Summer

Location: Idaho, Oregon, Wyoming

Accommodations: Tent

Years in Operation: 20

Religious Affiliation: Not relevant

STAFF

Student/Staff Ratio: 5:1

Staff Qualifications: Staff members average 27 years of age with a minimum age of 21 and are selected from hundreds of applicants based upon their proven outdoor skills and leadership backgrounds. While most have completed their undergraduate degrees, many are graduate students, full-time outdoor educators, secondary teachers, or college professors. They are excellent role models who exhibit positive life direction and who share a burning desire to have fun while teaching and facilitating groups of young adults.

PARTICIPANTS

Average Number of Participants: 10

For Participants Aged: 15–18

The Ideal Candidate: The ideal candidate for this expedition is a student who has a strong desire to participate in the activity offered. Students need not be super athletes—average physical condition and a positive attitude are all that are required!

Special Requirements for Participation: None.

COSTS

Average Cost: $4,290

Included in Cost: All food, lodging, activities, and group gear are included. The cost of airfare and personal gear is not included.

Financial Aid Available: Yes

HAWAII

THE PROGRAM

Description: Immerse yourself in the natural beauty of the Hawaiian Islands as we sea kayak along palm-lined coastlines, backpack through rain forest valleys, sail and snorkel spectacular bays, hike around an active volcano, backpack into a spectacular mountainous cloud forest, and learn about local Hawaiian culture and customs.

Specialty: We are special because of our experience, our low student/staff ratios, the comparable ages of our groups, our unmatched safety record, our personal attention, the enthusiasm of our participants, and the special places where we expedition.

Program Type: Outdoors/adventure

Classification: Coeducational, residential

Focus: Leadership/teamwork

Activities Center On: Outdoors/adventure

Intensity Level: 2

Duration: 2–4 weeks

Program Offered: Summer

Location: Hawaii

Accommodations: Tent

Years in Operation: 5

Religious Affiliation: Not relevant

STAFF

Student/Staff Ratio: 6:1

Staff Qualifications: Staff members average 27 years of age with a minimum age of 21 and are selected from hundreds of applicants based upon their proven outdoor skills and leadership backgrounds. While most have completed their undergraduate degrees, many are graduate students, full-time outdoor educators, secondary teachers, or college professors. They are excellent role models who exhibit positive life direction and who share a burning desire to have fun while teaching and facilitating groups of young adults.

PARTICIPANTS

Average Number of Participants: 12

For Participants Aged: 14–18

The Ideal Candidate: The ideal candidate for this expedition is a student who has a strong desire to participate in the activity offered. Students need not be super athletes—average physical condition and a positive attitude are all that are required!

Special Requirements for Participation: None.

COSTS

Average Cost: $3,990

Included in Cost: All food, lodging, activities, and group gear are included. The cost of airfare and personal gear is not included.

Financial Aid Available: Yes

HIGH SIERRA

THE PROGRAM

Description: This wonderful trip features two incredible backpacking trips; rock climbing in Yosemite, whitewater rafting, and inflatable kayaking; and snow and ice school, followed by an amazing summit climb of Mount Shasta.

Specialty: We are special because of our experience, our low student/staff ratios, the comparable ages of our groups, our unmatched safety record, our personal attention, the enthusiasm of our participants, and the special places where we expedition.

Program Type: Outdoors/adventure

Classification: Coeducational, residential

Focus: Leadership/teamwork

Activities Center On: Outdoors/adventure

Intensity Level: 3

Duration: 2–4 weeks

Program Offered: Summer

Location: California

Accommodations: Tent

Religious Affiliation: Not relevant

STAFF

Student/Staff Ratio: 6:1

Staff Qualifications: Staff members average 27 years of age with a minimum age of 21 and are selected from hundreds of applicants based upon their proven outdoor skills and leadership backgrounds. While most have completed their undergraduate degrees, many are graduate students, full-time outdoor educators, secondary teachers, or college professors. They are excellent role models who exhibit positive life direction and who share a burning desire to have fun while teaching and facilitating groups of young adults.

PARTICIPANTS

Average Number of Participants: 12

For Participants Aged: 14–18

The Ideal Candidate: The ideal candidate for this expedition is a student who has a strong desire to participate in the activity offered. Students need not be super athletes—average physical condition and a positive attitude are all that are required!

Special Requirements for Participation: None.

COSTS

Average Cost: $3,490

Included in Cost: All food, lodging, activities, and group gear are included. The cost of airfare and personal gear is not included.

Financial Aid Available: Yes

NORTHWEST

THE PROGRAM

Description: This fabulous trip was our first in 1973 and continues to offer the widest variety of wilderness environments and activities in one of the world's most beautiful and distinct regions. From the beaches of the Olympic peninsula to the mountain wilderness of Oregon to the placid water of Puget Sound, this adventure fulfills the expectations of every outdoor enthusiast.

Specialty: We are special because of our experience, our low student/staff ratios, the comparable ages of our groups, our unmatched safety record, our personal attention, the enthusiasm of our participants, and the special places where we expedition.

Program Type: Outdoors/adventure

Classification: Coeducational, residential

Focus: Leadership/teamwork

Activities Center On: Outdoors/adventure

Intensity Level: 3

Duration: 4–6 weeks

Program Offered: Summer

Location: Oregon, Washington

Accommodations: Tent

Years in Operation: 31

Religious Affiliation: Not relevant

STAFF

Student/Staff Ratio: 5:1

Staff Qualifications: Staff members average 27 years of age with a minimum age of 21 and are selected from hundreds of applicants based upon their proven outdoor skills and leadership backgrounds. While most have completed their undergraduate degrees, many are graduate students, full-time outdoor educators, secondary teachers, or college professors. They are excellent role models who exhibit positive life direction and who share a burning desire to have fun while teaching and facilitating groups of young adults.

PARTICIPANTS

Average Number of Participants: 10

For Participants Aged: 15–18

The Ideal Candidate: The ideal candidate for this expedition is a student who has a strong desire to participate in the activity offered. Students need not be super athletes—average physical condition and a positive attitude are all that are required!

Special Requirements for Participation: None.

COSTS

Average Cost: $4,890

Included in Cost: All food, lodging, activities, and group gear are included. The cost of airfare and personal gear is not included.

Financial Aid Available: Yes

OREGON

THE PROGRAM

Description: From the snow-capped volcanoes of Oregon's Cascades to the arid beauty of the state's desert canyons, this s16-day adventure offers a stunning variety of environments and experiences, all within a 30-mile radius.

Specialty: We are special because of our experience, our low student/staff ratios, the comparable ages of our groups, our unmatched safety record, our personal attention, the enthusiasm of our participants, and the special places where we expedition.

Program Type: Outdoors/adventure

Classification: Coeducational, residential

Focus: Leadership/teamwork

Activities Center On: Outdoors/adventure

Intensity Level: 2

Duration: 2–4 weeks

Program Offered: Summer

Location: Oregon

Accommodations: Tent

Years in Operation: 6

Religious Affiliation: Not relevant

STAFF

Student/Staff Ratio: 5:1

Staff Qualifications: Staff members average 27 years of age with a minimum age of 21 and are selected from hundreds of applicants based upon their proven outdoor skills and leadership backgrounds. While most have completed their undergraduate degrees, many are graduate students, full-time outdoor educators, secondary teachers, or college professors. They are excellent role models who exhibit positive life direction and who share a burning desire to have fun while teaching and facilitating groups of young adults.

PARTICIPANTS

Average Number of Participants: 10

For Participants Aged: 14–18

The Ideal Candidate: The ideal candidate for this expedition is a student who has a strong desire to participate in the activity offered. Students need not be super athletes—average physical condition and a positive attitude are all that are required!

Special Requirements for Participation: None.

COSTS

Average Cost: $2,590

Included in Cost: All food, lodging, activities, and group gear are included. The cost of airfare and personal gear is not included.

Financial Aid Available: Yes

Pacific Coast Bike

The Program

Description: Join our Pacific Coast bicycle adventure for the ultimate bicycle touring experience in the western United States. This classic route from Seattle to San Francisco follows one of the world's most beautiful coastlines, offering a spectacular seascape of sandy beaches, dramatic bluffs, redwood forests, and picturesque seaside villages. Along our way we'll stop for two days of whitewater rafting before concluding our ride by crossing the Golden Gate Bridge.

Specialty: We are special because of our experience, our low student/staff ratios, the comparable ages of our groups, our unmatched safety record, our personal attention, the enthusiasm of our participants, and the special places where we expedition.

Program Type: Outdoors/adventure

Classification: Coeducational, residential

Focus: Leadership/teamwork

Activities Center On: Outdoors/adventure

Intensity Level: 3

Duration: 4–6 weeks

Program Offered: Summer

Location: California, Oregon, Washington

Accommodations: Tent

Religious Affiliation: Not relevant

Staff

Student/Staff Ratio: 4:1

Staff Qualifications: Staff members average 27 years of age with a minimum age of 21 and are selected from hundreds of applicants based upon their proven outdoor skills and leadership backgrounds. While most have completed their undergraduate degrees, many are graduate students, full-time outdoor educators, secondary teachers, or college professors. They are excellent role models who exhibit positive life direction and who share a burning desire to have fun while teaching and facilitating groups of young adults.

Participants

Average Number of Participants: 12

For Participants Aged: 14–18

The Ideal Candidate: The ideal candidate for this expedition is a student who has a strong desire to participate in the activity offered. Students need not be super athletes—average physical condition and a positive attitude are all that are required!

Special Requirements for Participation: None.

Costs

Average Cost: $3,890

Included in Cost: All food, lodging, activities, and group gear are included. The cost of airfare and personal gear is not included.

Financial Aid Available: Yes

Pacific Northwest

The Program

Description: This wonderful three-week introduction to the Pacific Northwest will see us backpack through the spectacular "American Alps," sea kayak the placid waters of Puget Sound, raft the exciting Deschutes River, and rock climb at Smith Rock State Park.

Specialty: We are special because of our experience, our low student/staff ratios, the comparable ages of our groups, our unmatched safety record, our personal attention, the enthusiasm of our participants, and the special places where we expedition.

Program Type: Outdoors/adventure

Classification: Coeducational, residential

Focus: Leadership/teamwork

Activities Center On: Outdoors/adventure

Intensity Level: 2

Duration: 2–4 weeks

Program Offered: Summer

Location: Oregon, Washington

Accommodations: Tent

Years in Operation: 20

Religious Affiliation: Not relevant

Staff

Student/Staff Ratio: 5:1

Staff Qualifications: Staff members average 27 years of age with a minimum age of 21 and are selected from hundreds of applicants based upon their proven outdoor skills and leadership backgrounds. While most have completed their undergraduate degrees, many are graduate students, full-time outdoor educators, secondary teachers, or college professors. They are excellent role models who exhibit positive life direction and who share a burning desire to have fun while teaching and facilitating groups of young adults.

Participants

Average Number of Participants: 10

For Participants Aged: 14–18

The Ideal Candidate: The ideal candidate for this expedition is a student who has a strong desire to participate in the activity offered. Students need not be super athletes—average physical condition and a positive attitude are all that are required!

Special Requirements for Participation: None.

Costs

Average Cost: $3,290

Included in Cost: All food, lodging, activities, and group gear are included. The cost of airfare and personal gear is not included.

Financial Aid Available: Yes

Puget Sound Bike

The Program

Description: Explore the wonders of the Pacific Northwest and Puget Sound on this introduction to bicycle touring.

Specialty: We are special because of our experience, our low student/staff ratios, the comparable ages of our groups, our unmatched safety record, our personal attention, the enthusiasm of our participants, and the special places where we expedition.

Program Type: Outdoors/adventure

Classification: Coeducational, residential

Focus: Leadership/teamwork

Activities Center On: Outdoors/adventure

Intensity Level: 3

Duration: 2–4 weeks

Program Offered: Summer

Location: Washington

Accommodations: Tent

Years in Operation: 15

Religious Affiliation: Not relevant

Staff

Student/Staff Ratio: 5:1

Staff Qualifications: Staff members average 27 years of age with a minimum age of 21 and are selected from hundreds of applicants based upon their proven outdoor skills and leadership backgrounds. While most have completed their undergraduate degrees, many are graduate students, full-time outdoor educators, secondary teachers, or college professors. They are excellent role models who exhibit positive life direction and who share a burning desire to have fun while teaching and facilitating groups of young adults.

Participants

Average Number of Participants: 10

For Participants Aged: 14–18

The Ideal Candidate: The ideal candidate for this expedition is a student who has a strong desire to participate in the activity offered. Students need not be super athletes—average physical condition and a positive attitude are all that are required!

Special Requirements for Participation: None.

Costs

Average Cost: $3,590

Included in Cost: All food, lodging, activities, and group gear are included. The cost of airfare and personal gear is not included.

Financial Aid Available: Yes

Rocky Mountain

The Program

Description: Set in the northern Rockies, this fabulous whitewater rafting, backpackin, and sea kayaking program has been a favorite since 1975. Join us on a trek through the rugged and beautiful Teton Range and sea kayak Yellowstone Lake's placid waters. Then, cross the Continental Divide through Montana's breathtaking Anaconda-Pintlar Wilderness, and conclude your journey by whitewater rafting and inflatable kayaking Idaho's wild and scenic Salmon River.

Specialty: We are special because of our experience, our low student/staff ratios, the comparable ages of our groups, our unmatched safety record, our personal attention, the enthusiasm of our participants, and the special places where we expedition.

Program Type: Outdoors/adventure

Classification: Coeducational, residential

Focus: Leadership/teamwork

Activities Center On: Outdoors/adventure

Intensity Level: 3

Duration: 2–4 weeks

Program Offered: Summer

Location: Idaho, Montana, Wyoming

Accommodations: Tent

Years in Operation: 28

Religious Affiliation: Not relevant

Staff

Student/Staff Ratio: 5:1

Staff Qualifications: Staff members average 27 years of age with a minimum age of 21 and are selected from hundreds of applicants based upon their proven outdoor skills and leadership backgrounds. While most have completed their undergraduate degrees, many are graduate students, full-time outdoor educators, secondary teachers, or college professors. They are excellent role models who exhibit positive life direction and who share a burning desire to have fun while teaching and facilitating groups of young adults.

Participants

Average Number of Participants: 10

For Participants Aged: 14–18

The Ideal Candidate: The ideal candidate for this expedition is a student who has a strong desire to participate in the activity offered. Students need not be super athletes—average physical condition and a positive attitude are all that are required!

Special Requirements for Participation: None.

Costs

Average Cost: $3,490

Included in Cost: All food, lodging, activities, and group gear are included. The cost of airfare and personal gear is not included.

Financial Aid Available: Yes

Teton

The Program

Description: With the towering Tetons overhead, this 16-day adventure is action-packed: we backpack in the amazing Tetons, attend whitewater kayaking school on the Snake River, and explore the wonders of Yellowstone by kayak.

Specialty: We are special because of our experience, our low student/staff ratios, the comparable ages of our groups, our unmatched safety record, our personal attention, the enthusiasm of our participants, and the special places where we expedition.

Program Type: Outdoors/adventure

Classification: Coeducational, residential

Focus: Leadership/teamwork

Activities Center On: Outdoors/adventure

Intensity Level: 2

Duration: 2–4 weeks

Program Offered: Summer

Location: Wyoming

Accommodations: Tent

Years in Operation: 15

Religious Affiliation: Not relevant

Staff

Student/Staff Ratio: 5:1

Staff Qualifications: Staff members average 27 years of age with a minimum age of 21 and are selected from hundreds of applicants based upon their proven outdoor skills and leadership backgrounds. While most have completed their undergraduate degrees, many are graduate students, full-time outdoor educators, secondary teachers, or college professors. They are excellent role models who exhibit positive life direction and who share a burning desire to have fun while teaching and facilitating groups of young adults.

Participants

Average Number of Participants: 10

For Participants Aged: 14–18

The Ideal Candidate: The ideal candidate for this expedition is a student who has a strong desire to participate in the activity offered. Students need not be super athletes—average physical condition and a positive attitude are all that are required!

Special Requirements for Participation: None.

Costs

Average Cost: $2,490

Included in Cost: All food, lodging, activities, and group gear are included. The cost of airfare and personal gear is not included.

Financial Aid Available: Yes

Teton Crest

The Program

Description: This advanced outdoor leadership program is designed specifically for students who are seeking a challenging two-week wilderness experience and extensive backcountry skill training. Conducted in one of North America's most fabulous wilderness environments, this expedition is open to both former Wilderness Ventures participants and to new students without prior experience.

Specialty: We are special because of our experience, our low student/staff ratios, the comparable ages of our groups, our unmatched safety record, our personal attention, the enthusiasm of our participants, and the special places where we expedition.

Program Type: Outdoors/adventure

Classification: Coeducational, residential

Focus: Leadership/teamwork

Activities Center On: Outdoors/adventure

Intensity Level: 3

Duration: 2–4 weeks

Program Offered: Summer

Location: Wyoming

Accommodations: Tent

Religious Affiliation: Not relevant

Staff

Student/Staff Ratio: 5:1

Staff Qualifications: Staff members average 27 years of age with a minimum age of 21 and are selected from hundreds of applicants based upon their proven outdoor skills and leadership backgrounds. While most have completed their undergraduate degrees, many are graduate students, full-time outdoor educators, secondary teachers, or college professors. They are excellent role models who exhibit positive life direction and who share a burning desire to have fun while teaching and facilitating groups of young adults.

Participants

Average Number of Participants: 10

For Participants Aged: 14–18

The Ideal Candidate: The ideal candidate for this expedition is a student who has a strong desire to participate in the activity offered. Students need not be super athletes—average physical condition and a positive attitude are all that are required!

Special Requirements for Participation: None.

COSTS

Average Cost: $2,490

Included in Cost: All food, lodging, activities, and group gear are included. The cost of airfare and personal gear is not included.

Financial Aid Available: Yes

WASHINGTON MOUNTAINEERING

THE PROGRAM

Description: Join this phenomenal advanced leadership expedition and traverse the spectacular North Cascades for two weeks. Then, spend six days learning advanced snow and ice climbing skills on Washington's Mount Baker. Previous snow and ice climbing experience is not necessary.

Specialty: We are special because of our experience, our low student/staff ratios, the comparable ages of our groups, our unmatched safety record, our personal attention, the enthusiasm of our participants, and the special places where we expedition.

Program Type: Outdoors/adventure

Classification: Coeducational, residential

Focus: Leadership/teamwork

Activities Center On: Outdoors/adventure

Intensity Level: 3

Duration: 2–4 weeks

Program Offered: Summer

Location: Washington

Accommodations: Tent

Years in Operation: 20

Religious Affiliation: Not relevant

STAFF

Student/Staff Ratio: 5:1

Staff Qualifications: Staff members average 27 years of age with a minimum age of 21 and are selected from hundreds of applicants based upon their proven outdoor skills and leadership backgrounds. While most have completed their undergraduate degrees, many are graduate students, full-time outdoor educators, secondary teachers, or college professors. They are excellent role models who exhibit positive life direction and who share a burning desire to have fun while teaching and facilitating groups of young adults.

PARTICIPANTS

Average Number of Participants: 10

For Participants Aged: 16–18

The Ideal Candidate: The ideal candidate for this expedition is a student who has a strong desire to participate in the activity offered. Students need not be super athletes—average physical condition and a positive attitude are all that are required!

Special Requirements for Participation: None.

COSTS

Average Cost: $3,690

Included in Cost: All food, lodging, activities, and group gear are included. The cost of airfare and personal gear is not included.

Financial Aid Available: Yes

WYOMING MOUNTAINEERING

THE PROGRAM

Description: This empowering advanced leadership program in Wyoming is highlighted by a trek along the entire crest of the Teton Range in the Jedediah Smith Wilderness and a rock climbing adventure in the Bridger Wilderness of the Wind River Range.

Specialty: We are special because of our experience, our low student/staff ratios, the comparable ages of our groups, our unmatched safety record, our personal attention, the enthusiasm of our participants, and the special places where we expedition.

Program Type: Outdoors/adventure

Classification: Coeducational, residential

Focus: Leadership/teamwork

Activities Center On: Outdoors/adventure

Intensity Level: 3

Duration: 2–4 weeks

Program Offered: Summer

Location: Wyoming

Accommodations: Tent

Years in Operation: 20

Religious Affiliation: Not relevant

STAFF

Student/Staff Ratio: 5:1

Staff Qualifications: Staff members average 27 years of age with a minimum age of 21 and are selected from hundreds of applicants based upon their proven outdoor skills and leadership backgrounds. While most have completed their undergraduate degrees, many are graduate students, full-time outdoor educators, secondary teachers, or college professors. They are excellent role models who exhibit positive life direction and who share a burning desire to have fun while teaching and facilitating groups of young adults.

PARTICIPANTS

Average Number of Participants: 10

For Participants Aged: 16–18

The Ideal Candidate: The ideal candidate for this expedition is a student who has a strong desire to participate in the activity offered. Students need not be super athletes—average physical condition and a positive attitude are all that are required!

Special Requirements for Participation: None.

COSTS

Average Cost: $3,490

Included in Cost: All food, lodging, activities, and group gear are included. The cost of airfare and personal gear is not included.

Financial Aid Available: Yes

YELLOWSTONE FLYFISHING

THE PROGRAM

Description: From the world-renowned, blue-ribbon waters of the Snake, Madison, and Yellowstone Rivers, to the sparkling alpine lakes of the Beartooth Mountains, this marvelous adventure combines great backpacking with an opportunity to become a skilled fly-fisher in a setting without compare.

Specialty: We are special because of our experience, our low student/staff ratios, the comparable ages of our groups, our unmatched safety record, our personal attention, the enthusiasm of our participants, and the special places where we expedition.

Program Type: Outdoors/adventure

Classification: Coeducational, residential

Focus: Leadership/teamwork and skill-building

Activities Center On: Outdoors/adventure

Intensity Level: 2

Duration: 2–4 weeks

Program Offered: Summer

Location: Montana, Wyoming

Accommodations: Tent

Years in Operation: 5

Religious Affiliation: Not relevant

STAFF

Student/Staff Ratio: 5:1

Staff Qualifications: Staff members average 27 years of age with a minimum age of 21 and are selected from hundreds of applicants based upon their proven outdoor skills and leadership backgrounds. While most have completed their undergraduate degrees, many are graduate students, full-time outdoor educators, secondary teachers, or college professors. They are excellent role models who exhibit positive life direction and who share a burning desire to have fun while teaching and facilitating groups of young adults.

PARTICIPANTS

Average Number of Participants: 10

For Participants Aged: 14–18

The Ideal Candidate: The ideal candidate for this expedition is a student who has a strong desire to participate in the activity offered. Students need not be super athletes—average physical condition and a positive attitude are all that are required!

Special Requirements for Participation: None.

COSTS

Average Cost: $2,490

Included in Cost: All food, lodging, activities, and group gear are included. The cost of airfare and personal gear is not included.

Financial Aid Available: Yes

WORLD HORIZONS INTERNATIONAL, LLC

World Horizons sends high school students between the ages of 14 and 18 on three- to five-week community service trips during the summer. In addition, World Horizons also sends students on community service trips over Christmas and spring breaks.

Years in Operation: 16

Religious Affiliation: Not relevant

Price Range of Programs: $3,000–$5,400

For More Information:
  Contact: Stuart L. Rabinowitz, Executive Director
       PO Box 662
       Bethlehem, CT 06751
  Phone: 800-262-5874
  Fax: 203-266-6227
  Email: worldhorizons@att.net
  Website: www.world-horizons.com

WORLD HORIZONS INTERNATIONAL (CANADA)

THE PROGRAM

Description: This community service trip to a town outside Montreal will involve service projects ranging from working with children and senior citizens to helping with a recycling project, and may also include some painting and small building projects.

Specialty: This program is special because the students are working with the community, and learning about their culture. There is also the possibility of doing an individual internship.

Program Type: Community service, travel/cultural

Classification: Coeducational, residential

Goals: Participants should expect to improve their French speaking ability and learn about a different culture. Québec is a very European environment.

Focus: Community service and cultural

Activities Center On: Travel

Intensity Level: 2

Duration: 2–4 weeks

Program Offered: Summer

Location: Victoriaville, Québec

Accommodations: Other

Years in Operation: 2

Religious Affiliation: Not relevant

STAFF

Student/Staff Ratio: 5:1

Staff Qualifications: Program staff are fluent in French and have extensive background working with teens. Many leaders are teachers, and many are returnees from the Peace Corps.

PARTICIPANTS

Average Number of Participants: 10

For Participants Aged: 14–18

The Ideal Candidate: The ideal candidate is one who is interested in different cultures, anxious to do community service, and eager to improve his/her French.

Special Requirements for Participation: Participants should have had a few years of French.

COSTS

Average Cost: $3,900

Included in Cost: Program fee includes round-trip airfare from the departure city, transportation, accommodations, food, and sightseeing.

Financial Aid Available: Yes

WORLD HORIZONS INTERNATIONAL (COSTA RICA)

THE PROGRAM

Description: This community service program involves language and cultural immersion. Students work with day care centers, preschools, senior citizens, and projects for the community.

Specialty: This program offers immersion into a community in Costa Rica, the chance to work side by side with the local people, and the possibility of an individual internship.

Program Type: Community service, travel/cultural

Classification: Coeducational, residential

Goals: Participants should expect to learn about a different culture, improve their Spanish skills through language immersion, and help others less fortunate than themselves.

Focus: Community service and cultural

Activities Center On: Travel

Intensity Level: 3

Duration: 2–4 weeks

Program Offered: Summer

Location: Palmares and Chirraca, Costa Rica

Accommodations: Other

Years in Operation: 10

Religious Affiliation: Not relevant

STAFF

Student/Staff Ratio: 5:1

Staff Qualifications: All staff are fluent in Spanish and have an extensive background working with teens. Most are either teachers or returnees from the Peace Corps.

PARTICIPANTS

Average Number of Participants: 10

For Participants Aged: 14–18

The Ideal Candidate: Ideally, candidates should have an interest in helping others and learning about a new culture; they should also have had a few years of Spanish.

Special Requirements for Participation: Participants should have had a few years of Spanish language.

COSTS

Average Cost: $4,300

Included in Cost: The program fee includes round-trip airfare from the departure point, accommodations, transportation, food, and sightseeing.

Financial Aid Available: Yes

WORLD HORIZONS INTERNATIONAL (ECUADOR)

THE PROGRAM

Description: Participants in this community service program will be immersed in the language and culture of Ecuador while working with children and senior citizens and doing small building and painting projects for the community.

Specialty: This program offers language immersion, community service projects, and the possibility of an individual internship in the community, which will give a better insight into the local culture and life.

Program Type: Community service, travel/cultural

Classification: Coeducational, residential

Goals: Participants should expect to learn about a different culture and to improve their Spanish skills through language immersion.

Focus: Community service and cultural

Activities Center On: Language and travel

Intensity Level: 3

Duration: 2–4 weeks

Program Offered: Summer

Location: Cayambe, Ecuador

Accommodations: Other

Years in Operation: 10

Religious Affiliation: Not relevant

STAFF

Student/Staff Ratio: 5:1

Staff Qualifications: Staff are mostly teachers and also returnees from the Peace Corps. Leaders have had extensive experience working with and leading teens.

PARTICIPANTS

Average Number of Participants: 10

For Participants Aged: 15–18

The Ideal Candidate: The ideal candidate is a student interested in helping others, learning about a new culture, and improving his/her language skills.

Special Requirements for Participation: Students need to have has at least two years of Spanish to travel to Ecuador.

COSTS

Average Cost: $4,300

Included in Cost: Round-trip airfare from the departure point, accommodations, food, transportation, and sightseeing.

Financial Aid Available: Yes

WORLD HORIZONS INTERNATIONAL (ENGLAND)

THE PROGRAM

Description: This is a four-week program to the central part of England where the students will be working with a "riding for the handicapped" program and, possibly, with senior citizens.

Specialty: The experience of working closely with the local people and the possibility of doing an individual internship.

Program Type: Community service, travel/cultural

Classification: Coeducational, residential

Goals: The rewards of doing something for someone less fortunate than oneself; a feeling of accomplishment by helping the handicapped.

Focus: Community service and travel

Activities Center On: Travel

Intensity Level: 2

Duration: 2–4 weeks

Program Offered: Summer

Location: Kingston upon Thames, United Kingdom

Years in Operation: 2

Religious Affiliation: Not relevant

STAFF

Student/Staff Ratio: 5:1

Staff Qualifications: Program staff are usually teachers or returnees from the Peace Corps and have extensive experience working with teens.

PARTICIPANTS

Average Number of Participants: 10

For Participants Aged: 14–18

The Ideal Candidate: The ideal candidate is interested in doing community service, likes working with children, enjoys travelling and seeing other cultures, and is flexible.

Special Requirements for Participation: Patience with children.

COSTS

Average Cost: $4,800

Included in Cost: Program fees include round-trip airfare from New York, accommodations, transportation, food, and sightseeing.

Financial Aid Available: Yes

WORLD HORIZONS INTERNATIONAL (HAWAII)

THE PROGRAM

Description: On this community service trip to the island of Oahu, students will assist children doing day camp activities, work with senior citizens and terminally ill children, and participate in some painting and small building projects.

Specialty: The experience of working beside people of a different culture, the opportunity to learn about different ways of life, and the possibility of doing an individual internship.

Program Type: Community service, travel/cultural

Classification: Coeducational, residential

Goals: Participants should expect to learn a little about the culture of Hawaii and also about people in situations less fortunate than themselves.

Focus: Community service, cultural, and travel

Activities Center On: Travel

Intensity Level: 1

Duration: 2–4 weeks

Program Offered: Summer

Location: Honolulu and Kaneohe Bay, Hawaii

Accommodations: Dormitory, bunk/cabin

Years in Operation: 8

Religious Affiliation: Not relevant

STAFF

Student/Staff Ratio: 6:1

Staff Qualifications: Leaders have had extensive experience working with teens. Most leaders are teachers or returnees from the Peace Corps.

PARTICIPANTS

Average Number of Participants: 12

For Participants Aged: 14–18

The Ideal Candidate: Participants should be flexible and willing to live in conditions less comfortable than what they are used to. They should also be tolerant of others and of different ways of doing things.

Special Requirements for Participation: A desire to do community service and help others, and the ability to be flexible.

COSTS

Average Cost: $5,100

Included in Cost: Program fee includes round-trip airfare from departure city, transportation, accommodations, food, and sightseeing.

Financial Aid Available: Yes

WORLD HORIZONS INTERNATIONAL (ICELAND)

THE PROGRAM

Description: This is an environmental community service trip working with the Icelandic government on a reforestation project.

Specialty: The close involvement of our students with the local people of the area.

Program Type: Community service, travel/cultural

Classification: Coeducational, residential

Goals: Students should expect to learn about environmental issues and about the culture of Iceland.

Focus: Community service and cultural

Activities Center On: Travel

Intensity Level: 2

Duration: 2–4 weeks

Program Offered: Summer

Location: Reykjavik, Iceland

Years in Operation: 2

Religious Affiliation: Not relevant

STAFF

Student/Staff Ratio: 5:1

Staff Qualifications: Program staff are mostly teachers and returnees from the Peace Corps who have had extensive experience working with teens.

PARTICIPANTS

Average Number of Participants: 10

For Participants Aged: 15–18

The Ideal Candidate: The ideal candidate would be interested in community service, the environment, and different cultures.

Special Requirements for Participation: Flexibility: the ability to adapt to whatever task is required.

COSTS

Average Cost: $5,100

Included in Cost: The program fee includes round-trip airfare from the departure point (New York), all accommodations, food, transportation, and sightseeing.

Financial Aid Available: Yes

WORLD HORIZONS INTERNATIONAL (UTAH)

THE PROGRAM

Description: This trip goes to Best Friends Animal Sanctuary, the largest animal sanctuary in the United States. Students train animals, observe the vets, and help with construction of new buildings and fences. During the second half of the trip, the students go camping at Zion National Park and help rangers with trail maintainance.

Specialty: Working alongside the vets at Best Friends and gaining a real understanding of what it is like to work with animals.

Program Type: Community service, travel/cultural

Classification: Coeducational, residential

Goals: To learn how to train and care for animals, how to do some basic construction, and how to keep hiking trails in good condition.

Focus: Community service and travel

Activities Center On: Community service and travel

Intensity Level: 3

Duration: 2–4 weeks

Program Offered: Summer

Location: Kanab, Arizona; Nevada; Utah

Years in Operation: 8

Religious Affiliation: Not relevant

STAFF

Student/Staff Ratio: 6:1

Staff Qualifications: Program staff are usually teachers or returnees from the Peace Corps and have extensive experience working with teens.

PARTICIPANTS

Average Number of Participants: 12

For Participants Aged: 14–18

The Ideal Candidate: Participant should be interested in caring for animals, and hiking and working in the outdoors at Zion.

Special Requirements for Participation: An interest in the outdoors and animals.

COSTS

Average Cost: $4,100

Included in Cost: Program cost includes round-trip airfare from New York, accommodations, transportation, food, and sightseeing.

Financial Aid Available: Yes

World Horizons International, LLC (Dominica)

The Program

Description: This is a cultural immersion and community service program in which students will work with children and senior citizens. Tasks include tutoring, providing day camp activities, and participating in small building and painting projects.

Specialty: Cultural immersion into a community and the satisfaction of working for the warm and welcoming local people.

Program Type: Community service, travel/cultural

Classification: Coeducational, residential

Goals: Participants should expect to learn about a culture much different from their own.

Focus: Community service, cultural, and travel

Activities Center On: Community service and travel

Intensity Level: 2

Duration: 1–2 weeks, 2–4 weeks

Program Offered: Winter intersession/January term, summer

Location: Roseau, Dominica

Years in Operation: 6

Religious Affiliation: Not relevant

Staff

Student/Staff Ratio: 5:1

Staff Qualifications: All World Horizons leaders have extensive background working with teens, and most are either teachers or returnees from the Peace Corps.

Participants

Average Number of Participants: 10

For Participants Aged: 14–18

The Ideal Candidate: Ideal candidates should have a strong interest in learning about a different culture and helping people less fortunate than themselves.

Special Requirements for Participation: An ability to be flexible and an understanding that living conditions will differ greatly from what most participants are used to.

Costs

Average Cost: $4,300

Included in Cost: The program fee includes round-trip airfare from the departure point, all transportation, accommodations, food, and sightseeing.

Financial Aid Available: Yes

Xi'an Winning Training Center

Project management, business English, and other training; operates under the auspice of the Shaanxi Provincial Government, and trains Chinese professional managers.

Years in Operation: 3

Religious Affiliation: Not relevant

Price Range of Programs: $100–$2,000+

For More Information:
  Contact: David Schoon, USA Representative
        2150 44th Street SE
        Grand Rapids, MI 49508
  Phone: 616-281-0000
  Fax: 616-281-2118
  Email: dbschoon@attbi.com
  Website: www.usapmp.com

China Summer Learning Adventures

The Program

Program Type: Travel/cultural

Classification: Coeducational, residential

Focus: Cultural

Activities Center On: Cultural, history, and language

Intensity Level: 3

Duration: 2–4 weeks

Program Offered: Summer

Location: Shaanxi Province, China

Accommodations: Dormitory

Years in Operation: 1

Religious Affiliation: Not relevant

Staff

Student/Staff Ratio: 6:1

Staff Qualifications: College graduates with relevant work experience.

Participants

Average Number of Participants: 10

For Participants Aged: 16–19

The Ideal Candidate: Ideal candidates are social, adaptable, mature, and interested in academics. We prefer children with international travel experience, and we do not accept special-needs children, including handicapped, learning disabled, or those on medication.

Special Requirements for Participation: Applicant must have a valid Chinese tourist visa, and may bring a camera but not a laptop computer. Applicant may purchase Chinese phone card to call home. Any applicant who is disruptive is returned immediately to parents, who are responsible to pay for additional flight fees and other incidental costs. A pro rata refund for unused days less incidental costs will be sent to payor of record.

Costs

Average Cost: $1,950

Included in Cost: Cost includes food, lodging, tuition, materials, tours, local ground transportation, and 24/7 supervision. It does not include insurance, airfare to Xi'an, or other costs such as those for incidentals.

Financial Aid Available: No

PART THREE
INDEXES

UNITED STATES

Exploration Senior Program (at Yale University), Academic/pre-college enrichment 151
MITE, Academic/pre-college enrichment 307

DELAWARE
Conservation Crew Program (Delaware), Community service 267
Craft of Writing, Academic/pre-college enrichment 308
University of Delaware Summer College Program, Academic/pre-college enrichment 311

DISTRICT OF COLUMBIA
Business & Technology, Academic/pre-college enrichment 225
Capitol Classic Debate Institute, Academic/pre-college enrichment 108
Congressional Student Leadership Conference, Leadership/teamwork 188
Craft of Writing, Academic/pre-college enrichment 308
Eye on Engineering & Computer Science, Academic/pre-college enrichment 108
International Diplomacy, Academic/pre-college enrichment 226
Law & Advocacy, Academic/pre-college enrichment 226
Law Preview Law School Prep Course, Academic/pre-college enrichment 187
LeadAmerica, Leadership/teamwork 188
Mastering Leadership, Leadership/teamwork 227
Musiker Active Teen Tours, Travel 295
Opera Institute for Young Singers, Skill-building 109
Summer Discovery (Georgetown), Academic/pre-college enrichment 297
The Princeton Review College Discovery Experience, Academic/pre-college enrichment 295
Volunteers for Peace International Work Camp, Community service 318

FLORIDA
Conservation Crew Program (Florida), Community service 268
Craft of Writing, Academic/pre-college enrichment 308
Landmark Volunteers (Florida), Community service 173
Law Preview Law School Prep Course, Academic/pre-college enrichment 187
Musiker Active Teen Tours, Travel 295
Summer Scholar Programs, Academic/pre-college enrichment 311
Volunteers for Peace International Work Camp, Community service 318

GEORGIA
ASA at Emory University, Academic/pre-college enrichment 72
Caretta Research Project, Other 254
Conservation Crew Program (Georgia), Community service 268
Craft of Writing, Academic/pre-college enrichment 308
Early College Summer Program, Academic/pre-college enrichment 260

HAWAII
AAVE—Hawaii, Travel 90
Australian Outback + Hawaii, Travel 320
Conservation Crew Program (Hawaii), Community service 269
Craft of Writing, Academic/pre-college enrichment 308
Fire and Ice, Travel 86

WYOMING

UNITED STATES TERRITORIES

INTERNATIONAL

ACADEMIC/PRE-COLLEGE ENRICHMENT

Women in Engineering Workshops, MI   194
Women in the Sciences & Engineering Camp, PA   241
Young Investigators' Summer Program in Nuclear Science & Technology, NC   228

COMMUNITY SERVICE
Conservation Crew Program (Alaska), AK   263
Conservation Crew Program (Arizona), AL   264
Conservation Crew Program (Arkansas), AR   265
Conservation Crew Program (California), CA   265
Conservation Crew Program (Colorado), CO   266
Conservation Crew Program (Connecticut), CT   266
Conservation Crew Program (Delaware), DE   267
Conservation Crew Program (Florida), FL   268
Conservation Crew Program (Georgia), GA   268
Conservation Crew Program (Hawaii), HI   269
Conservation Crew Program (Idaho), ID   269
Conservation Crew Program (Illinois), IL   270
Conservation Crew Program (Indiana), IN   271
Conservation Crew Program (Iowa), IA   271
Conservation Crew Program (Kansas), KS   272
Conservation Crew Program (Kentucky), KY   272
Conservation Crew Program (Louisiana), LA   273
Conservation Crew Program (Maine), ME   274
Conservation Crew Program (Maryland), MD   274
Conservation Crew Program (Massachusetts), MA   275
Conservation Crew Program (Michigan), MI   275
Conservation Crew Program (Minnesota), MN   276
Conservation Crew Program (Mississippi), MS   276
Conservation Crew Program (Missouri), MO   277
Conservation Crew Program (Montana), MT   278
Conservation Crew Program (Nebraska), NB   278
Conservation Crew Program (Nevada), NV   279
Conservation Crew Program (New Hampshire), NH   279
Conservation Crew Program (New Jersey), NJ   280
Conservation Crew Program (New Mexico), NM   281
Conservation Crew Program (New York), NY   281
Conservation Crew Program (North Carolina), NC   282
Conservation Crew Program (North Dakota), ND   282
Conservation Crew Program (Ohio), OH   283
Conservation Crew Program (Oklahoma), OK   283
Conservation Crew Program (Oregon), OR   284
Conservation Crew Program (Pennsylvania), PA   285
Conservation Crew Program (Rhode Island), RI   285
Conservation Crew Program (South Carolina), SC   286
Conservation Crew Program (South Dakota), SD   286
Conservation Crew Program (Tennessee), TN   287
Conservation Crew Program (Texas), TX   288

CULTURAL

ABOUT THE AUTHOR

As the brave and lucky guinea pig of Neil Bull, founder of the Center for Interim Studies, Neill Seltzer is the veteran of many summer adventures in far-flung places, from Alaska to Africa, from the West Indies to the South of France. His summer experiences may have contributed to his unusual career path as a professional chef, actor, college professor, entrepreneur, consultant, and author. In his roles as teacher, writer, and vice president for The Princeton Review, Neill has advised thousands of teenagers and their families (in two continents and six states) on the difficult transition to college and beyond. Neill currently teaches, writes, and lives in Brooklyn, New York.

KNOW OF A GREAT SUMMER PROGRAM FOR TEENAGERS?

If you do and you do not find it in this guide, send us an email at surveysupport@review.com, with "Summer Programs" in the subject line. Tell us what the summer program is, any contact information (email addresses and websites are best) you have for it and why you think it ought to be included. We'll check it out, and if we think it's up to standards, we'll try to include it in the next edition of the book.

NOTES

NOTES

NOTES

NOTES

NOTES

www.PrincetonReview.com

The Princeton Review
Admissions Services

At The Princeton Review, we care about your ability to get accepted to the best school for you. But, we all know getting accepted involves much more than just doing well on standardized tests. That's why, in addition to our test preparation services, we also offer free admissions services to students looking to enter college or graduate school. You can find these services on our website, *www.PrincetonReview.com*, the best online resource for researching, applying to, and learning about how to pay for college.

No matter what type of program you're applying to—undergraduate, graduate, law, business, or medical—**www.PrincetonReview.com has the free tools, services, and advice you need to navigate the admissions process.**

Read on to learn more about the services we offer.

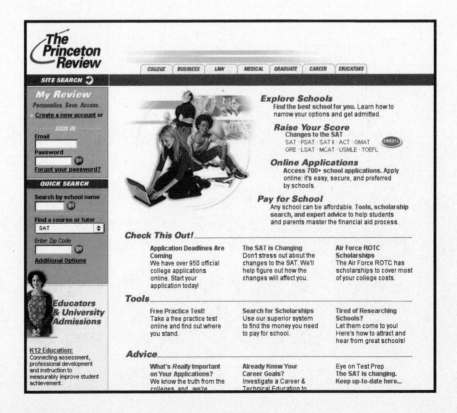

Research Schools
www.PrincetonReview.com/Research

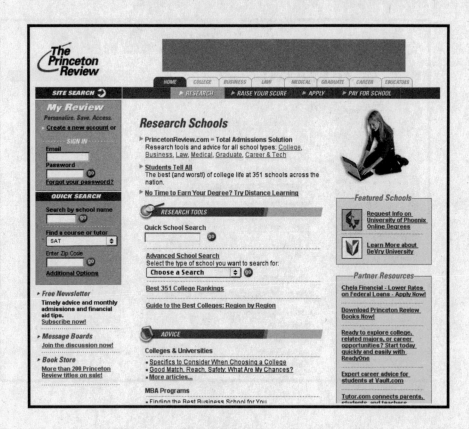

www.PrincetonReview.com features an interactive tool called **Counselor-O-Matic.** When you use this tool, you enter stats and information about yourself to find a list of your best match schools, reach schools, and safety schools. From there you can read statistical and editorial information about thousands of colleges and universities. In addition, you can find out what currently enrolled college students say about their schools. Once you complete Counselor-O-Matic make sure you opt in to School Match so that colleges can come to you.

Our **College Majors Search** is one of the most popular features we offer. Here you can read profiles on hundreds of majors to find information on curriculum, salaries, careers, and the appropriate high school preparation, as well as colleges that offer it. From the Majors Search, you can investigate corresponding careers, read **Career Profiles**, and learn what career is the best match for you by taking our **Career Quiz**.

No matter what type of school or specialized program you are considering, **www.PrincetonReview.com has free articles and advice, in addition to our tools, to help you make the right choice.**

Apply to School
www.PrincetonReview.com/Apply

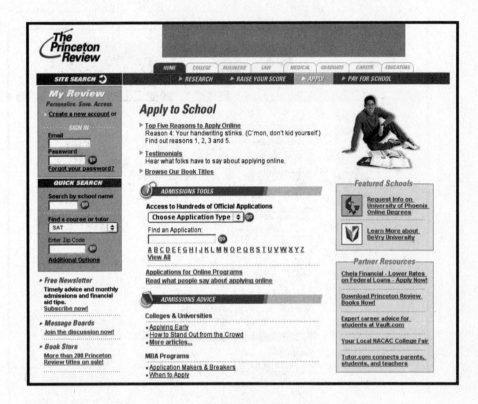

For most students, completing the school application is the most stressful part of the admissions process. www.PrincetonReview.com's powerful **Online School Application Engine** makes it easy to apply.

Paper applications are mostly a thing of the past. And, our hundreds of partner schools tell us they prefer to receive your applications online.

Using our online application service is simple:

- Enter information once and the common data automatically transfers onto each application.
- Save your applications and access them at any time to edit and perfect.
- Submit electronically or print and mail in.
- Pay your application fee online, using an e-check, or mail the school a check.

Our powerful application engine is built to accommodate all your needs.

Pay for School
www.PrincetonReview.com/Finance

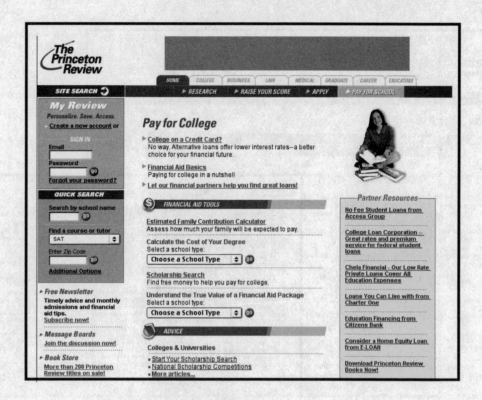

The financial aid process is confusing for everyone. But don't worry. Our free online tools, services, and advice can help you plan for the future and get the money you need to pay for school.

Our **Scholarship Search** engine will help you find free money, although often scholarships alone won't cover the cost of high tuitions. So, we offer other tools and resources to help you navigate the entire process.

Filling out the FAFSA and CSS PROFILE can be a daunting process, use our **strategies for both forms** to make sure you answer the questions correctly the first time.

If scholarships and government aid aren't enough to swing the cost of tuition, we'll help you secure student loans. The Princeton Review has partnered with a select group of reputable financial institutions who will help **explore all your loans options**.

If you know how to work the financial aid process, you'll learn you don't have to **eliminate a school based on tuition.**

Be a Part of the www.PrincetonReview.com Community

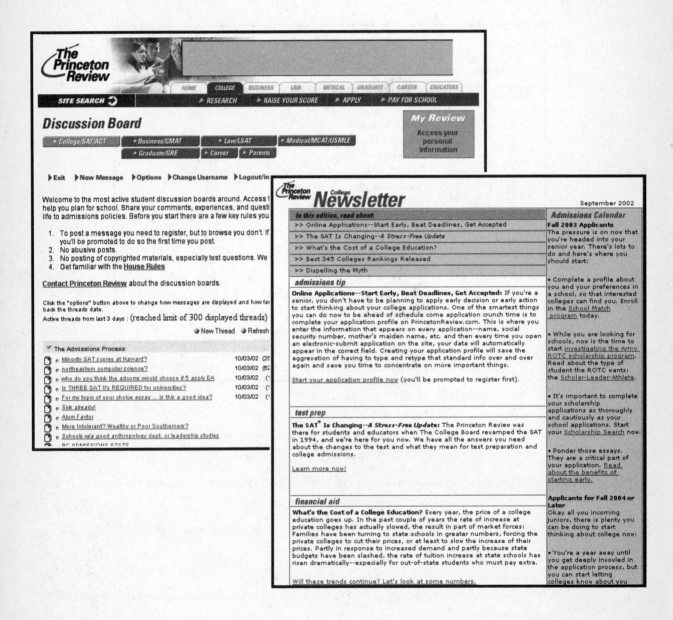

PrincetonReview.com's **Discussion Boards** and **Free Newsletters** are additional services to help you to get information about the admissions process from your peers and from The Princeton Review experts.

Book Store
www.PrincetonReview.com/college/Bookstore.asp

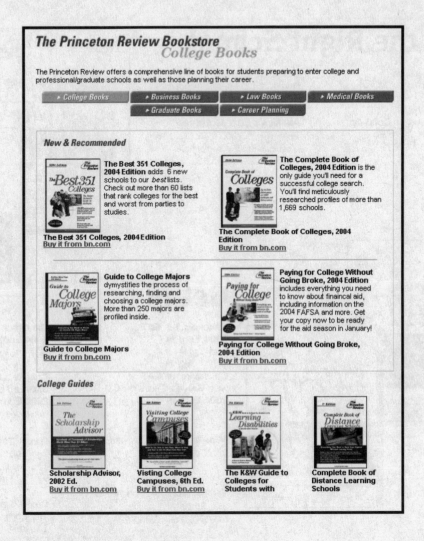

In addition to this book, we publish hundreds of other titles, including guidebooks that highlight life on campus, student opinion, and all the statistical data you need to know about any school you are considering. Just a few of the titles we offer are:

- Complete Book of Business Schools
- Complete Book of Law Schools
- Complete Book of Medical Schools
- The Best 351 Colleges
- The K&W Guide to Colleges for Students with Learning Disabilities or Attention Deficit Disorder
- Paying for College Without Going Broke

For a complete listing of all of our titles, visit our **online bookstore**:

www.PrincetonReview.com/college/bookstore.asp

Find the Right School

BEST 351 COLLEGES
2004 EDITION
0-375-76337-6 • $21.95

COMPLETE BOOK OF COLLEGES
2004 EDITION
0-375-76330-9 • $24.95

COMPLETE BOOK OF
DISTANCE LEARNING SCHOOLS
0-375-76204-3 • $21.00

AMERICA'S ELITE COLLEGES
The Smart Buyer's Guide to the Ivy
League and Other Top Schools
0-375-76206-X • $15.95

Get in

CRACKING THE SAT
2004 EDITION
0-375-76331-7 • $19.00

CRACKING THE SAT
WITH SAMPLE TESTS ON CD-ROM
2004 EDITION
0-375-76330-9 • $30.95

MATH WORKOUT FOR THE SAT
2ND EDITION
0-375-76177-2 • $14.95

VERBAL WORKOUT FOR THE SAT
2ND EDITION
0-375-76176-4 • $14.95

CRACKING THE ACT
2004 EDITION
0-375-76395-3 • $19.00

CRACKING THE ACT WITH
SAMPLE TESTS ON CD-ROM
2004 EDITION
0-375-76394-5 • $29.95

CRASH COURSE FOR THE ACT
2ND EDITION
The Last-Minute Guide to Scoring High
0-375-75364-3 • $9.95

CRASH COURSE FOR THE SAT
2ND EDITION
The Last-Minute Guide to Scoring High
0-375-75361-9 • $9.95

Get Help Paying for it

DOLLARS & SENSE FOR COLLEGE STUDENTS
How Not to Run Out of Money by Midterms
0-375-75206-4 • $10.95

PAYING FOR COLLEGE WITHOUT GOING BROKE
2004 EDITION
0-375-76350-3 • $20.00

THE SCHOLARSHIP ADVISOR
5TH EDITION
0-375-76210-8 • $26.00